THE RED SOX FAN HANDBOOK

COMPILED BY LEIGH GROSSMAN

UPDATED FOR 2005

THE RED SOX FAN HANDBOOK

COMPILED BY LEIGH GROSSMAN

UPDATED FOR 2005

Rounder Books

Cambridge, Massachusetts

The Red Sox Fan Handbook
Compiled by Leigh Grossman

Copyright © 2005 by Leigh Grossman

Published by Rounder Books

an imprint of
Rounder Records Corp.
One Camp Street
Cambridge, MA 02140

Printing history
First edition published in March 2001
Second edition published in March 2002
This edition published in March 2005

ISBN: 1-57940-110-4
Library of Congress Control Number:

Cover design by Jean Pierre Leguillou
Cover photo by Bill Nowlin
Designed and typeset by Swordsmith Productions

Grossman, Leigh Ronald, 1966–
The Red Sox Fan Handbook
1. Boston Red Sox (Baseball team) I Title

2005900949
796.357
ISBN 1-57940-110-4

10 9 8 7 6 5 4 3 2 1

Contents

An overview of the team, its players and management over the years, with all the highlights and lowlights

More than 400 of the players who people still talk about, and why they're important
Don Aase • Harry Agganis • Rick Aguilera • Israel Alcantara • Dale Alexander • Manny Alexander • Luis Alicea • Gary Allenson • Abe Alvarez • Larry Andersen • Brady Anderson • Mike Andrews • Luis Aparicio • Luis Aponte •

Tony Armas • Rolando Arrojo • Bronson Arroyo • Steve Avery • Carlos Baerga • Jeff Bagwell • Bob Bailey • Willie Banks • Marty Barrett • Don Baylor • Rod Beck • Hugh Bedient • Gary Bell • Stan Belinda • Gary Bell • Mark Bellhorn • Moe Berg • Dante Bichette • Max Bishop • Tony Blanco • Greg Blosser • Mike Boddicker • Wade Boggs • Lou Boudreau • Oil Can Boyd • Hugh Bradley • Darren Bragg • Eddie Bressoud • Ken Brett • Tom Brewer • Mike Brown • Tom Brunansky • Bill Buckner • Don Buddin • Damon Buford • Tom Burgmeier • John Burkett • Morgan Burkhart • Ellis Burks • Rick Burleson • George Burns • Juan Bustabad • Orlando Cabrera • Bill Campbell • Jose Canseco • Bernie Carbo • Bill Carrigan • Frank Castillo • Danny Cater • Orlando Cepeda • Ben Chapman • Robinson Checo • Bruce Chen • Eddie Cicotte • Jack Clark • Tony Clark • Mark Clear • Roger Clemens • Matt Clement • Reggie Cleveland • Alex Cole • Michael Coleman • Jimmy Collins • Ray Collins • David Cone • Billy Conigliaro • Tony Conigliaro • Gene Conley • Billy Consolo • Cecil Cooper • Scott Cooper • Wil Cordero • Rheal Cormier • Jim Corsi • Ted Cox • Doc Cramer • Paxton Crawford • Steve Crawford • Cesar Crespo • Lou Criger • Joe Cronin • Leon Culberson • Ray Culp • Midre Cummings • John Curtis • Johnny Damon • Danny Darwin • Brian Daubach • Andre Dawson • Rob Deer • Brian Denman • Juan Diaz • Dom DiMaggio • Lenny DiNardo • Big Bill Dineen • Joe Dobson • Pat Dodson • Bobby Doerr • John Dopson • Patsy Dougherty • Dick Drago • Walt Dropo • Joe Dugan • Mike Easler • Dennis Eckersley • Howard Ehmke • Alan Embree • Nick Esasky • Vaughn Eshelman • Dwight Evans • Carl Everett • Jeff Fassero • Rick Ferrell • Wes Ferrell • Boo Ferriss • Mark Fidrych • Lou Finney • Carlton Fisk • Bryce Florie • Cliff Floyd • Lew Ford • Mike Fornieles • Tony Fossas • Casey Fossum • Rube Foster • Keith Foulke • Chad Fox • Pete Fox • Jimmie Foxx • Joe Foy • Buck Freeman • Jeff Frye • Denny Galehouse • Rich Garces • Nomar Garciaparra • Larry Gardner • Wes Gardner • Rich Gedman • Gary Geiger • Jeremy Giambi • Billy Goodman • Tom Gordon • Jeff Gray • Craig Grebeck • Pumpsie Green • Mike Greenwell • Doug Griffin • Lefty Grove • Mark Guthrie • Jackie Gutierrez • John Halama • Erik Hanson • Carroll Hardy • Tommy Harper • Ken Harrelson • Greg Harris • Mickey Harris • Reggie Harris • Bill Haselman • Billy Hatcher • Scott Hatteberg • Dave Henderson • Rickey Henderson • Dustin Hermanson • Joe Hesketh • Pinky Higgins • Shea Hillenbrand • Butch Hobson • Glenn Hoffman • Harry Hooper • Sam Horn • Dwayne Hosey • Tom House • Elston Howard • Bobby Howry • Waite Hoyt • Long Tom Hughes • Tex Hughson • Bruce Hurst • Adam Hyzdu • Reggie Jefferson • Ferguson Jenkins • Jackie Jensen • "Indian Bob" Johnson • Earl Johnson • Sad Sam Jones • Todd Jones • Eddie Joost • Ed Jurak • Gabe Kapler • George Kell • Dana Kiecker • Byung-Hyun Kim • Sun-Woo Kim • Ellis Kinder • Jack Kramer • Roger LaFrançois • Carney Lansford • Mike Lansing • Bill Lee • Mark Lemke • Dutch Leonard • Curt Leskanic • Darren Lewis • Duffy Lewis • Tim Lollar • Jim Lonborg • Derek Lowe • Sparky Lyle • Fred Lynn • Brandon Lyon • Steve Lyons • Mike Macfarlane • Mike Maddux • Tom Maggard • Ron Mahay • Mark Malaska • Frank Malzone • Matt Mantei • Felix Mantilla • Josias Manzanillo • Juan Marichal • Mike Marshall • Pedro Martinez • Ramon Martinez • John Marzano • Carl Mays • David McCarty • Mickey McDermott • Willie McGee • Stuffy McInnis • Jeff McNeely • Sam Mele • Ramiro Mendoza • Kent Mercker • Lou Merloni • Catfish Metkovich • Doug Mientkiewicz • Kevin Millar • Rick Miller • Wade Miller • Doug Mirabelli • Bill Monbouquette • Bob Montgomery • Dave Morehead • Rogelio Moret • Ed Morris • Jamie Moyer • Bill Mueller • Rob Murphy • Buddy Myer • Mike Myers • Tim Naehring • Mike Nagy • Jeff Newman • Reid Nichols • Al Nipper • Otis Nixon • Trot Nixon • Hideo Nomo • Buck O'Brien • Jose Offerman • Ben Oglivie • Tomo Ohka • Bob Ojeda • Troy O'Leary • Steve Ontiveros • David Ortiz • Spike Owen • Jim Pagliaroni • Stan Papi • Freddy Parent • Mel Parnell • Marty Pattin • Jay Payton • Rudy Pemberton • Tony Peña • Herb

Pennock • Tony Perez • Robert Person • Johnny Pesky • Rico Petrocelli •
Hipolito Pichardo • Calvin Pickering • Jimmy Piersall • Phil Plantier • Dick
Pole • Curtis Pride • Carlos Quintana • Dick Radatz • Manny Ramirez • Jeff
Reardon • Jody Reed • Pee Wee Reese • Pokey Reese • Jerry Remy • Edgar
Renteria • Jim Rice • Dave Roberts • Alex Rodriguez • Frankie Rodriguez •
Billy Rohr • Brian Rose • Rich Rowland • Joe Rudi • Red Ruffing • Pete
Runnels • Ryan Rupe • Jeff Russell • Babe Ruth • Ken Ryan • Gene Rye •
Bret Saberhagen • Donnie Sadler • Joe Sambito • Freddy Sanchez • Rey
Sanchez • Jose Santiago • Scott Sauerbeck • Wally Schang • Curt Schilling •
Calvin Schiraldi • Pete Schourek • Don Schwall • Everett Scott • George Scott
• Tom Seaver • Diego Segui • Aaron Sele • Jeff Sellers • Ernie Shore •
Sonny Siebert • Al Simmons • Ted Sizemore • Heathcliff Slocumb • Lee Smith
• Reggie Smith • Tris Speaker • Bobby Sprowl • Chick Stahl • Jake Stahl •
Matt Stairs • Tracy Stallard • Lee Stange • Bob Stanley • Mike Stanley •
Mike Stanton • Dave Stapleton • Dernell Stenson • Gene Stephens • Vern
Stephens • Jerry Stephenson • Jeff Stone • Dick Stuart • Chris Stynes •
Frank Sullivan • Marc Sullivan • Jeff Suppan • Jim Tabor • Frank Tanana •
Jesse Tannehill • Jose Tartabull • Ken Tatum • Birdie Tebbetts • Lee Thomas •
Luis Tiant • Mike Timlin • Denny Tomori • Mike Torrez • John Tudor • Julio
Valdez • John Valentin • Jason Varitek • Mo Vaughn • Ramon Vazquez •
Wilton Veras • Mickey Vernon • Frank Viola • Clyde Vollmer • Hal Wagner •
Tim Wakefield • Todd Walker • Bill Wambsganss • John Wasdin • Bob Watson
• Earl Webb • Eric Wedge • David Wells • Billy Werber • Sammy White •
Ted Williams • Scott Williamson • Jim Willoughby • Earl Wilson • Rick Wise •
Tony Womack • Smoky Joe Wood • John Wyatt • Carl Yastrzemski • Rudy York
• Kevin Youkilis • Cy Young • Matt Young • Bob Zupcic

Preface

Most people don't think of baseball as a soap opera. A lot of baseball fans would probably be a little offended at the characterization. But in a few key ways, baseball plays the same role in the lives of its fans that soap operas do for their viewers. For six months a year there is a baseball game on almost every night, a refreshing comfort in a world where little else is constant. As in a soap opera, we know the cast of characters in a baseball game, but not who the hero or villain will be on that particular night. Sometimes we'll go out of our way to watch a game that guest stars someone especially famous, or a former cast member who is no longer with the team.

At a time where not much is certain in life there is certainty in baseball, and there is great comfort in that certainty.

And certainly the last few years have been particularly operatic times in the history of the Red Sox. The second edition of *The Red Sox Fan Handbook* came out in 2002. The team had just been sold, and nobody knew what to expect. The Red Sox were on their third manager since the preceding August, and a season that had started with high hopes had ended disappointingly . . . not an unusual occurrence for Red Sox fans.

Water passed under the bridge. Swordsmith Books, the publisher I ran at the time, stopped publishing its own books, a victim of a bankrupt distributor and life's disasters: deaths in the family, a divorce. Through the rough times the Red Sox brought continuity, hope. The disaster that might have followed the sale of the team never happened—the new owners proved to be terrific, the teams they put on the field very good. The 2003 playoffs brought heartbreak but also hopefulness. Unlike the fluke of 1986 this team did not have to be lucky to win, did not fall apart in the aftermath of another crushing loss. Like many of us, I drew great personal comfort from their resilience, and the triumph of 2004 was in many ways a triumph for all of new England—always a cliché when a regional sports team wins a championship but literally true in this case. This book is about that triumph, and about many other triumphs and tragedies, stories and soap operas, and all of the things that make the Red Sox New England's team, as well as the team of many non-New Englanders, as I was.

I'm 38 years old now, and I've been a Red Sox fan since 1979, when I was 12. I'm about average-aged for the contributors to this book, the oldest of whom saw his first Red Sox game in 1927. What made me a Red Sox fan? At the time, I wasn't even a *baseball* fan. No one in my family played baseball. I lived near Atlantic City, New Jersey, close to eight hours' drive from Boston. I'd been to a few Philadelphia Phillies games, in sterile Veterans Stadium, and had come away less than impressed.

My sister was in college in the Boston area, and I came up to visit her one summer. She and a bunch of friends dragged me to a Red Sox game. We sat in the bleachers, section 35. I was bored and being pretty obnoxious. Sometime during the game, something captured me. I don't know if it was Fenway Park, or the crowd, or something magical about the game itself, but by the time Dwight Evans broke open a tie game with a ninth-inning grand slam, I was hooked.

Two summers later I traveled to Boston again, for a week this time. I walked from Somerville to Boston to buy Red Sox tickets, and went to every game I could afford, sometimes walking instead of taking public transit so I could save my money to go to more games. The night before I had to leave town, the Red Sox got into a 19-inning duel with the Seattle Mariners. I couldn't bear to leave, even though the last bus back to Somerville left at 1:00 A.M.. After the game was finally suspended, I ended up walking back through Boston and Cambridge to my sister's apartment in Somerville, showing up around 3:00 in the morning. She never said anything.

I took to listening to the Red Sox on the radio. From Atlantic City, on a clear night, you can just barely pull in WTIC-AM 1080 from Hartford. I'd go up to the highest point in the house and listen on the ancient clock radio that had the best reception of all the radios in the house—making tiny adjustments to try and preserve the signal when it faded. I still listen to most of the Red Sox games on the radio, even though I live in New England now and could probably watch more of them. But the Red Sox captured my imagination as much as my heart, and listening to games on the radio allows my imagination to do much of the work.

What made me come up with the idea for this book? *The Red Sox Fan Handbook* is the book I wish I'd had when the team first captured my imagination. It's easy to find a book about stats, or a dry analysis of a baseball team's chances. It's much harder to find the folklore of a team—not just who the important players were, but why people still care about them, what brought them to life for other fans watching games last year, a dozen years ago—or a hundred years ago. This is a book about Ted Williams and Babe Ruth and Curt Schilling and Manny Ramirez, but it's also a book about Ed Jurak catching a rat in his glove, and Tom Maggard dying at the brink of the major leagues. There are stories about more than 400 players in this book—some of them famous, some of them funny, some of them tragic, some of them just about the lives of people that we care about, or that previous generations of fans cared about.

There is a history of the team in this book, but that history is part of an ongoing story of how the team and its fans became what they are today, not just an account of who won or lost or was traded.

There are questions and answers that I wanted when I first discovered the game—answers about the basic strategies of the game, about some of baseball's confusing rules and procedures, and about the Red Sox themselves.

There is an account of Fenway Park—not just how to get tickets or where to park or eat (although that's here) but what the experience of Fenway Park has been for other fans, and why a tiny, outdated facility is so beloved by so many people. There are stories by other fans of what captured their imaginations, in the same way that meaningless 1979 game captured mine.

And along the way there are all of the other things you would expect in a guide for Red Sox fans, new or long-suffering: a list of books and a guide to websites, information about visiting spring training or the Red Sox minor league teams.

Whether you read through or browse for favorite players and incidents, whether you are using this book to learn about the team for the first time or to relive a half-century of memories, this book is an attempt to capture the soul of a team that has captured the soul of New England and a good part of the nation.

This new edition has been updated through the 2005 preseason. More than 200 player entries were added or changed. (More than 400 players are profiled in all.) The history of the team is now complete through the 2004–05 offseason. The minor league prospects section has been completely revised and updated. The section on where to eat near Fenway Park has been expanded, as have the websites, quotes, and the bibliography of Red Sox books. Other sections have been updated or completely rewritten. Since the previous editions, many people have written in with their own stories, requests, or ideas. You'll see some of those ideas here—more on the minor leagues, stories about Jim Pagliaroni, Dernell Stenson, and other favorites, some new stories of how people became fans.

The Red Sox Fan Handbook was a team effort, with dozens of people participating to some degree. The primary contributors to this book include Lyford P. Beverage Jr., Dave Bismo, Keith R. A. DeCandido, Joe Kuras, Robert P. Machemer, Heather Anne Nicoll, Toine Otten, Paul Ryan, Neil Serven, Val Vadeboncoeur, Eric Van, Donald J. Violette, and Edward R. Zartler. Others who contributed stories, information, or corrections include Jon Diamond, Don Fisher, Jim Freid, Dan Golden, Lee Harris, Bill Kirk, James J. Lyons, Mario Martinelli, Chris Morth, Thomas S. Parrott II, Colin Smith, Richard Smith, Jim Tiberio, Daryl Jasper and Jeff Ouimette of the Pawtucket Red Sox, Chris

Cameron of the Portland Sea Dogs, Tripp Baum of the Wilmington Blue Rocks, Pete Ehmke of the Capital City Bombers, and Todd Stephenson of the Gulf Coast Red Sox. Bill Nowlin, publisher of Rounder Books (and a well-known Red Sox scholar and author), acquired this new edition of the book and contributed both editorial changes and a remarkable store of Red Sox lore. Val Smith, my wonderful agent, helped keep me focused and productive, and made me laugh when I needed to. Brad San Martin and Steve Netsky at Rounder Books helped shepherd the book through the editiorial and production process, while Jamie Johnson, Elizabeth Glover, Wendy Goldberg, Stacy Cortigiano, and Matthew Peck assisted with previous editions that this work evolved from. Gus Anderson, a longtime friend, workout partner, and source of many baseball conversations was in my thoughts while writing, though prior commitments in Iraq prevented him from helping in person. And of course I have to thank Penny, Jen, and the crew of the Pomfret XTramart, who patiently cope with both my need for Boston newspapers and my late-night snack runs.

—LEIGH GROSSMAN
February, 2005

Why to Buy This Book

It's early spring, and you've been tossed into a book store up in Boston.
While you eye their great selection
Boyfriend Joe is in the section
where the books discuss the Sox
from Freddy Lynn to Jimmie Foxx.
Your last night's date was not so hot
(he'd cooked you dinner, though he's not
a Paul Prudhomme or Fannie Farmer).
Still, he tried, the handsome charmer!
Date soon went from bad to worse
when you both failed to, well, converse.
"So whaddya think of Kennedy?"
you ask him with amenity,
while thinking of the man named Ted.
But Joe's reply is tainted Red:
"I used to like him well enough
I thought him made of sterner stuff
until I saw him pamper Mo.
By then I wanted him to go."
He pampered more? "More what?" you think.
You start to pour yourself a drink.
"I hated Nixon" you expound
while searching for some common ground.
"He's still quite young," your man replies,
"I like the way he catches flies."
Confused, you rule out politics
and think, "this date is hard to fix!"
You ask him for some more chianti
but instead get "El Tiante." He
talks of him and Tony C,
he quotes the loony Spaceman Lee.
He hints at Hughson and at Harris,
waxes eloquent on Ferriss,
on and on (he likes to talk!), he
has mixed thoughts on Thomas Yawkey.

Sammy White to Pumpsie Green!
He lectures you on Bill Dineen.
He talks of Roosters and of Bags
of '83 and no-hit Rags.
He calls Frazee, "A Yankee whore."
He talks of Yaz and Bobby Doerr
and Smoky Joe and Tris and Cy.
You're almost ready now to cry,
for every time you start anew
your date finds ways to misconstrue.
His mind and yours are not in tune
while you are normal, he's a lun-
atic whose main concerns
are baseball-ish. Like Doris Kearns
he seems quite normal, till he sees
the dark blue caps with bright red B's.
Within the store, you spy this book
and, what the hey!, you take a look.
You pick this book up off the shelf
surprising him, also yourself.
Your guy is nutty—sure that's true,
and yet, there's something else there too.
You're kinda moved by how he speaks
of Splinters and of Golden Greeks.
You like this man and how his eyes
light up each time you vocalize
some words like "Monster" and, (how droll!)
some other words like "Pesky's Pole."
You think it's cute to (when you're cozy),
whisper nothings like: "Dwayne Hosey."
It is time you learned the truth
on why the Sox sold G. H. Ruth.
You want to know about LeRoux
and Val and Wakes and Nomar too.
You'll see the heights of Morgan's Magic,
know the lows like Buckner's tragic—

never mind, just pay the clerk,
you'll make this Sox-fan romance work.
Your life with him will turn out great.
You'll be conjoined forever. Fate
decrees that Boston fans all must
stick by their loves till "Dust to dust."
For what else earthly lasts as long?
(Eight decades now and going strong).
Through good and bad he'll stand by you.
A Sox fan, if naught else, is true
when good times end and bad times come
through players poor and owners dumb.
He'll stay with you through thick and thin
through good guy's loss and bad guy's win.
So buy this. Read. You'll know your man
(as well as any woman can).
And maybe you'll become good friends
with our great team within the Fens.
Please note the poem's author knows
that women like the Scarlet Hose
as much as men, in cases more,
that men might also, in the store,
be seeking ways to know their mate
for when they're out upon a date.
So gay or straight, no one is banned
from buying this that's in your hand
(not even fans of Yanks or Mets—
I'll take their cash without regrets!)
and maybe soon we'll all give cheer
when "next year" comes. Is this the year?

—Robert P. Machemer

A Short History of the Boston Red Sox

1. The Cy Young Years: 1901–1908

In 1901 the Boston Americans were a charter member of the new American League. This first Boston team was largely built from star players enticed from other leagues like the established National League, and was very good. Superstar pitcher Cy Young was lured away from St. Louis, along with his personal catcher, Lou Criger. Jimmy Collins, Buck Freeman, and Chick Stahl (who would die bizarrely a few years later) had been the core of the National League's Boston Beaneaters' lineup before they joined the Boston Americans. Third baseman Collins would be the team's player-manager (a common practice in that period).

The Americans were in first place in August, but eventually faded to a close second behind the Chicago White Stockings (soon to be the White Sox). The Americans had terrific pitching; led by Cy Young's league-leading 33 wins and 1.62 earned run average, the team was second in the eight-team league in earned run average. Collins, Freeman, and Stahl all hit over .300, although the team was only in the middle of the pack offensively. The Americans also led the league in home runs—with only 37 in this deadball era, when the balls used were almost impossible to hit out of the park. Like all teams at the turn of the century, nearly everyone on the team stole a lot of bases. It wasn't until around 1930 that the Red Sox fabled lack of base-stealers took hold.

The 1902 team was even stronger, although they finished third in the league. (For a long time, it was thought that team had been renamed the Pilgrims in 1902, but recent research suggests that they never were.) The pitching staff, which had been inconsistent besides the veteran Cy Young and 23-year-old George Winter, was bolstered by rookie Big Bill Dineen (who led the league in losses despite pitching well). Boston was still a middle-of-the-road team offensively, but they now had the league's best pitching. For each of the next three years they would lead the league in earned run average—something the Red Sox would not do in consecutive years again until the Pedro Martinez-led, Joe Kerrigan-coached pitching staffs of 1999 and 2000.

Everything came together in 1903. With the war between the National League and the upstart American League settled, the leagues agreed to play a nine-game series to determine baseball's championship. Boston led the American League in pitching, hitting, and home runs, and romped to the league championship. Boston won 91 games, while the next-closest team in the league won 77. Cy Young led the league with 28 wins, and Bill Dineen and Long Tom Hughes both won at least 20. The Americans were underdogs in the first World Series, however, and fell behind the Pittsburgh Pirates three games to one. But Dineen (two shutouts in the series) and Young carried the team to an astonishing comeback, giving Boston the first World Series victory ever.

Another American League championship followed in 1904, but with it came troubling signs of things to come. New owner General Charles Taylor sold Patsy Dougherty (who had hit .342 and .331 the previous two seasons) and 20-game winner Long Tom Hughes to the New York Highlanders, forerunners of the soon-to-be-hated Yankees. Boston slipped offensively, but the league was increasingly dominated by pitching, and Boston still had the best pitching, with Jesse Tannehill filling Hughes's place on the pitching staff along with Cy Young and Bill Dineen. Dineen outdueled Highlanders' ace Jack Chesbro (who set a modern record with 41 wins that year) on the last day of the season to clinch the American League pennant, but there would be no second World Series title that year: Embarrassed by Boston's win the previous year, the National League champion New York Giants refused to play them.

Boston began to fade rapidly in 1905, and by 1906 they were a terrible team, losing 20 games in a row at one point. The offense, built from established National League stars, dwindled to nothing as those stars aged. The pitching staff, which had been the league's best, faded to average, and was the worst in the league by 1906, when Cy Young—nearly 40 years old—finally began to show his age. Late in the season player-manager Jimmy Collins was replaced as manager by outfielder Chick Stahl, who failed to improve the team as manager and then killed himself the following spring. The team went through four more managers in 1907 but kept playing badly. While the pitching improved to slightly above average (bolstered by Cy Young's 1.99 ERA at age 40), the hitters remained awful, batting .234 as a team (league average was .247) and scoring the fewest runs in the league. In December 1907 it was decided that a name change might help the club's increasingly chaotic image. From then on, the team would be called the Boston Red Sox, a name that dated back to the original Boston Red Stockings, who eventually became the Boston Braves (and who later moved to Milwaukee and then to Atlanta).

The Red Sox returned to near-mediocrity in 1908

Key Players, 1901–1908
Jimmy Collins, 3b-mgr
Lou Criger, c
Big Bill Dineen, p
Patsy Dougherty, of
Buck Freeman, 1b-of
Long Tom Hughes, p
Chick Stahl, of-mgr
Jesse Tannehill, p
Cy Young, p

with improved hitting and a miraculous season from Cy Young (21–11 with a 1.26 ERA at age 41). Young had the best earned run average of his career, although not his best season in the increasingly pitching-dominated game. (The league *average* was 2.39, which would have led the league in 2004, ahead of Johan Santana's AL-leading 2.61.) This would be Young's last 20-win season, and also his last year with the Red Sox. He was traded to Cleveland after the season ended for two mediocre pitchers and $12,500.

2. The Road to Fenway Park: 1909–1913

The Red Sox were firmly committed to a youth movement, and it showed immediate positive results. Boston won 88 games in 1909, and began building the core that would make the Red Sox first a good team and then a great team for the next decade. Like many Boston teams since, the rebuilt Red Sox team was built around a fine outfield and good hitting, with an average pitching staff (as the pitching staff improved, the Red Sox would go from contenders to champions). The Sox would lead the league in home runs for each of the next four years, with dead ball era *totals* of between 20 and 43 homers for the team (102 players hit at least 20 homers by themselves in 2000, and 9 of them hit 43 or more). By 1910 the Red Sox outfield contained future Hall of Famer Tris Speaker in center, rifle-armed Harry Hooper (who also made the Hall of Fame) in right, and cult favorite Duffy Lewis in left. All were good hitters and excellent defensively, with Speaker one of the all-time greats at his position. Pitcher Smoky Joe Wood also joined the starting rotation, although he showed few hints of the extraordinary Red Sox star he would become (for an all-too-brief period).

The 1911 Red Sox fell to 78–75 after first baseman Jake Stahl (not related to the late Chick Stahl) left the team to pursue a banking career. Stahl had led the league in home runs in 1910, and while the Red Sox still led the league in homers without him, his offense was missed on a team that had several other hitting stars but little depth. There were some good signs for the future, however; all three of the Red Sox star outfielders hit over .300, and Smoky Joe Wood emerged as a front-of-the-rotation starter, winning 23 games at age 21. More importantly, though, the team began construction of a marvelous new ballpark just off Kenmore Square in Boston.

The Red Sox moved into newly completed Fenway Park in 1912, with immediate and extraordinary results. With Jake Stahl lured back as player/manager and extraordinary seasons by Tris Speaker and Smoky Joe Wood, the Red Sox won a then-record 105 games. Speaker hit .383 (league average was .265) with a league-leading 53 doubles, 12 triples, 10 home runs (more than a third of the teams's league-leading total), 52 stolen bases, 82 walks, 136 runs, and 98 RBI, and was named the league's most valuable player. Wood went 34–5 with 10 shutouts and a 1.91 earned run average, leading a

Key Players, 1909–1913

Hugh Bedient, p
Bill Carrigan, c-mgr
Eddie Cicotte, p
Ray Collins, p
Harry Hooper, of
Dutch Leonard, p
Duffy Lewis, of
Buck O'Brien, p
Tris Speaker, of
Jake Stahl, 1b-mgr
Smoky Joe Wood, p

pitching staff with two other 20-game winners. The Red Sox met the New York Giants in the World Series, the same team that had refused to play them in 1904 (although no Sox players remained from the 1904 team). The seven-game series (reduced from the best-of-nine series the Sox had played in 1903) came down to the tenth inning of the seventh game. Boston fell behind in the top of the tenth, but scored twice in the bottom of the inning to win the World Series, helped by two Giants fielding misplays, "the $30,000 muff" by outfielder Fred Snodgrass, and a foul ball that went uncaught by first baseman Fred Merkle—already famous for his 1908 baserunning error, immortalized as "Merkle's boner," that cost the Giants a pennant.

The Red Sox followed their world championship with a season of chaos. With Smoky Joe Wood reduced to a part-time pitcher (by a broken hand and the previous season's overwork) and Jake Stahl retiring as a player at age 33, the team fell back to earth, finishing 79–71. The outfield continued to play well (Speaker hit .365), but without Wood as an anchor, the pitching staff was just average. The team hit only 17 home runs, although they led the league in triples and were close to the league lead in doubles. Stahl was fired as manager halfway through the season and replaced by catcher Bill Carrigan, who would soon lead the team to glory. But in a disturbing sign of the future, the team's ownership was in flux. Jimmy McAleer and Bob McRoy had purchased 50 percent of the club from General Taylor prior to 1912 (Jake Stahl also had a small share of the team), but sold the club to hotelier Joe Lannin after the 1913 season. (Lannin would also buy Buffalo of the Federal League and Providence of the International League.) Further, and disastrous, ownership changes would follow in the next decade— but before those changes would come some of the team's greatest moments.

3. The Coming of Babe Ruth: 1914–1919

The second half of the 1910s marked some of the greatest and some of the most tragic moments in Red Sox history. The team spent years as a powerhouse, built around great pitching staffs and decent (but not great) hitting. But the period would also lay the groundwork for the franchise's lowest moments—when Boston would function as the farm club out of which a great New York Yankees dynasty was built. And when the great team was sold off, the Red Sox would experience a decade and a half of humiliatingly bad teams.

The 1914 Red Sox bounced back from the 1913 fiasco, winning 91 games in Bill Carrigan's first season as manager and finishing second in the American League. (The team was overshadowed that summer by the National League Boston Braves' dramatic pennant chase.) The Sox were clearly built around pitching; although the team hit a lot of doubles and triples the offense was only average, carried by Tris Speaker. The major addition to the team's offense was shortstop Everett Scott, a fine fielder who helped steady the infield for the next eight years—but a terrible hitter. The pitching, on the other hand, was dramatically reinforced in 1914. Holdovers Dutch Leonard and Ray Collins were joined by new starting pitchers Rube Foster and Ernie Shore, more than making up for a fadeout by Hugh Bedient and Smoky Joe Wood's part-time status. Most importantly, a young lefthanded pitcher bought from the cash-strapped Baltimore Orioles (then a minor league team) joined the Red Sox as well—Babe Ruth. Ruth only played briefly with the Red Sox in his first season; with the Sox pitching already strong, owner Joe Lannin instead sent Ruth to Providence, to help the Providence Grays minor league team that Lannin also owned win the International League pennant.

Ruth moved into the rotation the next year and won 18 games, one of five Sox pitchers to win at least 15 games (including Smoky Joe Wood's last hurrah—he went 15–5 with a league-leading 1.49 ERA despite appearing in only 25 games, 16 of them starts). Ruth also led the team with four home runs in only 92 at bats. The rest of the team's hitters combined for 10 home runs, with Tris Speaker, Duffy Lewis, and first baseman Dick Hoblitzel the only decent offensive players. More offense wasn't really needed given the Boston pitching staff, however. The team won 101 games to edge a Detroit Tigers team that won 100 but failed to make the playoffs.

The World Series against the Philadelphia Phillies was one-sided. Philadelphia ace Grover Cleveland Alexander beat the Sox in Game 1, but the Phillies lost the next four games and the series. Strangely, the Red Sox had no real home games in the series; games in Boston were played on the Braves' home field, which had a larger seating capacity than Fenway Park (which has since been expanded). Seating capacity played another role in the series. The Phillies added temporary bleachers in the outfield to fit in more spectators, but lost the deciding game when Sox outfielder Harry Hooper—who had hit only two homers during the regular season—hit a pair of fly balls that carried into the extra seats for home runs.

In 1916 the Red Sox picked up right where they had left off the previous season. The team won nine fewer games, but that was enough to win in a well-balanced American League in which seven of eight teams won at least 76 games. The skew between hitting and pitching grew even more extreme; Boston's only hitting star, future Hall of Famer Tris Speaker, was traded to Cleveland after he refused to take a pay cut from owner Joe Lannin, who complained that Speaker's average had fallen to "only" .322 (Speaker was traded for yet another pitcher, future star Sad Sam Jones). The pitchers continued to excel despite the lack of offense. Babe Ruth won 23 games and led the league with a 1.76 earned run average (Ruth also tied for the team lead with three home runs). Four other pitchers won at least 14 games, with the departed Smoky Joe Wood replaced in the rotation by Carl Mays, a capable pitcher who is now remembered mostly for accidentally killing a batter with a pitch in 1920, after he was no longer with Boston. The Red Sox were helped by excellent defense as well. They committed by far the fewest errors in the league at a time when errors were rampant. The 1916 Red Sox were the first American League team ever to commit fewer than 200 errors in a season (they made 183), and they would lead the league in this category for the next six years (at which point the team had been stripped of most of its talent). Again the Red Sox won the World Series in five games, this time against the Brooklyn Dodgers.

A flurry of changes began with the end of the 1916 season. With the team coming off back-to-back World Series victories and its value at its peak, Joe

Lannin decided to sell the Red Sox. At the same time, player/manager Bill Carrigan—who was independently wealthy and involved with baseball for the fun of it—also decided to leave. The new owner was underfinanced theatrical producer Harry Frazee. While Frazee would be popular and successful at first, a series of cash shortages in his business empire would soon force him to slowly sell off the team's best players in order to pay his debts (including the notes he owed to Lannin) and keep his businesses afloat.

But the disasters to come were not yet apparent in 1917. Frazee replaced Carrigan as manager with second baseman Jack Barry. The team played about as well as it had the year before, with the hitting still mediocre and the pitching and defense superb. Babe Ruth won 24 games and Carl Mays won 22 to lead the pitching staff. The team won 90 games, one less than in 1916, but the Red Sox found themselves in a distant second place behind a Chicago White Sox team that won 100.

The 1918 season would unexpectedly turn out to be the last hurrah for the Red Sox dynasty, which was soon to be disassembled. Although the Red Sox would finish the season as winners of three of the previous four World Series, they would not have another winning season until 1935. Frazee brought in a new manager for the 1918 season (Jack Barry had enlisted in the Navy), former International League president Ed Barrow, who would later become general manager of the Yankees, joining most of the Boston stars who would be sold to New York.

The season was shortened by a month because of World War I, and stars Duffy Lewis and Dutch Leonard left to enter the military. Babe Ruth, who had recently married, stayed in Boston. Frazee found reinforcements by buying players from the financially troubled Philadelphia Athletics, including first baseman Stuffy McInnis and pitcher Bullet Joe Bush. (Frazee's own financial troubles had not yet become severe.) Manager Barrow was still faced with a shortage of outfielders, however, and a team with almost no offensive punch. He decided to make Babe Ruth, his best pitcher but also the best hitter on the team, his left fielder. Given more playing time, Ruth led the league in home runs (with 11; the rest of the team combined for only four) and hit .300, the only Boston player to do so. He also went 13–7 with a 2.22 earned run average as a part-time pitcher. The strategy led to a World Series victory against the Chicago Cubs, with Ruth pitching a shutout in Game 1 and winning the fourth game of the series as well—the last time he would pitch in a World Series.

The trouble began in 1919. Ruth got into a contract squabble with Frazee. By now Ruth was clearly the team's best player, and he asked to be paid a comparable salary—$10,000, a lot of money but less than what some other top players were making, and less than Tris Speaker had been paid. Frazee refused,

Key Players, 1914–1919
Ed Barrow, mgr
Bill Carrigan, c-mgr
Ray Collins, p
Rube Foster, p
Harry Frazee, owner
Harry Hooper, of
Sad Sam Jones, p
Joe Lannin, owner
Dutch Leonard, p
Duffy Lewis, of
Carl Mays, p
Stuffy McInnis, 1b
Babe Ruth, p-of
Everett Scott, ss
Ernie Shore, p
Tris Speaker, of
Smoky Joe Wood, p

telling Ruth, "I wouldn't pay one of my best actors that much." Eventually Ruth settled for $9,000.

The team never gelled in 1919. Although the players who had been in the military returned, everybody else's stars returned as well. Babe Ruth had an extraordinary season as a full-time outfielder and part-time pitcher, hitting .305 with 101 walks and a then-record 29 home runs, helping usher the dead ball era to a close. The previous American League record had been 16, while the major league record of 27 dated back to the 1880s. No one else in the major leagues hit more than 12 home runs. The rest of the Red Sox team hit only four home runs combined. Although the offense was improved with the return of Harry Hooper and good seasons from Stuffy McInnis and the previously punchless Everett Scott, and the defense remained excellent (leading the league in fewest errors committed and most double plays turned), the pitching staff faded from excellent to average. With Dutch Leonard traded to Detroit, Sad Sam Jones having an off year, and Babe Ruth in left field most of the time (he did go 9–5 in 15 starts), the pitching depth that had characterized Red Sox teams was no longer there. The Red Sox faded to 66–71 as a team, sixth place in the American League. Worst of all, when pitching star Carl Mays left the team under mysterious circumstances at midseason, Frazee's response was to sell his pitcher to the New York Yankees for $40,000. Few people realized at the time that Mays would be just the first of many to go.

4. The Selling of Babe Ruth and the Dark Ages: 1920–1932

The bombshell exploded in January 1920. Owner Harry Frazee, his financial situation shaky and his notes to Lannin coming due, sold his best player, Babe Ruth, to the New York Yankees. In return, Frazee got $125,000 and a $350,000 loan—secured by a mortgage on the Fenway Park bleachers. Worse was yet to come. Over the next three years, Frazee would sell the rest of his team's talent to the well-heeled Yankees in deal after deal. The remarkable pitching depth—Bullet Joe Bush, Waite Hoyt, Herb Pennock, George Pipgras, and others—all went to the Yankees. So did catcher Wally Schang, shortstop Everett Scott, third baseman Joe Dugan, outfielder Elmer Smith, and other useful players. The Red Sox dropped to last place in the standings; by 1923, the Sox were last in the league in hitting, fielding, and earned run average, and next to last in home runs. That year, the New York Yankees won their first World Series—with 11 former Boston players on their roster.

There is a common misperception that Harry Frazee sold Babe Ruth to the Yankees to finance *No No Nanette*, Frazee's big Broadway hit. However, the connection between the money Frazee got for the Babe and *No No Nanette* isn't that direct. Frazee sold

Key Players, 1920–1932
Dale Alexander, 1b
George Burns, 1b
Joe Dugan, 3b
Howard Ehmke, p
Harry Frazee, owner
Waite Hoyt, p
Sad Sam Jones, p
Stuffy McInnis, 1b
Ed Morris, p
Buddy Myer, ss-3b
Herb Pennock, p
Bob Quinn, owner
Red Ruffing, p
Earl Webb, of

the Babe in January 1920 in order to pay off debts which threatened to end his theater production business. The selling of the Babe was only one of many trades in which Frazee got cash for players, all in the hope of saving his theater business. Frazee eventually sold the Sox in 1923, after having gutted the club to stay in business on Broadway. *No No Nanette* came to the boards in 1925 and was the big hit Frazee had been longing for. So to say that Frazee sold the Babe in order to finance *No No Nanette* isn't really accurate, but without the sale of the Babe, Frazee might not have been around to finance *Nanette* a few years down the road.

Between 1922 and 1932, the depleted team finished last 9 times in 11 seasons and won barely a third of its games. Attendance fell from over 415,000 in 1919 to less than half that in 1932. By the time he sold the team to a group of investors headed by Bob Quinn in 1923, Frazee had gone from the saviour of the franchise to one of the most reviled men in Boston. (A few years later, Frazee supposedly showed up for a game at Fenway Park. Getting out of the cab, Frazee announced to his female companion at the time that "he had once owned this team." The cabbie asked "Are you Harry Frazee?" When Frazee said yes the cabbie knocked him to the ground.)

It would take 11 years, another new owner, and a succession of managers before the Red Sox would again win as many as half their games in a season. Although the talent drain stopped, the Sox did not have much left to build with; too many of their regulars were borderline major league players. And while Quinn didn't sell players off the way Frazee did, he was nearly as underfinanced, and couldn't spend the money to bring in top-tier players; he ran the team on a tight budget. Boston finished last in the league in both batting average and earned run average in 1923, 1925, and 1926. In fact, it wasn't until 1931 that the Red Sox again finished better than last place in hitting. After manager Lee Fohl had back-to-back 100-loss seasons, Quinn managed to lure manager Bill Carrigan—who had won back-to-back World Series a decade before—out of retirement. The team improved only marginally, losing 103, 96, and 96 games before Carrigan left. His replacement, ex-Sox shortstop Heinie Wagner, lost 102 games in 1930.

I was delivered into the hands of the Boston Red Sox. Or, to be exact, an ex-second-baseman for the Boston Red Sox, Andy Spognardi, who signed my birth certificate as the attending physician. The date was April 15, 1946, and the location was Faulkner Hospital in Jamaica Plain; my parents lived in Roslindale, a neighborhood of Boston. I became a Red Sox fan for life.

Andy Spognardi was captain of the Boston College baseball team in 1932. He was accepted into Tufts Medical School before signing with the Red Sox. He played 17 games at second base for the Red Sox starting on September 2, 1932, batting .294. The next year, he opted to attend medical school rather than return to the Red Sox because, as a story in the January 10, 1933 *Boston Post* put it, "A player grows less valuable over the years, while a doctor improves with age." He graduated from Tufts Medical School in 1936 and opened a general practice in Roslindale in 1939. While a student at Tufts, he played minor league baseball with Jersey City and Syracuse in the International League. Dr. Spognardi delivered hundreds of babies before his retirement in 1988. He died at the age of 91 on January 1, 2000.

—Gary N. Powell

The team hit rock bottom two managers later. The 1932 Red Sox lost 111 games and won only 43, finishing 64 games behind the New York Yankees. The Sox were again last in the league in batting (the next-worst team was 15 points better) and earned run average. Attendance fell to fewer than 200,000 fans—about 2,500 a game. Off the field, everything seemed to go wrong as well. Ed Morris, one of the team's better pitchers, was stabbed to death by a jealous husband. The team traded for Dale Alexander, who hit .372 for the Red Sox to win the batting title over future Sox star Jimmie Foxx—only to see Alexander's career ended when a mistreated leg injury turned gangrenous and the leg was almost lost.

The end of the losing was in sight, however. Quinn finally sold the team to a wealthy young lumber industrialist by the name of Tom Yawkey. Yawkey, who had inherited millions while still in his early twenties, would be the well-financed owner the Red Sox had lacked for years. It would be 60 years before a Red Sox team finished last again.

5. Enter Tom Yawkey: 1933–1937

Tom Yawkey had many character flaws, but unwillingness to spend money was not one of them. In his long tenure, the team would experience some of its brightest and most memorable moments—but it would never win the world championship he so desperately craved. The team's failure to win everything would be partly due to bad luck and partly to bad choices or management decisions. But perhaps the biggest factor was Yawkey's inability or unwillingness to overcome the racism that was deeply entrenched in Boston baseball (and, some would say, in Yawkey himself). Arguably Dan Duquette's greatest achievement as the Sox general manager over the last half-decade has been ridding the team of the lingering stigma of racism—the perception that black and Latino players were less welcome, less well treated, and more quickly dumped or traded away at the slightest sign of decline (while the team showed more loyalty and patience with its white stars).

But in 1933, integration of baseball was more than a decade—and another World War—away. Yawkey had bought a talent-thin, uninspired team at the bottom of a long decline. He was determined to reverse the Red Sox fortunes quickly, regardless of the cost. He immediately installed Eddie Collins (a former player who would eventually be selected to the Hall of Fame) as general manager, and gave Collins the authority to get the players he needed by whatever means necessary.

In a reversal of the Frazee era, Collins went about *buying* players instead of selling them. He had to buy players if he wanted to improve the team—the Red Sox didn't have players other teams wanted to trade for, and it would take a few years to replenish the team's talent base. He bought future Hall of Fame catcher Rick Ferrell from St. Louis in 1933, and his brother (and arguably the better player), pitcher Wes

Key Players, 1933–1937

Max Bishop, 2b-1b
Ben Chapman, of
Doc Cramer, of
Joe Cronin, ss-manager
Rick Ferrell, c
Wes Ferrell, p
Jimmie Foxx, 1b
Lefty Grove, p
Pinky Higgins, 3b
Roy Johnson, of
Bill Werber, 3b

Ferrell the next year. Infielder Billy Werber, bought from the hated Yankees, would lead the league in stolen bases twice for the Red Sox. He also obtained Lefty Grove and others from the cash-poor Philadelphia A's in 1934. Yawkey spent a fortune (in the height of the Depression) rebuilding the dilapidated Fenway Park, including the giant wall in left field that became known as the Green Monster. More improvements were to come. Yawkey wanted to win and he wanted to win in a hurry.

The Red Sox climbed out of last place in 1933. The next year they reached mediocrity. By 1938 they would be good.

In 1935 the Sox added another key player. Boston acquired shortstop Joe Cronin from the Washington Senators, who were sinking at the same time the Red Sox were rising. Cronin was made player-manager, replacing Bucky Harris as manager despite the team's first .500 season since 1918 in Harris's one season with the team. By 1935, the team had a mediocre lineup (a big improvement), but very little power or depth. They finished third in the league in pitching, but this was a little misleading. Boston had two terrific front-line pitchers in Wes Ferrell (who led the league with 25 wins) and Lefty Grove (who led the league in ERA), but not much else on the pitching staff. The next year Yawkey added two more key players from the Philadelphia A's, superstar first baseman Jimmie Foxx and center fielder Doc Cramer. Grove and Ferrell continued to pitch brilliantly, but the team still didn't gel, finishing in sixth place amid a rash of injuries and arguments. Wes Ferrell led a clubhouse faction that wanted Joe Cronin fired. In a game against the Yankees in August 1936, Ferrell stormed off the mound in the middle of a New York rally, making Cronin furious.

After the season both Ferrell brothers were traded to Washington for Ben Chapman (who would have two great years for the Sox) and Bobo Newsom, a serviceable pitcher, in what sportswriters dubbed "The Harmony Deal," because it was meant to reassert Cronin's power and ensure peace in the clubhouse. Billy Werber was sent to Philadelphia for Pinky Higgins, in a trade of third basemen. Boston finished eight games over .500 in 1937 (although still in fifth place, far behind the Yankees). By this time, the farm system was starting to produce talented players again, having recovered from the overfishing and underfinancing of the Frazee and Quinn years. The Red Sox would never turn into the dynasty that Yawkey hoped for, but they would be good—sometimes great—for most of the next 15 years, with the exception of the World War II years.

6. Ted Williams and the Dynasty that Never Happened: 1938–1942

For the first time in 20 years, the Red Sox had a good team. They weren't good enough to beat the Yankees yet—or even seriously threaten them—but the 1938 Red Sox had good hitting, decent pitching, and finished in second place in the American League with 88 wins. Six of the team's regulars hit over .300 as Boston led the league in hitting with a .299 *team* batting average. Jimmie Foxx had perhaps the greatest season of his great career—hitting .349 with 50 home runs and an astonishing 175 runs batted in, leading the league in batting and RBI and setting club records for home runs and RBI that still stand more than 60 years later. The Red Sox weren't serious contenders yet—the Yankees hit almost twice as many home runs and after the aging Lefty Grove the Red Sox pitchers were average at best—but there were good signs of things to come.

While the core of the team was still made up of players Yawkey and general manager Eddie Collins had bought or traded for, home-grown talent was starting to arrive. The new starting second baseman in 1938 was 20-year-old Bobby Doerr, who would anchor the position for the Red Sox for the next 14 years. And in 1939 The Kid would arrive.

Boston won 89 games in 1939 with 20-year-old Ted Williams replacing Ben Chapman in right field (Williams would move to left field after his rookie year). Again the team's hitting was good and its pitching was indifferent (Lefty Grove won the ERA title for the second year in a row but was only a half-time starter because of his age, and no one else on the staff could pick up the slack). Williams hit .327 with 31 homers and 107 walks, while leading the league in doubles and RBI (a rookie-record 145). Jimmie Foxx was even better, hitting .360 with a league-leading 35 home runs. Bobby Doerr, Joe Cronin, and Doc Cramer also hit better than .300, as did key reserve Lou Finney. It wasn't enough. The Yankees won 106 games.

In 1940 the Sox added yet another kid—Joe DiMaggio's 23-year-old younger brother Dom, who hit .301 in right field. (DiMaggio would move to center field the following year, replacing Doc Cramer.) Eight Sox regulars hit .285 or better, topped by Williams at .344. Five players hit more than 20 home runs, led by Foxx's 36. (Foxx was only 31, but alcoholism was starting to erode his talent and he would have only one more good year.) The team narrowly missed the league lead in hitting, and did lead the league in slugging. The Sox were entertaining, but they still couldn't win. In a year when the Yankees slumped to 88 wins, the Red Sox slumped even further, pulled down to 82–72 by their lack of pitching as the 40-year-old Lefty Grove could no longer carry the staff. Despite an extraordinarily gifted offensive team, no pitcher managed to win more than 12 games, and the Red Sox finished fourth.

The story would repeat itself in 1941, with the pitching-shy Sox finishing a distant second to the Yankees. The Sox wasted one of the greatest offensive seasons in history. In 1941 Ted Williams hit .406 (the last major league player to hit .400) and led the league in home runs, runs, and walks. He had an unprecedented .553 on base percentage—meaning he was on base in well over half his plate appearances. He drove in 120 runs and anchored a team that led the league in batting average, slugging, and runs scored. Just like the team as a whole, Williams ended up in second place, as Joe DiMaggio rode a 56-game hitting streak and the adulation of the press to the Most Valuable Player award. Williams, one of the greatest offensive players in history, was never able to master the media in the way he mastered hitting. Like many

Key Players, 1938–1942

Ben Chapman, of
Doc Cramer, of
Joe Cronin, ss-manager
Dom DiMaggio, of
Bobby Doerr, 2b
Lou Finney, of-1b
Jimmie Foxx, 1b
Lefty Grove, p
Tex Hughson, p
Johnny Pesky, ss
Jim Tabor, 3b
Ted Williams, of

Red Sox stars before and since, Williams was bitterly criticized by the media during his career, and only became an icon after his retirement.

Yet another second-place finish followed in 1942, but this time better things seemed to be on the horizon. The Red Sox won 93 games, their highest total since 1918. They led the league in hitting once again, and the pitching was dramatically improved—third in the league in ERA. The team's aging stars were being replaced by young talent as well. Joe Cronin continued to manage but only played occasionally. Jimmie Foxx was shipped off to the Chicago Cubs when his alcoholism finally got the best of him. Young stars Williams, Doerr, and DiMaggio were joined by Johnny Pesky, a 22-year-old shortstop who hit .331 and led the league with 205 hits. Williams won the Triple Crown—leading the league in batting average, home runs, and RBI (as well as walks and runs scored) but again finished second to a popular Yankees player (this time Joe Gordon) in the MVP balloting. Even better, the team had a young pitcher who seemed poised to replace Lefty Grove. Twenty-six-year-old Tex Hughson won 22 games in 281 innings pitched to lead the league in both categories.

But what looked like a dynasty in the making was about to be derailed. By the beginning of the next season, half the team would be at war.

7. The War Years: 1943–1945

Boston's young stars were among the first to enlist in the military for World War II. Ted Williams, Johnny Pesky, and Dom DiMaggio were all gone by the beginning of the 1943 season, as was any hope of contention. While Williams was flying planes for the Marines, the Red Sox were sinking to 68–84, a distant seventh place behind the Yankees. The next year the team was in pennant contention in September when Bobby Doerr, Tex Hughson, and catcher Hal Wagner (who was hitting .332) were all drafted into the military within a three-week period. The team went on a 10-game losing streak and finished well out of the race.

With most of the team's players in the armed services, the Red Sox turned to fill-ins like outfielder Catfish Metkovich, shortstop Skeeter Newsome, and pitcher Mike Ryba—players whose roles would be drastically curtailed (or whose careers would end) as soon as the war was over. Thirty-eight-year-old manager Joe Cronin—who hadn't played regularly in four years—inserted himself into the lineup in 1945 when the draft left the team without a third baseman. Three games later Cronin broke his leg, ending his playing career.

One bright spot did come out of the dismal 1945 season. The Red Sox, with little else going for them, came up with a ringer on the pitching staff. Boo Ferriss's asthma would limit his pitching at times—but it also earned him an early discharge from the military. Joe Cronin made the 23-year old righthander his ace. Ferriss started 31 games (10 more than any other Sox pitcher) and won 21 of them. He also made four relief appearances, saving two more wins. He threw 26 complete games—over 264 innings in all, a lot of strain on a young pitcher's arm.

Key Players, 1943–1945
Joe Cronin, manager
Bobby Doerr, 2b
Boo Ferriss, p
Tex Hughson, p
Hal Wagner, c

8. The Return to Glory: 1946–1950

The young Red Sox stars had lost three years of their careers to the war, but they returned as a strong, focused team that finally had the pitching to go with their extraordinary offense. The next four years would be some of the most exhilarating—and the most heart-wrenching—in Red Sox history. Three times in four years the Red Sox would reach the brink of glory, only to fall just short of their goal.

The 1946 team led the league in hitting and played terrific defense. The pitching was solid, with a four-man rotation of Tex Hughson (20–11), Boo Ferriss (25–6), Mickey Harris (17–9), and Joe Dobson (13–7). The Sox weren't deep, but their front line players were terrific: Ted Williams, Johnny Pesky, Bobby Doerr, Dom DiMaggio, and aging star Rudy York, imported from Detroit to play first base. Remarkably, the stars all stayed healthy and in the lineup all year (in a typical season about 70% of players are injured at some point), and Boston dominated the league. The Red Sox finished 104–50, 12 games ahead of their nearest competitor. The Yankees were a distant third, 17 games back.

In the World Series the Red Sox faced a St. Louis Cardinals club with deep pitching and two of the National League's most dangerous hitters, Stan Musial and Enos Slaughter. The series lead swung back and forth repeatedly, with the two teams proving extremely well matched. Boston won the first game, rallying in the ninth inning and winning on a York home run in the tenth. St. Louis came back to shut out Boston in Game 2, led by pitcher Harry Brecheen, who'd been mediocre (15–15) in the regular season, but would be dominant in this series. Boo Ferriss pitched a shutout of his own in Game 3, the fiftieth shutout in World Series history, and the teams continued to trade games. After 6 games, the series was tied, with Brecheen having won both his games for St. Louis.

The deciding Game 7 would hinge on a famous misplay that may not have been a misplay at all. After Boston had tied the game with two runs in the top of the eighth inning, St. Louis had Enos Slaughter on first base when Harry Walker dropped a bloop hit into center field. Slaughter was running from the moment the ball was hit, and never slowed down at third base. Leon Culberson, playing center field for the injured Dom DiMaggio, threw the ball weakly to shortstop Johnny Pesky who checked on the runner coming from first before throwing home. It's unlikely a quicker relay would have caught Slaughter, but all most fans remember is the myth that grew up in the media afterward: that Pesky held the ball. St. Louis had taken the lead. In the ninth inning Boston was shut down yet again by Harry Brecheen, who won his third game of the series while pitching in relief.

Things did not go as smoothly the next year. The Red Sox lack of depth, which hadn't been a problem in 1946, now haunted them. When Rudy York began to show his age and Dom DiMaggio missed time due to injury, there was no one to fill the gap. Williams and Pesky were both spectacular again, but in 1947 DiMaggio and Doerr were merely good, which negated the strong season of new catcher Birdie Tebbetts, who would solidify a position that had been in flux since Rick Ferrell was traded. The pitching was about average, but here, too, there were troubling signs. In an era when 20-game winners were much more common than today, no Red Sox pitcher won more than Joe Dobson's 18 (although 5 pitchers won at least 11 games). Boo Ferriss and Tex Hughson were both starting to show the results of overwork; they each won only 12 games—and they would combine for only 14 more wins in a Red Sox uniform. The Sox limped to the finish line in third place, 14 games behind the once-again-victorious Yankees.

Owner Tom Yawkey made changes after the disappointment of 1947. Joe Cronin—a fixture as manager since 1935—was moved into the front office, and Joe McCarthy replaced him as field boss. Reinforcements were brought in from the St. Louis Browns in the form of pitchers Ellis Kinder and Jack Kramer, and shortstop Vern Stephens, in return for 10 players and a huge amount of Yawkey's ready cash. Johnny Pesky moved to third, and rookie Billy Goodman—who'd played a few games in the outfield the previous year—took over at first base.

Although the team was not dramatically better on paper, the 1948 Red Sox played very well. Pesky's move to third base paid off, filling in one of the gaping holes in the lineup (right field was the other), and Stephens hit 29 home runs out of the shortstop position. Billy Goodman hit .310 at first. The bench played respectably. The team didn't lead the league in batting average or home runs, but *everyone* in the lineup was excellent at drawing walks, so there were constantly runners on base. Four players scored at least 114 runs, as Boston led the league in runs scored by a wide margin. The pitching was a little better than the year before, just a little better than league average. Ellis Kinder, Jack Kramer, and Mel Parnell filled the rotation behind Joe Dobson, taking the place of Tex Hughson and Boo Ferriss, neither of whom was effective. Earl Johnson won 10 games in relief.

The pennant race came down to the final days of the season, with both Boston and the Yankees close behind the surprising and powerful Cleveland Indians (who *did* lead the league in both batting average and pitching). Boston knocked the Yankees out by winning two straight, while the Indians lost two of their last three, leaving Boston and Cleveland tied with 96 wins on the last game of the season.

When two teams tie for the league lead there is a one-game playoff, with the winner moving on and the loser going home for the winter. Cleveland started rookie knuckleballer Gene Bearden, who had gone 19–7 and led the league in ERA. Most fans expected Boston manager Joe McCarthy to start young left-hander Mel Parnell, who had been the team's best pitcher down the stretch. But with four dependable starting pitchers to choose from, McCarthy selected none; he chose journeyman Denny Galehouse, pitching on fumes at the end of his career. Galehouse was shelled and the Indians went on to an 8–3 victory—and to the World Series.

The Red Sox began the 1949 season determined to make up for the near-miss of 1948. The lineup remained largely the same, except for an upgrade in right field, where incumbent Stan Spence was sent to St. Louis (along with more of Yawkey's cash) for Al Zarilla. If the offense had been very good in 1948, it was terrific in 1949. Despite the weak bench, the Red Sox led the league in batting average, runs scored, and home runs, all by a wide margin. Ted Williams and Vern Stephens tied for the league lead in RBI with 159, while Williams led the league in home runs. Four players walked at least 96 times. Four starters hit over .300, and two others hit .290 or better. The pitching was better than it had been—decent, not great—but this year it was led by two developing stars. Mel Parnell led the league with 25 wins (setting a record for a Red Sox lefty), a 2.77 ERA, and 27 complete games; Ellis Kinder was right behind with 23 wins, including 13 in a row going into the season's final weekend.

The Red Sox got off to a slow start, falling 12 games behind the Yankees. But as the pitching of Parnell, Kinder, and Joe Dobson clicked and the offense heated up, the Sox began to close the ground. They overtook the Yankees a week before the season's end, and went into the last two games of the season ahead by one game at 96–56, needing only a single victory to go to the World Series. The Yankees beat Parnell in the first game. In the second game, the Yankees took a 1–0 lead into the eighth against Kinder, who had been unbeatable for weeks. Desperate for runs, McCarthy pinch hit for Kinder (who was not a good-hitting pitcher), but the gamble failed. McCarthy, determined not to repeat his previous mistake of losing with someone who wasn't his best player, brought Parnell—the previous night's starter—in as a relief pitcher. But the exhausted Parnell had nothing left. Tex Hughson, brought in to try and rescue a failing situation, fared little better. The Red Sox lost 5–3. Once again 96 wins left them one game short of the pennant.

In 1950, the Red Sox again came close, despite an elbow injury to Ted Williams that would cost him half a season, and an early season injury to Billy Goodman. Instead of relying on the team's weak bench, minor leaguer Walt Dropo was called up to fill in for Goodman. Dropo responded by hitting .322 with 34 homers and a league-leading 144 RBI, winning Rookie of the Year in what, alas, would turn out to be a fluke season. When Goodman came back from his injury the Red Sox made him a utility player, filling in for injured or resting players at all four infield position as well as the outfield. Goodman thrived in his new position, hitting .354 and scoring 91 runs in only 424 at bats. Amazingly, he was only sixth on the team in runs—five players scored more than 100 runs. The 1950 Red Sox were the last team to average .300 as a team, hitting .302 and leading the league in slugging and runs by wide margins. It wasn't quite enough to overcome the thinness of the team's pitching, however. Parnell, Kinder, and Dobson were all solid once again, but no one else on the staff pitched very well. As it turned out, average pitching and extraordinary hitting were enough to combine for 94 wins. Boston finished a close third behind better-balanced teams in New York and Detroit.

It wasn't apparent at the time, but the Red Sox had missed their window of opportunity. It would be 17 years before the team won as many as 90 games again. The game was changing profoundly, but Tom Yawkey and his Red Sox were slow to adjust to that change. In

Key Players, 1946–1950

Joe Cronin, manager
Dom DiMaggio, of
Joe Dobson, p
Bobby Doerr, 2b
Walt Dropo, 1b
Boo Ferriss, p
Denny Galehouse, p
Billy Goodman, of-1b-2b-3b-ss
Mickey Harris, p
Tex Hughson, p
Earl Johnson, p
Ellis Kinder, p
Jack Kramer, p
Joe McCarthy, manager
Mel Parnell, p
Johnny Pesky, ss-3b
Vern Stephens, ss
Birdie Tebbetts, c
Ted Williams, of
Rudy York, 1b

1947 the Dodgers broke the major league color line by playing Jackie Robinson. Later that year, Larry Doby broke the American League color barrier with the Cleveland Indians. The Sox turned down chances to sign Robinson and Willie Mays. In 2000, Red Sox trustee John Harrington would claim it was not racism on Yawkey's part, but reluctance among the Red Sox minor league teams in the South to play blacks that caused the Sox to wait so long to sign black players. Regardless of whether it was racism or just stubborn resistance to change, the Sox paid and would continue to pay for their unwillingness to draw on the newly available talent pool of black players—while other teams benefited. Twice after the color barrier was broken, the Red Sox fell one game short of the World Series—at least in part because of how thin the team's talent was behind its frontline starters. In 1950 the Red Sox had the best offense in the world—but as those hitters began to age, there would be no one of comparable talent to replace them—and this time, Yawkey's money would not be enough to overcome his failings.

9. The End of the Era: 1951–1960

The Red Sox slide started slowly. The team managed to win 87 games in 1951, finishing a respectable third, but they were nowhere near as good as the previous four years' teams had been. Walt Dropo's batting average fell nearly 100 points, and he dropped from 34 home runs to 11. The hole in right field opened up again, despite one torrid stretch by Clyde Vollmer, who hit more than half his 22 homers in a single month. Catcher Birdie Tebbetts was traded, and the Sox tried to replace him with seven different players, six of whom hit less than .203 (the seventh hit a still-woeful .229). The core hitters—Ted Williams, Dom DiMaggio, Vern Stephens, Johnny Pesky, Bobby Doerr, and Billy Goodman—were still very good, but some of them were starting to age. Boston still led the league in runs in 1951, but the margin was no longer very large. The pitching staff had two great players and a bunch of maybes. Mel Parnell had another fine year, but he was the only starter to win more than 12 games. Ellis Kinder, his arm no longer able to take the strain of starting regularly, was converted to relief where he pitched brilliantly, leading the league in appearances and saves (with 14) and winning another 11 games in relief.

The early signs in 1952 were not good. Ted Williams, the best Red Sox hitter since Babe Ruth, and possibly the best ever, was recalled to military duty. The Red Sox would lose two more years of his career, and be lucky to see Williams again at all—twice in his 39 combat missions over Korea Ted Williams would have to bring a badly damaged plane down intact (one of those times in flames). Bobby Doerr, the team's second-best hitter, was forced to retire because of back problems.

As he had in 1947, Yawkey was determined to make changes to keep the Red Sox on top, but this time the changes failed. Joe McCarthy had quit as manager in the middle of 1950. Steve O'Neill, the man who replaced him, was fired after 1951, despite the team's 149–97 record in his season and a half at the helm. His replacement was fading Cleveland star Lou Boudreau, who would serve as player-manager. Johnny Pesky and Walt Dropo were traded. The team turned out to be mediocre in every way—average hitting, an average pitching staff on which only Mel Parnell won as many as 12 games, and a 76–78, sixth place record.

The team seemed to recover a little in 1953. The hitting was just average, led by Billy Goodman—now at second base—and third baseman George Kell. Fan favorite Jimmy Piersall took over for Dom DiMaggio in center field. Mostly, the pitching improved dramatically, with Parnell and Kinder returning to brilliance, and a great season from lefthander Mickey McDermott, who liked to sing in nightclubs in his spare time. When Ted Williams returned at the very end of the season there were great hopes that the team could build on its 84-win finish, and maybe become a real contender the following year. As it happened, they were false hopes. The team wouldn't win more than 84 games again until the Impossible Dream season of 1967.

Those hopes evaporated when Ted Williams broke his collarbone in spring training and Mel Parnell broke his arm during the season. Williams would come back at full strength, but Parnell was never able to handle a full-time starter's load again. The Sox pitching was second-worst in the league, and while the hitting was pretty good—led by Williams, Piersall, newcomer Jackie Jensen, and promising rookie Harry Agganis—the Sox finished a dreadful 69–85, an astonishing 42 games behind the powerhouse Cleveland Indians.

The Sox followed with three turbulent but respectable years before sliding into mediocrity. Lou Boudreau was fired as manager and replaced by Pinky Higgins. Ted Williams announced his retirement (almost certainly a divorce strategy), only to be talked out of it a month later. First baseman Harry Agganis, a Massachusetts native and former BU star, died suddenly of a pulmonary embolism. Ellis Kinder and Mel Parnell retired. Billy Goodman was traded. The pitching continued to be mediocre. Through it all, the Red Sox had enough hitting to keep them at 82 to 84 wins a year, led by the outfield of Ted Williams, Jackie Jensen, and Jimmy Piersall. In 1957 the 38-year-old Ted Williams hit .388 to win his fifth batting title. He would win another one a year later—battling throughout the season with Red Sox rookie second baseman Pete Runnels—but the team would drop a notch further, to 79 wins. It would be nine years before another Red Sox team would win as many as half its games.

More turbulence followed in 1959 and 1960. Joe Cronin left the front office to become league president. The Red Sox finally fielded their first black player, utility infielder Pumpsie Green, twelve seasons after the color barrier had fallen elsewhere. Ted Williams was hurt most of the year. Pinky Higgins— who had sworn he would never have a black player on his team—was fired as manager, and replaced by Bill Jurges, who rallied a bad team to a strong second half. The next season Jurges was fired and replaced by Higgins again, who had apparently reconsidered his position somewhat. The team finished 65–89.

Key Players, 1951–1960

Harry Agganis, 1b
Mike Fornieles, p
Billy Goodman, of-1b-2b-3b-ss
Jackie Jensen, of
George Kell, 3b
Ellis Kinder, p
Mickey McDermott, p
Bill Monbouquette, p
Mel Parnell, p
Jimmy Piersall, of-ss
Pete Runnels, 2b
Frank Sullivan, p
Sammy White, c
Ted Williams, of

Amid the chaos on the field, another era was coming to a close. Ted Williams hit .316 with 29 home runs as a 40-year-old part-time player in 1960, an amazing finish to an amazing story. In his last at bat at Fenway Park that year (which he had announced would be the last at bat of his career), he homered into right field. The moment has become a baseball legend, but only 10,484 people, die-hard fans of a seventh-place team, saw it at the time.

The Jimmy Fund

In 1947 the Variety Club of Boston, a social and charitable club set up by show business people in the Boston area, selected a charity. They decided to help Dr. Sidney Farber establish the Children's Cancer Research Foundation, affiliated with Children's Hospital in Boston. That year Dr. Farber had developed a treatment to enable certain cancer-stricken children to go into remission via chemotherapy. In 1947 the Variety Club raised $47,000 for the project, and early in 1948 they teamed with the Boston Braves to orchestrate a mass market fund raiser.

On May 22, 1948, the radio show *Truth Or Consequences*, hosted by Ralph Edwards, talked to a patient named "Jimmy" in a hospital in Boston and asked him whether he liked baseball, and which team was his favorite. Then he asked the boy who his favorite player was. When Jimmy answered that it was Johnny Sain, Sain walked into the hospital room and greeted the boy. As Edwards asked about other Braves players, they entered, one by one. They brought autographed baseballs, T-shirts, and tickets to the Braves doubleheader the next day, and manager Billy Southworth promised that they'd win at least one of the games. (They ended up winning both.) After the phone conversation, Edwards addressed the national radio audience and explained that Jimmy had cancer, but didn't know it. He asked people to send whatever they could to help Jimmy. Dr. Farber was present at the show and talked to Edwards. When the host suggested that the "Variety Club of Boston's Children's Cancer Research Foundation" was a bit unwieldy, Farber suggested just calling it the "Jimmy Fund." The name stuck. To this day, there are few things in New England with a higher name recognition and awareness than the Jimmy Fund.

When the Braves left Boston following the 1952 season, Braves PR man Billy Sullivan (who later owned the New England Patriots) approached Red Sox owner Tom Yawkey at the league meeting about having the Red Sox take over for the Braves in supporting the Jimmy Fund. Yawkey was initially hesitant but finally agreed. On April 10, 1953, the Boston Red Sox officially announced that they would join the motion picture industry as co-sponsors of the Jimmy Fund. Over the years, the Red Sox have helped to raise millions of dollars to fight childhood cancers. Many Red Sox players have been particularly noteworthy in their efforts. Ted Williams, whose own brother died of leukemia, devoted many hours to the cause. Mike Andrews, the second baseman on the 1967 Impossible Dream team, has been the executive director of the Fund since 1978. John Valentin is known to have spent many hours at the institute, visiting with sick kids.

In 1976 the Children's Cancer Research Institute became the Sidney Farber Cancer Institute, in honor of its founder. In 1983, as a result of many years of support from the Charles A. Dana foundation, it was renamed again, as the Dana-Farber Cancer Institute. That name is now nearly as well known as the Jimmy Fund itself.

There have been Red Sox players who have needed the services of the institute. Bob Stanley's son Kyle fought cancer with the help of Dana-Farber. *Boston Globe* sports columnist Dan Shaughnessy, known for the gloominess and cynicism in his writing, is not a cynic with regards to the Dana-Farber Cancer Institute. His daughter Kate has fought leukemia with the help of the Jimmy Fund.

The Jimmy Fund has become almost as much of an institution in New England as the Red Sox themselves. The two are bound to be intertwined, as the Red Sox are a large part of the reason that the Jimmy Fund has been so successful at raising money for the fight against cancer. To contact the Jimmy Fund, call 1-800-52-JIMMY, write to The Jimmy Fund, 375 Longwood Avenue, Boston, MA 02215, or go online to www.jimmyfund.org/jimmy/contribute/index.shtml

10. The Seeds of Rebirth: 1961–1966

Ted Williams's familiar place in left field was taken over by a 21-year-old rookie from Long Island, converted second baseman Carl Yastrzemski. Yaz hit .266 (a little better than league average) with 11 home runs, an inauspicious start to what would be a great career. The Red Sox were still pretty bad. They moved Pete Runnels to first base—turning him from one of the best-hitting second basemen in the game to an average first baseman, given his lack of power. Jackie Jensen soon left baseball, unable to conquer his fear of flying at a time when teams no longer traveled exclusively by train. Frank Malzone was pretty good at third base (as well as a brilliant defensive player), but that was about it for hitting. The pitching wasn't very good either. Bill Monbouquette anchored the rotation, followed by a cast of mediocrities. Pitcher Don Schwall was Rookie of the Year in 1961, but his control was so poor that the quick disintegration of his career surprised no one.

The Red Sox added two talented pitchers in 1962, and an enigmatic first baseman in 1963. Neither improved the club's fortunes much, any more than Yaz's improvement as a hitter did. Dick Radatz was the best relief pitcher in the league, and redefined the way short relievers were used. Before Radatz, most relief pitchers—even the best of them—were broken-down starters. But Radatz was purely a reliever, whose role was to come in and put out fires with his intimidating fastball. Until his arm burned out from several years of overuse, he was unhittable.

Earl Wilson was the team's first black pitcher. He was a solid starting pitcher, not a star but a talented player who could be dominant when he was at his best. In 1966 he complained about the unequal treatment accorded black and white Red Sox players, and was quickly traded to Detroit.

First baseman Dick Stuart was the most one-dimensional on a team of one-dimensional players. A slugging first baseman who was nicknamed "stonefingers" for his fielding ineptitude, he would have two great years with the Sox, averaging 38 homers and 116 RBI in an increasingly pitching-dominated era. In many ways, he was a forerunner of the slugging Red Sox teams of the 1970s—and like many of the players on those teams, he fought openly with his manager and was dumped because of it.

Despite some entertaining players, the Red Sox failed to improve much. They were actually a worse team than their record looked in the early 1960s. Because two expansion teams were added in 1961 and the schedule increased from 154 games a year to 162, the Sox record was inflated by their games against these new teams, which were largely built from minor leaguers and burned out major league retreads.

Pinky Higgins was made general manager after the 1962 season and replaced by longtime Red Sox star Johnny Pesky as field manager. The team had

Key Players, 1961–1966
Tony Conigliaro, of
Jim Lonborg, p
Bill Monbouquette, p
Rico Petrocelli, ss
Dick Radatz, p
Pete Runnels, 1b
George Scott, 1b
Dick Stuart, 1b
Lee Thomas, of-1b
Earl Wilson, p
Carl Yastrzemski, of

power, but not much hitting or pitching. Despite Yaz's first batting title, Radatz's relief dominance, and Bill Monbouquette's 20 wins, the team finished 76–85 in 1963, essentially the same record as the previous two years.

In the next three years the team went through two more managers (Billy Herman and Pete Runnels) and finished in eighth or ninth place each year. Dick Radatz burned out his arm, and both Earl Wilson and Bill Monbouquette were traded—Wilson after complaining about treatment of black players and Monbouquette after leading the league in losses. Despite eight consecutive losing seasons, however, things were beginning to point in the right direction. Between 1964 and 1966, a core of young players began to take over jobs on a team whose only star in his prime was Carl Yastrzemski.

First, 19-year-old Tony Conigliaro claimed an outfield slot, hitting .290 (league average was .247) with 24 homers as a rookie. The next year he would lead the league in home runs. Rico Petrocelli, a 21-year-old shortstop with power, moved into the lineup in 1965. Pitcher Jim Lonborg, age 22, came up in 1965. Lonborg narrowly avoided the league lead in losses that year, but he showed tremendous potential. George Scott, a 22-year-old rookie first baseman, hit 27 home runs in 1966 while sparkling defensively—leading the league in putouts and double plays. Before the 1967 season, the Red Sox hired a manager who they hoped could get the most out of all the team's young players. Dick Williams, winner of two consecutive minor league pennants, confidently predicted that the Red Sox would have a winning record in 1967. At the time, few of the team's dispirited fans agreed with him.

11. The Impossible Dream: 1967

Dick Williams was committed to playing the kids in 1967. Three more rookies played key roles on the team: second baseman Mike Andrews, center fielder Reggie Smith, and relief pitcher Sparky Lyle (who would figure in one of the worst trades in Red Sox history). More surprisingly, Williams kept his commitment to winning. Somehow, the perennially losing Boston Red Sox started to win.

In a year in which pitching was king, Boston would win with its bats. The Red Sox had terrific hitting. The average hitter in 1967 managed only a .236 batting average. The Sox were above average at eight positions, and had two key bench players who also hit well. Best of all of them was Carl Yastrzemski, who won the Triple Crown with his .326 batting average, 44 home runs, and 121 runs batted in. The Red Sox led the league in hitting, home runs, slugging percentage, and runs scored. They were third from the bottom in pitching.

Key Players, 1967
Mike Andrews, 2b
Tony Conigliaro, of
Jim Lonborg, p
Sparky Lyle, p
Rico Petrocelli, ss
George Scott, 1b
Reggie Smith, of
Dick Williams, manager
John Wyatt, p
Carl Yastrzemski, of

Somehow, no matter what the odds against them were, the Red Sox kept winning. Jim Lonborg was the only pitcher who was able to start more than 24 games, and his ERA wasn't all that much better than average, but he led a charmed life that year, and always seemed to find a way to win. Only one other starting pitcher had a winning record, but the team's deep bullpen (led by John Wyatt, Dan Osinski, and Sparky Lyle) found ways to win even when the starters foundered. In August Tony Conigliaro, who already had 20 homers in the season's first half, was hit in the head by a pitch from Jack Hamilton, ending his season. The Red Sox somehow overcame the loss and kept winning.

The 1967 pennant race was one of the closest ever. Four teams finished within three games of the lead, and all four of those teams still had a chance to win in the season's final days. Already having a great season, Yaz carried the team in the final days of the season, with 23 hits in his last 44 at bats (a .523 average). The Sox finished the season with two games against first place Minnesota, needing to win both games to have a chance at the pennant. Yaz went 7-for-8 in the final two games, and made an extraordinary throw to end a Minnesota rally in the eighth inning of the season's final game—preserving the Red Sox Jim Lonborg's league-leading twenty-second win. After an agonizing wait for the results of the Detroit game (a Detroit win would have meant a tie for first and a one-game playoff like in 1948 and later in 1978) the good news came in: The Red Sox had won the pennant.

Just like in 1946, the World Series would be a hard-fought, evenly matched battle. Just like in 1946, the series would extend to the full seven games. Unfortunately, the result would be the same as well. Boston faced a St. Louis team built on pitching and speed. Offensively, St. Louis was fronted by leadoff hitter extraordinaire Lou Brock, slugging first baseman Orlando Cepeda, former home run king Roger Maris, and Curt Flood, who would later sacrifice his career in an attempt to win fairer contracts for other players. The Cardinals had a terrific pitching staff, including future Hall of Famers Bob Gibson and Steve Carlton. They had won 101 games during the regular season, nine more than the Red Sox.

The series opened on an ominous note for the Red Sox, who got good pitching from Jose Santiago and still lost to Bob Gibson (Santiago homered for the only Boston run). Game 2 was more of what the Sox had hoped for, with Jim Lonborg allowing only one hit and Yaz hitting two homers. But the deep St. Louis pitching staff held Boston to two runs in the next two games, including a shutout by Gibson. Facing elimination, the Red Sox were again saved by Lonborg, who outdueled Steve Carlton in Game 5, allowing only a Roger Maris home run in the ninth inning. The Boston offense finally got going in Game 6 (setting a record with three homers in the fourth inning) and scored eight runs against a record-setting eight St. Louis pitchers.

Once again it would all come down to a seventh game. Bob Gibson and Jim Lonborg, each with two victories in the series, would face each other. However, Gibson was pitching with his normal three days' rest (in the days when teams used four-man rotations instead of today's five), while Lonborg was pitching on two days' rest. Too exhausted to be effective after a league-leading 39 regular season starts and two complete games in the series, Lonborg gave up seven runs in six innings. Gibson threw his third complete game of the series, giving up his second and third runs. He would go on to even greater glory the next year, while the Red Sox got to go home and wonder what might have been.

In some ways the Impossible Dream season was a fluke; the pitching-thin Red

Sox played over their heads in that glorious year, and were not serious pennant contenders again for some time. But in another sense, the 1967 season did usher in a sort of golden age. If the Red Sox weren't great, they were good, young, and talented. The Red Sox would have 15 winning seasons in a row beginning in 1967, including another World Series appearance, and several other memorable near-misses. They would have consistently exciting—if sometimes flawed—teams throughout the 1970s.

12. Good, But Not Good Enough: 1968–1974

In the 1968 season the pitching dominance got out of hand. The *league average* ERA was 2.98. By contrast, in 2004, Johan Santana was the only American League pitcher with an ERA that low. The average hitter managed a .230 mark, and the Red Sox Carl Yastrzemski was the only player in the league to hit .300. (The next best was Danny Cater at .290.) Things got so bad for hitters that the rules would be changed after the season, lowering the pitcher's mound and making alterations in the strike zone to give the hitters a chance.

The Red Sox were still a good team, but while they seemed to ride out every disaster in 1967, in 1968 they weren't as adaptable. The hitting was still pretty good, despite George Scott's inexplicable decline from .303 with 19 homers to .171 with 3 homers. Just about everybody's numbers were worse than in 1967, but that was true for the rest of the league as well, which helped even things out.

Ken Harrelson—picked up for free after he was dumped by the A's for criticizing their owner—hit .275 with 35 home runs and, for that season at least, helped the team handle the loss of Tony Conigliaro in the outfield.

The problem was pitching. In 1967 the Red Sox had decent pitching, led by Jim Lonborg and Jose Santiago. In 1968, Jim Lonborg was ineffective after trying to come back from a knee injury and Santiago went down after hurting his arm. What was left were three average starters—Ray Culp, Dick Ellsworth, and Gary Bell—and one terrific reliever in lefty Sparky Lyle. It wasn't enough, as the Red Sox went a respectable 86–76, but finished a distant fourth to the Tigers.

They were about the same in 1969, the first year of divisional play (the league split into Eastern and Western divisions, with the division winners playing each other for the right to go to the World Series). The Sox led the league in homers, and were a good- but not great-hitting club. The pitching staff once again had three solid starters, some good relief pitching, and a lot of lesser lights. The team was good, but never in serious contention, with the excitement for the year coming from Tony Conigliaro's successful (at least at first) comeback, the controversial trade of popular short-timer Ken Harrelson to make room for Tony C. (Harrelson didn't want to leave and refused to report to Cleveland at first), and the firing of manager Dick Williams. The team finished with 87 wins, the last five of them for new manager Eddie Kasko.

Between 1970 and 1974, the Red Sox would win between 84 and 89 games each year. They would be good, but not quite good enough, despite a playoff near-miss in 1972. Every year the Sox would have great hitting and a few good pitchers, but never enough pitching depth to seriously contend for the pennant.

Adjustments were made to change the composition of the team, including controversial trades of Mike Andrews to Chicago for end-of-the line fielding wizard Luis Aparicio; popular Tony Conigliaro to California; George Scott to Milwaukee for Tommy Harper; and Sparky Lyle to the hated Yankees for the now-ineffective Danny Cater. None of them helped or hurt much in the short run, as the team stayed about the same. (Sparky Lyle became a superstar for the Yankees, but the trade made a certain amount of sense at the time. The Red Sox had traded Scott to Milwaukee with the intention of having minor league sensation Cecil Cooper play first base, but Cooper turned out not to be ready. The Sox needed to trade for a first baseman and felt Lyle was expendable, since Bill Lee was coming off a great year as a lefty reliever as well.)

In 1972 the Red Sox fell half a game short of the American League Eastern Division title, robbed of a chance to win the title. Despite the disastrous Danny Cater at first base and a new center fielder who couldn't play center field (the speedy Tommy Harper, with incumbent Reggie Smith moved to right field), the Red Sox were a good hitting team in another great year for pitchers (league ERA was 3.07), leading the league in runs and slugging percentage. The team's pitching was among the league's worst, despite a magnificent addition to the starting rotation. Luis Tiant, cast off by Cleveland and Minnesota after a disastrous 1969 and an injury-plagued 1970, came all the way back in 1972, leading the league in earned run average with an extraordinary 1.91 and winning 15 games—despite spending only the second half of the year in the starting rotation.

The start of the 1972 season was delayed for a week by a player's strike. When the strike ended, a decision was made not to replay any of the lost games, even though it would leave teams with an unequal number of games played at the end of the season. The Red Sox missed seven games because of the strike, while the Detroit Tigers missed six. The season came down to a final series in Detroit, where the Red Sox lost two of three, to finish the season half a game behind the Tigers—with the margin of error the single extra game that the Tigers got to play (they finished 86–70 to the Red Sox 85–70).

Even in the lost hope of another failed playoff drive, there were signs of good things to come. Tiant looked like a rotation anchor for years to come. Young catcher Carlton Fisk, born and bred a Red Sox fan, hit .293 with 22 homers and won Rookie of the Year. An outfielder named Dwight Evans with a rifle arm was tearing up the minor leagues, and played a few games for the Sox late in the season.

Evans and fellow rookie outfielder Rick Miller both broke into the lineup in 1973. Tommy Harper, mercifully moved to left, had a terrific year, setting a team record with a league-leading 54 stolen bases. Reggie Smith hit .303 with 21 homers

Key Players, 1968–1974

Mike Andrews, 2b
Rick Burleson, ss
Tony Conigliaro, of
Ray Culp, p
Dick Drago, p
Dwight Evans, of
Carlton Fisk, c
Ken Harrelson. of
Darrell Johnson, manager
Eddie Kasko, manager
Bill Lee, p
Sparky Lyle, p
Roger Moret, p
Mike Nagy, p
Marty Pattin, p
Rico Petrocelli, ss-3b
George Scott, 1b
Reggie Smith, of
Luis Tiant, p
Dick Williams, manager
Carl Yastrzemski, of

despite battling injuries. Orlando Cepeda was imported from Oakland to have one last good year in the first year of the designated hitter, batting .289 with 20 homers. Yaz hit .296 and walked 105 times. The team once again led the league in slugging, and this time the pitching was able to carry some of the load as well. Bill Lee moved into the rotation and won 17 games with a 2.74 ERA (very good in a year when the league ERA was 3.82). Luis Tiant won 20 games, and Roger Moret went 13–2. The pitching staff wasn't exactly good, but it was above average. The Red Sox won 89 games, just enough to finish a strong second behind the Baltimore Orioles. Eddie Kasko was fired as manager at the end of the season and replaced by Darrell Johnson.

The 1974 team was built around youth. Luis Aparicio was replaced by rookie shortstop Rick Burleson, who hit .284 while fielding brilliantly. Orlando Cepeda was replaced as designated hitter by Tommy Harper. Reggie Smith was traded to St. Louis in a racially charged deal ostensibly designed to bolster the pitching staff. Dwight Evans moved into the lineup full time, with other young players like Mario Guerrero, Juan Beniquez, and Cecil Cooper given key roles. The team won five fewer games and finished in third place, with Luis Tiant (22 wins), Bill Lee (17 wins), and Kansas City retread Dick Drago the only consistent pitchers on a mediocre staff. But the Red Sox seemed to be a young, promising team. The next season they would be even younger—and would begin to fulfill some of that promise.

13. The Sixth Game: 1975

Two kids would join the team as starters in 1975. Fred Lynn would displace Rick Miller—who hadn't really developed as a hitter—in center field, while Jim Rice displaced Juan Beniquez and others in left field (Yaz had moved to first by then). Both played brilliantly, helping the Red Sox to lead the league in batting average, slugging percentage, and runs scored. As in 1967, the 1975 team seemed to have an ability to overcome misfortune. The season started with Tony Conigliaro's last, failed comeback attempt (he hit .123 in 23 games as the team's DH). Key starters Carl Yastrzemski, Rick Burleson, and Rico Petrocelli all had poor seasons. Catcher Carlton Fisk hit .331—but was injured and unable to play for nearly half the season. Petrocelli and Dwight Evans both also missed significant time to injury. None of the starting pitchers had an ERA below the league average, including the team's ace, Luis Tiant.

Somehow, none of those problems mattered. The Red Sox had a talented, mostly young ensemble cast, and other players filled in the gaps. Young first baseman Cecil Cooper, finally given consistent playing time, hit .311. Infielder Denny Doyle, a .250 career hitter, hit .310 as a platoon second baseman. Juan Beniquez hit .291 while filling in for injured players in the outfield and at third base. Bernie Carbo hit 15 home runs in limited playing time as a backup in the outfield. Light-hitting Doug Griffin, relegated to the bench much of the time by Doyle's hitting, turned into a terrific pinch hitter down the stretch. Roger Moret shuttled between the bullpen and the starting rotation, and somehow went 14–3. Tiant, Bill Lee, and Rick Wise all stayed healthy and won between 17 and 19 games—pitching steadily if unspectacularly in a hitters' ballpark that could make pitchers pay dearly for their mistakes. Dick Drago moved to the bullpen full time and saved 15 games. Relief pitcher Jim Willoughby pitched very well down the stretch.

More than anything, Fred Lynn and Jim Rice carried the team. Called the "Gold Dust Twins" in the media, the two became inextricably tied together in Red Sox lore: Rice, the working-class product of a segregated South who was inhumanly strong, shattering bats with his checked swing, and who doggedly worked on improving his poor defense in left field; Lynn, the Southern California kid who seemed to effortlessly run down everything in center field and whose marvelous throwing arm was overshadowed by Dwight Evans—with the best arm in baseball—beside him in right field. Rice hit .309 with 22 home runs and 102 runs batted in. Lynn was even better: A lefthanded line drive hitter with a perfect Fenway Park swing, Lynn hit .331 with 21 homers and 105 runs batted in, and led the league with 47 doubles and 105 runs. Lynn would win both Rookie of the Year and the league MVP.

At the season's end, when the Red Sox were nearing the division title over the Baltimore Orioles, their luck, pushed to the breaking point, began to run out. Jim Rice's wrist broke when he was hit by a pitch, and he was not available for the playoffs. It didn't seem to matter as the Red Sox swept the Oakland A's in the American League Championship Series (a sweep for which the A's would more than get revenge in 1988 and 1990), led by Tiant, who won Game 1, and Dick Drago, who saved the other two games. But Rice's loss would be felt in the World Series.

In the World Series the Red Sox faced a similar team to themselves, Cincinnati's Big Red Machine, filled with hitting superstars and with decent but unheralded pitching (six pitchers had won 10 or more games). The Reds won 108 games during the regular season, the Red Sox 95.

At first it looked like Luis Tiant would singlehandedly lead the Red Sox to victory. He shut out the Reds 6–0 in Game 1. After the Reds won on a ninth-inning comeback in Game 2 and a hitters' duel in Game 3 (there were six homers in the game, three by each team), Tiant came back to win Game 4, throwing 163 pitches to win a 5–4 complete game on a day when he didn't have his best stuff. The Reds then beat Reggie Cleveland in Game 5, pulling within one victory of a World Series win. After two days of rain delays, Tiant was brought back again in Game 6 to try and hold off disaster once more.

The sixth game of the 1975 World Series is considered one of the best baseball games ever played. Certainly it was one of the most exciting. The Red Sox took an early 3–0 lead, but Tiant couldn't hold it. After the Reds went ahead 6–3, the Red Sox came back on a pinch-hit three-run homer by Bernie Carbo in the eighth inning to tie the game. The Red Sox loaded the bases with no outs in the ninth, only to be stopped without scoring by Reds reliever Pedro Borbon. In the eleventh inning, Dwight Evans made a spectacular

Key Players, 1975

Rick Burleson, ss
Bernie Carbo, of
Reggie Cleveland, p
Cecil Cooper, 1b
Dick Drago, p
Dwight Evans, of
Carlton Fisk, c
Darrell Johnson, manager
Bill Lee, p
Fred Lynn, of
Roger Moret, p
Rico Petrocelli, 3b
Jim Rice, of
Luis Tiant, p
Jim Willoughby, p
Rick Wise, p
Carl Yastrzemski, of

catch of a seemingly uncatchable Joe Morgan drive, throwing out a startled Ken Griffey at first base when he failed to get back in time. (Interestingly, Griffey and Borbon both would have sons who played in the majors.) The game went on to the twelfth inning, where it finally ended in one of the most enduring images of the Red Sox: Carlton Fisk hitting a long fly, jumping up and down at the plate with his arms raised in the air as if desperately trying to wave the ball fair, and then triumphantly circling the bases with the game-winning home run after it landed just on the right side of the foul pole.

After Game 6, the last game of the World Series was almost anticlimactic, and it would end in controversy. The Red Sox were once again unable to hold a 3–0 lead, and Jim Willoughby—who had pitched extremely well all series—came in to put out the fire, leaving the game tied. With two outs in the bottom of the eighth inning, Willoughby was due at the plate (there was no DH used in the World Series that year), and manager Darrell Johnson sent up Cecil Cooper— mired in a 1-for-18 slump—to pinch hit. Cooper fouled out, and Johnson was forced to use rookie Jim Burton to pitch. (The extra-inning game the night before had drained the bullpen.) The Reds scored on a Joe Morgan single in the ninth and the Red Sox were unable to respond. Once again they had gloriously overachieved, but fallen just short of the prize.

14. The Years of the Gerbil: 1976–1980

Like the United States as a whole, baseball went through a transitional period in the mid-1970s, and the Red Sox would not handle this transition particularly well. The Red Sox had some extraordinarily talented teams in the 1970s, but those teams had to cope with extraordinary tensions. As a result, they would become another team of near misses, with the most famous near-miss of all in 1978.

Longtime owner Tom Yawkey was edging closer to death in 1976, and desperate to win a championship before he died. He took one last shot at winning the way he had 30 years before—turning a good team into a powerhouse by purchasing key players from struggling clubs. Yawkey paid $1 million each for Oakland A's stars Rollie Fingers and Joe Rudi (who much-hated Oakland owner Charlie Finley knew he was going to lose with the advent of free agency). Baseball commissioner Bowie Kuhn voided the sales, however, before Fingers and Rudi ever got to play for the Red Sox, ruling that the sale was not in the best interests of the game.

Despite good hitting and their best pitching in years, the Red Sox never got off the ground in 1976. Luis Tiant won 21 games, and the rotation was solid, despite the loss of Bill Lee (injured by a cheap shot from Yankees outfielder Mickey Rivers during a brawl that put his arm in a sling for most of the year). But Jim Rice and Fred Lynn, who had been superhuman in 1975, were merely very good in 1976. Cecil Cooper, Denny Doyle, and Carlton Fisk all came back to earth as well. Tom Yawkey died on July 9, leaving ownership of the team in the hands of his widow, Jean Yawkey, but control in the hands of two of the team's limited partners, Buddy Leroux and former Red Sox catcher Haywood Sullivan. Ten days after Yawkey's death manager Darrell Johnson was fired, with the team foundering at 41–45. The Red Sox righted themselves slightly the rest of the way, going 42–34 in the season's second half under their new manager, Don Zimmer.

Zimmer would prove to be a poor fit as manager. His record is certainly not a disaster—his first three teams won 97, 99, and 91 games—but his legacy is not reflected in that record. To most Red Sox fans he is remembered as the man who, when handed a supremely talented team, got into a power struggle with his players and eventually refused to play many of them, leaving the team shorthanded at a crucial moment. Zimmer made some good decisions and some poor ones, but was fated to have the poor ones haunt him forever in Red Sox lore.

Zimmer was a former catcher, an ex-Marine who had been wounded fighting in the Pacific during World War II, and part of a conservative old guard trying to forestall changes in baseball. He followed conventional wisdom. He wanted his orders followed without question. Many of his players were products of the 1960s, used to asking questions, testing new ideas, and to a certain extent, challenging authority (although Bill Lee, depicted as the ultimate antiestablishment figure, also served in the military).

The Red Sox in 1977 won 97 games, finishing in a second-place tie with Baltimore, just behind a New York Yankees team that won 100. The Sox were an offensive powerhouse, leading the league in home runs and slugging percentage by a wide margin, and narrowly missing the lead in batting average and runs scored. Cecil Cooper was traded to Milwaukee to get first baseman George Scott back—a terrible trade in the long run, but in 1977 Scott hit 33 homers. New third baseman Butch Hobson also hit 30, with Fred Lynn and Carl Yastrzemski not far behind. Perhaps most importantly, Jim Rice had a tremendous breakout season—hitting .320 and leading the league with 39 home runs and a .593 slugging percentage—and for the next three years Rice would be the most dangerous hitter in baseball.

The Red Sox pitching was about average, without a standout in the rotation (an aging Luis Tiant went 12–8) but with six pitchers winning 10 or more games. The leading winner was a reliever—Bill Campbell, the first major signee of the new free agent era. Zimmer rode his top reliever hard; Campbell threw 140 innings—an extraordinary total for a reliever—went 13–9, and led the league with 31 saves. The workload was far too heavy, and Campbell would never be consistently effective again.

Zimmer followed the same pattern with the rest of the team. He had starters and bench players, and the starters rarely rested, sometimes even if they were hurt. Only three bench players batted as many as 100 times during the season, and that was mostly because of injuries to Dwight Evans (costing him more than half the season), Denny Doyle, and Fred Lynn. The next year this would turn into a full-fledged disaster, with overplayed starters getting hurt by midseason

Key Players, 1976–1980

Tom Burgmeier, p
Rick Burleson, ss
Bill Campbell, p
Bernie Carbo, of
Dennis Eckersley, p
Dwight Evans, of
Carlton Fisk, c
Butch Hobson, 3b
Ferguson Jenkins, p
Bill Lee, p
Fred Lynn, of
Tony Perez, 1b
Jerry Remy, 2b
Jim Rice, of
George Scott, 1b
Bob Stanley, p
Luis Tiant, p
Bob Watson, 1b
Jim Willoughby, p
Carl Yastrzemski, of
Don Zimmer, manager

and bench players being so rusty they were unable to contribute.

Even more damaging was the open rift between the manager and many play-ers. Bill Lee christened Zimmer "the Gerbil," and the nickname stuck. Lee, Ferguson Jenkins (a future Hall of Fame starter for whom the Sox had traded Juan Beniquez to Texas), key reliever Jim Willoughby, and primary outfield back-up Bernie Carbo formed the core of a group called the "Buffalo Heads," which openly mocked Zimmer and derided his intellect. Zimmer responded by bench-ing them, or insisting that the team dump them for whatever they could get. His attempt to enforce discipline without gaining the players' respect failed badly, even though Zimmer did get his way. Carbo, Willoughby, and Jenkins were gone by the time they were needed in 1978, and Lee was demoted to the bullpen, leav-ing the Red Sox with no lefthanded starter.

The damage wouldn't be apparent until midseason. The Red Sox began the 1978 season with an extraordinary run. After trading with Cleveland for hard-throwing young Dennis Eckersley and signing free agent 20-game-winner Mike Torrez away from the Yankees, the Red Sox had a formidable rotation in the sea-son's first half, with Tiant and Bill Lee in the last two spots. Bill Campbell was a shadow of the reliever he'd been the previous year, but much of the slack was filled by Bob Stanley (who went 15–2, mostly in relief) and Dick Drago, in his second tour of duty with the Red Sox. With a powerful offense led by Jim Rice (who would finish the year at .315 while leading the league in triples, home runs, RBI, and slugging percentage), the Red Sox had a 14½ game lead over the Yankees at midseason. At that point, the cumulative effect of injuries and two years of overwork hit the Red Sox stars. Rick Burleson hurt his knee. Zimmer left him in the lineup as the steady .280 hitter saw his average fall to .248. Dwight Evans was beaned, and began having vision problems. Zimmer left him in the lineup. Evans, a superb fielder, had never dropped a fly ball in the major leagues, but now he did it twice in a week. His average dropped from .287 the previous year to .247. Butch Hobson had bone chips in his elbow that would cause it to

The Red Sox have long been a New England phenomenon, not just in Boston or even Massachusetts. Our yearly trip to Fenway from central Maine was a pilgrimage of sorts. Parking at Wonderland, Blue Line to Government Center, Green Line to Kenmore. But my most vivid memories are of games on the radio. Lying in bed when Lynn hit three home runs in Detroit. Having the radio on the boat while hauling lobster traps on a Saturday afternoon.

The strangest place that I listened to a game was on a football field. On October 2, 1978, the MCI Huskies JV football team played at Mattanawcook Academy, in Lincoln, Maine. We took the field in about the second inning of the Red Sox-Yankees playoff game. I don't know what the score of that football game was, and I didn't know that day. We were blown out, but nobody really want-ed to play—everyone was far more concerned with what was happening 5½ hours south. There was a radio on the sideline, and no one wanted to go in—everyone wanted to remain on the bench so that they could listen to the game. They had a radio playing over the speakers, but you couldn't really hear when you were playing.

I know that the Red Sox were down as we left the field, shortly after the Bucky Dent home run. We raced through the showers, radio blaring in the locker room. I vividly remember sitting on the bus, pulling out of the parking lot, when Yaz, always my all-time favorite, popped out to end the game. That was far more devastating than the thumping we had just taken on the field.

—Lyford P. Beverage

lock during games, and made throwing painful. Zimmer left him in the lineup until Hobson finally begged to be taken out, knowing he was hurting the team— but in the meantime Hobson would make a league-leading 43 errors at third base and drop from 30 home runs to 17. For the second straight year, Carlton Fisk played more than 150 games at catcher, the most physically demanding position on the field, and his numbers declined significantly. Thirty-four-year-old George Scott, overplayed in 1977, stopped hitting entirely by the middle of 1978.

The Red Sox foundered at midseason, and in one of the biggest collapses of all time allowed the Yankees to catch and pass them. With Bill Lee banished to the bullpen, Zimmer used terrified-looking rookie Bobby Sprowl in an attempt to stop the bleeding during the so-called "Boston Massacre." The Yankees swept the Sox in a four-game series at Fenway by a collective score of 42–9. The most talented Red Sox team since the 1940s looked utterly lost.

Somehow they righted themselves. The Red Sox miraculously won eight games in a row to end the season, tying the New York Yankees for the division lead. Just like 1948, there would be a one-game playoff to determine who went on to the American League Championship Series. Dennis Eckersley had gone 20–8 with a 2.99 ERA as the Red Sox ace. Luis Tiant and Bill Lee had both pitched very well. Zimmer passed over them both to start Mike Torrez, a steady but unspectacular pitcher who'd gone 16–13 with an ERA above the league average. The Red Sox took a quick lead on a Yastrzemski homer, only to fall behind on a cheap home run by light-hitting shortstop Bucky Dent, one of the most infamous moments in Boston history. After a furious comeback, the Red Sox found themselves with no one to use as a pinch hitter—Bernie Carbo, one of the heroes of the 1975 World Series and a power threat off the bench, had been dumped for his criticism of Zimmer. Zimmer sent up .191 hitter Bob Bailey instead, and the Red Sox season was ended in their eventual 5–4 defeat.

The 1979 season was more of the same. The hitting was again excellent. The Red Sox led the league in batting average, home runs, and slugging percentage. Although the overworked Fisk went down with a predictable shoulder injury for half the season, it was offset by a breakout year from Fred Lynn, who won the batting title at .333 and hit 39 home runs to nearly double his previous high. Jim Rice hit a career-high .325, and matched Lynn's 39 homers. Bob Watson, acquired from Houston after he started the year poorly, hit .337 in the last two-thirds of the season.

But the pitching was woefully thin. Bill Lee was dumped to the Montreal Expos for Stan Papi, a backup infielder who hit .188. (Lee won 16 games for the Expos.) Luis Tiant, an irreverent pitcher who'd also been critical of Zimmer, was allowed to go to the Yankees as a free agent. That forced the Red Sox to move Bob Stanley, their most effective reliever, into the rotation behind Dennis Eckersley and Mike Torrez, thinning out the bullpen behind Dick Drago and lefty Tom Burgmeier. The Red Sox won 91 games and were within shouting distance of the pennant race, but ended up in third place.

By 1980 the Don Zimmer era was clearly coming to a close, as everything seemed to go wrong for the Red Sox. Butch Hobson, Jerry Remy, and Fred Lynn each missed at least 50 games with injuries. Most damaging of all was Jim Rice's second broken wrist (again after being hit by a pitch), which would turn him from a great hitter into a merely good one. The team was still good offensively, but not nearly good enough to make up for its pitching, which utterly collapsed. Dennis Eckersley, troubled by alcohol problems, fell to 12–14, and he was the team's most consistent starter. The Red Sox fell to 83–77, the last four of those games (three of them losses) under interim manager Johnny Pesky, after the firing of Don Zimmer.

15. Chaos Descends: 1981–1984

The 1981 season was marred by off-field chaos, which would plague the Red Sox for years. The new ownership that had taken over since Yawkey's death was erratic, with the relationships between the team's limited partners clearly strained, and managing partner Haywood Sullivan sometimes as focused on avoiding having his position undercut as he was on beating the Yankees. In December, 1980, someone in the Red Sox front office committed an inexplicable error, mailing out the contracts for Fred Lynn and Carlton Fisk a day after the deadline had passed. The Players Association argued that Fisk and Lynn should be declared free agents (since they hadn't been tendered contracts in time), and the case went to arbitration. The Red Sox traded Lynn to the Angels in the meantime (as part of the trade he agreed to drop the appeal and sign a contract with the Angels), and hoped for the best with Fisk, who was a lifelong Red Sox fan. But in the midst of the chaos and growing bad feelings, even Fisk had had enough. Although collusion among the owners (soon to lead to another strike) kept most of them from making any offers to the All Star catcher, Chicago White Sox owner Jerry Reinsdorf finally did, and Fisk reluctantly moved on.

Key Players, 1981–1984
Luis Aponte, p
Tony Armas, of
Marty Barrett, 2b
Wade Boggs 3b-1b
Oil Can Boyd, p
Tom Burgmeier, p
Mark Clear, p
Roger Clemens, p
Dennis Eckersley, p
Dwight Evans, of
Rich Gedman, c
Ralph Houk, manager
Bruce Hurst, p
Carney Lansford, 3b
Bob Ojeda, p
Jerry Remy, 2b
Jim Rice, of
Bob Stanley, p
John Tudor, p
Carl Yastrzemski, of

There was more chaos awaiting manager Ralph Houk, "the Major," a well-respected former Yankees manager who was talked out of retirement to become a stabilizing force for the Red Sox. The middle of the 1981 season was disrupted by major league baseball's second players' strike. A third of the season was wiped out, and the decision was made to play the season's second half as a separate, "split" season, and have the first and second half winners play each other in the playoffs. The Red Sox, expected to fall below .500, actually played reasonably well despite the talent drain. The pitching was pretty bad, and no member of the starting rotation finished with a better than average ERA (with the exception of rookie sensation Bob Ojeda, who went 6–2 after being called up in the season's second half). The hitting, despite the loss of Lynn and Fisk, Rice's injury-related decline, and the age-related slides of 41-year-old Carl Yastrzemski and 39-year-old Tony Perez (who had helped hold the team together as a free agent pickup the previous year), was pretty good—the Sox led the league in batting average, slugging percentage, and runs scored. Young third baseman Carney Lansford and former Sox outfielder Rick Miller were obtained (along with pitcher Mark Clear) from California in what turned out to be a terrific trade for Rick Burleson and Butch Hobson. Lansford hit .336 to win the batting title and Miller hit a surprising .291 as a fill-in for the departed Lynn in center field. Even more surprising, 29-year-old Dwight Evans suddenly went from being a decent hitter known for his defense to a terrific hitter—batting .296 and leading the league in home runs and walks.

In 1982 the Red Sox got another amazing performance from manager Ralph Houk. He guided a weak team with only two good hitters for most of the year and no reliable starting pitchers to 89 wins and a remarkable third-place finish. Dwight Evans continued his late-career transformation into a hitting star with a .292 batting average, 32 home runs, 122 runs, and 112 walks. Defending batting champ Carney Lansford went down with an injury, which opened up a lineup spot for rookie Wade Boggs, who hit .349 in 104 games. Jim Rice hit .309 with 24 homers, but was a shadow of his previous self. Somehow, Houk held the pitching together by assembling a terrific bullpen consisting of role players Bob Stanley, Mark Clear, Tom Burgmeier, and Luis Aponte, all of whom had strong years.

By 1983 even Houk couldn't work any more magic, and the Red Sox tumbled to 78–84. The team was embroiled in chaos as Buddy Leroux attempted to take over the club from managing partner Haywood Sullivan, choosing the night of a memorial for heart attack–stricken Tony Conigliaro to announce the coup. (Eventually, Jean Yawkey would buy out Leroux and take control of the team through the Yawkey Trust, but the chaos took several years to resolve.) Carl Yastrzemski played his last season. The unsettled atmosphere was used by many to explain the Red Sox fall from the previous year, but the team just wasn't very good. Carney Lansford was traded for outfielder Tony Armas, a prodigious home run hitter who never walked and who was out of his league defensively in center field. Wade Boggs led the league with a .361 batting average at third, but none of the other infielders hit very well. Although the starting outfield combined for 97 home runs, no one else on the team hit very many. And the pitching wasn't good, despite Bob Stanley's 33 saves. On the positive side, the Red Sox were beginning to develop young players who could help the team rebuild. Boggs was the first. Catcher Rich Gedman was being worked into the lineup. Outfielder Reid Nichols hit well, and looked like the fleet center fielder the team needed. (As it turned out, with Armas in center field, Nichols would never be given the chance.) The team also had five promising young starting pitchers in John Tudor, Bruce Hurst, Bob Ojeda, Oil Can Boyd, and Al Nipper.

More young players worked their way into the lineup the next year, and the Red Sox began to look like a team on the rise. Marty Barrett, a rookie second baseman, hit .303, while fellow rookie Jackie Gutierrez hit .263 at shortstop. Boston traded one of its young starting pitchers, John Tudor, for Pittsburgh's Mike Easler, who hit .313 with 27 homers as the new DH. Dennis Eckersley, the former ace fallen on hard times, was sent to the Chicago Cubs for first baseman Bill Buckner, an ex-batting champion who had lost his job in Chicago. Buckner wasn't very good, but he replaced Dave Stapleton—who had been awful—at first base. More importantly, the young pitching began to show signs of coming through. Hurst, Ojeda, Boyd, and Nipper all won 11 or more games. And a young pitching phenom drafted out of the University of Texas went 9–4 before going down with an injury: Roger Clemens.

Ralph Houk retired, leaving behind a team that had gone 86–76 and seemed to be on the way up. His replacement would be another respected baseball man, John McNamara—who would unfortunately turn out to have more in common with Don Zimmer than with Ralph Houk.

16. Almost, Again: 1985–1987

John McNamara didn't seem to have the same magic Ralph Houk did. The Red Sox played sluggishly in 1985, and did not respond well to McNamara's conservative management. Like Don Zimmer, McNamara believed in picking starters and sticking with them. Only two bench players batted more than 100 times all season, and that was as a result of an injury that took Tony Armas out of the line-up for half a season and Jackie Gutierrez's ineffectiveness at shortstop. Older players like Dwight Evans and Mike Easler saw their production drop sharply. The Red Sox hit well—leading the league in batting average and on-base percentage, and coming in second in slugging. They had solid front-line pitching, both in the rotation and the bullpen. The pitching wasn't incredibly deep, but the team had a better-than-league average ERA, despite pitching in Fenway Park. Somehow that only translated into a disappointing 81–81 record.

They would go further with a less-talented team in 1986. The Red Sox made some minor moves: they traded lefthanded starter Bob Ojeda and minor league prospects to the New York Mets for pitchers Calvin Schiraldi, Wes Gardner, and other prospects; they also traded DH Mike Easler to the Yankees for DH Don Baylor. Late in the season, with Tony Armas hurt again in center field and a gaping hole at shortstop, they made another deal, trading with Seattle for shortstop Spike Owen and outfielder Dave Henderson, neither of whom would hit .200 over the rest of the season. The team fell to eleventh in the league in home runs, and declined in batting average, slugging, and on-base percentage. Backup catch-

I remember it was 1983, a cloudy afternoon, and I was lying on my beanbag chair watching the Sox play. I don't remember who was playing the Sox, but they had a great outfield of Rice, Armas, and Evans. Three bangers and three very good defensive players. The rest of the team was so-so. I don't remember the game, but I remember the ending. Sox were tied in the ninth, man on third, one out. I remember holding my hands, begging, praying for a sacrifice fly. Just deep enough to score the run and get a win. I was odd; most people would root for a base hit or home run, I liked the sac fly. Dewey came up. Sac Fly . . . Sac Fly . . . I secretly chanted, twisting my body in a pretzel-like knot, trying to use all the Force I could to help the Sox.

Then came his swing . . . Fly ball to left, going back . . . damn I thought, they always disappoint . . . back, back . . . left fielder against the wall . . . back . . . back . . . into the net. Sox win. Sox win! Dewey's two-run home run to win the game was an epiphany and a curse. Now I live and breathe for the Red Sox, and all because of a wind-aided fly to the net over the Green Monster.
—Teddy Zartler

er Marc Sullivan, who happened to be the owner's son, failed to hit .200 for the second consecutive year. The first baseman didn't hit at all and couldn't play defense because of his disintegrating ankles, despite which McNamara played him in 153 games.

Somehow they made it all the way to the World Series. The offense wasn't great but it was good, with Wade Boggs hitting .357 and walking 105 times, and Dwight Evans, Marty Barrett, and Don Baylor doing a good job of getting on base (despite poor batting averages from Evans and Baylor). Even the declining Jim Rice walked 62 times—about average for his number of plate appearances, but Rice's career high. Tony Armas and Bill Buckner were gaping holes in the lineup all year, but Buckner got hot in September to finish with superficially respectable stats.

The main reason the 1986 team won 95 games was pitching. For the first time since 1979, the Red Sox had a legitimate ace. In April, Roger Clemens set a major league record by striking out 20 batters in a game. He went 24–4 that season with a 2.48 ERA and won the Cy Young award. Bruce Hurst finally developed into the top pitcher he'd been projected as, going 13–8 with a 2.99 ERA despite missing time with an injury. Oil Can Boyd was a terrific third starter (despite a midseason emotional meltdown when he wasn't selected to the All Star team, that led to him being briefly institutionalized), finishing 16–10, 3.78. When fourth starter Al Nipper faltered, the Red Sox traded Steve Lyons to the Chicago White Sox for Tom Seaver, an end-of-the-line Hall of Famer who pitched well down the stretch before getting hurt. The Red Sox needed all the starting pitching they could get; their bullpen was terrible, despite some late-season heroics from minor league callup Calvin Schiraldi (1.41 ERA and 9 saves in 25 games).

It didn't look like the Red Sox were going to get very far in the playoffs. They quickly fell behind in the American League Championship Series, three games to one. In Game 5, they were one strike away from elimination when Dave Henderson hit a dramatic home run against Angels closer Donnie Moore (who went into a tailspin after the game and eventually killed himself). When the Red Sox bullpen blew the lead in the bottom of the ninth, Henderson came back to win the game in the eleventh with a sacrifice fly. Suddenly rejuvenated, the Red Sox went on to win the next two games of the series by a combined score of 18–5.

In the World Series, they faced a Mets team that had won 108 games, and clearly outclassed the Red Sox, at least on paper. The Mets had a terrific pitching staff, good power, and balanced hitting; they had led the National League in ERA, batting average, slugging percentage, and runs scored.

Roger Clemens was not available to pitch Game 1 (he'd pitched the last game against California), but Bruce Hurst shut the Mets down completely in their own park. Despite great pitching of their own, the

Key Players, 1985–1987

Tony Armas, of
Marty Barrett, 2b
Wade Boggs 3b
Bill Buckner, 1b
Ellis Burks, of
Oil Can Boyd, p
Roger Clemens, p
Steve Crawford, p
Dwight Evans, of
Rich Gedman, c
Mike Greenwell, of
Bruce Hurst, p
John McNamara, manager
Al Nipper, p
Bob Ojeda, p
Jim Rice, of
Bob Stanley, p

Mets lost 1–0. Clemens left Game 2 early, but the relief staff uncharacteristically shut the Mets down. The Red Sox won 9–3 and led the series two games to none, heading back to Fenway Park. After the Red Sox lost Game 3, manager McNamara made an odd decision—to start Al Nipper, who'd been ineffective all season, rather than bringing back Bruce Hurst on three days' rest (as the Mets did with Ron Darling). Predictably, Nipper lost 6–2, and the series was tied. Hurst was brought back a day too late and won again, 4–2, salvaging the last of the three games at Fenway. Boston went back to New York needing to win only one of the final two games to win the World Series.

The Red Sox jumped out to an early 2–0 lead, but Clemens couldn't hold on. It didn't matter; they scored again to give Clemens a 3–2 lead going into the bottom of the eighth. They might have scored more, but McNamara let Bill Buckner (who hit .218 against lefties) hit against tough lefty Jesse Orosco with the bases loaded in the top of the eighth, instead of pinch hitting Don Baylor, who killed lefties. Buckner, who because of a bad ankle was usually removed for defensive purposes late in games when the Red Sox had the lead, was left in the game at first base. At this point, the story gets murky. Clemens had a bleeding blister, and McNamara removed him from the game. To this day McNamara claims that Clemens asked out of the game and Clemens claims he left only under protest. Calvin Schiraldi came in and promptly gave up the tying run.

In the top of the tenth inning, playoff hero Dave Henderson hit a home run to put the Red Sox ahead. They led 5–3 going into the bottom of the tenth, with Schiraldi still pitching. After getting two quick outs and coming within one strike of winning, he fell apart, giving up three singles and a run. Bob Stanley came in to pitch to Mookie Wilson, with runners at first and third in a 5–4 game. Stanley also got within one strike of the win before Wilson fouled off his next three pitches. Stanley's seventh pitch was wild (although some people feel catcher Rich Gedman could have handled it). The runner scored from third and the game was tied. On the eleventh pitch of the at bat, Wilson slapped a weak grounder to first baseman Bill Buckner. The ball went under Buckner's glove and through his legs. The winning run scored. (McNamara later said that he had left Buckner out there rather than putting in a defensive replacement because he wanted Buckner to be on the field when the team won the World Series.)

There was still a seventh game to play, but this time it was the Mets who seemed rejuvenated. The Red Sox took an early 3–0 lead as Bruce Hurst

It's 1986, I'm 10 years old, and to tell the whole truth I didn't care too much for organized baseball. Like any good kid growing up on the Massachusetts border I pretended to be a Sox fan but couldn't tell you who was on the team. I remember coming home from school though, and for some reason impatiently waiting for the World Series games to start. It seemed that everyone was excited, and being 10, I loved taunting the few Mets fans that I would encounter. So for a week and a half I got to stay up late and watch my father scream at the players on the TV. I received a crash course in players like Wade Boggs and Roger Clemens. In the end I was disappointed, as we all were, but I couldn't wait for next spring to arrive; I needed to watch my new heroes correct their mistakes. That's when it started—the more I knew about the game, the more I wanted to watch.
—Paul Ryan

attempted to win his third game of the series. After the Mets rallied to tie, McNamara brought in Schiraldi again, only to see him give up a tie-breaking home run. The Mets, heavily favored all along, went on to win 8–5. The World Series was over.

The 1987 Red Sox went back to underachieving again. The team was loaded with talent, but McNamara didn't seem to know what to do with some of it. The Red Sox had terrific veteran hitters in Dwight Evans (.305 with 34 homers, 123 RBI, and 106 walks) and Wade Boggs (.368 with a career-high 24 homers and 105 walks). They brought up young hitters from the minors in response to injuries or ineffectiveness, and they all played well. Mike Greenwell hit .328 with 19 homers. Ellis Burks took over in center field and was far better than Armas had been, hitting .272 with 20 home runs and 27 stolen bases. Todd Benzinger hit .278 with decent power in about half a season of playing time. Sam Horn was called up and hit 14 homers in only 158 at bats. Jody Reed hit .300 in a brief infield trial. In Roger Clemens, the Red Sox had the best pitcher in the league, although after Clemens and Hurst the pitching staff wasn't very good. Still, the team wasn't as bad as it played, limping home at 78–84. One year after almost winning the World Series, a team filled with talented players looked entirely directionless.

17. Morgan Magic: 1988–1991

The Red Sox shored up one of the team's biggest weaknesses after the 1987 season, trading pitchers Al Nipper and Calvin Schiraldi to the Chicago Cubs for Lee Smith, one of the best relief pitchers in baseball. The confused ownership situation was resolved with Thomas Yawkey's widow Jean Yawkey buying out Buddy Leroux's stake in the team, leaving the Jean R. Yawkey Trust as majority owner. Day-to-day control of the team passed to John Harrington, an accountant and former controller of the American League who had been a trusted associate of the Yawkeys since 1973. Nevertheless, the team continued to struggle for the first half of the season.

In June, star third baseman Wade Boggs was hit with a palimony suit by his longtime mistress, real estate agent Margo Adams, who had been traveling with the team on road trips and claimed Boggs had promised to support her. This was news to Debbie Boggs, Wade's wife. It was also unwelcome news to many of Wade's Sox teammates, who knew that their own road-trip adventures were likely to be aired in any trials. (They eventually were revealed in a notorious *Penthouse* interview.) When a shouting match erupted on the team bus between Boggs and some of his teammates, it became clear that McNamara had lost control of the team. He was fired with the team mired at 43–42, and replaced on an interim basis by longtime Pawtucket manager and loyal organization man Joe Morgan (not the same Joe Morgan who starred in Cincinnati and is now an ESPN broadcaster).

The only major change that Morgan made was to insert Jody Reed into the starting lineup at shortstop, but Morgan's folksy-but-competent style was a huge relief after the directionless McNamara. The team won 12 in a row and 19 of 20. They set a new record by winning 24 straight games at home. Morgan made the team his own, even winning a brief fistfight with fading star Jim Rice, who was offended that Morgan had pinch hit for him. Jody Reed hit .293 as the starting shortstop. Wade Boggs, despite all the acrimony, hit .366. Mike Greenwell hit .325 with 22 homers and 119 RBI, and both Dwight Evans and Ellis Burks finished the year over .290. In Roger Clemens, Bruce Hurst, and midseason pickup Mike Boddicker, the Red Sox had three frontline starters, and Lee Smith and Bob Stanley both had great years in relief. The rest of the pitching didn't amount to much, but there was enough Morgan Magic to carry the team to 89 wins and victory in one of the closest division races ever—only 3½ games separated the first-place Red Sox from the fifth-place Yankees.

The Red Sox were swept out of the playoffs by a powerful Oakland Athletics team (they stopped using A's as a nickname) that won 104 games during the season. All four of the Oakland victories were saved by former Red Sox ace Dennis Eckersley, who had gotten control of his alcoholism and revived his career as a relief pitcher.

The Red Sox stayed competitive in 1989, although Wade Boggs and Mike Greenwell saw their hitting come back to earth a bit, and Ellis Burks, Dwight Evans and Marty Barrett missed time from injuries. (In Barrett's case, it was the beginning of the end of his career from a knee injury that had been mistreated by the club physician, right after he signed a longterm contract. Barrett would later sue the team.) Bruce Hurst, deeply religious and just as deeply offended by the sordid fallout of the Margo Adams scandal, left the club as a free agent, leaving Clemens, Boddicker, and newcomer John Dopson (in his single effective season with the Sox) as the only consistent starters. The relief pitching carried the team at times, led by another excellent season from Lee Smith and an equally strong one from lefthander Rob Murphy, obtained from Cincinnati for Todd Benzinger. Toward the end of the season, the Red Sox picked up 33-year-old ambidextrous reliever Greg Harris, who would be a key contributor for several years, after he was released by the Philadelphia Phillies. But the Red Sox just didn't have enough pitching to win any more than they did, with general manager Lou Gorman unable to patch the holes in the rotation that came from Hurst leaving and injuries to Oil Can Boyd. Morgan's welcome wore off a bit in 1989, and some of the players—especially Marty Barrett and fading pitcher Bob Stanley—grumbled about the roles Morgan was asking them to play. There was speculation that Morgan would never make it through the 1990 season. Morgan, for his own part, dismissed the speculations, and said that he planned to manage for three more years before retiring.

But the skeptics turned out to be wrong. Morgan

Key Players, 1988–1991

Marty Barrett, 2b
Mike Boddicker, p
Wade Boggs 3b
Ellis Burks, of
Oil Can Boyd, p
Jack Clark, dh
Roger Clemens, p
Danny Darwin, p
Nick Esasky, 1b
Dwight Evans, of
Rich Gedman, c
Jeff Gray, p
Mike Greenwell, of
Greg Harris, p
Bruce Hurst, p
Joe Morgan, manager
Rob Murphy, p
Tony Pena, c
Carlos Quintana, of-1b
Jeff Reardon, p
Jody Reed, ss-2b-3b
Jim Rice, of
Lee Smith, p
Bob Stanley, p
Mo Vaughn, 1b
Matt Young, p

still had an injury-prone lineup and a shortage of pitching in 1990, but found a way to win the division anyway. With a black hole at catcher replaced by free agent Tony Peña, a former National League superstar now reduced to a light-hitting defensive specialist, and 24-year-old longtime prospect Carlos Quintana taking over at first base for Nick Esasky, who had left as a free agent, the Red Sox still managed to lead the league in hitting and on-base percentage, although their offense was far from dominant. Dwight Evans was reduced to a designated hitter role by his bad back. In an attempt to fill the void in right field, GM Lou Gorman traded Lee Smith—the team's best relief pitcher—for Tom Brunansky, a former Minnesota slugger fallen on hard times in the National League, but Brunansky turned out to be mediocre. Smith's role in the bullpen was replaced

When I was about six or seven, I discovered baseball. I didn't discover it in the way that leads to collecting cards, learning mounds of trivia about the players, memorizing statistics and being able to rattle them off: I just discovered baseball.

I was raised in a nonreligious household: my parents were nonpracticing Red Sox fans. Or at least I suspect so; following the Sox is said to run in the female line in the Harringtons, and my father, while largely nonpartisan, did go to college at MIT and thus was exposed to the infectious bodies of such fandom. I suspect that I was raised by nonpracticing Sox fans for a specific reason, though—the only ballpark whose name I knew was Fenway. I remember peering through the sports section of *The Washington Post* as I grew up in Maryland, and deciphering the standings and the box scores. I remember the Sox second in the standings, though I do not remember which year that was, nor which month of the year, and I remember saying, "I was born in Boston. Therefore, I'm a Red Sox fan." Things are much simpler when you're seven.

For years, when asked where I was born, I have given the answer, "Fenway. The region, not the ballpark." (I was born in the Boston Lying-In, later Brigham and Women's.)

I remember sitting on the floor in my grandfather's house in Stoughton sometime before he died, watching the game, learning the rules by the process of osmosis that baseball uses to enter the minds of small children and never leave again. I remember that he gave me a baseball bat, and it was one of my most precious possessions until my father and my brother managed to lose it at one of my brother's Little League games, something which I have yet to forgive entirely.

I don't remember 1986. My grandfather died that year.

I remember 1990, though.

My kid brother also discovered baseball. And was born-again as a true, diehard, passionate Oakland fan. (He discovered baseball, I fear, while Oakland was running very high, but my respect for his loyalty has increased since he stuck with them when they weren't.)

I was twelve. He was eight. He had the baseball cards, quoted the statistics, praised the glories of Canseco and McGwire, prattled on at length. He was an Oakland fan through and through, and it was a good year to be an Oakland fan.

It was also a good year to be a Red Sox fan.

It was a bad year to watch the series for the pennant, when the two people in the house who really wanted to see it were banished to the guest bedroom and the crotchety old television that only nominally had color, and only when jiggered correctly. It was a bad year for siblings to watch the games together under such circumstances, especially with one of them a Red Sox fan, and the other rooting for the Athletics.

That was my first Red Sox heartbreak. But I did manage to avoid strangling my kid brother.

I continued as a Red Sox fan, stubborn and set in my ways: this was in my blood. I was born in the Fens.

Then I moved back to Massachusetts, and had come home, resting safe and secure in the Hub of the Red Sox universe. Here it was safe to pupate from casual fan into diehard; here I am and shall stay.

—Heather Anne Nicoll

by Jeff Reardon, an aging relief star who had been lured back to his native Massachusetts as a free agent.

With no real starting pitchers besides Roger Clemens and Mike Boddicker, manager Morgan turned to castoff reliever Greg Harris, ex-UPS driver Dana Kiecker—a 29-year-old rookie—and 28-year-old career minor leaguer Tom Bolton. Somehow, the three of them combined for a 31–23 record, and the patchwork pitching staff finished fourth in the league in ERA. Together with excellent years by Clemens (21–6) and Boddicker (17–8), it was enough to give the Red Sox an 88–74 record—just enough to squeak into the playoffs in a weak division. The close race led to a terrible trade, however. Rob Murphy had inexplicably self-destructed during the season, leaving the Red Sox very thin in the bullpen behind Jeff Reardon and rookie Jeff Gray. General manager Gorman wanted to pick up Larry Andersen, a 37-year-old middle reliever who was pitching well for Houston. Houston wanted AAA third base prospect Scott Cooper, but Gorman surprised them by counter-offering AA third baseman Jeff Bagwell, who had just won the Eastern League MVP award despite playing in a terrible hitter's park. Andersen would pitch well for the last three weeks of the season and then leave as a free agent, while Bagwell went on to become a likely Hall of Famer in Houston.

Once again, there was no magic in the playoffs. For the second time in three years, the Red Sox were swept by a more powerful (103–59) Oakland Athletics team. Eckersley pitched in the first three games for Oakland, picking up two saves. In the second inning of the fourth game, with the Red Sox down to their last chance at survival, Roger Clemens blew up at umpire Terry Cooney, who threw Clemens out of the game. The Red Sox went down in a 3–1 defeat.

The next year may have been Morgan's best year as a manager, and one of Lou Gorman's worst as a GM. Dwight Evans was forced to play his last season in Baltimore when the team refused to pick up his option, instead keeping Mike Marshall, who would only play 22 games in 1991. Mike Boddicker left as a free agent, signing with Kansas City. Gorman signed *three* big-money free agents to longterm contracts, only one of whom was much help in 1991. Jack Clark was a 35-year-old who had been one of the best hitters in the National League in his prime. After an awful start, he did manage 28 homers and 96 walks to go with a poor .249 batting average. Danny Darwin, a 35-year-old pitcher coming off an ERA title in a great pitcher's park in Houston, managed only 12 games before injuries ended his season. Matt Young, a 32-year-old pitcher with great stuff but astonishingly bad control, went 3–7 with an awful 5.18 ERA. After Roger Clemens and part-time starter Greg Harris, the team had *no* reliable starting pitching. The bullpen was better for the season's first half, with increasingly fragile 35-year-old closer Jeff Reardon and lefty specialist Tony Fossas supported by Jeff Gray, who was having an astonishing breakout season. Then, after pitching in 50 games, Gray suffered a career-ending stroke in July. After a terrible start, Morgan started playing kids ahead of the high-priced free agents. The team went on an incredible six-week run, going 31–10 and almost catching the Blue Jays for the division title. The Red Sox managed an 84–78 record and a third place finish, remarkable under the circumstances.

18. Return to Chaos: 1992–1994

After the 1991 season, the Red Sox fired manager Joe Morgan and promoted rising star Butch Hobson from the manager's job at Pawtucket (AAA), ostensibly because they feared he would be hired by the Yankees. It was a job that Hobson wasn't ready for. He came in, replacing a popular manager, to an aging, talent-depleted team that still thought it was good. The roster was filled with players that were past their prime (Wade Boggs, Tom Brunansky, Jack Clark), weren't ready yet (Mo Vaughn) or never were any good (Bob Zupcic, Luis Rivera). Things got off on the wrong foot quickly when the best player on the team, star pitcher Roger Clemens, was late for spring training, without making so much as a courtesy call to inform his new manager. But if things were bad before Clemens showed up, they got worse when he arrived. The first real footage of Hobson to be shown in Boston in the spring of 1992 was the manager following the star pitcher around, the pitcher wearing headphones and, to all appearances, completely ignoring Hobson. Despite surprisingly good pitching, the Red Sox plummeted in the standings, finishing 73–89—their first last-place finish in 60 years. The once-powerful hitting fell apart completely. Despite playing in a good hitter's park, the Red Sox hit .246 as a team, finishing thirteenth of the league's 14 teams in batting average and twelfth in home runs. Although the team would play better in the two years that followed, they would have losing records for three years in a row.

At the same time, other changes were going on. Owner Jean Yawkey died after a stroke at age 83. The terms of her will left her 53% of the team to the Jean R. Yawkey Trust, which was to continue to be run by John Harrington, and also was to continue to disburse millions of dollars to local charities every year, particularly the Jimmy Fund.

While the team continued to struggle, a transition was going on as well. Lou Gorman made two more big free agent signings, replacing Jack Clark with another ex-National League slugger, 38-year-old former MVP Andre Dawson, who'd had nearly a dozen knee operations, and bringing in 32-year-old former Cy Young Award winner Frank Viola to give the starting rotation the reliable lefthander it had lacked since Bruce Hurst's departure. Both players were troubled by injuries while in Boston. After Wade Boggs, the team's last hitting star, left as a free agent following the 1992 season, the Red Sox finally made a commitment to rebuild with young players, and the team began to improve.

First baseman Mo Vaughn, shortstop John Valentin, and third baseman Scott Cooper all moved into the lineup. Bob Zupcic was given a long audition for the center field job. The changes came too late

Key Players, 1992–1994

Wade Boggs 3b
Tom Brunansky, of
Ellis Burks, of
Jack Clark, DH
Roger Clemens, p
Scott Cooper, 3b
Danny Darwin, p
Dwight Evans, of
Mike Greenwell, of
Greg Harris, p
Butch Hobson, manager
Tony Pena, c
Paul Quantrill, p
Carlos Quintana, of-1b
Jeff Reardon, p
Jody Reed, ss-2b-3b
Aaron Sele, p
John Valentin, ss
Mo Vaughn, 1b
Frank Viola, p
Matt Young, p

for Lou Gorman, whose tenure began with a flurry of terrific personnel moves, but who would end up being remembered for the ones that came back to haunt him—the trade of Jeff Bagwell and the free agent signings of Matt Young, Jack Clark, Andre Dawson, and Danny Darwin. In January 1994 he was replaced by former Montreal Expos general manager Dan Duquette, a Massachusetts native, longtime Red Sox fan, and one of the youngest GMs in the major leagues.

Butch Hobson managed the team for three years, amassing a 207–232 record. This record was largely due to the lack of talent on the team. Despite that, there was never any confidence in Hobson among the fandom. He appeared to be overmatched by the job, unable or unwilling to make difficult player decisions, and not up to tactical decision making in game situations. The media called the team the "sons of Butches," at first as an affectionate tribute to Hobson, but later in a derogatory way. It was widely expected that he would be fired as soon as Lou Gorman was replaced by Dan Duquette, but Duquette left Hobson in place during the strike-shortened 1994 season. That would be Hobson's last managerial season at the major league level. After the 1994 season was officially canceled, Hobson was fired and replaced by Kevin Kennedy.

19. The Dan Duquette Era: 1995–2000

More than most general managers, Dan Duquette put his stamp on the team he ran. In seven years as Red Sox general manager, Duquette was both admired and reviled by fans and the media, sometimes almost simultaneously. A tremendously popular choice when he was hired by John Harrington, Duquette was hailed as a native New Englander and lifelong Red Sox fan who would understand the team and its fans in a way that no outsider could. Much of the media criticism of Duquette, however, came because of the very New England characteristics for which he was prized—he was seen as aloof and taciturn, guarded in his conversations, keeping his own counsel and not talking to the media unless he had something concrete to say. He was criticized as a New England intellectual who took unconventional approaches to the game of baseball, at the time dominated by Southern and Western traditionalists. He made a bunch of terrific player acquisitions (and a few not-so-terrific ones), rebuilt a Red Sox minor league system that he felt wasn't productive (in the process firing a number of popular media sources), mostly erased the lingering stigma of racism from the Red Sox system, and fielded strong if erratically managed teams. But he was not a great interview, and was frequently derided in the media for this lack of articulation, which was more conspicuous because Duquette followed Lou Gorman, who was comfortable with the media and at ease in interviews. One of the ways that Duquette tried to compensate for his lack of media presence was in the managers he chose—and that, too, came back to haunt him at times.

A Massachusetts native, Duquette came from Dalton and attended Amherst College. In 1991, after working his way through the Milwaukee Brewers organization, Duquette became the youngest GM in baseball with the Montreal Expos. There he assembled a talented team under tight financial restrictions, relying on player development and canny trading of mature talent for prospects.

Upon joining the Sox in 1994, Duquette announced a five-year plan for rebuilding the team and its minor league system. The heart of this plan was to remain competitive without signing major free agents who would cost the team draft picks or trading away high-level prospects. The team was to be rebuilt largely through the farm system and through economical signings. In 1994, Butch Hobson's last season, Duquette went about seeing what the Red Sox farm system had to offer. Unproductive players were quickly shuttled off the roster. Minor leaguers and other players—talented castoffs from other systems who had been injured or unproductive for reasons that could be fixed—were given chances to prove themselves, in what became a hallmark of Duquette's style.

The results were mixed in 1994. While the team was still bad, fans enjoyed seeing new players who had the potential to be very good, rather than following the previous few years' strategy of signing end-of-the road veterans who still had enough left to give the team the illusion of mediocrity (to use sportswriter Peter Gammons's phrase). The Red Sox used an astonishing 45 players in the strike-shortened 1994 season. (The 1995 season was also shortened before the labor problems were at least temporarily settled.) Some of those players, like catcher Damon Berryhill and center fielder Lee Tinsley, were just as mediocre as the people they replaced. Some, like catcher Rich Rowland, pitcher Scott Bankhead, and outfielders Wes Chamberlain and Andy Tomberlin, didn't justify the hype, or never regained skills that they had lost to injury. But while the first year's experiment didn't succeed, Duquette made it clear that the status quo was changing, that the team would emphasize young and undervalued players where possible, giving big-money contracts only to reward Sox players who had done well or to fill in a key missing piece, and to avoid trades of prospects for overvalued older players. That strategy would pay off in the years to come. The times when Duquette did not follow his own plan led to some of his biggest failures—such as signing Steve Avery and trading for Ed Sprague.

After the 1994 season, Butch Hobson was fired and replaced by former Texas manager Kevin Kennedy. Kennedy was polished with the media, gave a good interview, and was good at in-game strategy. His people skills would presumably allow Duquette to play a more behind-the-scenes role in rebuilding the Red Sox. Kennedy liked power-hitting teams, and Duquette went out and got him one, trading speedy center fielder Otis Nixon for slugging former MVP Jose Canseco, signing power-hitting catcher Mike Macfarlane, and bringing in underpriced sluggers such as Mark Whiten and Reggie Jefferson to complement the team's key hitters like Mo Vaughn, John Valentin, and Mike Greenwell. Once again Duquette auditioned other teams' castoffs—a record 53 players spent time on the major league roster during the season—and this time the strategy

Key Players, 1995–2000

Jose Canseco, of
Roger Clemens, p
Brian Daubach, 1b
Carl Everett, of
Nomar Garciaparra, ss
Tom Gordon, p
Mike Greenwell, of
Reggie Jefferson, 1b-of
Kevin Kennedy, manager
Derek Lowe, p
Pedro Martinez, p
Tim Naehring, ss-2b-3b
Trot Nixon, of
Jose Offerman, 2b-1b
Troy O'Leary, of
Aaron Sele, p
John Valentin, ss
Mo Vaughn, 1b
Tim Wakefield, p
Jimy Williams, manager

worked beautifully. Outfielder Troy O'Leary, a Milwaukee castoff, was inserted into the starting lineup and hit .308. Second baseman Luis Alicea stabilized the infield while hitting .270. Thirty-six-year-old former batting champion Willie McGee hit .285 off the bench. But most of all, Duquette found pitching. Knuckleball pitcher Tim Wakefield, released by the Pittsburgh Pirates, came up in May and carried the team for much of the year, going 16–8, 2.95 in a season when ace Roger Clemens and number two starter Aaron Sele were limited by injuries. Erik Hanson, picked up cheaply after a year of injuries in Cincinnati, went 15–5. Rheal Cormier, picked up in a trade for third baseman Scott Cooper (who had lost his job to Tim Naehring), filled in effectively as both a starter and reliever. Mike Maddux, forgotten older brother of National League superstar Greg Maddux, was very good in a middle relief role. Rule 5 draftee Vaughn Eshelman finished the year 6–3 after a surprisingly good start. Despite a lower payroll than the previous year the Red Sox went 86–58 and won the American League East before being swept out of the Division Series (a new round of play-offs introduced along with wild card teams) by a powerhouse Cleveland Indians team that had gone 100–44. (Boston would get its revenge a few years later.)

If everything had gone right for Duquette's system in 1995, things were not so smooth in 1996. Once again, he brought in a record number of players—54 this time—and once again he found some gems. Jeff Frye replaced Luis Alicea at second base and hit .286. Catcher Mike Stanley, signed away from the Yankees, hit .270 with 24 home runs. Reggie Jefferson, hobbled by injuries the previous year, returned to health and hit .347 in a platoon role. Tom Gordon was obtained from Kansas City and won 12 games, although he pitched inconsistently. But this year the team was never in the race. They started the season dreadfully, losing 16 of their first 20 games, before recovering to finish 85–77. There were accusations that Kevin Kennedy hadn't prepared the team properly during spring training, and whisperings about a caste system in the locker room. Kennedy was very popular among the team's star players, particularly Roger Clemens, Mike Greenwell, and Jose Canseco, but others claimed that Kennedy was quick to take credit for wins while always blaming the players for losses. Tensions grew as the season neared its end. Mike Greenwell, unhappy that the Red Sox wouldn't guarantee him a big new contract and a starting role the following season (despite his falling production), cleaned out his locker before the end of the season, even though the team was technically still in the pennant race. Clemens and Canseco both had harsh words for Duquette, and it was unclear how much Kennedy and bench coach Tim Johnson backed the players.

After the season Kennedy was fired, Canseco was traded to Oakland for pitcher John Wasdin, and Clemens and Greenwell were allowed to leave as free agents. Although Greenwell never played in the major leagues again, Clemens went on to revive his career (which had been limited by injuries for several years) in Toronto, New York, and Houston—winning four more Cy Young awards—and is still starring for Houston in 2005 at age 42. Although Tim Johnson was a media favorite to be hired as manager, he also was allowed to leave. (Johnson later became manager for Toronto, where he was fired after it was revealed that he had fabricated stories of wartime experiences in Vietnam—where he had never served—to inspire his players.) After reportedly being turned down in his pursuit of some high-profile managerial candidates, Dan Duquette settled on Atlanta third base coach Jimy Williams, whose folksy speaking style was slightly reminiscent of New England hero Joe Morgan. Williams was highly regarded as a coach but had been a conspicuous failure in his previous managerial position with the Toronto Blue Jays. He'd managed one team that had blown a seemingly insurmountable lead by collapsing at the end of the season. And in 1989 the Blue Jays were 12–24 when he was fired—then turned their season around and won the division. (The same thing would happen to Williams in Houston in 2004; the Astros were 44–44 when Williams was fired, then went 48–26 the rest of the way to make the playoffs.) Another key hire was also made, as Duquette replaced pitching coach Al Nipper with Joe Kerrigan, with whom he'd worked in Montreal (an unusual move, since managers generally select their own coaches).

In 1997 the player movements continued, with 46 more players seeing time with the Red Sox. Duquette had said the pace of change would slow down as the Sox minor league system began to contribute more longterm members of the team. However, the minors were slow to produce the players he needed. Although shortstop Nomar Garciaparra had a tremendous rookie year and catcher Scott Hatteberg developed into a valuable contributor, there wasn't the steady flow of talent Duquette had hoped for. The lack of frontline starting pitching to replace Roger Clemens forced Duquette to lavish money on former prized Atlanta pitcher Steve Avery, who was a disaster. The team's record actually worsened in Jimy Williams's first year, when the Sox went 78–84 despite leading the league in batting average.

Reacting to the lack of productivity from the minor leagues, Duquette made changes. Director of Player Development Bobby Schaefer was fired, as was Director of Minor League Operations Ed Kenney Jr., whose father had also run the minor league system for many years. Several other key minor league personnel either left as a result of the firings or were forced out. Duquette was harshly criticized for the firings, particularly by Peter Gammons, who began attacking Duquette in his weekly column in the *Boston Globe* and continued the practice when he moved on to ESPN. Gammons also attacked Duquette's emphasis on pursuing comparatively inexpensive Latin American and Asian players instead of players acquired through the amateur draft—who frequently commanded millions in signing bonuses—and others picked up the chorus.

As a manager, Jimy Williams turned out to be a mixed blessing. The press, at first hostile, and then bewildered, soon warmed to Williams's surreal quotes, which didn't always answer their questions but generally made for good copy. Unlike Kevin Kennedy, Williams never criticized his players publicly, which gave him the support of the team. But at times Williams's lineup selections would be just as surreal as his answers to interviewers' questions. And there were times when Williams and Duquette were clearly not on the same page. In the clearest example, Williams gave struggling pitcher Steve Avery—who was pitching dreadfully and had been pulled from the rotation—an additional start that guaranteed another year on Avery's bloated contract. Two years later he would play a declining Mike Stanley enough to guarantee an option year in Stanley's contract. These moves were popular with players, but made it more difficult for Duquette—working within a budget set by the Yawkey Trust—to construct a competitive team.

Williams wanted a better defensive team instead of the slugging team that Kevin Kennedy had favored, and Duquette gave it to him. Fleet center fielder Darren Lewis, a former Gold Glove winner, was signed. Another fast outfielder, Damon Buford, was obtained as part of a trade for Aaron Sele. Mike Benjamin was signed as a utility infielder. When Jeff Frye went down with an injury, Duquette bowed to Williams's request that he sign former Atlanta second baseman Mark Lemke. Speedy rookie infielder Donnie Sadler spent time on the roster. Except for Buford, none of these players hit very well, but the team's defense did improve. The team batting average fell from first in the league to third, despite excellent seasons from first baseman Mo Vaughn and shortstop Nomar Garciaparra.

The decrease in hitting was overshadowed by the surge in pitching, however. Pitching coach Joe Kerrigan had promised great results and he delivered them. Led by new acquisition Pedro Martinez—a wiry Dominican pitcher who Duquette had traded for both in Montreal and in Boston, and who won 19 games—the team surged to second in the league in ERA in 1998. Tim Wakefield won 17 games, and Bret Saberhagen, one of Duquette's reclamation projects who'd been picked up cheap after seriously injuring his arm, went 15–8. Tom Gordon, an inconsistent starter, was converted to the team's closer, where he was nearly invincible, setting a team record by saving 46 games. Derek Lowe (obtained along with catcher Jason Varitek in a steal of a trade from the Seattle Mariners) was erratic as a starter, but then developed into an outstanding middle reliever. Jim Corsi, repeatedly released by other teams, also pitched extremely well in relief.

The Red Sox won 92 games and a wild card spot. Once again, they faced the Cleveland Indians. After Pedro Martinez won the first game, the Red Sox lost two straight and were on the brink of elimination. There were widespread media calls for Jimy Williams to bring back Pedro Martinez on short rest for Game 4. Instead, he made the controversial decision to start erratic lefthander Pete Schourek, a late-season acquisition—reasoning that the Red Sox had to win two games, and they had the best chance of winning them both if they saved Martinez for Game 5, when he would be rested. Schourek pitched extremely well, but the gamble failed anyway. Tom Gordon, who hadn't blown a save in four months, was hit hard in the eighth inning and the Red Sox lost 2–1.

The offseason revolved around a contentious negotiation with the most visible Red Sox star, slugging first baseman Mo Vaughn. Duquette and Vaughn had been conducting on-again off-again contract negotiations for some time amid an atmosphere of growing distrust. Vaughn publicly criticized the team for not supporting him after he'd wrecked a car and been arrested on suspicion of driving while intoxicated. He also criticized the team for not locking up key players to longterm contracts. When Duquette responded by signing Troy O'Leary, Darren Lewis, and John Valentin to longterm deals (all of which would come back to haunt Duquette) and signed free agent second baseman and leadoff hitter Jose Offerman to a 4-year contract, Vaughn complained that signing other players first showed a lack of respect for him. Despite a series of offers from the Red Sox, Vaughn eventually signed a deal with the Anaheim Angels that briefly made him the highest-paid player in the game. Duquette drew harsh media criticism as the general manager who allowed both Roger Clemens and Mo Vaughn to walk away. There were derisive comparisons between Mo Vaughn and Jose Offerman in the media, especially when Duquette described Offerman as having replaced Vaughn's "on-base ability," which was true, but only further highlighted the loss of Vaughn's ability to hit 40 home runs a year. (Not re-signing Vaughn turned out to be an excellent move, despite the criticism Duquette received for it; Vaughn's batting average dropped 50 points in his first year in Anaheim, and his career soon succumbed to injuries and poor conditioning. He managed 79 at bats for the Mets in the 2003-04 seasons combined, but was paid more than $17 million each year.) Heading into the 1999 season there were widespread predictions that the Red Sox would do poorly.

Instead they won 94 games and returned to the playoffs. The hitting did fall off badly, with terrible seasons by Darren Lewis and Damon Buford and an injury-filled year by John Valentin having as much effect as Vaughn's loss. The Red Sox finished seventh in the league in batting average and ninth in home runs—despite solid seasons from the reviled Offerman and scrap-heap pickup Brian Daubach, and a batting title from Nomar Garciaparra (.357). But in 1999 the pitching was even stronger, finishing first in the league in ERA. Although the team had no consistent starters behind the astonishing Pedro Martinez, who went 23–4 and won the Cy Young Award, and Bret Saberhagen, who pitched brilliantly between repeated struggles with injuries, pitching coach Joe Kerrigan and manager Jimy Williams seemed to have an uncanny ability to get the most out of pitchers, pulling pitchers out quickly before they could get into trouble. When Tom Gordon was injured and missed most of the season, Williams plugged

It all started in September 1999. On a holiday to Boston with friends I had a choice of an afternoon shopping or doing my own thing. I was already aware of the legendary Sam "Mayday" Malone and his exploits with the Red Sox so opted for a tour of Fenway Park to see where it all took place.

I remember reveling in the history and quirkiness of the stadium and realizing that here was a ballpark with a history and tradition that could never be built into a newly erected space conscious structure. There was a story to every part we visited and I quickly realized I wanted to participate in the next chapter! I was hooked! However, in the first of many disappointments, my visit coincided with the team's longest road trip! I returned home to England without ever seeing my newly adopted club in the flesh.

I did some searching and managed to find a late night television program in the U.K. that covered baseball and so I was able to follow the ups and many downs of the Red Sox. A crash course in the rules meant I could appreciate the finer points of the game and despair as yet another challenge faltered. I soon learnt that following the Old Towne Team wasn't easy! Despite all this I vowed to return and see them for myself.

I was eventually able to return in July 2003 and August 2004 and this time made sure I bought tickets for Fenway. I have been fortunate to see some outstanding plays including a Trot Nixon grand slam, a Pedro complete game and a bottom of the ninth game-winning shot by Orlando Cabrera that caromed vertically off the scoreboard on the Green Monster, giving Johnny Damon valuable extra time needed to make it home safely! A brilliant finale! I hope my visits are to become annual from now on and I get to see many more similar plays from the newly crowned World Champions!

—Colin Smith

knuckleballer Tim Wakefield into the closer's role, and when Wakefield began to falter Derek Lowe took over as relief ace. Late in the season, Duquette traded with the Chicago Cubs for reliever Rod Beck, a former closer coming off an arm injury, who pitched extremely well down the stretch. Ramon Martinez, Pedro's older brother who had been the Dodgers' ace until hurting his arm, came back from injury rehabilitation to pitch well in the season's final weeks.

In the playoffs against the Cleveland Indians once again, the Red Sox appeared to be destined for a quick exit. Pedro had to leave the first game early with a pulled muscle in his back, and appeared done for the series. The Indians won the game 3–2 with a ninth-inning run. In the second game they hammered Saberhagen, who was pitching with a shoulder that would be operated on immediately after the playoffs. Facing elimination in Game 3 and needing to win three games in a row against a powerful Indians team, the Red Sox managed to stave off defeat by scoring six runs against a weak Cleveland bullpen to break open a tie game. In Game 4 the end appeared to be in sight when Boston starter Kent Mercker was knocked out in the second inning. Instead the Red Sox erupted for 23 runs, led by seven RBI from John Valentin, who'd had an injury-marred season up to that point. The fifth game was even more remarkable. Once again, Saberhagen was knocked out early, and this time Pedro Martinez was brought into the game in relief. Despite the back injury—which made him unable to throw his fastball effectively—he held the Indians hitless with a combination of off-speed pitches and pure guile. Twice Cleveland walked Nomar Garciaparra to face the slumping Troy O'Leary, and twice O'Leary homered, driving in seven runs. The Red Sox won 12–8 and moved on to face the World Champion New York Yankees in the American League Championship Series.

Seven years ago I suffered a stroke that partially paralyzed my left side. It severely limited my ability to walk, especially in crowded, uncertain conditions. At one time, something like a ball game at Fenway Park was out of the question.

On Sunday September 25, 2000, the last day of the home season for the Boston Red Sox, I attended my first post-stroke game.

We got lucky in the parking, getting a spot 50 yards or so from the main gates. I bought a traditional Sox cap before even entering the park and had pictures taken in front of the park by my brother, who apparently understood the significance of the event. Once through the turnstiles, I had to get a program and a yearbook. We went to our seats through the twisting, rising ramp. When I got my first sight of the field, tears came to my eyes. I hadn't expected this degree of emotion. We found our seats, which was tough, as going down steps is my biggest challenge. Got seated about 15 minutes before game time. Though it's work for me to stand, I did my duty and stood for the National Anthem (part of the whole experience).

The game got under way under threatening skies. It rained some early, but we stayed dry because we were in box seats just to the first base side of home plate. Ohka was very impressive for seven-plus innings, but Mussina was a little better. Baltimore scored its only run in the eighth. The Sox had a couple of good scoring chances late, but failed to score while having the game-tying run thrown out at the plate in the ninth. A disappointment, but it did not spoil the specialness of the day for this disabled fan from Vermont.

I've seen many games at Fenway, some very memorable for many reasons, but while I don't remember my first game, I'm never likely to forget this one.

—Don Violette

The tone of the heartbreaking series was set in the first game, when Rod Beck gave up a tenth-inning home run to Bernie Williams to lose a close game. Another close loss followed before Pedro, his back improving, shut the Yankees and ex-Sox star Roger Clemens down 13–1 in Game 3. The last two games dissolved from close games into Yankees blowouts as the Red Sox seemed to self-destruct amid a series of questionable umpiring calls (the most devastating one occurred when Jose Offerman was called out to end a rally, while replays show the tag missed him badly). The Yankees went on to another World Series victory, but Jimy Williams was awarded Manager of the Year.

Still, there were high hopes that the 2000 Red Sox would overtake the Yankees and challenge for the World Series. The Red Sox had the best pitching in baseball, and the single best pitcher in Pedro Martinez. A big hole in the lineup was filled over the winter when Dan Duquette traded minor league shortstop Adam Everett for Houston center fielder Carl Everett (no relation), a 28-year-old coming off a season in which he hit .325 with 28 homers and 27 steals, while playing great defense. Anticipating that offensive reinforcements would be needed during the season, Duquette stocked the Pawtucket minor league club with players like Israel Alcantara, Morgan Burkhart, and Curtis Pride: older minor leaguers with great hitting potential. Coming into the season, optimism was high. *Sports Illustrated* even picked the Red Sox to win the World Series.

The Red Sox started the season well, and took first place in May. Although the pitching was still the best in the league—with Pedro Martinez having one of the greatest seasons ever by a pitcher and Derek Lowe taking over the closer's role—the offense began to founder. Jimy Williams continued to emphasize defensive players above offense, even when the team's lack of offense reached critical levels. When John Valentin went down early with a knee injury, he was replaced by light-hitting Wilton Veras (.244 with no homers) and Manny Alexander (.211). Troy O'Leary, in the midst of a terrible divorce, didn't hit at all in the season's first half, but Williams kept playing him. Darren Lewis was awful at the plate (.241 with no power and a below-average number of walks), but Williams played him frequently, even if it meant benching a better-hitting player. Carl Everett started the season red-hot, but after a 10-game suspension (for making contact while arguing with an umpire) and a nagging injury, he was just average. Like Don Zimmer in the 1970s, Williams seemed to develop favorites and to put other players in the doghouse. When deaf outfielder Curtis Pride, who was tearing up the International League, was called up, Williams refused to play him, preferring to stick with Darren Lewis; Williams even gave weak-hitting second baseman Jeff Frye significant time in right field. Eventually Williams forced Pride's release. First baseman Morgan Burkhart was called up and hit outrageously well for two weeks, but the first time he had a bad game he was sent to the bench, and barely played the rest of the year—even after first baseman Brian Daubach was injured and unable to hit effectively during the season's last month. Israel Alcantara, leading the International League in home runs, was called up and hit well. But after a terrible defensive game in Chicago in which Alcantara committed several rookie mistakes, Williams buried him on the bench, giving him only sporadic playing time the rest of the year.

Duquette's options were limited. With the team trying to negotiate a deal with the city of Boston and the state of Massachusetts for a new ballpark, and with the team for sale (the convoluted sale eventually took more than 18 months to complete), firing a popular manager coming off a Manager of the Year award would be difficult. At the same time, with the Yankees looking vulnerable and the rest of the division playing poorly, the Red Sox were letting a narrow window of opportunity slip away, because of his manager's reluctance to entrust playing time to unproven minor leaguers in the heat of the pennant race—no matter how badly his other players fared. In an attempt to add offensive players who Jimy Williams would actually use, Duquette began doing what he had always avoided in the past—trading young prospects for older, declining veterans with good reputations. He sent two prospects to the San Diego Padres for third baseman Ed Sprague, a former All Star who was having a good first half (but was a notoriously poor second-half hitter). He sent two more to Cincinnati for Dante Bichette, a 36-year-old slugger who had a $6 million contract. He signed veterans Bernard Gilkey and Rico Brogna, aging sluggers with good defensive reputations. The gamble failed badly. Williams gave playing time to most of the new acquisitions, but only Bichette hit decently (and even he provided less production than Alcantara and Burkhart combined, in almost exactly as much playing time). Although the Red Sox finished within 2½ games of the Yankees, the race wasn't really that close—a late losing streak by the Yankees closed the gap after the playoff hunt was already all but decided. The Red Sox finished thirteenth in the league in batting average, and eleventh in home runs.

20. End of the Yawkey Era: 2001–2002

After the 2000 season, GM Dan Duquette reverted to his previous style and set about addressing the team's weaknesses. Although he had a poor-hitting team with a great pitching staff (including promising young pitchers such as Tomo Ohka and Paxton Crawford), there was a clamor in the media for Duquette to sign another frontline starting pitcher, such as 32-year-old Baltimore free agent Mike Mussina. Duquette was criticized for his halfhearted pursuit of Mussina—although the effect of that pursuit was to cause the Yankees to pursue Mussina forcefully and sign him to a huge contract. With the Yankees having spent their free agent budget, Duquette turned to pursuing the best hitter available—Cleveland superstar Manny Ramirez, who was only 28. After signing Ramirez to an eight-year $160 million deal, Duquette signed two starting pitchers who'd been forgotten in the free agent madness, Toronto's Frank Castillo and Detroit's Hideo Nomo. Both had pitched about as well as Mussina in 2000, although Duquette signed both of them combined for about half what the Yankees would pay Mussina. At that point, Duquette announced that there would be no more trades of young players before the season. Having patched up the weaknesses in the lineup—

Key Players, 2001
Brian Daubach, 1b-of
Carl Everett, of
Nomar Garciaparra, ss
Joe Kerrigan, manager
Derek Lowe, p
Pedro Martinez, p
Trot Nixon, of
Hideo Nomo, p
Manny Ramirez, of
Jason Varitek, c
Jimy Williams, manager

and with one of the highest payrolls in baseball—the 2001 Red Sox were going to give young players like Trot Nixon, Tomo Ohka, and Paxton Crawford a chance to help the team's core of Nomar Garciaparra, Pedro Martinez, Carl Everett, Manny Ramirez, Derek Lowe, and company go after the World Series in 2001. Duquette's differences with manager Jimy Williams were patched over, at least on the surface, with most of the media taking Williams's side.

For a while it looked like the strategy would work, despite a chaotic spring training. Although Nomar Garciaparra showed up to camp with a wrist injury that would eventually wipe out most of his season and there was grumbling when Jimy Williams benched veterans Jose Offerman and Dante Bichette at the start of the season, the Red Sox got off to a good start. Newcomer Hideo Nomo threw a scintillating no-hitter in the season's second game. Manny Ramirez, though slowed by a hamstring injury for most of the season, homered in his first Fenway at bat and opened the season on a hitting tear, and rookie third baseman Shea Hillenbrand emerged from nowhere to have a terrific first month. The loss of Nomar (who was replaced by a patchwork committee of infielders, none of whom hit well) was offset by the arrival of Ramirez and breakout seasons from Trot Nixon and Jason Varitek, and the team's pitching remained excellent. Williams's control of the team (always based on the players liking and respecting him, which many of them apparently no longer did) seemed to be wavering, and his surreal lineup selection continued, but the team kept winning.

In June the wheels started to come off. A *Sports Illustrated* cover story exposed nationally what had already been widely rumored locally—most of the players on the team had tuned out the manager (even if many still liked him personally) and a few weren't even on speaking terms with Williams. A series of disasters hit the team in the following weeks. Nomar's injury was more serious than originally thought, and his return date was pushed back to August. Jason Varitek, hitting .293 and on a home run hitting tear, broke his elbow while making a spectacular sliding catch. Pedro Martinez developed a sore arm. Bret Saberhagen and John Valentin were only able to play briefly before injuries ended their seasons. Starting pitcher Frank Castillo was in and out of the rotation with a number of injuries. Reliever Hipolito Pichardo, unhappy with his role on the team, abruptly retired. Carl Everett was embroiled in a number of controversies—including an open war with several members of the press corps—and his hitting never returned to the level of the previous year. Rookie Hillenbrand stopped hitting, as did outfielder Troy O'Leary.

For a while the team continued to win anyway. Christened the "Dirt Dogs" (a term coined by ex-Red Sox pitcher Paul Quantrill and popularized by announcer Jerry Remy and others) for their hard-nosed play, Red Sox hitters managed to score enough runs for the team's deep and resilient pitching staff to win more than their share of games. Rolando Arrojo and Tim Wakefield—both exiled to the bullpen during spring training—stepped into the rotation to fill in for injured starters. Although closer Derek Lowe was inconsistent, Rod Beck and Rich Garces anchored a strong bullpen. The thinking was that if the team could stay close to the top, then when Nomar, Pedro, and Varitek returned in August, the Red Sox could make a run at the division-leading Yankees.

August began with Nomar's dramatic return to the lineup and a trade for Expos closer Ugueth Urbina. But instead of being revitalized, the team seemed to fall into a malaise, and Dan Duquette decided that the Red Sox weren't going to be able to win if Williams remained as manager. Taking advantage of Williams's fading popularity and the team's slump, Duquette fired Williams and replaced him as manager with pitching coach Joe Kerrigan—who was heralded for his handling of pitchers, but had no previous managerial experience. Duquette's hope was that the change in managers would spark something akin to the "Morgan Magic" of 1988.

Kerrigan promised to restore stability to the team's lineup, but the continuing rash of injuries prevented him from doing so. Nevertheless, the team seemed to respond at first. Buoyed by Nomar's return to the lineup, the Red Sox started playing well on a West Coast road trip. After winning six of their first nine games under their new skipper, they seemed primed to take off.

It didn't happen. Nomar's comeback had seemed to be progressing well, but suddenly he was hurting again. The team lost a disheartening 18-inning game in Texas, and the next night Nomar played his last game of the season. Those games were the start of a nine-game losing streak which essentially took the team out of the pennant race. Not only was Nomar gone, but the injuries to Jason Varitek and Pedro Martinez were more severe than initially thought (there were whispers that both might be career-threatening); Varitek was lost for the season, and Martinez barely pitched again. When it became clear that the three star players would not be returning, the rest of the team (with the very visible exception of Trot Nixon and a few others) seemed to almost give up on the season. Manny Ramirez, playing on a sore hamstring most of the season, aggravated the injury. Carl Everett, the talented outfielder whose frequent clashes with Jimy Williams had created a rift between Williams and Duquette (who had sided with Everett) the previous year, picked a fight with his new manager as well, and was eventually suspended. Everett's timing—immediately after the September 11 terrorist attacks on the World Trade Center and the Pentagon—reinforced the notion that many players were caught up in petty and personal concerns, rather than the goals of the team as a whole. Only a season-ending winning streak kept the team from finishing below .500 on the year; the Red Sox ended the season in second place at 82–79, a distant 13½ games behind the Yankees.

Dan Duquette—who could do no wrong at the beginning of the season after signing Manny Ramirez—was heavily criticized in the media for the team's collapse. Anti-Duquette signs appeared at games, and an anti-Duquette website received a lot of publicity. With the sale of the team in its final stages, it was widely assumed that Duquette would be out of a job when the new owners took over. When John Harrington, who ran the team for the Jean R. Yawkey Trust set up after owner Jean Yawkey's death, gave Duquette a three-year contract extension, it was seen as a sort of golden parachute.

Nevertheless, Duquette set about rebuilding the team. He traded Everett—who had completely worn out his welcome—to Texas for Darren Oliver, an expensive pitcher coming off two bad seasons, but with none of Everett's emotional baggage. He picked up All Star first baseman Tony Clark for nothing from

Detroit when the Tigers decided they didn't want to pay his $5 million contract. When Hideo Nomo turned down a three-year $22 million contract, Duquette let him leave and replaced him with starting pitchers John Burkett and Dustin Hermanson. Star center fielder Johnny Damon, thought to be out of reach because of his contract demands, was signed to a longterm deal when his price fell, replacing Everett in the lineup. Underachieving and unhappy players like Mike Lansing, Troy O'Leary, Dante Bichette, and Darren Lewis were not re-signed, and were replaced by players with a reputation for maintaining clubhouse harmony. Former Red Sox star Dwight Evans replaced Rick Down as hitting coach, and Mike Stanley—a clubhouse leader when he played with the team— was hired as bench coach.

But all of the offseason moves were overshadowed by the sale of the team, which reached its final stages after years of maneuvering. A huge number of groups had expressed interest in buying the Yawkey Trust's controlling share (53 percent) of the team, which also included Fenway Park and an 80 percent ownership in the New England Sports Network (NESN) regional cable station. More than 10 groups reportedly paid the $50,000 fee to be allowed to bid on the team (each potential bidder also required clearance from Major League Baseball before they were allowed to look at the team's books). By the time the dust cleared and the first round of bids was in, many groups had merged or dropped out, and four serious bidders remained: a group led by Florida Marlins owner John Henry (who would have to sell the Marlins to finance his bid), former Padres owner Tom Werner, and Larry Lucchino, a longtime baseball executive; a local group led by real estate developer Steve Karp and concessionaire Joe O'Donnell; and groups led by New Yorkers Miles Prentice, an investment banker, and Charles Dolan, owner of a media empire, brother of the Cleveland Indians owner, and reputed archenemy of Yankees owner George Steinbrenner. It was an open secret that Major League Baseball preferred Henry's group, because it would facilitate a complicated plan of Commissioner Bud Selig's that involved Henry selling the Marlins to Expos owner Jeff Loria and the league taking over the Expos and either folding the team or moving it.

When the bids came in, Dolan's—which included not only the team, but also an offer to buy out the remaining limited partners if they so chose—was by far the highest. Although there wasn't supposed to be a second round of bidding, Dolan's price was immediately leaked to the media, and the other bidders demanded a right to submit new bids. O'Donnell and Karp's group—the only remaining local bidders—dropped out when it was revealed that John Harrington had extended the contract of team concessionaire Aramark by 10 years. (O'Donnell was a competing concession owner, and not being able to control the team's concessions made his bid financially unworkable.) There were grumblings in the media about the contract extension—especially since it looked like it might be a quid-pro-quo for limited partner Aramark's vote to approve a sale.

After the second round of bidding, Henry and Werner's bid worth $700 million (in cash and assumed debt) was declared the winner. Dolan—who had also bid $700 million but was not given a chance to raise his offer—and Prentice—who had bid an astonishing $790 million—both cried foul. The Massachusetts attorney general got involved, publicly stating that he thought the sale to Henry and Werner's group had been orchestrated by Major League Baseball, and claiming jurisdiction since the sale was held to benefit charitable organizations, which fall under the state's authority. Several congressmen threatened to hold hearings on the status of baseball's antitrust exemption. Harrington claimed that Prentice had been disqualified because his financing had contingencies (although the winning bid was contingent on Henry's sale of the Marlins). When Dolan raised his offer to $750 million and Prentice to $755 million with no contingencies, Harrington said that they were too late and the sale was already closed (although Henry and Werner's winning bid was also received after the bidding had been closed). When Henry and Werner's group agreed to increase the percentage of the sale money that would go to the charitable trust, the attorney general withdrew his protest and the sale was quickly approved at a meeting of baseball owners—despite the fact that the sale of Henry's Marlins had not yet been completed.

After the sale, it was widely rumored that Duquette would be fired as soon as the new owners took control, but as spring training approached he remained the team's GM. Bizarrely, one of the names floated as a potential replacement for Duquette was his own cousin, Jim Duquette, an executive with the New York Mets. Joe Kerrigan, whose candor was refreshing after the impenetrable Jimy Williams—but whose team collapsed down the stretch—hoped for a chance to prove that the collapse was a fluke. But on February 28, the day after the new owners closed the sale, Duquette was fired, with Kerrigan losing his manager's job a week later.

21. Cowboy Up!: 2002–2003

Although the way in which the sale was conducted left a bad taste in many fans' mouths, the new owners' moves quickly seemed to justify Selig's actions. Where John Harrington and Dan Duquette always seemed to mean well but communicate poorly, the new administration had a flair for making just the right gesture, seemingly impossible in Boston's fractured political and media environment. The always-controversial plans to replace Fenway were put on hold, and then scrapped. Plans to change Fenway and add seating incrementally (including right and left field roof seats, premium seats near the dugouts, and most controversially, seats that replaced the netting above the Green Monster) were grudgingly accepted at first—and then received with enthusiasm when they proved to fit in perfectly with the character of the park. Rather than being standoffish absentee owners, the new ownership group quickly became a vocal and visible part of the community, and their clear passion to win (and dislike for the Yankees) won over skeptical fans.

For the time being, general manager Dan Duquette was replaced by Mike Port, who was named interim GM for the season with assurances that he'd be interviewed for the job on a permanent basis. The manager's job went to Grady Little, a 52-year-old former Cleveland coach who was one of the game's hottest managerial prospects. Because Little was hired so late in spring training, however, he was stuck managing a team that had been built for Joe Kerrigan's managerial style, and would also be working with Kerrigan's coaches. (Kerrigan resurfaced as pitching coach for his hometown Phillies; he resigned under pressure from the ownership after the 2004 season when many Phillies pitchers didn't like his unorthodox methods.)

The 2002 team was never as good as it looked on paper, though when the parts clicked, there were some electric performances. Derek Lowe's transformation from reliever to starter proved to be an astonishing success (at least in 2002), and he electrified Boston fans by throwing a near no-hitter in his first start and following it with an actual no-hitter at Fenway Park in his second start, on April 27. Lowe, Pedro Martinez, and a revitalized Tim Wakefield (who rejoined the rotation late in the year) dominated the league, finishing 1–2–4 in the league in ERA and combining for a 52–17 record. The rest of the pitching was shaky, though: Beyond the top three, Boston pitchers dropped off to 41–52 and despite Ugueth Urbina's 40 saves, he and the rest of the relievers were inconsistent. Pitcher Rich Garces, a fan favorite who had anchored the team's middle relief for the previous 2½ years inexplicably lost his effectiveness, finishing the season with a career-killing 7.59 ERA. Dustin Hermanson, expected to be the team's third starter, pulled a hamstring in his first start and took four months (rather than the usual couple of weeks) to heal; when he came back, he pitched ineffectively. John Burkett, the 37-year-old who'd earned a big contract with his 2001 season in Atlanta, was merely average in 2002.

The hitters, too, provided a mix of terrific performances and poor ones. The team finished second in the league in hitting and third in on-base percentage, but only seventh in home runs. Manny Ramirez was the dominant hitter the team had signed him to be, winning the batting title with a .349 average, hitting 33 home runs, leading the league in on-base percentage—but he missed a quarter of the season with injuries. Nomar came back strongly from his lost 2001 season, hitting .310 with 24 homers, though not as strong as he had been before the injury. Newcomer Johnny Damon proved to be a reliable leadoff hitter and had a good season, chipping in 31 steals, hitting 14 homers and drawing more than his share of walks, exactly what the team had expected (though a little short of their hopes, perhaps). Brian Daubach had a nearly identical year to his 2001 season.

But a number of hitters had years ranging from disappointing to terrible. Jason Varitek came back from his elbow injury to anchor the team emotionally, but his power stroke was slow to return, and his walk totals plummeted as well. Trot Nixon, expected to have a breakout year after his promising 2001 season, had trouble adjusting to a full-time role (and facing lefty pitching on a regular basis); Nixon hit 24 homers and drove in 94 runs, but his .256 batting

Key Players, 2002–03

John Burkett, p
Frank Castillo, p
Johnny Damon, of
Brian Daubach, 1b-of
Alan Embree, p
Cliff Floyd, of
Nomar Garciaparra, ss
Shea Hillenbrand, 3b-1b
Byung-Hyun Kim, p
Derek Lowe, p
Pedro Martinez, p
Kevin Millar, 1b-of
Doug Mirabelli, c
Bill Mueller, 3b
Trot Nixon, of
David Ortiz, 1b-DH
Manny Ramirez, of
Mike Timlin, p
Ugueth Urbina, p
Tim Wakefield, p
Scott Williamson, p
Jason Varitek, c
Todd Walker, 2b

average was the lowest of his career. Shea Hillenbrand had a hot start and ended up hitting .293 with 18 homers in his second season, but he only marginally improved on his hideous walk totals. Tony Clark, an All Star with Detroit in 2001, completely lost his batting eye, hitting .207 with only three homers before losing his starting spot. Jose Offerman's knees proved to be completely shot, and the team finally released him midway through the season, despite his hefty contract. Cliff Floyd, the Montreal star obtained in a stretch-drive trade, hit .316 with 7 home runs in 47 games—but only managed to drive in a baffling 18 runs. Role players like light-hitting second baseman Rey Sanchez and 43-year-old future Hall of Famer Rickey Henderson were forced into much bigger roles than the team envisioned. And Grady Little proved to be a much more traditional manager than his reputation had led the team to expect.

Despite its extraordinary individual performances, the 2002 team was less than the sum of its parts. The Red Sox had seven All Stars, but while they played well enough to make the playoffs at times, they never looked like the league's best team. (The All Star Game in 2002 ended in a 7–7 tie when both teams ran out of players, causing an uproar which forced Major League Baseball to change the game's structure to make it more competitive. Among those changes was the decision that the league which won the All Star Game would have home field advantage in the World Series, which benefited the Red Sox in 2004.)

The 2002 team was never really out of the race, but not seriously in it either. Their early-season lead proved ephemeral, and a late-season charge wasn't enough to catch an extraordinary Angels team, on its way to a World Series victory, for the Wild Card. It would have taken 100 victories to win the Wild Card in 2002, and the Red Sox won 93—disappointing considering the new ownership's high hopes and the team's high payroll, but still 11 more wins than in the 2001 season. It seemed like something to build on, and the new ownership intended to do so.

While Port had done a creditable job as the interim general manager, the team wanted someone less traditional, more forward-looking, and more comfortable with the ways the game was becoming increasingly driven by technology and statistical analysis. By November, the Red Sox search focused on Oakland GM Billy Beane, the subject of the influential *Moneyball*, which advocated the importance of on-base percentage and developing inexpensive talent, much as Dan Duquette had. (The difference was that Bill James, Duquette, and others were ahead of the curve and were portrayed in mainstream media as reactionaries, while Beane, with better timing, was seen as the herald of a new era in baseball. Bill James, one of the heroes of the new movement, was quietly hired by the Red Sox as well.) Oakland reluctantly gave Boston permission to talk to Beane, and after he agreed to a 5-year, $12.5 million contract with the Red Sox, Beane's last act as Oakland GM was to be negotiating the compensation the Red Sox would owe the A's for his services (reportedly third baseman Kevin Youkilis, championed in *Moneyball* as "the Greek god of walks"). After thinking about the deal overnight, Beane decided to stay in Oakland, and the Red Sox finally settled on the in-house candidate whose thinking was most like Beane's: 28-year-old assistant GM Theo Epstein. Epstein was the youngest GM in baseball, and the choice was greeted with widespread bemusement, but he proved to be a strong fit for the job, combining Dan Duquette's knack for finding inexpensive talent with a much more laid back, personable demeanor. (Epstein immediately became the most eligible bachelor in Boston.)

The 2003 team was built to be a World Series contender; the feeling in the front office and among ownership was that there was a narrow window of opportunity, both in terms of the team's talent level and because many core players (Pedro Martinez, Nomar Garciaparra, Derek Lowe, and Jason Varitek) would be free agents after the 2004 season, and the team wouldn't be able to afford to keep all of them. With that in mind, Theo Epstein went about systematically plugging the team's holes. First base was filled by jettisoning Clark and obtaining Kevin Millar (coming off a .306 season) from the Florida Marlins, though not before causing a moderate international scandal by blocking the Marlins' attempted sale of Millar to a Japanese team. For depth, Epstein cheaply signed lefty slugger David Ortiz—a 27-year-old who'd hit .272 with 20 homers as a part-timer in Minnesota before the Twins released him in favor of a cheaper option—and Jeremy Giambi, another strong hitter and the younger brother of superstar Jason Giambi. The open wound at second base was filled with Todd Walker, who'd hit .290 or better in five of the previous six seasons, but who had priced himself out of small-market Cincinnati. He signed Bill Mueller, a fine defensive third baseman with good on-base percentages, who was available cheaply because he was coming off two years of injuries; if healthy, Mueller could supplant Hillenbrand at third, but there was little risk in signing him. The relief pitching was shored up by signing Ramiro Mendoza, a former All Star as a swingman with the Yankees, picking up young pitcher Brandon Lyon off waivers from Toronto, and for pitching depth Epstein gave low-risk contracts to a number of underpriced, high-upside veterans coming off injuries or bad situations, such as Mike Timlin, Chad Fox, Robert Person, Ryan Rupe, and Bobby Jones.

The 2003 Red Sox looked like a World Series team, and they certainly hit like one. With the exception of Giambi (who hit .197, lost his job, and later got caught up in a steroid scandal) all of Epstein's hitting acquisitions worked beautifully. The team led the league in hitting (.289), on-base percentage (.360), slugging (a record .491), runs (961), and doubles, and finished second in triples and home runs. Not only did Mueller take over the third base job, he won a surprise batting title, hitting .326 to narrowly edge out teammate Manny Ramirez's .325. Mueller also hit a career-high 19 home runs—which placed him only seventh on a team that had 6 players who hit 25 or more, led by Manny's 37. After Epstein acquired outfielder Gabe Kapler to take some of Trot Nixon's at bats against left-handers, Nixon had the breakout season everyone had expected the year before, hitting .306 with 28 homers, a .396 OBP and a .578 slugging percentage (fourth in the league, right behind Manny). Minnesota castoff David Ortiz forced himself into a full-time job by hitting .288 with 39 doubles and 31 homers, despite starting the season on the bench behind three other players. Even Shea Hillenbrand, who got off to his usual hot start before being supplanted by Mueller at third and Ortiz and Millar at first, contributed when Epstein was able to trade him for All Star pitcher Byun-Hyung Kim.

The pitching was talented but inconsistent, especially in the bullpen, expected to be a strength of the team. Before the season, Epstein had decided not to re-sign Urbina, reasoning that a good-but-not-great closer wasn't worth $8 million or so of the team's resources, and that the Red Sox would be better off with a variety of pitchers who brought different strengths to the table. At worst the manager would have a lot of pitching flexibility, and ideally one of those pitchers would emerge into a closer. When Epstein used the phrase "closer by committee" to describe the arrangement, the media ridiculed the unconventional term, and though Grady Little never actually followed the committee approach—using first Chad Fox, then Robert Person (very briefly), then Brandon Lyon as his closer until Kim took over the role in midseason—the bullpen was a source of instability. Lowe, Wakefield, and Burkett all pitched worse in 2003 than they had the previous year (though all remained effective), and while Pedro Martinez led the league in ERA for the second year in a row he required frequent extra rest and a strict pitch count (which is why he made 29 starts but had a 14–4 record). Pitching coach Tony Cloninger was unable to coax the same magic from his staff that Joe Kerrigan had; when Cloninger was diagnosed with cancer and had to leave the team, he was replaced by former Dodgers coach Dave Wallace (whose results weren't much better); Cloninger was offered a lesser position when he returned from chemotherapy.

Yet somehow the feeling that, for the second year in a row, the team was less than the sum of its parts persisted. The hitters were not only record-setting, they remained remarkably injury-free all year; the pitching wasn't bad, with a nice blend of talent; the chemistry was great, with the entire team playing hard and working together—yet late in the season the Red Sox were in a struggle to win a Wild Card spot, rather than running away with the division. Rumors abounded that anything less than a World Series victory would cost manager Grady Little his job.

The Boston media, always pessimistic, gave up on the team by August, but the players didn't. In particular, Kevin Millar stepped forward, famously announcing that it was time to "cowboy up," and that the team had every intention of winning. His words proved either prophetic or inspirational, and the Red Sox started to win convincingly. An FBI agent friend of Millar's unearthed a video of him as a teenager, singing Bruce Springsteen's "Born in the USA." As a joke, the video was played on the scoreboard during a game the Sox were losing; when they came back to win, the "rally karaoke" was born, and Millar gamely allowed the embarrassing video to be played whenever the Sox fell behind at home.

Theo Epstein traded for pitching reinforcements, bringing in Kim (who helped a lot) as well as starter Jeff Suppan and relievers Scott Williamson and Scott Sauerbeck (none of whom helped much during the regular season); gradually, the pitching stabilized, and by late in the season Little had figured out an effective bullpen rotation. The Red Sox didn't catch the Yankees for the AL East title, but they didn't fold to the charging Seattle Mariners either. When the dust cleared, the team had another second-place finish; at 95–67 the Red Sox were two games better than the previous year, and six games behind the Yankees, but this time it was enough to nudge them into the Wild Card slot.

The playoffs opened in Oakland, site of the Sox one-sided playoff losses in

1988 and 1990. And the 2003 best-of-five series opened on a similar note. The pitching-rich A's won the first game on a bizarre twelfth-inning bunt single by catcher Ramon Hernandez, wasting Todd Walker's four hits and two homers. Then Oakland lefty Barry Zito outdueled Tim Wakefield 5-1, with all of the A's runs scoring during the second inning when Wakefield's dancing knuckleball had *too* much movement: Oakland scored five runs with only two hits because of two walks, a hit batter, a diving knuckleball that catcher Doug Mirabelli couldn't handle, and a Todd Walker throwing error. Wakefield struck out seven in six innings, but Red Sox hitters were shut down by Oakland pitching. Amid the gloom, there was a sign of good things to come, however. Boston's bullpen, unreliable for most of the season, had now given up only two runs in 7⅔ innings, with one of those runs scored off Derek Lowe, normally a starter.

Boston faced long odds in its return to Fenway, needing to win three games in a row to avoid elimination. Oakland had now won 10 consecutive playoff games against the Red Sox. But strangely, there was no sense of defeat among Red Sox players, who by now firmly believed they could "cowboy up" to overcome any odds. Many employees at Fenway Park wore cowboy hats to emphasize the sentiment.

Game 3 again went into extra innings with a 1–1 score, thanks to two Oakland runners thrown out in the sixth inning: Eric Byrnes failed to touch home plate on a slide despite a missed relay throw, allowing Jason Varitek to retrieve the ball and tag him out, and later in the inning Miguel Tejada, awarded third base on an interference call against Bill Mueller, was tagged out when he mistakenly believed he could advance home as well. (The A's argued, but under the rules, the umpires had called it correctly.) The lone Red Sox run also scored strangely, when Eric Chavez was called for interfering with Varitek on a rundown at third, allowing him to advance home. Derek Lowe, who had lost Game 1 in relief, came back on short rest to start Game 3 and pitched masterfully, allowing only an unearned run in seven innings. And the bullpen, suddenly the strength of the team, outdueled Oakland's vaunted pitching for another four innings, until Trot Nixon won the game with a two-run pinch hit homer in the eleventh.

The Red Sox went with fourth starter John Burkett to oppose Oakland ace Tim Hudson in Game 4, rather than bringing back Pedro Martinez on short rest, and the gamble seemingly failed. Although Hudson was forced to leave the game after one inning with a strained muscle, Burkett did not pitch well, giving up four runs on nine hits in 5⅓ innings. The bullpen again was perfect—Tim Wakefield and Scott Williamson holding the A's scoreless the rest of the way—but Boston was down 4–3 in the bottom of the eighth inning when David Ortiz, who had been hitless in the series, rifled a two-run double to deep right field off A's All Star closer (and future Sox hero) Keith Foulke. After a long standing ovation, Williamson retired Oakland in order in the ninth, collecting his second consecutive win.

The series returned to Oakland, with Pedro on the mound against Game 2 winner Barry Zito. Pedro pitched well for seven innings, but in a dangerous sign of things to come, Grady Little left him in the game to start the eighth. Two sharp Oakland hits and a run later, he finally removed Martinez. Boston went into the ninth with a 4–2 lead, thanks to Manny Ramirez's three-run homer in the sixth (after striking out his first two appearances against Zito), but short it's center fielder, after Johnny Damon had to be carried off the field following a collision with backup second baseman Damian Jackson. In the ninth, the Boston bullpen seemed to sag, with a tiring Williamson walking two. Former closer and Game 3 starter Derek Lowe came in and added another walk to load the bases, but instead of losing his composure (which had cost him the closer's job previously) he struck out pinch hitter Terence Long looking to send the Red Sox to the ALCS, and a matchup with the "evil empire," as Red Sox president Larry Lucchino referred to the hated Yankees.

Tim Wakefield, who had pitched so well both as a starter and in relief during the ALDS, got the call as the opening game starter in New York. Once again his knuckleball stayed effective; he pitched six shutout innings before losing his control in the seventh, and got the 5-2 win when David Ortiz, Todd Walker, and Manny Ramirez all homered off Yankees starter Mike Mussina, who had flirted with the Red Sox before signing with the Yankees in 2001. Game 2 starter Derek Lowe was unable to build on his ALDS heroics, giving up six runs in 6⅔ innings while the Red Sox were held in check by Yankees lefty Andy Pettitte. The Red Sox lost 6–2, but there was room for optimism as the series moved to Fenway Park tied 1–1, with Pedro starting Game 3 against former Red Sox star Roger Clemens.

Johnny Damon returned from his ALDS collision and had three hits, but his performance was overshadowed by a series of fights, as tensions between the two teams reached the boiling point. In the fourth inning, Pedro Martinez threw a pitch over Yankee Karim Garcia's head, and Garcia was awarded first base amid Yankees accusations that Martinez had intentionally thrown at Garcia. When the next batter grounded out, Garcia slid hard into second, as if to take out Sox second baseman Todd Walker, and both benches emptied onto the field, but the teams were restrained without further fighting. In the bottom of the inning, Clemens threw a head-high pitch on the inside part of the plate to Manny Ramirez. Ramirez started to the mound, bat still in his hand; he was restrained from going after Clemens, but a general melee broke out between the teams in the meantime. In a surreal moment, 72-year-old Yankees coach (and former Sox manager) Don Zimmer, an ex-Marine, charged Pedro Martinez. Martinez pushed Zimmer to the ground, but it was really a no-win situation for Pedro: either he could be seen as assaulting a 72-year-old, or he could allow himself to be assaulted by a 72-year-old. In the ninth inning, two Yankees pitchers in the bullpen got into a fight with a member of the Red Sox grounds crew, when they objected to him rooting for the Sox. Garcia got involved again—injuring his hand when he vaulted over the wall separating the outfield and the bullpen—and had to leave the game. The final score hardly seemed to matter but in the end Clemens had outdueled Pedro, who blew a 2-0 lead, for a 4-3 victory.

After a rainout delayed the next game by a day, Wakefield came to the rescue again in Game 4, although he flirted with danger all night, only to have the Red Sox defense bail him out with several terrific plays. He allowed only one run in seven innings, striking out eight. Todd Walker hit yet another home run—breaking a team record with his fifth postseason home run, and Trot Nixon had three hits and a homer. (Yankees reliever Felix Heredia hit Walker with a pitch in the eighth inning, but both teams remained calm after bloodcurdling warnings from the league.) The Red Sox held a 3–1 lead entering the ninth before Ruben Sierra's pinch hit homer off Scott Williamson (the first run given up by Red Sox relievers in 19⅓ innings) increased the tension level at Fenway Park. But Williamson came back to strike out the next two hitters, evening the series at 2–2.

Game 5 was dominated by Yankees lefthander (and future Red Sox pitcher) David Wells, who allowed a Manny Ramirez home run but not much else. Derek Lowe pitched decently but fell to 0–3 in the postseason with the 4–2 loss, and the Red Sox returned to Yankee Stadium on the brink of elimination, and with their weakest starter, John Burkett, slated to pitch Game 6. Still the team remained confident, especially given the recent example of their ALDS comeback.

Played in a swirling wind that made fielding an adventure, Game 6 turned into a hitter's duel, which played to the Red Sox greatest strength. Burkett was gone in the fourth after giving up five runs, but the Sox bullpen held the Yankees to one run the rest of the way, while piling up 16 hits, including homers by Trot Nixon and Jason Varitek and a wind-assisted triple by Nomar Garciaparra. The Red Sox came from behind with a three-run seventh inning and ended up winning 9–6, setting up a climactic seventh game that everyone had expected: Pedro vs. Roger Clemens in a one-game showdown with the pennant on the line.

The expected pitchers' duel did not materialize; Trot Nixon and Kevin Millar homered, giving the Red Sox a 4–0 lead and chasing Clemens from the game after three innings. Mike Mussina quieted the Red Sox bats, but Pedro was pitching his best game of the postseason. After seven innings, he had only allowed two Jason Giambi homers (steroid-aided, as it turned out later) and had a 5–2 lead, thanks to an eighth-inning David Ortiz homer. The Red Sox bullpen had been spectacular throughout the playoffs (as they would be again in Game 7), and Pedro was supposed to be on a strict pitch count, which he had already exceeded. But Grady Little—perhaps haunted by the legacy of John McNamara's decision to remove Clemens from the fateful Game 6 of the 1986 World Series—left Pedro in. After three doubles and a single, the game was tied. Alan Embree and Mike Timlin stopped the bleeding, but the damage was done.

The season came down to a duel between Yankees closer Mariano Rivera and the Red Sox bullpen. Grady Little brought Tim Wakefield in to pitch the tenth inning. Wakefield already had two wins in the series; if the Red Sox had scored in the tenth he would have won the game and probably been named series MVP. Instead, Rivera continued to hold the Sox in check for three innings—almost unprecedented for a short reliever in the present day. On the first pitch in the bottom of the twelfth, one of Wakefield's unpredictable knuckleballs failed to dance, and Yankees third baseman Aaron Boone lined it into the stands in left for a game-winning home run.

It was a crushing defeat for what had seemed to be a team of destiny. But unlike in 1986, where a flawed team had lost a rare shot at World Series victory, this was a strong team that would have another shot—and the Red Sox would get their revenge on Rivera in 2004.

Grady Little was widely criticized for leaving Pedro in the game too long, but in the end, it wasn't that single decision that cost him his job. His option was not picked up for the simple reason that he had a supremely talented Red Sox team—and a flukily injury-free one, which would not be repeated in 2004—and failed to win. The team expressed its appreciation to Little for bringing them as far as he had in two years, and paid him a $250,000 bonus, which was not required contractually, but announced that they would be going in a new direction in 2004, with a manager who shared the front office's vision of what it would take to finally bring the World Series trophy back to Boston. (Little interviewed for managerial jobs with several teams, but ended up spending the 2004 season as special assistant to the GM for the Chicago Cubs.)

When the playoffs started, I was absolutely sure, convinced, that the Sox would win it all. Even at 2-0 down to Oakland I made sure to post a message on the board to that effect. It was all about "one game at a time" (a phrase I'd have a lot of fun with in 2004!). When we got back to 2–2, it only confirmed to me that this was all going to plan, and as Derek Lowe put the seal on an incredible comeback (and lucky in many ways!), it was the big Sox-Yankees showdown for the AL pennant. We started well, but found ourselves needing to win two in New York. Again, I was sure they would do it, no doubt in my mind, I could see it all before me, so when we made it 3–3, it was just Oakland all over again.

However, that's when the "Curse" struck. Of course, I don't believe in curses, except in the way that they creep insidiously into the minds of fans and players, such that at key moments when clear thinking is required, you can feel the collective intake of breath, the terrible, and morbid tension as a thousand minds collectively feel that this is the moment when "something bad's going to happen". I think that's a very real effect. Anyway, having been glued to the TV, or Gameday throughout the season and watching every playoff game live, it came down to Game 7, a game which could take the glorious Red Sox over the hump of almost a century of disappointment.

And then it happened. That intake of breath, that morbid certainty that something was going to go wrong. I didn't feel it, but somehow the Curse reached out across the ocean and caused a problem on the train line between Edinburgh and Sheffield, meaning that I was stuck in Leeds where I work. Oh yes, you can check the facts for yourself. On only one day in the whole of 2003 was there a major fault on that line, causing a delay of more than four hours. By the time I got home, having burned the candle at both ends slipped off to bed for a quick nap before the game started at midnight.

And then it happened again. A power cut. You don't need to ask if my alarm clock was electric or not. And so that's how I slept through the biggest Red Sox game in my brief tenure as a Red Sox obsessive. Distraught, I resigned myself to watch the "as live" (a key point) replay the next morning. We all know what happened next. At 5–2 ahead, I joined the collective screams (delayed in my case) for Grady to "PULL PEDRO," "PULL PEDRO," "PULL PEDRO." It just made no sense. The bullpen had been lights out during the post season. Pedro was tiring, he'd gone over his pitch limit, Matsui was coming up, a dangerous lefty. It was truly sickening to watch, and to see those swirling winds sweep paper round in cyclones on the Yankee grass. You knew those clever boys at Fox wouldn't let talk of the Curse go that easily, did you? The most awful moment came during the Boone inning, looking at the clock on the TV, there were only 5 minutes left of the program, it was the start of the Yankee inning. There was no way there'd be enough time for a Red Sox inning. So I knew this was it even before it happened.

My first taste of the dreadful disappointment, the gut-wrenching pain of seeing the team not only lose, but lose after playing so well, so beautifully, fighting back from the dead time and time again, putting themselves into position to win, only to inexplicably throw it away with what seemed even to my novice baseball mind to be a bizarre choice by Grady *** Little. The agony was intense. It just felt wrong. It *was* wrong. And I remain convinced that had I managed to get home in time, squeezed in a nap before Clare went to bed, got up in plenty of time for the game and watched it live, then we would have won that game, and beaten the Marlins. Still, there was always next year, right?

—Lee Harris

22. Cowboys and Idiots: 2004

The Red Sox offered extensions to all four of their potential big-name free agents before the 2004 season, and all of them declined. It looked pretty certain that Nomar Garciaparra and Derek Lowe would be going elsewhere after the season, while the odds of re-signing Pedro Martinez and Jason Varitek appeared somewhat better. (The Red Sox did manage to sign Trot Nixon and David Ortiz to longterm deals by early in the season, but they would have more than a dozen players file for free agency following the 2004 season.) With the powerful team that Dan Duquette, Mike Port, and Theo Epstein had assembled potentially in its last year, the Red Sox decided to roll the dice and try to increase their odds of winning. First Epstein traded young pitchers Casey Fossum and Brandon Lyon to Arizona in return for veteran pitching ace (and former Sox farmhand) Curt Schilling, visiting Schilling and his wife at Thanksgiving in order to work out the contract extension that the deal hinged on. Then Epstein signed free agent closer Keith Foulke, the most effective reliever on the market (but a pitcher that a lot of teams shied away from because he didn't have extraordinary velocity).

Epstein also considered the previously unthinkable: moving Nomar Garciaparra and Manny Ramirez to other teams. Although an extraordinary hitter, Ramirez had mused openly about playing in his hometown of New York and seemed regretful he had signed with the Red Sox, and his contract (more than $22 million in 2004) ate up a tremendous percentage of team resources. At one point the Red Sox placed Ramirez on irrevocable waivers—offering the league's best pure hitter for $50,000 to anyone who would take on his salary—but there were no takers. The point was made clearly to Manny: He was going to have to learn to love playing for the Red Sox, since he didn't have any other options. (To his credit Manny did so, opening up more to fans and the media and seeming to genuinely enjoy playing in Boston in 2004.)

Nomar, who had always seemed so joyful playing with the Red Sox, was becoming increasingly estranged from the team, however. He reportedly turned down a four-year, $60 million contract offer, after the 2003 season, but by the time the market for shortstops proved weaker than he and his agent expected, the Red Sox had reduced their offer. While unwilling to re-sign with the Red Sox, Nomar seemed shocked and hurt when the Red Sox tried to trade him as part of a complex series of deals that would have sent Manny Ramirez to Texas for shortstop Alex Rodriguez and Nomar to the Chicago White Sox for outfielder Magglio Ordoñez. The trade fell through, but Nomar seemed to sulk his way through spring training, then spent months recovering from what the team had thought was a minor injury.

By spring training the Red Sox had a new manager: Terry Francona, a former backup outfielder for five teams from 1981–1990 who'd quickly become a major league manager for four unsuccessful years with bad Phillies teams from 1997–2000. Although he had an excellent major league pedigree (his father is former All Star Tito Francona), Terry Francona seemed like an unlikely candidate for as high-profile a job as managing the Red Sox. After a terrific interview (and showing that he could handle the Boston media, with years of experience in the equally tough Philadelphia market), he landed the job. It didn't hurt that he'd managed Schilling in Philadelphia.

Francona's first spring training with the Red Sox was a difficult one, however, with Pedro Martinez reporting on his own schedule, Manny initially aloof, Nomar sulking and then injured, and Trot Nixon arriving in camp with a back injury that would cost him most of the season. When the season started, Pokey Reese, expected to play second, was the starting shortstop, with utility player Mark Bellhorn starting at second. Gabe Kapler—a light hitter despite his hulking physique—was in Nixon's spot in right field. Bill Mueller's knee was hurting. Kevin Millar, who had started the previous season red-hot, was ice-cold at the beginning of this one. Derek Lowe was complaining vocally that the Sox didn't want him and hadn't made him a real offer (even though he'd turned down the same three-year, $27 million contract that White Sox ace Freddy Garcia had signed) and pitching dreadfully. Byung-Hyun Kim, counted on to be the fifth starter, mysteriously lost velocity and effectiveness, and soon lost his job to Bronson Arroyo. Perhaps most worrisome of all, ace Pedro Martinez had also lost velocity, struggling to reach 90 MPH on his fastball in the spring, and getting hit hard early in the season. And despite public words to the contrary, Pedro seemed unhappy sharing the pitching limelight with Curt Schilling.

There was a lot to like about the 2004 team, however, even if it didn't look as strong as the 2003 edition. Even with two starters out and another one hobbled, the offense was still very good. David Ortiz was even better than he had been the previous year, combining with Manny Ramirez for a deadly middle of the lineup. Johnny Damon put together his best offensive season in Boston, and with Mark Bellhorn's suprising ability to get on base (he drew a ton of walks to go with a decent batting average, while setting a club record for strikeouts) there were a lot of people for Ramirez and Ortiz to drive in. Jason Varitek 's elbow was now fully recovered from injury, and his power returned, along with a surge in batting average. Keith Foulke was absolutely unhittable, anchoring a strong bullpen, and the starting pitching was injury-free.

Key Players, 2004

Bronson Arroyo, p
Mark Bellhorn, 2b-3b-ss
Orlando Cabrera, ss
Johnny Damon, of
Alan Embree, p
Keith Foulke, p
Nomar Garciaparra, ss
Derek Lowe, p
Pedro Martinez, p
Kevin Millar, 1b-of
Doug Mirabelli, c
Bill Mueller, 3b
Trot Nixon, of
David Ortiz, DH-1b
Manny Ramirez, of
Curt Schilling, p
Mike Timlin, p
Tim Wakefield, p
Jason Varitek, c
Kevin Youkilis, 3b

But high expectations accompanied the acquisitions of Foulke and Schilling to bolster what was already a very good team. And while the team started well (15–6 in April), they were soon mired in a sort of malaise, playing well enough to stay above .500, but not in serious playoff contention. May opened with five straight losses, and the team went 55–52 in May–July. Some of the underperforming was because of the injuries to Nixon and Garciaparra (both of which lingered beyond expectations), Bill Mueller (who needed minor surgery during the season), and reliever Scott Williamson (who was pitching extremely well before his injury). Even the staff was not exempt, with first base coach Lynn Jones nearly losing an eye in an accident at home with a screwdriver. Some of the problem was the team's porous defense, although many of the weakest defenders were players who'd been very good in that area in the past, such as Nomar. But injuries and defense alone didn't account for how the team was playing, and the media began to search for targets, focusing largely on sulking shortstop Garciaparra and on manager Francona, who refused to publicly criticize his players.

By July, much of the Boston media had given up on the team, which fell as far as 10½ games behind the Yankees, and at one point was in danger of falling behind the surging Devil Rays and the Orioles in the division as well. There were calls for Francona's ouster. Other than disgruntled players Nomar and Derek Lowe, however, the rest of the players certainly weren't giving up. Led by Kevin Millar's "cowboy up" ideology, a newly puckish Manny Ramirez, David Ortiz and his "cookie monster" clubhouse persona, and shaggy Johnny Damon, who proclaimed "We are not the cowboys anymore—we are just the idiots this year," the 2004 Red Sox seemed to have more fun playing the game than any Red Sox team since the 1940s, and seemed confident that the results would turn around in the season's second half. And some of the omens seemed good, especially when Ortiz and Manny hit homers in the All Star Game to win it for the American League— giving the AL home-field advantage in the 2004 World Series.

A late-July series against the Yankees at Fenway looked like it could potentially end the Red Sox season, especially after the Red Sox lost a heartbreaker of a first game on a ninth-inning single by almost-a-Red Sox shortstop Alex Rodriguez. Tensions ran high in the second game, on July 24. The Red Sox arranged to have a local band, the Dropkick Murphys, do a live performance of "Tessie," the fight song used by the Royal Rooters in 1903 to intimidate opposing teams. When Sox starter Bronson Arroyo hit Rodriguez with a pitch, the Yankees shortstop screamed at Arroyo all the way up the first base line, with Jason Varitek blocking Rodriguez's path to the pitcher. When Rodriguez yelled at Varitek to "come and get it," Varitek obliged, shoving A-Rod's face with his catcher's mitt and setting off a cathartic melee and a series of ejections. By the time Bill Mueller, recently returned from surgery, won the game with a ninth-inning homer off Yankees closer Mariano Rivera, something seemed to have changed. Things changed even more a week later, when Theo Epstein pulled the trigger on a four-team deal sending Nomar Garciaparra and a prospect to the Cubs in return for Montreal shortstop Orlando Cabrera and Minnesota first baseman Doug Mientkiewicz. Neither was a star of Nomar's caliber, but both had been good hitters in the past and were excellent defensive players—and both of them were happy to play for a World Series contender. A second trade brought speedy outfielder Dave Roberts from the Dodgers.

Almost immediately the defense stabilized and the offense flourished. The Red Sox began to win, first a little, and then a lot. In mid-August the Sox went on a 20–2 run, including a 10-game winning streak. They opened September by going 10–3 in a tough stretch against the teams competing with them for the Wild Card spot. Things that had gone wrong earlier in the season started to break right: Bronson Arroyo, who had pitched decently but had a 2–7 record in the first half suddenly couldn't lose; Derek Lowe found his confidence with a rejuvenated defense behind him; Pedro began pitching like Pedro again, despite his iffy fastball. Schilling was dominant and ageless, leading the league in wins. Millar caught fire and Ortiz, who had been hot all season, got even hotter. Trot Nixon came back from two injuries and looked as if he'd been playing all season, hitting as well as he ever had. While the media focused on the Red Sox hunt for the Wild Card berth, the players weren't willing to concede the division crown, and in an exhilirating stretch managed to close within two games of the Yankees. Throughout the pressure of the pennant race, the team remained lighthearted but intense, clowning in the dugout and coming up with wild hair arrangements—from shaved heads to Kevin Millar's multiple colors to Johnny Damon's caveman look to Manny Ramirez's wild Afro to Bronson Arroyo's elaborate cornrows.

In the end they fell just short, as Francona repeated Grady Little's mistake and left Pedro Martinez in too long in a September series against the Yankees. Martinez, frustrated and in the midst of losing his last four decisions of the year, responded with an unfortunate quote of "I just tip my hat and call the Yankees my daddies," which guaranteed that he would be greeted with derisive "whose your daddy?" chants every subsequent time he pitched against the Yankees in New York. The Sox finished the season at 98–64, three games behind the Yankees, and with a better record than either of the other division winners. They led the league in batting (tied with Anaheim), on-base percentage, and slugging, and finished fourth in homers. The pitchers were third in the league in ERA and led the league by allowing the fewest hits and fewest home runs. All five starters won at least 10 games, led by Schilling's 21–6 record.

The ALDS against the Anaheim Angels was far less dramatic than the previous year's series against Oakland, much to the relief of Red Sox fans. Boston's offense continued to roll, sweeping the series by scores of 9–3, 8–3, and 8–6, the last game only close because of a late grand slam by Angels slugger Vladimir Guerrero that forced it into extra innings. Derek Lowe, fuming over being dropped from the starting rotation, ended up pitching a shaky but scoreless tenth inning and got the win when David Ortiz homered off Angels left Jarrod Washburn. Unlike in 2003, the Sox starting pitching was as dominant as the hitters: Curt Schilling (pitching despite an ankle injury) and Pedro Martinez easily won their games and Bronson Arroyo had a 6–1 lead when the bullpen took over in Game 3. Boston hit .302 in the series and held Anaheim hitters to a .226 average.

Against the Yankees in the ALCS, however, things did not go so smoothly. "Father's Day" was the headline in one New York paper, reminding everyone of Pedro's indiscreet remark. Game 1 starter Curt Schilling was clearly bothered by his ankle injury, which affected his delivery; he gave up six runs in only three innings, while Yankees starter Mike Mussina shut down the Red Sox. By the time the offense woke up, scoring seven runs in the seventh and eighth innings, it was too late. The Yankees won 10–7. Even worse, it was announced after the game that Schilling's ankle injury would probably prevent him from pitching again in the series. Red Sox hitters were similarly handcuffed by Yankees reclamation project Jon Lieber in Game 2. Although Pedro Martinez pitched decently, the

Yankees won 3–1 and the series moved to Fenway Park with the Red Sox down 2–0, not a good sign.

Game 3 was a debacle. Although the Sox hitters were able to get to Yankees starter Kevin Brown early, knocking him out of the game with a four-run second inning, none of the Red Sox pitchers could get anybody out. They gave up 22 hits and 18 earned runs, losing 19–8, on a night where Tim Wakefield volunteered to give up his Game 4 start in order to save the rest of the pitching staff for a last stand the next day.

No team in baseball history had ever come back from being down three games to none in a seven-game series.

Derek Lowe, bumped from the rotation for the ALDS, started the last-ditch Game 4 as a result of Wakefield's sacrifice. The players toasted each other with Jack Daniel's before the game for luck, refusing to bow to the inevitable. Lowe gave up two early runs, but the Red Sox hitters bailed him out with three in the fifth, only to see Lowe and Mike Timlin both suddenly ineffective by the sixth inning. Manager Francona brought in closer Keith Foulke with one out in the seventh to keep the game from getting away, but by that time the Yankees had a 4–3 lead, and superb closer Mariano Rivera ready to end the game and the series. Leading off the ninth, Millar managed to work a walk, and Dave Roberts pinch ran for him. Everyone in the park knew that Roberts was going to try to steal second, and Rivera threw over repeatedly. When Roberts ran, he just barely beat a close throw. Bill Mueller, who had beaten Rivera in the fight game on July 24 came up and did it again, singling cleanly to score Roberts. The Yankees bullpen relied heavily on Rivera and two former Red Sox players who set him up, Tom Gordon and Paul Quantrill. All had terrific seasons in 2004, but had been heavily used. (The 35-year-old Quantrill led the league with 86 appearances, while 36-year-old Gordon was second with a career-high 80. Rivera had 74, seventh in the league.) That overuse was beginning to take its toll. When Quantrill came in to pitch the twelfth he had nothing on his pitches. Manny Ramirez singled to lead off the inning and David Ortiz quickly followed with a game-winning home run. For one more night, the Red Sox remained alive.

Pedro Martinez started Game 5 (after another Jack Daniel's toast, in what became a pre-game tradition for the rest of the playoffs), and the Red Sox scored two quick runs to give him a lead off Mike Mussina. That was all Mussina gave up however, and the Yankees scored three times in the sixth off Pedro to turn a 4–2 lead over to the Yankees bullpen. This time Gordon and Rivera combined to cough up the lead. David Ortiz led off the eighth with a home run, cutting the Yankees lead in half, and when Millar followed with a walk, Roberts again pinch ran for him, setting up a repeat of the previous night. This time Roberts didn't go, as Gordon was clearly preoccupied by his presence at first; Trot Nixon's single sent Roberts to third and brought Rivera into the game to no avail. Jason Varitek's fly ball to center brought home the tying run. Once again the game went into extra innings and this time the Red Sox bullpen pitched as it had in 2003, contributing eight scoreless innings. Tim Wakefield—the seventh Red Sox pitcher of the game—went three scoreless innings, including an inning in which Jason Varitek, unused to catching Wakefield's knuckleball (Doug Mirabelli usually caught Wakefield's starts), gave up three passed balls but still prevented the Yankees from scoring. In the bottom of the fourteenth David Ortiz once again came through, singling in Johnny Damon with two outs to win the game.

The series returned to New York for Game 6, but Yankees fans were growing restive. Somehow the air of inevitablity had turned the other way, especially when Curt Schilling returned from the lost to start the game. Schilling's ankle would require surgury after the season ended, but team doctor Bill Morgan temporarily stabilized it by suturing a tendon to the bone (he tested it on a cadaver first, but otherwise the procedure was medically untried), then removing the sutures at the end of the game. With blood seeping through his sock on every pitch, Schilling threw seven strong innings, leaving with a 4–1 lead. (The bloody sock would later be donated to the Hall of Fame.) The key blow was a three-run homer by Mark Bellhorn, who'd been dropped to the ninth spot in the batting order because he was having a terrible offensive series. The ball bounced off a fan and back onto the field, and an umpire initially ruled it a double before correctly changing the call to a home run. In the eighth inning, Bronson Arroyo came in to pitch, setting up another memorable encounter with Alex Rodriguez. With one out and a run home, Rodriguez grounded weakly to Arroyo, but as the pitcher approached first base to make the tag Rodriguez, running down the line, batted the ball out of his glove. The first base umpire, who was blocked on the play, initially called Rodriguez safe when he saw the ball come loose, but once again the umpires reversed the call, calling A-Rod out for interference, and the play was widely portrayed as childish and unsportsmanlike, even in New York.

Derek Lowe drew the Game 7 start on only two days' rest, with the rest of the pitching staff depleted. But with victory in sight, Lowe pitched like the pitcher he'd been two years previously. Kevin Brown was hit hard again and then left

During the 2003 post-season, my wife became a Diehard. She was up and down, every emotion, every pitch. "They have to win, they just have to." I smiled and her, "Now you are truly a fan." During Game 7 of the ALCS, as I paced the whole game, and held my breath in the seventh as hit after Yankee hit after Yankee hit got rung up, she screamed at no one, and everyone, "Bubba Gump's gotta pull Pedro." As the game was tied, going into extra innings, I said, "if the Sox win this game, and win the World eries, I want to name our next child after the winning pitcher." "Sure, sure, whatever," she said, chomping her nails and waiting for Aaron Boone to come to bat.

(Fast forward to 2004. Sox win the World Series. She's pregnant. "Erica, dear, What do you think of the name Derek?")

At the beginning of spring training in 2004, she said, "What would it take to get the Red Sox games on our TV?" I said, "well, digital cable, the MLB package, its too expensive, blah blah." And thought nothing further. A few weeks later, I got a call at work, "Well, there's a special on digital cable," she started. "And the MLB package is 160 bucks. " And so on. "Sweetheart, I think we can do it, we'll have to look at our budgets, though."

"That's good, " she said. " They're coming tomorrow to install everything."

I knew then my wife was perfect.

My son and my wife and I had a great summer watching the Red Sox. Into the post-season, every meal was in the family room listening to the game. My son, whose birthday is the now famous October 27 (he turned three), has some difficulty with speech production and can be very difficult to understand. During the ALCS, he was on the phone talking to his grandfather, when clear as a bell, he blurted out: "Yankees poop in their diapers." As it turned out, the Yankees did.

—Teddy Zartler

with a sore back, and the Red Sox hit four homers (two by Johnny Damon, along with another homer by Bellhorn and one by David Ortiz) to open up a huge lead. With the Red Sox up 8–1 and the crowd out of the game, Terry Francona bowed to Pedro Martinez's request and brought him into the game, to an immediate chorus of "Whooooo's your dad-dy" and two quick Yankees runs. The Red Sox bullpen held on the rest of the way however, and Derek Lowe won the series clincher for the second time in 2004.

The World Series provided a rematch with the 105–57 St. Louis Cardinals, who had bested the Red Sox in 1946 and 1967. The team invited key members of the 1946, 1967, 1975, and 1986 teams to help cheer the team on, and Carl Yastrzemski, star of the 1967 Impossible Dream team threw out the first pitch of Game 1. With the Red Sox rotation depleted by the Yankees series, Tim Wakefield drew the start, but the magic of ALCS Game 5 was gone; he gave up five runs in 3⅔ innings, but Cardinals starter Woody Williams was worse, giving up seven runs in only 2⅓ innings, in a wild game that evoked the Fenway Park slugfests of the 1970s, before new construction made it less of a pronounced hitter's park. Boston made four errors and saw its 7–2 lead turned into an 8–8 tie in the eighth inning, before Mark Bellhorn's two-run homer won the game.

It proved to be the high water mark for the Cardinals, as Boston pitching allowed only two more earned runs for the rest of the series. Curt Schilling again pitched with his ankle tendon sutured to the bone, allowing only one unearned run in six innings. The Red Sox made another four errors, but again the mistakes were mostly harmless—the eight errors in two games led to only two runs. Once again Mark Bellhorn had a key hit, doubling in two runs to make the score 4–1, and becoming an unlikely playoff hero in the same way his fellow second baseman Marty Barrett had in 1986.

In Game 3, Pedro Martinez looked like the Pedro of old, helped by surreal Cardinal baserunning. Manny Ramirez threw out Larry Walker trying to score on a shallow fly in the first inning. In the third inning, Cardinal starting pitcher (and Red Sox flop in 2003) Jeff Suppan couldn't decide whether to try to score on a groundout or to return to third. he ended up doing neither and was thrown out, so instead of having runners at second and third with one out, the Cardinals had a runner at second with two outs. The Cardinals didn't score at all until Walker's homer in the ninth, by which time they were already down 4–0.

By Game 4, Red Sox fans were trying not to celebrate prematurely, as they had in 1986. After all, there was their own recent example of a comeback from a three-games-to-none deficit. But it didn't look good for the Cardinals when Johnny Damon led off the game with a home run, and Derek Lowe once again pitched like the no-hit pitcher of 2002. Jason Marquis pitched better than any of the other starters, but the Cardinals never mounted a serious threat, and the Red Sox won 3–0. For the third time this postseason, Derek Lowe had won the series-clinching game.

The city of Boston went insane with celebration. Fans mobbed the streets in impromptu festivities. The celebrations after the ALCS had been marred by the accidental police killing of Victoria Snelgrove, a college student who was hit in the face with a round fired from a pepper pellet gun. But this time there was no trouble. Millions of Red Sox fans from around the world converged on Boston and braved rainy weather as the players paraded through the streets on amphibious duck boats, finishing with a cruise on the Charles River for the benefit of additional fans who lined the shoreline. The parade turned into a daylong celebration, and this time there were no fan incidents at all—astonishing for a college town jammed with millions of additional celebratory fans. The only major arrest came when someone tried to take advantage of police distraction to rob a bank, only to be caught easily when his getaway vehicle was trapped in heavy traffic.

For the first time in 86 years, the Red Sox were World Champions.

23. The Aftermath: 2005

There was no way the 2004 Red Sox team could remain intact for another run, but the euphoria lingered for a while. Players who were willing to take less playing time to win a World Series couldn't be expected to sacrifice their careers indefinitely, and other players would see their value rise beyond what the team's budget could sustain. But Theo Epstein and the Red Sox owners had promised to remain a World Series contender in 2005, and despite many free agents the Red Sox still had a formidible core.

The first moves revolved around minor players: Gabe Kapler went to Japan where he could be a starting center fielder, and the Red Sox obliged ALCS hero Dave Roberts's request that the Sox trade him to a team where he could start, sending him to San Diego in return for outfielder Jay Payton and utility infielder Ramon Vazquez. Scott Williamson underwent career-threatening surgery, and fellow reliever Curtis Leskanic retired. Doug Mirabelli, Tim Wakefield's personal catcher and part of what was arguably baseball's best catching tandem turned down offers to start elsewhere in order to return to the Red Sox.

But the success or failure of the offseason would hinge on the Red Sox ability to re-sign or replace the team's major free agents: Pedro Martinez, Derek Lowe, Jason Varitek, and Orlando Cabrera.

There was never much chance of Derek Lowe coming back, and postseason comments about how unappreciated he was didn't help. Lowe was coming off a terrible season, but his terrific postseason had raised his value. He ended up signing with the Dodgers (for about the same salary that the Red Sox had offered), where he will pitch in a park that is a lot more forgiving of pitchers' errors than Fenway is.

Orlando Cabrera had played very well for the Red Sox, hitting close to .300 and playing top-flight defense. He wanted to return to the Red Sox but also wanted a longterm deal, something the Sox were reluctant to give him with top prospect Hanley Ramirez, also a shortstop, only a year or so away. The issue became a moot point when the Sox found they could sign Cardinals shortstop (and recent World Series opponent) Edgar Renteria to a four-year deal for about $10 million a year—about a third less than Nomar had turned down for an equivalent player. Ironically, Renteria and Cabrera had grown up together and are good friends. Cabrera ended up getting his longterm deal from ALDS opponent Anaheim. (The triangle was completed when Anaheim shortstop and former Sox minor leaguer David Eckstein signed with St. Louis to replace Renteria.) As for Nomar, his value had decreased significantly because of his injury-plagued season, and he ended up returning to the Cubs with a one-year, $8 million deal.

The oddest free agent situation involved Pedro Martinez, not surprising for a Red Sox hero who had always played on his own terms. Concerned about his tattered shoulder and declining numbers (Pedro's 2004 ERA was his highest with the Red Sox by a huge margin, though he remained one of the league's better pitchers), the Red Sox nonetheless offered Martinez the same two-year, $27 million contract that Curt Schilling had signed, then agreed to guarantee a third year when Pedro implied that he would re-sign with the team if they did so. Instead, he used the Red Sox offer to get a guaranteed four-year contract offer from the Mets, which he signed when the Red Sox refused to offer a fourth year. Surprisingly, he then took shots at the team's administration after leaving, claiming that Epstein's not re-signing him showed a lack of respect. Unlike Mo Vaughn's similar charges against Dan Duquette, which fans found troubling, the reaction in Boston was more bemused and baffled than anything else; few fans were critical of Epstein's decision not to give Pedro a fourth year. Epstein and Francona mostly refused to get drawn into the criticism, but Epstein's on-field response quickly ended the controversy. He signed three starting pitchers for a

I've been a Red Sox fan since I began to play Little League baseball in the late fifties. My life is marked by memorable events that play in real time just by closing my eyes. Here are some scenes from the full-length feature.

When I was eight and living in Scituate, Rhode Island I played for a minor league team sponsored by a local pharmacy. We were known as the Rx Sox. Itchy uniforms did not diminish my excitement when our team got to go to Fenway to take in a game. I got lost and tearfully approached a peanut vendor outside the park. After being reunited with my team I saw the Red Sox lose to Cleveland in fourteen innings. It didn't matter. I had seen Fenway Park and I was hooked.

Before reaching the age when being with your parents is akin to a social disorder, my parents took my best friend and me to a Sox game. My dad, frugal as he was, parked in a Sears lot to save money. He bought a tablecloth to legitimize the deal. The Red Sox won and a favorite player, Gary Geiger, hit a home run. The next day his lung collapsed. Somewhat deflated by this turn of events, I soldiered on.

Fast forward to 1967. I leave for college in the midst of an unexpected quest for the pennant. My dad sends me clippings and I watch the Red Sox lose to the Cardinals with some new friends. I knew that Jim Lonborg, pitching on two days' rest, was not going to get it done. It was okay, though. The Impossible Dream team scene is a highlight.

1975. Newly married and living in Maine. My wife and I watch Game 6 and I'm jumping as high as Fisk. I act out Dewey's catch of Morgan's drive in the living room and scare the cat. I'm admonished.

1986. A plan to whoop it up outside with a neighbor is put into motion. In bare feet in the same living room, I watch Game 6 alone. As the Sox seemingly have it wrapped up in the ninth, I decide to put on my shoes and sock, one out at a time. I manage to get both socks on, but never have a chance to lace one sneaker. I curl up in a corner and cry. My wife doesn't understand.

2004. Newly married and newly living in Kentucky, I watch in wonder as Foulke snags Renteria's chopper to the mound. A quick flip to Mientkiewicz and I'm jumping, screaming and revealing to my amused wife that I'm going outside to howl, an 18-year-old plan still fresh in my mind. Lots of phone calls to friends in New England. My daughter calls from Italy. I'm crying again. My wife is, too. We're both looking forward to the sequel.

—Skip Mowry

combined total of what Pedro got: flamethrowing 30-year-old Matt Clement, Wade Miller, a young top starter with Houston coming off a shoulder injury that had not required surgery, and David Wells, the ageless former Yankees nemesis (who had to update some of the negative things he'd said about pitching at Fenway Park over the years).

Jason Varitek was the player the Sox were most determined to re-sign, seen by the pitching staff as the heart and soul of the team. Although Varitek was represented by agent Scott Boras, famous for his tough negotiating, Varitek insisted that Boras give the Red Sox every chance to come to an agreement before even talking with other clubs. In the end, the contract came down to the Red Sox unwillingness to extend a no-trade clause to any player (especially since several other team members have clauses that will take effect if the Sox give one to anyone else). Boras and Epstein worked around the issue by creating a new policy that grants no-trade privileges to anyone with eight years of service with the Red Sox, which Varitek will reach by the middle of the 2005 season.

The Red Sox continued to make other changes to separate the team from the old way of doing things. For the first time, the team hired a psychologist (former pitcher and TV analyst Bob Tewksbury) to work with young players and help them deal with the stresses of being a professional baseball player. And a group of the team's top minor league prospects were brought to Boston on an extended visit to learn some of the ins and outs of living in New England, and to increase their chances of successfully making the transition to major league athletes.

By the opening of spring training, euphoria still lingered in New England, but much of the irascilibility that defines the Boston media—and to a certain extent, is treasured by its fans—had returned. *Boston Globe* writer Dan Shaughnessey stirred up a minor controversy when he found out that Doug Mientkiewicz had kept the ball that he'd been thrown for the final out of the World Series. (He had every right to it, and the team had never asked Mientkiewicz for it, but it made for quirky headlines, especially when he was traded to the Mets for a prospect. Eventually, the team and Mientkiewicz agreed that the ball would be loaned to the team so they could display it for a year after which, presumably, the controversy will have been overtaken by newer issues.) Alex Rodriguez began publicly complaining that Curt Schilling talked too much, which didn't do much for Rodriguez's already-fraying reputation as a superstar, and was such an irresistible comment that it led to a lot of funny responses, both by Schilling and others. Yankees owner George Steinbrenner, alarmed at being beaten by the Red Sox, traded several of the Yankees best young players and prospects to Arizona for Randy Johnson, a devastating lefthander who was the National League's best pitcher in 2004, but who also is a 43-year-old with a history of back problems. The trade sent the Yankees payroll soaring over $200 million, by far the highest in baseball.

The Red Sox-Yankees rivalry remains as strong as ever. But for the first time in most of our lives, the talk of a curse has been put to rest.

The Players

This isn't intended to be a list of the all-time greatest Red Sox players, although you'll find those players in this section. What you'll also find here are the players who are most talked about—the heroes and villains and cult favorites and quirkiest players who have appeared with the Boston Red Sox in the last 100 years. Many of the players here were great. Some were tragic, or bizarre, or funny, or some combination of all four. Taken one at a time, they are fascinating stories, little pieces of lives that interacted with a baseball team and its fans at a particular moment. Taken together they are the fabric of Red Sox history—the people who shaped the team and were in turn shaped by the city, its ballpark, and most of all—its fans.

Don Aase—after a promising rookie season as a starting pitcher with the Red Sox, Aase was sent to the Angels in 1977 in return for second baseman Jerry Remy. After three less-than-successful seasons as a starter, Aase was converted into a reliever, and was one of the league's better relievers for the next six years. He saved 34 games and was an All Star in 1986, a year when bullpen failures cost the Sox the World Series.

Harry Agganis—a well-loved New England athlete, "The Golden Greek" fit the true definition of a hometown hero. Agganis was born in Lynn, Massachusetts in 1930, excelled in baseball and football at Lynn Classical High School, and continued those sports at Boston University. While his football career seemed slightly more promising (he won All-American football honors and was later drafted as the first pick of the Cleveland Browns in 1952), he chose to stick with baseball, and after just one minor league season he was promoted to the Red Sox in 1954.

Though he was a young player performing among the likes of Ted Williams and Jimmy Piersall, Agganis, because his local roots and BU success were well documented, was adoringly embraced by the New England community. With good looks, a boyish charm, and fervent loyalty to his home and heritage, he was often called an Adonis. In competition for the first base job with Dick Gernert and later Norm Zauchin, Agganis finished a moderately successful rookie season with a .251 average and 11 home runs. Shortly into the 1955 season, however, he was hospitalized with pneumonia, which caused an embolism in his lung. His death at age 26 shocked a region that had perceived Agganis as an immortal hero. Forty-five years later, however, his legend lives on, especially along the North Shore. A football award for the top senior college player in New England was named in his honor, as well as a scholarship, a road outside the BU campus, and a new ice hockey arena for BU, opened in 2005.

Rick Aguilera—Boston traded prized pitching prospect Frankie Rodriguez during the 1995 season in order to bolster their bullpen with the 33-year-old Aguilera, Minnesota's relief ace and a three-time All Star. Aguilera saved 20 games down the stretch with the Red Sox and helped them make the playoffs, but then left as a free agent at season's end in order to re-sign with the Twins. He retired after the 2000 season, in which he saved 29 games for the Chicago Cubs at age 38.

Israel Alcantara—in a bizarre story, 27-year-old rookie Alcantara played well in limited duty during the 2000 season but was scapegoated for a collapsing team's problems. Alcantara, a third baseman recently converted to the outfield, was leading the International League in home runs when he was called up to the Red Sox, who were in a tailspin and desperately needed hitting. He hit well, but in a game against the Chicago White Sox (fellow Pawtucket call-up Paxton Crawford's first major league start) Alcantara's tentative fielding turned two fly balls that a more experienced (or more confident) outfielder could have caught into hits. He was also thrown out on the bases. Inexplicably, Alcantara—who had spent nearly a decade of hard work trying to get to the major leagues—was widely accused by Boston media outlets of not hustling or caring about the game, all based on his single bad game. There were calls for him to be released or sent back to the minors (which would have meant losing him, since any other team could have claimed him on waivers). Manager Jimy Williams buried Alcantara on his bench, essentially going with one fewer offensive player even while the team languished near the bottom of the league in hitting. On the rare occasions Alcantara played, he hit well (slugging .578 in 21 games, one of the best figures on the team).

Ironically, during the 2000 World Series, Mets rookie outfielder Timo Perez made several questionable fielding plays and a glaring baserunning mistake evocative of Alcantara's play in Chicago—but in a much more crucial situation. However, it was reported in the media as just a rookie misplay, the kind of mistake inexperienced major leaguers make.

Alcantara was released by the Red Sox after the season, but was re-signed to a minor league contract. In 2001, he again tore up the International League, hitting .297 with 36 homers while winning the league MVP. Again, he didn't get a chance to show his stuff in The Show: Alcantara appeared in only 14 games (38 at bats) for the Red Sox. Again, he made the headlines in a way one does not want to make the headlines: During a AAA game in which he felt the opposing pitcher was trying to bean him, he kicked the opposing catcher square in the facemask before charging the mound. This got him suspended for seven games and thrown off the International League All Star team. He was not offered a contract for the next season.

Alcantara played in the Brewers organization in 2002, appearing in 16 games for Milwaukee. For the past two years, he has played for the Vaqueros Laguna (Laguna Cowboys) in the Mexican League.

Dale Alexander—a hitting star whose career ended prematurely. Alexander had been a terrific hitter with the Detroit Tigers as a 26-year-old rookie first baseman in 1929, hitting .343 with 25 home runs and 137 runs batted in. Over the next two years, however, the Tigers became frustrated with Alexander's defense (he also led the league in errors his rookie year), and early in the 1932 season they traded him to the Red Sox for outfielder Earl Webb. Alexander, who'd been riding the bench in Detroit, went on a season-long hot streak as soon as he arrived in Boston, finishing the year at .367 and nosing out Jimmie Foxx (who would later play for the Sox) for the batting title. Early the next year Alexander injured his knee and was treated with hydrotherapy, then a new technique. The water was much too hot, and his leg was essentially boiled, leaving Alexander with third-degree burns. He was able to play again late in the season (hitting .281, the only time in five major league seasons that he hit less than .325), but not well enough to offset his defensive liability to the team. He never played in the major leagues again.

Manny Alexander—a utility infielder who played for the Red Sox in 2000, Manuel De Jesus Alexander came up through the Baltimore system as a highly regarded shortstop prospect, first appearing in the major leagues in 1992. In 1996, the Orioles thought enough of him to move future Hall of Famer Cal Ripken to third base, but the move didn't last long; Alexander went 1-for-18 and was traded after the season, and Ripken reclaimed his position. In 2000, one of the Red Sox batboys was found in Alexander's car with steroids. Alexander was out of town at the time, and a criminal case for steroid possession had to be dropped because he couldn't be directly tied to the drugs. Alexander hit .211 with the Red Sox, and his poor hitting has kept him from landing major league playing time on a steady basis. After leaving the Sox, he played in the minor league organizations of Seattle, Detroit, Milwaukee, and Texas, as well as in the Mexican League, before resurfacing sporadically with the Texas Rangers in 2004. Alexander signed a minor league contract with the Rangers for the 2005 season.

Luis Alicea—a switch-hitting middle infielder with good range and speed but little power, Alicea got a fair amount of playing time in a variety of roles in his lone season with the Sox in 1995, getting into 132 games, and contributed 44 RBI and 13 stolen bases. In a 13-year MLB career with five teams, Alicea played every position except pitcher, catcher, and center field.

In 2004, Alicea was named manager of the Red Sox short-season Lowell Spinners team. As a minor league manager, Alicia proved to be a switch-thrower as well as a switch-hitter, throwing batting practice with his left arm when his right arm got sore. (Alicea had thrown lefthanded as a child but his father switched him to the right side of the plate at age 12 because he wanted to play in the infield.)

Gary Allenson—a weak-hitting catcher with a good defensive reputation, "Muggsy" played six years with the Sox at a time when the team's catching depth was poor. Because of injuries to other catchers, he often played more than his abilities warranted. Allenson was never a full-time starter, but he split time with Mike O'Berry at the position in 1979 when Carlton Fisk was hurt most of the year, and in 1982–83 he competed with an up-and-coming Rich Gedman for the starting job. Allenson hit just .221 over his major league career (all but the last 14 games of it spent with Boston), foiled by an inability to hit the curve ball.

Allenson coached for the Red Sox during the forgettable Butch Hobson years (1992–94) and has also coached in the Orioles, Yankees, and Brewers organizations. In 2004, he joined the Reds as a minor league catching coordinator.

Abe Alvarez—the only lefthanded pitcher to start a game for the World Series–winning 2004 Red Sox, Alvarez was a highly touted 21-year-old pitching in AA ball when the Sox called him up to pitch the first game of a doubleheader on July 22, to avoid disturbing the team's pitching rotation. Alvarez pitched five innings, giving up five runs, and was returned to AA immediately after the game. The Red Sox starting pitching remained flukily healthy throughout the 2004 season, while the rest of the team was riddled with injuries. Other than Alvarez's start, three starts by Byung-Hyun Kim (who started the season in the rotation before being bounced for ineffectiveness), and a late-season fill-in by Pedro Astacio, the same five pitchers (Pedro Martinez, Curt Schilling, Derek Lowe, Tim Wakefield, and Bronson Arroyo) started every game for the 2004 Red Sox, and each won at least 10 games. Alvarez remains a prospect in the Red Sox minor league system.

Larry Andersen—in one of the worst trades in history, Andersen, a 37-year-old pitcher who had settled into a niche as one of the National League's best middle relievers, was obtained from Houston late in the 1990 season for third baseman Jeff Bagwell. Although Andersen pitched very well in 15 games for Boston, he was declared a free agent at the end of the season because of previous collusion by major league owners and signed with San Diego. Boston came back and made a significantly better offer than the one Andersen's agents initially proposed to them, but that was turned down. Andersen signed with the San Diego Padres. Bagwell, converted to first base by the Astros, turned into one of the best players in baseball and a future Hall of Famer. Andersen was known around the league as a practical joker and free spirit, but in Boston he is remembered only as the player who spent three weeks in Boston in return for Jeff Bagwell.

After retiring, Andersen spent some time as a minor league pitching coach for the Philadelphia organization. He later became a color commentator for the Phillies after the sudden death of Richie Asburn in 1997.

Brady Anderson—lefthanded-hitting outfielder who debuted with the Sox to start the 1988 season. He had a gaudy minor league reputation, particularly for his speed, but found it difficult to break into an outfield that included veteran

Dwight Evans and solid young players Mike Greenwell, Ellis Burks, and Todd Benzinger. Anderson briefly covered center field while Burks was injured, then was traded to the Baltimore Orioles along with then-minor-league pitcher Curt Schilling for starting pitcher (and former 20-game winner) Mike Boddicker.

The Orioles patiently kept Anderson in their outfield through four mediocre offensive seasons before he finally found his home run stroke in 1992, when he hit 21. Anderson's combination of power, defense, and speed made him an outfield fixture in Baltimore throughout the 1990s, and his good looks (with trademark long sideburns) made him a gay icon. In 1996 Anderson took full advantage of the short right field porch in Baltimore's new Camden Yards by launching an anomalous 50 home runs—a total he would never approach again. While Boddicker made a significant contribution to the Red Sox playoff runs in 1988 and 1990, Anderson (along with Schilling) was listed for years by grumbling Sox fans as one of many highly touted players who were sacrificed for veteran help during contending seasons, only to have success with their new teams. In the 2004 off-season, steroids became a burning issue (several star sluggers admitted steroid use to a grand jury, and their slugging tailed off dramatically once drug testing was implemented), and the since-retired Anderson's lone 50 home run season was sometimes cited as possibly a steroid-produced season. (Anderson was not involved in the 2004 cases, however.)

Mike Andrews—solid-hitting second baseman on the Impossible Dream team of 1967. Andrews played briefly with the Sox in 1966, then took over at second base for new manager Dick Williams in 1967. He hit .263 (at a time when the league batting average was only .236), and walked frequently. His best year was 1969, when he hit .293 (tenth in the league) with 15 home runs, excellent for a second baseman at the time. His fielding was solid, if not extraordinary. Andrews was a favorite of Dick Williams, but a year after Williams was fired as manager, Andrews was traded to the White Sox for aging shortstop Luis Aparicio, a deal that helped neither team. Andrews, troubled by a chronic back injury, floundered with the White Sox before being picked up by Williams, then managing the Oakland A's, in 1973. During the 1973 World Series Andrews made two errors in the same game—leading to an extra-inning loss—and A's owner Charlie Finley tried to circumvent baseball rules to dump Andrews in mid-series. Andrews was reinstated by baseball commissioner Bowie Kuhn, and received a standing ovation when manager Williams, against the orders of his owner, brought him into a game to pinch hit. Williams managed the A's to victory in the World Series, then resigned afterward to protest how his player had been treated.

Andrews played in Japan the following season, then retired. Andrews's brother, Rob, was also a major league infielder.

Luis Aparicio—Hall of Fame shortstop, 10-time All-Star and winner of nine Gold Gloves, all for the Chicago White Sox and Baltimore Orioles. Aparicio was, in his prime, one of the best fielding shortstops ever, and not a bad hitter for the position. He singlehandedly reintroduced the stolen base into American League play, leading the league in steals his first nine seasons. Though he was used as a leadoff hitter, he didn't walk often enough to be great in that role.

Aparicio had far and away the best year of his career for the White Sox in 1970—at the age of 36. At the time, the Red Sox had a vacancy at one of two hitter's positions, third base or first base (depending on where they wanted to play George Scott), and a terrific incumbent shortstop in Rico Petrocelli. Rather than trade for another hitter, the Sox moved Petrocelli to third and traded second baseman Mike Andrews for Aparicio as part of a disastrous offseason shuffling.

Predictably, Aparicio fell off the table offensively. He had an 0-for-44 slump early in the season that earned him a condolence call from President Nixon. Defensively, he was still better than average, but not any better than Petrocelli had been, and his anemic bat was a drain on the Sox offense for three seasons. Aparicio was released at the end of spring training in 1974, having lost his job to rookie Mario Guerrero (with Rick Burleson waiting in the wings).

Aparicio is best remembered by most Boston fans for a baserunning blunder. Playing the Detroit Tigers with the pennant on the line in the last series of the 1972 season, Aparicio fell down partway to home and went back to third base. Unfortunately, Carl Yastrzemski was arriving there from the opposite direction and was promptly tagged out, ending a Boston rally. That game proved to be the margin in the pennant race, as the Sox finished half a game behind the Tigers.

Luis Aponte—Venezuelan relief pitcher who didn't pitch in the major leagues until he was 27, after having been out of baseball for three years. After brief appearances in 1980 and 1981, Aponte made the Red Sox staff full-time in 1982, and pitched well in middle relief for the next two years; his unusual forkball kept hitters off balance. Aponte was traded to Cleveland for a minor leaguer and pitched decently in 1983, but he was out of baseball at age 31.

Tony Armas—a slugging outfielder who played in Boston for four years in the mid-1980s. Armas was a well-regarded 29-year-old hitter with a reputation as a fine defensive right fielder when Boston acquired him and Jeff Newman from Oakland for former batting champion Carney Lansford and two others after the 1982 season. As a hitter, Armas struck out a lot and seldom walked, so he was never as good as his home run numbers made him look; he also had defensive problems in center field, which worsened as his speed and throwing ability declined. In 1983 he hit a then-career-best 36 home runs and drove in 107 runs—but with a .218 batting average and a disastrous .258 on-base percentage. He was much better in 1984, leading the league with 43 home runs and 123 RBI. Armas had leg injuries in 1985 (when he hit 23 homers in two-thirds of a season) and again in 1986, making him a defensive liability in center field and prompting GM Lou Gorman to trade for Dave Henderson from Seattle for the playoff drive. Age and frequent injuries sapped Armas's power; he finished 1986 with only 11 home runs, and never hit more than 13 again. He left the Sox after 1986 and finished his career with three more injury-plagued seasons with the California Angels.

Armas also has a connection to the Sox of the late 1990s. His son, Tony Armas Jr., was a top pitching prospect acquired from the Yankees for Mike Stanley. Armas Jr. was later traded to the Expos with Carl Pavano for superstar Pedro Martinez, and was developed into one of the NL's best young pitchers before injuries derailed his career.

Rolando Arrojo—Cuban pitcher who arrived late in the 2000 season from Colorado (along with infielder Mike Lansing) in exchange for Jeff Frye, John Wasdin, and Brian Rose. Arrojo was a member of the Cuban national team for many years, before defecting during the 1996 Olympics in Atlanta. There was some question about his age, as Major League Baseball listed him as being 32 in 2000, while news reports at the time of his defection indicated that he was four years older.

Arrojo signed as a free agent with the expansion Tampa Bay Devil Rays, and was the winning pitcher in the Devil Rays' first win in 1998. He was the first rookie pitcher ever to make the All Star team while pitching for an expansion team, and the first pitcher ever to win 14 games for an expansion team. His 1999 season, however, was injury-plagued, and not successful. Tampa Bay traded him to Colorado prior to the 2000 season. He was the key player, from the Red Sox point of view, in the trade that brought him from Colorado to Boston and pitched well for Boston after arriving from the Rockies.

Despite this, Arrojo lost his spot in the starting rotation in 2001, and reluctantly went to the bullpen, where he was terrific—far better than he had been as a starter. When Pedro Martinez was injured in midseason, Arrojo stepped back into the rotation temporarily and pitched well, though not as well as he had in relief. In 2002, Arrojo again was primarily used as a reliever, but pitched poorly. He was not re-signed by the Red Sox after the 2002 season and has been out of baseball since then.

Bronson Arroyo—few noticed when the Red Sox claimed the tall (6-foot-5), skinny righthander off waivers from the Pittsburgh Pirates shortly before spring training in 2003, but within a couple of years the move paid major dividends for the Sox. A third-round draft selection by the Pirates in 1995, Arroyo progressed steadily through Pittsburgh's minor league system, then struggled with the major league club in parts of three seasons (2000–02), compiling a 9–14 record with a 5.47 ERA. In 2003 with Pawtucket he went 12–6 with a 3.43 ERA in 24 games, his most notable win coming on August 10 when he pitched a perfect game against the Buffalo Bisons, just the fourth perfect game in International League history. He was called up to the Boston squad shortly afterward, appearing in six games with a 2.08 ERA. He was kept on the postseason roster as a reliever and pitched well in three games of the ALCS against the Yankees.

Coming into the 2004 season, Arroyo was in strong contention to capture the fifth slot in the Red Sox starting rotation, but eventually lost out to Byung-Hyun Kim, who had just signed a two-year, $10 million contract during the off-season. Arroyo started the season in the bullpen, but was quickly moved into the rotation when Kim struggled, and he remained there the rest of the way. Partly because of poor run support, Arroyo struggled to a 2–7 record in late June, but was terrific the rest of the year, finishing with a 10–9 record and a 4.03 ERA—excellent for a fifth starter.

Terry Francona rewarded Arroyo's fine year by including him in the starting rotation at the beginning of the 2004 playoffs. Arroyo pitched well in the Division Series against the Angels, but had a poor outing in Game 3 of the ALCS against the Yankees, after which a shortage of available arms necessitated his move back to the bullpen. He worked key innings in Games 5 and 6 of that series, during the Red Sox improbable comeback. Kept in the bullpen for the World Series against the Cardinals, Arroyo worked ⅔ inning in Game 4, allowing a walk.

Named for the movie actor Charles Bronson, the 27-year-old Arroyo blended with the rest of the colorful personalities on the 2004 Red Sox team. He is an accomplished guitarist, and by the middle of the season he was sporting cornrows on his head. On the mound, Arroyo is known for a windup with an extremely high leg kick, as well as for his willingness to pitch inside to hitters without fear. (His 20 hit batsmen in 2004 led the American League.) The most notable of those plunked was Yankees third baseman Alex Rodriguez, which triggered a memorable brawl between Rodriguez and Jason Varitek on July 24, considered by many to be the turning point in the 2004 season for the Red Sox.

Steve Avery—former lefty pitching prodigy with the Atlanta Braves who was signed as a free agent after the Sox lost Roger Clemens. Avery had looked like the next Koufax through age 23 but then lost his fastball and had three mediocre-to-poor seasons in a row. Sox manager Jimy Williams was familiar with Avery from his days as an Atlanta coach, and the Sox gambled on his returning to form.

It didn't happen. Avery, who would finish the 1997 season with a dreadful 6.42 ERA, was yanked from the starting rotation in mid-season. Unfortunately, he had 17 starts at that point and his contract called for a second guaranteed year to kick in if he made 18. Avery's agent threatened to file a grievance against the team, but that was rendered moot when Williams, reportedly against the orders of the front office, gave Avery the extra start in the last days of the season.

Avery's 1998 was somewhat better, as he begrudgingly experimented with new mechanics, showed occasional flashes of effectiveness, and finished 10–7 (but with a poor 5.02 ERA). His most glorious moments came on a couple of occasions when Williams used Avery as a pinch runner in the late innings of games. In one of those games he scored the winning run.

Avery was about the same for the Reds in 1999, then was out of the majors until 2003, when he pitched poorly as a reliever for a dreadful Tigers team. He did not pitch in 2004.

Carlos Baerga—a onetime rising star who reportedly ate his way out of the big leagues for several years, the switch-hitting Baerga played with the Red Sox in 2002. Baerga first came to the majors as a 20-year-old utility infielder in 1990, but soon settled into the Indians' second base job. He hit at least .312 for four straight years (with 15–21 home runs each year), from 1992–95, but was traded to the New York Mets in 1996 after his average (and apparent physical fitness) plummeted. Although Baerga hit .281 for the Mets in 1997, his power and speed were gone, and they dropped him after another disappointing season. After brief unsuccessful stops with the Padres and back to the Indians, he seemed to be out of baseball at age 30. Baerga did not give up though, playing for the Samsung Lions in Korea in 2001 and the Long Island Ducks in the independent Atlantic League. The Red Sox signed Baerga after he returned to playing condition and hit .346 for a team in the Puerto Rican winter league that he owns. Baerga hit

.286 as a part-time player in 2002; his main role on the team seemed to be acting as a friend and sometime spokesman for otherworldly superstar Manny Ramirez. His performance priced him out of the utility role on the Sox, and Baerga ended up with the Arizona Diamondbacks in 2003, where he hit .343 with a club-record 19 pinch hits. Arizona paid him $1 million to return for the 2004 season, but Baerga could not follow up on his 2003 success, hitting only .235.

Jeff Bagwell—righthanded hitting first baseman, a future first-ballot Hall of Famer. While the sale of Babe Ruth to the Yankees in 1919 remains the worst personnel move in baseball history, the 1990 trade of Jeff Bagwell by the Red Sox to the Houston Astros is one of the worst non-financially motivated, talent-for-talent trades of all time.

Bagwell was born in Boston, grew up a Sox fan in Middletown, Connecticut, and was the Sox fourth-round draft pick in the 1989 draft out of Hartford College. He hit .310/.384/.419 for the class A+ Winter Haven Sox that year and followed it with a remarkable .333/.422/.457 MVP season for AA New Britain. This was especially remarkable, because New Britain's Beehive Field was one of the worst parks for hitting in the history of organized baseball.

The Sox were clinging to first place at the end of August 1990 and badly needed another bullpen arm to fend off the charging Toronto Blue Jays. They decided on Houston's Larry Andersen, an effective veteran. According to journalist Peter Gammons, the Astros' asking price was one of three lefty pitching prospects: Kevin Morton, Scott Taylor, or Dave Owen. Sox GM Lou Gorman was unwilling to trade any of them, apparently because none was a sure-fire prospect and he wanted to maximize his chances of developing at least one lefty for the rotation. On the other hand, the Sox had an incumbent All Star at third base in Wade Boggs and two can't-miss third base prospects in Bagwell and Scott Cooper, so Gorman was willing to trade one of the kids because, as Gorman saw it, they were less needed. Cooper was a year older and had hit .266/.334/.393 at Pawtucket, even if he did have a rocket arm and better range at third. The Sox seemed unaware of the New Britain park effect, despite the fact that Cooper's batting average had fallen from .298 to .247 when he made the jump there and (four years earlier) Sam Horn's home runs had gone from 21 to 11. Gorman had never seen Bagwell play in person.

It's fashionable to say that the Sox had no idea that Bagwell would be this good, but analyst Bill James ran his system for converting minor league numbers to big league numbers that winter, and famously came up with the "prediction" that Bagwell could win the NL batting title while jumping from AA to another severe pitcher's park—the Astrodome. That didn't happen, because Bagwell traded some of his average for power, but he did win Rookie of the Year. Despite having played most of his career in the Astrodome, Bagwell has hit .297/.408/.542 lifetime in 14 seasons while playing first-rate defense; he even stole 30 bases twice.

In 2000 there was a short period during which there were rumors that Bagwell might consider returning to the Red Sox. In december of 2000 however he signed a five-year, $83 million deal with the Astros, making him effectively an

Astro for the rest of his major league career. Though his stats have dropped in the last four years, Bagwell still is a top 10 first baseman in most categories.

Meanwhile, Larry Andersen's Sox career consisted of 22 innings of pretty good relief during the last month of the season, as the Sox held off the Blue Jays only to be swept out of the playoffs in four games by the A's.

Bob "Beetle" Bailey—a 35-year old outfielder/third baseman at the end of the line by 1978, his only full season in Boston. Bailey was originally a prized prospect signed by the Pittsburgh Pirates to a contract with a huge bonus and rushed to the major leagues at age 19, years before he was ready. He'd later had some very good years with the Montreal Expos, but hit only .191 for the Sox in 94 at-bats in 1978, mostly as a DH. Because of the trade of power-hitting reserve outfielder Bernie Carbo, who had fallen into manager Don Zimmer's doghouse, Bailey was all that was left to pinch hit in the one-game playoff in 1978, where he made a key out.

Willie Banks—a righthanded reliever who joined the Red Sox late in the 2001 season, after being out of the major leagues for three years. The third overall choice in the 1987 draft, Banks made his big league debut as a much-hyped 22-year-old starting pitcher with Minnesota in 1991 and pitched unimpressively for parts of two years before becoming a full-time starter in 1993. He had the best ERA among any of the team's starters, and his 11–12 record was pretty good for a terrible (71–91) team, but Banks soon found himself a baseball nomad. He was sent to an equally terrible Chicago Cubs team the following year and lost his job despite pitching decently. After that, he bounced up and down between the majors and minor league teams (the Red Sox were his seventh team in eight years in the majors). After pitching well in Pawtucket, the 32-year-old Banks made 10 appearances with the Red Sox in 2001, and gave up only one run. He continued to pitch well in 2002, with a 3.23 ERA in 29 games, although the team never seemed to have much confidence in him except in mop-up roles. He was re-signed by the Sox for 2003, but released during spring training. Texas signed him to a minor league contract in 2004 but also released him before the season started. Banks pitched five games for the independent Newark Bears in 2004, going 1–3 with a 9.64 ERA.

Marty Barrett—a righthanded-hitting second baseman, Barrett hit second for the Red Sox behind Wade Boggs for most of the mid-to-late 1980s, and won the American League Championship Series MVP for the 1986 AL champions. A solid defensive player, Barrett was not the most physically talented player, but was very sound fundamentally. He fooled opposing baserunners into easy outs three times with the hidden ball trick (where an infielder fools a baserunner into thinking he doesn't have the ball, then tags the runner out when he steps off the base). Barrett was not a great hitter, but managed to hit .280 to .300 most years and put up better-than-league-average on-base percentages during the time when he was the everyday second baseman for the Red Sox. Barrett hurt his knee in 1989 and never played in more than 80 games again, finishing his career with 12 games in San Diego in 1991. He sued the Red Sox and then-team doctor

Arthur Pappas for mistreatment of his knee injury, and eventually won $1.7 million in court. Barrett's brother, Tommy, was a longtime minor leaguer who also played briefly for the Sox in 1992 (while Marty was in litigation with the team).

Don Baylor—a former American League MVP (in 1979, when Fred Lynn was robbed of the award) with the California Angels, Baylor spent a single year in Boston as the designated hitter on the Sox 1986 World Series team. Baylor was always dreadful in the field (although his drop of an easy popup in Roger Clemens's 20-strikeout game gave the Rocket an extra out to set the record) and his batting average fluctuated dramatically from year to year, but he had excellent power and got on base frequently. Although he only drew an average number of walks, he had an uncanny ability to be hit by pitches (eventually setting the major league record for being hit by pitches). Boston traded Mike Easler for Baylor prior to the 1986 season in a rare swap with the Yankees. Although the 37-year-old Baylor hit only .238 for the 1986 team, he hit 31 home runs and drove in 94 runs. Perhaps most important was the appearance Baylor *didn't* make, however: In Game 6 of the World Series, with the bases loaded, two outs, and the Red Sox clinging to the lead in the potential deciding game of the series, manager John McNamara did not pinch hit Baylor for Bill Buckner (who hit only .218 against lefties) against lefty Jesse Orosco (who held lefthanded hitters to a .187 average)—even though the hobbling Buckner would normally have left the game for a defensive replacement anyway. Buckner was out, and the Red Sox lost the lead, the game, and eventually the Series.

Rod Beck—in his prime, Beck was the prototypical closer. Not only was he larger and fiercer looking than the average baseball player, he also had an above-average fastball and excellent control. Together, these factors led to him being a dominant closer for both the Giants and Cubs, amassing more than 260 saves in the 1990s. In 1999, Beck's fastball lost some of its zip, and it was revealed that he had bone spurs in his elbow, likely from overwork. Beck pitched poorly after the surgery, lost the closer's job with the Cubs, and was shipped to the Red Sox late that year.

Beck arrived at Fenway in the third inning of a game in which he eventually earned his first American League save. Beck helped the team to the playoffs by pitching very well down the stretch in 1999, but the image fans remember is that of Beck giving up a tenth-inning homer to Bernie Williams in Game 1 of the ALCS. Beck spent time on the disabled list with a pinched nerve in his neck in 2000, but when able to pitch, he was an effective setup man for Red Sox closer Derek Lowe. While he no longer had the overpowering fastball that was once his bread and butter, he could still be an intimidating figure on the mound, and he used guile to compensate for his physical shortcomings.

Many Red Sox fans were surprised when the team picked up Beck's $4.5 million option for the 2001 season, but Beck got off to a terrific start, again as a setup man for Lowe, ranking among the league leaders in appearances. The heavy workload seemed to catch up with him, and late in the season Beck began to give up homers at an extraordinary rate. When Lowe lost his closer's job, he was replaced not by Beck—who made no secret that he wanted to return to the job of relief ace—but by newly acquired reliever Ugueth Urbina. After 68 appearances (and 15 home runs allowed), it was discovered that the 32-year-old Beck had a serious arm injury. He underwent tendon-transplant surgery shortly afterward and did not play in 2002.

In 2003, Beck returned to professional baseball as a member of the Chicago Cubs' Triple-A team in Iowa. He shaved his head, kept his Fu Manchu mustache, and lived behind the right field wall of Iowa's Sec Taylor Stadium in his motor home. Beck signed later that year with the San Diego Padres and converted all 20 save opportunities while star closer Trevor Hoffman was on the disabled list. He left the Padres briefly in 2004 to take care of some unspecified off-the-field issues, and rejoined the club in May. In August of 2004, the Padres released him.

Hugh Bedient—a righthanded pitcher who spent three years with the Red Sox from 1912–14. He went 20–9 as a 22-year-old rookie in 1912, and beat Christy Mathewson and the Giants 2–1 in the fifth game of the World Series. Mathewson and Bedient matched up again in Game 8 (Game 2 ended as a 6–6 tie), and the rookie pitched seven strong innings in a game the Sox won in the tenth to clinch the Series. The 1912 season proved to be Bedient's best, however. After steadily declining over the next two years (finishing 8–12 in 1914 with a much worse than league average ERA), Bedient finished up in 1915, pitching one season for the Buffalo Blues of the Federal League. He died in 1965 at 75 years old.

Stan Belinda—a righthanded pitcher with an unusual sidearm motion, Belinda will probably be best remembered for giving up the home run that cost the Pittsburgh Pirates the National League Championship Series in 1992. After several mediocre seasons in Kansas City, Belinda signed with Boston in 1995, and pitched well as the setup man for closer Rick Aguilera. He was frequently injured in 1996, and the Red Sox eventually released him. Belinda continued to be plagued with physical problems, including being diagnosed with multiple sclerosis in 1998, although he managed to stay in the major leagues through the 2000 season. He once said that while the NLCS homer bothered him for years, the MS put it in perspective.

Gary Bell—trade acquisition who stabilized the pitching staff in 1967, helping the Red Sox achieve their Impossible Dream. The 30-year-old Bell was in his tenth season with Cleveland, where he had several pretty good years both as a starter and a reliever. After pitching a career-high 254 innings in 1966, Bell started 1967 slowly (1–5 record), and the Indians feared that he might be washed up. In June, the Red Sox took a chance on him, trading veteran Don Demeter and prospect Tony Horton. Bell immediately proved his detractors wrong, winning 12 of his 20 decisions for Boston, with a fine 3.16 ERA. He even saved three games in five emergency relief appearances. In the World Series, he lost Game 3, but saved Game 6. Bell pitched well again in 1968, winning 11 games, with a 3.12 ERA (excellent by today's standards, but about average in that notoriously pitcher-friendly season). He made the All Star team, but his pitching tailed off in the second half. The Red Sox left Bell exposed in the 1969 expansion draft, and the Seattle Pilots (now the Milwaukee Brewers) took him. (Bell and his Pilots teammates were immortalized in Jim Bouton's classic, controversial book, *Ball Four*.) Bell struggled with his new team, and did even worse after a trade to the White Sox. After the 1969 season, he retired.

Mark Bellhorn—a versatile switch-hitting infielder and former Auburn University standout, the Boston-born Bellhorn was acquired before the 2004 season to add depth to the Red Sox infield, but ended up as a starter and playoff hero. After several partial seasons as a utility player (he played every position except pitcher and catcher) Bellhorn's first full major league season came in 2002 for the Cubs, in which he hit 27 homers in 146 games but only managed to drive in 56 runs. He was unable to repeat those numbers the following year (hitting only .209 for the Cubs with two home runs), and in midseason he was traded to the Rockies, again relegated to a utility role. The Red Sox acquired him during the off-season in exchange for a player to be named later. Despite a poor spring training in 2004, Bellhorn opened the season as Boston's starting second baseman when an injury to Nomar Garciaparra moved Pokey Reese, who was expected to start at second base, to shortstop.

Bellhorn has an unusually patient batting approach (often seeming to keep the bat on his shoulder and dare the pitcher to strike him out) and surprising power. Despite playing part-time early in the 2004 season and time on the disabled list in August with a fractured thumb, Bellhorn finished third in the AL with 88 walks—but also led the American League with a startling 177 strikeouts, which shattered a team record previously held by Butch Hobson (1977). Bellhorn's .373 on-base percentage was 33 points above the league average, and he rediscovered his power stroke, hitting 17 homers and driving in a career-high 83 runs.

When Bellhorn struggled to hit in the first five games of the American League Championship Series against the Yankees, many fans called for his benching in favor of the slick-fielding Reese. Manager Terry Francona stuck with Bellhorn, however, and the move immediately paid off. Bellhorn, batting lefthanded, hit an opposite-field three-run homer off Jon Lieber in Game 6 at Yankee Stadium, a hit that was initially ruled a double but then was correctly reversed by the umpires. (Replays showed that the ball had cleared the left field wall and ricocheted off the chest of a fan in the front row and back onto the field.) He followed that up with an eighth-inning homer that struck the right field foul pole in Game 7. In Game 1 of the World Series, with the score tied 9–9 in the eighth inning, he hit a two-run shot off Cardinals reliever Julian Tavarez (again off the foul pole) that put the Red Sox ahead for good.

Moe Berg—a light-hitting, much-traveled backup catcher better known for his work as a spy for the United States in World War II. Berg played the last five of his 15 seasons with Boston (1935–39), but only appeared in 148 games. The Princeton-educated Berg spoke at least 12 languages (the running joke was "Moe Berg speaks 12 languages and can't hit in any of them"), was the star of a radio quiz show, and was dubbed "The Professor."

Dante Bichette—righthanded power-hitting outfielder-DH, acquired late in the 2000 season in a desperate attempt to get enough offense to enable the Red

Sox to squeeze into the playoffs. It didn't work, though it wasn't Bichette's fault—he hit 7 home runs in his 30 games in a Sox uniform, with a good .518 slugging percentage. The trade was controversial, as Bichette had been one of the most overvalued (by traditional statistics) of all players in baseball for the previous eight years. (He spent seven of those years playing in the thin air of Colorado, probably the most conducive environment to hitting in the history of the major leagues.) Some Sox fans, looking at his averages of 32 home runs and 132 RBI and batting averages between .298 and .340, thought it was a great trade—while others, looking at his weak hitting outside of his home park and his inability to draw walks, thought that the at-bats Bichette got could have been given more productively to similar Sox players, without trading young pitching, or taking on a $7 million salary obligation for the following season. There was an upside, though: Unlike some big-name players who shunned Boston, Bichette talked glowingly of the chance to play in Fenway Park (he met his wife across from Fenway), and of his admiration for Red Sox icon Ted Williams.

At the end of 2001 spring training, manager Jimy Williams shook up the team by benching Bichette, claiming he hadn't performed well enough in spring training to keep his job. Bichette seemed stunned by Williams's decision, saying that if he had known in advance that spring training was to be an audition he would not have experimented with hitting toward the opposite field and using a heavier-than-usual bat. This lack of communication between Jimy Williams and his key players would recur and trouble the team throughout the season. Bichette eventually regained his spot in the lineup, but his playing time was intermittent, and he seemed to sulk when he wasn't playing. After Williams was fired, Bichette played more regularly, but an injury took away much of his home run power. He finished the year with a .286 batting average but only 12 home runs in 391 at bats, and was not offered a new contract by the Red Sox. He signed a minor league contract with the Dodgers for 2002, but retired during spring training when it became clear he would not be given a starting role. At the urging of his two sons, the youngest of whom had never seen him play, the 40-year-old Bichette came out of retirement in 2004 to play the outfield and pitch for the Nashua Pride of the independent Atlantic League.

Max Bishop—a light-hitting second baseman with an extraordinary ability to draw walks, the lefthanded Bishop was nicknamed "Camera Eye." A longtime member of the Philadelphia A's before finishing his career in Boston, Bishop never played more than 130 games in any of his 12 years in the major leagues—but still drew more than 100 walks seven times (leading the league with 128 in 1929) and scored more than 100 runs four times. As a 34-year-old part-time player for the Sox in 1934, Bishop hit only .261, but walked 82 times—almost a quarter of his plate appearances, and more than any full-time Sox player in 2000—and had an extraordinary .442 on-base percentage. Bishop retired after the 1935 season.

Tony Blanco—Once considered a can't-miss prospect, the 21-year-old third baseman was traded to Cincinnati (with minor league pitcher Josh Thigpen) for Todd Walker after the 2002 season. Blanco was the best player on Boston's Dominican Summer League team in 1999, and followed by an amazing season at

Rookie-level Fort Myers (.384, league-record 13 homers). *Baseball America* rated him the league's best prospect, raving about his cannon arm, lightning-quick righty bat, and work ethic. In 2001, he jumped to low-A Augusta, posting mildly disappointing numbers. Still, Blanco was very young, and he had a sore shoulder, so Boston remained optimistic. But Blanco was disastrous in 2002. Playing 65 games for high-A Sarasota in between disabled list stints, he hit only .221, with 70 strikeouts and only six walks, leading to an atrocious .250 OBP. He showed little power (six homers), and made 30 errors at third base. For all his tools, Blanco had regressed dramatically, and his poor strike zone judgment hardly fit into Theo Epstein's and Bill James's vision of the team's future. With Cincinnati, Blanco continued to fight injuries and a low walk rate, but in 2004 hit .306 with terrific power in class-A Potomac, before hitting poorly when promoted to AA. Cincinnati left Blanco unprotected, and Washington selected him in the the Rule 5 Draft (meaning he has to be kept on Washington's 2005 major league roster or returned to Cincinnati).

Greg Blosser—the Sox used the first-round draft pick they got from San Diego as compensation for free agent Bruce Hurst to make Blosser, a lefthanded hitting outfielder, the sixteenth overall pick in the 1989 draft—seven slots ahead of Mo Vaughn. The pick seemed savvy a year later when Blosser hit .282 against competition three years older, as a 19-year-old on a high class A team. But the next year, Blosser got eaten alive by the huge ballpark in AA New Britain, and his career never recovered. Blosser was later reported to have a drinking problem, which certainly didn't help him to cope with this (in part illusory) setback.

Blosser hit .228 for Pawtucket in 1993 and had an excruciating 2-for-28 cup of coffee with the Red Sox in September. But the next spring he hit the ball consistently hard and played fine defense in right field, showing a strong arm. He made the team, sat on the bench behind Billy Hatcher, made three errors in three games and went 1-for-11, and was never seen again in the big leagues. He bounced around the minor leagues for nine more years, before retiring on May 20, 2003 as a member of the Atlantic League's Somerset Patriots.

Mike Boddicker—obtained in a trade that has since become controversial, Boddicker helped pitch the Red Sox to two division titles. Boddicker never threw very hard, although his breaking pitches were effective—he once struck out 18 in a minor league game, and had 14 strikeouts as an Orioles rookie in 1983. Boddicker was second in the Rookie-of-the-Year voting in 1983, and won 20 games in 1984, when he led the league in both wins and ERA. He followed with three inconsistent seasons, however, and when he started off the 1988 season 6–12, the Orioles traded Boddicker to the Red Sox for two young prospects, outfielder Brady Anderson and pitcher Curt Schilling.

In his new setting, Boddicker turned his career back around. He went 7–3 with a 2.63 ERA in 15 games with the Red Sox in 1988, won 15 games in 1989, and then went 17–8 in 1990 to help the Red Sox to another division title. A free agent after the 1990 season, the 33-year-old Boddicker chose to sign with Kansas City instead of returning to the Red Sox, a decision that hurt both team and player. After an average season in 1991 and a slow start in 1992, the Royals gave up

on Boddicker and dropped him from the rotation. He played briefly and ineffectively for Milwaukee the next year before retiring.

The Boddicker trade has become controversial because both Andersen and
Schilling went on to become stars, but it's misleading to call the trade a bad one.
Both players took years to develop—and Schilling was traded repeatedly—before
they became effective major leaguers, and in 1988 the Red Sox couldn't wait for
pitching help. And Boddicker was everything the Sox had hoped for when they
gave up two prospects to get him—the second best starting pitcher on the team
(after ace Roger Clemens) for three years and two playoff appearances.

Wade Boggs—one of the greatest hitters to ever don the uniform of the Boston
Red Sox. A third baseman, Wade got a late start to what would eventually be a
Hall of Fame career, not making the majors until 1982 at the age of 24, and only
then because of an injury to incumbent third baseman Carney Lansford. Boggs
hit .349 that year—not an American League record for a rookie, as is commonly
reported, but an impressive first season for a player who, after his fifth minor
league season, was left off the 40-man roster and was available to any major
league team that wanted to claim him during the Rule 5 draft (none did). It was-
n't that Boggs didn't hit well in the minors; his minor league numbers were terrific, but the kind of hitter he was (high average, lots of walks, but not much
home run power or speed) was not well thought of at the time—though it's
become exactly the kind of player today's Red Sox organization values most highly, in part because Boggs did so much to overcome the conventional wisdom of
what good hitters should look like: either fast singles hitters, or big, slow sluggers.

He went on to lead the American League in hitting five times during his years
with the Red Sox (and finished in the top five another four times), making the All
Star team every year from 1985 to 1992. Drawing copious walks (he led the
league twice) and banging doubles off Fenway's Green Monster (also a two-time
league leader), Boggs was one of the best hitters in the American League—
arguably the best—during the 1980s (during which he hit over .350), despite his
lack of speed or home run power. Boggs's career .328 average, 3,010 hits, and
.415 on-base percentage, accumulated over an 18-year career with the Red Sox,
Yankees, and Devil Rays, place him among the best third basemen of all time.
(His .338 average while with the Red Sox is second only to Ted Williams's .344.)

Boggs had a variety of superstitions that he followed religiously—always eating chicken on game days, for instance, and always drawing the same symbol (the
Hebrew word חי, which means life) in the dirt with his bat before hitting, and
never altering his route to and from the playing field so that by late summer his
footprints were often clearly visible in the grass in front of his home dugout.
Boggs fielded exactly 150 ground balls during infield practice before virtually
every game. (The person hitting fungoes used to count for him, but after a minor
league teammate told him one night that he had only fielded 149 grounders,
Boggs always insisted on doing his own counting.) Boggs also had a fixation on
the numbers 7 and 17. He signed his 1984 contract for $717,000. During night
games, Boggs stepped into the batting cage at 5:17 and ran wind sprints at exactly 7:17. Boggs once reportedly vomited in Toronto when the scoreboard techni-

cian intentionally changed the clock from 7:16 to 7:18. His superstitions helped endear him to Sox fans in the same way Bill Lee, Luis Tiant, and Nomar Garciaparra captured Boston fans with quirky personality traits that separated them from other athletes. Boggs was also respected as a hard worker who devoted himself utterly to baseball—both in mastering the strike zone in a way few others since Ted Williams have and in countless hours spent improving his fielding at third base. (Boggs made a lot of errors at third base early in his career, but always covered a lot of ground; he did win two Gold Gloves for fielding when he was 36–37 years old, though he was never really considered a great fielder.)

And yet, despite Boggs's great contributions to the successful Red Sox teams of the late 1980s, his name has become, if not anathema in Boston, at least not nearly so revered as his on-field achievements suggest he deserves. His reputation took a hit in 1986 when he sat out the last few days of the season in order to protect his lead in the American League batting race. Boggs's reputation was further sullied in 1988 when his much-publicized extramarital affair with real estate agent Margo Adams seemed to distract a team which should have been fighting for the division lead (and yet which did not, in fact, begin to fight until after the All Star break of that year). Boggs's wife stuck with him, but his public defense that his mistress accompanied him on road trips because he was "addicted to sex" didn't elicit a lot of sympathy—and teammates were even less sympathetic when Adams, in a *Penthouse* interview and pictorial, named names and described many of their own extramarital sexual inclinations. A later incident between Boggs and an official scorer (in which Boggs asked that an error charged to himself be changed to a hit—threatening teammate Roger Clemens's pursuit of the ERA title because it caused additional runs to be charged to Clemens) helped solidify Boggs's reputation as a me-and-my-stats-first player.

Finally, Boggs did little to endear himself to Boston fans when he signed with the New York Yankees after the 1992 season. Although Boston offered him more money than anyone else following his first subpar season, it was not the longterm deal Boggs wanted, and he complained about the team's lack of respect for his accomplishments when he left. Many Boston fans have a single rule for their idols—don't play for the Yankees—and when Boggs violated that rule willingly, he lost those fans. For many New Englanders, the sight of Wade Boggs riding a horse around Yankee Stadium in celebration of their 1996 World Series win severed the emotional ties to the best third baseman in team history.

After he retired, there was some controversy regarding the Hall of Fame for Boggs. A story was circulated that the Devil Rays paid Boggs $1 million to wear their hat on his Hall of Fame plaque (which would make him the first Devil Rays Hall of Famer). The Hall finally pointed out that they, and not the player, decide which hat will appear on the player's plaque. In 2004, Boggs was elected to the Hall of Fame with in the first year he was eligible (just the 41st player inducted in his first year of eligibility), and the Hall did, in fact, choose a Red Sox hat for his plaque. The timing of Boggs's election to the hall reminded Red Sox fans once again of his superstitions: Boggs wore #12 for the Yankees and Devil Rays, and #26 for the Red Sox. The telephone call to inform him of his election to Hall came at exactly 12:26 P.M.

Lou Boudreau—Hall of Fame shortstop who ended his playing career with the Red Sox, after many years as one of Boston's fiercest rivals. Boudreau played for the Indians from 1938–50, combining outstanding defense and solid hitting (.295 lifetime average, with lots of doubles and walks). In 1942, at age 24, Boudreau was named Indians' player-manager, making him the youngest man ever to manage a full season in the majors. In 1946, he began employing the "Boudreau Shift" against Ted Williams, a dead-pull hitter (meaning he almost always pulled the ball to the right side when he was hitting). Boudreau put six fielders to the right of second base, daring Williams to bunt down the third base line or hit the ball to left field. Williams foiled the shift later that year, hitting an inside-the-park homer to clinch the American League pennant. (A similar shift would later be used against Sox star Mo Vaughn.) Two years later, Boudreau got his revenge. Not only did he win the MVP (.355, 18 homers, 106 RBI, 98 walks, and only 9 strikeouts), but he singlehandedly led Cleveland to an 8–3 win against Boston in a one-game playoff for the American League championship. (The two teams finished the regular season tied at 96–58, forcing a playoff.) Boudreau surprised many by starting rookie Gene Bearden, and was hailed as a genius when the lefty knuckleballer won. (To be fair, Bearden won 20 games and led the league in ERA, so he was hardly unproven.) Cleveland really didn't need to worry about pitching that day anyway, since Boudreau had four hits, including two homers. And just so Boston's National League fans didn't feel left out of the carnage, Boudreau then led Cleveland to a World Series victory against the National League Boston Braves.

But 1948 was Boudreau's last hurrah. Injuries had taken their toll, and he was released after the 1950 season. The Red Sox signed him as a backup shortstop and third baseman in 1951, and he hit .267 in 82 games, with only five homers. Boudreau took over as manager the following year, though he retired as a player after four appearances. He managed the Sox for three seasons, never finishing above fourth place. Boudreau later managed the Kansas City A's and Chicago Cubs, and spent many years as a Cubs broadcaster. His daughter was once married to Denny McLain, prior to the former pitching star's well-publicized arrest and drug problems. Boudreau was elected to the Hall of Fame in 1970, and died in 2001.

Oil Can Boyd—one of a trio of young starting pitchers who came up with the Sox in the early 1980s (along with Bruce Hurst and Bobby Ojeda), Dennis Boyd's unpredictable temperament sometimes overshadowed his talent as a pitcher. Boyd was never considered a great prospect the way Bruce Hurst was. Son of a Negro League player and one of 14 children, Boyd came from a small southern town and was so scrawny (only 160 pounds, although he was over six feet in height) that he didn't look like he could possibly be a major leaguer. As a result he had to prove himself at every minor league level before he made it to the majors.

Boyd first appeared with Boston in 1982, then made the team for good during the 1983 season, when the 23-year-old pitched well despite a 4–8 record (3.28 ERA). He was a fixture in the rotation from 1984 to 1986, with his win totals increasing to 12, 14, and 16. Boyd had good control, which allowed him to be effective even though he was sometimes hit hard. In 1986, he joined with Roger Clemens and Bruce Hurst to form a potent top-three starters on the World Series team. In July of that year, Boyd was upset at being left off the All Star team despite his 11 wins at the time. His inexplicable reaction resulted in a suspension, a disputed scuffle with police officers, a series of drug tests (all of which came up clean), and a brief hospitalization.

In 1987 Boyd developed a recurring blood clot in his shoulder, which sent him to the disabled list frequently. After three injury-marred seasons, he signed with the Montreal Expos as a free agent. He had a great 1990 season with the Expos, but was out of baseball after the next season, at age 31. Before the 2005 season Boyd announced that he was attempting a comeback, and signed with the independent Brockton Rox.

The nickname *Oil Can* is slang for *beer can*.

Hugh Bradley—a part-time first baseman and utility player, Bradley hit the first home run over the Green Monster at the new Fenway Park on April 26, 1912. It was the only home run Bradley would hit that year, and one of only two in his five-year career in the major leagues. When Fenway was built, some experts predicted it would be years before anyone would hit a ball over the massive left field wall. It took six days.

Darren Bragg—a lefthanded-hitting outfielder, Bragg was a Connecticut native who came up with Seattle in 1994. Despite a reputation as a hard worker, Bragg never consistently hit at the levels a major league outfielder needs to hit. When Seattle was gearing up for the stretch run in 1996, the Sox, who felt they were out of things after being buried by a terrible start, traded pitcher Jamie Moyer for Bragg. (This turned into a seriously lopsided trade when Moyer, who the Red Sox had picked up as an unheralded 33-year-old free agent, went on to win 13–21 games in each of the next nine years.) Boston needed young outfielders, and Bragg was a good defensive right fielder who approached the game aggressively. But he still didn't hit enough, and when he hit free agency following the 1998 season, the Sox did not re-sign him. After a serious injury, Bragg has bounced around as a part-time player with six teams since leaving the Sox. He hit .188 with San Diego and Cincinnati in 2004.

Eddie Bressoud—mediocre shortstop whose bat came alive after moving to Fenway in 1962. Bressoud had spent six indistinguished seasons as a utility man with the Giants, who traded him to Boston for another shortstop, Don Buddin. Bressoud got to play regularly for the first time, and he responded with a .277 average, 40 doubles, 9 triples, and 14 homers. Never known as a good fielder, Bressoud led American League shortstops with 28 errors, but his bat made up for his defensive shortcomings. As an encore, he set a career high with 20 homers in 1963, though his average fell to .260. In 1964, Bressoud had his best season, setting career highs in average (.293), on-base percentage (.374), slugging (.456), walks (72), and doubles (41). He also hit 15 homers, and was selected to the All Star team. For a shortstop in that pre-Cal Ripken Jr., pre-Nomar era, Bressoud's offensive numbers were outstanding. But in 1965, he reverted back to his pre-Boston days, batting a paltry .226 with only eight homers. By midseason, Bressoud was benched in favor of rookie Rico Petrocelli. By late November, he was a New York Met, having been traded for Joe Christopher. Bressoud ended his career as a utility man on the 1967 World Champion St. Louis Cardinals, and he played two World Series games against his former team.

Ken Brett—a lefthanded pitcher and the older brother of Kansas City's Hall of Fame third baseman George Brett, Ken Brett is one of the great might-have-been stories in Sox history. He was a much bigger star at California's El Segundo High School than his kid brother was five years later, and legendary Sox scout Joe Stephenson never hesitated in naming him the best prospect he ever saw—as a center fielder. The Sox took him fourth overall in the June 1966 minor league draft. But alas for the Sox, Brett was also a lefty who threw close to 100 MPH, though without much polish. Since the parent club had a young outfield of Yaz, Reggie Smith, and Tony Conigliaro but a dearth of pitching, they didn't hesitate to project Brett as the next Koufax rather than the next Musial. Brett fanned 219 batters in 189 innings pitched in A and AA ball in 1967 (truly eye-popping numbers 35 years ago in general, let alone for an 18-year-old), got a late-season call up to the parent club, and became the youngest pitcher in World Series history when he pitched twice in relief, retiring four batters and walking one.

He was hurt for most of 1968 and spent most of the next year in AAA, but had a promising rookie season in 1970, fanning 155 batters in 139 innings and going 8–9 with a 4.08 ERA. He also hit .314 with power in his first 51 big league at-bats, despite having had little hitting practice in the minors.

Unfortunately, that was the high point of his career. He never did have much command (79 walks in 1970), lost a crucial few MPH off the fastball, and was hit hard in 1971. After the season he was included in the disastrous trade of George Scott to the Milwaukee Brewers—ironically, the key player the Sox got, Tommy Harper, was supposed to fill a void in center field—where Brett might have been playing. Brett then became a baseball nomad, pitching for nine other teams in the next 10 years before retiring with an 83–85 record and a 3.93 ERA, a bit worse than average for those days. He set a record for pitchers by homering in four straight starts for the Phillies in June 1973; after the 1974 season he still had lifetime numbers of .276/.309 /.434 in 272 at bats (to put this in perspective, today's best hitting pitcher, Mike Hampton, was a career .231/.296/.277 before moving to Colorado and hitting the first seven homers of his career). To this day both George Brett maintains that "Kemer" (that was young George's attempt at saying "Kenneth") was flat-out the better hitter. After his career, Brett was a long-time radio and TV analyst with the Angels, before moving to Spokane to run minor league baseball and hockey teams with his brothers Bobby and George. Ken Brett died of brain cancer in 2003, at age 53.

Mike Brown—a perpetual pitching prospect who never quite made it as a major leaguer. Brown jumped from AA to the big leagues in 1982, then was decent as a rookie starter in 1983, going 6–6. He then went 1–8 with a 6.85 ERA in 1984 and spent most of 1985 pitching poorly in the minors before making the team again in 1986. After a poor start he was traded to Seattle in midseason as part of a deal for Dave Henderson and Spike Owen.

Tom Brunansky—slugging outfielder who played a pivotal role in the Red Sox pennant drive during the 1990 season. When GM Lou Gorman failed in his attempts to land a starting pitcher for unneeded reliever Lee Smith, Gorman shipped him to St. Louis for Brunansky, to fill a power hole in the lineup. Brunansky never hit for a high average, but he drew an above-average number of walks, and had been a solid power hitter in the mid-1980s with the Twins, twice topping the 30-homer mark before struggling in his 2+ years with the Cardinals. Bruno responded mightily to the new environment, including a 5-for-5, two-homer, five-RBI game against his former team, the Twins, during his first week at Fenway. Although he ended up hitting only .267 for the rest of the season with 15 homers, he is best known for his diving catch of an Ozzie Guillen line drive in Fenway's right field corner on the final day of the season to clinch the American League East title. Brunansky played for two more years as a regular with the Sox, never hitting more than 16 homers. After two years in Milwaukee, he returned to play briefly with the Sox again in 1994, and retired after that season with 271 career homers.

Bill Buckner—lefthanded first baseman, acquired from the Cubs early in the 1984 season for starting pitcher Dennis Eckersley (both teams were dumping ex-stars who had worn out their welcome, although Eckersley would eventually return to stardom as a reliever). Buckner played parts of five seasons in two different stints with the Red Sox, mostly with very bad ankles that made him look like every step was a special effort. He was a solid hitter for most of his career, but not as good as his batting average and RBI totals made him seem. (Although Buckner won a batting title for the Cubs, he seldom walked and had limited power.)

Buckner is best remembered for the ground ball hit by Mookie Wilson of the Mets that went through his legs in the bottom of the tenth inning of Game 6 of the 1986 World Series, the play on which the winning run scored for the Mets. Though widely derided and blamed for the loss (for instance, an old joke was revived: "Say, did you hear about Bill Buckner? He tried to commit suicide by jumping in front of a bus . . . but it went through his legs . . . ") many thought that the sore-ankled Buckner couldn't have made the play even if the ball had been fielded cleanly. And others think that the game was lost already, with the two-run lead having been blown. He was released by the Red Sox in the middle of the 1987 season, and then signed with California.

Despite the public vilification which eventually led to him moving out of Massachusetts several years after his retirement, he signed as a free agent with the Red Sox prior to the 1990 season, and was greeted with a standing ovation from the crowd on opening day. He played 22 games, hitting badly, before being released.

Don Buddin—long remembered as a symbol of mediocrity, the name Don Buddin conjures up memories of the poor Red Sox teams of the late 1950s to early 1960s, a lean time indeed for Sox fans old enough to remember it. But in many ways, Buddin was a victim of his times: He was a solid offensive and defensive shortstop in an era when the most important measures of quality were batting average, runs batted in, and errors made—and when his strengths as a player were invisible. Buddin hit for a decent average, but walked a lot (more than he struck out over his career, which is very rare), giving him a strong on-base percentage for a shortstop at a time when most middle infielders were light-hitting defensive specialists. He made a lot of errors, but he also had excellent range, making plays that many other shortstops wouldn't. As a result, his fielding percentage was about average, even with his high error totals.

Buddin's reputation also suffered because he played for bad teams, and because of the Pumpsie Green fiasco, where Buddin ended up being caught in the the crossfire between a racist management team (in particular, manager Pinky Higgins) and everyone else, especially the local media. Buddin was the incumbent shortstop who was "blocking" the progress of Pumpsie Green, who eventually became the first black Red Sox player, although at second base. Writers of the time tended to play up the weaknesses of Buddin while downplaying his positives in making a case for the Sox promoting Green. (Although as it turned out, Green wasn't nearly the player Buddin was, either with the bat or with the glove.)

Damon Buford—righthanded-hitting center fielder who had two tours of duty in the Red Sox organization. The light-hitting Buford (he hit lefthanded pitching well, but struggled against righties) was obtained from Texas in the Aaron Sele trade after the 1997 season. He hit a surprising .282 in 1998 with 10 home runs as a part-time player, and played excellent defense in center field. The next year, manager Jimy Williams increased his playing time against righthanders with disastrous results: Buford's batting average fell 40 points and his on-base percentage and power dropped even further. Buford was traded to the Chicago Cubs where he became the starting center fielder for a year without improving his hitting much, then lost his job when he hit .176 in 2001. He signed a minor league contract with the Red Sox after the 2001 season, but never made it back to the majors. Buford's father, Don Buford, spent 10 as a major league player (and is now a coach) and was an All-Star in 1971.

Tom Burgmeier—lefthanded reliever who played a key role in the Sox bullpen in the late 1970s and early 1980s. Burgmeier was already 34 and a veteran of 10 big league seasons when the Sox obtained him from Minnesota in 1978. Although he didn't pitch particularly well that year, he was excellent for the next four years, including 1980 when he saved 24 games as the team's closer and made the All Star team. He pitched two more strong years with Oakland before retiring at age 40. Burgmeier didn't have much of a fastball, but had great control and pitched aggressively, though off the field he was famously laid back. ("You can tell an awful lot about a person by what's on the back of his baseball card," was one famous quote.)

Burgmeier was the last Red Sox pitcher to play another position in the field. He played the outfield in 1980 as part of a double switch, when Skip Lockwood was brought into the game to pitch to a righthanded hitter. After retiring,

Burgmeier coached in the Baltimore and Kansas City organizations, including a sting as Royals bullpen coach that was interrupted for two months when a car ran into Burgmeier while he was bicycling to the ballpark. Most recently, Burgmeier served as pitching coach of the Single-A Burlington Bees in 2003.

John Burkett—soft-throwing veteran righthanded starting pitcher signed as a free agent by the Red Sox after the 2001 season. Burkett pitched over 200 innings in a season five times in his career, and put up winning records in each of his first four full years in the majors. He appeared on his way to stardom in 1993, when he finished with a 22–7 record and 3.65 ERA. But a string of mediocre seasons followed, and Burkett drifted from the Giants to the Marlins to the Rangers to the Braves.

At age 36, Burkett enjoyed a renaissance with the Braves in 2001. Supported by a strong rotation and a winning atmosphere, he pitched 219 innings with an impressive 3.04 ERA (third-best in the National League), despite finishing with a 12–12 record. A free agent after the season, Burkett at first seemed unwilling to play in Boston, but after meeting with manager Joe Kerrigan—who shared Burkett's analytical approach to pitching—he changed his mind. Some confusion followed when Burkett's agent announced that he had been signed and the team insisted that he hadn't, but eventually, a two-year deal was agreed to. (Burkett never actually got to pitch for Kerrigan, who was replaced by Grady Little before the 2003 season began.) Burkett pitched two so-so seasons for the Sox, with a total of 25 wins and 17 losses, before retiring from baseball.

While Burkett never pitched a no-hitter, he does have a number of perfect games to his credit—as an accomplished tenpin bowler. He also set a dubious major league record as a San Francisco Giants rookie in 1989, by leaving the most free tickets for friends and family at a single baseball game: 147.

Morgan Burkhart—a switch-hitting first base-DH type, Burkhart arrived in Boston after an unusual and winding journey. Burkhart wasn't drafted out of college, probably because (a) he went to an obscure Division II school, and (b) he doesn't look athletic and is short for a first baseman. Instead he ended up in the independent Frontier League, where he won the MVP award three years in a row. In 1998 he hit .404, had 36 homers (a league record), and drove in 98 runs in just 280 at bats—but because the league does not allow any players over 26, he was forced to move on. Burkhart signed with Boston, who sent him to minor league clubs in Sarasota (where he dominated) and Trenton. He continued to get on base constantly, and finished the season with 36 homers, 108 RBI, and 96 runs scored. He played that winter in the Mexican League, leading the league in RBI, on-base percentage, slugging percentage, runs scored, home runs, and extra base hits. Not surprisingly, he was named league MVP.

Burkhart split the 2000 season between AAA Pawtucket and Boston. He made an immediate impression on Red Sox fans by getting a hit in his first big league at bat, and by going on an extraordinary tear in his first couple of weeks in the majors. After a tough game in Baltimore in which Sidney Ponson struck him out four times, however, manager Jimy Williams seemed to lose confidence in Burkhart, and he rarely played the rest of the year, even though the Sox other first basemen were either injured or playing poorly. In 25 big league games, Burkhart hit .288, with an extraordinary .442 on-base percentage. Sent to the minors again in 2001, the 29-year-old Burkhart got off to a poor start, and spent only limited time with the Red Sox, hitting poorly in 33 at bats. He was released after the season ended, and played only six more major league games, for Kansas City in 2003.

Ellis Burks—came up to the Red Sox in 1987 along with fellow rookie outfielders Mike Greenwell and Todd Benzinger, all of whom put up welcome first-season performances. Burks had a rare combination of power, speed, and solid defense; his development allowed the Sox to include prized young center fielder Brady Anderson in the trade for Mike Boddicker, who helped the team win division titles in 1988 and 1990. Burks finished the 1987 season with 20 home runs and 27 stolen bases; but while his power remained relatively consistent, his supposed speed was an enigma. Often plagued by injuries and not a gifted basestealer despite his speed, Burks's steal totals declined to 25 in 1988, 21 in 1989, and remained in single digits for every year until 1996. Not so his power: In a game against the Indians in 1990, he accomplished the rare feat of hitting two home runs in the same inning.

Burks was not re-signed by the Sox after injuries limited him to just 66 games in 1992. (His relationship with Boston fans had frayed amid frustration that he'd never turned into the star many people expected). He spent the 1993 season with the White Sox, but went on to enjoy great success with the Colorado Rockies, taking advantage of the thin air at Coors Field. His best season came in 1996, when he hit .344 with 40 homers and 128 RBI, while stealing 32 bases. Burks was traded to the Giants in 1998, and hit .344 for the NL West champs in 2000. He signed with Cleveland as a free agent in 2001, helping to fill the vacancy left when Manny Ramirez signed with the Red Sox by hitting .280 with 28 homers at age 36. With Cleveland in 2003, Burks sprained his wrist in spring training. The veteran designated hitter tried to play through the injury until June 7, when the muscles in his right hand affected his ability to swing the bat. He underwent season-ending surgery to repair nerve damage in his right elbow on June 23.

As a 40-year-old outfielder-designated hitter, Burks returned to the Red Sox as a free agent for the 2004 season, hoping to make a last hurrah in the town where he'd started before retiring. Although greeted warmly by fans and regarded by other players as a role model and positive influence on the World Championship team, Burks's final season was a frustrating one: He spent nearly five months on the disabled list after two operations on his left knee and a steady rehabilitation effort. Burks appeared in just 11 games, hitting only .182 before retiring at season's end.

Rick Burleson—"The Rooster" was a popular shortstop on the great slugging Red Sox teams of the late 1970s. Burleson was a slick-fielding shortstop with speed and a decent bat, although he didn't walk much. Although he was one of the weakest hitters in the lineup, he usually hit near the top of the order, because he *looked* like a traditional leadoff hitter—a fast guy who hit .280 but didn't have much power—and Boston managers such as Don Zimmer tended to be very conservative. In spite of batting more than 600 times a year in powerhouse lineups, he never got on base enough to score more than 93 runs in a year, and averaged about 75. Burleson was considered one of the best fielding shortstops of his day, and was an All Star from 1977–79, also winning the Gold Glove in 1979.

After seven years in Boston, Burleson was traded to California, where he tore his rotator cuff, and reinjured it while attempting to come back. He finished his playing career with Baltimore before going into coaching, including stints as hitting coach and third base coach with the Red Sox. He is currently manager of Cincinnati's Single-A club in the Pioneer League.

George Burns—a righthanded first baseman who spent two of his 16 major league seasons with the Red Sox. Burns was a decent fielder and (in the context of the era) a better than average hitter during his time with the Sox. He also has a very rare accomplishment to his credit, one that is almost always done by second basemen or shortstops. During 1923, his last season in Boston, he turned an unassisted triple play from first base, moving with a baserunner, catching a line drive, tagging the runner, and outracing the runner from second to the bag. He played for five different teams during his career, and had two stints each with Cleveland and the Philadelphia A's.

Juan Bustabad—a frequently hyped shortstop prospect who was going to be the next star of the Red Sox in the early 1980s. He never made it to the big leagues. He was hitting coach for the Vero Beach Dodgers minor league team in 2004.

Orlando Cabrera—Colombian shortstop who joined the 2004 Red Sox in a blockbuster midseason trade. Cabrera hit .294 in his half-season for the Sox, and solidified a shaky infield defense. Cabrera first came to the majors with the Expos in 1997, and had his breakout year in 2001, when he hit .276, with 14 home runs and 96 RBI, stole 19 bases, and won the Gold Glove for fielding excellence at shortstop. The next two years were also very good for Cabrera, and he peaked in 2003 when he hit .297 with 17 home runs and 24 stolen bases. He had established himself as a very good shortstop, just below the top tier of players at the position.

In 2004, Cabrera got off to an indifferent start. Superstar Vlad Guerrero had left the Expos the previous off-season, the ownerless, nomadic team played in front of fewer than 7,000 people per night, and Cabrera's hitting seemed to reflect that lack of enthusiasm (though his fielding remained excellent). So it came as a reprieve of sorts when playoff-contender Boston acquired him (along with Minnesota first baseman Doug Mientkiewicz) in a 4-team trade in which the Red Sox gave up star shortstop Nomar Garciaparra. Cabrera hit a home run in his first game for Boston, hit well after an initial adjustment period, and played superb defense as the Red Sox made their push for the postseason.

A free agent at the end of the 2004 season, Cabrera expressed interest in remaining with the Red Sox, but signed a deal with the Angels after the Sox signed former Cardinal star (and fellow Colombian) Edgar Renteria as their starting shortstop. (There was a three-team chain reaction, as incumbent Angels shortstop and ontime Sox farmhand David Eckstein signed with the Cardinals to replace Renteria.)

Cabrera's older brother, Jolbert, also drafted by the Expos originally, spent seven seasons in the major leagues, and now plays in Japan.

Bill Campbell—the first big-name free agent signed by Boston, after going 17–5 with 20 saves and a 3.01 ERA for Minnesota in 1976. Campbell was even better for the 1977 Sox, going 13–9 with a 2.96 ERA, and temporarily setting a team record for saves (31). He hurt his arm the following season (after two years of ridiculous overuse by his managers), and was never the same pitcher, though he hung on with Boston until 1981. After leaving the Red Sox Campbell drifted to five teams in six years before retiring from baseball after the 1987 season.

Jose Canseco—rarely has any one player evoked such a mix of emotions from Red Sox fans as has Jose Canseco. Fans hated him as a foe, liked his power in a Sox uniform, and despised him again when he moved on. Canseco was glamorous (at one point romantically linked with Madonna), deadly with his bat, but also outspoken, critical, and prone to reckless decisions (and sometimes reckless driving) wherever he went—which contributed to frequent changes of teams as soon as his skills began to decline.

Canseco started his career as one half of the "Bash Brothers" along with Mark McGwire in Oakland in 1985, where he won Rookie of the Year. In 1988 he won the American League MVP award, and became the first player ever to hit 40 home runs and steal 40 bases in the same season. By the time he was traded to Boston in 1995, injuries had reduced Canseco to a one-dimensional player, and injuries continued to plague him during his time in Boston. He still hit well when he was able to play, hitting over .300 for the first time since 1988, slugging well over .500 both years, and drawing more than his share of walks—but he batted fewer than 400 times in either season (a typical starter bats 500–600 times a year). By this point Canseco's speed was gone, and he was used in the field only as a last resort. (Before coming to Boston, Canseco was once hit in the head by a fly ball he was attempting to catch.)

One of Canseco's more bizarre injuries occurred in Fenway Park in 1993, while he was playing for the Texas Rangers. Texas (and future Boston) manager Kevin Kennedy tried to save his beleaguered pitching staff by putting Canseco in to pitch late in a game that Texas was losing badly. Canseco hurt his "pitching" arm and was lost for the rest of that year.

Boston traded for Canseco at Kevin Kennedy's request shortly after he was hired as Boston manager. The two were friends off the field, and to a certain extent Kennedy protected Canseco, a frequent critic of then-Sox general manager Dan Duquette, from management criticism. After Kennedy was fired following the 1996 season, Canseco was traded back to his first team, the Oakland A's. He played for four teams in a five-year span from 1998 through 2001, before deteriorating skills forced him to abandon his quest for 500 home runs at 462.

Canseco's identical twin brother, Ozzie, also played in the major leagues for four years, but in his case without notable success. The difference in size between Ozzie and the bulked-up Jose led to speculations of steroid use by Jose. The speculation was confirmed when Canseco was arrested in June 2002 after testing positive for steroids. This violated his probation stemming from a nightclub brawl in 2001. Since Canseco had already violated his probation by leaving Florida for several weeks and failing to start community service and anger management classes, he was sentenced to 30 days in jail and two years of house arrest. In a 2005 book, Canseco openly admitted to the allegations, and claimed he had used steroids with many other prominant players.

Bernie Carbo—journeyman outfielder who spent time with six different teams during a 12-year major league career, including two stints with the Red Sox. His biggest moment of glory came in the eighth inning of the sixth game of the 1975 World Series. The lasting memories of that game are the play that Dwight Evans made in the eleventh inning, catching a deep drive off the bat of Joe Morgan and doubling Ken Griffey off first base, and, of course, the Fisk home run that ended the game in the twelfth. But none of the other heroics would ever have happened without Carbo pinch-hitting for Roger Moret with two outs in the bottom of the eighth and the Red Sox trailing 6–3. With two strikes, Cincinnati reliever Rawley Eastwick threw a pitch that Carbo barely got a piece of with a horrible swing, fouling it into the dirt on the third base side. Then Carbo drove the next pitch into the center field bleachers for a three-run homer to tie the game, and set up the drama that was to follow.

A fan favorite and frequent pinch-hitter during the five seasons which he spent (all or part of) in Boston, after retirement, Carbo was an occasional presence on Boston radio, and well known for running a beauty salon in his native Detroit. After struggling with alcohol and drug dependency, he founded the nondenominational Diamond Club Ministry, and now devotes much of his free time speaking to church and other groups, as well as managing the independent Pensacola Pelicans and running a fantasy camp every November.

Bill "Rough" Carrigan—starting catcher on the 1912 World Champions. He was named player-manager in 1913, and piloted the Sox to back-to-back World Series titles in 1915 and 1916. He resigned after Harry Frazee bought the team, and went back to Maine to work in banking. Carrigan returned as manager for three unsuccessful seasons in the post-Ruth era (1927–29).

Frank Castillo—inconsistent starting pitcher who was a Red Sox regular during the 2001–02 seasons. In 10 years in the majors as a full-time starter (mostly with bad teams) the oft-injured Castillo managed to pitch more than 200 innings only once, and won 10 or more games only five times (including once with the Sox). In 26 starts for Boston in 2001 Castillo went 10–9 with a 4.21 ERA—but was limited to just 136 innings after missing all of July with a strained right latissimus and being pulled for a reliever early in a number of his starts. In 2002, he was 6–15 in a variety of roles.

The normally mild-mannered Castillo managed to get suspended twice in 2002. On May 3, the Red Sox beat the Devil Rays in a game that saw Rays (and future Red Sox) pitcher Ryan Rupe hitting Nomar Garciaparra and Shea Hillenbrand with a pitch in the same inning, Trot Nixon throwing his bat at Rupe to start off the very next inning (Nixon claimed the bat "slipped"), Castillo getting his one-thousandth career strikeout, and Castillo being tossed (and later suspended for five games) after hitting Tampa Bay's Randy Winn with a pitch. In June he was suspended again for five games, after umpire Bill Welke called a balk on Castillo, allowing the Padres' Tom Lampkin to move into scoring position. Following a run-scoring double by Julios Matos, Castillo charged Welke, stepping on the umpire's left foot. After being out of the major leagues in 2003, Castillo signed a minor league contract with Boston in 2004, but pitched only ⅔ of an inning with the Sox in April, spending the rest of the season with their AAA Pawtucket club.

Danny Cater—the product of one of the worst trades in Red Sox history, the 32-year-old Cater was a light-hitting utility player (he hit for a decent batting average but had no power and rarely walked) who the Red Sox gave up left-handed relief ace Sparky Lyle to get in 1972. Lyle went on to have eight consecutive strong seasons for the Yankees. Cater, installed at first base, hit .237 and lost his job by midseason; he played two more seasons as a backup for the Sox before being traded to St. Louis—his seventh team over a 12-year career.

Orlando Cepeda—the 1958 National League Rookie of the Year and 1967 National League MVP, Cepeda was a first baseman who had a borderline Hall of Fame career with the San Francisco Giants, St. Louis Cardinals, and Atlanta Braves. He was elected to the Hall by the Veterans Committee in 1999. A post-career conviction for marijuana smuggling may have had something to do with the writers not electing him to the Hall, though he missed by just seven votes during the 1993 voting. Cepeda and Roberto Clemente are the only native Puerto Ricans in the Hall of Fame.

Cepeda (whose father was nicknamed "the Bull" and sometimes called the "Babe Ruth of Puerto Rico") was nicknamed "the Baby Bull." He hit 25 homers or more eight times, and finished with 379. When the American League implemented the DH rule following the 1972 season the Red Sox signed Cepeda, and he was their first DH. He was just a shadow of what he had been, and not much of an asset. He hit 20 homers but that was about all, as he didn't walk much, and couldn't run well on worn out and damaged knees. He did have one moment of glory as he tied a major league record by hitting four doubles in a game against Kansas City in August. The Red Sox released Cepeda in March of 1974 and he signed on with Kansas City. He played badly in 33 games for the Royals before retiring.

Ben Chapman—a speedy outfielder who never hit for much power, but played well enough to play 15 seasons over 17 years in the big leagues, playing for 7 different clubs. He broke in with the Yankees in 1930 and hit at least 10 home runs in each of his first three years, then never hit double figures again. Tom Yawkey tried to purchase his contract from the Yankees prior to the 1936 season, when Chapman was in trouble in New York for making anti-Semitic remarks following a run-in with a Jewish fan. The Yankees didn't want him going to a competitor, and refused.

The Yankees traded him to Washington early in 1936, however, and the Red Sox acquired him from the Senators in June of 1937, along with Bobo Newsom, for the Ferrell brothers (Rick and Wes) and an outfielder named Mel Almada. Chapman spent the next year and a half in Boston, hitting well and playing a good outfield. But the Red Sox had Ted Williams coming, and after the 1938 season, Chapman was traded to Cleveland for Denny Galehouse.

His 1938 season in Boston, when he hit .340, was his last good one. He bounced around for a couple more years, coming back after the war to play ineffectively in 58 games for Brooklyn and Philadelphia. In the middle of the 1945 season he went from Brooklyn to Philadelphia, where he played and managed the Phillies through the 1948 season. He was widely known and remembered for the racial slurs he threw at Jackie Robinson from the Phillies dugout during Robinson's rookie season in 1947. He is alleged to have repented before his death in 1966, but his playing and managing days are known as much for his bigoted and controversial behavior as for his playing ability.

Robinson Checo—a young pitching star in Japan, where he had a 19-9 record and 3.16 ERA over two seasons with the Hiroshima Carp, Checo was signed to an expensive free agent contract by Red Sox general manager Dan Duquette in the mid-1990s. When Checo failed to live up to his promise, the media ridiculed Duquette for the unconventional signing. (Checo was dubbed "The Dominican Mystery Man" by *Boston Globe* writer Gordon Edes, for instance.) Checo did pitch briefly for the Red Sox in 1997 and 1998, before moving on to the Dodgers organization in 1999.

Bruce Chen—lefthanded pitcher who at age 27 has already pitched for seven major league teams. At one point, Chen was a much-hyped Braves prospect, expected to be next in a long line of starting pitchers produced by the Atlanta system. He first appeared with the Braves as a 21-year-old in 1998, and had what turned out to be his best year in 2000 (7–4, 3.29 ERA), when he was traded to the Phillies in a deal for Andy Ashby. After that he went through six teams in two years (including five games for the Red Sox in 2003), intriguing all of them with his talent without impressing any of them enough for an extended stay. He pitched well enough with pitching-desperate Baltimore at the end of the 2004 season to get re-signed for 2005, so he may have finally found a home.

Eddie Cicotte—righthanded pitcher who spent just over four years with the Sox, ending in the early 1910s. Cicotte went on to have a career that warranted Hall of Fame consideration as a member of the White Sox, leading the league by winning 28 games in 1917 and 29 in 1918. He is best known, however, for being one of the "Black Sox," the eight members of the Chicago White Sox team that intentionally threw the 1919 World Series. He was banned from baseball late in the 1920 season, after being indicted by a grand jury investigating the scandal.

Jack Clark—a veteran righthanded power hitter signed as a free agent by the Sox before the 1991 season, Clark was known for his batting eye (he'd led the league in walks three of the previous four seasons). Clark's signing was one of three big-money acquisitions made by general manager Lou Gorman at that time, along with acquiring pitchers Matt Young and Danny Darwin. He joined the Sox with 16 seasons of baseball experience behind him, the first 10 of those with the San Francisco Giants. Despite hitting a grand slam on Opening Day against the Toronto Blue Jays, Clark, a notorious slow starter, did not hit consistently until the second half of the season, finishing 1991 with a disappointing .249 average, 28 homers, and 87 RBI (although he did walk 96 times). Clark retired following the 1992 season after hitting only .210 in 81 games. He also made news during his time with the Sox by filing for bankruptcy despite his huge contract.

Clark was fired as hitting coach for the Los Angeles Dodgers in 2003, and ended up managing the independent Frontier League's Mid-Missouri Mavericks in 2004. When the team struggled, he was shifted to the front office and replaced as manager by Jim Gentile. Clark also sidelined in 2004 as the hitting coach of the McKinney Marshals of the Texas Collegiate League, a summer wood-bat college league.

Tony Clark—tall, switch-hitting first baseman who went from All-Star in Detroit to huge flop in Boston. Clark came up with the Tigers in 1995 and became a regular in 1996, when he hit 27 home runs in only 376 at-bats. The next year the 6-foot-7 Clark was a full-time starter, and improved dramatically, raising his batting average from .250 to .276, hitting 32 home runs, and going from a below-average 29 walks to 93 walks, seventh in the league that year. He continued to hit well (with slugging percentages over .500 for five consecutive years), but in 2000 and 2001 his playing time was limited by injuries and by a logjam at first base in Detroit, which began to see him less as a hitting star and more as an expensive contract obligation.

After the 2001 season, in which he hit .287 with 16 home runs and a high walk total the Tigers put Clark on waivers, hoping to get someone else to take on his $5 million contract, and he was snapped up by Red Sox GM Dan Duquette. On Opening Day in 2002, everybody jumped on the Clark bandwagon after he went 3-for-5 with a homer. After that, Clark looked like a completely different player, batting just .207 with three home runs and a poor walk total in 90 games before losing his job. Clark regained some of his power after leaving the Red Sox (16 home runs each of the last two years) but not his ability to hit for average. He helped the Red Sox in another way in 2004: As a fill-in for injured Yankees star Jason Giambi, Clark hit only .143 with nine strikeouts against the Sox during the 2004 ALCS. Clark signed a one-year deal to play for his hometown Arizona Diamondbacks in 2005.

Mark Clear—an overpowering relief pitcher with a great curve who struggled with his control. Clear had a great year as the Sox closer in 1982. After being obtained from California along with Carney Lansford and Rick Miller in what turned out to be a great trade for Butch Hobson (who was at the end of the line) and Rick Burleson (who suffered a career-ending injury shortly afterward), Clear spent five years with the Red Sox, but was only effective in the first two years. He went 8–3 with 9 saves in 1981, and 14–9 with 14 more saves in 1982, when he also made the All Star team. Clear was always difficult to hit, but his control gradually got worse; his last year in Boston he walked nearly a batter an inning. Boston gave up on Clear and traded him to Milwaukee before the 1986 season, which turned out to be a mistake—Clear went on to have one last good year, and the pennant-winning Red Sox would fail in the World Series primarily because of the weakness of their bullpen.

Roger Clemens—nicknamed "The Rocket" for his blazing fastball, Clemens was that rarest of Red Sox commodities: a pitching prospect who lived up to his potential. In fact Clemens surpassed any reasonable expectations in his 13 seasons with the Red Sox, although his reputation has been tarnished in some fans' eyes by the bitterness that surrounded Clemens's departure from the team. Drafted out of the University of Texas, Clemens made the major leagues at age 21, less than a year after he was drafted. He pitched 18 utterly dominant games in the minor leagues for Winter Haven, New Britain, and Pawtucket, where he combined for a 1.55 earned run average and gave up only 92 hits in 128 innings (anything less than one hit per inning is considered good, especially for a pitcher with Clemens's excellent control).

A rookie in 1984, Clemens stepped right into the rotation with very few of the struggles most young pitchers encounter. Clemens survived early surgery on his pitching arm and went 16–9 in limited action his first two seasons. He blossomed into the league's best pitcher in 1986, when his 24–4 record led the Sox to the World Series. Clemens won both the Cy Young Award and MVP in 1986. He would win two more Cy Youngs with the Red Sox, in 1987 and 1991. Over the next seven seasons Clemens won between 17 and 21 games every year, leading the league in earned run average 3 times over that span.

Clemens struggled from 1993 to 1996, averaging just 10 wins a year in an injury-plagued four-year stretch, with losing records in two of those years. While he pitched well over much of that period, he no longer seemed to be the staff-carrying ace he had been while in his twenties (Clemens turned 30 in 1993). Some of this perception was based on his won-lost record with teams that had declining offensive punch. Despite his 40–39 record from 1993–96, however, Clemens was among the league leaders in ERA in two of those years—and nearly won the ERA title in 1994. (The ERA title would instead go to Steve Ontiveros, who later came out of retirement to pitch briefly for the Sox. The title was controversial because Ontiveros seemed to sneak in through the back door, only barely pitching enough innings to qualify.) Clemens's relationship with the media also deteriorated during this period, and there were speculations in the media that his injuries and declining effectiveness were due to his gaining weight or otherwise being out of shape. Clemens was a great pitcher but not a great communicator, and once his superstar luster faded, some sportswriters delighted in poking fun at his sometimes-confusing statements and criticizing his perceived selfishness and his high salary. (Clemens had signed a longterm contract that made him the best-paid pitcher in the game before his performance declined.) Clemens was also criticized for failing to lead the Red Sox to the next level—although he was the ace of playoff teams in 1986, 1988, 1990, and 1995, Clemens was only 1–2 in nine postseason starts. Clemens left the sixth (and potentially winning) game of the 1986 World Series because of a blister, only to see the bullpen blow the lead and lose the infamous "Bill Buckner" game. He also lost his temper and was thrown out of a key playoff game against Oakland.

Clemens's contract with the Sox was set to expire after the 1996 season, and attempts to extend the agreement proved fruitless. Clemens wanted a longterm deal that rewarded him as the best pitcher in the game, while Sox management was concerned about signing a 33-year-old coming off four good-but-not-great seasons to a big-money deal. GM Dan Duquette made an ill-considered remark about Clemens being in "the twilight of his career" that helped doom an increasingly contentious negotiation, although the Red Sox eventually made a substantial offer. Clemens, for his part, made a series of seemingly contradictory statements—first he would only re-sign with the Red Sox, then only with the Red Sox or a Texas team (to be close to his Texas home), then only with a World Series contender, then only with a team that played in a different division than the Red Sox. Throughout all his statements he insisted that winning was more important than money. Instead, he ended up signing with a mediocre Toronto team (in the same division as the Sox) that offered to make him the best-paid pitcher in the game. Many Sox fans felt betrayed by Clemens's seeming about-face, especially after months of media-fueled controversy and acrimony. (Circumstantial evidence of an illegal agreement between the Toronto front office and Clemens's agents while Clemens was still Sox property surfaced in 2000, but nothing was ever proven.)

Whether it was a result of injuries healing or escaping the now-hostile Boston media, Clemens seemed to be more driven and in better shape in Toronto then he had been the previous years in Boston. He went 41–13 in two years with the Blue Jays, leading the league in earned run average both years and winning his unprecedented fourth and fifth Cy Young awards. He was then traded to the New York Yankees, where he was an important part of two World Championship teams. In 2001, at age 38, Clemens went 20–13 to win yet another Cy Young award. After two more good years in New York, Clemens signed a discounted contract with his hometown Astros (there were brief rumors he would return to the Red Sox), and at age 41 went 18–4 with a 2.98 ERA to win his seventh Cy Young award. After flirting with retirement, Clemens re-signed with the Astros for $18 million, to once again become the highest-paid pitcher in the game.

Clemens is the all time Red Sox leader in victories; 192 of his 328 wins came in a Boston uniform. He leads all active pitchers in strikeouts with over 4,300, and is second on the all-time strikeout list. He set the record for strikeouts (20) in an 1986 game against the Mariners in an electrifying performance and tied his own record in a 1996 game against the Detroit Tigers, confounding bitter Boston fans who thought he was playing out the string at the end of his Red Sox contract. He played in 10 All Star games, six of them for the Red Sox. He is certain to be a Hall of Famer as soon as he is eligible.

Boston fans' love/hate relationship with Roger Clemens peaked during his years with the Yankees, but has diminished somewhat now that he's with the Astros. Wildly popular in his first eight years in Boston, and still popular in his last years in the city, when Clemens left for Toronto blame was split between Clemens and Duquette, the GM who failed to re-sign him. When Clemens orchestrated a trade to the archrival Yankees, he became a player many fans loved to hate. Clemens was booed when he pitched badly against the Red Sox in the 1999 American League Championship Series. Perhaps the greatest highlight of the disappointing 2000 season was an epic pitching duel between Clemens and Sox ace Pedro Martinez. Clemens remains a contentious figure in Boston, sometimes booed, sometimes cheered, but always drawing attention.

I was a Wellesley chick. Wellesley, being a women's school, was not exactly chock-full of diehard baseball fans, but I knew one. Her name was Leanne, and her team was the Padres. The year was 1996, which was, I seem to recall, not a good one for San Diego. She did, however, acknowledge the Red Sox as a poor American League substitute for her team, and in the late spring organized a trip to Fenway.

We got our tickets at the gate, and filed into the depths of Fenway, the shadowed corners, the booths and gates. Our seats were, of course, obstructed-view—I could see the pitcher's mound, and the batter if I leaned.

"Who's pitching?" That was what I wanted to know.

The answer, as it happened, was Roger Clemens.

Roger Clemens!

My first game at Fenway, and I was going to see Roger Clemens pitch. My brother was the person who knew the stats, the names of the players. But even I knew the name of Roger Clemens. Roger Clemens!

And, to make this even the more sweet, he was pitching against Oakland—Oakland, my brother's team, Oakland, whose players I knew because my brother recited their names to me: Giambi, McGwire, Canseco.

Except Canseco was . . . playing for Boston. A name I knew.

With Roger Clemens!

Boston got a run in the second.

Then Oakland racked up two in the third. It was a horrible sight to see.

Then Roger Clemens began to pitch like Roger Clemens could: he sent men down in rapid succession. I do not recall a man from the Athletics reaching base for three, maybe nearly four innings.

And Boston racked up three runs in the fourth. 4–2.

Seven and a third innings into the game, Roger Clemens sat down. I don't know why, if he was hurt, if the manager saw something I didn't see: I just know that he had been unhittable since the unfortunate third inning, with a number of Ks to his credit, and he went and sat down.

McGwire was one step from on deck when the manager sent out the new pitcher. I looked up at the scoreboard to see who this person was who was coming in to replace Roger Clemens.

Gunderson, the name was. ERA: 0.00. Not bad.

Except that. . . . Innings pitched: 0.

Gunderson lasted a third of an inning. He got the guy he came in to face, and gave up a home run to Giambi.

Slocumb came in then, and got McGwire. Phew.

The score was 4–3. It was a narrow margin, but it could hold. Only one inning left to go.

The Red Sox did not score in the bottom of the eighth.

Stanton pitched the top of the ninth. Got Plantier. Got Berroa.

Gave up a home run to a pinch hitter. 4–4.

The Red Sox did not score in the bottom of the ninth.

Garces pitched the tenth. And gave up two runs to go with his three strikeouts.

The Red Sox scored in the bottom of the tenth.

One run.

Final score: 6–5. In 10 innings.

There are times when one comes to a visceral understanding of what it can be to be a baseball fan in general, a Red Sox fan in specific. What if Clemens had pitched through the eighth? What if one or another of those nail-biting scoring opportunities had come through? What if, what if, what if. There are times when one knows in one's heart that that game could have been won, if only if a little more prayer had been applied, a little more hope, a little less that-ump-is-blind, a little more hey batter batter and a little less wind blowing out.

Maybe next game.

—Heather Anne Nicoll

Matt Clement—a lean righthanded pitcher with great stuff but inconsistent control, Clement joined the Red Sox as a free agent in December 2004, just days after losing Pedro Martinez to the Mets. Calling Clement (69–75, 4.34 ERA lifetime) a replacement for Pedro is grossly unfair to both pitchers, but the big righty has shown flashes of dominance during his up-and-down career.

San Diego drafted Clement in the third round of the 1993 draft, and *Baseball America* named him their best prospect after the 1997 and 1998 seasons. The Padres thought so highly of Clement that they refused to include him in a proposed trade for superstar pitcher Randy Johnson. He made his big league debut in September 1998, and joined San Diego's rotation full-time the following spring. Clement had a promising rookie year in 1999 (10–12, 4.48), but stumbled as a sophomore, due mainly to control problems (13–17, 5.14, NL-leading 125 walks). At the very end of spring training in 2001, he was sent to Florida in a deal for outfielder Marc Kotsay and future Red Sox utility player Cesar Crespo. He didn't pitch well for the Marlins (9–10, 5.05), and was beginning to look like he'd never harness his potential.

The Cubs thought they could turn Clement around, and they acquired him (with closer Antonio Alfonseca) in a controversial trade for minor leaguers. (Fans accused Florida of dumping salary, but one of the minor leaguers, Dontrelle Willis, won the Rookie of the Year for the 2003 Marlins.) Clement responded to the change of scenery, giving the Cubs three solid seasons. He went 12–11 in 2002, setting career bests in ERA (3.60) and strikeouts (215), while cutting his walk rate down a bit. Clement's ERA rose to a still-respectable 4.11 in 2003, though he had 14 wins, 177 strikeouts, and only 169 hits allowed in 201.2 innings. In 2004, he was outstanding for the first four months (3.03 ERA), and was rumored to be a trade target of Theo Epstein (who had worked in the Padres' front office when Clement pitched there). In fact, early reports said Clement was part of the Nomar Garciaparra trade, with Derek Lowe headed for Minnesota. Reportedly, Red Sox players pleaded with Epstein to keep Lowe, and the GM acquiesced. Considering how well Lowe pitched in October—and how poorly Clement did down the stretch (6.10 ERA, partially attributed to a nagging neck strain)—the Red Sox were lucky the swap never occurred. Still, Clement's overall 2004 numbers were impressive, except for his unlucky 9–12 record. He had a 3.68 ERA, struck out 190 batters in 181 innings, while allowing only 155 hits. Oddly, he was much more effective in Wrigley Field, a notorious hitters' park (7–6, 3.19), than on the road (2–7, 4.50).

In each of the last three seasons, Clement has been among the NL leaders in most strikeouts and fewest hits per inning, thanks to his combination of a 95-MPH fastball, devastating slider, and decent changeup. He's also been durable, starting 30 or more games in each of his six full seasons. The key issues for Clement have always been control and consistency. While it's unlikely that he'll improve the former, the Red Sox hope pitching coach Dave Wallace, ace Curt Schilling, and catcher Jason Varitek can help with the latter. With Pedro, Brad Radke, and Carl Pavano off the market, Clement was generally regarded as the best available free agent, and Boston rewarded him with a three-year, $25.5 million contract.

Reggie Cleveland—a righthanded starting pitcher acquired by Boston in December of 1973 from St. Louis, where he'd spent the first five years of his career. In 1973, Cleveland had had the best season of his career, going 14–10 in 32 starts for the Cardinals, with an ERA much better than league average. In Boston, the Red Sox got the pre-1973 version, who was worse than league average. He made 27 starts for the Sox, as well as 14 appearances out of the bullpen. He pitched slightly better in 1975, and that October, he was the first native Canadian to start a World Series game. He had another very good season in 1976, mostly out of the bullpen. In 1978, he made one appearance for the Sox, pitching just ⅓ inning and taking a loss, before being traded to Texas as part of manager Don Zimmer's purge of the team. He finished his career in 1981 with Milwaukee, pitching entirely in relief.

Alex Cole—a speedy lefthanded-hitting outfielder, Cole hit .280 for five teams over seven seasons with good on-base averages. Although he had a center fielder's speed (he stole 40 bases as a part-time player his rookie year and 148 in his career), Cole was not a good fielder, and he played poorly in limited at-bats during his only season with the Red Sox in 1996. Cole played in various independent leagues after the Sox released him; in 2001, he was arrested at the stadium before a Bridgeport Bluefish (Atlantic League) game and charged with conspiracy to distribute heroin. He was later sentenced to 18 months in jail.

Michael Coleman—a former high school football star, Coleman had a great 1997 season in the minors (.305, with 21 homers and 24 steals) and was anointed Boston's center fielder of the future—but alienated teammates, who derisively referred to his self-given nickname, "Prime Time." Coleman had a poor season in AAA in 1998, but hit 30 homers for Pawtucket in 1999. Expected to finally make the big club in 2000, Coleman was again sent to Pawtucket (Sox manager Jimy Williams made cryptic comments about Coleman's maturity at the time), where a wrist injury cost him most of the season. Coleman was traded to Cincinnati after the 2000 season, then after a great spring training with the Reds, was abruptly sent to the Yankees. (A Reds official made cryptic comments about Coleman "parking in Pokey Reese's spot.") With the Yankees, Coleman had three very good games filling in for Bernie Williams in April before tailing off. On April 13, he left a game at Fenway Park with an pulled hamstring and was never a real factor for New York afterward. Eventually he was released and in November 2001 was signed by the Red Sox—to the surprise of nearly everyone, given Coleman's seeming ability to burn bridges (teams have been quick to drop him despite his talent, and vague and unsubstantiated rumors have swirled around at every stop) and his seeming unpopularity with teammates during his previous stint in Boston. Still a talented outfielder gifted with speed, power, and good defense, Coleman played for Pawtucket in 2002, then drifted to the independent Newark Bears in 2003 and 2004, before signing a minor league contract with the Washington Nationals (formerly the Montreal Expos) for 2005.

Jimmy Collins—Hall-of-Fame third baseman who jumped from the Boston Braves to the brand-new Red Sox in 1901 as player-manager. Collins hit .332 with

108 runs and 94 RBI for the first Red Sox team. He helped the Sox win the first World Series in 1903, as well as an American League title in 1904 (when the National League's Giants refused to play Boston in the World Series). Collins was relieved of his duties as manager during the 1906 season, and left Boston for the Philadelphia Athletics during the following season. He is often credited with being the first third baseman to position himself far off the base, enabling him to range further for balls hit to his left, and was the first third baseman to be elected to the Hall of Fame, in 1945.

Ray Collins—a lefthanded pitcher known for his ability to get Hall of Famer Ty Cobb out, Collins pitched for the Red Sox from 1909–15. During several of those years, he pitched a large number of innings, and was better than league average in ERA. He went 20–13 for the 1914 team, while throwing over 270 innings, and was limited to 104 innings in 1915, the worst season of his career, and the last.

David Cone—Signed unexpectedly by the Red Sox before the 2001 season at the ripe age of 38, veteran righthander Cone was coming off an awful season with the New York Yankees (who managed to win the World Series despite his terrible year). His 4–14 record and 6.91 ERA in 2000 resulted from a mix of shattered confidence, lost command, and rotten luck; Cone had won 20 games just two years previously.

Cone had first reached the major leagues in 1986 and enjoyed a long career as a front-line starter for the Royals, Mets, Blue Jays, and Yankees—although his frequent moves to contending teams looking for an ace to put them over the top gave him something of a "hired gun" reputation. He won the Cy Young Award in 1994 with Kansas City, but his most glorious moments came in Yankees pinstripes. In just over five seasons with New York, Cone had collected four World Series rings (a fifth came with Toronto in 1992), and on July 18, 1999, he threw a perfect game against the Montreal Expos at Yankee Stadium.

Although Cone became a folk hero for helping put several teams over the top, he was involved in a number of controversies. While with the Mets Cone was accused by three women of exposing himself—and pleasuring himself—in their presence during a 1989 game. (Cone was in the bullpen at the time.) They sued him for $8.1 million in 1992, but the case was later dismissed. The New York City papers had a field day, with headlines like WEIRD SEX ACT IN BULLPEN. In 1991, a woman accused Cone of raping her the night before he struck out 19 Phillies (tying an NL record). Police investigated and said the accusations had no merit. In the spring of 1992, Cone was peripherally linked to another rape accusation. A woman in Florida said that Cone's teammates Vince Coleman, Doc Gooden, and Darryl Boston gang-raped her at a house Cone rented. Cone himself was absolved by police; he wasn't there and had no knowledge of the incident.

Instead of retiring after his dreadful year in 2000, Cone attempted a comeback with the organization that had developed a reputation for giving final chances to fallen stars. Just three years earlier, Red Sox pitching coach Joe Kerrigan had helped to resurrect the career of another veteran starter, Bret Saberhagen. Under Kerrigan's tutelage, Cone found a semblance of his former self in 2001, stepping into the rotation after injuries to Frank Castillo and Pedro

Martinez. He overcame an early-season injury to post a 9–7 record in 25 starts with a decent 4.31 ERA. Any doubts about his ability to return were quelled when he won seven straight decisions in a span of less than two months. After the season, the 39-year-old Cone once again became a free agent, but found no big-money offers waiting for him. He sat out 2002 and then attempted another come-back with the Mets in 2003; after only five games, he was diagnosed with chron-ic bursitis in his hip which forced his retirement two months later.

Billy Conigliaro—Tony C's kid brother, a center fielder with good power, was the fifth player taken overall in the very first MLB draft in 1965. He forced his way into the crowded Sox outfield picture in 1970 with an impressive rookie sea-son for a 22-year-old (.271 with 18 home runs, at a time when offense was much lower than today). Unfortunately, the Sox way of making room for Billy C. in cen-ter the next year was to trade his brother to the Angels and move Reggie Smith to right field. Billy accused Carl Yastrzemski and Smith of engineering the trade and spent the 1971 season as an outspoken malcontent. When his production dropped slightly that year as well, the Sox decided they just didn't want him around, and that winter they traded George Scott to the Brewers for a new cen-ter fielder, Tommy Harper (who had never played the position), and tossed Billy C into the deal. The Brewers had an incumbent veteran in center and didn't want to give playing time to a kid; instead, they platooned him in right with Joe Lahoud (also obtained from the Sox in the deal). Billy didn't hit as a platoon player and was so unhappy with his new city, limited playing time, and poor performance that he quit baseball at the end of June. Two attempts at comebacks with the Oakland A's (in 1973 and 1977) were aborted by knee injuries, and he ended his career as just another in the Sox long list of hugely talented might-have-beens.

Tony Conigliaro—a youthful, aggressive power-hitting outfielder with local roots whose life and career were marred by tragedy. Born in Revere in 1945 and raised in Swampscott, East Boston, and Lynn, Tony C came from a well-liked family. He signed with the Red Sox for $20,000 in 1963 and spent one season at Class A ball; Sox manager Johnny Pesky was so impressed by the young ballplay-er that he immediately gave him a spot on the 1964 club. Conigliaro arrived in the majors with an ambitious attitude and no fears; in his major league debut at Yankee Stadium he even accused legendary pitcher Whitey Ford of throwing the spitball. A couple of weeks later, he lit up the Fenway Park opener with a home run on the first pitch he saw in his new home yard, a towering shot to left field off Joel Horlen in front of an audience of prestigious names present to honor slain president John F. Kennedy.

Despite being one of the youngest players in the league, Tony C possessed a quick swing and a brazen face, a combination that led to immediate success but also made him very unpopular among American League pitchers. He crowded the plate and challenged pitchers to throw inside, and missed many games early in his career from injuries to his right arm and left wrist after being hit by pitch-es. He finished his rookie season with 24 homers, and hit 32 in 1965 to lead the league at age 20. He also capitalized on his newfound popularity by signing a recording contract with RCA-Victor.

Early on, however, the Red Sox were unable to take advantage of their young star's success. Conigliaro was provided with little help in the lineup, and the pitching on the Sox teams of the mid-1960s was too mediocre to help turn his homers into wins. That changed in the Impossible Dream season of 1967, when the Sox got outstanding pitching from Jim Lonborg and consistent hitting from a lineup that featured Rico Petrocelli, George Scott, and Carl Yastrzemski. Conigliaro made his first and only All Star appearance in July of that year.

The Red Sox were in the thick of an unbelievable pennant race when the Sox met the California Angels for the opener of a weekend series at Fenway on the night of Friday, August 18. The game stayed scoreless into the fourth inning when, moments after Scott was thrown out at second trying to stretch out a single, a fan threw a smoke bomb into left field, delaying the game for 10 minutes. Fans and players in attendance were still buzzing about that surreal moment as Tony C stepped up to face Jack Hamilton with the bases empty and two outs. Hamilton's first pitch sailed up and caught Tony C in the face. Conigliaro barely moved when the pitch arrived; there would later be speculation that he could not see the ball against the background of white shirts in center field. The pitch broke Conigliaro's left cheekbone and damaged the retina in his eye. The Fenway crowd grew furious at Hamilton, as did Sox players who were convinced that the pitch was a spitball. A famous newspaper photo of Tony shows him sitting up in bed hours after the accident, his left eye swelled shiny like a plum.

His vision remained blurred for the rest of the season and into 1968. The rest of his career consisted of a series of comeback attempts in which he was forced to adjust to his weakened eyesight. He struggled in 1969 under manager Dick Williams, with whom he had constant disagreements, but came through with a 36-homer season under Eddie Kasko in 1970. The Red Sox helped ease Conigliaro's comeback when they acquired his younger brother Billy to join him in the outfield that year. Just as things were settling back into normalcy, however, a series of disagreements between the team and Conigliaro's father, Sal Conigliaro, led to the Sox' decision to trade Tony C to the Angels that October, a decision that alienated the family from the team even further.

Adversity continued to follow Conigliaro after he left Boston. His vision worsened in 1971, leading to his premature retirement at age 26. An attempted return in 1975 proved unsuccessful. He finished an eight-year career with 166 home runs and a .264 batting average (a respectable average in the low-offense 1960s). In 1982, his efforts to secure a job as a commentator for Boston's WSBK-TV 38 ended after he suffered a massive heart attack. This setback debilitated Conigliaro for the rest of his life; he required chronic nursing care up until his sudden but quiet death on February 24, 1990 at the too-young age of 45. The Red Sox honored Conigliaro by wearing black armbands on their uniform sleeves that season, as they captured the eastern division title.

Gene Conley—a righthanded pitcher who started his career in Boston with the Braves, finished his career in Boston with the Red Sox, and played basketball for the Boston Celtics in between. In 1954 (the Braves' second season in Milwaukee), Conley, who hadn't pitched enough during the 1952 season to lose his rookie status, came in second in the Rookie of the Year balloting. That was probably his best season overall (14–9 with a 2.96 ERA for the Braves).

After five seasons in Milwaukee Conley pitched in Philadelphia for two years before finishing up with the Red Sox from 1961–63. He won 15 games for the Sox in 1962. He also briefly deserted the team on one bizarre occasion. In a New York city traffic jam Conley and infielder Pumpsie Green got off the team bus. Green reported to the team hotel that night, but Conley was gone for three days. For reasons that remain unclear, he had tried to fly to Israel, but was unable to because he didn't have a passport.

Conley won a World Series ring in 1957 in Milwaukee with the Braves. He also won three NBA championship rings as a backup center for the Boston Celtics. He blew out his arm in 1963 and was released by the Sox after the season. Although Conley had a tryout with the Indians before the 1964 season, his days of professional athletics were over.

Billy Consolo—a very weak-hitting infielder. In 1952, baseball implemented a rule to discourage the large bonuses that Tom Yawkey had been paying players, requiring that any player who received a bonus of $30,000 or more remain on the major league roster for two years. Billy Consolo was the first victim of this rule. Whether he would ever have developed is unknowable, but it can't have helped to make the jump from high school to the majors without the option of any minor league seasoning (at the ages of 18 and 19 he was sitting on the bench and playing intermittently for the 1953–54 Red Sox). He never did learn to hit, finishing his 10-year career with nine home runs and a paltry .315 on-base percentage. Boston finally gave up on him during 1959, and he played for five different teams over the next three years before his career ended in 1962 at the age of 27. Consolo went on to be a longtime coach, as well as a licensed barber.

Cecil Cooper—a fill-in player at first base and designated hitter for six seasons with the Red Sox, Cooper went on to become an offensive and defensive star with the Milwaukee Brewers. Cooper hit well in part-time play in Boston, batting between .275 and .311 with decent power in the three seasons he was given at least 300 at bats by the Red Sox, from 1974–76. But the red Sox wweren't happy with his devlopment as a hitter, and traded Cooper to Milwaukee for aging first baseman George Scott before the 1977 season. Scott turned out to have one last good season left in him, hitting .269 with 33 home runs before fading into oblivion. Cooper, installed as Milwaukee's starting first baseman, would hit over .300 for each of the next seven years on his way to a .298 lifetime batting average, 241 career home runs, and five All Star Game appearances. He is now bench coach for the Houston Astros.

Scott Cooper—lefthanded-hitting third baseman during the dismal Hobson era of the early 1990s. Cooper was a highly thought of prospect who had the misfortune of being asked to replace Wade Boggs at third base. He once hit for the cycle in a game in Kansas City, and made two All Star teams as a member of the Red Sox (mainly because the rules state that each team *has* to have at least one All Star) but never really lived up to his promise. Cooper's main point of notoriety for Sox fans is that GM Lou Gorman wouldn't part with him in a trade for reliever Larry Andersen, and gave up future Hall-of-Famer Jeff Bagwell instead. Cooper was traded to St. Louis for Rheal Cormier after the 1994 season but lasted only one season with the Cardinals, hitting just .230 with 3 homers and 15 RBI. He resurfaced as a part-time player with the Kansas City Royals in 1997, but his major league career was over before he turned 30.

Wil Cordero—a promising young infielder acquired by the Red Sox before the 1996 season to fill their second base hole. The Sox sent pitcher Rheal Cormier to the Montreal Expos for the 25-year-old shortstop. Wilfredo Cordero was a poor defender at shortstop (he committed 33 errors in 1993), but he was fast and athletic, and had good offensive potential. The Sox hoped that moving him to second base (a slightly easier defensive position than shortstop) would help him defensively, and that he would develop into a powerful offensive threat. The plan didn't work; Cordero committed 10 errors in only 37 games at second base in 1996 before suffering a freak injury (he broke his leg after being spiked by a runner sliding into second) in May. Jeff Frye, who was brought in from Texas to fill in, played brilliantly while Cordero was out, ending Cordero's second base experiment. When Cordero came back he was a left fielder and designated hitter. The injury robbed Cordero of much of his speed, and he never developed into the star he was projected to be. His hitting was decent for a second baseman (a position that emphasizes defense, so it is hard to find good hitters who can play) but not for a left fielder (one of the easiest positions to play).

Cordero is mostly remembered by Red Sox fans for the 1997 season, in which he was arrested in a domestic abuse incident. Although his wife refused to press charges and there were conflicting accounts of what happened, many fans were outraged by the perception that Cordero didn't take the charges seriously. Cordero was eventually suspended and ordered by the team to undergo counseling. While he was suspended and supposedly dealing with the problem (and just as the furor was dying down, with many fans arguing that he should be given a second chance), Cordero appeared on an ESPN interview, relaxing at poolside in a bathing suit, and said that he and his wife didn't need counseling and didn't have any problems.

Unpopular with fans, mediocre at the plate, and a headache to the front office, Cordero was released by the Red Sox after the season. Interestingly, despite his problems in Boston, Cordero retained ties to Boston's Latino community and was reportedly instrumental in convincing superstar outfielder Manny Ramirez to sign as a free agent with the Red Sox after the 2000 season. Since his two seasons with the Red Sox, Cordero has played for the White Sox, Indians, Pirates, and Expos. In 2004, a knee injury sidelined him for much of the season, and Cordero appeared in only 27 games for the Marlins, primarily as an outfielder/first baseman.. In August 2004, a jury acquitted Cordero of drunken driving in a highway accident the previous December. He had caused a two-car crash in which his sport utility vehicle rolled onto its side.

Rheal Cormier—lefthanded pitcher who enjoyed two stints with the Red Sox, the first as a starter and the second as a reliever. A French-speaking native of

Canada, Cormier came up with the St. Louis Cardinals as a starter and pitched decently before being traded to the Sox after the 1994 season (for marginal All Star third baseman Scott Cooper, soon to be out of baseball). Cormier went 7–5 in 48 games for the Sox in 1995, before being traded to Montreal for infielder Wilfredo Cordero (Montreal wanted him because he was a French speaker), but only pitched one full season for the Expos. He returned to the Sox in 1999 as a free agent reclamation project following a severe injury that took almost two years to recover from. The Sox worked around Cormier's permanently weakened arm by converting him into a lefty bullpen specialist. He did relatively well in this role, appearing in 124 games over two seasons as part of a relief corps that was one of the most effective in the league. The Red Sox declined his request for a substantial raise after the 2000 season, and Cormier signed a high-priced free agent contract with the Philadelphia Phillies, where he established himself as one of the NL's most solid (if underrated) lefty relievers. Cormier was great in 2003, going 8–0 with a terrific 1.70 ERA, and finishing second in the NL in stranding inherited runners. He remained strong in 2004 (4–5, 3.56 ERA), prompting the Phillies to sign the now-38-year-old reliever for two more years.

Jim Corsi—righthanded relief pitcher, Corsi is a Newton, Massachusetts, native who bounced around the majors for 10 seasons over 12 years (including three separate stints with the Oakland A's) but never had a secure grip on a major league job. He was a generally effective middle reliever, without the wins of a starter or the saves of a closer. He relied on guile and control rather than an over-powering fastball. Corsi signed with Boston prior to the 1997 season and, given the chance to pitch in his hometown in the twilight of his career, Corsi responded with the two best seasons of his life. In 1999, at age 37, he pitched very badly and was released yet again. He signed on with Baltimore but pitched only briefly for the Orioles, then retired after going to spring training with the Arizona Diamondbacks before the 2000 season.

Ted Cox—a much-heralded third baseman who had burned his way through the Sox minor league system, Cox was called up in September of 1977 and had hits in his first six at bats, setting a major league record. The Red Sox reluctantly agreed to include Cox in a trade to Cleveland for pitcher Dennis Eckersley the next spring. Cox never turned into the star he was projected to be, however. He made stops in Cleveland, Seattle, and Toronto but hit only .245 for his career; Cox was out of baseball at age 26.

Doc Cramer—leadoff hitter and center fielder in the 1930s and 1940s, Cramer played for 20 years in the major leagues, five of them with the Red Sox during the heart of his career (1936–1940). He was already a star when the Red Sox bought him and Jimmie Foxx from the cash-strapped Philadelphia A's before the 1936 season. Cramer was a five-time All Star, with four of those appearances coming as a Red Sox player. He was remarkably consistent with the Red Sox, hitting between .292 and .311 every year and providing excellent defense. (A Philadelphia sportswriter nicknamed him Flit, after an insecticide, because Cramer was deadly against fly balls.) He rarely homered (once in his five years with the Sox), but was usually among the league leaders in doubles and triples, although this was more a product of how many times he came to the plate than any actual power; since Cramer led off for good offensive teams, stayed healthy, and seldom walked, he was close to the league lead in at bats and hits every year. He holds a major league record by leading the league in at bats seven times. He also twice tied a major league record by going 6-for-6 in a game.

Paxton Crawford—righthanded starting pitcher called up by the Red Sox for the first time in 2000. He pitched well in limited appearances just before the All Star break, then was sent back to the minor leagues so he wouldn't get rusty during the break, with the expectation that he would be called back up 10 days later. Instead, he suffered a freak injury when he rolled out of bed and landed on a glass, cutting open his back. (The team's explanation seemed incomplete, and unsubstantiated but lurid rumors of how the accident actually happened circulated around the Internet.) Crawford wasn't able to return to the Sox until September, when he once more pitched well, but again battled injuries in 2001 and spent most of the season in Pawtucket. He appeared in only eight games for the Red Sox, and has not resurfaced in the major leagues. Crawford pitched for the Cincinnati Reds' AA team in Chattanooga in 2004, after spending 2003 in the independent Atlantic League.

Steve Crawford—a hulking righthanded pitcher who spent most of the 1980s with the Red Sox, Crawford came up as a starting pitcher. Despite his imposing size and menacing appearance, Crawford was not a strikeout pitcher. He always gave up a lot of hits, and relied on good control for his success. In 1981 he lost all five decisions in 11 starts. He only got to start one more game over the rest of his 10-year career. Sent back to the minors, Crawford didn't return for good until 1984. He pitched solidly for the next three years as one of the only reliable relievers on teams with terrible bullpens. He filled in as closer for a while in 1985 and led the team in saves (with only 12; Bob Stanley was second with 10). He pitched well in the 1986 playoffs, winning Game 2 of the World Series in relief of Roger Clemens, but not well enough to overcome the rest of the bullpen's failings. After a poor season in 1987 Crawford was sent to Kansas City, where he pitched for three more undistinguished years.

Cesar Crespo—a journeyman utility player acquired by the Red Sox in 2003, Crespo had shown plate discipline, speed on the basepaths, and good baserunning instincts in the minor leagues, but displayed none of those things when pressed into emergency service with the Sox. A native of Puerto Rico, Crespo appeared to be a happy-go-lucky veteran minor leaguer who was making the best of playing in cold-climate cities like Boston and Pawtucket. Crespo's biggest asset was his versatility: He has played every position except pitcher, catcher, and first base. His 2004 season was an emotional whirlwind as Crespo made the Red Sox roster as a backup shortstop while Nomar Garciaparra was on the disabled list, started a game in center field for the injured Johnny Damon and went 2-for-4, started a game at second base with Mark Bellhorn shifting over to third while Bill Meuller was out with a sore knee and went 2-for-5 with a double, stolen base, and

RBI—but finally was demoted to Pawtucket after batting just .165 (13-for-79) with 2 RBI in 52 games for the Red Sox. Crespo signed a minor league deal with the Pirates for 2005

Lou Criger—Cy Young's personal catcher, Lou Criger played for 16 years, eight of them with the Red Sox (1901–08). He played with Young in Cleveland and St. Louis as well as Boston. Criger was a terrible hitter, batting .221 for his career and hitting below .200 in nine different seasons (league average was around .250 for most of those years.), although he did have a high walk total for the period. Not surprisingly, his career in Boston ended at the same time Young's did.

Joe Cronin—one of the greatest shortstops in baseball history, and one of five men to have his number retired by the Red Sox. During a remarkable 58-year career, Cronin did it all: superstar player, pennant-winning manager, general manager, American League President, and American League Chairman. He spent 24 of those years with the Red Sox, and was one of the key Tom Yawkey acquisitions (along with Lefty Grove and Jimmie Foxx) who brought the franchise back to respectability. Cronin is one of the giants of Red Sox history, though some of his decisions as an executive would haunt the team for decades.

He began his big league career with Pittsburgh in 1926, but the Pirates already had an outstanding shortstop in Glenn Wright. The Washington Senators acquired Cronin in 1928, and he became a regular a year later. In 1930, Cronin had his best season, batting .346 with 41 doubles, 13 homers, and 126 RBI, plus 72 walks and 17 steals. He won the MVP, though some sources don't consider the award official (the modern MVP award began in 1931). Cronin continued to play at a high level for Washington from 1931–34, batting over .300 three times, with over 100 RBI each year. His home park, Griffith Stadium, had the deepest left field in baseball (407 feet down the line), and it undoubtedly cost Cronin many homers, though he usually hit over 40 doubles and 10 triples a year. Reports on Cronin's defense vary. Statistical methods indicate that he was excellent in Washington, but not as good in Boston. Observers were split on his fielding, though shortstops who hit well are often assumed to be subpar defensively no matter how well they play.

In 1933, Cronin became player-manager and piloted the Senators to their last pennant, though they lost the World Series. He also played shortstop in the first All Star Game, the first of his seven All Star appearances. Late in the 1934 season he married the daughter of Washington's owner, Clark Griffith. During Cronin's honeymoon, new Red Sox owner Tom Yawkey offered Griffith $250,000 and shortstop Lyn Lary for his son-in-law. Griffith frantically called Cronin, who agreed that it was "an offer he couldn't refuse." The deal was finalized, and Yawkey fired manager Bucky Harris to let Cronin continue doing double-duty.

But 1935 was a frustrating season for Cronin. He hit .295 with 95 RBI, but the shift to Fenway only raised his home run total from 7 to 9. As a manager, he improved Boston's record by just two games. Cronin's year was epitomized by a September 7 game against Cleveland at Fenway. The Sox trailed, 5–1, with the bases loaded and no outs in the bottom of the ninth. Cronin, the tying run, hit a bullet off the third baseman's forehead. The ball caromed directly into the shortstop's glove, and he started a triple play to end the game. 1936 was even worse for Cronin, as injuries limited him to 81 games (and 2 home runs).

Cronin finally figured out Fenway in 1937, and he began an outstanding five-year stretch. During that span, he hit .307 with 99 homers and 517 RBI. In 1940 he hit a career-high 24 homers, and the Red Sox became the first big league team to have each infielder hit more than 20 (first baseman Jimmie Foxx had 36; second baseman Bobby Doerr hit 22; third baseman Jim Tabor had 21). Cronin continued to hit extremely well in 1941, his fifth standout season in a row. However, he couldn't run well anymore, and his defense was deteriorating. He played only 119 games at shortstop in 1941, while appearing in 22 at third base. The following spring, the 35-year-old Cronin decided to bench himself in favor of impressive rookie Johnny Pesky, who wound up hitting .331. For the next four years, Cronin devoted himself almost entirely to managing. (He managed the Sox to second place finishes in 1938, 1939, and 1941, and the team was clearly on the rise.) Cronin had only 355 at bats from 1942–45, and rarely played the field (54 games at first, 24 at third, and just 1 at shortstop). He was, however, a superb pinch hitter; in 1943, he hit an American League record five pinch homers. He managed the Sox to another second place finish in 1942, but the team struggled in 1943–45.

After the players serving in World War II returned, Cronin felt there was no need to remain on the active roster. (His 1945 season had been ended after only three games by a broken leg.) He retired with a .301 average, 170 home runs, and 2,285 hits, eventually earning him election into the Hall of Fame in 1956, with a Red Sox "B" on his plaque, though his stats were slightly better in Washington. 1946 was his first year as a nonplaying manager, and everything came together—at least until the World Series. Cronin's Red Sox won 104 games, the second-most in team history (the 1912 edition had 105), and took the American League pennant by 12 games. But after an excruciating World Series loss to the Cardinals in October, the team limped to an 83–71 mark in 1947, and Cronin's managerial career came to an end. His 1,071 wins are still the most of any Red Sox skipper, though he was often criticized for overusing his pitchers and wasting his team's potent offense.

Owner Tom Yawkey kicked Cronin upstairs, and he became the Red Sox GM, serving in that capacity from 1948–58. The team went downhill in the 1950s. A commonly cited reason was the Red Sox long delay in integrating the team. While Cronin was manager, the Red Sox gave tryouts to Jackie Robinson and Sam Jethroe (later a National League Rookie of the Year with the crosstown Braves), but failed to sign either player. During Cronin's tenure as GM, they also passed on a golden chance to sign Willie Mays. The Red Sox didn't have a black player until the year Cronin left. It is unclear how much of this was the fault of Cronin, who was generally described as a kind, funny, friendly man. But the fact remains that this unfortunate period happened under his watch. Cronin had other personnel problems as well. In 1937, he instigated the trade of star pitcher Wes Ferrell, the leader of an outspoken anti-Cronin clique in the clubhouse. Also in the late 1930s, he convinced Yawkey to sell minor league shortstop Pee Wee Reese to the Dodgers, where he became a Hall of Famer. Some accounts say Cronin was jealous of the young infielder, while others indicate that he merely thought Reese wasn't good enough. Even though the Sox had another fine young shortstop in Johnny Pesky, Cronin's decision on Reese was shortsighted.

In any case, Cronin's association with the Red Sox ended in 1959, when he was elected President of the American League. He served in that role until 1973, and was nominated for Commissioner at least once in the interim. In 1974, Cronin took a largely ceremonial position as American League Chairman of the Board, a position he held for the remainder of his life. Early in the 1980s, Cronin became seriously ill, and the Red Sox decided to retire his #4 in May 1984. A Joe Cronin Night was hastily assembled, and the great shortstop watched the proceedings from a private box. Four months later, Cronin died.

Leon Culberson—a backup outfielder who took an injured Dom DiMaggio's place in the outfield late in the seventh game of the 1946 World Series. His weak throw to cutoff man Johnny Pesky allowed Enos Slaughter to score from first with what proved to be the deciding run of the series. Culberson was a righthanded-hitting outfielder who had been a fill-in player while most of the stars were in the military in World War II. Although he was a decent backup (hitting .313 as a part-timer in 1946), he is mainly remembered for the throw that cost the Series. He hung on in a limited role in Boston until 1947, and was out of baseball after 1948, at age 29.

Ray Culp—a righthanded starting pitcher who was a former Rookie of the Year in the National League, Culp spent the last 6 years of his career in Boston, from 1968–73. He was acquired in the winter following the "Impossible Dream" season, in hopes of providing a boost for the pitching staff and helping the team build on the success of 1967. Interestingly enough, the same offseason saw the Red Sox add Dick Ellsworth. The previous offseason, Ellsworth and Culp had been traded for each other, with Culp leaving the Phillies that he had come up with to go to the Cubs, and Ellsworth going from Chicago to Philadelphia.

Culp hadn't pitched well in either of the 2 seasons prior to coming to Boston. He had experienced arm problems the year before, but recovered and added a palm ball to his arsenal. This led to a 16–6 record and career-best 2.91 ERA in his first year in Boston. At one point during the 1968 season, he threw four consecutive shutouts. In 1969, Culp's 17–8 record and 3.81 ERA led to an All Star Game berth. In 1970, he tied a major league record when he struck out the first six men that he faced in a game in May. The 1970 season was probably his best, as he went 17–14 with a 3.04 ERA in a league where the average ERA was 3.97. Culp struggled badly in 1972 and in 1973 he only threw 50 innings before retiring.

Midre Cummings—lefthanded-hitting outfielder with tremendous talent and terrible baseball instincts. Cummings, the ninth of 10 major leaguers hailing from the U.S. Virgin Islands, spent parts of two seasons with the Red Sox, primarily as a pinch hitter, in 1998 and 2000, although the Red Sox did not re-sign him at the end of either season. Although he could hit and was a fast runner, Cummings's fielding was erratic, and he ran into outs frequently on the bases. He has not been able to hold onto a job at any of his many major league stops. He played in only 22 major league games in 2004 as an outfielder for the Devil Rays, and signed a minor league deal with the Orioles for 2005.

John Curtis—A local hero from nearby Newton, Massachusetts, Curtis was considered a can't-miss prospect, but settled for a respectable 15-year career. Curtis starred at Clemson University, where he pitched three no-hitters. In the 1967 Pan Am games, he became the first American to defeat the Cuban National Team. The lefthander joined the Sox as a 22-year-old, pitching one game in 1970. After a terrific September performance in 1971 (2–2, 3.12, 19 strikeouts and 6 walks in 26 innings), Curtis was expected to be a mainstay in Boston's rotation. He had a solid rookie year in 1972 (11–8, 3.73), and an even better sophomore season (13–13, 3.58, 221 innings). But in December 1973, Curtis was traded to St. Louis in a six-player deal (the Red Sox got Reggie Cleveland and Diego Segui). He pitched until 1984, mainly as a spot starter and long reliever, but never matched his early success.

Johnny Damon—speedy, free-spirited lefthanded-hitting outfielder signed by the Red Sox before the 2002 season to replace the traded Carl Everett. Damon broke into the majors with the Kansas City Royals in 1995 as a popular player with All Star potential, quirky good looks (he's half Thai), and a rock star moniker to match, displaying flashy defense (though a weak arm) and solid baserunning skills. In three years he established himself as a solid leadoff hitter with some power, and in 2000 had his best season, hitting .327 with 16 home runs and a .382 on-base percentage, while leading the American League with 46 steals and 136 runs scored. Knowing they would be unable to afford to sign the soon-to-be free agent, the Royals traded Damon to Oakland in a three-way swap after the 2000 season, a move that seemed to provide the final piece to a talented young Athletics team. Damon struggled in the first half of 2001, however, with a batting average that hovered around .200; he finished the season with a .256 average.

With Boston's prolific offense Damon wasn't counted on to be a star, just a good defensive outfielder who got on base as a leadoff hitter. For the next two years he did just that, hitting about .280 with decent power, stealing about 30 bases a year and rarely getting caught, drawing his share of walks. Damon made his first All Star team in 2002, when he also broke Ken Griffey Jr.'s American League record for outfielders by not making an error in 576 straight chances. In 2003 he tied former Sox outfielder Gene Stephens's modern major league record by recording three hits in a single inning.

Damon showed up to spring training in 2004 with shaggy long hair and a beard that made him look vaguely Cro-Magnon, signaling what would become a teamwide hair fixation; along with Kevin Millar, Damon was a leader of the unconventional, carefree but intense approach to the game that characterized the 2004 World Series winners. (When asked how the team was able to weather disasters, he responded, "We're just a bunch of idiots.") Damon had a terrific season, shaggy hair and all, hitting .304 with 123 runs scored and career highs in homers (20), RBI (94, terrific for a leadoff hitter who gets fewer opportunities to hit with men on base), and walks. Women began showing up to the park in false beards, shaggy wigs, and Damon jerseys; at one point during the season he had his hair cut and beard shaved on live TV for charity, but soon reverted to his former wild look. Damon hit two home runs and drive in six runs in Game 7 of the 2004 ALCS, which essentially won the game and clinched the American League Pennant for the Red Sox.

After the season, Damon—shaggy hair and all—married longtime girlfriend Michelle Mangan. Damon's his 5-year-old twin daughters from a previous marriage participated in the ceremony. And the long hair will remain at least through the spring of 2005—Damon co-authored a book, and the publisher contractually insisted that he keep the long hair until the end of the book tour.

Danny Darwin—an injury-prone 35-year-old pitcher, Darwin was signed to a four-year deal as a free agent by Sox GM Lou Gorman. Darwin was coming off a terrific year—he had won the ERA title with Houston in 1990, going 11–4 while shuttling between the starting rotation and long relief. He did pitch well for Boston while healthy, which was about half the time. He went 15–11 as a full-time starter in 1993, but it was the only year out of the four that he was able to make more than 15 starts. Remarkably, Darwin continued to pitch for years after he left the Red Sox, playing for more than 20 years in the big leagues altogether. In some ways, Darwin was symbolic of the free agent signings Gorman made toward the end of his tenure as Sox GM—aging, expensive players signed to try to keep the club marginally competitive rather than rebuilding with young players.

Brian Daubach—minor league free agent signed by the Red Sox shortly after the departure of Mo Vaughn who became a fan favorite. Formerly a replacement player in the Mets' system, the 27-year-old rookie first baseman attracted attention by putting up strong numbers during spring training in 1999. He continued his strong performance during the season after an injury to Reggie Jefferson opened up playing time for him. Daubach finished the year with a .294 average, 21 homers, and 73 RBI as a lefthanded-hitting platoon first baseman, DH, and occasional outfielder. His numbers were good enough for him to finish fourth in Rookie of the Year balloting and to become a fan favorite, with his distinctive sideburns that made him look, as one reporter put it, like a 1970s porn star.

Fears that Daubach would become a one-year wonder grew when Daubach sunk into a horrible tailspin late in the 1999 season (his average was about .340 in August) before recovering at the end of the season and in the playoffs. However, Daubach opened 2000 by hitting homers in his first two at bats. Despite shaving the sideburns early in the 2000 season, he remained a fan favorite, with a penchant for the key late-inning hit. In one thrilling game against Oakland in 1999, he rocked a bases-clearing double off the left field wall in the ninth inning after just barely missing a game-winning grand slam by hooking the previous pitch a few inches foul past Pesky's Pole.

Though he earned him a reputation as a streaky hitter, Daubach managed over 20 homers and 70 RBI in all four seasons when he received regular playing time, two of them marred by unlucky injuries: good enough to be a solid contributor, but not a star or a player with a secure hold on a major league job. Daubach hurt his elbow and hand in a brawl against Tampa Bay in 2000. (He was repeatedly attacked—and later threatened—by Tampa Bay players, possibly over his role as a replacement player while a minor leaguer, which also caused him problems with some Red Sox players and with the Players Association, which refused to admit him.) The injuries clearly weakened his swing, and he also missed several weeks of 2001 when he contracted a staph infection in his shin that required hospitalization. Following the 2002 season in which Daubach lost his job to Tony Clark, regained it when Clark flopped, and was once again solid but not great (.266 with 20 homers) the Red Sox failed to tender Daubach (who was arbitration-eligible and would have received a substantial raise) a contract, and he signed with the White Sox as a free agent. After a frustrating season on the White Sox bench, Daubach returned to the Red Sox, but with David Ortiz now starring at first, Daubach ended up spending most of the 2004 season in the minor leagues.

Andre Dawson—a righthanded-hitting outfielder, the Hawk had been a star ballplayer for years: a Gold Glove outfielder who could hit for average and power, and could steal bases. But not for the Red Sox. When GM Lou Gorman signed Dawson to a lucrative free agent contract prior to the 1993 season, he was a 38-year-old full-time DH with 17 major league seasons of wear and tear on his failing knees (he'd already had more than 10 knee operations, and would have several more while with Boston) who had already hit 399 of his 438 career home runs. He played two injury-plagued years for Boston before finishing his career with the expansion Marlins.

Rob Deer—a big righthanded outfielder, Deer came up with the San Francisco Giants but made his name as a member of the Milwaukee Brewers in the late 1980s. The Sox acquired him from Detroit late in the 1993 season. At the time they made the trade, Andre Dawson was unable to play the field anymore because of the condition of his knees, and Boston was alternating Carlos Quintana, Ivan Calderon, and Bob Zupcic in right field. They were also last in the league in home runs, and hoped that Deer would address that. In his 38 games for the Sox, Deer did hit seven home runs, including one in his first Fenway Park plate appearance in a Boston uniform. But he hit .196 and only walked 20 times. The Red Sox finished in fifth place in the AL East, and did not re-sign Deer following the season.

Deer still holds the American League record for strikeouts in a season, with his 186 whiffs in 1987. (Red Sox infielder Mark Bellhorn approached the mark with his team-record 177 in 2004, most ever by a switch hitter.) As Deer was going through the minor leagues, he won home run titles at three different minor league levels, but also led leagues in strikeouts four times. He was in the top 10 in the American League in strikeouts during all eight seasons in which he played more than 100 games in the major leagues. He also walked frequently, so that his on-base percentages were not as bad as his batting averages. Deer developed a cult following and fan club on the Internet, as the modern master of the so-called "Three True Outcomes," because his plate appearances so frequently ended in a strikeout, a home run, or a walk. They are the only three outcomes in which the pitcher-batter confrontation, which is the heart of baseball competition, is determined only by the pitcher and batter, with no help from the rest of the team. After finishing the 1993 season with Boston, Deer was out of the majors for two years. He finished his career hitting .180 for the San Diego Padres, with 30 strikeouts in only 64 plate appearances, in 1996.

Deer currently oversees all of San Diego Padres' minor league hitters. Nowadays, he wants hitters aiming at the top of the ball instead of trying to lift it out of the park; steady line drives are more important to him as a coach than the all-or-nothing approach that used to characterize Deer as a player.

Brian Denman—a Sox minor league phenom after going 15–3 in AA in 1981, Denman started nine games in the majors in 1982, and pitched decently— including a shutout against the Yankees in his final game. The following year in spring training he lashed out at manager Ralph Houk after being sent back to the minors without being given what he thought was a fair chance to make the team. Houk was not amused, and Denman was never seen in the major leagues again.

Juan Diaz—oversized, overhyped Cuban refugee who looked like a promising righty slugger, but never overcame injuries, weight problems, and poor strike zone judgment. Diaz defected to the United States in 1996 and signed with the Dodgers, but Major League Baseball later ruled that the contract was illegal, making him a free agent. Boston signed Diaz before the 2000 season, and he sky-rocketed through the farm system. He played at three minor league levels in one season, hitting .301 with 28 homers and 82 RBI in only 77 games, while showing surprisingly good defense for a man his size. A severe ankle injury ended his season before Boston could call him up, and the already bulky Diaz reportedly ballooned to 295 pounds in the spring of 2001. Diaz hit 40 homers in Pawtucket in 2001–02, but his other stats were unimpressive. To make matters worse, it turned out that Diaz was two years older than previously thought, thus changing his status from 26-year-old prospect to 28-year-old journeyman. (After the terrorist attacks of September 11, 2001, greater scrutiny was placed on foreign players' documentation.) Though Diaz had a cup of coffee with Boston in 2002 (2-for-7 with a home run), he was taken off the 40-man roster after the season. Most recently Diaz played for the Rochester Red Wings in the Twins organization.

Dom DiMaggio—younger brother of Joe DiMaggio and Vince DiMaggio, Dom played his entire career for the Red Sox, mostly as starting center fielder and leadoff hitter. Dom DiMaggio wasn't a superstar like his brother Joe, but he played 10 years in the major leagues (1940–52, with the 1943–45 seasons spent in the military during World War II and three token appearances during 1953) without ever having a bad season. His lowest batting average was .283 (he hit as high as .328, and batted .298 for his career) and he walked frequently. As the table setter for several terrific offensive teams, DiMaggio scored more than 100 runs six times in his career, leading the league in runs scored twice and averaging over 100 runs a year for his career. He also led the league in stolen bases in 1950 with only 15 steals, at a time when stolen bases were rare.

Lenny DiNardo—lefty reliever acquired in the Rule 5 Draft who made 22 mop-up appearances for the 2004 Red Sox. DiNardo was drafted out of high school by the Red Sox in 1998 (tenth round), but elected to attend Stetson University instead. Three years later, he was taken by the Mets in the third round. He pitched well as a starter in the Mets' system, but the team didn't protect him on their 40-man roster after the season. There were doubts about DiNardo's lack of velocity (his fastball peaks around 85–87 MPH), even though he had good control and a knack for avoiding the long ball, and the Mets figured he was too far from the majors to be an attractive Rule 5 target. But the Red Sox snagged DiNardo, and he showed enough in spring training to make the team, though he began the season on the DL with a sore shoulder. He made his big league debut on April 23, and wound up pitching a total of 27⅔ innings, usually when the Red Sox were far ahead or getting blown out. As a result, he had no decisions, though his 4.23 ERA was respectable. After the All-Star break, he developed a blister and went on the DL again, never to return the rest of the season. Cynics accused the Red Sox of stashing DiNardo to avoid having to offer him back to the Mets (who reportedly would've jumped at the chance to reacquire him). In any case, he spent enough time on the active roster to meet the Rule 5 requirement, and the Red Sox may send the 25-year-old back to the minors for more seasoning.

Big Bill Dineen—though normally overshadowed by Cy Young, this reliable #2 starter was the hero of the Red Sox first World Series victory in 1903. (His name is often spelled as Dinneen, but he spelled it Dineen, as did the newspapers in his time.) Dineen pitched a three-hit shutout against Pittsburgh in Game 2, and clinched the Sox first championship with a four-hit shutout in Game 8. (The 1903 World Series, the first of the modern era, was a best-of-nine). Overall, Dineen was 3–1 with a 2.06 ERA in the 1903 Series. Dineen had jumped to the Red Sox from the Boston Braves in 1902. He won 21 games or more in each of his first three seasons with the Red Sox, but this was not as rare or prestigious a feat as it is today. Dineen slipped a bit in 1905 and 1906, and was shipped to the St. Louis Browns early in 1907. After retiring as a player, Dineen umpired in the American League for 29 seasons (from 1909–37).

Joe Dobson—a righthanded pitcher who spent two years with the Indians before being traded to the Red Sox prior to the 1941 season. With the exception of the 1942–43 seasons which he spent in the military, Dobson was one of the members of the Red Sox starting rotation through the 1950 season. He was never a great pitcher, but he was good and consistent for a long time. Dobson won 76 games for the Sox over the span of 1946–1950, a time when they went to the World Series once and just missed on a couple more occasions. He threw a four-hitter (though three unearned runs scored) in Game 5 of the 1946 World Series to give the Sox a 3–2 lead in the series.

He was traded to the White Sox in December of 1950, and had what might have been his best season in 1952, going 14–10 with a 2.51 ERA. But that was close to the end of the line. In 1953 half of his appearances came out of the bullpen, then usually a home for declining pitchers. In 1954 he was back with the Red Sox, but pitched less than three innings in two games before his career ended.

Pat Dodson—a much-heralded slugging first base prospect who never quite made it. Dodson put up terrific minor league numbers, but didn't hit well in three brief major league appearances from 1986–1988, totalling only 99 at bats. He struck out in a third of his at bats, but also walked frequently. He didn't make it to the majors until he was 26, and was never given more than 45 at bats in a season to prove himself.

Bobby Doerr—a very good second baseman for the strong Sox teams of the 1940s. After making the team at the age of 19, Doerr became the regular second baseman in 1938 at age 20, a job he would not relinquish until 1951. An excellent fielder, Doerr showed steady improvement in his hitting through his first few years in the league, reaching highs in many major categories in 1940, when he finished seventh in the league in total bases and RBI (with 105, the first time he topped the 100 RBI mark). The next season, Doerr made the first of his nine All Star appearances, although his overall numbers were not quite as good as the year before.

As the major league ranks began to be depleted by the war, Doerr continued to show considerable pop for a second baseman. (Since it's a key defensive position and it's hard to find players who are good both offensively and defensively, many second basemen are light hitters.) From 1942 to 1945, Doerr finished in the top 10 in doubles twice, in home runs three times, in RBI twice, in slugging percentage three times, in on-base percentage once, in hits once, and in runs once. His best wartime season was 1944, when he led the league in slugging, finished second in batting average, finished third in on base-percentage, and enjoyed top-10 status in runs, triples, home runs, and RBI. His average, on-base percentage, and slugging numbers all set career highs.

With the return of the regulars at the end of the war, Doerr was an important part of the 1946 team which blew away the competition to reach the World Series. In that World Series, while players such as Pinky Higgins, Johnny Pesky, and the injured Ted Williams had great difficulty with Cardinal pitching, Doerr was the unofficial MVP in the Sox losing effort, hitting .409, with a .458 on-base percentage, and a .591 slugging percentage. (To be fair, Doerr's hitting stats may be a little misleading. He hit .315 with 145 homers at Fenway Park, but only .261 with 78 homers on the road, so he was a great Fenway hitter, but just a good hitter away from home.)

From 1946 to the end of his career in 1951, Doerr continued to play excellent defense and hit well. In four of those six years, he had over 100 RBI (setting a career high in 1950 with 120) and twice he reached 27 home runs, putting him in the top 10 for the American League. He also led the American League in fielding percentage four times, in putouts four times, and in assists three times. He led the league in double plays turned five times, a record. He also holds the big league record with eight double plays (fielding) in a doubleheader (in 1950). In 1948, he handled 414 consecutive chances without an error.

Doerr retired young in 1951 because of major back problems. At that time, his 1,865 games played were the most in Red Sox history. After his retirement, Doerr's excellence as a fielder and slugger were belatedly recognized when he was elected to the Hall of Fame in 1986 (he used to appear frequently on "Why isn't he in the Hall of Fame" columns). His #1 was subsequently retired by the Sox, honoring the player who was the best all-time Red Sox second baseman.

Doerr made an additional contribution to the Sox as well. Dick Williams hired him as first base coach in 1967, and Carl Yastrzemski credited Doerr with helping him turn into a Triple Crown hitter that year. Doerr coached with Boston until 1969, and also coached for Toronto in that team's first five years (1977–81).

John Dopson—talented righthanded pitcher acquired from Montreal for Spike Owen after the 1988 season. Dopson first appeared in the majors briefly in 1985, but due to injuries did not resurface until 1988, when he went 3–11 with an excellent 3.04 ERA for a bad team. His first year for Boston was his best as a major leaguer; he started 28 games and went 12–8. Dopson was neither a hard thrower nor a control artist, and after more injuries (the next two years he appeared in a total of five games) he lost his ability to fool hitters. (He had "Tommy John" tendon transplant surgery on his elbow, but was never the same pitcher afterward.) In 1992 and 1993, Dopson started 53 games and went a combined 14–22 for bad Red Sox teams. He finished his career in 1994 with the California Angels.

Patsy Dougherty—righthanded-hitting outfielder who spent the first 2½ seasons of his 10-season career with the Red Sox (actually the Boston Americans) from 1902–04. He hit .342 and .331 in his first two years with the Red Sox, but never hit higher than .285 over the rest of his career (although he led the league in stolen bases in 1908). In 1903 he hit two home runs in Game 2 of the first World Series. The Red Sox sent him to the New York Highlanders midway through 1904 in a terrible trade for Bob Unglaub (who hit .251 in parts of three seasons with the Sox). Dougherty was later traded to the Chicago White Sox after getting into a fistfight with the New York manager.

Dick Drago—former ace starting pitcher of the expansion Kansas City Royals, Drago had begun to break down from overwork by the time Boston traded pitcher Marty Pattin for him after the 1973 season. After a mediocre 1974 season, the 30-year-old righthander moved into the bullpen in 1975, and took over as the Sox relief ace down the stretch, saving 15 games. In the playoffs he pitched well, saving two games and only giving up one run in four appearances—but it was a big run, costing the Sox Game 2 of the World Series. Drago was traded to California after the season and then to Baltimore the next year before returning to the Red Sox as a free agent. He pitched very well for the Sox in 1978 (saving seven games to finish second on the team) and 1979 (when he won 10 games in relief and saved 13 more) and decently in 1980, when he was pressed into use as an emergency starter at times. The Sox traded him to Seattle during spring training in 1981, where Drago pitched poorly and then retired.

In 1976, while pitching for California, Drago gave up Hank Aaron's 755th and final home run.

Walt Dropo—"The Moose from Moosup" was a hulking first baseman from northeast Connecticut who was Rookie of the Year in 1950. Called up to replace the injured Billy Goodman early in the season, Dropo hit .322, with 36 homers and a league-leading 144 runs batted in. He dropped to .239 his second year, and never hit better than .281 in the major leagues again (he only hit more than 19 homers once more in 13 seasons). Boston traded him to Detroit in 1952, and he drifted from team to team for years but never recaptured the magic of his first season in the majors.

Jumpin' Joe Dugan—a righthanded infielder who played in 85 games with the Red Sox in 1922. An alumnus of Holy Cross College in Worcester, Dugan was acquired in a three-way deal before the 1922 season. Members of the Boston press, by this time critical of every move that owner Harry Frazee made (after Frazee had sold the core of his team to the New York Yankees), claimed that the Sox had only traded for Dugan because the Yankees wanted him, and that he'd never play a game in a Boston uniform. They were wrong. He played 85 of them before being traded (along with Elmer Smith) to the Yankees on July 22 for a couple of backup players and cash. Dugan went on to become one of the key members of the Yankees' first dynasty. The trade caused some commotion in baseball since it seemed to give the Yankees—who were in the midst of a tight pennant race—an unfair advantage, and led to a June 15 trading deadline the following season.

Mike Easler—"The Hitman" was a lefthanded hitting specialist who played for the Sox in the mid–1980s and later was a controversial hitting coach. Easler had bounced up and down between the major and minor leagues for years before finally sticking with the Pittsburgh Pirates in 1980, at age 29. He was a poor outfielder, but a deadly hitter against righthanded pitching. Pittsburgh platooned Easler with a righthanded-hitting outfielder, never batting him more than 475 times in a season, but after Boston traded pitcher John Tudor for him, the 33-year-old Easler was given a shot as a full-time DH and occasional outfielder or first baseman. Easler excelled at the plate in 1984, hitting .313 with 27 home runs, but tailed off the next season (especially against lefty pitching). He was traded to the Yankees for Don Baylor, who would be the DH on the 1986 World Series team.

Ironically, Easler had been Red Sox property prior to the Tudor trade. In the late 1970s, the Sox claimed him off the Pirates roster in the Rule 5 Draft. Easler was on the Sox 40-man roster and played in spring training, but didn't make the team, and the Pirates got him back. Considering how good a hitter Easler was, he could have helped out in the late 1970s and early 1980s, and wouldn't have cost the Sox Tudor.

Easler returned to the Red Sox as hitting coach after the 1992 season, and was immediately successful. He was credited with helping Mo Vaughn's development (and Vaughn continued to work with Easler after his firing, which caused some controversy). However, Easler fell out with the Red Sox front office, first over new GM Dan Duquette's perceived failure to back him in a dispute with Sox pitching coach Al Nipper during the 1994 winter league season (the dispute led to Easler being fired as manager of Caguas in the Puerto Rican league), then over Easler's reluctance to coach replacement players during the 1995 strike. When the bad feelings escalated into a salary dispute, Easler was replaced as Red Sox hitting coach by Jim Rice. Easler, an ordained minister, is currently the manager of the Independant League's Florence Freedom.

Dennis Eckersley—righthanded pitcher who had two stints with the Sox, during totally disparate incarnations of his career. He came up as a fireballing starter, winning the American League Rookie Pitcher of the Year award in 1975 as a member of the Cleveland Indians. After three seasons in Cleveland, Eck was traded to Boston in March of 1978 and went on to have the best starting season of his career. He went 20–8 with a 2.99 ERA for the 1978 Red Sox team that won 99 games but lost the division title to the Yankees in a one-game playoff. (He won four games down the stretch as the Red Sox caught the Yankees to force that playoff.) He pitched just as well in 1979, but after that he slowly spiraled downward, as overuse, excessive drinking, and marital problems (involving an ex-Cleveland teammate) took a toll on his fastball. Early in the 1984 season Boston traded Eckersley to the Chicago Cubs for Bill Buckner.

For a time he seemed to be rejuvenated by the change of scenery, but after a decent (though not great) 1985 season, he struggled badly in 1986, and seemed to be at the end of the road. On the eve of the 1987 season, Eckersley was traded from Chicago to Oakland in a deal involving minor leaguers. Oakland planned to use him in long relief, to shore up their bullpen. But when Jay Howell was injured, they stuck Eck into the closer's role, and he went on to record at least 33 saves in each season from 1988 to 1993, leading the league twice. He became a dominant closer, famous for his stunning control. In 1989, he pitched 57⅔ innings and walked only three batters. The next season, he pitched 73¼ innings and walked four. In 1992 he won the American League Cy Young and the American League MVP, as he saved 51 games and had a 7–1 record. Unfortunately, one of the most dramatic moments of his career was also one of his few failures as the A's closer, when he gave up a two-out, pinch hit home run to Kirk Gibson of the Dodgers to lose Game 1 of the 1988 World Series.

In 1996 he rejoined former A's manager Tony LaRussa in St Louis. He saved 66 games in two years with the Cardinals, but was no longer the same dominant factor he had been. He lost 11 games, more than in his first five years as the Oakland closer. In 1998, Dan Duquette signed the 43-year-old Eckersley as a free agent to join the Sox bullpen. Eckersley had never moved away from the Boston area, where he remained popular, and was glad to pitch near his home. Though he said he still wanted to close, everyone knew he was being brought in to support Tom Gordon, who was making the transition from starting to closing. Eckersley provided 39⅔ innings of roughly league average work before retiring. He finished with 197 wins and 390 saves.

In his early days as a player, Eckersley was famous for making up words, and was a popular interview. After his retirement, Eckersley occasionally filled in as a color commentator on Red Sox radio broadcasts, where his candor, engaging style, and knowledge of the game made him an excellent analyst. He currently works for NESN as a studio analyst for pregame and postgame shows. Dennis Eckersley was inducted into the Hall of Fame in 2004 (albeit wearing an Oakland

A's hat). He was also inducted into the Boston Red Sox Hall of Fame in 2004. Today, Eckersley remains popular as a hero who fell, then rebuilt his life (overcoming alcoholism and other problems) and became a hero again.

Eckersley was not the only hero in the family. His 5-year-old son came to his mother's rescue in 2000 when a fire in the fireplace got out of control. Eck's son, who had recently learned lifesaving techniques at school, instinctively yelled, "stop-drop-and roll," and Eckersley's wife Nancy escaped serious harm. Eckersley repaid the lifesaving lessons by volunteering as the national spokesman for Fire Prevention Week in 2001.

Howard Ehmke—a rare bright spot on the terrible post-Babe Ruth teams of the early 1920s, and later an unlikely World Series hero for the Athletics. Ehmke broke in with Buffalo of the Federal League, and then signed with the Detroit Tigers when the Federal League folded. He was a journeyman righthanded pitcher for Detroit from 1916–22, but blossomed after being traded to the Red Sox. He won 20 games in 1923 and 19 in 1924, with decent ERAs. In 1925, Ehmke fell to 9–20, even though his ERA was still better than average (the Red Sox were an atrocious 47–105 that season). In 1923, while pitching for the Red Sox, Ehmke pitched a no-hitter. The feat was in jeopardy in the seventh inning when A's pitcher Slim Harriss hit a ball to the wall and ended up on second, but was ruled out for missing first base. His next outing was a one-hitter, with the only hit a disputed call on a ball that third baseman Howard Shanks, ordinarily an outfielder, failed to field cleanly.

Ehmke was traded to the Philadelphia Athletics in mid-1926. His most famous performance was probably Game 1 of the 1929 World Series, when Philadelphia A's manager Connie Mack shocked the baseball world by starting Ehmke against the Cubs. He had only pitched 11 games for the A's that year, but was secretly sent by manager Connie Mack to scout their likely World Series opponents, the Chicago Cubs. Just prior to Game 1, Mack named Ehmke his surprise starter—and the 35-year-old beat the Cubs, 3–1, setting a World Series record (since broken by Bob Gibson) with 13 strikeouts.

Alan Embree—hard-throwing lefthander who overcame frequent injuries to become a successful reliever. Embree was drafted by the Indians in 1989 after not pitching his senior year of high school due to a shoulder impingement. He made four starts for the Indians in 1992, before missing the entire 1993 season when he tore an elbow ligament and underwent replacement surgery. By 2002 he'd become a 32-year-old major league nomad, pitching for his sixth team (the Padres) after yet another round of arm surgery. Finally healthy, he had an extraordinary first half with San Diego, allowing only three runs in 36 appearances for an astonishing 0.94 ERA. The Red Sox traded two prospects to the Padres, hoping Embree would bolster the team's bullpen for the stretch drive. While he hasn't reprised his San Diego dominance, he's been a strong, consistent reliever—and largely injury-free.

Embree has a career playoff ERA of 2.11 in 30 appearances, 19 of them with the Red Sox. In the 2003 ALDS against Oakland, Embree pitched in three games, allowing only one hit and helping the Sox win the series. In the famed

2003 ALCS against the Yankees, Embree was even better, pitching in five games without giving up a run, and winning the crucial Game 6. Controversially, Embree was not used in the dramatic seventh game, though he was available to face the Yankees in the seventh inning when Pedro Martinez was left to founder on the mound. In the 2004 postseason, Embree pitched in 11 of 14 games, and got the last out against the Yankees in Game 7 of the ALCS, concluding the most dramatic comeback in baseball history.

Nick Esasky—power-hitting first baseman acquired by the Sox from the Cincinnati Reds in December 1988 in a four-player deal involving Todd Benzinger and Rob Murphy. After six National League seasons in which he hit for good power but an inconsistent average in limited playing time, Esasky found Fenway Park—and American League pitching—to his liking in 1989. He hit .277, while leading the Sox with 30 home runs and 108 RBI. The excitement did not last for long, however, because following the season the free agent Esasky chose to sign with the Atlanta Braves. Shortly afterward his baseball career ended abruptly when he was struck by a severe case of vertigo; he played only nine more games after leaving the Sox.

Vaughn Eshelman—lefthanded pitcher acquired by the Red Sox from Baltimore via the Rule 5 Draft prior to the 1995 season. Eshelman made an initial splash by pitching two outstanding games against the Yankees early in the year, but never lived up to the initial promise. He burned his pitching hand on a candle in his hotel room during spring training in 1997 and started the year on the disabled list. He pitched poorly that season, mostly in relief, and hasn't been in the major leagues since, although he continued to pitch in the minors.

Dwight Evans—a tremendous defensive outfielder and one of the classiest players in baseball, who became an offensive force later in his career. "Dewey" Evans (who reportedly hated the nickname fans gave him, but tolerated it anyway) played all but one of 20 years for the Sox. After an extraordinary run through the minor leagues, Evans first appeared with the Sox in 1972, and became a starter in 1973 (when he hit only .223). He settled into the Sox lineup as a solid hitter with some power who had an extraordinary ability to field Fenway Park's difficult right field, and had perhaps the best outfield arm the team had seen since Harry Hooper. (He used to finish his warmups in the outfield with a cannon throw to the plate every game.) In the slugging Boston lineup of the mid- to late-1970s, Evans didn't have to be a great hitter, and he eventually won eight Gold Gloves for his fielding.

From 1972 to 1977, Evans was a .275 hitter who averaged about 15 home runs a year (good but not great by the offensive standards of the time). From 1978–80, his power started to increase, but without much sign of the sudden improvement in hitting that was to come. Up to that time, Evans was best known for a great defensive play, his game-saving catch of Joe Morgan's blast in Game 6 of the 1975 Series. Deep in right field, Evans reached into the Sox bullpen and caught the ball. Turning, he wheeled and threw back into the infield, doubling the runner off. The runner was so amazed that the ball was caught that he was out by a mile.

Evans was a devoted disciple of Sox hitting coach Walt Hriniak, who finally got Evans to stop changing batting stances frequently and hit in a consistent manner. Evans responded by becoming a hitting star at an age when most players are starting to decline. In the strike-shortened 1981 season, Evans tied for the league lead in home runs while hitting .296 with 85 walks, easily his career high in both categories. He followed up by hitting .292 with 32 homers and 112 walks the next year, and remained a consistently deadly hitter through 1989, when he was 37. After a so-so year in 1990, the Red Sox chose not to exercise a contract option on Evans for what he'd announced would be his last season. Sadly, Evans had to finish his career in Baltimore, where he hit .270 as a part-timer.

When the tawdry Margo Adams scandal broke and it was revealed that many of the team's players were running around on their wives, Evans was one of the few players who was not caught up in the mess. It became known fairly early in his career that he was raising a severely disabled son, but Evans refused to make a big deal of it, or of any of his community involvement. He continues to live in New England.

Evans was a three-time All Star, who led the league in OPS twice and in walks three times, despite his late start as a hitter. For his career he hit 385 home runs, scored 1,470 runs, and drove in another 1,384. He also had 151 outfield assists, a total that would have been higher if runners hadn't stopped taking chances against him because of his intimidating arm. Evans was overshadowed when he first appeared on the Hall of Fame ballot, and his name was quickly dropped from the ballot. Because of a rule in effect at the time, it appeared that Evans would never be eligible to the Hall of Fame (since he failed to get at least 100 votes in the initial stage of balloting). However, the rule was changed in 2001 to restore his eligibility—although Evans's Hall of Fame chances are still unclear. Reportedly estranged from the team because of the way his career ended, Evans was wooed back by GM Dan Duquette in 2001. Following the 2001 season, Evans was named Sox hitting coach, only to be replaced by Ron Jackson after the 2002 season, when Grady Little announced his 2003 major league staff. The Red Sox then made Dewey a player development consultant.

Carl Everett—switch-hitting centerfielder, obtained from Houston before the 2000 season. The trade for Everett was expected to replace some of the offensive punch the Red Sox had lost when Mo Vaughn left via free-agency before the 1999 season, as well as fill the center field position which had become a revolving door of players since the departure of Ellis Burks after the 1992 season (and by far the Sox weakest position the previous year). The trade and subsequent long-term signing of Everett were somewhat of a risk. Everett was coming off a great year in Houston (.325 average and 25 home runs in a hitters' park, as well as 27 stolen bases and good defense) but he had struggled before coming to the Astros two years previously. At age 28, he was already joining his fifth organization (having been exposed to an expansion draft by the Yankees and traded by the Marlins and Mets). He'd run into legal trouble while with the Mets (he was exonerated of charges of child neglect) and left that organization under a cloud. But after getting off to a terrific start both with the bat and his outspoken comments

(Everett hated the Yankees, who had given up on him, with a passion that resonated for many Red Sox fans), Everett quickly joined Nomar Garciaparra and Pedro Martinez as one of the team's most popular players.

In his first season in Boston, Everett put up impressive numbers, hitting .300 with a career-high 34 homers. He also played a spectacular and occasionally adventurous center field. The offensive numbers were in spite of a second half dropoff brought on by a hand injury, and a 10-game suspension for a confrontation with an umpire that led to accidental physical contact (which was depicted in the media as a "head bump"). Everett also clashed with manager Jimy Williams at least twice, and with teammate Darren Lewis once. The Williams incidents exposed a rift between the manager and GM Dan Duquette that persisted well past the end of the season. At the heart of this conflict was the perception that Duquette was backing his player rather than the manager, and this perception led to widespread media attacks on both Everett and Duquette. Everett and Williams eventually met at the winter meetings, purportedly to clear the air, and Everett agreed to suggestions that he work on anger management. But the 2001 season was more of the same. Everett was limited by a knee injury that affected both his hitting and defense, but he continued to clash with Williams and then with new manager Joe Kerrigan. Kerrigan suspended Everett for lateness, after which Everett accused the manager of racism and public drunkenness. By this time the last of Everett's support from the front office had vanished. He didn't play again in 2001 and was traded to the Texas Rangers after the season.

Everett has played for the Rangers, the White Sox, the Expos, and the White Sox again in the last three years. Though he is still an above-average player, his 1999 and 2000 seasons remain his best ones. Everett exercised a $4 million option to stay with the White Sox for the 2005 season.

Jeff Fassero—much-traveled lefthanded pitcher who was very effective for Montreal during the early 1990s, but mostly unhappy in his year in Boston. Fassero had elbow surgery after the 1998 season (when he'd pitched for Seattle), and pitched horribly in 1999. Seattle traded him to Texas, where he attempted to regain his form working out of the bullpen. Prior to the 2000 season, Dan Duquette, who had been the general manager in Montreal when Fassero came up, signed him and reunited him with his Montreal pitching coach, Joe Kerrigan. Fassero started 23 games for the 2000 Sox but was inconsistent, occasionally very effective and occasionally shelled. Toward the end of the season, he made 15 appearances out of the bullpen and pitched very well, but was unhappy about losing his starting role. He signed with the Chicago Cubs after the 2000 season where he remained in the bullpen and pitched very well as a 38-year-old in 2001, filling in as Cubs' closer for part of the season when Tom Gordon was injured. After a stint in St. Louis, Fassero found himself in Coors Field (a terrible pitcher's park) for the 2004 campaign. He went 3–8 for the Rockies, before being released in September after a discussion with manager Clint Hurdle about Fassero's ability to start a game after not having pitched for 11 days. (Hurdle thought he could, Fassero thought he couldn't.) The Diamondbacks snatched him up for the remainder of the season, but after they declined to offer him salary arbitration, the 41-year-old Fassero signed a minor league deal for 2005 with the Giants, his ninth team.

Rick Ferrell—One of the most controversial Hall of Famers ever, Ferrell played very well for the Red Sox in parts of five seasons (the last four of them with his younger, more famous brother Wes). An outstanding defensive catcher, Ferrell hit for solid averages, drew a good number of walks, and rarely struck out (never more than 20 times in a season for Boston), but had little power. He began his career with the St. Louis Browns in 1929, and was traded to Boston early in the 1933 season. With the Sox that year, Ferrell batted .297 with 72 RBI, and caught all nine innings in baseball's first All Star Game. (Ferrell was named to the first six American League All Star Teams.) He hit .297 again in 1934, .301 in 1935, and .312 with a career-high 8 homers in 1936.

Early in 1937, the Ferrell brothers were traded to Washington for Bobo Newsom and Ben Chapman. Rick got some nice press with the Senators in 1945, when he caught a staff of four knuckleballers (a notoriously hard pitch for a catcher to handle). He retired in 1947 with a .281 average and 28 homers (Wes, a pitcher, hit .280 with 38 home runs), and little expectation of ever making the Hall of Fame. Ferrell only earned a grand total of three votes from the baseball writers, but was a surprise selection by the Veterans Committee in 1984, when he was 79 years old. Many writers blasted the Veterans Committee for picking elderly ex-teammates instead of more qualified candidates from other eras. Some writers wondered if the Veterans Committee had meant to select Wes instead, and others called for the abolishment of the Committee altogether. But the unassuming Ferrell handled the controversy gracefully, and lived his last 11 years with the satisfaction of having a plaque in Cooperstown, deserved or not.

Wes Ferrell—temperamental but talented pitcher who starred (along with his older brother and catcher Rick) on the Red Sox teams of the mid-1930s. Ferrell began his career with Cleveland, winning 21 or more games in each of his first four full seasons (1929–32). Known for his blazing fastball, occasional control problems, and power-hitting (he hit nine homers in 1931, and his 38 career home runs are the most of any pitcher), Ferrell was one of the game's best young pitchers. But a sore arm limited his effectiveness in 1933, and new Red Sox owner Tom Yawkey took a chance on him the following season, trading two bit players and $25,000 to Cleveland for Ferrell. Ferrell responded with a 14–5 record and a deceptively good 3.63 ERA (the American League ERA that year was 4.50). In 1935 Ferrell tied a career high with 25 wins, leading the league, while batting .347 with seven homers. He had his sixth 20-win season in 1936, leading the league with 301 innings pitched and 28 complete games.

After a disastrous 3–6, 7.61 start in 1937, Wes and his brother Rick were traded to Washington. Ferrell had some success with the Senators, but arm problems forced him to retire at age 33 with only 193 career wins. His 4.04 lifetime ERA seemed high to Hall of Fame voters, but was actually excellent for an American League pitcher of the 1930s. Ferrell has sometimes been mentioned as a possible Hall of Fame candidate, especially in light of his brother's surprise selection, but remains a longshot.

Boo Ferriss—a shooting star of a pitcher, the righthanded Dave "Boo" Ferriss won 21 games as a 23-year-old rookie newly discharged from the military in 1945. He followed it up by going 25–6 to lead the league in winning percentage and made the All Star Game the next year. Ferriss threw almost 540 innings those two years for the pitching-starved Sox, and hurt his arm from the overwork. He managed to win 12 games in 1947, but was only able to start nine games in 1948. He never won another major league game after 1948. He later coached for the Red Sox before becoming baseball coach at Mississippi State.

Mark Fidrych—eccentric righthanded pitcher who was the American League Rookie of the Year in 1976 while pitching for Detroit. Nicknamed "The Bird," Fidrych was known for exaggerated motions on the mound and for talking to the baseball before throwing it. He won 19 games in 1976 while leading the league in ERA, but after throwing 250 innings and 24 complete games at age 21, he never threw more than 81 innings in a season in the majors again. Fidrych, a Worcester, Massachusetts native, is of note to Red Sox fans because he finished his pro career with two seasons in Pawtucket, retiring in June 1983 with a 9.68 ERA. Two years later, the guy who once said that "The only time Lady Luck smiles on me is when she spits in my face" was diagnosed with two major tears in his rotator cuff.

Lou Finney—a key reserve for the Red Sox in the early 1940s, Finney was a lefthanded-hitting outfielder/first baseman who hit for a good average but without much power or ability to draw walks. Boston picked Finney up from the Philadelphia A's early in the 1939 season, and he hit .325 the rest of the way, leading the league with 13 pinch hits. He hit .320 the following year—playing almost every day because of injuries to other players—and made his only All Star appearance. Finney hit in the .280s his remaining three years in Boston (interrupted for a year by wartime military service). His brother, Hal Finney, also played in the major leagues.

Carlton Fisk—Pudge (a nickname he acquired as a child) is arguably the definitive Red Sox player—not just because he is a native New Englander (born in Vermont, raised in New Hampshire), but also because of his strange relationship with the organization. Though he played high school and American Legion baseball, his sport of choice was basketball, and his dream was to one day play for the Celtics. Fortunately for baseball, as Fisk himself put it, "I didn't grow into a power forward." In 1967, he was drafted as the fourth pick in the first round of the amateur draft by the Red Sox. Reportedly, the only reason he lasted that long was that the three teams drafting ahead of Boston knew Fisk would never sign with any team except the Red Sox.

In 1969 Fisk made his big league debut, appearing in two games without reaching base. He appeared in 14 games in 1971, getting his first two home runs and six RBI. Fisk became a regular in 1972, appearing in 131 games and hitting .293, with 22 home runs and 61 RBI. He was named Rookie of the Year, the first to win that award unanimously. He also won his only Gold Glove in that year.

In 1975 Pudge hit a walk-off home run in the twelfth inning of Game 6 of the

World Series, which many consider to be one of baseball's greatest moments. It is remembered because it won what was already a great game, and for the visual of Fisk frantically waving the ball fair. (This is among the most replayed baseball moments ever, and helped reignite interest in the game of baseball.)

In 1980, in a situation that is to this day shrouded in some mystery, the Red Sox mailed Fisk's new contract to him two days late, making him a free agent. So after more than a decade in the Red Sox organization, Carlton Fisk signed a contract with the Chicago White Sox, for whom he played until he retired in 1993.

By the time that retirement came about Fisk's name riddled the record books. His major league records include 2,226 games as a catcher, 72 home runs after age 40, and 351 home runs as a catcher. He also holds the American League record for most home runs by a catcher in a single season, 37 in 1985. He was named to 11 All Star teams. As a Red Sox player, Fisk hit 162 home runs and had 568 RBI. His highest batting average was .331 in 1975.

Fisk was inducted into baseball's Hall of Fame on July 23, 2000, in his second year of eligibility (a victim of a glut of talented first-year eligibles the previous year, including Nolan Ryan, George Brett, and Robin Yount). On August 4, 2000, his number 27 became only the fifth uniform number to be retired by the Red Sox. (The number 72 that he wore in Chicago was also retired by that team.) The number retirement was somewhat controversial, as Red Sox policy had been to retire a number only for a player who was in the Hall of Fame and had ended his career in Boston. General Manager Dan Duquette got around that rule by appointing Fisk as a consultant in the Red Sox front office. There are likely few longtime Red Sox fans who would not include Carlton Fisk on a list of their favorite Red Sox players, or the 1975 home run as one of their favorite baseball memories.

Bryce Florie—an unlucky righthanded reliever, Florie was an unheralded veteran when he came to Boston to support the Sox bullpen in the middle of 1999. In August 1999, when manager Jimy Williams refused to start volatile ace Pedro Martinez because he arrived late to the ballpark, Florie was the pitcher chosen to start in Pedro's place. Florie pitched well for 4⅔ innings (just short of the five innings needed for a win), before Pedro relieved and ended up getting a controversial win—though Williams tried to nurse the out-of-gas Florie through the fifth for the win.

On September 8, 2000, in the eighth inning of a game against the Yankees, Florie took a line drive to the face off the bat of Ryan Thompson, in an incident eerily reminiscent of Dick Pole's injury in 1975. Florie never lost consciousness, but it was a bloody, gruesome event that shattered his eye socket and ended his season. There was concern for a time that he would lose the sight in his right eye. Florie recovered enough vision to attempt a return to the Red Sox in 2001, but the team seemed reluctant to go along with the attempt and refused to activate him until threatened with a union grievance. After a couple of decent relief appearances, Florie was again struck by a batted ball. Though not injured, he was understandably shaken. His remaining stints were less than effective, and after appearing in a total of seven games, Florie was released.

In 2002 Florie had surgery to remove bone chips from his elbow, but started 16 games for Oakland's AAA affiliate in Sacramento. He was out of professional baseball in 2003, then while attempting a comeback in 2004 with the Marlins, Florie strained a rib cage muscle. That night, he cut his chin so badly in a "sleep-walking accident" that it required 15 stitches. He didn't make it back to the majors.

Cliff Floyd—a powerful but injury-prone outfielder who Boston acquired at the 2002 trading deadline, Floyd's career has always been star-crossed. He was the Expos' first-round draft pick in 1991, back when Dan Duquette was Montreal's Assistant GM, and was quickly hailed as one of the best prospects in all of base-ball—a lefty slugger with a good batting eye and great speed. Though he had been a center fielder, the Expos needed help at first base, so the 6-foot-4 Floyd switched positions when he reached the majors in late 1993. But on May 15, 1995, Floyd's career nearly ended after he shattered his wrist in a gruesome col-lision at the first base bag. He returned later that year (as an outfielder), but the injury sapped his power, and he was traded to Florida for future Red Sox pitch-er Dustin Hermanson in 1997. Floyd earned a World Series ring as a Marlins reserve in 1997, and joined their starting lineup after Florida's infamous post-championship salary dump. Though he missed chunks of the 1999 and 2000 sea-sons with knee injuries, Floyd was a very productive hitter with the Marlins, par-ticularly in 2001 (.317, 31 homers, 103 RBI, 123 runs, 44 doubles, 18 steals). In 2002, Florida wanted to get something for Floyd before he left as a free agent. They traded him back to the Expos (a surprise contender that year) on July 11, getting several young players, including ex-Red Sox prospect Carl Pavano, in return. When Montreal didn't move up in the standings, they decided to reverse course and trade their newly acquired star. Meanwhile, the Red Sox were des-perately trying to secure a wild card spot, but needed another bat to help Manny Ramirez and Nomar Garciaparra. On July 30, Boston traded top pitching prospect Seung Song (who later got hurt, and hasn't made the majors) and two other minor leaguers for Floyd.

Floyd's statistics with Boston were terrific: .316 average, .374 OBP, .561 slug-ging, 7 home runs and 21 doubles in 171 at-bats. Yet he rarely seemed to come up with men on base, and he only drove in 18 runs—and the Red Sox failed to make the playoffs. After the season, Floyd became a free agent. The Red Sox offered arbitration, but Floyd refused, and he signed a four-year, $26 million con-tract with the Mets. Many fans were upset that GM Theo Epstein didn't keep Floyd, and some accused ownership of being cheap. But Floyd was disappoint-ing in New York, missing 101 games with various injuries, while the bargain pick-ups who replaced him (David Ortiz, Kevin Millar, Bill Mueller) have been major factors in Boston's success. Boston also got two draft picks as compensation for Floyd, and both have already made an impact: pitcher Abe Alvarez is one of the team's top prospects, and outfielder Matt Murton was sent to the Cubs in the controversial but pivotal Garciaparra trade of 2004.

In an interesting side note, the Red Sox supposedly offered the Mets Manny Ramirez for Floyd after the 2004 season. (The idea was that the Red Sox would save more than $65 million over four years, and would be able to spread the money around several positions, instead of just giving it to one great but limited player.) New York GM Omar Minaya turned down the trade, and then shocked the baseball world by signing Pedro Martinez a few days later. Meanwhile, Floyd remains the Mets' left fielder—at least until his next trip to the disabled list.

Lew Ford—former Red Sox minor leaguer who was practically given away to the Minnesota Twins, where he blossomed. Boston drafted Ford in the twelfth round in 1999 (a year when, coincidentally enough, they had a "Lewford" center field platoon: Darren Lewis and Damon Buford). Ford had a fantastic 2000 season for low-A Augusta (.315, 122 runs, 52 steals), though skeptics said he was old for his league and had unremarkable tools. Shortly after Augusta's season ended, Boston sent Ford to the Twins for journeyman reliever Hector Carrasco—a trade that made little sense. Carrasco was acquired too late to make a playoff roster, though his atrocious pitching (9.45 ERA) helped ensure the Red Sox failed to make the playoffs at all, and he never pitched for Boston again. Meanwhile, Ford fought his way up Minnesota's minor league ladder, eventually reaching the majors as a backup in late 2003, where he batted an eye-opening .329 in limited action. He was set to begin 2004 in the minors, but the Twins had a rash of outfield injuries, and Ford simply hit too well to be benched. Playing all three outfield spots and DH, he batted .299 with a .381 OBP, 15 homers, and 20 steals. Only a technicality (too many days on the roster in 2003) kept Ford from winning the Rookie of the Year Award. Hindsight is always 20/20, but Red Sox fans can't help wishing they still had Lew Ford—or at least got more than Hector Carrasco for him.

Mike Fornieles—a righthanded relief pitcher, the Cuban-born Fornieles spent all or part of seven seasons with the Red Sox. He was generally an average, or slightly below average, pitcher during his career. In 1960, however, he led the American League in appearances with 70, and in saves with 14. He made the All Star team in 1961, when he had 15 saves, though his ERA skyrocketed to 4.68. Relief pitching star Dick Radatz (the Monster), who came up with Boston in 1962, later credited Fornieles with teaching him the batters in the American League, and how to close out games effectively.

Tony Fossas—Cuban-born, Boston-raised reliever who practically defined the term "lefty specialist." In 1991, after spending most of his career in the minors, Fossas achieved his boyhood dream of pitching for the Red Sox. Since Fossas was very tough against lefty hitters, but struggled mightily against righties, Boston gave him as narrow a role as possible. Whenever a tough lefthanded hitter came up in a key situation, Fossas entered the game. Very often, he'd depart after facing just the one batter. During Fossas's four years in Boston, he appeared in 239 games, yet only pitched 161 innings. Because of his limited role, it's hard to judge Fossas by traditional statistics, but he was generally effective against lefties (though righty pinch-hitters murdered him). The Red Sox had mixed feelings about Fossas, and continually searched for a more complete pitcher to replace him. He was taken off the 40-man roster in 1993 and 1994, but the Sox couldn't find anyone better, and re-signed him both years. Fossas finally left in 1995, had three good years with St. Louis, and retired after the 1999 season. Fossas is currently pitching coach for Florida Atlantic University.

Casey Fossum—skinny (160-pound) 24-year-old lefty pitcher with a great curve who pitched well as a rookie in 2001, after a brief but brilliant minor league career. Fossum, a star at Texas A&M, was drafted in 1999 with a compensation pick for the loss of free agent pitcher Greg Swindell. The Red Sox, impressed with Fossum's intelligence and poise, put him on the fast track to Fenway. He spent his first full season with Class A Sarasota, where he had a great second half, including a 16-strikeout no-hitter. The lefthander jumped to AA Trenton in 2001, where an astonishing lack of run support led to a misleading 3–7 record. (Fossum's 2.83 ERA was seventh in the Eastern League, and his other stats were just as good.) The Red Sox, battered by pitching injuries, called Fossum up to the majors, and the rookie acquitted himself reasonably well (3–2, 4.87 ERA in 13 appearances). As a starter, Fossum often ran out of gas (batters hit .220 in the first 60 pitches of his games, but .372 afterward); he was better as a reliever. Fossum spent the next two years juggling between starting and relief, not quite pitching well enough to claim a job, but showing tantalizing ability that made him the first choice when another pitcher was lost to injury or ineffectiveness.

Other teams were tantalized as well, and by 2003, Fossum had a trade bait status. He was discussed as part of a potential deal for Montreal's Bartolo Colon over the offseason, but the Red Sox refused to include him with third baseman Shea Hillenbrand. Despite the Red Sox reluctance to part with him, they found a deal they couldn't refuse: Fossum was sent to Arizona as a part of the trade that brought Curt Schilling back to the Red Sox organization. Injuries hindered Fossum's performance for his new team in 2004; he went 4–15 with an 6.65 ERA for a terrible Arizona club, then was traded to Tampa Bay before the 2005 season.

George "Rube" Foster—a little righty who pitched exceptionally from 1913–17, before retiring with arm problems. Foster only appeared in 19 games as a rookie, but came into his own in 1914, going 14–8 with an amazing 1.70 ERA (second in the league to teammate Dutch Leonard's incredible 0.96). In 1915 the Sox had perhaps their best pitching staff ever; Foster and Ernie Shore led the way with identical 19–8 records. (Rookie Babe Ruth was 18–8, while Leonard and Smoky Joe Wood each won 15.) The Sox easily beat the Phillies in the World Series, and Foster won both his starts, including the clinching game. Boston defended its title in 1916, but injuries limited Foster to 14 wins (including a no-hitter against the Yankees on June 21). He planned to retire after the World Series, but was talked into returning. Foster, in constant pain, struggled through 17 games in 1917, going 8–7. Unable to continue pitching, he retired to his ranch in Oklahoma, leaving the game at age 29 with a 58–33 record and a 2.36 ERA.

Another Rube Foster—born Andrew Foster—was a star pitcher who helped create the Negro League, and is in the Hall of Fame.

Keith Foulke—durable righthanded reliever who overcame the prejudice against non-power pitchers to become one of the best closers in baseball. Foulke has an above-average fastball but relies on an excellent changeup (actually, he throws two kinds of changeup with different movement) and very good control (only 2.1 walks per 9 innings over his career). Drafted by the Giants in 1994 out of Lewis and Clark State College in Idaho, Foulke pitched poorly as a 24-year-old rookie starter for San Francisco before being shipped to the White Sox as part of a package of young players for three veteran pitchers for the Giants' playoff run. The White Sox quickly converted Foulke to a reliever, and he was extremely effective for the next 5½ years, first as a setup man, and then as a closer. Although Foulke saved 34 games in 2000 and 42 in 2001 (with excellent ERAs both years), the White Sox never seemed to trust his less-than intimidating pitches, and took the closer's job away from him in 2002, although Foulke had another strong year (and an 0.74 ERA in the second half). When Oakland offered hard-throwing closer Billy Koch to the White Sox for Foulke, Chicago jumped at the deal. In Oakland, Foulke had his best year yet in 2003, making the All Star team, winning the Rolaids Relief Award, saving a league-leading 43 games with a 9–1 record and 2.08 ERA, and only allowing 57 hits in 86⅔ innings. (Koch had a dreadful 5.77 ERA with the White Sox and lost the closer's job.) After the season, Foulke became a free agent and signed a four-year contract with the Red Sox. (Ironically, the last game Foulke pitched for the A's was Game 5 of the ALDS, in which he blew a save to the Red Sox.)

With the Red Sox, Foulke continued to pitch just as well as he had with the A's. Unlike most contemporary closers, he frequently worked more than one inning at a time. Foulke won 5 games and saved 32 during the regular season (the high-scoring Red Sox had fewer save opportunities than the A's and White Sox, since they had fewer close games). He was unhittable for most of the year (2.17 ERA, except for 2 brief stretches of ineffectiveness, when he acquired nearly all of his 7 blown saves and 3 losses. In 11 postseason appearances (including all four World Series games), Foulke allowed only one run, and threw out Edgar Renteria on a groundball back to the mound for the final out of the World Series. He won one game and saved three others, pitching more than one inning six times, including 2⅔ scoreless innings in the do-or-die Game 5 of the ALCS.

Chad Fox—an injury-plagued righthanded reliever, Fox pitched well over parts of three seasons with the Braves and Brewers, but had to have two separate surgeries to reconstruct his elbow. Finally healthy, he had a terrific season as a 30-year-old in 2001 (5–2 with a 1.89 ERA in 65 games for a terrible Brewers team). The Brewers planned to make him a closer the following season, but a strained ligament in his elbow followed by a strained rotator cuff limited him to three major league games. Frustrated with Fox's injuries, the Brewers removed him from their roster, and he signed with the Red Sox as a free agent.

Fox was maddeningly unreliable with the Red Sox, blowing a game for Pedro Martinez in his first appearance of the 2003 season, and walking 17 batters in 18 innings. Desperate for bullpen consistency, the Red Sox released Fox. He was picked up by the Florida Marlins, where he immediately regained his old form, helping solidify the Marlins bullpen with a 2.13 ERA and making nine postseason appearances as a key member of the World Champion Marlins' pitching staff. Fox signed a minor league deal with the Cubs before the 2005 season.

Pete Fox—though never a great hitter, this righthanded outfielder did hit for a good average several times. Fox spent the first eight years of his 13 year career in Detroit, before coming to Boston in 1941, and finishing in 1945. He had a reputation as a solid outfielder, and was considered a key part of the successful Tiger teams of the mid-1930s. He started the season in left field in 1941 in place of Ted Williams, who had a bone chip in his ankle and couldn't run or field to start the year. He was an All Star during the war-depleted 1944 season.

Jimmie Foxx—unquestionably one of the greatest hitters ever to play the game, "Double X" was the heart of the Philadelphia A's lineup that dominated baseball from 1929 through 1931. Red Sox owner Thomas Yawkey acquired Foxx in 1936 as A's owner/manager Connie Mack sold off his best players in a Great Depression–related firesale. Acquisitions like Foxx and pitcher Lefty Grove led to the 1930s Red Sox being nicknamed "the Gold Sox," a moniker meant to mock Yawkey's attempts to use his vast financial resources to transform one of the worst teams of the 1920s into a contender overnight.

A catcher when he debuted in the majors in 1925 at the age of 17, Jimmie Foxx spent his first three years in the majors enjoying limited playing time at several positions (catcher, third base, first base, and the outfield) before Connie Mack decided to give him a more regular role. Finally given the chance to establish himself at first base in 1929, Foxx responded by leading the league in on-base percentage, finishing third in slugging percentage, and placing in the top 10 in a number of other major statistics while leading the A's to the World Championship. Knowing a good thing when he saw it, Mack left Foxx at first base. Foxx continued to hit as well as anyone in the league, and the A's proceeded to win the World Series in 1930 and 1931, the first team ever to win three consecutive World Series.

Jimmie Foxx's batting accomplishments are too many to list here. He hit for average and power, walked constantly, and was durable. He spent all or part of 20 seasons in the majors, and hit over .300 in 14 of those seasons (winning two batting titles along the way). He hit 30 or more homers in a season 12 times, leading the league in homers four times and in slugging percentage five times. He had seven seasons with more than 100 walks (and another with 99), and led the league in walks twice. He scored more than 100 runs 11 times and drove in more than 100 runs 13 times, leading the league three times in RBI (with astonishing totals of 169, 163, and 175 those years). Some highlights include Foxx's 58 home runs in 1932, which led to a .749 slugging percentage and the first of his three MVP awards; his winning the Triple Crown in 1933 which earned him his second MVP; his selection to the American League All Star team every year from its inception in 1933 through 1941; his nearly winning his second Triple Crown in 1938 when he led the league in average, RBI, on-base percentage, slugging percentage, total bases, and walks—although he hit 50 home runs that year, he finished second to Hank Greenberg (who had 58) in that category; and his third MVP in 1938 for leading the Red Sox to a second-place finish behind the Yankees.

It is said that when Ted Williams joined the Red Sox to start the 1939 season, a teammate, struck by his brashness, told the young Williams to be more humble with the line, "Wait till you see Foxx hit." Williams's response was "Wait till he sees me hit!" His one-liner is even more daring when one keeps in mind that Foxx had won his third MVP in the previous season.

As it happened, Foxx's career was almost over at this point. He continued to hit quite well in 1939 (his .360 average and .694 slugging percentage), but his heavy drinking was about to derail his career. In 1940, his average fell below .300 and his slugging below .600 (still good numbers, but a subpar season for Double-X). In 1941, his slugging percentage fell to .505 (his lowest mark since he was 18). In 1942, after 30 games (with a slugging percentage in the mid-.400s), Boston put Foxx on waivers. He was picked up by the Cubs, but his numbers continued to plummet. The Cubs gave Foxx another 15 games (in 1944) to see if he could straighten out his life enough in order to hit as he once did, but he had nothing left. Foxx retired.

World War II was still being waged, however, and he was able-bodied enough to fill major league ranks, so the last-place Phillies asked Foxx to come back, perhaps hoping he could recover his stroke, or at least draw fans from his old Philadelphia A's past to come to the ballpark to watch him in his swan song. The prodigious power was no longer there, but his arm was still live enough that the Phils tried him as a pitcher—Foxx compiled a 1.59 ERA in 22 innings.

Foxx retired for good following the 1945 season (after which major league regulars returned from wartime duty). His 534 home runs were second only to Ruth (despite hitting only 42 home runs after age 32). He was elected to the Hall of Fame in 1951, a great player whose numbers could have been even greater had his addiction to the bottle not caused his career to go south at age 33. (Fans of the movie *A League of Their Own* will recognize that Tom Hanks's character, was based on Jimmie Foxx, who really did manage in the All-American Girl's Professional Baseball League).

Joe Foy—a righthanded-hitting third baseman and minor league phenom, Joe Foy spent the first three years of his career with the Sox and played decently. He was the starting third baseman on the 1967 Impossible Dream team, and led the league in both double plays and errors twice while with the Sox. His batting averages are unimpressive today, but he played at a time when pitching was king. He had some power, could steal bases (fifth in the league in 1968), and walked frequently (among the league leaders in two of his three years with the Sox). Foy developed a weight problem and when he failed to deal with it, Red Sox management shipped him to Kansas City.

Foy is mostly remembered for being part of a terrible trade a year after he left the Red Sox. After stealing 37 bases for Kansas City in 1969, Foy was traded to the New York Mets for Amos Otis and Bob Foster. Foy, troubled by substance abuse problems, never played full-time again and was out of baseball at age 28, while Otis went on to an illustrious 17-year career. Foy's drug problems may have contributed to his early death in 1989, at age 46.

Buck Freeman—had he been born 30 years later, the now-forgotten John "Buck" Freeman might have been regarded as one of the game's greatest sluggers. But at the turn of the twentieth century, home runs were rare, and Freeman was seen as more of a curiosity than a star. The 5-foot-9 lefty swinger became a regular out-fielder with the National League's Washington team in 1899, hitting .318 with 25 triples, a league-leading 25 homers, and 122 RBI. No other National Leaguer hit more than 12 home runs that year, and Freeman's 25 were tied for the second-most in a nineteenth-century season. Freeman moved to the National League's Boston Braves in 1900, and jumped to the Red Sox in their inaugural 1901 season.

Freeman's first three seasons with the Red Sox were excellent. He hit a career-high .339 as the team's first baseman in 1901, with 15 triples, 12 homers, 114 RBI, a .400 on-base percentage, and a .520 slugging percentage (outstanding in the dead ball era). Freeman moved back to right field in 1902, and led the American League with 121 RBI, while hitting .309 with 19 triples and 11 homers. His average slipped to .287 in 1903, but Freeman's league-leading 13 homers and 104 RBI helped the Sox win the first modern World Series. During the 8-game Series, Freeman hit three triples and batted .281. Freeman led the American League in triples in 1904, with 19, but his other numbers began to slip. He played regularly in 1905 and 1906, and briefly in 1907, but only hit five more major league home runs.

Modern historians have had difficulty judging Freeman. His power numbers were among the best of his era, but his era was marked by pitching, defense, bunting, and daring baserunning—"inside baseball," rather than the station-to-station style of today's game. Never much of a fielder or baserunner, Freeman was often criticized by his peers, yet may have helped pave the way for Babe Ruth and the home run revolution. If nothing else, Freeman began the Red Sox tradition of high-power, low-defense outfielders.

Jeff Frye—righthanded-hitting second baseman, signed as a free agent by the Red Sox off of Texas's Oklahoma City team early in the 1996 season. The injury-prone Frye had hit very well in Texas before being buried in the minors after one of many knee injuries, and was picked up by the Red Sox on the recommenda-tion of manager Kevin Kennedy, his former manager on the Rangers. Frye hit well for the Sox and ended up as the team's starting second baseman. Although he had little power, Frye always hit for a good average and did a decent job of getting on base, while playing an acceptable second base. The Red Sox reward-ed Frye for his performance with the first multiyear contract of his career fol-lowing the 1997 season, but he blew out his knee again in the first baserunning drill of the spring in 1998, and was lost for the season. He came back to play intermittently in the 1999 and 2000 seasons before being traded to Colorado in the Rolando Arrojo deal. Frye spent 2001 with Toronto, where on August 18 he became the second player in Blue Jays history to hit for the cycle. A free agent after the season, Frye signed a minor league contract with the Reds. He hit .297 for the Reds' AAA Louisville team, but when he hadn't been called up to the major league club by August, chose to retire. Frye lives in Fort Worth, Texas with his wife and three children, where he helps baseball professionals with career planning, contract negotiations, and professional endorsements.

Denny Galehouse—righthanded pitcher who was a surprise starter in one of the biggest games in Red Sox history. Galehouse was a 36-year-old veteran pitching on fumes at the end of the 1948 season, which he had spent as a decent fill-in behind five other starting pitchers. He had a 109–117 career record, and had won more games than he lost in only three of his 14 big-league seasons. With the Red Sox and Cleveland Indians tied for the league lead on the last day of the season, manager Joe McCarthy inexplicably chose Galehouse to start the one-game playoff that would decide who went to the World Series. To no one's surprise, the Red Sox lost the game, and the pennant, 8–3. Galehouse played in only two more major league games. He died on October 14, 1998 in Doylestown, Ohio.

Rich Garces—hefty righthanded relief pitcher from Venezuela. Garces, a converted center fielder despite his oversized appearance, spent most of the early 1990s pitching in the Minnesota farm system. He split time in 1995 between the Cubs and Florida Marlins before joining the Sox as a free agent for the 1996 season. In 1996 and 1997, he continued to be an unimpressive and injury-prone middle reliever for the Sox, spending a good portion of 1997 in AAA Pawtucket. Garces fared better in 1998, and became an excellent setup man (with an extraordinary 1.55 ERA) in 1999. By the 2000 season he was a fan favorite, affectionately called "El Guapo" (the beautiful one) in response to his roly-poly body and unkempt appearance on the mound. Garces was one of many workhorses in a heavily worked bullpen for the next two years, and continued to pitch well.

After the 2001 season, Garces expressed anger about not being offered a multiyear contract by the Red Sox, who remained concerned about his health and weight. Garces settled for a one-year, $2.2 million contract, and reported to spring training 35 pounds lighter than he had been. His improved physique didn't pay off though; he had a disastrous 2002 season, hampered by a persistent hamstring injury. He appeared in only 26 games with a ghastly 7.59 ERA. Garces was designated for assigment to Pawtucket, but refused to report there and was released.

Garces signed with the Colorado Rockies for the 2003 season, but then missed his physical and the first part of camp. Visa problems were blamed for delaying his trip from Venezuela. After finally arriving at his Florida home, Garces decided at the last minute to retire. (His agent claimed there were health concerns in his family.) In 2004, Rich Garces was the closer out of the bullpen for Magallanes in the Venezuelan winter league. In January 2005, Garces disappeared after a game, and there were fears that he had been kidnapped like the mother of former Sox pitcher Ugueth Urbina. But Garces later turned up unharmed; reportedly he had gone to a 10-day beach party without telling his team or agent (though other accounts of the disappearance cited family problems).

Nomar Garciaparra—for years the cornerstone of the Red Sox, Garciaparra was one of three extraordinary shortstops who all came to the major leagues around the same time (along with Alex Rodriguez and Derek Jeter, both of whom now play for the Yankees). Garciaparra was a so-called "five tool" player; he hit for power, average, had good speed, a strong arm, and was a good defensive player. Although he was a free swinger—like Mike Greenwell before him, Garciaparra frequently swung at the first pitch he saw—Garciaparra hit for high averages with good power and seldom struck out. In the field his great range and strong throwing arm led to both spectacular plays and occasional wild throwing errors (particularly since he threw to poor defensive first basemen for much of his career).

Anthony Nomar Garciaparra ("Nomar" is his father's name spelled backward) was selected in the first round of the 1994 draft, the first pick by new Red Sox GM Dan Duquette. Garciaparra had been a member of the 1992 U.S. Olympic Baseball Team, and had starred on a Georgia Tech team alongside catcher (and Red Sox teammate) Jason Varitek and outfielder Jay Payton (who joined the Red Sox the season after Nomar left). The Milwaukee Brewers had tried to sign Nomar as a teenager, but Garciaparra had insisted on going to college for three years—where he studied business management—in case something went wrong in his baseball career. As a youth, baseball was not even his best sport— Garciaparra was a southern California soccer standout.

Despite an early season injury, Garciaparra was called up to the majors at the end of the 1996 season after posting impressive numbers at AAA Pawtucket. Garciaparra was immediately thrust into the starting lineup, replacing shortstop John Valentin, one of the team's most valuable players, who was slowed by nagging injuries. (Later rumors claimed that manager Kevin Kennedy told Valentin that GM Duquette was forcing him to play Nomar over Valentin.) Garciaparra played in 24 games for the Sox that year, driving in 16 runs and hitting 4 homers.

The controversy continued into the spring of 1997. New manager Jimy Williams first said that the shortstop job was Valentin's to lose, then said that Valentin and Garciaparra would openly compete for the job, but then handed the job outright to Garciaparra after only a few spring training games had been played. Valentin was moved to second base (displacing Jeff Frye) and then to third base after an injury to incumbent Tim Naehring. This shuffling disrupted the clubhouse and angered Valentin, who briefly left the team before settling down to play well at both second and third.

The clubhouse rumblings quieted when it became evident that Nomar was the shortstop of the future. Batting first on a team without a natural leadoff hitter, Garciaparra hit .306 with 30 homers (a rookie shortstop record), led the league in total bases, and set a record for a leadoff hitter (since broken by Anaheim's Darin Erstad) with 98 RBI. He shattered the record for extra base hits by a rookie shortstop, which had stood since 1924, as well as records for runs, doubles, total bases, and slugging percentage by a rookie shortstop. Garciaparra also hit in 30 straight games, the second-longest streak ever by a Red Sox player, on his way to being a unanimous selection for American League Rookie of the Year.

In the years that followed, Garciaparra continued to put up exceptional numbers. His 24-game hitting streak in 1998 was the longest in the majors that year. After Mo Vaughn left as a free agent following the 1998 season, it was widely speculated that pitchers would be able to pitch around Garciaparra in the weakened Sox lineup and his production would decline. Instead, he won the batting title in 1999, hitting .357, and won it again in 2000 by hitting .372—the first righthanded batter in 60 years to win back-to-back batting titles. Garciaparra hit two grand slams in a game against the Seattle Mariners on May 10, 1999. While his home run totals diminished from a career-high of 35 in 1998 to 21 in 2000, he continued to be a dangerous power hitter, among the league leaders in extra base hits.

In many ways Nomar was indicative of the problems the Red Sox faced on and off the field in 2001. Early in spring training he aggravated a wrist injury that originally occurred during the 1999 playoffs. Both the team and player waffled as to whether surgery was needed. The operation was performed on Opening Day, which turned out to be a bad omen for the season.

He returned on July 29 with two dramatic home runs in his first game back. At first the comeback seemed to be progressing well, with the Sox giving him every fourth day off to keep the still-sore wrist from worsening. On August 16, he was hitting .309/.356/.582, numbers very close to his 1998 season. But after that he stopped hitting for power (though he was still getting on base with walks and singles), and it became clear the wrist was still bothering him.

On August 24, the Sox beat the Rangers in Texas to run their record under new manager Joe Kerrigan to 6–3; Nomar went 2-for-4 with a walk. The next day was Nomar's scheduled day off, and it was reported that the wrist was seriously bothering him as the Sox lost a devastating 18-inning game. The next night he went 0-for-4 in obvious pain and the Sox lost again. He never played another inning, and the Sox went into a season-destroying tailspin. Many Sox players seemed to have invested a great deal of mental energy into keeping their heads above water, staying within striking distance of the Yankees, until Nomar could return; when he went down for a second time—combined with injuries to Pedro Martinez and Jason Varitek—the team seemed to lose all heart.

(Interestingly, this was exactly the psychological spin several Sox put on the season afterward. Yet the Boston media, never shy about rewriting history, spent the rest of the season portraying the Sox as a team of quitters who collapsed when Joe Kerrigan took over. Of course, these were the same writers who were saying that the team was showing great character by playing way above their heads in July and most of August without Nomar, Pedro, and Varitek, and the same writers who had nothing but good things to say about Kerrigan's first nine games.)

Nomar came back from the injury to have good (but not great) seasons in 2002–03, hitting just over .300 with good power although his walk totals, which had risen from poor to merely below-average dropped back down to poor. After his outstanding rookie season, the Red Sox had signed Garciaparra to a multiyear contract, a bold and risky move considering the team could have kept him at a much lower price for several years and would have been liable if Garciaparra became hurt or ineffective. The gamble paid off when Garciaparra became a superstar and was already signed at far less then his potential market value. But as that contract reached neared its end, it became clear that re-signing Nomar would be very difficult for the Red Sox. While he had been that rare Red Sox player who is popular in the media for most of his career, by 2003 critical articles had begun to appear, and Nomar didn't help the situation by responding with comments like "no wonder no one wants to play here." When Nomar turned down a four-year, $60 million extension (higher than his market value) in 2003, the team began to seriously consider trading him rather than losing Nomar to free agency after the 2004 season. A much publicized series of trades that would have sent Nomar to the White Sox and brought Alex Rodriguez (then with the Rangers) to the Red Sox fell through, but Garciaparra was clearly upset that the team would think about trading him and even more upset when the team lowered its contract offer as a result of a declining market.

Nomar injured his Achilles tendon in a spring training game, and was slow to recover; there were reports that his heart wasn't in the rehab because of his breach with the team. Other injuries to his groin and wrist meant he got a late start on the season, didn't cover much ground in the field, and was only sporadically available when he was playing. Whether it was because of injury or unhappiness, Nomar's malaise seemed to reflect the team's malaise, and when he wasn't available to play in a key game against the Yankees during which Yankees shortstop Derek Jeter sacrificed his body to make a defensive play, it highlighted the growing problem to everyone. In a four-way trade on July 31, the Red Sox gave up Nomar and prospect Brad Baker in return for Montreal shortstop Orlando Cabrera and Minnesota first baseman Doug Mientkiewicz. (Nomar ended up with the Cubs.) Whether it was because Nomar had been affecting the team's chemistry, or because the new players exactly filled the team's holes, or just coincidence, the Red Sox began their charge to the World Series at about the same time Garciaparra left, leaving an unfair legacy for a player who gave so much to the team and its fans for so many years. (He was still voted a three-quarter share of playoff money by his former teammates.) Nomar played about the same for the Cubs as he had for the Red Sox—pretty well, but nowhere near his normal level of play—as the Cubs fell just short of the playoffs. He ended up signing a one-year, $8 million contract to return to the Cubs in 2005, far below the contract he'd turned down with the Sox.

During his years with the Red Sox, Garciaparra was one of the most superstitious ballplayers in baseball, with an array of rituals he followed every game that rivaled those of former Sox star Wade Boggs. He climbed the steps out of the dugout almost sideways, stepped with both feet on each step, kissed his bat, and crossed himself repeatedly. While in the batter's box, he would continually tug at his batting gloves and tap his toes with his bat (both holdovers from his youth, when he had to adjust his older brother's hand-me-down equipment). He always wore a decaying warmup jersey from Georgia Tech under his uniform, and he reportedly played the same music on the way to the park every game.

Until 2003, Garciaparra was as popular with the media as he was with fans. He combined an all-out playing style and vigorous work ethic with a self-deprecating manner and boyishly enthusiastic speaking style. While Derek Jeter received more national attention, Nomar made appearances on *Saturday Night Live* and the sitcom *Two Guys and a Girl*, attended and sometimes interacted with wrestlers during WWF shows, and was romantically linked at various times with actress Lauren Holly and hockey player Cammi Granato before marrying longtime soccer star Mia Hamm, a longtime friend.

Nomar's younger brother, Michael Garciaparra, was drafted by the Seattle Mariners in 2003. He hit .226 in 2004 while playing shortstop for the Mariners' Inland (high-A) farm team, but missed much of the season with a wrist injury.

Larry Gardner—one of the best third basemen of the 1910s and early 1920s, Gardner was a key member of three World Series winners for Boston. The lefty-swinging Vermont native joined the Red Sox in 1908, a year after Hall of Fame third baseman Jimmy Collins departed. Gardner became the team's regular second baseman in 1910, and moved to third midway through the following season. A .289 lifetime hitter with little power and average speed, Gardner's statistics aren't overwhelming by today's standards. But in the deadball era, third base was much more of a defense-oriented position, thanks to the greater emphasis on bunting and baserunning. Hitting was considered a bonus, making a player like Gardner extremely valuable. Gardner had his best Red Sox season in 1912, batting .315 with 86 RBI and 25 steals for the World Champions. He also played for the 1915 and 1916 champs, hitting .308 in the latter season. In 1918, Gardner and Tilly Walker were traded to the Philadelphia Athletics for star first baseman Stuffy McInnis. (Walker went on to tie Babe Ruth for the league lead in homers, with 11.) A year later, Gardner joined his ex-Sox teammate Tris Speaker in Cleveland. In 1920, Gardner won his fourth World Series ring, driving in 118 runs and batting .310 for the Indians. The advent of the lively ball helped Gardner's numbers, and he put up nearly identical stats in 1921.

Gardner ended his 17-year career in 1924, and later returned to the University of Vermont, his alma mater, as baseball coach and athletic director.

Wes Gardner—righthanded pitcher acquired with Calvin Schiraldi from the Mets in the Bobby Ojeda trade. He had a great arm, but never lived up to what people expected from his physical skills. After teasing Red Sox fan with glimpses of potential for five years, Gardner finished his career in 1991, splitting 26 innings between Kansas City and San Diego. In five years in Boston, he recorded 20 wins and 12 saves.

Rich Gedman—a rare lefthanded-hitting catcher, Gedman worked hard to turn himself from an undrafted, overweight first baseman into one of the league's premier catchers before abruptly flaming out. Gedman debuted in September 1980 (as a pinch hitter for Carl Yastrzemski) and spent most of the next three years platooning with light-hitting Gary Allenson. Although Gedman hit for a good average, he wasn't productive as a hitter, since he drew a below-average number of walks and hit only 11 home runs combined in those three years. In 1984 Gedman blossomed as a hitter under the tutelage of unorthodox Sox hitting coach Walt Hriniak, playing in 133 games and hitting 24 home runs. The next year he hit a career-best .295 with 18 homers. He began to struggle at the plate in 1986 but was still productive, hitting 16 homers while batting .258.

That year, however, was the year the Sox made the World Series and Gedman was the catcher behind the plate for Bob Stanley's wild pitch that allowed the Mets to tie Game 6. Gedman had developed a fine throwing arm, but he was at best an average defensive catcher; many other catchers could have prevented Stanley's pitch from getting away—and if Stanley had gotten out of the inning without the wild pitch, the Sox would have won the World Series. In 1987 Gedman appeared in only 52 games because of injuries and ineffectiveness. His hitting deteriorated to the point where he looked helpless at the plate, a caricature of the odd swing that Hriniak advocated. The Sox finally gave up and released Gedman in 1990. He played sparingly for Houston and St. Louis until

1992, but never recovered his batting ability. Gedman is now a coach with the independent North Shore Spirit.

Gary Geiger—speedy lefthanded-hitting outfielder obtained from Cleveland (with Vic Wertz) in 1958 when the Red Sox traded the popular Jimmy Piersall. Geiger had been a pitcher in the minor leagues before being converted to the outfield in 1957. The 22-year-old Geiger wasn't Piersall, but he was talented: He didn't hit for a high average but he walked a lot and had good power, and his stolen base totals were excellent at a time when stolen bases were unpopular. (He was among the league leaders in steals three times with Boston, though he never stole more than 18 bases in a season.) He was a good fielder with a strong, accurate arm, but unlike Piersall, he was never going to be a star, just a solid player on a series of bad Red Sox teams. After five full seasons with Boston, first as a good platoon player, then as a so-so starter, Geiger lost his job to developing star Tony Conigliaro, and spent most of the 1964–65 seasons in the minors. Left unprotected by Boston, Geiger was selected by Atlanta in the Rule 5 Draft in 1965, and spent four seasons as a part-timer in Atlanta and Houston before retiring. In 1966, he hit the first double ever in Busch Stadium. Geiger died in 1996.

Jeremy Giambi—the less-heralded brother of slugger Jason Giambi, the 28-year-old outfielder/first baseman was acquired from the Phillies before the 2003 season. (He had previously played in Kansas City and with his brother in Oakland.) Giambi's on-base percentage (.413 in 2002, .381 career), ability to get into a hitter's count, and hit with power to all fields made him attractive to the Boston front office. Giambi struggled with injuries and hit only .197 without much power (though he still walked quite a bit), and has not played in the major leagues since. After the 2004 season, grand jury testimony was leaked to the press in which Giambi admitted to having taken steroids while playing.

Billy Goodman—versatile singles hitter who played for the Red Sox in the late 1940s and 1950s. A lifetime .300 hitter (.306 with Boston), Goodman also drew a fair number of walks, but had only 19 homers in a 16-year career. He debuted in 1947, and became the team's regular first baseman in 1948. Goodman made the All Star team in 1949 (hitting a rather empty .298), but he lacked the power of his predecessor, Rudy York. After an injury to Goodman early in 1950, slugger Walt Dropo took over at first base and went on a seasonlong tear. Although Goodman no longer had a regular position when he returned to the team, he got into 110 games at five different positions and won the batting title (.354). He was a backup at first and third base, and took over in left field after Ted Williams got hurt in the All Star Game. When Williams returned, Goodman resumed his utility role, until another Hall of Famer got hurt. Bobby Doerr had a career-ending back injury in 1951, and Goodman replaced him at second base. He continued to hit near or above .300 each year, though his defense didn't remind anyone of the great Doerr. He made the All Star team again in 1953, when he hit .313 and struck out only 11 times in 514 at bats. Early in 1957, the Red Sox traded Goodman to Baltimore for young reliever Mike Fornieles. The following year he was traded to the Chicago White Sox, where he played four seasons, including five games in the 1959 World Series. He finished his career with the expansion Houston Colt 45s in 1962, mainly as a backup. He didn't have enough power for a first baseman or left fielder, or enough defense to be a top second baseman, but the easygoing Goodman was certainly good to have around. His last major league role was with the Atlanta Braves in 1976, when he was an instructor and coach. Goodman died of cancer in 1984, at age 58.

Tom Gordon—righthanded reliever who had an extraordinary transition from starter to reliever, only to see his stardom sidetracked by injury. Gordon made a splash as a 21-year-old rookie with the Kansas City Royals in 1989, going 17–9 with a good 3.64 ERA. He never developed into the star the Royals hoped, however; Gordon pitched consistently but won 12 games or fewer in each of the next six seasons. Although he had one of the best curves in baseball and a good fastball, Gordon didn't have control of any additional pitches that would allow him to fool hitters consistently. Traded to the Red Sox in 1996, he won 12 games again but pitched inconsistently. Sox pitching coach Joe Kerrigan suggested that Gordon might be more successful as a relief pitcher—where he would only face each batter once and his curve would be most effective.

Gordon began pitching in relief late in the 1997 season, and recorded 11 saves. The next season Gordon became the full-time closer, with fading star Dennis Eckersley signed to the pitching staff to help tutor Gordon in the role. Gordon's contract was restructured as well, essentially giving him a new three-year deal with lucrative incentives if he was successful in his new role. Gordon responded with an extraordinary 1998 season, saving a league-leading 46 games and going months without blowing a save—until his luck ran out with a heartbreaking loss in the playoffs against the Cleveland Indians. Gordon won the Rolaids Relief award, and achieved another kind of immortality when Stephen King's short novel, *The Girl Who Loved Tom Gordon*, came out the following spring.

Unfortunately, Gordon's good fortune didn't last (at least not with the Red Sox). An injured elbow cost him most of the 1999 season. He feuded with the team's management and medical staff over his course of treatment (the team wanted him to try resting rather than season-ending surgery), pitched poorly on his return, and then was forced to have surgery after all—which meant he would miss the entire 2000 season as well. Although his relationship with the team was mended somewhat, the Red Sox did not pick up Gordon's $4.5 million contract option for the 2001 season. Gordon ended up continuing his comeback with the Chicago Cubs (for whom he saved 27 games in 2001). But when Gordon missed half of the following season to a torn shoulder muscle, the Cubs traded him to Houston. He pitched for the White Sox in 2003, mostly as a setup man. In 2004, Gordon signed with the Yankees, where he was heavily used as a setup man to closer Mariano Rivera. Although Gordon pitched very well (posting a 9–4 record and 2.21 ERA and being selected to his second All Star team) the career-high 80 appearances wore the 36-year-old pitcher down by the end of the season; he was used by the Yankees in six of their seven ALCS games against the Red Sox but pitched ineffectively.

While Gordon pitched for the Red Sox in 1995–96, his cousin, Clyde "Pork

Chop" Pough, played with the team's AAA club in Pawtucket. Gordon and Pough shared an apartment halfway between Pawtucket and Boston.

Jeff Gray—promising, often-dominating reliever whose career abruptly ended after he suffered a stroke. Gray, a college teammate of former Red Sox infielder Jody Reed at Florida State, put up excellent minor league numbers in the Reds' system. However, he wasn't regarded as a prospect, and only appeared in five big league games (in 1988). The Reds traded Gray to the Phillies in 1990, but he was released after spring training. Gray signed a minor league deal with the Red Sox, and pitched well in Pawtucket, earning a promotion to the majors. Though Gray's stats weren't great (2–4, 4.44 ERA), he was an unsung hero for the Sox, earning nine saves while closer Jeff Reardon recovered from a serious back injury. He entered 1991 as Reardon's setup man, and was superb, allowing only 39 hits and 10 walks in 61 innings, while posting an outstanding 2.34 ERA. Gray did the dirty work, stifling seventh and eighth inning rallies, while Reardon got the glory, setting a team record (since broken by Tom Gordon) with 40 saves.

Then tragedy struck. Sitting in the clubhouse before a July 30 game against Texas, Gray started to feel dizzy, with numbness on his right side, and his speech became slurred. He collapsed, and doctors later revealed that Gray had suffered a stroke. The news was shocking, since Gray was only 28 years old, and had appeared to be in perfect health. The tough reliever promised to come back, and spent months rehabilitating. Gray had to relearn many motor functions, and could only get his fastball back to the 80 MPH range. He pushed himself as far as he could, and tried to pitch in the minors in 1992, but it became sadly evident that Gray would never regain his old form. The Red Sox hired him as a minor league pitching coach, and he remained in the organization until 1999, when he moved to the Reds' system. Most recently (2003) Gray was the pitching coach for the Rookie-Level Gulf Coast League Reds. Gray also operates the highly successful Beef O'Brady's restaurant in Sarasota, Florida with Jody Reed. He is a member of the Florida State University Hall of Fame.

Craig Grebeck—a utility infielder whose career evaporated with the Red Sox. Grebeck was a 36-year old career backup with a reputation as a good fielder when he signed with the Sox before the 2001 season. He was coming off two of his best seasons as a hitter (.295 and .363 batting averages, in a total of about 400 plate appearances) and had been a decent hitter throughout his career. In 2001 he started the season in a hideous slump, however, and ended it on the disabled list. His final numbers with the team were 2–41, for an .049 batting average. He was released by the Red Sox at the end of the season and retired from the game.

Pumpsie Green—the first black player to play for the Red Sox, who were the last team in the major leagues to integrate. Although the Red Sox had tried out Willie Mays and Jackie Robinson in the 1940s (and then chosen not to sign them) it wasn't until 1959 that a black player was signed. Elijah "Pumpsie" Green spent four years with the Sox as a utility infielder and pinch hitter, never batting more than 260 times in a season or hitting higher than .260. Although Green ended the Sox white-only policy, tinges of racism toward black and Hispanic players persisted for many years, and the last vestiges were only rooted out in the 1990s under general manager Dan Duquette. (In a welcome sign, when superstar free agent Manny Ramirez chose to sign with the Red Sox in December 2000, he did so partially because of the team's diversity and welcoming climate toward players of all races.)

Mike Greenwell—"Gator" was a Red Sox outfielder from 1985–1996. Called up as a pinch hitter for the stretch drive in 1986, the lefthanded-hitting Greenwell replaced a fading Jim Rice in the lineup in 1987 and seemed to be the next great Red Sox left fielder. At the time there was a great deal of media attention focused on the nearly unbroken succession from Ted Williams to Carl Yastrzemski to Jim Rice to Mike Greenwell, although the talk gradually died down when it became clear that Greenwell would not be a Hall of Famer. In 1987 Greenwell hit .328 with 19 home runs in limited playing time, and he followed with a .325, 22 home run season as a full-time starter in 1988 (when he finished second in MVP voting to future Sox outfielder Jose Canseco); Greenwell was an All Star in 1988 and 1989. Although he continued to hit for average (a .303 lifetime batting average), his power gradually decreased (only 130 home runs over 12 seasons, despite his strong start), and the lack of production made it harder to overlook his weak defense.

Although he started out as a fan favorite and remained popular in Boston even as he declined as a player, Greenwell left under acrimonious circumstances, cleaning out his locker before the end of the 1996 season when he was told he would only be brought back as a reserve, not a starter. As an injury-plagued free agent with little power and poor defense, he drew little interest from other teams, and finished his career in Japan in 1997 with the Hanshin Tigers, hitting .231 in only 26 at-bats. Greenwell worked as a hitting coach in the Cincinnati organization for a while, but now owns a cattle ranch and "Mike Greenwell's Family Fun Park" in Florida.

Doug "Dude" Griffin—an excellent defensive (but light-hitting) second baseman with big sideburns, Griffin came to Boston from California after the 1970 season, along with pitcher Ken Tatum and outfielder Jarvis Tatum, for Tony Conigliaro. Ironically, the 1974 team lost Griffin when he was hit in the head by a pitch from Nolan Ryan. (Conigliaro had also been the victim of a famous beaning.) Griffin spent the last seven years of his career in Boston, never hitting higher than .266 in a season.

Lefty Grove—an utterly remarkable pitcher who some analysts consider the best ever. Like Pedro Martinez, Grove posted mind-boggling numbers in an offense-dominated era. He pitched from 1925–41 and had a career ERA of 3.06; during that time the average American League ERA ranged from 4.02 to 5.04. Grove won 300 games—with nine seasons of 20 or more wins—and led the league in ERA a record nine times. He only lost 141 games, and his .680 winning percentage is fourth all-time among retired pitchers. Early in his career, just to pass the time between starts, Grove was one of baseball's first "closers," saving 55 games. He had his greatest years with the Philadelphia Athletics, but had plenty left after joining Boston in 1934. In eight seasons with the Red Sox, Grove had an excellent 105–62 record and 3.34 ERA. He still ranks among the team's all-time leaders in several pitching categories.

Born Robert Moses Grove (the family name was originally Groves, and many writers used the pluralized version), Lefty joined the minor league Baltimore Orioles in 1920—six years after they sold a lefthander named Babe Ruth to the Red Sox. Grove was outstanding with Baltimore, winning 108 games in five years, but owner Jack Dunn refused to sell the overqualified pitcher to the majors until he was 25 years old. Connie Mack of the Athletics bought Grove for a then-record $100,600, but was mocked when the young pitcher struggled as a rookie. He led the American League in strikeouts (as he did in each of his first seven seasons), but went 10–12 with a 4.75 ERA. Grove also led the league in walks, and developed a reputation for immaturity. His temper tantrums angered teammates, especially after he blamed them for making errors—Lefty always made sure to use his right hand, though, when he punched walls or lockers.

Grove's control improved in 1926, and he won his first ERA title. He followed that with three 20-win seasons. But in 1930, Grove took his game to a new level, winning pitching's Triple Crown (a league-leading 28–5 record, 2.54 ERA, and 209 strikeouts—not to mention an American League–best 9 saves), and leading the A's to their second consecutive world championship. Grove was even better in 1931. He repeated his Triple Crown, going 31–4 with a 2.06 ERA and 175 strikeouts, while completing 27 of his 30 starts (and saving 5 games in 11 relief appearances). Only one pitcher has won 30 or more games since (Detroit's Denny McLain, 31–6 in 1968), and Grove was rewarded with the MVP Award. At one point in 1931, he tied an American League record by winning 16 games in a row—though he forever blamed Hall of Fame teammate Al Simmons for ending the streak. (Simmons was injured, and his replacement misjudged a fly ball, leading to a 1–0 loss.)

Grove won 25 and 24 games in 1932 and 1933, but the Great Depression put the Athletics in dire financial straits. Manager/owner Connie Mack had broken up a great team in 1915, and he was forced to do the same in the 1930s. New Red Sox owner Tom Yawkey, eager to spend big money on the biggest stars he could get, gladly gave Mack $125,000 for Grove. (Yawkey would later acquire another Hall of Famer from Mack: first baseman Jimmie Foxx.)

Red Sox fans were eager to see their new star, but there was one problem: Grove's workload, which typically included 10–15 emergency relief appearances, had taken a toll. With the Athletics, he had relied almost exclusively on his blazing fastball, but he was now 34 years old. Grove's velocity was down, and his arm was bothering him for the first time. Expectations were high, but Grove couldn't get on track in the spring of 1934. Doctors first thought his sore arm was caused by dental problems, but it still hurt even after three abscessed teeth were removed. The stubborn Grove decided to pitch through his pain, while teaching himself a now-needed curve ball, but he had a disastrous season (8–8, 6.50 in only 109 innings).

Thought to be washed up, Grove rebounded in 1935, winning 20 games and leading the league in ERA for the sixth time (2.70). He repeated the ERA title in

1936 (his 2.81 was over two runs better than the American League's 5.04) and won 17 games. Grove won 17 games again in 1937, the last season in which he pitched more than 200 innings. By this time, Grove almost never pitched in relief, and he needed more days off between starts. But while his workload was diminished, Grove was still a very valuable spot starter, winning 29 games (and his eighth and ninth ERA titles) in 1938–39. His performance declined as a 40-year-old (7–6, 3.99), leaving him 7 wins shy of 300.

A myth has persisted that Grove was horrendous in 1941, and that the Sox kept sending him out there, even if he was bombed, until he won 300. This isn't entirely true, as his 4.37 ERA was near the league average. Grove started the season well enough, going 6–2, but lost his next two starts. Finally, on July 25, 1941, Grove beat Cleveland for number 300, but it wasn't pretty: a complete-game 12-hitter in a 10–6 slugfest. His longtime teammate Jimmie Foxx had the game-winning triple. Though overshadowed by Ted Williams's quest for .400 and Joe DiMaggio's 56-game hitting streak, Grove's achievement was duly celebrated. He was the twelfth pitcher, and the first modern lefthander, to win 300 games. Uncharacteristically, he even threw a big champagne party for his teammates at a luxury hotel.

Unfortunately, that was Grove's final victory. He lost two more games before injuring his ribcage. Though urged to retire, Grove came back to pitch the season's final game (the second game of the famous doubleheader in which his good friend Ted Williams went 6-for-8 to finish at .406). He lost, though few noticed or cared, and finished the year at 7–7.

Grove contemplated coming back for another season, but Yawkey gently talked him out of it, since Grove had already achieved so much. He officially retired in December 1941, though he again thought about a comeback in 1942, when World War II thinned out the Red Sox pitching staff. Yawkey offered Grove a job as pitching coach, but he decided to return to his Maryland hometown, where had several business interests (and later coached youth baseball). Grove was elected to the Hall of Fame in 1947, and he died in 1975.

Mark Guthrie—inconsistent lefthanded relief pitcher who flopped with the Sox in 1999. Guthrie signed as a free agent after having a good year with the Dodgers (the year before that he'd been terrible, but the year before that he'd been outstanding), and celebrated Red Sox pitching coach Joe Kerrigan expected to make Guthrie even more successful by changing his pitching mechanics and adding more movement to his pitches. It didn't work, and Guthrie struggled through a terrible year before being sent to the Cubs with prospect Cole Liniak in return for injured former closer Rod Beck. Like many lefthanded specialists who don't face a lot of hitters, Guthrie's performances can vary wildly from year to year, since a few bad games can skew a season't worth of stats when a pitcher only faces one or two batters a game. Guthrie pitched for five teams in the next three years, finally having two good years in a row in 2002–03. But in 2004 he was pounded during spring training with the Pirates, abruptly ending his career.

Jackie Gutierrez—flashy, Colombian-born shortstop, best known for his habit of whistling loudly during games. Gutierrez joined the Red Sox in late 1983, and replaced Glenn Hoffman as the regular shortstop the following year. He had spectacular defensive tools, including speed and a fine arm, but often botched routine plays. The rookie hit .263 and stole 12 bases, but had only 17 extra base hits and 15 walks. Still, the Sox had high hopes for Gutierrez, and fans loved his enthusiasm. But while his defense was more consistent in 1985, his average sank to an unacceptable .218. Hoffman regained the starting job in the second half, and Gutierrez was traded to Baltimore after the season for reliever Sammy Stewart. The Orioles had Cal Ripken Jr. at shortstop, so Gutierrez barely played—and never learned how to hit. By 1988, his once-promising big league career was over.

John Halama—lefty swingman who signed a free agent contract with Boston in December 2004. The 33-year-old Halama, a Brooklyn native, had a great minor league career, including a combined 25–6 record in AAA in 1997–98. Halama made his big league debut for Houston in September 1998, but was sent to Seattle after the season as the player to be named later in a controversial Randy Johnson trade. (Houston also sent future stars Freddy Garcia and Carlos Guillen to the Mariners. Johnson was dominant for the Astros, but failed to deliver a championship and soon left as a free agent.) Halama had a solid rookie year for Seattle in 1999 (11–10, 4.22), but was mediocre for the next two seasons (24–16, 4.94). While Halama has been a nomad the last three years (pitching for Seattle, Oakland, and Tampa Bay), he has found a niche as a long reliever/spot starter (2.63 ERA in the bullpen, as opposed to 5.30 in the rotation). He's also been very effective against lefty batters. Halama doesn't throw hard or strike many batters out, but he has excellent control, and his versatility makes him helpful to a pitching staff.

Erik Hanson—a righthanded pitcher, Hanson started six games with Seattle in 1988, then went 27–14 over the next two years—including an 18–9 mark in 1990, establishing himself as one of the American League's best starters. Injuries and inconsistency plagued him after that season, and he lost 17 games for Seattle in 1992. After the 1993 season, he signed with Cincinnati, where despite continuing arm problems he pitched for the Reds until the 1994 strike hit.

When the labor dispute was settled in the spring of 1995 Hanson, along with many other players who had been without contracts, went through a free agent spring training session in Homestead, Florida. Dan Duquette signed Hanson out of the Homestead camp, and he went 15–5 for the 1995 American League East–champion Boston Red Sox. Noted for a biting curveball and a nasty forkball, chronic elbow problems made throwing the curve nearly impossible in Hanson's year with the Red Sox. He fought constant elbow problems to strike out 139 batters, and his record greatly benefited from excellent run support. (His gaudy won-loss record helped him to the All Star team.) In the playoffs, he started Game 2 at Jacobs Field in Cleveland, and pitched fairly well, giving up four runs over eight innings to the powerhouse Indians, who had managed to win 100 games even in the strike-shortened season, but the Red Sox were shut out by Cleveland righty Orel Hershiser and Hanson took the loss.

In the offseason, Hanson's salary demands were more than Boston was willing to pay, and he signed as a free agent with the Toronto Blue Jays. After a 1996 season in which he was basically a league average starter for the Blue Jays, injury problems struck again. He pitched only 15 innings in the 1997 season, and finished his career with 41 innings in 1998.

Carroll Hardy—a righthanded journeyman outfielder who began his major league baseball career in 1958 in Cleveland, Hardy was never a good hitter, though he did have a couple of memorable pinch-hitting at-bats. He had played defensive back for the San Francisco 49ers during the 1955 National Football League season before the Red Sox acquired him in 1960, and he became the answer to a couple of trivia questions. In September of 1960, Hardy became the only man to ever pinch-hit for Ted Williams, who had fouled a ball off his ankle and had to leave the game in the middle of his at bat. Hardy bunted into a double play. Six days later, Williams hit a home run in his last major league at-bat at Fenway. After Williams went out to left field in the top of the ninth, Hardy replaced him, and Williams left the field to a standing ovation. In his career, Hardy also pinch-hit for a young Roger Maris (hitting a three-run homer) and for Carl Yastrzemski. He also played for the Twins and Padres in an eight-season career that spanned 10 years.

Tommy Harper—speedy outfielder who holds the Red Sox record for steals in a season. Harper played three seasons for the Sox toward the end of his career. In 1973 he stole 54 bases while hitting .281 with 17 home runs and an above-average number of walks (league average was .259). He was an average hitter for most of his career, though (career batting average of .254), and slumped to .237 with 28 steals the following year.

After his playing career ended, Harper coached for the Red Sox (1980–84), but left the team bitterly after he spoke out against a team policy which allowed only white employees of the team to go to an Elk's Lodge near the team's spring training camp in Winter Haven, Florida. (The Equal Employment Opportunity Commission concluded that Harper was wrongfully dismissed by the Red Sox.) Harper went on to work for an auto body shop near Fenway Park, and also was a hitting coach for the Montreal Expos.

Harper returned as Red Sox first base coach for the 2000 season, and was a source of controversy when many players preferred to go to Harper for hitting advice rather than to batting coach Jim Rice. He remained as first base coach and unofficial batting coach through the 2002 season, outlasting both Rice and Rick Down as hitting coaches. More recently, he has been employed by the Red Sox as a player development consultant.

Ken Harrelson—Nicknamed "Hawk" by catcher Duke Sims, for his large, hooked nose (Harrelson even took to wearing "Hawk" on the back of his uniform, instead of the customary last name) the always-flamboyant Ken could easily have been baseball's poster child for 1960s fashion and style.

Harrelson began his big league career in 1965 with the A's. In 1967, Harrelson publicly called A's owner Charlie Finley a menace to baseball. This so enraged Finley that he released Harrelson, who was then courted by seven teams. The contract he eventually signed with Boston included a then-enormous $73,000 bonus. The Red Sox were in the thick of a pennant race, and Harrelson helped some, appearing in 23 games and hitting 4 homers, with 16 runs batted in. In 1968 Harrelson hit 35 home runs and drove in a league-leading 109 runs. He was extremely popular with the fans, and when he was traded to Cleveland in early 1969 fans picketed Fenway Park. (Harrelson was also unhappy with the trade, and threatened to retire instead of accepting it.)

George Will's book *Bunts* tells a possibly apocryphal story that on the day of a night game in which he didn't expect to play, Harrelson played 36 holes of golf. Finding himself in the lineup, Harrelson wore his golf gloves to protect his blistered hands when he came to bat. Thus the origin of batting gloves, a staple for today's players. (Ted Williams had worn batting gloves occasionally, though not during games.)

Harrelson broke his leg in 1970, missed most of that season, and remained unhappy playing in Cleveland. He quit baseball in 1971 to become a pro golfer, something he had threatened to do repeatedly. This attempt ultimately failed; since then "Hawk" has spent time as an outspoken (as always) but popular (as always) broadcaster for the Chicago White Sox, and even served a short, rocky stint as the White Sox general manager in the mid-1980s.

Greg Harris—ambidextrous pitcher who revived his career with the Red Sox in the early 1990s. Harris was a much-traveled player who'd been a failure as a starter but a very successful middle reliever throughout the 1980s. Boston picked the 33-year-old up on waivers in August 1989, after the Phillies (his sixth team) decided they didn't need him. Over the next five years Harris pitched well in a variety of roles for the Sox, playing the same kind of swingman role on the pitching staff that Bob Stanley had before him and Tim Wakefield would after him. He spent most of 1990–91 in the starting rotation, then as a reliever was among the league leaders in appearances in 1992–93. The workload seemed to catch up with him in 1984, when he pitched terribly at age 38, and the Red Sox released him. He went on to pitch for two more teams, including an excellent 1995 season, after which he retired.

Harris threw righthanded with the Red Sox, but was truly ambidextrous, and claimed he could pitch equally well from either side. He had a special six-fingered glove made that could be used with either hand, to allow him to switch hands during games. Red Sox GM Lou Gorman, however, refused to allow Harris to throw lefthanded during a game, feeling it would make a mockery of the game.

Mickey Harris—a righthanded pitcher who came up with Boston in 1940 and pitched poorly (and unluckily) in limited innings. In 1941, even though the Red Sox were the top scoring team in the league, he managed to go 8–14, despite having an ERA significantly better than league average. He was one of the first Red Sox players to be drafted into the military in World War II, and was gone from 1942–45. When he came back in 1946, he went 17–9 for the first Red Sox pennant winners in 28 years. He was the losing pitcher in two games of the 1946 World Series, though he didn't pitch particularly badly.

But that was the only season of his career in which he won as many as 10 games. He pitched extremely well in 1947, but arm injuries limited him to only 51⅓ innings pitched. In 1949 he was traded to Washington, and was eventually moved to the bullpen full time. In 1950 he led the American League in both saves (with 15) and games appeared in (with 53). He pitched two more years, for Washington and Cleveland, pitching entirely out of the bullpen, and not particularly well. His career ended with Cleveland in 1952.

Reggie Harris—injury-prone pitcher who has been in the major leagues off-and-on since 1990 with little to show for it, Harris was the Sox first round draft choice in 1987, but was lost to Oakland in the 1989 Rule 5 draft. This meant that the 21-year-old Harris had to be kept on Oakland's roster all season or returned to Boston, but because of injury he only got to pitch in 16 games (in which he was pretty good) before getting hurt again the next season. After he was removed from Oakland's major league roster, Seattle took him in the 1992 Rule 5 draft, though he didn't make the major league club. Harris didn't resurface in the majors until 1996, when he returned to the Red Sox as a 27-year-old, but only pitched in four games. He pitched 50 games for Philadelphia the next year, his only full season in the majors (he was also suspended for five games for intentionally hitting a batter that year), then ended up as a nomad, signing with eight major league teams in all, though he has only played in 86 major league games amid frequent injuries (including surgery on his arm and shoulder, and an inflamed elbow that cost him another season). After missing all of 2003 with a torn groin, Harris signed a minor league contract with the Sox, only to have his spring training derailed by a severe case of food poisoning. The 36-year-old Harris ended up pitching for the independent Newark Bears in 2004 before being picked up by the Astros late in the season (though he didn't appear in any games).

Bill Haselman—former backup catcher who's currently Boston's bullpen coach—and who has been mentioned as a future managerial candidate. Haselman played 13 seasons in the major leagues, and was a reliable backup for the Red Sox from 1995–97. The highlight of his career came on September 18, 1996, when Haselman caught Roger Clemens's 20-strikeout masterpiece against Detroit. Boston re-signed Haselman as a minor league free agent in 2003, but he hit only .225 at Pawtucket (though he was praised for his work with pitchers like Bronson Arroyo). Nevertheless, he was called up in September as an emergency catcher, and he went 0-for-3 in four appearances. After the season, he retired and became a scout—until May 2004, when Sox first base coach Lynn Jones nearly lost his eye in a freak household accident. Haselman spent two months filling in for Jones, and rejoined the Red Sox in September, when teams can add an extra coach. During the offseason, Boston decided not to bring back bullpen coach Euclides Rojas (who turned down an offer to be AA Portland's pitching coach), and the popular Haselman was tapped as his replacement.

Billy Hatcher—an outfielder with an inconsistent bat and a reputation as a base stealer with Cincinnati and Houston, he was traded to Boston in 1992, where his speed and hitting both deserted him. (He hit .238, and was thrown out on 6 of his 10 stolen base attempts.) His lone great moment in Boston came on a scintillating straight steal of home, one of the highlights of the dreary 1993 season. Hatcher is currently a coach for the Tampa Bay Devil Rays.

Scott Hatteberg—after short visits in 1995 and 1996, the lefthanded-hitting Hatteberg came to the Red Sox to stay in 1997. A top catching prospect valued for his defense, Hatteberg had not hit particularly well in the minors, and only made the team because he was out of options, and the Red Sox could not return him to the minors without the risk of losing him. To everyone's surprise, he hit well for a catcher (primarily as a platoon player), with decent power and the ability to walk frequently. Ironically, because he was a strong offensive catcher, many people assumed that Hatteberg's defense was poor and he was in the major leagues just for his bat—even though his defense got him to the majors.

Hatteberg started the 2001 season in an awful slump in limited playing time, and was publicly unhappy about his lack of at-bats. When platoon-partner Jason Varitek went down with a season-ending injury in June, Hatteberg became the full-time starter and his hitting improved, but he had difficulty throwing baserunners out and ended up splitting playing time with newly acquired Doug Mirabelli. With Hatteberg eligible for a big raise through salary arbitration, the Red Sox traded him to Colorado for Pokey Reese in the off-season, and in a bizarre sequence both players became free agents when their new teams failed to offer them contracts. Hatteberg eventually signed with Oakland, where he has spent the past three seasons at first base. Hatteberg was prominently featured in the best-selling book *Moneyball: The Art of Winning an Unfair Game* as the kind of player who has more value than it would seem based on his raw stats.

Dave "Hendu" Henderson—very few players made such an impact in a short period of time in a Sox uniform. He arrived in May 1986, coming (along with Spike Owen) from the Seattle Mariners in exchange for Mike Brown, Mike Trujillo, and Rey Quinones. Henderson played only 111 games for Boston (and 12 more in the postseason) before being traded to the San Francisco Giants early in the 1987 season. He had already become part of Boston history, even before joining the team, as he was the victim of three of Roger Clemens's 20 history-making strikeouts against the Mariners in April.

But his moment to shine came in Game 5 of the 1985 American League Championship Series in Anaheim against the California Angels. Though he managed only one hit in 9 at bats during the American League Championship Series, that hit was a doozy. In the ninth inning of Game 5, with the Red Sox one strike away from losing the game and the series, Hendu hit a two-out, two-run homer off Angels' relief ace Donnie Moore to vault the Sox into the lead. Then in the eleventh inning he drove in the winning run with a sacrifice fly. The home run in the ninth was probably one of the three most dramatic home runs in Red Sox history (along with Carbo's and Fisk's in Game 6 of the 1975 World Series). Henderson followed with another huge home run that was overshadowed: His homer in Game 6 of the World Series would have been the game winner if the Red Sox relievers hadn't failed to hold the lead.

In the late 1980s Hendu played several years as a key component of the powerhouse Oakland A's before finishing with a year in Kansas City. Tragically,

Donnie Moore went into a tailspin after giving up Henderson's home run. In July 1989, Moore shot his estranged wife and himself, in front of their 10-year-old son. Moore died, but his widow eventually recovered.

Rickey Henderson—probably the greatest leadoff hitter in major league history, but a player who has perpetually felt underappreciated, Henderson spent the 2002 season with the Red Sox on what the team felt was a farewell tour. Henderson, the all-time leader in runs, walks, and stolen bases was a 43-year-old platoon outfielder and pinch runner in his 72 games with the Red Sox, in which he hit .223 (though he walked enough to have a good on-base percentage). Nevertheless, he still felt he should be a starter, and spent much of the season complaining about his contract (and arguing with umpires when he was playing). Despite this, as a sure Hall of Famer he remained popular with his teammates, fans, and even the hypercritical Boston press. At the end of the season, the Red Sox awarded Henderson a new car in appreciation of his career achievements (which include over 3,000 hits, more than 2,000 walks, over 1,400 stolen bases, nearly 300 home runs, and 10 All Star appearances, as well as a lifetime .401 OBP). Henderson changed his mind about retiring, and when he couldn't find another major league job he signed with the independent Newark Bears in 2003, where he tore up the Atlantic League until several major league clubs took notice, and finished the season by hitting .208 in 30 games for the Los Angeles Dodgers, whose outfield had been riddled with injuries. In 2004 he returned to the Newark Bears and hit .281 with a .462 OBP, but major league lightning failed to strike again for the 45-year-old outfielder.

Butch Henry—talented but injury-prone lefthanded pitcher. Henry pitched for the Red Sox in 1997 when he posted a 7–3 record in 36 games. He returned in 1998, but was only able to pitch a total of nine innings, and left on poor terms when the Sox would not guarantee a contract for the following season (in which he was again injured, this time for Seattle). Henry pitched tantalizingly well for five different teams when healthy, but was never healthy enough to match the 165⅔ innings he threw as a rookie in 1992. He signed a minor league contract with the Red Sox as a 33-year-old in 2002, but was unable to make the team.

Dustin Hermanson—talented but inconsistent righthanded pitcher who had a single, lost season with the Red Sox. Hermanson, a star at Kent State University, had been one of the top young pitchers in baseball, both as a starter and reliever, but his performance had fallen off over several years, several trades, and several role changes. The Red Sox, looking for a durable, solid #2 or #3 starter, traded three minor leaguers (including promising first baseman Luis Garcia and former first round draft pick Rick Asadoorian) for the 29-year-old Hermanson during the 2001 Winter Meetings. But in his first start, on a cold rainy April night at Fenway, Hermanson slipped on the wet grass and pulled a hamstring. (The game was eventually canceled.) Hamstring injuries usually take a couple of weeks to heal. Hermanson's took nearly four months. He returned on July 20, and was immediately thrust into a tight relief situation in a game against the Yankees. He surrendered three runs in one inning, aiding in disheartening back-to-back 9–8 loses to New York. Hermanson spent the balance of the year pitching in relief, and not very well. After the season, the team declined to pick up his $7 million option and then declined to offer him arbitration, making him a free agent. Since leaving Boston he has regained his effectiveness somewhat, but still hasn't become the star it looked like he would develop into. He divided 2004 between the starting rotation and closing for the San Francisco Giants, and signed with the White Sox for 2005.

Joe Hesketh—lefthanded pitcher who joined Boston for the pennant drive in 1990 and stayed for four more mostly undistinguished years. He did pitch well in 1991, when he went 12–4, splitting time between starting and relief. He once got so distracted arguing with an umpire that he allowed a baserunner to steal second, third, and home.

Pinky Higgins—Higgins was a hard-hitting and steady-fielding third baseman, who in his 12-year career twice drove in 106 runs. Today he is better remembered for his unfortunate racial views than for his baseball skills. After starting his career with the A's (where he hit for the cycle in 1933), Higgins was traded to Boston for the 1937 season. In 1938 Higgins had 12 consecutive hits (the last 8 in a doubleheader) to break Tris Speaker's 18-year-old major league record of 11. In a 1940 World Series game he set a record by handling 10 chances at third base.

Higgins retired as a player after playing in all seven games of the 1946 World Series for the Red Sox. He returned to Boston to manage the Red Sox from 1955 to 1959, was kicked upstairs, then managed again from 1960 to 1962. His low-key manner and patience with young players made him popular with some, although his teams never finished higher than third place. Higgins also served for a while as the Red Sox Vice President and GM. He was fired as GM on September 16, 1965, the day Dave Morehead threw a no-hitter.

As a manager and administrator, Higgins was closely tied with the Red Sox reluctance to integrate. Author Al Hirshberg interviewed Higgins in the 1950s and claimed that Higgins said, "There'll be no niggers on this ballclub as long as I have anything to say about it." Earl Wilson, Boston's first black pitcher, was particularly vocal about Higgins's treatment of black players—and was traded after speaking out.

In 1969 Higgins was convicted of negligent homicide and jailed in Louisiana after killing someone in a DUI incident. He ran over four highway workers, one of whom died. Higgins served only two months of a four -year sentence. Two days after he got out of prison he died of a heart attack.

Shea Hillenbrand—few Red Sox players have inspired more vigorous debate among fans than this free-swinging third baseman, who played for Boston from 2001–03 (before being traded for another controversial figure, reliever Byung-Hyun Kim). His fast starts, high averages, and solid RBI totals garnered lots of praise, but also masked some glaring deficiencies, including low on-base percentages and inconsistent defense.

Hillenbrand's improbable rise to the major leagues began in his hometown of Mesa, Arizona, where he gained attention not as a baseball player, but as a soccer star. In 1993, he was named Arizona High School Soccer Player of the Year, but he decided to pursue a more lucrative career in baseball. After two years as a shortstop in Mesa Community College, the Red Sox drafted Hillenbrand. He hit .315 and .293 in his first two seasons, displaying an unusual ability to make hard contact with just about any pitch, no matter how far out of the strike zone it was. But by the same token, he hardly ever walked and didn't hit many homers. Defense was even more of a problem: he made 14 errors in 10 games at short-stop, and was shaky after switches to first and third base. In 1998, the Red Sox decided to try Hillenbrand at catcher, since he had a strong arm and good ath-leticism. Initially, the experiment was a success; he hit .349 with 19 homers (albeit in a low-A league he'd already played in), and showed potential behind the dish. However, a serious knee injury ended Hillenbrand's catching career in AA the next year. He returned to AA in 2000, playing both infield corners, and hit .323 (though he only had 11 home runs and 19 walks).

In 2001, after a red-hot spring training (.423, but no walks), Hillenbrand was handed the starting third base job by Jimy Williams. It was part of a chain reac-tion of surprising choices by Williams, who benched Jose Offerman and Dante Bichette, while moving Chris Stynes to second). Hillenbrand hit very well in April, but quickly declined (his great start kept his average at a respectable .263, but he hit only 12 homers, drew only 13 walks, and had an unacceptable .291 OBP). He also befriended a motley crew of characters: Johnny Pesky (who said Hillenbrand was like a son to him), Manny Ramirez (who showered the rookie with expensive gifts), and Carl Everett (who, for better or worse, took Hillenbrand under his wing).

Hillenbrand got off to another fantastic start in 2002, highlighted by a game-winning homer off Yankees closer Mariano Rivera on April 13, and a game-win-ning pinch-hit grand slam off the catwalk in Tampa Bay's Tropicana Field on May 4. New hitting coach Dwight Evans preached the virtues of working counts and being more patient, and Hillenbrand did improve in those areas early on, before reverting to his stubborn, free-swinging ways (and nearly driving Evans crazy). Fans voted him the starting third baseman for the American League in the All Star Game, sparking protests from many "statheads," who argued that Hillenbrand was vastly overrated. As with the previous season, he faded in the second half, though his final numbers were solid: .293, 18 homers, 83 RBI, 43 doubles (but only 25 walks and a .330 OBP).

When Theo Epstein took over as GM in 2003—and hired sabremetricians Bill James and Voros McCracken as advisors—it was widely assumed that the Red Sox would trade Hillenbrand, who didn't fit their philosophy. Once Boston signed Bill Mueller, the writing was on the wall for Hillenbrand. However, he was still on the roster on Opening Day, and played just about every day, rotating between third and first. As usual, he got off to a hot start, hitting .303 with 38 RBI in 49 games (but only seven walks and a .335 OBP). However, three circumstances made Hillenbrand expendable. Boston desperately needed to bolster its belea-guered relief corps (derided by the media as the "bullpen by committee experi-ment"). Mueller was having a career year and deserved to play third every day. And David Ortiz was wasting away on the bench. Hillenbrand didn't make matters easier by publicly mocking Epstein. In an unfortunate and inexcusable moment, Hillenbrand appeared on a local "morning zoo" radio show, called Epstein a homosexual epithet, and dared him to make a trade. On May 29, Epstein obliged, sending Hillenbrand to his hometown Arizona Diamondbacks for the talented but enigmatic Byung-Hyun Kim. Kim was two years younger than Hillenbrand, and while he had two infamous blown saves in the 2001 World Series, he had been a terrific closer—and would help stabilize Boston's bullpen in 2003 (before hurting his arm in the playoffs).

The Diamondbacks were one of baseball's worst teams during the last two years, but Hillenbrand was one of their few bright spots. His slashing swing didn't produce much power at Fenway Park, since the Green Monster knocked down many of his line drives. Arizona's park was much more to his liking, and Hillenbrand had 17 homers and 59 RBI in only 85 games with the Diamondbacks in 2003 (though his average slipped to .267—and his OBP was a terrible .302). Last season, he set career highs in batting average (.310) and OBP (.349), while hitting 15 home runs and driving in 80 runs. Due to Richie Sexson's injury, Hillenbrand spent most of the season at first base, a position many people feel is his best (though his productivity is below-average at that spot). He made a nice play to help preserve Randy Johnson's perfect game against the Braves on May 18, 2004 (the third no-hitter he's been a part of, having started at third base for Derek Lowe's gem in 2002, and for Hideo Nomo's a year earlier).

Hillenbrand was traded to Toronto in January 2005. His flaws have been well-publicized by sabremetricians, and even his supporters are often frustrated by his refusal or inability to be more patient at the plate. Then again, it's not easy to find talent at third base these days, so a player like Hillenbrand—who provides average production for the position, with adequate defense—will always find work.

Butch Hobson—former Alabama quarterback who was a popular, gritty third baseman for the Red Sox during the late seventies. One of the reasons that the Red Sox lineup looked so strong during the 1978 season was that Clell Lavern "Butch" Hobson, hitting ninth, had hit 30 home runs in 1977. He was never good, however, at actually getting on base, finishing his career in 1982 with a terrible .297 on-base percentage. He was a fan favorite for the way he played the game (with reckless abandon), several times falling down dugout steps to go after foul popups. This led to severe problems during the 1978 meltdown, however, as he played the season in incredible pain, constantly readjusting loose bone chips in his throwing elbow. During that 1978 season he hit only 17 home runs and committed an astounding 43 errors at third base—mostly on poor throws from his unresponsive elbow—before he was finally benched in late September.

Hobson later managed the team for three unsuccessful years, amassing a 207–232 record. Later, he was serving as the manager of the Phillies AAA team, the Scranton Wilkes-Barre Red Barons, when he received a package from someone in his hometown. The police arrested him that night for cocaine possession. He claimed that he must have received the package by mistake, and many fans were extremely surprised, but the word from the beat writers who covered the team was that no one was surprised by the arrest. The Red Sox connection to the cocaine story? When he received the package and was arrested his team was play-ing in Pawtucket against the Pawtucket Red Sox. Hobson has managed the Nashua Pride, an independent team in New Hampshire, since December 1999. As of 2005, Hobson will partly own the team, which last year fielded former Red Sox players Cole Liniak and Dante Bichette.

Glenn Hoffman—strong-armed, weak-hitting infielder who replaced Rick Burleson as the Red Sox starting shortstop in the early 1980s. A highly touted minor league prospect, Hoffman made the team as a backup infielder in 1980, and got significant playing time at third base because of Butch Hobson's injuries and ineffectiveness. Hoffman fielded well and hit an encouraging .285, though he lacked power. After Burleson and Hobson were traded for third baseman Carney Lansford, Hoffman moved back to his natural shortstop spot. But while Hoffman was a very capable fielder, his bat regressed (.231 and .209 in 1981–82). By 1984 Hoffman lost his starting job to Jackie Gutierrez, but regained it the following year, when he hit a surprising .276, with more power than usual—only to lose most of the 1986 season to an irregular heartbeat.

Hoffman was traded to the Dodgers early the next year, though he returned to Boston's AAA team in Pawtucket in 1988, before finished his major league career as a utility infielder with the California Angels. He became a player-coach for the Dodgers' AAA team in Albuquerque in 1990, and his playing career ended when he was hired to manage Great Falls, the Dodgers' Rookie League team. Hoffman managed Dodgers affiliates for four of the next eight seasons and was named interim manager of the major league team in June 1998 when Bill Russell was fired. (He managed 10 games against his younger brother Trevor, a star reliever on the San Diego Padres.) More recently, Hoffman has served as third base coach for the Dodgers; he interviewed for the Red Sox manager's posi-tion prior to the 2004 season.

Harry Hooper—part of an extraordinary defensive outfield on the great Sox teams of the 1910s (along with Duffy Lewis and Tris Speaker), Hooper was known for his excellent throwing arm. Hooper would later draw comparisons to another outstanding Sox right fielder, Dwight Evans, who also had a great arm and was a similar offensive player in many ways. Hooper was one of the Sox few good hitters on the pitching-dominated teams of the teens. (He played for the Red Sox from 1909 to 1920). Although he was inconsistent from year to year, he hit .281 over a 17-year career with a little power (usually 10–15 triples and 3–4 home runs a year, pretty good in the dead ball era when the league leader in homers usually hit 9 or 10 and the league batting average was in the .240s), drew a lot of walks, seldom struck out, and was a prolific base stealer. Hooper is still the Red Sox career leader with 300 stolen bases and 130 triples, and is among the leaders in walks and runs. He played for four Red Sox World Series-winning teams (in 1912, 1915, 1916, and 1918), and is remembered for his remarkable running barehanded catch in the eighth game of the 1912 Series.

Hooper was selected to the Hall of Fame in 1971, but there was some criti-cism of his selection, since he was seen as a very good—but not necessarily great—player. This perception may come from years playing in the shadow of center fielder and fellow Hall of Famer Tris Speaker, a career .344 hitter who outshone Hooper in nearly every facet of the game. After his career ended, Hooper coached at Princeton University, and served as a postmaster, but he died in poverty in 1974.

Sam Horn—slugging first baseman who was dumped in the Red Sox house-cleaning of the late 1980s. Horn was slow and a poor fielder, but he had a ton of power. When he was called up as a 23-year-old in 1987, he hit 14 home runs in only 158 at bats (a pace of about 50 for a full season) and looked like the next great Boston power hitter. He walked frequently, but he also struck out at an astonishing pace—almost a third of hit plate appearances ended in strikeouts. He hit poorly in very brief appearances over the next two years, and was released without ever being given a chance to earn more playing time. Horn played well as a part-timer for two seasons in Baltimore, and then appeared sporadically in the major leagues until 1995.

His name has since been immortalized to serious Red Sox fans through the Sons of Sam Horn (SOSH) website and online forum (www.sonsofsamhorn.com); the discussions in the forum were credited by Curt Schilling (who took part in some SOSH discussions) as a factor in convincing him to come to Boston in 2004. The name Sons of Sam Horn is both a play on words (The Son of Sam serial killer, and also Daughters of the American Revolution-style organizational names) and an ironic homage to a cult player. Horn himself had no knowledge of or affilia-tion with the site at first. When he first learned about it, he was reportedly wary (and supposedly considered legal action). But now he's become something of an ambassador to SOSH, and has done some charity events with them. On the *Faith Rewarded* DVD, Horn wears a SOSH T-shirt. Horn currently works for NESN, doing pre- and postgame shows.

Dwayne Hosey—a 28-year-old career minor leaguer (he'd missed his big break with Kansas City because of the 1994 strike), the speedy Hosey hit .338 with 12 extra base hits and 3 steals late in 1995, although his defense in center field was adventurous. He was given a shot as the starting center fielder the next year, but when he failed to hit in the first 28 games of the 1996 season, Sox management gave up on him and gave the job back to incumbent center fielder Lee Tinsley and Milt Cuyler. (Hosey did hit two home runs in the same inning that August while hitting .297 for the Sox AAA team in Pawtucket.) Curiously, all three center field-ers who played regularly for the Sox that year were switch hitters. A former gang member who became a devoutly born-again Christian without losing any of his boisterousness, Hosey was eventually sold to the Yakult Swallows in the Japanese League, where he hit 38 home runs in a tempestuous 1997 season. (The Japanese press didn't know what to make of his ebullient behavior, or his unconventional full-speed ahead playing style, and alternated between admiring him and loathing him.) Hosey played a second year in Japan before returning to North American, where he spent several more years in the minors before retiring as a player. He was hitting coach for Anaheim's Cedar Rapids minor league team in 2001 before making a comeback with the independent Bridgeport Bluefish in 2002. Hosey now works for the Nebraska-based Strike Zone Academy.

Tom House—a lefty reliever, House's biggest moment in baseball was as a footnote. On April 8, 1975 he was in the bullpen in Atlanta and caught Hank Aaron's 715th home run. This home run set a new career home run record. House was unimpressive in 1976 and part of 1977 with the Red Sox, winning two games and losing three.

Elston Howard—a righthanded-hitting catcher, Howard spent the vast majority of his 13-year career with the Yankees, making the All Star team nine times and winning the American League MVP award in 1963. He was still playing for the Yankees when the 1967 season started and broke up Billy Rohr's no-hit bid in Yankee Stadium in April. Traded to the Sox during that season, he was a backup on the 1967 pennant winners. He finished out his career by playing in 71 games for the Sox in 1968.

Bobby Howry—hard-throwing reliever who joined Boston's bullpen at the 2002 trading deadline, but was hampered by injuries. Howry built a reputation as a very good relief pitcher with the White Sox from 1998–2002. He served as their closer in 1999, saving 28 games, but lost the job to current Boston star Keith Foulke the following season. On July 31, 2002, Boston sent two minor leaguers to Chicago for Howry. (One of the prospects, reliever Frank Francisco, is now on the Texas Rangers—and gained notoriety for throwing a chair at a fan during an altercation in Oakland last year.) While Howry didn't do much during the 2002 stretch run (1–3, 5.00 in 20 games), Boston hoped he'd play a key role in their "bullpen by committee" in 2003. But after only four games—and a gruesome 12.46 ERA—he was optioned to Pawtucket to work on his mechanics. He pitched well in AAA, but his season ended prematurely after he underwent elbow surgery. Howry signed with Cleveland in December 2003, and pitched well for the Indians in 2004 (4–2, 2.74 in 37 appearances). He re-signed with them for the 2005 season.

Waite Hoyt—Hall of Fame pitcher, best known as the ace of the powerful 1927 Yankees, who pitched for the Red Sox in 1919 and 1920. The Brooklyn-born Hoyt was signed by New York Giants manager John McGraw as a 15-year-old, but pitched only one game for the Giants before being sent to Boston. Still a teenager, Hoyt went 4–6 as a spot starter with the Sox in 1919, and was 6–6 in the same role the following year. After the 1920 season, he and catcher Wally Schang were traded to the Yankees for second baseman Del Pratt. Along with ex-Sox like Babe Ruth and Herb Pennock, Hoyt helped the Yankees begin their long string of championships. He won 237 games during his 21-year career, and was elected to the Hall of Fame by the Veterans Committee in 1969. Hoyt is often cited as one of the least-deserving Hall of Famers, but his 45 wins in 1927–28, along with his engaging personality, inflated his reputation. A gifted storyteller and part-time vaudeville singer, Hoyt was one of the first ex-jocks to go into broadcasting, doing Cincinnati games on the radio for 24 years.

Long Tom Hughes—a righthanded pitcher, Hughes spent 1½ of his 13 seasons with the Red Sox. At the age of 24, Hughes went 20–7 for the 1903 Red Sox team that won the first World Series. He only threw two innings in the World Series, giving up two runs and taking the loss in Game 3. He was called "Long Tom" because of his height.

Tex Hughson—one of a number of good pitchers for the Red Sox in the 1940s whose career ended prematurely due to arm trouble. Debuting in 1941, Hughson led the league in wins (22) and innings (281) the next year at age 26. For this, Hughson earned his first trip to the All Star Game, an honor he earned each of the next three years. Over this three -year period, Hughson pitched 750 innings, with ERAs of 2.59, 2.64, and 2.26. Missing the next season because of World War II, Hughson did not pitch again until 1946, when he won 20 games (fifth in the league) while pitching 278 innings (third in the league) with a 2.75 ERA. With Hughson and Boo Ferriss (25 wins) leading the staff, the Red Sox won the American League pennant, but lost to the Cardinals in the World Series.

Unfortunately, what looked like a potential juggernaut was damaged when both Hughson and Ferriss developed arm trouble. Hughson declined to a 3.33 ERA in 189 innings in 1947, and then only threw 96 more innings over the next two years before retiring at age 33. Those fans who believe that managers should be wary of having their pitchers throw too many innings point to Hughson to support their argument. Red Sox fans, meanwhile, can only wonder at what Red Sox history might have been had the foursome of Hughson, Ferriss, Ellis Kinder, and Mel Parnell been able to stay healthy throughout the latter half of the 1940s and early 1950s. Certainly, it seems likely that the Sox would at least have won pennants in 1948 and 1949 (in both seasons they finished second by a single game).

Bruce Hurst—one of a group of young starting pitchers the Red Sox developed in the early 1980s, along with John Tudor, Bob Ojeda, Al Nipper, Oil Can Boyd, and Roger Clemens. He debuted in 1980, but did not make the majors full-time until 1982. Although he was considered a better prospect than Boyd or Ojeda (who came up about the same time), Hurst struggled badly at first. (He was 3–7 in 1982 with a 5.77 ERA.) But Hurst gradually blossomed into a good pitcher (if not a star), and started 30 or more games in 8 of the next 9 seasons. In 1986 (when Hurst started only 25 games because of injury) he went 13–8 with a 2.99 ERA and was a huge factor in helping the Sox get to the World Series. Hurst pitched well in the Series as well, starting Game 1 against the Mets (staff ace Roger Clemens had started Game 7 of the American League Championship Series against the Angels and was unavailable) and winning the game 1–0 for the Sox in the Mets' home stadium.

Hurst continued to pitch well for the Sox for the next two years, and had his finest year (18–6) in 1988, when the Sox once again made the playoffs. However, Hurst, a devoutly religious man, was deeply offended by a number of sordid scandals involving Red Sox players (including the very public allegations made by Wade Boggs's mistress, Margo Adams) and left the team as a free agent following the season.

Adam Hyzdu—the ultimate "AAAA player," a journeyman outfielder who had three separate stints in the Red Sox organization before finally played in the majors for them last September. Hyzdu, the Giants' first round pick in 1990, has spent most of his 15-year pro career in the minors, where he's slugged 239 homers. He joined the Red Sox system in 1996 and had his best season, hitting .337 with 25 homers for AA Trenton. Hyzdu had another fine year in 1997, batting .276 with 23 home runs for Pawtucket, but left the organization as a minor league free agent afterward. He returned to Pawtucket briefly in 1999, but spent 2000–03 in the Pirates' system, shuttling back and forth between the minors and majors. Overall, he hit only .218 in 173 games with Pittsburgh, though he had 18 homers and played solid defense. Hyzdu reunited with the Red Sox yet again in 2004, nearly made the team in spring training, and hit .301 with 29 home runs in Pawtucket. Rewarding both his persistence and productivity, Boston recalled Hyzdu in September, and he went 3-for-10 with two doubles and a monstrous home run against Tampa Bay. He's still on the 40-man roster, but at age 33, Hyzdu is primarily an insurance policy—a player the Red Sox can stash at Pawtucket, but would call up if a big league outfielder goes on the disabled list.

Reggie Jefferson—lefthanded-hitting first baseman who spent five seasons with the Red Sox. Jefferson spent time with Cincinnati, Cleveland, and Seattle before signing with the Red Sox prior to the 1995 season. Never a good defender, he spent most of his time in Boston as a platoon DH. He hit righthanded pitching well, but was never able to hit lefties. (Jefferson actually started his major league career as a switch hitter, but eventually abandoned righthanded hitting entirely.) During the later parts of the 1997 season he complained in the media that he wasn't going to get a chance to win the batting title, even though he was leading the league in hitting, because he wasn't getting enough at-bats. That changed after his platoon partner Mike Stanley was traded to the Yankees, but Jefferson slumped badly down the stretch, and finished up eighth in the league in batting. After that season, his playing time was limited by recurring back problems.

Jefferson was left off of the postseason roster in 1999 (with third baseman John Valentin questionable because of injury, the Sox opted to carry a second third baseman instead of Jefferson), and after complaining loudly in the press, he left the team. He might have been added prior to the Yankees series had that not happened, and he might have made a difference. Jefferson played for a year in Japan, then retired when he failed to make the Pittsburgh Pirates' major league roster in 2001.

Ferguson Jenkins—Hall of Fame pitcher who won 284 games in 19 major league seasons, but only 22 in his two years with the Red Sox. Fergie Jenkins became a star with the Cubs, winning 20 or more games every season from 1967–72. In 1971 he won the National League Cy Young Award, with a 24–13 record and a 2.77 ERA (excellent for a pitcher in Wrigley Field, a hitter's park). He was traded to Texas in 1974 and promptly won a career-high 25 games. After a disappointing 17–18 season in 1975, Jenkins was traded to Boston for promising outfielder Juan Beniquez.

He appeared to be a perfect addition to a team that nearly won the World Series, yet needed another starter. But Jenkins, who had pitched over 300 innings five times in his career, wasn't as durable or dominating with Boston. He pitched

209 innings in 1976, going a mediocre 12–11 though his ERA was a very solid 3.27. In 1977 Jenkins was 10–10 with a 3.68 ERA (good in a particularly high-offense season). But he only pitched 193 innings and only struck out 105 hitters (he had seven prior 200-strikeout seasons). More importantly, he never got along with Red Sox manager Don Zimmer, a conservative, old-school, often uptight man. Jenkins was a member of The Loyal Order of Buffalo Heads, a faction of anti-Zimmer players led by Bill Lee, Bernie Carbo, Jim Willoughby, and Rick Wise. The name was initiated by Jenkins, who said that the buffalo was the dumbest animal, and thus reminded him of Zimmer. The manager barely pitched Jenkins down the stretch in 1977, despite the close pennant race, and the veteran was sent back to Texas after the season for pitcher John Poloni, who never appeared in a game with Boston. Jenkins, who would surely have come in handy for the Red Sox in 1978, spent the season with the Rangers, going 18–8 with a 3.04 ERA—exactly the kind of year he usually had before joining Boston.

In 1980, while still with Texas, Jenkins was arrested for drug possession at a Canadian airport. He denied the charges, saying he was set up, and the judge dismissed the case citing the pitcher's strong record of community service and status as a Canadian sports hero (he was born in Chatham, Ontario, and was arguably the best Canadian-born player in baseball history). Jenkins rejoined the Cubs for his final two seasons, and retired in 1983 as the only pitcher ever to have over 3000 strikeouts, yet under 1000 walks.

In 1991, he became the first (and so far, only) Canadian to make the Hall of Fame. He was first eligible in 1989, but suffered because Yaz, Johnny Bench, and Gaylord Perry were also on the ballot for the first time. Also, since he was so consistent, yet never played for a pennant-winner, Jenkins was underrated for most of his career—especially compared to peers like Bob Gibson, Tom Seaver, and Steve Carlton.

Shortly after his making the Hall of Fame, Jenkins's wife died of injuries from a car accident. Two years later, his live-in girlfriend killed herself and Jenkins's young daughter at their ranch. A deeply religious man, Jenkins has done his best to persevere after these tragedies. He has since remarried, and has returned to baseball as a coach and minor league instructor.

Jackie Jensen—a righthanded hitter who excelled at both football and baseball at the University of California-Berkeley. A gifted athlete with numerous talents, the "Golden Boy" earned several honors in both sports at Berkeley. As a freshman fullback he played in the East-West Shrine All Star game, and he went to the Rose Bowl as a junior, finishing fourth in voting for the Heisman trophy that year.

Jensen's baseball talents were diverse as well. He excelled as both a hitter and a pitcher for the Golden Bears, and even played against Yale first baseman and future US president George Bush in the first NCAA World Series. He is in fact the only man in history ever to play in an East-West football game, a Rose Bowl, a baseball All Star game, and a major league World Series.

In 1949 Jensen decided to forgo his senior year to play professional baseball. He made his major league debut with the New York Yankees the following year, on the brink of Joe DiMaggio's retirement. He hit .249 in parts of three seasons with New York (including a promising .298 with 8 homers in limited action in 1951) before the Yanks sent Jensen to the Washington Senators, opting to go with future legend Mickey Mantle instead.

In Washington Jensen enjoyed playing time and production, averaging 82 RBI in his two seasons there. The Red Sox were impressed by his play and traded Marty McDermott and Tom Umphlett to get him before the 1954 season. Jensen's offensive numbers exploded with the Sox, as he launched over 20 homers in each of his first six seasons in Boston (including 35 in 1958), and topped 100 RBI five times. More impressively, his contact hitting was terrific for a power hitter. In an 11-year career, Jensen's season high for strikeouts was just 69, and he walked frequently. Despite this ability he hit over .300 just once, in 1956. He was a player of many tools, including speed (he reached double digits in stolen bases seven times, including a league-leading 22 in 1954 at a time when stolen bases were uncommon). His 35 homers, along with a .286 average and 122 RBI, earned Jensen American League Most Valuable Player honors in 1958. The following year he won his only Gold Glove award.

As Jensen flourished through the 1950s, so did postwar baseball. The game expanded to the West, eventually taking teams such as the Dodgers and Giants to California. With this expansion came the more frequent use of airplanes to transport teams around the country. This presented an emotional problem for Jensen, who could not overcome his fear of flying. Based on this fear, Jensen surprised the baseball world by choosing to retire at age 32, despite a successful 1959 season (he'd led the league in RBI for the second straight year). He attempted a brief comeback with the Red Sox in 1961 but retired again after a disappointing performance. He finished his short career with a .279 average and 199 home runs.

"Indian Bob" Johnson—one of the most underrated players in major league history, Johnson never seemed to be on the right team at the right time. In his 13-year career, Johnson made eight All Star teams and drove in 100 or more runs eight times, while playing consistently good defense in left field. But despite his fine stats and colorful (if politically incorrect) nickname, Johnson is largely forgotten today.

Johnson, a half-Cherokee, joined the Philadelphia Athletics in 1933, replacing Hall of Famer Al Simmons. Connie Mack would soon dump three more all-time greats (Lefty Grove, Mickey Cochrane, and Jimmie Foxx), and the A's began a 4-decade tailspin. But Johnson continued to play extremely well, hitting around .300 with 25–30 homers and 85–90 walks a season. He was traded to the Washington Senators in 1943 for Bobby Estalella (the grandfather of the current catcher), but had a subpar season.

Tom Yawkey bought Johnson from Washington in 1944, and Indian Bob filled in ably for Ted Williams, who was in the military. Johnson led the American League with a .431 on-base percentage and batted .324, with 40 doubles, 17 homers, and 106 RBI. To be fair, the quality of baseball during World War II was weak, as stars like Williams were in the service. But Johnson was still one of the league's best hitters, and he started in the All Star game. Johnson didn't do as well in 1945, when he slipped to .280, with only 12 homers, though he made the All Star team again. After the season, the 39-year-old Johnson retired. As usual, his timing was horrible. Just as he joined the A's too late to play on their great teams, he left the Red Sox too soon to enjoy their great 1946 season. Several statisticians have lobbied for Johnson's inclusion in the Hall of Fame, and he was clearly better than several outfielders who are in in the Hall. However, he'll likely remain on "best players not in the Hall" lists.

Johnson's brother Roy, also a fine hitter, played outfield for the Red Sox from 1932–35.

Earl Johnson—a lefthanded pitcher who went 40–32 with Boston over the course of seven seasons, from 1940–50. Johnson was one of the first Red Sox players lost to military service (in the fall of 1941), and when he came back, he was the war hero in the Boston clubhouse. In the Battle of the Bulge, his actions earned both Bronze and Silver Stars, and at one point he received a battlefield promotion to lieutenant.

Over three-quarters of his appearances were out of the bullpen. He was the winning pitcher, in relief, of Game 1 of the 1946 World Series. Johnson had his best season in 1947, throwing 142⅓ strong innings and winning 12 games. In 1951, he finished his career pitching 5⅔ weak innings for Detroit.

Sad Sam Jones—righthanded pitcher who is a footnote to the worst moment in Red Sox history. In 1921, Jones was the last in a long line of players sold to the Yankees. In 1918, Jones went 16–5 with a 2.25 ERA for the World Champion Red Sox. He followed that up in 1919 by going 12–20, and 13–16 for the now-Ruth-less Sox in 1920. In 1921 he went 23–16 before being sold to the Yankees. Jones pitched 14 more seasons in the majors, but his best was in a Sox uniform.

Todd Jones—Much-traveled reliever who spent the second half of 2003 with the Red Sox. Jones has saved 186 games in 12 major league seasons, playing for seven different teams. He had his biggest success as Detroit's closer from 1997–2001. In 2000, Jones and Boston's Derek Lowe tied for the AL lead with 42 saves apiece. However, by July 2003 Jones seemed to be washed up. He was 35 years old, and Colorado had just released him (thanks to a terrible 8.24 ERA pitching in deadly-to-pitchers Coors Field). But Boston needed long relief help, so they decided to give Jones a chance. He earned wins in two of his first four appearances for Boston, but finished the season poorly, and only appeared in one postseason game. Jones pitched fairly well for the Reds and Phillies in 2004 (career-high 11 wins), and signed a free agent contract with Florida after the season.

Eddie Joost—played but one season for the Red Sox, the rather forgettable 1955 season in which, at the age of 39, he played in 55 games, batting a lowly .193. As had been a trademark throughout his 17-year career, his good batting eye allowed him to draw walks even when his ability to hit the ball was in question. Thus, though he hit only .193, he got on base at a .299 clip (which is not actually all that good in and of itself, but is amazing considering the man could not really hit the ball anymore). Thus the man who walked over 100 times in six consecutive seasons in the heart of his career, despite never hitting well enough to really warrant pitchers' actually pitching around him, left the game the same way he entered it—walking.

Ed Jurak—a utility infielder who spent four years with the Red Sox from 1982 to 1985. His big moment of glory came when he caught, in his glove, a rat which was running around on the field during a game at Fenway.

Gabe Kapler—more famous for his sculpted physique than for his baseball skills, Kapler was a highly regarded prospect and looks like a superstar, but became a backup outfielder on the 2003–04 Red Sox. Kapler was the prototypical five-tool player when he came up with the Tigers in 1998, and hit 18 home runs in his first full season. He was a key player in the Tigers' trade for Rangers' star outfielder Juan Gonzalez after that season, and when he hit .302 with 14 home runs the next year for the Texas, it seemed like he had arrived as a hitting star. As it turned out, those would be his high-water marks for average and home runs, and Kapler was traded first to Colorado and then to Boston, each team hoping that his output would match his sculpted physical appearance.

While Kapler preferred a starting role, he settled comfortably into a position as the fourth outfielder for a playoff contending Red Sox team, playing well defensively at all three outfield positions, hitting for a decent average (though surprisingly little power), and providing veteran depth in the outfield that was crucial when Trot Nixon went down for most of the 2004 season. Interestingly, with Kapler and Kevin Youkilis both on the roster, the Red Sox were the only team to have two Jewish players in 2004. After winning the World Series with the Red Sox, Kapler signed with Japan's Yomiuri Giants, where he could return to a full-time role as a starting center fielder.

George Kell—Hall of Fame third baseman who played in 15 major league seasons, all in the American League. Kell, a contact hitter with consistently low strikeout numbers (his high total for a full season was 37), spent the prime of his career with the Detroit Tigers before joining the Red Sox in 1952. In parts of three seasons with the Sox he hit .305, and his season high of 12 home runs came in 1953. He was traded to the White Sox in 1954. He retired in 1957 with a .306 career average and 10 All Star appearances, and was inducted into the Hall by the Veterans Committee in 1983. On December 31, 2004, the 82-year-old Kell miraculously survived a car accident with a tractor trailer, escaping with a broken arm and leg.

Dana Kiecker—an ex-UPS driver who came out of nowhere to win a spot as a 29-year-old rookie and folk hero on the 1990 Red Sox. He pitched reasonably well for a thin pitching staff, and was a surprise starter in the playoffs against Oakland (where he pitched well in a losing cause). He didn't have overpowering stuff, and the next year he wasn't fooling anybody anymore. Kiecker's ERA nearly doubled in 1991, and he was out of baseball at age 30.

Byung-Hyun Kim—righthanded sidearm/submarine pitcher from Kwangsan-Ku Songjunsdon, Korea who was traded to the Red Sox by the Arizona Diamondbacks during the 2003 season for infielder Shea Hillenbrand. Kim came to the Red Sox as a 24-year-old with tremendous upside potential and major league experience as both a starter and a reliever. He'd made the Diamondbacks as a 20-year-old in 1999, become the full-time closer two years later, and been an All Star in 2002, when he saved 36 games with a 2.04 ERA. Kim's sidearm and underhanded deliveries to the plate overpowered hitters with fastballs, sliders, and curves that defied the laws of physics. His strikeout totals with the Diamondbacks (380 strikeouts in 323 innings) earned the 5-foot-11 righthander the nickname "The Little Unit," in reference to his 6-foot-10 teammate and fellow strikeout king, "The Big Unit," Randy Johnson. His onetime Arizona teammate Matt Williams once commented on his assortment of gravity-defying sliders, "He's got one that drops and one that rises. He's amphibious." But Kim was dogged by questions about his ability to pitch under pressure, after consecutive blown saves against the Yankees in Games 4 and 5 of the 2001 World Series, and in 2003 he lost his closer's job in Arizona to future Sox reliever Matt Mantei, and was converted to a starter.

Boston traded for Kim as a starter and he pitched well in that role (2–1, 3.10 in five starts), before the Red Sox imploding bullpen forced them to return Kim to the closer's role. He did stabilize the bullpen and pitched very well at times (16 saves, 3.22 ERA), but had a terrible August and was erratic enough that he didn't induce confidence even when he pitched well. Kim blew a save in Game 1 of the 2003 American League Division Series versus the Oakland A's, which inevitably brought reminders of 2001, and he did not react well to those reminders, making an obscene gesture to Boston fans who booed him during pregame introductions. He was then left off the roster of the American League Championship Series with the Yankees.

Kim was signed to a two-year, $10 million contract by Boston after the 2003 season with the idea that he would come back as a starter. The team hoped he would outgrow his reputation as an aloof, boyish, and shy player (with an amazing ability to sleep often and anywhere, such as naps in the laundry room of the clubhouse) but it wasn't an encouraging sign when that November Kim was questioned by Korean police about allegations that he assaulted a South Korean newspaper photographer who refused to stop taking his picture. Kim opened the 2004 season as the team's fifth starter before hip and back injuries—along with a puzzling loss of pitching velocity—sent him to the disabled list and then to Pawtucket. The team was concerned that Kim's intense workouts were part of the problem, and after what seemed to be a breakdown in communication, Kim was granted a leave of absence from the minor league team to return to Korea to see a specialist, with no timetable to return. He was recalled by Boston in September but pitched ineffectively, and was not on the Boston roster for the 2004 playoffs or World Series.

Sun-Woo "Sunny" Kim—a hard-throwing righty pitcher from Korea who was once regarded as Boston's most talented Asian prospect, Kim's major league performances never matched his great "stuff." Kim pitched on the Korean Olympic Team in 1996, and was MVP of the 1995 World Baseball Championships, which were played in Fenway Park. Reportedly, Kim liked the park so much that he not only signed with Boston, but also insisted upon an unofficial no-trade clause. He had a 31–23 record in his first three pro seasons (1998–2000), with excellent strikeout-to-walk ratios, but his ERAs went from bad to worse (4.82, 4.89, 6.03). Kim impressed manager Jimy Williams as a reliever in spring training 2001, and nearly made the Opening Day roster. Despite a 5.36 ERA at Pawtucket, Kim was recalled to the majors when injuries hit the staff. He got bombed in two starts and pitched mainly as a reliever, going 0–2 with a 5.83 ERA, while allowing a staggering 75 baserunners in 42 innings. Kim made the team as a reliever in 2002, and had a 7.45 ERA on July 30 when he was traded to the Expos (along with Seung Song) for Cliff Floyd. Kim is still with the Expos, where he went 4–6 in 43 games during the 2004 season.

Ellis Kinder—one of many young men whose careers were abbreviated because of contributions to his country during World War II, Ellis Kinder did not begin his major league career in baseball until 1946, by which time he was already 31. Kinder began his career with the St Louis Browns, for whom he toiled for two seasons before being acquired by the Red Sox in a trade.

Kinder's arrival, along with the emergence of young lefthander Mel Parnell, helped spark the dormant Red Sox who, after winning the pennant in 1946, languished at a distant third in 1947. The 1948 team finished tied for first with the Cleveland Indians. To start the all-important one-game playoff to determine the pennant, manager Joe McCarthy passed over Kinder and Parnell, as well as Joe Dobson (who led the team in innings pitched) and Jack Kramer (who led the team in wins) in order to pitch journeyman Denny Galehouse. The Indians went on to win the game handily (and thus the pennant), depriving Boston of its best chance for a streetcar series (since the Boston Braves were the National League pennant winner). As it happens, Cleveland has not won a World Series since beating the Braves 4–2 in 1948.

Kinder had an even better season in 1949, going 23–6 with a 3.36 ERA in 252 innings, providing a 1–2 punch along with the 25–7 Mel Parnell that gave the Red Sox a chance to clinch the pennant on the final weekend of the season. Unfortunately, needing only one win to make it to the World Series, the Red Sox were swept in a two-game series by the hated New York Yankees.

Perhaps influenced by the Yankees' use of reliever Joe Page, the Red Sox moved Kinder to a prominent role in the bullpen, where he continued to pitch well and blaze trails for the emerging role of bullpen ace. In 1951 he was 11–2 with a 2.55 ERA and a league-leading 14 saves. In 1953 Kinder was even better, going 10–6 with a 1.85 ERA and again leading the league in saves (with 27).

Two subpar seasons followed, after which Kinder was waived. His career was nearly over: He pitched briefly (though effectively) for the Chicago White Sox and St Louis Cardinals before retiring in 1957. Fondly remembered by the parents of the baby boomers, Ellis Kinder was a very good pitcher for Red Sox teams that twice finished within a game of making the World Series. He also helped usher in the new era of the bullpen ace with some excellent years in the pen.

Jack Kramer—righthanded pitcher who began his career with the St. Louis Browns in 1939. In the early part of his career, Kramer struggled badly with his control, and only made it to the majors for good in 1944 during the player short-age. In 1948 he came to Boston in the same trade that brought Vern Stephens and Ellis Kinder. He was a three-time All Star in St. Louis, but never made it to the All Star Game again. In his first season in Boston, he went 18–6 and led the league in winning percentage despite having an ERA that was virtually league average, because he played for a powerhouse offensive team. He pitched badly in 1949, 1950, and 1951, finishing up his career pitching mostly out of the bullpen for the New York Giants and then the New York Yankees. In his final sea-son he actually pitched for each of the pennant winners, but didn't last long enough on either roster to make it to the postseason.

Roger LaFrançois—a Connecticut native, LaFrançois was a catcher who spent the entire 1982 season with the Boston Red Sox, but got only 10 at bats in 8 games—one of the reasons that few teams carry three catchers any more. That was his only time in the major leagues. LaFrançois did get 4 hits in those 10 at bats, making him the last player to spend a full season on the Red Sox roster and hit .400.

Carney Lansford—third baseman who played two strong seasons for the Red Sox before losing his job. Lansford (along with Mark Clear and Rick Miller in his sec-ond tour of duty) was obtained from California for Rick Burleson (who was about to blow out his arm) and an end-of-the-line Butch Hobson after the 1980 season. As the starting third baseman in 1981, the 24-year-old Lansford hit .336 and won the batting title in a strike-shortened season. He hit .301 the following season, but Wade Boggs's development into a star hitter left him without a position (since the Sox wanted to play Boggs at third, rather than first base, where he spent most of his rookie year). Lansford was traded to Oakland as part of a deal for Tony Armas after the 1982 season, and went on to a long career with the Athletics.

Lansford was a very good player, but he was never a star with the Red Sox—he didn't have much power (although he hit 19 home runs three times for other teams) and drew a below-average number of walks. He had excellent speed for a third baseman but the Sox rarely stole bases as a team (he stole as many as 37 for the A's, though). As a fielder his reputation was better than his actual skills—he was notorious for acrobatically diving to stop balls that fielders with more range would field standing up.

Mike Lansing—a one-time power-hitting infielder acquired along with Rolando Arrojo from the Colorado Rockies in the 2000 season. This trade was viewed negatively by many Red Sox fans since Lansing had not hit well since undergo-ing back surgery in 1999 and continued to hit poorly (.194 with no home runs) after the trade—and the Red Sox were obligated to pay him a $7 million salary in 2001. Viewed as an afterthought on the roster, the 33-year-old second baseman was pressed into service at shortstop—a position he hadn't played regularly for eight years—when Nomar Garciaparra was injured in spring training. Lansing wasn't great, but he played better than most people expected,and his poor hitting improved after the All Star break. He signed a minor league contract with the Indians for 2002, but never played in the major leagues again.

In a minor footnote to Red Sox history, Lansing—who looked like he was going to be an offensive star early in his career—was the reason that Montreal was able to trade Delino DeShields for Pedro Martinez in 1994. Had Martinez remained in Los Angeles and blossomed the way he did in Montreal, he would never have been available when the Red Sox acquired him (since the Expos could not afford to pay a superstar like Martinez, while the Dodgers could). The Montreal general manager who traded DeShields for Martinez? The same one who later acquired him for Boston: Dan Duquette.

Lansing is from Casper, Wyoming, and when professional baseball returned to Wyoming after nearly a half century away, the home park of the minor league Casper Rockies was Mike Lansing Field. Lansing pledged $50,000 to help the field get built; it opened in 2002 after the team spent its first year in a borrowed high school stadium.

Bill Lee—there is an adage in baseball that two factors contribute to being a "flake," being a lefty pitcher, and being from California. Lee was both, in addition to being highly intelligent and frequently misunderstood. Upon seeing the Green Monster for the first time, Lee asked, "Do they leave it there during games?" This comment is said to have earned him his nickname of "Spaceman," which stuck. Lee was also responsible for nicknaming onetime Red Sox manager (and Lee nemesis) Don Zimmer "the gerbil," which also stuck.

Never an overpowering pitcher, Lee relied on the excellent control he had of his average fastball and above-average curveball. He also occasionally threw a pitch that was dubbed the "Leephus" pitch, basically a slow-pitch softball pitch that batters often found impossible to time. Lee never had what would be called a great season, but had several very good years, including a 9–2 season as a reliever in 1971, three straight 17-win years as a starter with the Red Sox (1973–75) and a 16-win season with Montreal in 1979, his first year there after being traded.

Lee's ongoing feud with Don Zimmer—an old-school manager who wanted nothing to do with the free-spirited Lee—escalated badly, and Zimmer's inability to handle Lee arguably cost the Red Sox a pennant in 1978. Lee was seen as the leader of a group of independent-minded players called the Buffalo Heads (among them Jim Willoughby and Bernie Carbo) who were embraced by fans. Zimmer, unable to cope with the Buffalo Heads, refused to play them—even when his talented team began breaking down from injuries and overwork. When Bernie Carbo's reliable bat was dumped at midseason, Lee left the team briefly in protest, which further infuriated Zimmer. Lee was the only lefthanded starter on the team, but Zimmer left him in the bullpen and used terrified rookie Bobby Sprowl in a key series against the Yankees, to disastrous results. After the season, Lee was given away to the Montreal Expos for infielder Stan Papi, who hit .188 in his only full season with the Red Sox. Lee continued to be a controversial free-thinker in Montreal. He retired early in the 1982 season, at least in part as a protest to the Expos for releasing his friend Rodney Scott.

Lee's history of being controversial has showed up in many areas, and he still occasionally expresses these opinions. He has publicly expressed a dislike for several of baseball's innovations over the years, including domed stadiums and the designated hitter. He once told journalists that he used marijuana "sprinkled on cereal," then later claimed he was putting them on. Lee now lives in rural central Vermont, where he played semi-pro baseball for years after retiring.

Mark Lemke—a light-hitting second baseman who manager Jimy Williams insisted on having for his 1998 Red Sox team—the first of a bunch of light-hitting middle infielders who crowded the Red Sox roster over the next several years. Lemke had briefly been a starter for the Atlanta Braves while Williams coached there, and had built a reputation based on hot streaks in the 1991 and 1996 playoffs. By 1998, Lemke was unemployed—mainly because he didn't hit much (he'd only hit above .255 once in 10 seasons) but wanted a substantial salary. When Red Sox starting second baseman Jeff Frye suffered a season-ending knee injury, GM Dan Duquette finally gave into Williams's public campaign and signed Lemke to a $1 million contract. Lemke hit .187 in 31 games before a concussion ended his season. Unable to find a major league job after his contract with the Red Sox expired, Lemke had a brief stint as a knuckleball pitcher for the New Jersey Jackals, an independent league team, before becoming a radio analyst for the Braves. Although never a star as a player, Lemke has been immortalized in another way, with recurring references in the cult favorite online cartoon *Homestar Runner*.

Dutch Leonard—though Bob Gibson's 1.12 ERA in 1968 is commonly cited as the single-season record, the modern mark actually belongs to Hubert "Dutch" Leonard, an overlooked star from the deadball era. (The all-time ERA record belongs to Hall of Famer Tim Keefe, with a 0.86 in the 85-game 1880 season, but conditions were very different.) The lefthanded Leonard joined the Red Sox in 1913, going 14–17, despite a 2.39 ERA. But it's fair to say he improved in his sophomore season. Leonard had a 19–5 record, including 7 shutouts, and his ERA was an incomprehensible 0.96. The American League had a very low 2.73 ERA in 1914, but Leonard's numbers are still remarkable. He allowed only 139 hits and 60 walks in 225 innings (anything less than one hit an inning is good), while fanning 176.

Leonard never approached his landmark 1914 season, but he was a valuable member of the 1915–16 championship staffs, winning 33 games, plus another in each World Series. His ERA jumped to a more human 2.36 in 1915, and remained the same in 1916. On August 30, 1916, Leonard pitched a no-hitter against the St. Louis Browns. He won 16 games in 1917 and eight more in 1918, including a no-hitter against Detroit on June 3. Three weeks after his no-hitter, Leonard left the Red Sox to enlist in the U.S. Navy, and he missed the remainder of the season, including the World Series. After World War I ended, Boston traded Leonard to the Yankees, along with Duffy Lewis and Ernie Shore. The Yanks promptly sold Leonard to Detroit, where he spent five mediocre seasons. He retired with 139 wins and a 2.76 ERA.

In 1926, Leonard found himself at the center of one of baseball's biggest scandals. He gave American League President Ban Johnson copies of two letters he got in 1919. One was from his then-teammate Ty Cobb; the other was from ex-Red Sox star Joe Wood, then with Cleveland. The letters allegedly proved that

Cobb and Cleveland's Tris Speaker (both were player-managers) fixed a meaningless late-season game, though Speaker's name wasn't directly mentioned. But when Johnson asked Leonard to testify at a hearing, the ex-pitcher refused. He recanted his story, supposedly because he feared Cobb's wrath. Commissioner Landis refused to suspend anyone, due to lack of evidence. Angry and embarrassed, Johnson decided to ban Cobb and Speaker from managing, but allowed them to sign with the Philadelphia Athletics as free agent players (as opposed to player-managers).

In 1933, another Dutch Leonard began a successful 20-year pitching career. Emil "Dutch" Leonard was a righty knuckleballer, and was no relation to Hubert, though the two are often confused for one another.

Curt Leskanic—veteran righty reliever picked up for the 2004 stretch drive. Leskanic came up with Colorado in 1993 and was a mainstay of the Rockies bullpen from 1995–99—leading the league in appearances in 1995—though his stats looked worse because of the thin air in Coors Field, which makes it a hitter's paradise. Traded to Milwaukee for future Sox reliever Mike Myers, Leskanic's stats improved dramatically; he was a popular prankster, and unflappable enough that a teammate had "Don't panic, we've got Leskanic" T-shirts made. A rotator cuff injury wiped out his entire 2002 season, and the shoulder surgery to repair it alleviated the injury, but not the pain. Determined to play anyway—with the philosopy that he'd be in pain anyway, so he might as well be doing something he enjoyed—Leskanic made a nice comeback in 2003; he was having a very good year for a very bad team when the Brewers traded him in midseason to Kansas City, which was unexpectedly in contention and looking for bullpen help. He pitched brilliantly in a losing cause for the Royals, and the Royals talked him out of retiring because of the continuing pain in his shoulder. However the Royals foundered early the next year and when Leskanic struggled with tendonitis, Kansas City inexplicably released him. (The Royals weren't rebuilding or making room for a young prospect, and Leskanic was a popular player who'd been pitching better as his arm recovered.) The 36-year-old Leskanic signed with the Red Sox, where he mostly pitched well (3.58 ERA in 32 games), but not consistently (a recurrence of the tendonitis made him harrowingly ineffective at times, and led to another stay on the disabled list). Leskanic pitched three times against the Yankees in the ALCS, and won Game 4 in the twelfth inning, when the Red Sox faced elimination. With a World Series championship in hand, and a shoulder that remains painful, Leskanic is reportedly planning to retire.

Darren Lewis—a light-hitting center fielder who was a favorite of manager Jimy Williams for four years. Signed to a short-money contract almost as an afterthought in 1998, the 30-year-old former Gold Glover brought defense and speed to the Sox. He won the starting center field position when he had a hot first half. Receiving the most playing time of his career (585 at bats in 155 games), Lewis cooled off in the second half of the season but nevertheless put up his best offensive numbers (.352 on-base percentage and .362 slugging percentage, still mediocre for a center fielder). After the season, Lewis was signed to a surprising longterm contract (given his age and his poor offense in previous seasons); there were suggestions that GM Dan Duquette gave Lewis a contract as part of a campaign to re-sign Mo Vaughn, who was close with Lewis.

Lewis struggled offensively in 1999 and became a role player when the Sox traded for Carl Everett before the 2000 season. Manager Jimy Williams liked Lewis's defense and attitude, however, and used him as a platoon right fielder (despite his weak throwing arm), to rest starters, and as a late-inning defensive replacement. Lewis still saw plenty of playing time in 2000—arguably far too much playing time, given the erosion of his speed and batting eye. His notable 2000 moment was a loud clubhouse confrontation with Everett—the outspoken star center fielder who took Lewis's job—during Everett's problems with Jimy Williams. Lewis's playing time was cut significantly in 2001 by the emergence of Trot Nixon and the late-season firing of Williams; he played only sporadically after Joe Kerrigan took over as manager and was not re-signed. Lewis spent the 2002 season as a spare part with the Chicago Cubs before retiring in midseason rather than accept a trade to Pittsburgh.

Duffy Lewis—left fielder who joined Tris Speaker and Harry Hooper in one of baseball's most famous outfields. Lewis played eight seasons with Boston, winning three World Series. He hit over .300 twice, with a high of 109 RBI on the 1912 World Champs, but is best remembered for his defensive skills. The original Fenway Park had a small hill in left (where the Green Monster is now) nicknamed "Duffy's Cliff" because of Lewis's deftness in playing it. He went to the Yankees in 1919, a year before Babe Ruth.

Lewis died in 1979 and was buried in an unmarked grave in Londonderry, New Hampshire. After a story appeared in the *Manchester Union Leader* about Lewis's grave, fans donated money for a gray granite headstone with an image of the old Fenway Park and Duffy Lewis, which was erected in June 2001.

Tim Lollar—a lefthanded relief pitcher who, during the 1986 season, accomplished the rare feat of finishing the year with a 1.000 winning percentage and a 1.000 batting average. He was 2–0 out of the bullpen, despite pitching very badly. Then during a game in Kansas City lineup moves forced him to pinch-hit, and he singled up the middle in his only at-bat. He spent only two years in Boston, and 1986 was his last year in the majors.

Jim Lonborg—though many players contributed to the miracle, when Red Sox fans think of the Impossible Dream year of 1967, they usually think of three men: pitcher Jim Lonborg, slugger Carl Yasztremski, and manager Dick Williams. Lonborg tied for the league lead in wins that season with 22, was second in the league in innings pitched with 273, and won the American League Cy Young for his efforts. He won two games in the World Series (including the amazing Game 2 effort in which he nearly recorded the second no-hit game in World Series history). Pitching Game 7 on only two days' rest, Lonborg had nothing left, and Bob Gibson and the Cardinals won the game and thus the Series. Still, the future seemed bright for the Sox that winter—the team had come out of nowhere, a half game out of last place in 1966, to win the pennant in 1967 with a young, talented team. Unfortunately, over the winter Lonborg broke his leg in a skiing accident and it took a number of years for him to regain the fine form which he enjoyed in that 1967 season (by which time he was no longer pitching for the Sox). He pitched for Milwaukee in 1972, then spent seven years with the Philadelphia Phillies, during which he finally regained his effectiveness, winning 17 games in 1974 and 18 in 1976. Lonborg returned to New England after his playing career ended, and went on to a second successful career—as a dentist.

Derek Lowe—tall, lanky righthanded pitcher acquired by general manager Dan Duquette in one of the great heists of all time. As the Red Sox fell out of contention before the trading deadline in 1997, he managed to turn shell-shocked reliever Heathcliff Slocumb, who everybody wanted him to just release, into Derek Lowe and Jason Varitek from the Mariners, who were desperate to upgrade their bullpen. (Why they thought that Slocumb would accomplish that remains unclear.)

Lowe had struggled as a starter in Seattle and also struggled initially as a starter in Boston. But he pitched well in short and medium relief, and clearly had great stuff. His big strength was a sinking fastball, and he threw a lot of ground balls. In 1999, he was one of the most valuable pitchers in baseball, setting up first Tom Gordon, and then Tim Wakefield after Gordon was injured. He then settled into the closer's role himself, and finished the season with 15 saves. In 2000, he started as the team's full-time closer, and saved 42 games over the course of the season. Though he saved 24 games in 2001, Lowe struggled in the middle of the season and seemed to lose his confidence, en route to posting a 5–10 record. Some critics questioned his ability to dominate hitters without the intimidating mound presence that marks many other successful closers. (ESPN writer Bill Simmons described the "Derek Lowe face," in which Lowe's defeated-looking body language presaged things about to go wrong on the mound.) The acquisition of Ugueth Urbina at the trading deadline dislodged Lowe from his closer's role; he was soon moved back to the starting rotation, where he flourished in the final month of the season.

By the 2002 season, Lowe had come full circle, moving into the starting rotation where he had begun his career. In his first game of the season, Lowe retired the first 15 hitters he faced, and took a no-hitter into the eighth inning. On April 27, Lowe pitched the first no-hitter at Fenway in 38 years. He joined an elite group of pitchers with 40 saves and a no-hitter (Dennis Eckersley and Dave Righetti), and was the first of this group to save 40 before throwing the no-hitter. Amazingly, this was also Lowe's first career complete game. Lowe had an awesome first half, going 12–4 with a 2.36 ERA and starting the All-Star Game for the AL. (This game was also famous for being called a tie after both sides used up all of their pitchers in extra innings.) He finished the season at 21–8 with a 2.58 ERA, and along with teammate Pedro Martinez finished 2–3 in the Cy Young voting that year.

In 2003, the Sox had high expectations, considering themselves legitimate contenders with a strong pitching rotation. Lowe did go 17–7 and again topped 200 innings. However, where in 2002 he was virtually unhittable, in 2003 he gave up 50 more hits and walked 24 more in 16 fewer innings, increasing his ERA from an excellent 2.58 to an about-average 4.47. Lowe also seemed to have the same problems with focus on the mound that he'd had as a reliever, seeming to lose confidence in key moments, and was clearly not the pitcher he had been the season before. However, Lowe pitched frequently in the playoffs and had some memorable outings. In Game 1 against Oakland, Lowe was called upon in extra innings of a tie game, and ended up losing the game for the Sox. Lowe came back to start Game 3 and dueled Ted Lilly. In seven innnings, Lowe gave up only one unearned run, laying the groundwork for a Red Sox victory in extra innings. In Game 5, with the Sox clinging to a one-run lead in the ninth Lowe was brought in to save the game, something he hadn't done for two years, after Scott Williamson walked the first two batters he faced. The first batter Lowe faced laid down a sacrifice bunt, moving both runners into scoring position. After striking out Adam Melhuse on a tailing fastball for a called third strike, Lowe walked the next batter to load the bases. Facing Jermaine Dye, Lowe struck him out looking, ending the game. In the ACLS against the Yankees, Lowe started Game 2 on two days rest and didn't pitch well. He also started the crucial Game 5 and pitched decently, but took his second loss of the series. (The Sox went on to lose the series in a dramatic Game 7.)

In 2004 the Sox again fielded a World Series contender, but Lowe did not return to his 2004 form. Lowe was in the last year of his contract, and though he turned down a four-year, $36 million offer, he complained that the Red Sox weren't seriously interested in re-signing him. His 14–12 record was a product of pitching for a team that scored a lot of runs; Lowe showed flashes of brilliance but pitched poorly overall, finishing with a 5.42 ERA (36th out of 40 who qualified for the ERA title). Lowe complained when he was dropped from the postseason rotation in favor of Bronson Arroyo, who'd been hot. However, in Game 3 of the ALDS against the Angels, Lowe was asked to enter the top of the tenth inning and hold the Angels. Lowe pitched a scoreless inning, winning the game (and the series) when David Ortiz hit a two -run homer. Lowe didn't pitch in the first three games of the ALCS, but started Game 4 (with the Sox down 0–3 in the series), and pitched well, though he was long gone by the time the Sox won dramatically in the twelfth inning. After the Sox went on to win Games 5 and 6, Lowe was tabbed to start Game 7 on two days' rest and pitched brilliantly, earning his second series-clinching win of 2004. In the World Series, Lowe started Game 4, with the Sox up 3–0 in the series. In seven innings, he gave up three hits, a walk, and no runs: his third series-clinching win of 2004. Lowe became the first pitcher to get the win in all three of his team's postseason series-winning games.

In January 2005, Lowe signed a four-year contract with the Dodgers for roughly the same money he'd turned down from the Sox, then repeated his complaint that the Sox hadn't wanted to keep him.

Sparky Lyle—a lefthanded reliever whom the Red Sox gave away in a truly awful trade. Lyle pitched 27 games for the 1967 Impossible Dream team as a 23-year-old rookie, and gradually developed into the team's top reliever, saving an average of 18 games from 1969 to 1971 with an ERA below 3.00 in four of his five years with the Sox. After the 1971 season he was deemed expendable (fellow lefty Bill Lee had gone 9–2 in relief that year, and the team's conservative management disapproved of Lyle's pranksterish nature) and was traded to the Yankees for Danny Cater, a journeyman infielder who would hit .237 as a replacement for the also-traded George Scott at first base. Lyle, 27 years old when he was traded, was just entering his prime, and would have eight good-to-great years in a row before losing effectiveness. He saved a league-leading 35 games for the Yankees in 1972; Bill Lee and Bobby Bolin tied for the Sox team lead with five each.

Fred Lynn—in 1975, lefthanded centerfielder Lynn and fellow "Gold Dust Twin" Jim Rice proved to be possibly the best tandem of rookies that a team ever put together. Lynn, in addition to winning the first of his four Gold Gloves, became the only major leaguer to win the Rookie of the Year award and the Most Valuable Player award in the same season. He was second in the league in batting average, fifth in on-base percentage, first in slugging, and first in OPS. On one memorable June night in Tiger Stadium he hit three home runs and drove in 10 runs. Those accomplishments—at age 23—heralded the advent of an outstanding career. Lynn was an excellent fielder, almost to the point of being reckless in the outfield. (Lynn's collision with the outfield wall at Fenway during the sixth game of the 1975 World Series led to the padding that now covers those walls.)

Lynn played well for the Red Sox for six years, including a 1979 season even better than his rookie campaign. After starting to use then-obscure Nautilus weight training machines, Lynn led the league in batting average, on-base percentage, and slugging. He was fourth in RBI and in runs scored. He hit 39 home runs (his previous season high was 22) and drove in 122 runs, while winning another Gold Glove for his defense in center field—but somehow he lost the MVP award to Don Baylor of California.

Following the 1980 season, the Red Sox made one of the great unexplained baseball screwups. They mailed out the contracts of Lynn and catcher Carlton Fisk a day after the deadline for offering player contracts. Knowing that Lynn would almost certainly be declared a free agent, the Sox were forced to trade him at a fire sale price to the California Angels, with whom Southern California native Lynn signed a longterm contract. The trade helped neither Lynn—the ultimate Fenway Park hitter—nor the Sox. Lynn played well, but never again had a great season after 1979. He did win another Gold Glove in 1982 and was the All Star Game MVP in 1983, hitting the first grand slam in All Star game history (a homer that essentially ruined the career of pitcher Atlee Hammaker, who never got over throwing the bad pitch in front of millions of fans). But Lynn was frequently hampered by injuries. He tore up knees and bruised ribs with his reckless style of defense, but he also lost time to muscle pulls and strains that led people in some quarters to question his toughness.

After four years in California he signed a free agent contract with the Orioles following the 1984 season. Still a good player but no longer a star, Lynn spent three full years in Baltimore, during which he hit 23 home runs in each season. He was traded to Detroit late in the 1987 season, and eventually finished up by playing 90 games for the San Diego Padres in 1990. His career never fulfilled the promise it had shown in the beginning: He finished his 16-year career with 306 home runs and 1,111 RBI. He never made it to the Hall of Fame, though, interestingly enough, his college roommate at USC, Pittsburgh Steeler Hall of Fame wide receiver Lynn Swann, did.

Lynn continues to live in California, but makes appearances for both the Red Sox and Major League Baseball. For the Red Sox, Lynn hosts corporate clientele in the Legends Skybox several times a year—most notably when the New York Yankees are in town.

Brandon Lyon—young righthanded pitcher who won a spot in Boston's bullpen in 2003, spent two months as closer, and was then involved in two controversial trades. Lyon was drafted by Toronto in 1999, signed a pro contract in 2000, and was in the Blue Jays' starting rotation by the end of 2001. He looked good in his first big league trial (5–4, 4.29), but had a disastrous 2002 season (6.53 ERA in the majors; 5.11 in AAA). Although they had lousy pitching depth, the Jays put the 23-year-old Lyon on waivers, and he was claimed by the Red Sox. He pitched well as a long reliever in April 2003, showing excellent poise and control, while bigger names (Chad Fox, Alan Embree, Ramiro Mendoza, Robert Person) battled injuries and ineffectiveness. Manager Grady Little gave Lyon a chance to close in May; he converted his first nine save opportunities and had a 3.07 ERA entering June 28. But on that night, he blew his first save, giving up a crushing game-winning homer to Florida's Mike Lowell. He had a loss and a blown save in his next two appearances, and soon lost his job to Byung-Hyun Kim. Few fans minded when Lyon and Anastacio Martinez were traded to Pittsburgh on July 22 (for lefty relievers Scott Sauerbeck and Mike Gonzalez). However, the Pirates claimed that an MRI showed that Lyon had elbow damage, even though Boston said he was healthy enough to pitch. After a tense nine-day standoff, the Red Sox and Pirates reworked the deal. Boston took Lyon and Martinez back, and also got pitcher Jeff Suppan; Pittsburgh got Gonzalez back, plus Red Sox infield prospect Freddy Sanchez. Lyon spent August on the disabled list, didn't do well in September, and was omitted from Boston's playoff roster. Shortly after Thanksgiving, Lyon, Casey Fossum, and two minor leaguers were traded to Arizona for ace Curt Schilling. The deal was blasted by Arizona fans as a pure salary dump, and it looked even worse for the Diamondbacks when Lyon missed all of 2004 with elbow problems (while Fossum had a 4–15 record and 6.65 ERA). Lyon has had nerve transposition and Tommy John surgeries on his elbow, and while he's only 25 years old, his future remains very much up in the air.

Steve Lyons—"Psycho" was a highly thought of third base prospect who never really panned out for the Red Sox (career average of .253), although he had four separate stints with the team. He came up in 1985 and was used mostly in the outfield, then was traded to the White Sox for Tom Seaver in 1986. After four-plus seasons with the White Sox, Lyons resigned with Boston as a free agent in April 1991. In 1992 he signed with the Braves and then the Expos, but later had his contract purchased by Boston in midseason. Lyons signed with the Cubs in 1993, but never made it out of spring training with Chicago that year, and signed with Boston for a fourth and final time in May 1993.

Lyons's most famous moment in the major leagues came in 1990 when he slid into first base safely in a cloud of dust, got up, called time, and unthinkingly dropped his pants in front of 30,000 spectators to shed the dust and grit. He is now a sportscaster for the Dodgers and Fox Sports.

Mike Macfarlane—a longtime Kansas City catcher with a good bat, Macfarlane came to Boston amid great fanfare in 1995. Things never really worked out for him in Boston, and he ended up as a part time catcher, hitting 15 home runs while driving in 51 runs. A steady if unspectacular performer, Macfarlane had one memorable moment as a member of the Red Sox. In a 2–2 game he hit a ninth-inning walk-off home run to near dead center field against the Yankees on a Sunday afternoon. In Game 1 of the 1995 playoffs, he dropped a throw to home plate, costing the Red Sox at least one run. (He wasn't charged with an error, but it was a catchable ball, and helped cost Boston the game.) After the 1995 season Macfarlane returned to Kansas City and went back to being a productive player. He retired after the 1999 season, and is now an ESPN commentator.

Mike Maddux—a righthanded relief pitcher who came up with the Phillies in 1986. In his 15-year career in the majors, he pitched mostly out of the bullpen (he came up as a starter, but got only spot starts after 1988). Despite his long career, he was only the second-best pitcher in the Maddux family, overshadowed by his younger brother Greg, a four-time National League Cy Young Award winner and future Hall of Famer. When Mike and Greg faced each other for the Phillies and Cubs in September of 1986, it marked the first time in baseball history that rookie brother pitchers had faced each other.

He signed with Pittsburgh prior to the 1995 season, but was released when he refused to accept a minor league assignment. The Red Sox picked him up (becoming his sixth team and his first in the American League), and he pitched very effectively for the team. He was 4–1 in 89 innings for the Sox, as that 1995 team won the American League East by seven games over second place New York. He pitched in two games against the Indians in the Division series, allowing no runs. He was also effective in 1996, though not as effective, and for fewer innings. The Red Sox did not re-sign him following 1996, and he pitched for four more teams over the next four years. Maddux retired after the 2000 season. He spent 2004 as pitching coach for the Milwaukee Brewers.

Tom Maggard—the Red Sox top draft pick in 1968, Maggard was a promising catching prospect. He was playing in AAA Pawtucket in September, 1973 when his arm swelled up after being bitten by an insect. After treatment attempts didn't improve the injury, he was sent home to California, where he died two weeks later. Maggard was 21 years old.

Ron Mahay—because he had agreed under pressure to participate as a replacement player during the 1994 strike, young center fielder Mahay was ostracized in his brief time with the Red Sox as an emergency callup in 1995, particularly by pitchers Roger Clemens and Tim Wakefield. After being sent back to the minor leagues, the Red Sox converted the light-hitting Mahay into a pitcher—a conversion he took to surprisingly quickly. By 1997 he was back with the team as a

26-year-old lefthanded relief pitcher, and pitched very well in limited duty. Mahay shuttled between Pawtucket and the Red Sox the following year, then failed to win a job in 1999. (He was out of minor league options and so could not be sent back to Pawtucket without giving other teams a chance to claim him.) Mahay was picked up by Oakland, then bounced between three teams while hampered by shoulder and bicep injuries in 2001 and 2002. He signed a minor league contract with the Texas Rangers for the 2003 season and by the end of the season had established himself as a key member of the Rangers bullpen. Given regular work for the first time as a 33-year-old in 2004, Mahay had a terrific season for the Rangers, appearing in 60 games with a 2.55 ERA.

Mark Malaska—lefty reliever who spent most of the 2004 season driving back and forth on Interstate 95, between Pawtucket and Boston. The Red Sox claimed Malaska on waivers from Tampa Bay in December 2003. The Devil Rays' decision to part with him was curious, since he had been a good minor league starter, did well after being converted to the bullpen, and had a 2.81 ERA in 22 major league relief appearances in 2003. Boston hoped Malaska would be a second left-hander in the bullpen, freeing Alan Embree to pitch in a wider variety of situations. However, Malaska was a victim of a numbers game in spring training, losing his role to mediocre veteran Bobby M. Jones (who, in a disastrous appearance on April 8, walked four straight Orioles to lose the game). After Jones's meltdown, Malaska was called up from Pawtucket, and he had an outstanding April (five scoreless appearances). But he struggled after that and soon went back to the minors, though he was recalled two more times during the summer. Though he's only 27 years old and has pretty good stuff, Malaska doesn't appear to be a big part of Boston's plans in 2005. But if any Red Sox pitchers go on the DL, he'll only be a 41-mile drive away in Pawtucket.

Frank Malzone—one of the best third basemen in Red Sox history, Malzone's steady hitting and excellent defense endeared him to Fenway fans for 11 seasons. From 1957–64, Malzone made eight All Star teams and averaged 84 RBI a season, making him one of the few bright spots on an otherwise dreary ballclub.Though he was born near Yankee Stadium, Malzone signed a contract with the Red Sox in 1948. He struggled for a while in the minors, and then missed two seasons while serving in the Korean War. Malzone didn't make his big league debut until late 1955, at age 25. He won the third base job in 1956, but was sent back to the minors after batting only .165. (During the previous offseason, Malzone and his wife had lost an infant daughter, and the grief may have contributed to his poor play.)

In 1957, Malzone reclaimed his spot as the starting third baseman. He responded with arguably his best season (.292 average, 15 homers, a career-high 103 RBI). His defense won raves, and he set a record for third basemen (since broken) with 10 assists in a game against Washington. Malzone also became the first player to lead his position in games played, putouts, assists, errors, fielding percentage, and double plays in the same season. (Despite the errors, he made enough plays to lead in fielding percentage.) He earned the brand-new Gold Glove Award, a trophy honoring the best defensive players at each position.

(Malzone won the first three Gold Gloves for American League third basemen, until Brooks Robinson came along in 1960. Robinson then won the award an amazing 16 straight years.) Though he'd have been considered a rookie under today's rules, Malzone was ineligible for the Rookie of the Year award, based upon his limited experience in 1955–56. Several Boston writers filed a petition to make him eligible, but the Baseball Writers Association of America rejected the protest. As a result, Yankees shortstop Tony Kubek, whose numbers were inferior to Malzone's, won the award. (One writer voted for Malzone anyway, to protest the BBWAA's ruling.)

Malzone continued to be among the best American League third basemen for the next few years. His 1958 and 1959 numbers were nearly identical to his "rookie" stats. He slumped a bit in 1960 and 1961, hitting .271 and .266, with 14 homers each year. Malzone rebounded in 1962, hitting a career-high 21 homers, and hit .291 the following season. Looking beyond the solid batting averages and RBI totals, Malzone was somewhat overrated as a hitter. His home run totals weren't that impressive for a third baseman, not to mention a righty hitter in Fenway Park, and he didn't walk a whole lot. But Malzone was extremely consistent and durable, and his defense was a major asset.

However, he showed signs of slipping in 1964. Malzone hit a weak .264, with only 13 homers and 56 RBI, and a poor .372 slugging percentage. He slumped to .239 in 1965, with only 3 homers, and ended the year platooning with young Dalton Jones. At 35, and clearly on the decline, Malzone was no longer in the team's plans, and the Red Sox released him after the season. He played another year as a backup with the California Angels, but retired after batting .206.

After his playing career ended, Malzone rejoined the Red Sox organization, serving in several roles, most notably as a scout. Still active at age 75, Malzone is now a special assignment instructor in the organization. He was inducted into the Red Sox Hall of Fame in 1995 for his contributions to the franchise, on and off the field. He was invited with a number of former Red Sox players to ride in the "legends" duck boat during the 2004 World Championship celebration in Boston.

Malzone's youngest son John played minor league ball for the Red Sox, advancing as far as AAA Pawtucket in 1993 and 1995. The younger Malzone later became a hitting instructor for Red Sox minor league teams.

Matt Mantei—flamethrowing but fragile righty reliever who signed a free agent contract with the Red Sox in December, 2004. Like the pitcher he replaced, Scott Williamson, Mantei is a former closer with devastating stuff (including a fastball that approaches 100 MPH), although early in his career his terrifying walk rates made him more closely resemble ex-Sox closer Mark Clear. The 31-year-old Mantei came up with the Florida Marlins in 1995, and first established himself as a quality reliever three years later. He took over as Florida's closer in 1999, was traded to Arizona in a midseason blockbuster, and finished the season with a career high 32 saves, a 2.76 ERA, and an astonishing 99 strikeouts in 65⅔ innings. However, he missed much of the 2000–02 seasons due to various injuries, including Tommy John surgery on his elbow (enabling his setup man, future Sox disappointment Byung-Hyun Kim, to step in as closer). In 2003,

Mantei was finally healthy again and had a fine season (29 saves, a 2.62 ERA, 68 strikeouts, and only 18 walks in 55 innings). But history repeated itself in 2004, and after shoulder problems limited him to 12 appearances—and an awful 11.81 ERA—the former $7 million a year closer had to settle for a 1-year, $750,000 contract with the Red Sox.

Felix Mantilla—used mostly as a reserve in his 11 seasons with the Milwaukee Braves (1956–61), the Mets (1962), the Red Sox (1963–65), and the Astros (1966), Felix Mantilla hit only 89 career home runs, and had a .261 lifetime batting average. In the conventional wisdom he was a utility infielder, a useful guy to have as a backup in the field, but not someone who should bat very often. Yet in his three years with Boston he would shatter that image.

Mantilla was primarily a shortstop with the Braves, but he was versatile. He played second, third, the outfield, and even some first base in the majors. In 6 seasons with Milwaukee he was regarded as a "good field, no hit" player. From 1957–61 he hit between .215 and .257 while averaging only 180 at bats a season. He totaled 18 home runs in those years. Then in 466 at bats with the Mets in 1962 he hit .275 with 11 home runs. That winter he was traded to Boston for two noteworthy if not illustrious players, Tracy Stallard and Pumpsie Green.

When Mantilla got to Boston perspectives changed quickly. First, he was a good hitter. Second, he wasn't a good shortstop. In 1963 he played only 27 games at short, 11 in the outfield, and 5 at second. He hit .315 with 6 home runs in 178 at bats, walked 20 times, struck out only 14, and made no errors at second or in the outfield. His career years were to come in 1964–65 when the Red Sox realized they needed to get his bat in the lineup.

Mantilla hammered an amazing 30 home runs in 1964. He played in 133 games, had 425 at bats and hit .289, with a .553 slugging percentage. He also was close to flawless in the field, making only one error in 48 games in the outfield, one error in 45 games at second base, and none in six games at shortstop. (He did make three errors in seven games at third.) In 1965 he had a career high 534 at bats and his power dropped, although he still hit .275 with 18 home runs and 92 RBI—very respectable for a second baseman, where he played 123 games that season. On the eve of the 1967 season he was traded to Houston for future Red Sox manager Eddie Kasko.

Josias Manzanillo—a great Red Sox pitching prospect in the late 1980s, Manzanillo blew out his elbow from pitching too much at age 18. After missing two years recovering from the injury, he was never the same pitcher, although he eventually made it to the big leagues for one game with the Red Sox as a 23-year-old in 1991. He drifted in and out of the major leagues for six different teams, including three separate stints with the Mets, but never won more than three games in a season. Manzanillo's injury woes also continued. While pitching for Seattle in 1997, he was hit by a line drive off the bat of Manny Ramirez, and had to have surgery to remove a testicle. Manzanillo finally established himself as a solid middle reliever for Pittsburgh at age 32, appearing in 43 games in 2000 and a career-high 71 in 2001. He has struggled with elbow problems and pitched only intermittently in the big leagues since then, appearing in 26 games for the

Marlins in 2004. Manzanillo signed a minor league contract to return to the Red Sox in 2005.

Juan Marichal—known as "The Dominican Dandy," this Hall of Famer pitched 11 games with Boston in 1974, his next-to-last season. Marichal, who had won 20 games six times with the Giants, went 5–1 with a 4.87 ERA (a poor ERA at a time when the league average was about 3.60). Although he was near the end of the line when the Red Sox picked him up to help fill out a thin pitching staff, Marichal finished his career at 243–142 with a 2.89 ERA, and became the first Dominican to make the Hall of Fame.

Mike Marshall—outfielder/first baseman who played most of his career with the Los Angeles Dodgers. Although Marshall had been a much-heralded prospect, he never became a great hitter (or even a very good one) but he did have some "pop in his bat," hitting 20 or more home runs three times. The Red Sox picked Marshall up late in the 1990 season to strengthen the bench for the stretch run and the playoffs. Marshall contributed very little, hitting just four homers in 112 at bats. He had only one hit in three games in the 1990 playoffs as the Red Sox were swept by the Oakland A's. He started the 1991 season in Boston but played badly and was released early in the year. There's a sad irony to this, since the Red Sox kept Marshall on the roster instead of longtime star Dwight Evans, who was forced to finish his career in Baltimore. Marshall was picked up briefly by the Angels, but he appeared in only two more games before retiring.

Marshall was an odd hitter, because he had a rare "reverse platoon," meaning that he hit righthanded pitchers better than lefties, even though he was righthanded.

Pedro Martinez—flamboyant and articulate (but physically and emotionally fragile) starting pitcher who dominated the American League for six of his seven years with the Red Sox. Born in the Dominican Republic, Martinez was the middle of three pitching brothers, all of whom once pitched in the Red Sox organization. The wiry Martinez made his major league debut for the Los Angeles Dodgers (for whom he had signed when he was 16) and was immediately tagged as too slight to start in the majors by then-Dodgers manager Tommy Lasorda, a normally astute judge of baseball talent. This led to Martinez pitching mostly in middle relief during his stay with the Dodgers—although as a 21-year-old he pitched extremely well in that role.

Traded to the Montreal Expos for highly thought of second baseman Delino DeShields in 1994, Martinez blossomed as a starter; at one point that season he pitched nine perfect innings before giving up a hit in the tenth inning of a scoreless game. In 1997 Martinez won the National League Cy Young Award with 18 wins, finishing the season with more than 300 strikeouts and an ERA under 2.00 (a combination that had only been done by one other pitcher, Sandy Koufax, since 1912). He also received the third-lowest run support of all National League starters, accounting for his low win total. (Ironically, Montreal traded DeShields to make room for Mike Lansing, later a backup infielder with the Sox, who they thought would be a bigger star.)

After the 1997 season, Montreal was forced to dump salary and traded Martinez to the Red Sox for top pitching prospects Carl Pavano and Tony Armas Jr. There was a short period where it appeared that Martinez—who was a year away from free agency—might not sign a contract with the Red Sox. But within days, GM Dan Duquette convinced Martinez to sign a contract that would make him a Red Sox player for up to seven years—and, at that time, the highest paid player in the game.

Martinez's reception in Boston was slightly mixed in 1998. Enthusiastic fans, happy to have a new ace after Roger Clemens's departure following the 1996 season, were eager to show their support. However, a midseason stretch of less-than-stellar performances (later blamed on illness), made fans uneasy as it reminded them of the failed Steve Avery experiment of the year before. The criticism of Martinez by some fans and media weighed heavily on him, to the point that during off-season negotiations between the Red Sox and Ramon Martinez (Pedro's older brother), Pedro cautioned Ramon about the unforgiving Boston media. Martinez went on to post very good numbers in 1998, going 19–7 with a 2.89 ERA and 251 strikeouts—excellent but not quite the dominance he showed in 1997 or would show in the following years. On the strength of Martinez's year the Red Sox made the playoffs as the wild card. Playing against the Cleveland Indians, the team that had dismissed them from the 1995 playoffs, the Red Sox could only manage to win one of four games—the game Martinez started.

During the off-season the Red Sox signed Pedro's brothers, Ramon and Jesus, both pitchers. Ramon, the older brother, had been the Dodgers' ace before a serious injury. (There was some debate over whether Ramon was signed for his pitching skills or for his potentially stabilizing effect on the emotional Pedro.) Ramon was hurt for most of the regular season, but pitched well for the Sox in the playoffs before a disappointing 2000. Jesus, the youngest of the three, pitched poorly in the low minors and has since bounced around several organizations.

Martinez's 1999 season was incredible. Starting the All Star Game in Boston, Martinez struck out five of the first six opposing hitters and was named the All Star Game MVP. He won the Triple Crown for pitchers, leading the league with a 23–4 record, a 2.07 ERA, and 313 strikeouts (making him the only pitcher to strike out more than 300 hitters in a season in both leagues). His 313 strikeouts in 213⅓ innings meant that an incredible 48.9% of his outs came by way of the strikeout. He won four Pitcher of the Month awards.

In 17 postseason innings Martinez allowed no runs, struck out 17, and had a 2–0 record—despite battling injury. The highlight of that postseason was a stunning relief appearance in which Martinez shut down a potent Cleveland offense on guile alone. Obviously in pain (and unable to lift his arm above his head) Martinez used his pinpoint accuracy and kept the Indians' lineup off guard by changing speeds and arm angles. Martinez pitched six perfect innings, defeating the Indians and sending the Sox to meet the Yankees in the American League Championship Series. The Red Sox lost that series, plagued by poor fielding, poor relief pitching, and bad calls by the umpires—the only win being a much-hyped matchup between Martinez and Roger Clemens at Fenway Park. Martinez was the unanimous Cy Young winner, and would have won the league

MVP, but he was entirely left off the ballots of two writers (who believed that pitchers shouldn't be MVPs, despite explicit rules from the BBWAA that pitchers must be considered).

In 2000 Martinez was even better, posting an 18–6 record with a 1.74 ERA. He was again victimized by poor run support, or his won-lost record would have been better. In May, Martinez would again be matched against Roger Clemens, winning 2–0 on national TV in the season's best pitching duel. In the beginning of September, Martinez's reputations for dominance and intimidation would collide. (Early in his career Martinez, who pitches inside a lot, gained a reputation as a "head hunter," a rep that has followed him his entire career, with good and bad consequences. Ironically, he got the reputation as a *batter* in the National League when he went after a pitcher who hit him. Pedro never actually hit anyone in the head, but he freely used his reputation to intimidate batters.) In a game against the Tampa Bay Devil Rays, Martinez hit the first Tampa Bay batter of the game, Gerald Williams. Williams rushed the mound, touching off a brawl. Following the fight, four different Devil Ray pitchers tried to hit Red Sox batters. After another bench-clearing skirmish, attention turned to the fact that while Martinez was not retaliating (Tampa Bay seemed to be trying to get him thrown out of the game) he was pitching a no-hitter. The no-hitter would be broken up in the ninth inning—immediately following Martinez placing his crucifix in his back pocket because the chain had broken on the previous pitch.

2001 began much as 2000 ended, with Pedro dominant. Through April and May, he was once again the best pitcher in baseball. On May 30, he threw eight shutout innings in a 3–0 win in his second of three consecutive starts against the Yankees. This performance lowereed his ERA to 1.44 over 81 innings in his first 11 starts. But it would be nearly the last "Pedro" performance of the season.

His next start occurred on June 4, and it turned out to be a turning point in the season. In a game that was the makeup of an earlier rained-out game, the pitching rotations lined up Martinez vs. Mike Mussina of the Yankees for the third consecutive outing in two weeks. But manager Joe Torre pushed Mussina back a day, to ease the stress on Mussina. The Red Sox pitched Martinez, and he ended up leaving after six innings and only 90 pitches with a 4–3 lead. But the bullpen failed to hold it, and despite Manny Ramirez beating Mariano Rivera for the second time in the 2001 season, this time with a two-run homer to tie it in the ninth, the Yankees won 7–6.

More important than the result of that game, however, was the fact that Pedro felt pain in his shoulder, the beginnings of an injury that would limit his physical availability to pitch for the rest of his time with the Red Sox. He pitched six strong innings in his next start against Philadelphia before giving up four runs in the seventh inning of a 5–2 loss. After skipping a turn in the rotation, he went five good innings against Tampa Bay, but in his next start, on June 26, also against the Devil Rays, he had to leave in the fifth inning. He was out for two months, and there were conflicting news reports about the diagnosis. There were reports of a tear in the rotator cuff, and other reports of "thinness" or "weakness." In any event, the team did not shut him down, and he took to the mound again on August 26.

But his season was, for all intents and purposes, over. He only pitched three games after he came back, two of which were short outings and not especially effective, certainly not by Pedro standards. He threw six scoreless innings against the Yankees on September 1, but, once again, he got no run support and they lost. He made his last start on September 7, going three innings and finishing the year with 18 starts and a 2.39 ERA.

From the 2002 season on, there were questions about Pedro that hadn't been there before. Even though he'd usually missed a couple of starts during the course of his seasons, for the first time, there were serious questions about the structural integrity of his pitching shoulder. He also seemed more emotionally fragile and moody, less often the lighthearted prankster, and more often the pitcher who sulked when the Sox, worried about the state of his shoulder, were slow to guarantee the $17.5 million option year on his contract for 2004. Though he came back to lead the league in ERA in both 2002 and 2003, he frequently pitched with extra days of rest and was rarely allowed to pitch deep into a game. While he had once been very effective in the late innings of games (leading the league in complete games in 1997), his effectiveness now diminished rapidly after about 100 pitches. This came back to haunt the Red Sox in the heartbreaking seventh game of the 2003 ALCS when manager Grady Little stayed with Pedro too long in a game Martinez had pitched brilliantly, only to see him abruptly lose his dominance, the game, and the season. (The decision to keep Pedro in the game despite his high pitch count, reportedly against the direct orders of the front office and the team's medical staff, arguably cost Little his job.)

Through 2003, several things set Martinez apart from other pitchers. Martinez had near-total mastery of three pitches. His best pitch was a fastball that sometimes hit 96 on the speed gun. He backed this up with a sharp curve and a devastating changeup. This triple mastery led to pinpoint control—the reason for the high strikeout and low walk totals. Martinez's long slender fingers allowed him to be creative with his pitches, changing his grips to get more movement on his fastball, or to change his curve from a sharp break to a more looping "lollipop curve." He mixed in occasional sliders and changed his arm angle, altering the action of the pitch and forcing the batter to change his line of sight.

But in spring training of 2004, much of Pedro's velocity had disappeared. While he gained back some of his pitching power as the season went on, he was never consistently overwhelming—still a very good pitcher, but no longer the ace of the staff (a role that fell to new arrival Curt Schilling) or a pitcher who consistently dominated the opposition. Martinez went 16–9 with a solid 3.90 ERA. But that ERA was more than a run higher than his previous worst in Boston, and the 26 home runs he gave up was more than the previous three seasons combined. What's more, Pedro seemed to be getting even more emotional, having a hard time adjusting to his new lack of dominance. After losing to the Yankees during a crucial late-September game, he vented by saying "I just tip my hat and call the Yankees my daddies," which predictably led to taunting chants of "Whoooooo's your dad-dy?" from Yankees fans every time Pedro faced them from then on. During the 2004 playoffs Pedro appeared in five games, four starts and one inexplicable relief appearance in Game 7 of the ALCS on short rest, in which he gave up two runs in front of a mocking Yankees home crowd (and singlehandedly seemed to bring a listless Yankee Stadium back to life). He pitched seven innings giving up three runs in Game 2 of the ALDS, and a marvelous seven shutout innings in Game 3 of the World Series, winning both those games. Against "his daddies" in the ALCS he twice pitched six innings, giving up four and three runs, and was the losing pitcher in Game 2.

Throughout his career in Boston, Pedro was tremendously popular among fans, his teammates, and most surprisingly, by-and-large among Boston's notoriously negative press. His popularity with the Dominican community in Boston was such that the *Boston Globe* reported on his games in Spanish as well as English. Fans posted K signs to record his strikeouts—not just at Fenway, but in other parks as well. (This also used to be true of Roger Clemens.) During games when Pedro was not on the mound he was an enthusiastic cheerleader, and a boisterous prankster (one game to such an extent that his teammates taped him to a dugout pole and gagged him; Nomar of course stood guard so that no foul balls would hit the team's ace). In another favorite moment Martinez wore a Yoda mask with his uniform, and during the 2004 drive to the World Series, he brought a 26-inch-tall friend, Nelson de la Rosa, into the clubhouse to become the team's unofficial mascot and deputy clown behind Pedro.

Martinez also played a role in breaking down Boston's reputation as an unwelcoming city for minorities. The city welcomed Martinez, and his popularity gave exposure to the area's thriving and vibrant Latin community. One of the reasons superstar free agent Manny Ramirez signed with the Red Sox was that his mother urged him to go to Boston because Martinez was there—even though she didn't know anything about baseball.

Martinez always spoke candidly but sometimes without thought to the consequences of his words, such as in 2000, when he was one of the few players to publicly support center fielder Carl Everett after the media turned on him. (Like Everett, Martinez feuded with manager Jimy Williams, particularly after Williams bumped him from an August 1999 start for being late to the ballpark.) Pedro's 2001 season ended with a much publicized (but never clearly described) conflict with new manager Joe Kerrigan. In 2004, manager Terry Francona refused to be drawn into public controversy when Pedro's relationship with team rules became increasingly erratic, publicly taking the heat for his star while privately trying to keep Pedro focused and effective.

Because of that outspokenness, the way Martinez left Boston was somehow unsurprising. Although concerned about his diminished effectiveness and fragile shoulder, the Red Sox initially offered a two-year deal with an option year at $13.5 million a year, then guaranteed a third year when Pedro gave the impression that he would re-sign with the Sox if they did so. Instead, he used the Red Sox offer as leverage to get a four-year offer from new Mets GM Omar Minaya (who was trying to make a splash upon his arrival in New York), then claimed the Red Sox failure to offer him a four-year deal showed a lack of respect, adding gratuitous criticisms of Sox manager Francona and GM Theo Epstein. The ungracious exit was stunning to a Red Sox Nation still basking in the afterglow of the 2004 World Series victory, but was shrugged off more as another instance of

Pedro's overexuberance rather than the sort of open wounds left behind by Roger Clemens or Wade Boggs or Mo Vaughn. He remains a hero in Boston, a future Hall of Famer, and one of the best pitchers in Red Sox history.

Ramon Martinez—tall, lanky righthanded pitcher, now known as Pedro Martinez's big brother. When Pedro started, he was known as Ramon's little brother. In 1990 at the age of 22, Ramon had a tremendous season for the Dodgers, going 20–6 while leading the National League in complete games, and making the top 10 in numerous other pitching categories. He looked like the next great pitcher in the National League, but never quite lived up to the standards that he set that season. He has never had another 20-win season, or another year with an ERA under 3.00.

He was hurt in the middle of the 1998 season and had to have shoulder reconstruction surgery. Sox GM Dan Duquette signed him as a free agent in the off-season, and he joined the Red Sox prior to the 1999 season, though he wasn't healthy enough to pitch until late in the year. He made four effective starts in September of 1999, helping the Red Sox wrap up the wild card. In the playoffs, he pitched well in 1 start against the Indians and one against the Yankees. Many Sox fans were encouraged and felt that he would be back in form for the 2000 season, but that did not turn out to be the case. His first start of 2000, in Seattle, turned out to be a precursor of the season to come, when he gave up five runs in the first inning, capped by a Jay Buhner three-run homer. He occasionally pitched well but frequently got into serious trouble early in the game. He finished the season averaging fewer than five innings per start, with an ERA over 6.00. The Red Sox declined to pick up his $8 million contract option for the 2001 season. Martinez drew little interest as a free agent, and wound up returning to his original team, the Dodgers. The Dodgers, however, had depth in the rotation. After being told that he'd have to start the season in the minors, Ramon asked for, and received, his release. He signed with the Pirates in April and started four games, pitching badly, before announcing his retirement on May 2, finishing his career with a 135–88 record and a 3.85 ERA.

John Marzano—a light-hitting catcher who debuted with the Sox in 1987. Marzano had been heavily publicized as a college star at Temple University and as a member of the US Olympic team, but in the majors he was a perpetual free swinger who displayed only occasional power. He shuttled back and forth between Boston and Pawtucket for six seasons, serving as backups to such players as Rich Gedman, Rick Cerone, and Tony Peña. After his release from Boston following the 1992 season, he was out of the major leagues until he resurfaced with the Texas Rangers in 1995. He spent parts of the next 3 seasons with the Seattle Mariners.

Marzano's most memorable moment came in a 1991 game against the Tigers, in which he may have saved the career of ace pitcher Roger Clemens. After being hit by a Clemens fastball, Tigers outfielder John Shelby charged the mound—with the bat still in his hand. With his pitcher a sitting duck, Marzano sprung from his catching position and, loaded with gear, caught up to Shelby and tackled him from behind.

Carl Mays—a starting pitcher who played for three World Series winners in his four-plus years in Boston (winning 18, 22, and 21 games as a full-time starter from 1916–18). In 1919, he left the club under mysterious circumstances. Two weeks later, new team owner Harry Frazee sold him to the Yankees for $40,000, in a portent of things to come (Frazee would soon sell Babe Ruth and many other Sox stars to the Yankees).

Mays is best known for killing a man during a baseball game. Mays threw underhanded, but had a devastating fastball. On August 16, 1920, he hit Cleveland shortstop Ray Chapman with a pitch; Chapman died 12 hours later without ever recovering consciousness (batters did not wear protective helmets at the time, or for many years afterward). Mays played nine more years in the big leagues after the incident, three times winning 19 games or more.

David McCarty—righthanded hitting first baseman/outfielder and former top prospect for Minnesota who ended up as a defensive replacement, pinch hitter, role player, and occasional lefthanded pitcher for the Red Sox. McCarty never developed into the hitting star the Twins envisioned when they drafted him third overall out of Stanford University in 1991. (His last year at Stanford, McCarty hit .420 with 24 homers and was *Baseball America*'s player of the year; his sophomore year he hit .445, a school record at the time.) McCarty was rushed to the big leagues, but hit poorly in his rookie year, and didn't get another sustained opportunity for seven years, by which time he'd drifted all over the major leagues. McCarty played for Minnesota, San Francisco, Seattle, Kansas City, Tampa Bay, and Oakland, before being claimed off waivers by the Red Sox in August 2003. McCarty appeared in 16 games for the 2003 Red Sox down the stretch, batting .407 (11-for-27) while playing well defensively. In 2004, McCarty made the club as a nonroster invitee after batting .410 (25-for-61) with 7 homers and 18 RBI in 26 spring training games. He played 89 games in 2004, losing some of his playing time (and his spot on the playoff roster) after Doug Mientkiewicz was obtained from Minnesota.

McCarty bats right but throws lefthanded (he has an 88 MPH fastball), and had always pitched a little. Following the 2003 success of Milwaukee's Brooks Kieschnick, a marginal 31-year-old outfielder who extended his value (and career) by filling in as a mop-up pitcher, McCarty pitched in three games during the 2004 season with a 2.45 ERA. (Kieschnick pitched in 42 games during 2003 and another 32 in 2004, but unlike Boston, Milwaukee wasn't in a pennant race and had many more games that were either meaningless or where the team ran out of pitchers.)

McCarty is thought of as a future baseball administrator and excellent judge of talent, and reportedly turned down a chance to oversee the Dodgers' minor league scouting system in order to keep playing with the Red Sox. He signed a minor league contract to return with the Red Sox in 2005.

Mickey McDermott—a lefthanded pitcher who looked like he was going to become a star, Maury "Mickey" McDermott first played for the Red Sox at age 19. He was an average pitcher for several years, before breaking out with an 18–10 season as a 24-year-old in 1953. When McDermott was traded that offseason for

Jackie Jensen, many fans were outraged: McDermott was a rising star, extremely popular in Boston's Irish community, and known for singing in Boston nightclubs. The trade turned out to be a good one, however—Jensen became a star for the Red Sox and McDermott never won more than 10 games in a season again.

Willie McGee—a singles-hitting outfielder with a good arm, range, and speed, McGee is as famous for the year he didn't join the Red Sox as the year he did. In 1990, when the Red Sox were fighting for a playoff berth and McGee (hitting .335) was available in a trade, Red Sox GM Lou Gorman famously said "What would we do with Willie McGee?" McGee went to the Oakland A's instead—a team that would go on to beat the Red Sox in the playoffs.

McGee had a long career with the St. Louis Cardinals (where he hit .353, the highest average ever for a switch hitter, in 1985) and the San Francisco Giants before joining the Red Sox in 1995. By this time the 36-year-old McGee was well past his prime due to age and injuries. In 67 games as a pinch hitter, late inning defensive replacement, and occasional starter, McGee hit .285, but walked just nine times. He stole only five bases (he averaged 25 a year over his career, and once stole 56 in a season) and was caught stealing nine times. It was his only year in Boston. After 1995 he returned to St. Louis, where he was a part-time player until age 40, retiring in 1999.

Stuffy McInnis—a Gloucester native, Jack "Stuffy" McInnis joined the Philadelphia Athletics as a teenage shortstop in 1909, but became a star after moving to first base two years later. Though the characterization seems ridiculous in the Manny Ramirez/Alex Rodriguez era, McInnis was part of the Athletics' great "$100,000 Infield" (with Hall of Famers Eddie Collins and Home Run Baker, and shortstop Jack Barry). McInnis hit for high averages in Philly (over .300 in six of his seven full seasons) and virtually never struck out, though he had little power and rarely walked. He was a legendary defensive player, and the first first baseman to go into a split when stretching for throws.

In 1918, the rebuilding Athletics traded McInnis to his hometown team for longtime third baseman Larry Gardner and outfielder Tilly Walker. McInnis wasn't as effective with Boston, where he slumped to .272, but he earned his third World Series ring. He hit .305 in 1919 and .297 in 1920, though his lack of power became a liability with the advent of the lively ball. In 1921 McInnis hit .307 and set 2 notable records. He had 584 at bats, but only struck out 9 times—the fewest ever of any Red Sox player with over 500 at bats. McInnis only made one error, and his .999 fielding percentage set a big league record for first basemen that stood for 63 years (Steve Garvey was a perfect 1.000 in 1984). Despite the records, McInnis was traded to Cleveland after the season for George Burns, a first baseman with more power. He retired after the 1927 season with 2,405 hits and a .307 lifetime average.

Jeff McNeely—once highly thought of as a prospect, Jeff McNeely was an outfielder who played a total of 21 innings in the majors, all during the 1993 season. He was one of the fastest players that the Sox have had, stealing six bases without being caught during his brief stint in the majors.

Sam Mele—outfielder/first baseman who came up with the Red Sox in 1947 then bounced around baseball for 10 years. He spent time with six separate teams, not counting two stints with the Red Sox. (He was traded in midseason four different times.) He was never a great hitter for average or for power, with a career high of 16 homers in 1952 (though his 36 doubles did lead the American League in 1951, while he was playing for Washington). He once drove in six runs in the fourth inning of a game against Boston while playing for the White Sox, hitting a three-run homer and a three-run triple. After his playing career ended, he managed the Minnesota Twins for seven seasons, leading them to the World Series in 1965. Mele was also a longtime scout for the Red Sox (serving the Boston area), and is currently a scouting consultant for the team.

Ramiro Mendoza—a Panamanian sinkerball pitcher who spent seven years as a key swingman on New York Yankees' pitching staffs (playing in three World Series along the way), Mendoza signed with the Red Sox as a 30-year-old free agent in 2003. The Sox had high hopes that he would be a stabilizing core pitcher in their bullpen, as Mendoza had been for the Yankees, but instead he had a disastrous, injury plagued 2003 season. (His 6.75 ERA was more than two runs worse than the league average.) The team lost confidence in Mendoza when another injury sidelined him during 2004 spring training and he was slow to recover effectiveness in minor league rehab stints, but manager Terry Francona was forced to use him late in the season after a rash of injuries to other pitchers. Mendoza pitched very well in 27 games, shoring up the team's middle relief during the Red Sox remarkable second-half playoff drive, holding opposing batters to a .225 average. He signed a minor league deal with the Yankees for 2005.

Kent Mercker—a lefthanded pitcher remembered by Boston fans for his role in the 1999 playoff drive, but whose career is more remarkable for an astonishing comeback after nearly dying during a game. A 31-year-old veteran starter in 1999, Mercker was traded to Boston where he pitched extremely well in five starts down the stretch, including winning the game in which the Red Sox clinched the American League Wild Card berth in September. He was ineffective in the playoffs, getting shelled in only 1⅓ innings in Game 4 of the Division Series (though Boston ended up winning the game 23–7). After the season Mercker signed with the Anaheim Angels. On May 11, 2000, he suffered a cerebral hemorrhage while pitching against Texas. He spent 12 days in the hospital, including four days in intensive care. Remarkably, he was pitching again in only three months, starting against the Yankees on August 12. On August 22, he beat the Red Sox in Fenway Park, his first win since he had clinched the Wild Card for the Sox the previous September. In January 2001, Mercker was honored at the Boston Baseball Writers' annual dinner as a co-winner of the Tony Conigliaro award, given annually to "the player who best overcomes an obstacle and continues to thrive through the adversity." A free agent once again after the 2000 season, Mercker signed a minor league contract with Boston in January, but didn't make the team. After changing his pitching motion, however, Mercker made an improbable late-career renaissance as a lefthanded relief specialist. He had a 1.95 ERA for 2 teams in 2003, and a 2.55 ERA in a career-high 71 games for the Cubs in 2004 (despite missing time with back soreness and a three-game suspension for intentionally hitting a batter). He signed a two-year contract with the Reds following the 2004 season.

Lou Merloni—a native of Framingham, Massachusetts, and Nomar Garciaparra's close friend and former AAA roommate, it's probably too strong to call Merloni a "local kid made good," but in limited play he became popular, attested to by the chants of "Lou, Lou, Lou" that accompanied him to the plate when he played at Fenway. Though his skills are average for a major leaguer, Merloni has a hard-nosed attitude that Red Sox fans appreciated. Merloni saw action at several infield positions in 1998 and 1999, hitting .281 after a hot start in 1998 (including a homer in his first Fenway Park at bat), but slumping to .254 in 1999. With his chances of making the major leagues slim in 2000, the Red Sox sold the 29-year-old Merloni's contract to the Yokohama Bay Stars of the Japanese Pro Baseball League, where he could make more money than as a fringe player in the United States. Merloni met with little success in Japan, hitting a measly .213. After being released he returned midway through the season to sign to a minor league contract with the Red Sox. It was good timing for both Merloni and the team, due to an early season-ending injury to third baseman John Valentin, and the failure of everyone else who had tried to replace him. Though not flashy, Merloni provided stability at that position with steady defense and hit .320 down the stretch. But over the next two years Merloni was used sparingly, eventually expressing his frustration at being shuttled between Boston and Pawtucket every time the team faced a roster crunch. Since he didn't figure in the team's plans but had a sort of folk hero status, the Red Sox agreed to release him the spring (rather than sending him to the minors or trading him) to allow him to find a favorable job. He played most of the season with the San Diego Padres before being reacquired by the Red Sox (who needed an experienced infield backup who was used to Boston pressure) in late August, in an attempt to bolster their infield depth for the playoff drive. After the season he signed with Cleveland, where he had a solid 2004 season (.289), established himself as the same sort of fan favorite he was in Boston, and was getting the most playing time of his career—until an August elbow injury curtailed his season. In seven major league seasons, he has played every position except pitcher, catcher, and center field. He signed a minor league contract with the Angels before the 2005 season.

Catfish Metkovich—center fielder for the Red Sox during World War II, when most of the team's regular players were in the military. George Michael Metkovich was an undistinguished hitter with some speed as a baserunner; he was good enough to remain a part-time player in the major leagues after the war ended. He played as a part-timer in 1946 after Dom DiMaggio returned to reclaim his job in center field, then drifted to five other teams in the next six years

Doug Mientkiewicz—a lefthanded-batting first baseman and former hitting star with Minnesota who played a key defensive role on the 2004 World Champion Red Sox. Mientkiewicz was acquired, along with shortstop Orlando Cabrera, in the trade that sent Nomar Garciaparra to the Chicago Cubs in 2004.

The Red Sox, approaching the trading deadline, were concerned both about their defense and about Kevin Millar's prolonged hitting slump. Because Millar went on a tear just after Mientkiewicz was obtained, Mientkiewicz didn't play a lot in Boston, though he finished a lot of games as a defensive replacement, and played most of the time behind groundball-inducing pitcher Derek Lowe (helping steady the emotional Lowe, who was frustrated by a lack of defensive support in the first half of the season but much better in the second half, and terrific in the playoffs).

Mientkiewicz started his career in Minnesota, where he won a Gold Glove at first base in 2001. Although never much of a power hitter for a first baseman, Mientkiewicz hit for a high average (over .300 in 2001 and 2003) with good plate discipline. He struggled at the bat in 2004 before the trade, and then struggled even more after joining the Red Sox. He did demonstrate the good glove that the Sox had expected, though. And actually played second base, and played it well, in a game when Bellhorn, Reese, and Youkilis were all hurt.

Mientkiewicz made it clear that while he was willing to play a bench role in a quest for a championship, ultimately he wanted to return to the starting lineup, so January 2005, the Red Sox traded him to the Mets for first base prospect Ian Bladergroen. The lasting memory of many Sox fans have of Mientkiewicz may be a story that was written by the *Boston Globe*'s Dan Shaughnessy, in which he seemingly took some quotes from both Mientkiewicz and team president Larry Lucchino out of context to generate a small controversy over the fate of the ball that Edgar Renteria grounded to Keith Foulke for the last out of the 2004 World Series. Mientkiewicz, as the first baseman at the time, made the last out and ended up with the ball, and the article implied that the ownership of the ball was in dispute (which apparently hadn't occured to anyone until the article brought it up, but for sentimental reasons Mientkiewicz was loathe to part with it, jokingly referring to it as his "retirement fund.")

Kevin Millar—free-spirited first baseman-outfielder who was a key rallying point both on and off the field for the 2003–04 Red Sox. The righthanded-hitting Millar put in a long minor-league internship (including an independent league stint) before making the Florida Marlins for good as a 27-year-old in 1999. Given a full-time job in 2001, he hit .314 with 39 doubles and 20 homers, and followed

How Many Millers?

With the signing of pitcher Wade Miller, the Red Sox have Miller, Millar, and Mueller (pronounced Miller) all on the same team. They toyed with signing catcher Damian Miller in the offseason as well. The team had 3 Martinez's in 2004, with Pedro, Anastacio, and Sandy but the record for most players with a single last name in one seson almost certainly belongs to the Pawtucket Red Sox And in one game in 1995, they all played at the same time!

    Steve Rodiguez, 1994–95
    Carlos Rodriguez, 1994–95
    Frank Rodriguez, 1994–95
    Tony Rodriguez, 1994–97
    Victor Rodriguez, 1995

Also, there was

    Ruben Rodriguez, 1992–94

it up by hitting .306 with 41 doubles and 16 homers the next year. The Red Sox tried to trade for Millar (who the Marlins felt they couldn't afford to keep), but instead they sold him to the Chunichi Dragons in the Japanese League, according to some sources telling Millar that no one in the U.S. wanted him. When it became clear that Boston wanted him very much—even submitting a waiver claim to block the sale to the Dragons—Millar balked at going overseas, citing the danger to his family from rising anti-American sentiment as a result of the unpopular war in Iraq. Finally, Florida bought out his contract with Chunichi in a face-saving deal, and sold Millar to the Red Sox.

Millar had a great first half for the 2003 Red Sox (he tailed off late in the season, finishing at .276 with a career-high 25 homers and 96 RBI) but his greatest contribution to the team was in a morale-boosting role. When most of the media and other players seemed to feel the playoffs were unattainable, Millar was the one who coined the slogan that helped rally the team into the postseason when he said it was time to "cowboy up" (borrowing the phrase from several country songs). When an FBI agent friend of Millar's provided the team with footage of Millar, as a teenager, doing an embarrasing karaoke to Bruce Springsteen's "Born in the USA," Millar gamely allowed the team to show it over the scoreboard—and when the team started rallying to win when it was played, the video became a late-inning staple on days the Sox were losing at home.

After a slow start in 2004 (to the point where the team traded for Doug Mientkiewicz as a possible replacement), Millar got red-hot in the second half of the season (finishing at .297 with 18 homers and a career-high 383 on-base percentage), and again publicly helped rally a team that seemed to be going nowhere . . . but ended up in the World Series. Once again he was in the news for his part in a ritual when he jokingly mentioned that during the playoffs team members did shots of Jack Daniel's before their improbable comeback against the Yankees, and continued to do so for luck before each World Series game.

Rick Miller—lefthanded-hitting outfielder who served two stints with the Red Sox, Miller had a long career as a platoon and backup player without ever being a full time starter. He batted more than 400 times only twice in 12 years with the Red Sox. (Most full-time players bat 500–600 times in a season.) Miller was a fine center fielder (he won a Gold Glove for the Angels in 1978), fast runner (although only an average base stealer), and a decent hitter who drew more than his share of walks but didn't have much power (his career high in home runs was six). Despite his lack of power, Miller tied a major league record by hitting four doubles in a game. (Three other Sox players, Billy Werber, Al Zarilla, and Orlando Cepeda have also tied the record.) Miller played for the Sox from 1971–1977, and during this time married the sister of teammate Carlton Fisk. Miller signed with the Angels as a free agent, then was traded back to the Sox in the ill-fated Fred Lynn trade before the 1981 season. He played until 1985, the last few years mostly as a pinch hitter.

Wade Miller—righthanded pitcher who signed with the Red Sox as a free agent in December 2004, after being nontendered by the Houston Astros. If healthy, Miller could turn out to be one of the biggest bargains of the 2004–05 offseason. He's got 3 above-average pitches (95 MPH fastball, curve, slider), and when he's on, he's very tough to hit (as evidenced by his low hit rates and high strikeout totals). Miller had been one of the National League's best starters, but missed the second half of 2004 with a frayed rotator cuff. Ironically, he was brought to Boston to help replace Pedro Martinez, who had a similar injury in 2001—and who, like Miller, went on a new workout program instead of undergoing surgery.

The 28-year-old Miller is the only player from Alvernius College (located in his hometown of Reading, Pennsylvania) to make the major leagues. Houston selected him in the twentieth round of the 1996 draft, and Miller quickly established himself as a top prospect. He went 15–5 with a 2.38 ERA in his first full minor league season, and reached the majors in 1999. Miller joined Houston's rotation for good in mid–2000, and while his rookie numbers weren't great (6–6, 5.14), he struck out nearly a batter per inning and showed enormous potential.

The Astros had high hopes for Miller in 2001, but never expected him to become an elite pitcher so quickly. He had a 16–8 record and 3.40 ERA, striking out 183 batters and allowing only 183 hits in 212 innings—and also had an outstanding start against Atlanta in the playoffs. Miller was even better in 2002 (15–4, 3.28), though he missed the beginning of the season with a pinched nerve in his neck. His 2003 season was hampered by a forearm strain, but he still put up solid stats (14–13, 4.13, 161 strikeouts in 187.1 innings). Last season began very well for Miller, who was 7–7 with a 3.35 ERA after 15 starts, but the rotator cuff injury ended his season in late June.

While reports on his prognosis have been optimistic, the Astros had a difficult financial decision to make. Miller earned $3.4 million in 2004 and was eligible for arbitration in the offseason. Under the rules, Houston had to offer him at least $2.7 million—and would likely have paid closer to $4 million. Since the Astros were trying to re-sign free agent center fielder Carlos Beltran (and lure back ace Roger Clemens), they didn't want to tie up too much money on a pitcher who might miss part of 2005. Instead, the Astros did not tender Miller a contract, making him a free agent. The Red Sox, who already had inquired about a possible trade for Miller, outbid seven other teams (including Houston), with a one-year deal for a guaranteed $1.5 million, plus another $3 million in potential incentives. Boston also has the right to keep Miller in 2006, since he's not eligible for free agency after 2005 (though the team will have the option of non-tendering him, as Houston did, if he doesn't pitch well).

Doug Mirabelli—after spending parts of five seasons as a backup catcher with the San Francisco Giants, Mirabelli started the 2001 season in possibly the most unenviable position in all of baseball—as the backup to ironman catcher Ivan Rodriguez in Texas. After Jason Varitek suffered a broken elbow, the Red Sox traded highly regarded pitching prospect Justin Duchscherer to get Mirabelli, who had a great defensive reputation but was hitting only .102 in limited playing time. Mirabelli was much better with the Red Sox, hitting .270 and slugging .518 in 54 games to go along with his vaunted defense and throwing arm, and eventually taking the bulk of the playing time away from the Red Sox incumbent back-up catcher, Scott Hatteberg, who was traded after the season ended.

Mirabelli has thrived in another unenviable niche in Boston: as personal catcher to knuckleballer Tim Wakefield, whose dancing pitches are almost impossible to handle. As a result of catching Wakefield's 65 MPH offerings, Mirabelli doesn't catch many runners stealing anymore (although he has a terrfic arm) and regularly leads the league in passed balls, but he made just two errors in 2004. (Sox catchers had the league's top fielding percentage, at .997.) He also has a potent bat, surprising given his sparse usage against lefthanded pitching, which he devours: in about a full season's worth of plate appearances (spread over four years in Boston), Mirabelli has 40 doubles and 31 home runs, and draws more than his share of walks. In 2004 he set career highs in batting average (.281), runs, RBI, on-base percentage (.368) and slugging (.525). A free agent in considerable demand after the World Series, Mirabelli signed a two-year, $3 million contract to remain with the Red Sox.

Bill Monbouquette—"Monbo" was a native of Medford, Massachusetts, who was the ace for very weak Red Sox teams from 1958 to 1965. Without an over-powering fastball, Monbouquette relied on changing speeds and on pinpoint control. He had at least 13 wins each year from 1960 to 1964, including a 20–10 record in 1963—quite an accomplishment on a team that finished 76–85. He tied for the league lead in losses on a dreadful (62–100) team in 1965, but with a decent 3.70 ERA.

A four-time All Star, Monbouquette's career highlights include striking out 17 Senators in 1961 (at the time the second-best ever in the American League), and a 1–0 no-hitter against Early Wynn of the Chicago White Sox on August 1, 1962. After the 1965 season Monbouquette was traded to Detroit. After a brief stay he moved on to the Yankees in 1967 (where he pitched well), and the Giants in 1968 (where he retired after going 1–7).

Monbouquette was a pitching coach for the New York Mets from 1982 to 1983 and in the Toronto organization in the 1990s. In 2004, he was pitching coach for the short-season Oneonta Tigers. He is also the director of the pitching clinic for the Cooperstown Diamonds National Youth Baseball Center. Monbouquette was inducted into the Red Sox Hall of Fame in 2000.

Bob Montgomery—a 10-year career backup catcher with the Sox, from 1970–1979, never batting more than 254 times in a season. "Monty" was a weak-hitting backup to Pudge Fisk and Jim Rice's golfing partner. Like many career backups, he was a favorite of underdog-rooting fans. After his playing career ended he spent several years as an English-butchering color analyst on Red Sox television broadcasts.

Dave Morehead—righthanded pitcher signed by the Boston Red Sox as an amateur free agent before the 1961 season. Until Derek Lowe's no-hitter in 2002, Morehead's claim to fame was throwing the last no-hitter at Fenway Park in 1965 (a year in which he led the league in losses with 18). Only 1,247 fans attended the game with the Cleveland Indians. The Red Sox announced the firing of GM

Mike Higgins after the game, overshadowing Morehead's achievement.

As a promising 19-year-old rookie Morehead threw a shutout in his first game in 1963 and lost a no-hitter against the Indians that year on an eighth-inning single. But Morehead would have only one winning season in his eight-year career; he went 5–4 as a part time player on the 1967 Impossible Dream team. His overall record in six years with the Sox was 35–56. The Sox lost Morehead to the Kansas City Royals in the 1968 expansion draft. He pitched two years for the Royals, then left baseball when the Royals released him in spring training 1971.

Rogelio Moret—talented, rail-thin (6-foot-4, 170 pound) Puerto Rican left-hander whose career was tragically undermined by mental problems. Moret, better known as Roger to Boston fans, reportedly had an IQ so low that it bordered on mental retardation, and never made any kind of adjustment to living in a foreign culture. The Sox couldn't decide whether the sidearmer should start or relieve, and he never really learned to throw strikes, but he had more than enough talent to be effective, actually leading the league in winning percentage in both 1973 (13–2) and 1975 (14–3), and throwing a scintillating near no-hitter against the White Sox in 1974. (Dick Allen beat out a grounder to short in the seventh that was controversially called a hit.) He pitched a scoreless sixth inning of Game 2 of the 1975 ALCS and got credit for the win, but was mostly ineffective in the Series, giving up Joe Morgan's tenth-inning game-winning single in Game 3 and an RBI single to Pete Rose in the seventh inning of Game 7. He is the answer to two trivia questions, however: He is the person whom Bernie Carbo pinch-hit for in Game 6, and the pitcher that Jim Willoughby relieved (getting out of a bases-loaded, two-out jam) in Game 7. The Sox traded Moret to Atlanta after the 1975 season and his career fell apart from a series of injuries and reported heavy drinking. In late June of 1978, still just 28, he went into a catatonic state while in the Texas Rangers' clubhouse, and was sent to a psychiatric hospital. Moret went to spring training with the Rangers in 1979 and the Indians in 1980, but never pitched in the major leagues again.

Ed Morris—top pitcher on terrible Sox teams in the 1930s who suffered a macabre death. Morris had played briefly with the Cubs in 1922 but didn't resurface in the major leagues until 1928, when he went 19–15 as a 28-year-old rookie on a team that lost 96 games. He led an equally bad team in wins again the next year. He was stabbed to death by a jealous husband at a fish fry just before spring training of 1932.

Jamie Moyer—a lefthanded starting pitcher and the son-in-law of ex-Notre Dame University basketball coach Digger Phelps, Moyer was an undistinguished, soft-throwing, 33-year-old veteran on his fifth team when the Red Sox signed him as a free agent prior to the 1996 season. He'd never won more than 12 games in a season, and had a lifetime 59–72 record. The 1996 Red Sox, defending American League East champions, started the season at 6–19, and were never realistically in the race. Moyer pitched well for Boston, and took advantage of strong run support in his games to go 7–1 as of July. Sensing a chance to get a high-upside player for a journeyman pitcher having what looked like a fluke season, the Red Sox sent him to Seattle for Darren Bragg. Since the trade to Seattle, Moyer continued his late-career blossoming process, becoming one of the best starters in the American League by 1997. In 2001, the 38-year-old Moyer won 20 games for the first time in his career, going 20–6 for Seattle. In 2003 he did it again at age 40, posting a 21–7 record for the Mariners and making his first All Star appearance.

Bragg was gone from Boston after 1998, and was never better than mediocre. Moyer has won 126 games by himself in the eight years since leaving the Red Sox, while Boston has had a total of 81 wins from all its lefthanded pitchers combined during those years.

Time seemed to catch up with Moyer in 2004, when he went 7–13 with a 5.21 ERA, and gave up 43 home runs, fifth most in major league history (though he pitched very well at times for a bad team). He's signed with the Mariners through the 2005 season.

Bill Mueller—an unheralded third baseman who won a surprising batting title for the Sox in 2003. Mueller (pronounced Miller) started his career with the Giants in 1996. In 55 games, he hit .330 with a .401 OBP, then hit over .290 in 3 of the next 4 years with the Giants. Mueller acquired a reputation as an excellent defensive third baseman who got on base a lot, but didn't have much of the power-hitting ability traditionally associated with the position. In 2001 he was traded to the Cubs (who perennially need a third baseman). He got off to very good start, then in June he shattered his kneecap against the tarp while sliding to make a catch (he didn't) in foul territory. Mueller missed the rest of that season and the beginning of 2002, though his hitting seemed to have suffered. He was traded back to the Giants, but too late to be on their postseason roster (as the Giants lost the World Series). He became a free agent and was signed by the Red Sox to a two-year $4.5 million contract, much less than Mueller would have commanded had he been healthy.

The 32-year-old switch-hitter flourished at Fenway Park, starting most of the time at third and occasionally filling in at second base. Staying largely healthy, he hit .326 to edge out teammate Manny Ramirez (who hit .325) for the batting title. Mueller also set career highs in homers (with 19; he'd never hit more than 10 before) doubles (45; 29 had been his high), and RBI (85; 59 was his previous best). In a game against Texas on July 29, Mueller became the only player ever to hit grand slams from both sides of the plate in the same game; he had three homers and nine RBI in the game in all.

In 2004 he started slowly, bothered by a recurring knee injury that eventually required surgery. Prized Red Sox prospect Kevin Youkilis filled in well while Mueller was out, raising questions about whether Mueller would be able to reclaim his position. On his return, Mueller played very well both offensively and defensively however, giving the team a huge boost in its championship run. His ninth-inning home run against Yankees closer Mariano Rivera won the game that arguably turned the team's season around, the late-July game in which Jason Varitek's confrontation with Yankees star Alex Rodriguez touched off a brawl. He also hit .321 during the 2004 playoffs, including a game-tying single in the bottom of the ninth in Game 4 of the ALCS, again burning Rivera. (He did have a defensive meltdown in Game 2 of the World Series, committing three errors and forcing a gimpy Curt Schilling to work extra-hard for the win.) After the season, Boston exercised its option to bring Mueller back in 2005.

Rob Murphy—a lefthanded reliever obtained from Cincinnati as part of the Nick Esasky trade, Murphy had a terrific season in 1989. Murphy was 29 and coming off three good seasons, but was still not well known as a player (not unusual for a middle reliever). Murphy and Lee Smith held together a bad relief corps in 1989, with Murphy appearing in 74 games and posting a 2.74 ERA. In 1990, with talk of Murphy being moved into a closer's role, everything fell apart. His ERA more than doubled (opposing hitters hit over .400 against him), and he was ineffective all year. The Red Sox traded him to Seattle during spring training the next year for pitcher Mike Gardiner. Although Murphy would recover some of his effectiveness and pitch decently again, he never had another year like 1989.

Buddy Myer—lefthanded-hitting infielder who played third base for the Red Sox in 1928. They Red Sox acquired Myer from Washington late in the 1927 season, and in 1928, he led the American League with 30 stolen bases while playing for the Red Sox. The Senators were so convinced that they'd made a mistake, they traded five players to the Sox after the 1928 season in order to get Myer back. He did eventually play on two All Star teams in 1935 and 1937. In 1935 he won the American League batting title by going 4-for-5 in the season's final game, while Cleveland's Joe Vosmik was sitting out the game to protect his average. With the exception of the one season in Boston, he spent his entire 17-season career in Washington, retiring after the 1941 season.

Mike Myers—much-traveled lefty reliever who was picked up for the stretch run of the Red Sox 2004 championship season. Myers has a sidearm delivery that makes him very tough for lefthanded batters to hit, but righthanded hitters feast on him; as a result, he has found steady work as a situational reliever, but has not been able to build that success into a larger role. The 35-year-old Myers pitched similarly for the Red Sox, his seventh team in a 10-year major league career: He appeared in 25 games, but totaled only 15 innings of work since he often faced only a single lefty hitter before being replaced.

Because Myers has the same name as the villain in the *Halloween* horror movies, there were many jokes about him pitching in Game 7 of the World Series, which would have fallen on Halloween night if the Sox hadn't already beaten the Cardinals. Apparently, Myers found St. Louis to his liking, though; he signed with the Cardinals for the 2005 season.

Tim Naehring—talented righthanded-hitting infielder whose eight-year career with the Sox was riddled by injuries. The 23-year-old Naehring came up to the Sox in 1990 touted as a guy who could hit for good power, a rare commodity at that time for middle infielders, and played well in his initial tour of duty. Handed the starting shortstop's job the next spring, Naehring hit a ghastly .109 in 20 games, including an 0-for-39 slump, before the Red Sox shut him down to see what was wrong. Back and leg trouble kept stifling his development (he hit .231

the following year) until it was discovered that one of his legs was actually short-er than the other. To curb this problem he was fitted with a platform to wear in his shoe, to readjust the discrepancy and take the pressure off his lower back. The adjustment helped, and Naehring hit .331 in 1993. By this time, however, John Valentin was already established at shortstop, so Naehring moved to the less lat-erally demanding third base (where he was terrific defensively), allowing the Sox to trade Scott Cooper. Finally given the chance to play regularly, Naehring put up solid numbers for the Sox, hitting over .300 in 1995 (he led the league in hit-ting going into June) and launching a career-high 17 homers in 1996. An elbow injury in 1997 effectively ended Naehring's Red Sox career, shortly after he had turned down more money from the Cleveland Indians to re-sign with the Red Sox as a free agent. Because of a quirk in the free agent rules, it would have cost the Red Sox more than $4 million to keep him. Although the Sox offered him other jobs in the system, Naehring did not want to retire, and reluctantly signed with his hometown Cincinnati Reds. After two years of failed comeback attempt, Naehring took a position in the Reds' front office in 1999, working in the Reds organization in the player develpoment and scouting departments, as well as being an assistant to the general manager. In October 2000, Naehring assumed the title of director of player development.

Naehring was an active community leader during his time with the Sox, involv-ing himself in numerous local charity events, and even leading the construction of a Little League field shaped as a miniature Fenway Park in Cincinnati (for a picture, see www.redsoxdiehard.com/players/naehring.html).

Mike Nagy—a righthanded pitcher, Nagy came up with Boston in 1969 as a 21-year-old phenom, and went 12–2 for the Sox with a very good ERA. However, as with many pitchers that are successful at an early age, arm injuries resulted, probably because of the excessive workload for his age. He pitched 128⅔ innings in 1970, and never threw more than 41 in any season after that. After 4 years in Boston, he spent a year in St. Louis and another year in Houston. He was done at the age of 26 after the 1974 season.

Jeff Newman—one of many poorly thought out acquisitions in the early 1980s, Newman was a 34-year-old righthanded-hitting catcher with some power (he'd hit 22 home runs in a terrible hitter's park in 1979, in his only year as a full-time starter). He was heralded by the Sox front office as a natural Fenway hitter who would shower doubles off the Green Monster. He hit .189 with three home runs, and quickly lost his job to light-hitting Gary Allenson. In a way, this was a bless-ing in disguise; if Newman had been adequate as a starting catcher, Rich Gedman, then a 23-year-old part-time player, would probably never have been given the chance to develop into the key starter he would be from 1984 to 1986.

Reid Nichols—a center fielder who looked like a rising star in the mid–1980s. Nichols had a reputation as the fastest player in the Red Sox system, and had call-ups with the team in 1980 and 1981 without hitting much. In 1982, as a 23-year-old, he was finally given real playing time in the outfield and blossomed, hitting .302 with mid-range power for a team with light-hitting Rick Miller in center and beginning-to-fade Jim Rice in left. Instead of increasing Nichols's playing time in 1983, the Sox traded for one-dimensional power hitter Tony Armas, who hit only .218 to go with his with 36 home runs, rarely walked, and was overmatched in center field. Nichols again hit well as a fourth outfielder, batting .285, drawing walks about twice as often as Armas, and increasing his power slightly. The next year his playing time was cut in half and he was ineffective. Traded to the White Sox in 1985, Nichols never batted more than 150 times in a season again and was out of baseball before his thirtieth birthday. He remains a what-might-have been—a player who performed well in the only times he was given regular work (on mediocre teams that could have used an infusion of speed and youth), but who was never given a shot to develop into a full-time player.

Nichols has been much more successful in his front office career. He's currently Milwaukee's farm director, overseeing their entire minor league system. He also held the same title with Texas for several years, though he returned to the field as the Rangers' first base coach for the 2001 season.

Al Nipper—righthanded pitcher who came through the Red Sox farm system and debuted in the majors in 1983. He outpitched fellow rookie and close friend Roger Clemens during their rookie seasons in 1984. Never overpowering, he was a middle-of-the-rotation starter for the Red Sox from 1984–87, although he never had another winning season after 1984. John McNamara was heavily criticized for starting Nipper in Game 4 of the 1986 World Series, despite Nipper's 10–12 record and terrible 5.38 ERA (league average was 4.18), a game that Nipper predictably lost. Nipper threw a beanball at Darryl Strawberry in the first Red Sox-Mets game after the 1986 World Series, during 1987 spring training. Apparently, Nipper had vowed to get back at Strawberry for the Series, and his attempt to keep his word was popular with some fans.

After 1987, Nipper and Calvin Schiraldi were traded to the Cubs for Lee Smith (a great trade for the Red Sox), but he never pitched regularly in the major leagues again. Nipper later worked as a pitching coach in the Sox system, including a stint as the major league pitching coach during the musical-pitching-coaches phase of the Butch Hobson era in the early 1990s. He was supposed to be the next great pitching coach, but instead left the Red Sox organization under acrimonious circumstances, after several disagreements with general manager Dan Duquette. Nipper resurfaced as Kansas City's pitching coach for parts of 2001 and 2002, but soon found himself out of work. With his nemesis Duquette no longer running the show, Nipper returned to the Red Sox in 2003. He served as Sarasota's pitching coach for two seasons, and was recently promoted to the key role of minor league pitching coordinator.

Otis Nixon—speedy, switch-hitting outfielder signed as a free agent by the Sox prior to the strike-shortened season of 1994. The veteran Nixon was the long-desired leadoff hitter with speed sought by a club dragged down by an unproductive, singles-hitting offense. The sight of speed on the basepaths was a refreshing one for Sox fans, and Nixon gained an early popularity with the Fenway crowd. In his only season with Boston he hit .274 (while stealing 42 bases in 52 attempts, in just 103 games). Despite the strong numbers, the 35-year-old Nixon was part of the trade that brought Jose Canseco to Boston after Kevin Kennedy (who wanted a team of sluggers) was signed on as manager. Nixon, who didn't hit above .263 until his ninth year in the majors, continued to play well for years after most of his contemporaries were forced to retire. He spent 17 years in the majors with nine different teams, during which he hit .270 with 620 career steals.

Since his playing career ended, Nixon has had a number of legal difficulties, including separate accusations in 2004 that he raped a 25-year-old woman and that he threatened his own bodyguard with a knife.

Trot Nixon—lefthanded-hitting outfielder drafted by the Sox in the first round in 1993 (Lou Gorman's last draft). Christopher Trotman Nixon was a highly touted, five-tool prospect, a great high school quarterback as well as a baseball star (and a neighbor to Hall of Famer Catfish Hunter). Back problems plagued Nixon's minor league career, however, and it was uncertain if he would ever live up to his expectations. After showing great strides in improving his offense at AAA Pawtucket in 1997 and 1998, Nixon won a platoon right field job with Boston in 1999. Replacing Darren Bragg, a good fielder and gritty player but only a so-so hitter, Nixon showed that he also went all out on every play. This approach to the game put him in good graces with manager Jimy Williams, who stuck with Nixon despite his .105 batting average in April. (Nixon was out of options and couldn't be sent back to the minors unless the Sox wanted to risk losing him to another team). Nixon turned things around and hit well the rest of the year, bringing his average up to .270 with 15 home runs (12 of them in the season's second half).

As was the case with several Sox hitters in 2000, Nixon had an up and down season with the bat, finishing at .276 with 12 homers—similar to his first season rather than the dramatic improvement many people projected. He did play terrific defense in the outfield, with the strong throwing arm one might expect of a former quarterback, and a patient batting eye. Inconsistent playing time seemed to affect Nixon's timing, however; while there was talk of making him the full-time right fielder, he continued to platoon with light-hitting Darren Lewis, even against lefthanders who were better against righthanded hitters. When he did get to face lefty pitching, he was much improved from his 1999 struggles. Nixon's 2000 highlight came in the top of the ninth inning of a nationally televised pitching duel between Pedro Martinez and Roger Clemens at Yankee Stadium. With the score 0–0, Trot belted a Clemens pitch for a two-run homer that was the eventual game-winning hit.

In 2001 Nixon finally got to play more or less every day, and posted career high numbers in batting average (.280), runs (100), RBI (88), home runs (27), and many other categories. His hard-nosed play and increasingly vocal leadership earned him the team MVP award over Manny Ramirez. Because of injuries and the chaos surrounding fellow outfielder Carl Everett, Nixon split time between right field and center field, and was a steadying presence on a team rife with distractions and injuries. An injury-plagued 2002 was highlighted by an incident in Tampa Bay, after Devil Rays pitcher Ryan Rupe had hit both Nomar Garciaparra and Shea Hillenbrand in the first inning of the game. In his first at bat, Nixon swung at a Rupe delivery and his bat "accidentally" (Nixon's claim) flew from his hands and went in the general direction of the mound. (In an odd quirk of fate, during the off season the Red Sox acquired Rupe in a waiver deal and he and Trot were briefly be teammates in 2003.) In 2003, Nixon finally established himself as a very good player (rather than a potentially very good one) and an important part of the Red Sox record-setting offense, reaching career highs in batting (.306), home runs (28), on-base percentage (.396), and slugging (.578), signing a three-year, $6.5 million contract following the season.

Nixon expected to build on his breakout season in 2004, but arrived at spring training with what seemed to be a mild back injury, originally attributed to the car ride to Ft. Myers. It turned out to be a herniated disk, later aggravated by a strained quadriceps from pushing his rehab too hard. Nixon missed the first 63 games of the season, returned briefly in late July, then had another stint on the disabled list until September 7. By that time, no one expected anything from him, but Nixon was a force for his abbreviated 48-game season, hitting .315 and slugging .510 while playing his usual aggressive defense. His major postseason contribution was a bases loaded two-run double in the third inning of Game 4 of the World Series, a clinching game the Sox won 3–0.

Trade rumors have hovered around Nixon every year since at least 2000, but GMs Dan Duquette, Mike Port, and Theo Epstein have all refused to part with Nixon. He's popular with fans, both because he's a gritty player who helped give birth to the "dirt dog" notion, and because Nixon has developed something of a "Yankee-killer" reputation. He's also seen as a stabilizing player in the clubhouse, very much in the tradition of another strong-throwing, good-hitting right fielder who was often overshadowed by more flamboyant teammates, Dwight Evans. Nixon's wife Kathryn runs in the Boston Marathon each year and is very active in community charities.

Hideo Nomo—righthanded pitcher and onetime star who threw a scintillating no-hitter in 2001, his lone season in Boston. It was the first no-hitter by a Boston pitcher since Dave Morehead threw one in 1965. Nomo had been a star in Japan as a member of the Kintetsu Buffaloes. Nomo reached the 1,000-strikeout mark faster than any other player in the history of Japanese professional baseball, and the 500 strikeout mark in only 444⅔ innings pitched, faster than any other pitcher in major league history. After signing with the Dodgers, Nomo became the first Japanese All Star, and went on to be the National League Rookie of the Year. His long, twisting delivery, in which he turned his back to the hitter much as El Tiante did, reminded Dodgers fans of Fernando Valenzuela's eccentric delivery. (Although his wildness placed him among the league leaders in walks allowed in 8 of his 10 seasons in the majors.) Nomo's 1996 sophomore season was filled with highlights (an astonishing no-hitter against the Rockies at Coors Field, the worst pitcher's park in baseball) and lowlights (he was caught in an embarrassing mid-season revelation of an extra-marital affair with a Japanese television reporter), but his performance declined as his fastball lost a couple of miles per hour. By 2001 he had regained some of his effectiveness, but had drifted through five more teams, elbow surgery, and a lot of erratic performances.

The Red Sox hoped to help him regain his consistency, but it didn't really happen. Nomo had a dreadful spring training, but in his first Red Sox start, on April 4, Nomo pitched a no-hitter against the Baltimore Orioles, winning 3–0, making him the fourth pitcher in history to hurl no-hitters in both the NL and AL. It was also the earliest no-hitter, by date, in history. Nomo followed that with a one-hitter on May 25, defeating the Toronto Blue Jays, 4–0. He was a consistent starter for the team during the first half of the 2001 season, but struggled down the stretch. (Nomo's falloff in productivity coincided with the loss of his regular catcher Jason Varitek, to injury.) He led the AL in both strikeouts and walks allowed, finishing with a 13–10 record and a league-average ERA. Nomo was offered a three-year, $22 million contract to stay with the Red Sox during the 2001 season, but turned it down on the advice of his agent and amid confusion surrounding the Sox front office. (Reportedly Nomo had wanted to stay in Boston, where his floundering career had revived.) No other team made a comparable offer, and he signed a deal to return to the Dodgers for the 2002 season. There, he finally did regain his consistency, putting together two strong 16-win seasons, and pitching as well as he had his first couple of years in the league before stumbling through an injury-marred 4–11, 8.25 ERA season in 2004. Nomo signed a minor league deal with Tampa Bay for the 2005 season.

Buck O'Brien—righthanded pitcher, O'Brien came up for five starts with Boston in 1911. A native of Brockton, Massachusetts, O'Brien's specialty was a spitball, still legal at the time. In 1912 he went 20–13 for the World Series champion Red Sox, throwing over 275 innings. However, O'Brien went 0–2 in the 1912 Series that the Sox won in eight games.

The most controversial loss came in Game 6. With the Sox leading the Series 3–1–1 (Game 2 had ended in an 11-inning 6–6 tie), Smoky Joe Wood was expected to start in the Polo Grounds. But the owner of the team, James McAleer, approached manager Jake Stahl and convinced him to hold Wood back. Had Wood won, the series would have been over that day, but a Sox loss meant that Wood would pitch in Fenway, to a tremendous gate, the next day. Stahl relented, and O'Brien got the start. He may have been out drinking late the previous night, not expecting to play, certainly not to start. Everyone on the team expected Wood to start. But whatever the cause, O'Brien gave up five runs in the first inning and the Sox lost 5–2. On the train back to Boston, Joe Wood's brother Paul, who had lost $100 by betting on a game he expected his brother to start, got into a fight with O'Brien and gave him a black eye. The whole sequence of events also exacerbated tensions that had been present on the team all year between the Catholic players, including O'Brien, and the Protestants, including Wood. The newspapers had even referred to the groups as "knights" and "masons."

After the season, Buck spent the winter touring with Hugh Bradley and two former teammates as a vaudeville act called the "Red Sox Quartette." They toured all of New England, featuring novelty tunes such as "Buck O'Brien, The Spit-ball Artist," and O'Brien came to camp out of shape in 1913. After 12 starts and 3 relief appearances, in which he went 4–9, he was traded to the White Sox, where he went 0–2 to finish the season, and his career.

Jose Offerman—switch-hitting second baseman acquired as a free agent following the 1998 season who became a major millstone on the Red Sox roster. Although Offerman was one of the best-hitting second basemen in baseball when they signed him (though not, as it turned out, for the last three years of his contract), the Red Sox were widely ridiculed for signing him to a four-year contract for $6 million a year—mainly because Offerman had never quite lived down the reputation he built early in his career for being an overhyped and underachieving player. (The joke was picked up by the national media, and actor Samuel Jackson made fun of the signing during the Espy Awards ceremony.) Offerman was signed around the same time the Red Sox lost powerful first baseman and local icon Mo Vaughn to free agency. Although the two players were very different, many fans saw the Offerman signing as a feeble attempt to replace Vaughn. General manager Dan Duquette didn't help matters when he said that Offerman would replace Vaughn's "on-base ability," which only highlighted the fact that Offerman lacked both Vaughn's power and his charisma. Offerman did temporarily convert many of his critics when he started the 1999 season with a blazing hot streak.

Offerman started his career as a shortstop with the Dodgers in 1990. He quickly gained a reputation as a poor fielder (and the nickname "Awfulman"), committing 42 errors in his first full year, and following with other 35+ error seasons. Throughout most of his years in L.A. Offerman was a poor offensive player as well. He reached double digits in steals only twice in six years (although he did steal 30 bases in 1993). In 1995 he showed flashes of what he could do offensively, posting respectable numbers for a shortstop, including an on-base percentage of .389.

Moving on to Kansas City, he had a fine offensive year in 1996, posting an on-base percentage of .384 and stealing 24 bases. That season also marked the beginning of his move away from shortstop. He would get about 30 starts each at both short and second base, and 80 starts at first base. (While his offensive numbers were good for a middle infielder, they were below-average for a first baseman.) He committed 10 errors at shortstop but only one at second base. In 1997 Offerman was strictly a second baseman, committing only nine errors in 101 games. He continued to hit as well, and in 1998 he established himself as a great leadoff hitter, scoring 102 runs, stealing 45 bases, and posting a .403 on-base percentage—effectively pricing him out of small-market Kansas City's budget. Offerman started the 1999 season under intense media pressure. Early reports out of spring training had manager Jimy Williams thinking of using him at first base and DH while letting Jeff Frye play second. An injury to Frye and the emergence of first baseman Brian Daubach put an end to the unfortunate experiment (paying a good offensive second baseman $6 million is one thing, while paying that same player to be a poor offensive first baseman is altogether different). Offerman eventually posted a .391 on-base percentage and scored 107 runs (although his steals dropped to 18 with manager Williams reluctant to let Offerman run). A knee injury drastically reduced Offerman's effectiveness in 2000—dropping his on-base percentage by almost 40 points and his stolen bases to zero (he was caught eight times), while limiting his ability to play second base.

Offerman was widely expected to make a comeback in 2001 but once again he found himself embroiled in controversy when manager Jimy Williams benched him at the end of spring training in favor of Chris Stynes. An injury to Stynes returned Offerman to the lineup, but he played inconsistently both offensively and defensively, finishing the year at .267, with only a .342 on-base percentage and five stolen bases—not good for a leadoff hitter in an offense-oriented period (although about average for a second baseman). The Red Sox openly shopped for a second baseman and leadoff hitter after the season ended, but were stuck with Offerman—who had another year on his contract and $6 million owed to him—on the roster. The team finally cut its losses and released Offerman during the 2002 season, after he hit only 232 in 72 games, mostly at first base. He caught on with Seattle, but didn't play any better, and was out of the major leagues in 2003. Offerman spent 2004 as a part-time player for Minnesota, where he didn't hit or run particularly well, but did walk enough to post his best OBP since 1999. He signed a minor league deal with the Phillies for 2005.

Ben Oglivie—an outfield prospect who seemingly wasn't going to pan out, the lefty-hitting Oglivie was inconsistent and not very good in parts of three seasons for the Red Sox, who gave him to Detroit for a washed-up Dick McAuliffe after the 1973 season. With Detroit and Milwaukee, Oglivie blossomed as a hitter, although he always remained inconsistent. In 1980, when the powerhouse Red Sox of the late 1970s began to fade, Oglivie had his best season, hitting .304 with 41 home runs for Milwaukee.

Tomo Ohka—the first Japanese player in Red Sox history came to the club as an afterthought. GM Dan Duquette had been sending older minor leaguers to Japanese teams for several years, and the Yokohama BayStars gave him the obscure Tomokazu Ohka, a righthanded control pitcher, to return the favor. Little was expected from Ohka, but he surprised everyone with a perfect 15–0 record (2.31 ERA) at Trenton and Pawtucket. He pitched briefly in the majors in 1999, but returned to Pawtucket the following year, making headlines with an astounding 76-pitch perfect game. This led to another big league audition, and the 24-year-old was the team's second-best pitcher down the stretch in 2000. (He posted a 3–6 record, due to the team's poor hitting, but an excellent 3.12 ERA.)

I got my curse from my Dad. He grew up a Brooklyn Dodger fan. He entered the Navy upon grad-uating college and upon coming home found an empty Ebbets Field. As a Dodger fan he had a natural animosity toward the Yanks. In the sixties his baseball interest waned as a result of the move of his team and a lack of national coverage. In the seventies his interest picked up again and while he never lost his venom toward the Skanks he found it hard to root for a team on the other coast. Since the Sox already had a natural rivalry with the Yanks he began to follow them and as an impressionable youngster I did too. My brother is also afflicted and me, my Dad, and my broth-er will do our best to teach my young (two-year-old and nine-month-old) nephews about the hor-rors of King George. My first Sox game at Fenway was in 1981 and Ojeda was a rookie. It was versus the Yanks in August or September and Ojeda brought a no-hitter into the ninth with the Sox up 2–0. At this point Oscar Gamble or someone doubled off the wall. The no-hitter was gone but the Sox held on.

—Jim Tiberio

Ohka was traded to the Montreal Expos for Ugueth Urbina during the 2001 season. In 2002, Ohka was reunited with former Pawtucket teammate Sun Woo Kim when Kim was traded by Boston to Montreal for Cliff Floyd. Ohka and the Korean-born Kim had been in the news together before, when they were involved in a shoving match during a Pawtucket Red Sox rain delay, and again the next morning in their hotel. Ohka has established himself as a solid starter in the National League, despite losing most of the 2004 season when his right forearm, broken by a line drive hit by Astro Carlos Beltran, had to be surgically repaired.

Bob Ojeda—one of a group of pitchers developed by the Sox in the early 1980s who went on to long careers. (Bruce Hurst, Oil Can Boyd, and John Tudor were the others.) Ojeda was a soft thrower who never overpowered hitters but got them out with smarts, location, and a variety of deceptive pitches. After a brief stay with the Sox in 1980, Ojeda was called up from the minors at the end of the strike in 1981, and had a terrific second half, leading to tremendous expectations. He had a terrible year in 1982 (not surprising for a young lefthanded pitcher in Fenway Park, at the time a paradise for righty sluggers), but established himself as a solid, consistent starter over the next three years (with nearly identical ERAs around 4.00 each year). Ojeda's best year for the Sox was in 1984, when he went 12–12 in 216⅔ innings.

Ojeda was traded to the Mets in 1986 for four minor leaguers, including prospects Calvin Schiraldi and Wes Gardner (Red Sox GM Lou Gorman was a former Mets GM and knew the organization that the Sox would face in the World Series later that year very well). Ojeda went on to brief stardom in New York, going 18–5 with a 2.57 ERA for the World Champions and starting two games against his old team in the World Series.

Ojeda missed the last three weeks of the 1998 season when he severed his left middle finger while trimming his hedges at home. The tip of the finger was intentionally re-attached at a crooked angle. Although Ojeda lost strength and feeling and in the finger, the different angle allowed him to throw his curveball with the same effectiveness as in prior seasons. In 1989 he dispelled fears that his career was over, and posted a 13–11 record with a respectable 3.47 ERA.

He spent five years with the Mets, never winning more than 13 games after 1986. In 1993, after two years with the Dodgers, he joined the Indians. During spring training he was badly injured in a speedboat accident in which teammates Steve Olin and Tim Crews died. He appeared in only nine games in 1993, two more for the Yankees in 1994 and then was out of baseball at age 36.

Ojeda returned to professional baseball in 2001 as the pitching coach for the Mets' short-season Single-A team, the Brooklyn Cyclones, and in 2003 was promoted to pitching coach in Binghamton of the AA Eastern League. Ojeda left the organization (which wanted him to stay) following the 2003 season, citiing frustration with decisions made by the Mets ownership and philosophical differences over how to develop young pitchers.

Troy O'Leary—an outfielder with a good bat, the 25-year-old O'Leary was snatched off waivers from the Milwaukee Brewers in 1995. He quickly took over in right field for the outfielder-poor Red Sox, but his difficulties with Fenway's enormous right field caused him to be moved to left, where he eventually developed into an excellent fielder. O'Leary's quiet manner and strong work ethic made him a key supporting player in the late 1990s teams, built around a few star hitters like Nomar Garciaparra and Mo Vaughn. O'Leary was a solid player, but not a star; he hit over .300 twice with the Sox, but had below-average power for a left fielder and didn't walk much.

In 1999 O'Leary hit a career-best 28 home runs and seemed on the verge of stardom. He played an extraordinary role in Boston's American League Division Series victory against the Cleveland Indians that season. Boston was on the verge of elimination in Game 5, especially when starter Bret Saberhagen was knocked out of the game in the second inning. Twice that night Nomar Garciaparra was intentionally walked with men on base to pitch to O'Leary (who had a career playoff average of .094 at the time). Both times O'Leary followed with a home run, driving in a series-record seven runs (tying teammate John Valentin, who had done it the game before). Later in the game with Garciaparra at bat, a man on base, first base open, and O'Leary waiting on deck, players from the Red Sox dugout could be heard saying, "Go ahead, walk him again!"

O'Leary got off to a terrible start in 2000 amid a difficult divorce. (It was rumored that a Sox minor leaguer was involved). After a trip to the disabled list to get his head together O'Leary played well the second half of the season but his hitting fell off even further in 2001. He was not re-signed when his contract expired at season's end, and ended up as a part-time player for the Montreal Expos in 2002 and for the Chicago Cubs in 2003. Unable to find a major league job in 2004, O'Leary signed with the Samsung Lions of the Korean Professional Baseball League, but was released after just 63 games.

Darren Oliver—lefthanded veteran pitcher obtained by Boston in a trade with the Texas Rangers for controversial outfielder Carl Everett after the 2001 season. Everett had to be traded and in order to get rid of him, the Sox had to take on someone else's problem. Texas's problem was Oliver, a $6 million-a-year pitcher coming off two terrible seasons. Red Sox manager (and former star pitching coach) Joe Kerrigan planned to work with Oliver to break down his mechanics and make him a more effective pitcher. But Kerrigan was fired during spring training 2002 and barely had an opportunity to work with him. Oliver looked promising at the beginning of the season, with a 4–1 record. He had a strong outing against the Yankees on April 12 and a shutout against the Orioles on April 30. But by June his record had dipped to 4–5 with a 4.66 ERA (still better than his career norm) and the Red Sox designated Oliver for assignment. Oliver has continued to find major league work without notable pitching success (pitching for three teams in the last two years), mostly because lefthanded pitching is a relatively rare commodity. His father is Bob Oliver, an outfielder/first baseman who played for six major league teams from 1965–75.

Steve Ontiveros—a righthanded pitcher, Ontiveros edged out Red Sox Roger Clemens for the American League ERA crown in strike-shortened 1994. Pitching mostly out of the bullpen for the Oakland A's, Ontiveros barely qualified with his 115⅓ innings. After being out of the majors for over four years, he signed with the Red Sox in August of 2000, and in a critical September start in Detroit, he started instead of hot rookie Paxton Crawford. Ontiveros got only three outs while giving up six runs, and the Red Sox lost badly. Less than a week later, however, he earned a measure of redemption when he pitched 2⅓ scoreless innings against Cleveland in a vital game when starter Rolando Arrojo was knocked out early. Ontiveros was awarded with the win when the Red Sox came back for a 9–8 win. Ontiveros signed a minor league contract with the New York Mets following the season, but did not pitch in the major leagues in 2001.

David Ortiz—easygoing Dominican first baseman-DH who became a slugging star and cult hero with the 2003–04 Red Sox. The hulking Ortiz was signed by the Mariners as an amateur free agent just after he turned 17, and was in the majors less than five years later with the Twins, who'd acquired him as the player to be named later in a trade for Dave Hollins. He spent several years as a platoon player for the Twins, hitting reasonably well (and drawing a surprising number of walks), but not as well as the Twins hoped. In 2002 he had his best season, hitting .272 with 20 homers and a .500 slugging percentage, but the Twins decided that he wasn't worth the several million dollars an arbitrator would award him and didn't tender Ortiz a contract. The Red Sox then signed him as insurance behind three other first baseman-DHs, Shea Hillenbrand, Kevin Millar, and Jeremy Giambi. However, Giambi quickly flamed out and Ortiz hit so well in his limited appearances that the Red Sox traded Hillenbrand and handed Ortiz a full-time job. Although he only played in 128 games he hit .288 with 31 homers (72 extra-base hits in all), slugged .592 (third in the league), and finished fifth in the MVP voting. He capped off the performance with two more homers in the ALCS against the Yankees.

The Red Sox signed Ortiz to a longterm contract early in the 2004 season. He rewarded the team's gamble by having an even better season than the previous year, hitting .301 with career highs in on-base percentage (.380), home runs (41), and RBI (139), and a fourth-place finish in the MVP balloting. Ortiz built an increasing reputation as a big-game hitter and powerful slugger (more than half his Boston hits have gone for extra bases), and his performance in the 2004 playoffs cemented that reputations. Ortiz hit a walk-off home run in extra innings to win Game 3 of the ALDS from the California Angels. He did the same thing in the eleventh inning of Game 4 of the ALCS against the Yankees, a game in which the Sox faced being swept out of the postseason. The next day his hit in the fourteenth inning won Game 5 for the Red Sox, winning him the ALCS MVP. Overall Ortiz hit .400 in the 2004 postseason, with 5 homers, 19 RBI, and an astonishing .515 on-base percentage.

Ortiz's popularity with fans is based as much on his gentle giant reputation as on his hitting, both as the affable "Papi" who helps keeps fellow Dominican star Manny Ramirez and the rest of the clubhouse on an even keel and as the "Cookie Monster," the nickname his three-year-old daughter game him that stuck.

Spike Owen—shortstop acquired along with Dave Henderson in the stretch run of 1986 from the Seattle Mariners for four players. Owen had been a teammate of Roger Clemens at the University of Texas, and earlier in 1986 he had been Clemens's nineteenth strikeout victim in the game in which Clemens set the record with 20 whiffs. Known more for his glove than his bat, Owen would hit just .183 for the Sox for the remainder of the season, before churning out a .429 in the playoffs against the Angels and .300 against the Mets in the World

It started with baseball cards.

On Christmas Day 1987, when I was 12, I came downstairs to find a baseball card starter kit. I had never asked for one; up until that point my experience with baseball had been limited to a few wiffle ball games with the neighborhood kids and one failed attempt at Little League when I was nine. (I bailed out on every pitch fearing the pitcher was more interested in killing me than getting me out. After three games I realized that no nine-year-old boy could throw a hard ball consistently for strikes. So I kept the bat on my shoulder for the remainder of the season and led the league in walks. "Good eye!" my coaches cheered, not realizing I had already given up on this confounding game.)

The kit itself was far from a gold mine, but it interested me enough to start buying baseball cards with my allowance. At the time most baseball cards came in wax-coated packages that gave off a sugary smell from the stale sticks of gum included inside. It didn't take me long to grow into the collecting habit; I eagerly memorized the information on the backs of the cards and organized them first by team then by player. Having gotten to know all about the players on the cards, I quickly yearned to see them in action, so I patiently waited for the baseball season to begin.

I already knew the basics surrounding the Red Sox. I knew that they had come astonishingly close to winning the World Series in 1986, and I knew all about Roger Clemens, Wade Boggs, Bob Stanley, Dwight Evans, Jim Rice, and Rich Gedman. Those guys had all been around a while so they needed little introduction. But as I watched more seriously I came across names that I had never seen before. They had just traded for a burly relief pitcher named Lee Smith. A lefthanded-hitting outfielder named Mike Greenwell got off to an early home run tear. By combining my fondness for underdogs and for players with interesting names, I settled my eyes on the team's starting short-stop, the light-hitting Spike Owen.

There was nothing dazzling about Owen's style of play, but that didn't stop him from becoming my favorite player. He wasn't very powerful but he ran pretty hard and was solid with the glove. While guys like Greenwell and Evans were hitting the ball all over the yard, I silently hoped for Owen to come up with some big hits on his own. Unfortunately, as the #9 guy in the order, he rarely got the chance.

For the Sox as a whole the 1988 season got off to a disappointing start. Oil Can Boyd went down with an injury early and much of the lineup struggled to hit in the clutch. At the All Star break manager John McNamara was fired and replaced by Joe Morgan.

The move took me by surprise for 2 reasons. For one thing, I didn't know that managers could be fired. I wasn't sure why they decided to blame the manager when the players weren't getting the hits and getting the other team out. As the season continued, however, I learned a great deal about the role of the manager on a baseball team. Under Morgan's command the Sox went on to have one of the more exciting halves in team history, winning 12 in a row and 24 straight at home en route to the division title.

As for Owen, he didn't get to play as great a role as would have happened had I written the sea-son's script. He lost his starting shortstop job to Jody Reed, and was traded after the season. But he did have a couple of noted moments that year. Owen was the player Morgan pinch-hit for Jim Rice in a bunting situation during Morgan's first week as manager, leading to a shoving match between Rice and Morgan in the dugout. Spike also came through with a key late-inning pinch hit to win a game at Yankee Stadium in September that helped ice the division.

Sometimes I think I might have been spoiled by Morgan Magic. After a season filled with improbable comebacks keyed by players like Todd Benzinger and Kevin Romine, I felt a little disillu-sioned in following years when the Sox didn't catch similar breaks. Now with over a decade's worth of seasons under my belt, and my baseball cards still hibernating in my bedroom closet, I think I'm better adapted to the emotional seesaw that comes with being a Red Sox fan.

—Neil S. Serven

Series. In August he tied an American League record by scoring six runs in a nine-inning game, during a 24–5 Sox rout of the Cleveland Indians. Owen played 2½ years with the Sox before being traded to the Expos in December 1988. He also played with the Yankees and Angels before retiring after the 1995 season.

Jim Pagliaroni—a hulking catcher from Dearborn, Michigan, Pagliaroni made his major league debut for the Sox in 1955, when he was only 17. He didn't resurface in the majors for another five years, but was the regular catcher for bad Red Sox teams in 1961–62. He was an average hitter, drawing a fair number of walks and with decent power—pretty good for a catcher at the time. Pagliaroni was on deck when Ted Williams hit his last home run in 1960, and was the first to greet Williams as he crossed home plate. After the 1962 season Pagliaroni and pitcher Don Schwall were traded to Pittsburgh for colorful slugger Dick Stuart. He played seven more years in the majors before finishing up with the expansion Seattle Pilots (where his lifestyle was immortalized in Jim Bouton's *Ball Four*) in 1969. He currently lives in the Sacramento area, where he is active with local charity and school athletic programs.

Stan Papi—utility infielder whom the Sox traded pitcher Bill Lee (who manager Don Zimmer was determined to dump) to Montreal for after the 1978 season. Papi was not considered a prospect; at age 28 he was coming off a .230 season, and not yet an established major leaguer. He went on to hit .188 in his only full season with the Red Sox, while the banished Lee won 16 games for Montreal.

Freddy Parent—an excellent-fielding infielder, the diminutive (5-foot-5) Parent was the starting shortstop for the Red Sox first World Series winner. He was a fast runner and one of the team's best hitters from 1901–04, after which his average plummeted and his power vanished. He remained in Boston as a utility player until 1907, and in the major leagues until 1911, but he never hit well again. Parent lived to be nearly 100 years old, dying in his native Maine in 1972.

Mel Parnell—a dominant lefty, Mel Parnell was the best pitcher for the Red Sox from 1948 through 1953. A rookie in 1947, Parnell led the 1948 team in ERA. His emergence as a dominant pitcher, along with the acquisition of Ellis Kinder over the winter, helped transform the third-place 1947 team into the excellent 1948 team which finished tied atop the standings with the Cleveland Indians. Because of the tie, a one-game winner-take-all playoff was played between the two teams. Instead of Parnell, who had led the team with a 3.14 ERA (good for fourth in the league) and who had finished second on the team in innings pitched, manager Joe McCarthy opted to start journeyman Denny Galehouse, who promptly lost the game, allowing the Indians to advance to the World Series and depriving the Sox the chance to play their crosstown rival, the Boston Braves.

Parnell followed up his excellent 1948 performance with an even better one in 1949. He led the league in wins (25), innings pitched (295), and complete games (27). He was second in the league in ERA (2.77), second in winning percentage (his .781 was only bettered by teammate Ellis Kinder), and fourth in shutouts (4). It was likely the best performance by a Sox pitcher since Lefty Grove in 1936, and the best any would see from a Sox pitcher (give or take Frank

Sullivan in 1955) until Roger Clemens in 1986. And yet, despite Parnell's hero-ics, despite Kinder chipping in 23 wins, and despite Ted Williams winning the Triple Crown, the Sox finished second to the hated New York Yankees by a sin-gle game. With a chance to win the pennant by winning one of its final two games, the Sox lost both games to the Yankees, and with them the pennant.

Though he never had another season to match 1949, Parnell continued to be the ace of the Red Sox staff into the 1950s. He finished in the top ten in the league in ERA, wins, and innings pitched in 1950, 1951, and 1953. An All Star in 1949, Parnell made the All Star team again in 1951. Unfortunately, injuries to fel-low pitchers, losing Ted Williams to injury and the Korean War, and other factors combined to waste Parnell's excellence—the team finished third in the league in 1950 and 1951, sixth in 1952, and fourth in 1953. By 1954 Parnell's run of domi-nance was over as his arm gave out. After winning 21 games and pitching 241 innings in 1953, Parnell would win only 12 more games over the next three years while pitching only 269 innings. His 10-year career ended after the 1956 season. Red Sox fans would not see a pitcher as good for as sustained a period until Roger Clemens's emergence in the late 1980s.

Marty Pattin—a righthanded pitcher, "Bulldog" spent 13 seasons in the major leagues, coming up with California in 1968. He was taken by the Seattle Pilots in the expansion draft after the 1968 season, and went with Seattle to Milwaukee when they became the Brewers in 1970. After the 1971 season, Pattin was trad-ed to Boston with Tommy Harper in a 10-player trade that sent Jim Lonborg, Ken Brett, and George Scott to Milwaukee. Pattin won 17 and 15 games in his two seasons with Boston, with an ERA at about league average levels. His 17 wins in 1972 led the staff for the Sox team that finished just half a game behind Detroit. Pattin was traded to Kansas City following the 1973 season, and he fin-ished his career there seven years later.

Jay Payton—athletic, slick-fielding, righty-hitting outfielder who the Red Sox acquired from San Diego in December 2004. Though he was traded (with Ramon Vazquez and minor league RHP Dave Pauley) for the now-legendary Dave Roberts, Payton is viewed more as a replacement for reserve outfielder Gabe Kapler (who signed with a Japanese team), as a key righthanded bat com-ing off the bench, filling in for injured players, as well as platooning in right field with Trot Nixon, who struggles against lefties. Over the last three years, Payton has hit .275 with a .346 OBP and 18 homers in 447 at bats against lefties. While he's only played six major league games in right field, sabremetric defensive measurements rank Payton very highly in center and left, and his range will come in handy in Fenway's cavernous right field.

Payton, who's now 32 years old, was once considered a can't-miss prospect. He was an All-American (and also an Academic All-American) at Georgia Tech, where his teammates included Jason Varitek and Nomar Garciaparra. (Since he and Nomar are very close friends, Payton was often mentioned in trade rumors whenever the Red Sox needed outfield help. Also, like Nomar, Payton is an aggressive player and a line-drive hitter who doesn't walk much—but also does-n't strike out a great deal.) The Mets drafted Payton 29th overall in the 1994

Draft, and he made an immediate impact in the minor leagues, hitting .365 in short-season class A ball. New York jumped Payton to AA in 1995, and even though he only played 82 games at that level, he was so good that he won the Eastern League MVP. However, he struggled after a promotion to AAA, and then missed large chunks of the next four years with injuries. He played 28 games for the Mets in 1998–99, but was regarded by most people as a bust heading into the 2000 season. To everyone's surprise, a finally healthy Payton won the starting center field job, played strong defense, and hit .291 with 17 homers (though his .331 OBP was nothing to write home about). He was also one of the few Mets to do well in the World Series, hitting .333 in a loss to the hated Yankees.

However, Payton struggled in 2001, batting an unproductive .255 in between trips to the disabled list with hamstring problems. He rebounded to his 2000 level the following year, but really took off after a July trade to the Colorado Rockies (who play in baseball's best hitters' park). Overall, he hit .303 with 16 home runs, and followed that with his best season in 2003: .302, 28 homers, 89 RBI. Although Coors Field inflated Payton's stats, he hit more homers on the road (15, along with a solid .281 average). But the Rockies let Payton leave as a free agent, and he signed a contract with the Padres—whose new park, Petco Field, is extremely favorable to pitchers. So while Payton's numbers with San Diego last year look mediocre (.260, 8 homers, .326 OBP), his road numbers remained about the same as they'd been in 2003 (.275, with all 8 of his homers).

The Padres felt that a speedy player like Roberts would be a better fit for their lineup and ballpark, and the Red Sox preferred to have a righty-hitting fourth outfielder (and also needed a utility infielder), so the trade made sense from both sides. Boston originally tried to get San Diego to take Byung-Hyun Kim (a bust for the Sox who is due $5 million in 2005), but the Padres decided to pass and give Boston $2.65 million instead—which covers most of Payton's $3.5 million salary, effectively making him the same price that Kapler was in 2004.

Rudy Pemberton—a former Detroit prospect who had been sent to the Red Sox (via Texas) as the player-to-be-named later to complete a minor trade, the 26-year-old Pemberton was called up late in 1996 and went on an extraordinary tear, hitting .512 with 9 extra-base hits and 3 steals in 13 games. He won a job as a platoon right fielder the following spring, but after a slow start at bat and an erratic time in the field, manager Jimy Williams grew disenchanted with Pemberton. He was sold to a Japanese team and never resurfaced in the major leagues. He was a Mexican League All Star in 2004, and in 2005 will be a teammate on the Laguna Vaqueros of another ex-Sox slugger who never got a real chance, Israel Alcantara.

Tony Peña—an All Star catcher with Pittsburgh and St. Louis, Peña came to the Red Sox as a 32-year-old in 1990, and was credited with helping stabilize the Sox pitching staff. Peña was popular for his distinctive catching stance—he stuck one leg out, instead of the squat most catchers use—and for his unpredictable snap throws to first base. Peña had been a good hitter and great fielder early in his career, winning Gold Gloves from 1983–85, and going to the All Star Game five times between 1982 and 1989. He still fielded well with the Red Sox, but his once-lethal throwing arm was less deadly than it had been, and he no longer hit well. Peña hit .261 in 1990, but faded to .181 in 1993, his last year in Boston. After losing his starting job in Boston, he continued playing as a backup catcher for Cleveland (for whom he hit a game-winning home run against the Red Sox in the 1995 playoffs) and Houston until 1997, when he retired at age 40.

In 1998, Peña immediately moved to managing. He managed the White Sox team in the Arizona Fall League and also served as their Coordinator of Dominican Operations. He guided Aquilas, a Dominican team, to the Caribbean Series title that winter. For the next three seasons, Peña managed the New Orleans Zephyrs of the Pacific Coast League, winning the Pacific Coast League title in 2001 and being named PCL Manager of the Year in 1999, 2000, and 2001 despite a losing record over the three years. In 2002, Peña returned to the major leagues as Jimy Williams's bench coach in Houston. When Kansas City Royals manager Tony Muser was fired in April 2002, Peña (with zero major league managing experience and about six weeks of major league coaching experience), was named to replace him. (Muser had a brief Red Sox history, hitting .111 in two games for the Sox in 1969 before moving on to the White Sox, Orioles, and Brewers.) Peña's infectious enthusiasm didn't cheer long-suffering Royals fans; when the team finished 49–77 under Peña (62–100 overall), it was widely expected that he wouldn't retain the job. He did, however, and in 2003 the Royals players seemed to buy into Peña's enthusiasm and unexpectedly went 83–79, remaining in playoff contention until a late-season swoon. Peña won the AL Manager of the Year Award in 2003, though his thin Royals team returned to earth in 2004 with a 58–104 record.

Herb Pennock—Hall of Fame lefthanded pitcher who, like so many other young Red Sox stars, was sold to the hated Yankees during Harry Frazee's Reign of Error. Known as "The Knight of Kennett Square" (his Pennsylvania hometown), Pennock began his career as a teenager with the Philadelphia Athletics. Ironically, Pennock came to the Red Sox in the same way he left. Connie Mack was losing money during World War I, and he sold many of his best players, giving Boston the promising Pennock in 1915. The lefty pitched sparingly from 1915–17, and served in the war in 1918. In 1919 Pennock blossomed, going 16–8 with a 2.71 ERA. He won 16 more games in 1920, but the Sox had already begun their descent into two decades of futility. Pennock pitched valiantly for two more years, winning 23 games total, with ERAs near the league average (low 4.00s).

Prior to the 1923 season, Boston gave Pennock to the Yankees (as if Ruth hadn't been enough), where he rattled off win totals of 19, 21, 15, 23, 19, and 17. Pennock pitched for three Yankees World Champions, and was 5–0, with three saves and a 1.95 ERA, in World Series play. He rejoined the Red Sox for his final year, 1934, going 2–0 with a 3.05 ERA as a long reliever. Pennock finished his 22-year career with 241 wins, and he made the Hall of Fame in 1948, earning more votes than anyone on the ballot that year, including such greats as Al Simmons, Jimmie Foxx, and Dizzy Dean.

Tony Perez—longtime Cincinnati Reds star first baseman (and Hall of Famer) who helped hold together a collapsing Red Sox team in 1980. Considered washed up at age 38, Perez played a surprising 151 games in 1980 and led the team in home runs as the last Don Zimmer-managed Sox team fell apart amid injuries and internal discord.

Perez played two less-than-successful years as a part-timer with Boston before moving on to the Philadelphia Phillies in 1983. At age 41, Perez played just one season for the Phillies, batting .241 in a part time role for the National League champions. He returned to Cincinnati and played three more years for the Reds before retiring in 1986.

Perez became the manager of the Reds after the 1992 season when Lou Piniella resigned as the skipper. By May 1993, he was gone, replaced at the helm by Davey Johnson. Perez then joined the Marlins' front office. He was the Marlins' interim in 2001, and remains a special assistant with the team.

Robert Person—a reclamation project that never really panned out, Person had bounced around between six different organizations, mostly as a starting pitcher, before breaking through with a 15–7 season for the Phillies as a 31-year-old in 2001. He had operations on his shoulder and elbow the next year, wasn't re-signed by Philadelphia, and was picked up by Boston off the scrap heap and signed to a minor league contract in the hopes that he'd be able to help the starting rotation. When it became clear that his slowly recovering arm (slowed further by shoulder and ankle injuries) would no longer support the rigors of starting pitching, Person was briefly made the closer of the Red Sox flailing bullpen, but Person's arm wasn't really resilient enough for relief pitching either. A hip injury ended his season after seven appearances. Person tried another comeback with the White Sox in 2004, but a ruptured achilles tendon ended that season as well.

Johnny Pesky—playing on Red Sox teams with Ted Williams, Johnny Pesky tended to be somewhat overshadowed, but indelibly marked the team's history as a slick-fielding shortstop, a fine contact hitter, and a longtime coach and mentor of players. Although he was a great hitter, John Paveskovich (who eventually changed his legal name to his nickname of Johnny Pesky) only hit 17 homers in his 13-year career. Several of those hit in Boston curled around the foul pole down the very short right field line in Fenway Park, which eventually became known affectionately as "The Pesky Pole." Perhaps the most amazing Pesky stat is that he struck out only 218 times in his entire career.

As a rookie in 1942, Pesky amassed a then–Red Sox rookie record 205 hits and a .331 batting average, finishing second in the batting race to Williams. He then left for service in the armed forces. World War II would cost him the next three seasons, from 1943 to 1945. Upon his return in 1946, Pesky picked up right where he had left off, helping to lead the Red Sox to the 1946 pennant by again leading the league in hits and batting .335. In one stretch, he had 11 hits in a row, and once scored six times in a game, an American League record at the time.

In 1947 (marriage and a 30-pound weight gain didn't seem to cause him to miss a beat) he led the league in hits for the third straight year. He also had a 27-game hitting streak that year.

Pesky was moved to third base in 1948, and while his average dropped to .281, he adapted well in the field, leading the league in double plays. He returned to shortstop in 1951, but was traded during the 1952 season.

In an example of how history can sometimes be unfair, despite a very good career, Pesky is perhaps best remembered for two plays he didn't make. In Game 7 of the 1946 World Series with the game tied, Enos Slaughter was on first when a bloop double was hit to center. Slaughter ran on the pitch, Pesky took the relay from weak-armed Leon Culberson with his back to the plate, checked the runner at first, and threw late to the plate, allowing Slaughter to score. The rest, as they say, is history. The media conception that "Pesky held the ball" grew over time and eventually became accepted as a misplay that cost the game.

In 1952, while playing in Detroit, Pesky had trouble getting a ground ball out of his glove in the third inning of Virgil Trucks's attempt at a second straight no-hitter. Originally called a hit, Pesky admitted to misplaying the ball, and the play was changed to an error, preserving Trucks's no-no.

After his playing days were over, and after spending some time elsewhere, Pesky returned to the Boston organization in 1961 as a minor league manager, and managed the parent club for the 1963 season and most of the 1964 season. He was interim manager after Don Zimmer was fired late in the 1980 season. From 1969 to 1974, Pesky was color man for Red Sox TV and radio broadcasts.

Pesky remained an organization employee in different roles for many years, and there was public outrage from fans when the team attempted to curtail his on-field duties in recent years; the image of Pesky still in uniform hitting fungos to players before games is a powerful one. After the Red Sox World Series victory in 2004, Pesky was one of the first people sprayed with champagne in the clubhouse, and was singled out as an inspiration and connection with Red Sox history by Curt Schilling (who mentioned Pesky first before anyone else), Theo Epstein, and others after the victory. Pesky is now in his eighties, and remains a Red Sox employee as well as a part of Red Sox history.

Rico Petrocelli—regardless of what effect future players named Rico may have on Red Sox history, the name "Rico" will likely always refer to one man to long-time Red Sox fans . . . Rico Petrocelli. (And despite the pronunciation of the Judd Hirsch TV detective show, *we* know how it's really said.) An infield mainstay for the Red Sox for over a decade, Petrocelli was a rarity of the day, an infielder who combined a very good glove and a bat loaded with power. This was best displayed in 1969 when Rico hit 40 homers, a record for a shortstop at the time, while making only 14 errors, tying another shortstop record at the time.

The lasting image that most fans likely hold of Petrocelli is of him catching what appears to be a routine popup. The reason it is frequently played as a part of highlight shows is that it was also the final out of the final game of the regular season of the 1967 "Impossible Dream" pennant drive. Along with Yaz and Reggie Smith, Petrocelli was part of a first in the 1967 World Series: three home runs in one inning. Petrocelli hit two homers that game, the only two he would hit in 14 World Series games.

In 1971 Petrocelli uncomplainingly moved to third base when the Sox acquired slick fielding Luis Aparicio. The move didn't faze Petrocelli, who led the league in fielding at third base that year.

A series of injuries began to slow Petrocelli down in the mid-1970s. Elbow problems in 1974, and a leg injury and beaning in 1975 all limited his playing time (though he appeared in all seven games of the 1975 World Series, hitting .308). Inner ear problems led to his retirement in 1976. Petrocelli was a two-time All Star during his career, which was spent entirely in a Red Sox uniform (another rare feat, both then and now). In the years since his retirement, Rico has played several roles in the Red Sox organization, including managing and announcing for minor league teams.

Hipolito Pichardo—a slender righthanded pitcher from the Dominican Republic, Pichardo came up with the Kansas City Royals, pitching decently in a variety of roles from 1992–98. Generally he was around league average or slightly better. He had elbow surgery following the 1998 season and missed all of 1999. Red Sox general manager Dan Duquette signed Pichardo to a minor league free agent contract in February of 2000 as a reclamation project, and called him up to Boston in May. Despite injury problems he pitched extremely well for the Red Sox out of the bullpen, throwing 65 innings in 38 games, with the best ERA of his career. He was expected to be a key component of the Sox bullpen in 2001, but started the year hurt and didn't appear until May 16. After three months of up-and-down performances, he shocked his teammates and coaches when he followed a bad performance against the Orioles by walking into manager Joe Kerrigan's office and retiring. (Pitching coach Kerrigan had replaced Jimy Williams as manager only the week before.) Pichardo was reunited with Williams the following season, signing with the Houston Astros in 2002. Recovering from a sore elbow, he started the year in the minors and had little success when he was called up, pitching ⅓ of an inning and giving up three earned runs. Pichardo retired again in May 2002.

Calvin Pickering—once a big prospect (literally and figuratively) with Baltimore, this lefty first baseman/DH was picked up on waivers from Cincinnati late in the 2001 season, and hit well in limited action. Pickering, a native of the Virgin Islands, is one of the heaviest players in big league history (listed at 283 pounds). He had excellent seasons in the Orioles' system in 1996–97 and won the Eastern League MVP in 1998, at age 21. Pickering was only okay in AAA in 1999, and was awful in a September callup (5-for-40). He infuriated the Orioles by being out of shape the next spring, and was sent back to AAA, where he hit .218 in an injury-shortened season. He rebounded in 2001, hitting .282 with 22 homers, while leading the International League with 99 RBI. Despite Big Cal's solid season, the Orioles put him on waivers in late August, and the Reds picked him up. After only four at bats with the Reds, he was waived again and claimed by Boston. A quadriceps injury cost him the entire 2002 season, and when he struggled with offseason injuries as well the Red Sox also gave up on him. Pickering, who is still only 28, resurfaced in the major leagues with the Royals in 2004, hitting seven home runs in only 35 games.

Jimmy Piersall—righthanded-hitting outfielder who enjoyed a productive but somewhat inconsistent 17-year career, mostly in the American League. Piersall came up to the Red Sox in 1950 and spent his first nine seasons in Boston, hitting about .275 (at a time when the league average was about .255) with decent power numbers. He never hit more than 19 homers in a season, but did lead the league in doubles in 1956. A solid defender and above-average baserunner, he reached double figures in steals three times while with the Sox, and five times in his career.

Piersall possessed a dynamic personality and was known for some bizarre habits, including one episode of talking aloud to Babe Ruth's monument while playing outfield at Yankee Stadium. Often he would attempt to loudly distract opposing players, a tactic that led to his frequent ejection from games. On one occasion late in his career he tried to defend Ted Williams by roaming wildly in his outfield position, a trick he called "The Williams Shift." Both Piersall and his manager protested vehemently after Piersall was ejected.

Piersall was plagued by well-publicized emotional troubles at the beginning of his career that culminated when he suffered a nervous breakdown during the 1952 season. He spent part of that year in a sanitarium, and made a successful comeback the year following. Rather than shy away from his ordeals, Piersall spoke openly about them, and did so with a brave sense of humor. He went on to document his experiences in the book *Fear Strikes Out*, which was later made into a motion picture starring Anthony Perkins. Piersall was actually disappointed with the lead actor's portrayal of him, claiming that Perkins "threw a baseball like a girl."

Piersall went on to become a two-time All Star with the Sox, and later enjoyed success with the Cleveland Indians before winding down his career with the Washington Senators and the Los Angeles/California Angels. He hit a career-high .322 for Cleveland in 1961.

A bizarre moment of baseball history occurred on June 23, 1963, during his brief stint with the New York Mets. After hitting the one-hundredth home run of his career into the right field stands at the Polo Grounds, Piersall took his trot around the bases—backward. This quirkiness didn't impress manager Casey Stengel, who cut Piersall two days later. Piersall remained in baseball after his retirement in 1967, working as a coach, in the front office, and in the broadcast booth. He later enjoyed some small acting roles, including a television appearance on *The Lucy Show*.

Phil Plantier—power-hitting lefthanded outfielder who came to the big leagues with the Red Sox at a time when the minor leagues were bare. Plantier tore up the minor leagues, but team officials were skeptical that he could hit major league pitching with his crouched hitting stance (once described as looking like he was sitting on a toilet). Plantier could generate a lot of power and a lot of air, striking out about a quarter of the time. Called up in 1991, Plantier appeared in 53 games and hit .331 in only 148 at bats, with excellent power. Plantier seemed poised for big things at the major league level. (He was often linked with Yankees slugger Kevin Maas, who came up about the same time and had similar early success, although neither turned into stars.)

The next year Plantier struggled in 108 games, hitting only .246 in 349 at bats, with an awful .361 slugging percentage. The Red Sox, not convinced he could hit, shipped Plantier to San Diego for promising reliever Jose Melendez (who was only able to pitch 32 innings over the next two years). Plantier went on to hit 34 home runs and drive in 100 runs for the Padres. Injuries and lack of confidence in his unorthodox batting stance soon undermined Plantier's career, however. Over the next few years he played with Houston, San Diego (two different times), Oakland, and ended his career in 1997 with St Louis.

Dick Pole—a promising righthanded pitcher in the mid-1970s, Pole was International League MVP while playing for AAA Pawtucket in 1973, leading the league in ERA and strikeouts. Pole pitched briefly with the Sox in 1973 and 1974, then joined the rotation full time in 1975. On June 30, Tony Muser hit a line drive that shattered Pole's face, and cost him most of his vision in one eye. (A scarily similar accident happened to Sox reliever Bryce Florie in 2000.) Although Pole came back to pitch again (even appearing briefly in the 1975 World Series) he never regained his effectiveness, and retired at age 27 with a 25–37 career record. Pole went on to a long coaching career, including stints in the Red Sox organization as bullpen coach and Pawtucket pitching coach. He is now pitching coach for the Cleveland Indians.

Curtis Pride—a deaf center fielder signed three times by GM Dan Duquette (twice for the Red Sox and once for the Expos, where Pride made his major league debut in 1993). Pride was a serviceable outfielder and lefthanded hitter who played well in starting roles, but not coming off the bench, over the course of his career. Pride was called up from AAA Pawtucket in 2000 during a stretch when the Sox outfield was riddled by injury and ineffectiveness (Pride was tearing up the International League at the time), but Sox manager Jimy Williams barely played him, preferring to go with light-hitting Darren Lewis and slumping Troy O'Leary. After getting into only nine games in the 2000 season, Pride was released to make room for returning players. He continues to be too good a hitter for the minors, but has had only limited sucess in the majors, always as a pinch hitter or sparsely used backup; in 2004 he was hitting .431 when the Angels called him up, but only hit .250 in 40 at bats spread over 35 major league games.

Carlos Quintana—righthanded-hitting first baseman and outfielder who put up promising numbers for his first two full seasons before fate sadly intervened. Upon the loss of power-hitting Nick Esasky to free agency following the 1989 season, rookie outfielder Quintana competed with Bill Buckner and Billy Jo Robidoux for the first base job in 1990 before taking over the position full time in May. Chubby and likable in a quiet way, Q could not replicate Esasky's power numbers, though he proved to be a solid run producer throughout 1990 and 1991, and had a terrific defensive reputation. That offseason, however, Quintana was involved in a hideous car accident in his home country of Venezuela while racing his brothers to the hospital after a shooting, and he missed the entire 1992 season. Ironically, manager Butch Hobson had just announced that Quintana would be the starting first baseman that season, rather than talented prospect Mo Vaughn. Quintana unsuccessfully attempted to return in 1993, and his retirement paved the way for Vaughn to become a star.

Dick Radatz—an intimidating relief pitcher who dominated the league for three years before breaking down from overuse, "The Monster" helped define the modern closer's role. As a 25-year-old rookie in 1962, the 6-foot-6 Radatz led the league in appearances, saves, and wins in relief. The next two years his workload increased; Radatz went 31–15 with 54 saves those two seasons, leading the league in relief wins both years and saves in 1964. He made the All Star team both years; in the 1963 game he struck out Willie Mays, Duke Snider, Willie McCovey, and two others in two innings of work. Radatz's *worst* ERA in those first three years was 2.29 (league average was about 3.60). He was almost unhittable, with a blazing sidearm fastball that helped him post astonishing strikeout totals. By 1965, after three years of pitching two or three innings at a time several games in a row, he was much less effective, finishing with a losing record (9–11) and a 3.91 ERA. He never recovered his effectiveness, drifting from the Red Sox to four other teams over the next 4 seasons with a 3–11 record. He is now a Boston-area radio show host. Ironically, he is one of the leading opponents of pitch counts and other measures thought to protect pitchers from overuse.

Manny Ramirez—one of the best and most feared righthanded power hitters in baseball while playing for the Cleveland Indians, the Red Sox made him the second-highest paid player in baseball following the 2000 season (the first big-time free agent signing for the team since they signed reliever Bill Campbell in 1977). Ramirez was one of the most desired free agents in baseball, a complete hitter who was still only 28 years old. In his final two seasons in Cleveland, he had led the league in both slugging percentage and OPS—exactly what the offensively anemic Red Sox needed.

Ramirez posted impressive numbers in his first season in Boston, although somewhat below his previous years' stats. A spring training hamstring injury (a frequent past problem for Ramirez) nagged him all year and limited him to DH duties more often than not, keeping him out of the lineup altogether in the final weeks of the season. Still, his numbers—a .306 batting average, 41 home runs, 125 RBI, and an excellent on-base percentage—combined to make him the team's clear offensive leader. Among his highlights were a home run in his first Fenway Park at bat, an early season game-winning single against the Yankees, and several tape-measure home runs. These included one in Toronto that was estimated at 491 feet, the longest ever hit there, and one off the Coke bottles in Fenway that was conservatively estimated at 501 feet—which would make it a foot shorter than the longest ever hit by Ted Williams.

As with most Red Sox stars, some controversy followed Ramirez around. When he expressed discomfort for playing left field rather than right, it was spun by some members of the Boston press corps as refusing to do what was best for the team. It was later suggested that Manny quit on the team as it collapsed late in the season, especially when he refused to talk about an outpatient medical procedure that he missed a game to undergo. He later expressed concerns with the small size of the Red Sox clubhouse—a frequent complaint of players unhappy with the lack of privacy or forced intimacy with members of the media—but it was spun into the second-highest paid player in the game complaining about his working conditions. Despite some attempts by the press to tarnish the very private Ramirez, the fans like him, and all indications are that his teammates respect him. Manny spent his first Boston season living in a pricey Boston hotel (more fodder for the local press). During the offseason, in a quiet ceremony, he married one of the hotel employees.

In 2002, Manny again was the focus for both the offense (winning the batting title at .349, and chipping in 33 homers and a .467 on-base percentage) and controversy. In Seattle, Ramirez made an ill-advised headfirst slide into home (he was out) and collided with the catcher, fracturing a finger. (He repeated the maneuver during his minor league rehab stint.) He was out six weeks and less than full strength for some time after his return. Ramirez also angered many fans when he hit an easy ground ball, took a step toward first, and abruptly turned to the dugout, resurrecting a media debate about whether or not he hustled enough (an odd debate to be having over someone who hits .349). He almost won another batting title in 2003 (falling one point short of teammate Bill Mueller), but seemed unhappy in the harsh media environment of Boston, where no amount of good hitting could make up for the microscope that his eight-year, $160 million contract put him under. After Manny mused about playing in New York City (where he'd grown up), the Red Sox actually put him on irrevocable waivers, meaning that anyone willing to pick up Ramirez's contract could have him for the $50,000 waiver price. No one did, and a trade that would have sent him to Texas also fell through, primarily over money. The point was made: Manny was going to stay with the Red Sox, so he might as well learn to enjoy it.

That's exactly what he did in 2004. Instead of taking the trade talk as a slight (as teammate Nomar Garciaparra did), Ramirez remained a consistent offensive force, and seemed to enjoy playing in Boston much more—even before winning the World Series. Perhaps it was the number of exuberant players surrounding him, or the support of fellow Dominican teammate David Ortiz, but for the first time, Ramirez seemed comfortable opening up to the press, and the Boston media responded by depicting his quirky behavior as charming and exuberant, rather than oblivious and uncaring as they had previously. It didn't hurt that Ramirez led the league in home runs (43) while hitting .308 and driving in 130 runs. In the playoffs he turned his game up a notch, hitting .350 with two homers and 11 RBI (though oddly, none in the ALCS), and winning the World Series MVP.

Jeff Reardon—righthanded relief pitcher who was one of several different pitchers to break the all-time saves record during the early 1990s, when the roles of relief pitchers were changing and save totals skyrocketed. A native of Massachusetts, Reardon had already had a long and productive career, mostly for the Expos and Twins, when the Red Sox signed him as a free agent prior to the 1990 season. The Red Sox already had Lee Smith as a closer, but GM Lou Gorman thought that the team could be upgraded by trading Smith for an outfielder and signing Reardon. Shortly into the season Smith was traded to St. Louis for the soon-to-be-disappointing Tom Brunansky.

Reardon pitched for the Red Sox for 2½ years, recording 88 saves. His high for the Sox was 40 saves in 1991. With his seventh save of 1992 he passed Rollie

Fingers to become the all-time MLB leader in career saves (though he has since been passed by Lee Smith, Dennis Eckersley, and John Franco.) But despite the gaudy save numbers, Reardon was not dominating, and before the trading deadline in 1992, the Sox traded him to Atlanta. He pitched for three teams over the next three years, retiring after the 1994 season.

Jody Reed—a heralded shortstop prospect who was a key part of the 1988 "Morgan Magic." Reed had played briefly for the Sox in 1987 and was a reserve early in 1988. When Joe Morgan replaced John McNamara as manager, he moved the 25-year-old Reed into the starting lineup, replacing Spike Owen at shortstop (Reed played a few games at second as well). Reed hit .293, walked frequently, and hit a lot of doubles to help key a Sox resurgence that led to the Eastern Division title. Reed finished third in the Rookie of the Year voting that year.

Because of Marty Barrett's declining knees, Reed was moved to second base midway through the following season. He remained remarkably consistent for the next three seasons, hitting better than .280 with 40 or more doubles each year. After an off year in 1992 (.247 with only 27 doubles), Reed was left unprotected in the 1992 Expansion Draft. Colorado drafted Reed then traded him to the Dodgers, where his batting average returned but his power did not. Reed rejected a lucrative free agent contract from the Dodgers only to find that no one else was willing to make a long-term commitment to him. He drifted between three teams over the next four years, playing decently until his bat failed him in 1997 and he was released. He now runs a baseball school in Tampa, Florida.

Pee Wee Reese—Hall of Fame shortstop for the Brooklyn Dodgers in the 1940s; Reese came up through the Red Sox system but never played for the team. Supposedly, player-manager Joe Cronin (also a shortstop) was jealous of Reese, and he was sold to Brooklyn for next to nothing.

Pokey Reese—a slick-fielding (but light-hitting) shortstop and second baseman who was involved in a surreal trade with the Sox, and later played a supporting role on the 2004 World Champion team. The South Carolina native won back-to-back Gold Gloves in 1999 and 2000 with the Reds (1999 was by far his best year; he also hit .285 with 38 steals), but after five years in Cincinnati, Reese "played" for three teams in three days. He was traded by the Reds to the Rockies on Dec 18, 2001. The next day, the Rockies traded him to Boston for Scott Hatteberg. Both teams failed to tender a contract to the players and on Dec. 21, Reese became a free agent. (The Red Sox wanted Reese, but not at the salary an arbitrator would award him, so when they couldn't reach a quick agreement with him they let him go.)

Reese played two seasons in Pittsburgh, but after a thumb injury cost him his starting job, signed with the Red Sox, hoping to fill the second base position left open by the loss of Todd Walker. Instead, Reese opened the seson at shortstop, filling in for an injured Nomar Garciaparra, and though he didn't hit particularly well (except for May 8, when he hit two of his three home runs for the year), his flashy defense made him a fan favorite. Reese ended up on the disabled list himself with a rib injury, and by the time he came back, his starting role was gone; Mark Bellhorn had stepped in at second and was having a terrific year, and Orlando Cabrera had taken over at short. Reese played sparingly for the rest of the season (batting .221 in 96 games), but was involved in some postseason controversy when fans called for him to replace the splumping Bellhorn against the Yankees in the ALCS. Bellhorn stayed in and hit two crucial home runs, and followed that with a strong World Series. Reese played 10 in playoff games as a defensive replacement, but only batted twice, going 0-for-2. Unlike 2001, the Red Sox offered Reese arbitration after the 2004 season, but he signed with Seattle (which offered him more playing time) instead.

Jerry Remy—a lefthanded-hitting second baseman, Remy hit leadoff for the great slugging Red Sox teams of the late 1970s and the weaker early 1980s teams. Remy was obtained as a 25-year-old veteran from the California Angels for pitcher Don Aase before the 1978 season, and was expected to shore up the Sox weakness at second base. Remy was a good but not great hitter (especially against righthanded pitching) and a solid defensive player. He batted .280 to .300 every year, though with little power and a below-average number of walks for a leadoff hitter. In his three years with the Angels Remy stole from 34 to 41 bases a year, but he was never a great base stealer (he had above-average, but not great, speed and was caught stealing a lot). He stole 30 bases his first year with the Red Sox, but persistent knee injuries and the team's lack of emphasis on base-stealing limited him to 16 steals a year or fewer for the rest of his career.

Remy had a reputation as a great bunter, and frequently bunted for base hits. He usually attempted to bunt for a hit at least once a game, and experimented with different bunting techniques throughout his career. His combination of speed (on a lead-footed team) and scrappiness (as a hustling but undersized infielder who played well even though he didn't look like a major league hitter) made Remy a fan favorite, and he remains popular in New England. Although injuries cut his playing career short (four of his seven Boston seasons were shortened by injuries) he continues to be involved with the Red Sox as a television color commentator.

Jerry Remy began as NESN's Boston Red Sox color analyst in March of 1988, teaming up with veteran play-by-play announcer Ned Martin. He has also worked with Sean McDonough, Bob Kurtz, and Don Orsillo. Prior to the 2003 season, Remy signed a four-year contract to continue broadcasting all Red Sox games on the Red Sox cable, VHF, and UHF stations. Over the years, Remy has enjoyed a growing cult status with Red Sox fans both at home and on the road. Posters for Remy and the TV station broadcasting the game are omnipresent at MLB ballparks during Sox games. Remy is known to his fans as "The Remdawg" (a product of his commentary on the 2003 "dirt dogs" team) and he has his own web site, The Remy Report (www.theremyreport.com).

Edgar Renteria—slick-fielding 29-year-old shortstop with an excellent clubhouse reputation (he was nicknamed "the Captain" in St. Louis). Renteria, a Colombian native and childhood friend of the shortstop he's replacing, Orlando Cabrera, made his major league debut for the Florida Marlins at age 20. He finished second in the NL Rookie of the Year balloting in 1996; since then he's been a four-time All Star, and his teams have made it to postseason play in five of his nine seasons, including four of his last five.

Renteria was a key member of the 1997 World Series championship team in Florida, and of the 2004 St. Louis Cardinals team that won 105 games en route to the National League pennant. Renteria was one of the few Cardinals to hit well in the 2004 World Series, but his ground ball to Keith Foulke ended the Series. It also earned him a place in an interesting trivia question, as he joined Goose Goslin as the only players in major league history to drive in a run to end a World Series (1997) and to make an out to end a World Series (2004).

Renteria is an excellent fielder (two Gold Glove awards), and a good hitter (.330 in 2003, and a lifetime average of .289), with decent plate discipline, good speed (he stole 41 bases one year), and some power—a very good hitter for a shortstop. He was clearly the best shortstop, and one of the best players at any position, available on the free agent market. However, his signing to a four-year contract was somewhat surprising because Boston was expected to sign a stopgap player, leaving the position open for prospect Hanley Ramirez in 2006.

Renteria is the youngest of 14 children. Unlike many players who turn out to be older than their official age, it's widely rumored that Renteria is a year *younger* than listed. He supposedly lied about his age to sign a pro contract with the Marlins (claiming to be 16 when he was really 15). That means he was probably 19 as a rookie, and is only 28 now.

Jim Rice—star left fielder who had the unenviable task of replacing Hall of Famer Carl Yastrzemski (who had replaced Ted Williams). Jim Ed Rice was a high school star from South Carolina drafted in the first round by Boston in 1971. Reportedly he was such a good athlete in his mostly segregated hometown that the school board redrew the school zones so that Rice could attend the primarily white high school (the line passed through his bedroom) and compete in several sports—but not his little sister. Rice was noted for great strength; on at least one occasion a bat snapped in half when he checked his swing, as if it had been smashed into a wall.

Rice debuted with the Sox in 1975 as one of "The Gold Dust Twins," with fellow rookie sensation Fred Lynn. Rice helped lead the Red Sox to the postseason in 1975, but late in the season was hit by a pitch which broke his arm, causing him to miss the American League Championship Series and the World Series. Rice hit .309 with 22 homers and 102 RBI that year (at a time when hitters were not as dominant as today), and finished second to Lynn in the Rookie of the Year balloting. (Lynn also won the league's Most Valuable Player award.)

Rice continued to blossom as a hitter, and from 1977 to 1979 was arguably the best hitter in baseball, averaging about .320 (league average was about .265) with at least 39 home runs each year. In 1978 Rice was named league MVP, and was the first player in 37 years to amass 400 total bases in a season. In 1980, Rice was hit by a pitch that broke his wrist. While he came back to play well, he was never the league's dominant hitter again; although Rice played 10 more years in the majors, he only reached 30 home runs once more (after doing it the previous 3 years) and reached .300 in only three of those years. Since Rice didn't walk much, hit into a lot of double plays, and was never a great defensive player (he worked hard to go from being terrible early in his career to decent as the years went on), he needed to hit for both power and average to be effective. Rice later experienced vision problems and became a singles hitter for his last few years in the majors (only 31 homers in his last three years combined), before retiring after the 1989 season. He finished his career with a .298 lifetime batting average and 382 home runs, just short of the .300 average and 400 homers that would have made him a near-certain Hall of Famer.

Rice remained a Red Sox employee after his 16-year career ended. He served as the minor league hitting instructor from 1992 to 1995 and Boston's hitting coach from 1997–2000. After a huge initial improvement in hitting, the team's batting average declined for three straight years, and many players seemed to prefer being coached by first base coach (and ex-Expos hitting coach) Tommy Harper rather than the aloof Rice. Rice is now a roving instructor for the Red Sox. He also spent time as an occasional NESN studio analyst.

As a player, Rice was uncomfortable in interview situations (he sometimes came off as being surly or unapproachable), and like many Boston stars was not particularly popular with the press. (Rice was very popular with fans, however.) Although he is eligible for the Hall of Fame and a fairly strong candidate, Rice has not done especially well in voting—which some people have blamed on his poor relationship with the media (since the voting is done by longtime baseball writers). In 2005, Rice fell short of the 75% requisite for entry to the Hall, but received his highest percentage of votes (59.5% on 307 out of 516 ballots) since first being eligible for voting in 1995.

Dave Roberts—speedy outfielder who played a key role in the 2004 playoffs for the Red Sox. The lefthanded-hitting Roberts, who is half-Japanese and was born in Okinawa, first came up with the Indians in 1999, and played sparingly against the Sox in the playoffs that year. He established himself three years later as a speedy but light-hitting outfielder with the Dodgers. He stole 45 bases in 2002, another 40 in 2003, and already had 33 steals (with only one caught stealing) when the Red Sox acquired him on July 31, 2004. With Boston, the 32-year-old Roberts was used mostly as a pinch runner or substitute who could bring galvanizing speed off the bench in the late innings of a close game.

He played that role twice in the ALCS against the Yankees, with the Red Sox having lost the first three games of the series and facing elimination. In the ninth inning of Game 4, with the Sox trailing 4–3 and three outs away from elimination, Kevin Millar walked. Roberts pinch ran for him, and drew multiple throws to first from Yankees closer Mariano Rivera (since Rivera and everyone else in the park knew that Roberts would be stealing). Roberts stole second in a harrowingly close play, and Bill Mueller then singled off the rattled Rivera to score Roberts and tie the game, which they eventually won in the twelfth inning. In Game 5 of the ALCS, the Red Sox were down, 4–2, in the bottom of the eighth inning. David Ortiz hit a solo homer off Tom Gordon to cut the lead to one run. Then Kevin Millar again walked, and Roberts was again sent in to pinch-run.

While Roberts didn't have a dramatic stolen base like the night before, he clearly rattled Gordon, who kept looking over his shoulder at first base. Finally, Roberts took off on a hit-and-run, and Trot Nixon singled up the middle. Roberts easily scampered to third base, and soon scored the tying run on Jason Varitek's sacrifice fly off Mariano Rivera. Six innings later, Ortiz's single gave the Red Sox another dramatic win, making their improbable ALCS comeback suddenly seem possible.

While the Red Sox might have kept Roberts as a reserve outfielder, he preferred to play for a team where he had a chance to start; since there was considerable demand for his services, the Sox obliged Roberts by sending him to San Diego for Jay Payton, Ramon Vazquez, and cash. Ironically, Henri Stanley, the minor league outfielder the Sox sent to the Dodgers for Roberts, had been picked up off the waiver wire from San Diego the previous year, meaning the Red Sox essentially got three players, plus two months of Roberts's speed, for the price of a waiver claim.

Alex "A-Rod" Rodriguez—star infielder who was almost a member of the Red Sox, but became an archenemy instead. Rodriguez was the first pick in the 1993 draft for Seattle, and was in the majors the next year, at age 18. In 1996, his first full season, he won the batting title, and soon established himself as arguably the game's best player: a terrific fielder at a difficult position and a great hitter with speed and 40-homer power. A free agent by the time he was 25, Rodriguez signed a 10-year, $252 million contract with the Rangers, by far the game's richest contract. He won the home run title for the next three years, and tacked on two Gold Gloves and a league MVP, but the Rangers, their payroll handcuffed by his salary, were never in contention.

After the 2003 season, Rodriguez asked to be traded from the Rangers to a contender, and the Red Sox—because they were a big-market team with huge contracts they wished to unload—seemed to be the only possible suitor. (Very few teams could afford A-Rod's contract, and the Players Association refused to allow him to lower the value of the contract to make it more trade-friendly.) The deal took a number of twists and turns, eventually evolving into a trade in which Rodriguez would go to the Red Sox, Sox outfielder Manny Ramirez (who made $20 million a year himself) and cash would go to the Rangers, and the Red Sox would follow by trading incumbent star shortstop Nomar Garciaparra (who was a year away from free agency and had declined Sox overtures at a new contract) and pitcher Scott Williamson to the White Sox for outfielder Magglio Ordoñez. Rodriguez very much wanted to be a member of the Red Sox. His wife has family in the area. He visited Harvard and seemed intrigued with the idea of taking extension courses there. A-Rod was willing to take a pay cut of about $25 million to play in Boston, which the Players Association refused to allow him to do. After that, the trade foundered over how much additional money the Red Sox were willing to pay the Rangers, and the Yankees—whose third baseman, Red Sox 2003 ALCS nemesis Aaron Boone, had blown out his knee playing basketball—swept in and traded second baseman Alfonso Soriano for Rodriguez. While Ramirez took the trade talks (made public by the Rangers) in stride and had a terrific season with the Red Sox, Garciaparra did not, and seemed unhappy about returning to the Red Sox. (Garciaparra, Williamson, and Ordoñez all ended up hurt for much of the season.)

Rodriguez moved to third base for the Yankees, and though he made the All Star team for the eighth time, he wasn't $20 million better than Soriano, who nearly duplicated A-Rod's .286 average, 36 homers, and 28 steals. More importantly for Red Sox fans, Rodriguez triggered two of the season's most bizarre and intense moments. During a late July game (with the Yankees in first and the Red Sox in the midst of a long malaise) Rodriguez started screaming at Sox pitcher Bronson Arroyo after being hit by a pitch. Sox catcher Jason Varitek stepped between the two, and A-Rod taunted Varitek, telling him to "bring it on," which Varitek did, mauling A-Rod in the face with his glove hand. The ensuing brawl, along with the game-winning walk-off home run by Bill Mueller off Yankees closer Mariano Rivera, was the moment when the 2004 team started their remarkable run to the 2004 World Series. (A possibly apocryphal story has Varitek telling Rodriguez, who was slumping at the time, "We don't hit .260 hitters.")

A-Rod found himself in the spotlight again during the ALCS, when he hit a one-hopper back to the pitcher (ironically again Arroyo). Rather than be tagged out, Rodriguez chopped at Arroyo's left arm, knocking the ball out of the pitcher's glove. Not only did A-Rod reach second but a run scored, making the game a one-run affair. The first base umpire (whose view of the play was blocked) initially called Rodriguez safe, but after the umpires conferred they correctly changed the call: Rodriguez was out and the runner was returned to first, and A-Rod's display of poor sportsmanship was heavily criticized even in the New York press. In some ways, this felt like a turning point for Sox fans, who were used to having odd calls go against them in big games against the Yankees, and expected another call like the phantom tag on Jose Offerman in 1999.

Frankie Rodriguez—a onetime top prospect of the Red Sox (although when they drafted him, they were unsure whether he was a pitcher or a shortstop). Rodriguez and the team finally decided to bring him along as a pitcher, and he was in the majors in 1995 at age 22. He pitched badly for Boston before being traded to Minnesota for ace reliever Rick Aguilera, on the night of the trading deadline. The deal had been much talked about, and many fans knew about it before it was announced (the Sox were playing in Minnesota that night, and during the game Rodriguez and Aguilera both were called in from their respective bullpens, and disappeared into the clubhouses). Rodriguez never lived up to his expectations, although his talent got him nine major league seasons worth of opportunities with four teams, during which he only once posted an ERA below 5.00. His major league career was over at age 28.

Billy Rohr—lefthanded pitcher who made one of the most memorable debuts in major league history. In April of the Red Sox magical Impossible Dream season of 1967, Rohr made his first major league start at Yankee Stadium and took a no-hitter into the bottom of the ninth. Yastrzemski kept the no-hitter alive in the seventh with a great catch of a ball hit by Tom Tresh. Elston Howard singled with two outs in the ninth and Rohr had to settle for a 3–0 shutout win. He beat the

Yankees again in his next start, and then never won another game in a Sox uniform. He won one game for Cleveland in 1968 and retired with a 3–3 major league record.

Brian Rose—much-heralded starting pitcher from New Bedford, drafted by the Sox in 1994. In the minors he was often compared with Carl Pavano, another great Red Sox pitching prospect, and the Montreal Expos were given their choice of Rose or Pavano (they picked Pavano) in the Pedro Martinez trade. A control pitcher, Rose had excellent minor league numbers, but struggled with inconsistency at the major league level. Called upon to fill in for an injured Juan Peña in May 1999, Rose pitched brilliant games against the Yankees and Indians, two of the best teams in the American League (he allowed only one earned run in his first three starts). But after two months of solid pitching he became ineffective (he went five straight starts without lasting more than four innings) before going on the disabled list with a "tired arm." He continued to struggle in 2000, pitching brilliantly at times but ineffectively at others—and pitching especially badly with runners on base.

Rose was sent back to the minor leagues in June 2000 to regain his form then was traded to Colorado—a nightmarish pitcher's park—as part of a deal for pitcher Rolando Arrojo in July. After that, his career seemed to disintegrate. Rose pitched briefly for both the Mets and the Devil Rays in 2001 before experiencing elbow problems subsequently having Tommy John surgery. Since then, Rose, now 29 years old and a spare part, rather than a prospect, has pitched in the minor leagues for Kansas City and Cincinnati; the Reds signed him to a 2005 minor league contract.

Rich Rowland—a power-hitting catcher, the Sox acquired Rowland from the Detroit Tigers in April of 1994, trading John Flaherty in an exchange of catching prospects who were to become free agents following the season. Both were players that had bounced up and down in their organizations, spending time in the majors but not figuring in their teams' plans. Rowland was reputed to be a lumberjack in the offseason. At the time of the trade, Rowland's age was listed as 27, but a month later *Globe* reporter Nick Cafardo discovered that he was actually 30. Rowland appeared in 46 games for the Sox in 1994, hitting the only nine home runs of his career. After appearing in 14 more games for Boston in 1995, his major league career ended.

Joe Rudi—a good-glove, decent-hit outfielder, Rudi made his name as a key member of the Oakland A's teams that won three straight World Series in the mid-1970s. He won three Gold Gloves while in Oakland, and led the American League in both doubles and total bases in 1974. When A's owner Charlie Finley began dismantling the team because he didn't want to meet the players' salary demands, the Red Sox acquired Rudi and relief pitcher Rollie Fingers for $2 million. But commissioner Bowie Kuhn stepped in and halted the sale, on the grounds that it was not in the best interest of the game. Rudi signed with the Angels as a free agent following the 1976 season.

When the Red Sox were faced with losing Fred Lynn in 1980 because they hadn't mailed out his contract in time, Lynn agreed to accept a trade to California. Joe Rudi finally became a member of the Red Sox in this trade. But he was basically done as a player. He hit dreadfully for the Sox, and re-signed with the Oakland A's after only one season in Boston. He only played one more year for Oakland before retiring at age 35.

Red Ruffing—Hall of Fame pitcher who began his career on a horrid Red Sox team, but became a star with the Yankees. Charles "Red" Ruffing pitched for Boston from 1924–30, pitching about as badly as his team played (39–96, with ERAs around the league average). He lost a staggering 25 games in 1928, though his 3.89 ERA was respectable, and he lost 22 more decisions in 1929. After an 0–3 start, the Sox sent him to the Bronx for Cedric Durst and $50,000. Going from a last place team to a nascent dynasty did Ruffing good; as a Yankee he was a fabulous 231–124 (adding seven World Series wins as well). From 1936–39 the Yanks won four straight championships—and Ruffing won 20 or more games each season. He was also one of the best hitting pitchers in history, finishing with a .269 average and 36 homers. Had he not lost four toes on his left foot as a child, costing him his speed, Ruffing might have achieved his dream of being a big league outfielder. Instead, he had to settle for a 273-win career, earning him election to the Hall of Fame in 1967.

Pete Runnels—one of the most unlikely batting champions ever, Runnels was a 30-year-old middle infielder (an age at which most players are declining) with the Washington Senators when he was traded to Boston for Albie Pearson and Norm Zauchin after the 1957 season. Runnels had only hit over .300 once in seven years with Washington, and was coming off a .230 season. In Fenway Park—a left-handed line-drive hitter's paradise—Runnels found an ideal home; in five years with the Red Sox Runnels never hit below .314, and he won batting titles in 1960 and 1962. Although he didn't have much power, Runnels walked quite a bit, and was one of a few bright spots on mediocre Red Sox teams in the twilight of the Ted Williams era. Runnels played all over the infield for the Red Sox, splitting his time between second and first base, as well as filling in at shortstop and third base. He was traded to Houston for Roman Mejias after the 1962 season. After leaving Fenway, his batting average dropped 70 points, and he was out of baseball the following year. (The trade was bad for both players; Mejias was also gone after the 1964 season, his average dropping nearly 60 points on coming to Fenway.)

Ryan Rupe—tall righthanded starting pitcher whose waiver claim was GM Theo Epstein's first player transaction as general manager. Rupe had spent his entire four-year major league career with awful Tampa Bay Devil Rays teams, but was best known to Red Sox fans for his role in Tampa Bay's on-field attacks and off-field threats on Sox player (and former replacement player during the 1994 strike) Brian Daubach in 2000, when Tampa pitchers repeatedly threw at him and his hand and elbow were hurt in an on-field melee. Sox player Trot Nixon later retaliated by nearly braining Rupe when his a bat flew out of his hands toward Rupe on a swing. (Nixon maintained that the bat was accidental, but allowed that "I dislike that boy.") Rupe gave up four home runs in four games with the 2003 Red Sox before they'd had enough. He pitched poorly for Japan's Hokkaido Nippon Ham Fighters in 2004, and signed a minor league deal with the Dodgers for 2005.

Jeff Russell—talented but inconsistent closer who saved 33 games in his only full season with the Red Sox. Russell signed with Boston as a free agent in 1993, after an up-and-down 10-year career. He began as a promising starter with Cincinnati, was traded to Texas, and eventually became a pretty good reliever. Russell saved 38 games in 1989, with a 1.98 ERA. He posted similar numbers in 1992, but was part of a blockbuster August 31 trade to Oakland for Jose Canseco. The A's used Russell as a setup man for Dennis Eckersley, and he held opponents scoreless in his eight appearances. But Toronto beat Oakland in the American League Championship Series, and the A's decided that Russell was too expensive to re-sign. Boston, after trading Jeff Reardon the previous year, needed a closer, and Russell fit the bill. He had a terrific 1993 season (33 saves, 2.70 ERA), though an ankle sprain caused him to miss most of September. Coincidentally or not, Russell was never the same pitcher after the injury. He saved 12 games for the Red Sox in 1994, but his 0–5 record and 5.14 ERA didn't sit well with Dan Duquette. In July, Russell was traded to Cleveland for two pitchers: reclamation project Chris Nabholz, and washed up Steve Farr (who had once been a good closer). Neither player contributed to the Red Sox, and Russell retired after two more seasons.

Babe Ruth—lefthanded pitcher, lefthanded-hitting outfielder. The two best hitters in baseball history have played for the Red Sox. The second best, Ted Williams, spent his entire career in a Boston uniform. The best hitter in baseball history spent the majority of his six years in Boston in the pitching rotation, winning 89 games and helping to lead the Red Sox to World Series victories in 1915, 1916, and 1918.

The 21-year-old George Herman "Babe" Ruth started 41 games for the Red Sox in 1916 and pitched 323 innings while leading the league with a 1.75 ERA. He was on a career path that might well have led to the Hall of Fame as a pitcher if he hadn't converted to the outfield. His .671 won-lost percentage is still the ninth highest in baseball history. His career ERA of 2.28 is 14th all-time. His shutout in the opening game of the 1918 series extended his World Series scoreless inning streak to 29 innings, a record that stood for 43 years. (It was broken in 1961 by Whitey Ford.)

Over the 1918–19 seasons he made the transition from pitcher and occasional outfielder to pretty much full-time outfielder. Some anecdotes indicate that the impetus for this was Hall of Famer Harry Hooper, the Red Sox captain at the time, suggesting to manager Ed Barrow in 1918 that Ruth play the outfield on days when he wasn't pitching. Hooper had apparently noticed an increase in attendance on days when Ruth was pitching. In 1919 the left field position opened up for Ruth to play full time when Broadway producer and Red Sox owner Harry Frazee traded Duffy Lewis, along with Ernie Shore and Dutch Leonard, to the Yankees for players and cash.

Following the 1919 season Frazee sold the contract rights to Babe Ruth to the New York Yankees in order to pay off debts which threatened to end his theater production business. The Yankees owner, Colonel Jacob Ruppert, in return for Ruth, paid Frazee $100,000 and lent him $350,000 more, with Fenway Park and the land it was sitting on as collateral. (Yes, the New York Yankees held a mortgage on the Boston Red Sox stadium until Tom Yawkey paid it off in 1933.)

Ruth went on, of course, to become the greatest slugger in the history of the game. When he retired he held the records for highest career slugging percentage, highest career on-base percentage, most home runs in a season, most home runs in a career, and numerous others. He literally changed the way the game was played. In 1919 Ruth hit 29 home runs. There were three players tied for second in the league, with 10 apiece. The Red Sox had only four that were not hit by Ruth. Four out of the eight teams in the league had fewer than Ruth's 29 home runs. In 1920 George Sisler of the Browns hit 19 home runs to finish second behind Ruth. Ruth hit 54. No other *team* hit 54 home runs. The fact that his name has become almost a cliché sometimes takes away from what he actually accomplished.

Babe put up most of these numbers while playing for the New York Yankees. If Red Sox fans actually have a complex with regards to the Yankees, this is the source. The best player in baseball, playing in the age of the reserve clause, had no power to leave. His entire career could have been played in Boston. But Boston's owner considered the Red Sox a secondary concern to his Broadway shows, and sold off the Red Sox assets to finance his stage productions.

In fact, the first Yankees World Series winners in 1923 had *11 players* on the roster who had been acquired from Boston between 1919 and 1922. Sixty-four of their 98 wins went to pitchers who had pitched for the Red Sox during their last World Series win in 1918, and 17 more went to Waite Hoyt, who joined the Red Sox in 1919 and was sent to the Yankees in 1921. The Yankees' dynasty was basically founded as Red Sox South because Harry Frazee was more interested in financing musicals than fielding a baseball team. Of the eight position regulars for the World Series champion 1918 Red Sox, all were gone from Boston by 1922, including Hall of Famers Harry Hooper and Babe Ruth. Two of them, Ruth and Everett Scott, went directly to New York. The four members of the starting rotation were all gone by 1922, all of them directly to New York. (Dutch Leonard never actually pitched for the Yankees, though, being immediately traded to Detroit.)

Babe Ruth is still the all-time major league leader in slugging percentage (.690) and OPS (1.164), and his career .474 on-base percentage is second only to Ted Williams. Ruth's numbers are staggering, but the bottom line is this: Babe Ruth was a great pitcher who developed into the greatest hitter in the history of the game. The Red Sox had him and sold him. And Red Sox fans had to lament what could have been for 86 years, until the 2004 Red Sox won their first World Series since 1918.

Ken Ryan—a hard-throwing righthanded relief prospect who never turned into the star many fans expected. Ryan pitched briefly with the Sox as a 23-year-old in 1992, then pitched well but inconsistently in limited action in 1993, going 7–2. In 1994 Ryan took over the closer's role for half a season, saving 13 games with a 2.44 ERA. But the following year he pitched inconsistently again, struggling badly with his control. The Sox, in need of a closer and unsure how long it would take Ryan to develop into one, packaged him with outfielder Lee Tinsley in a trade to the Philadelphia Phillies for reliever Heathcliff Slocumb. With the Phillies, Ryan followed the same pattern before injuries derailed his career—one great year followed by two inconsistent seasons.

Gene Rye—lefty-hitting outfielder who played for the Sox in 17 games during the 1931 season, his only stint in the majors. He's worth mentioning because of a feat he accomplished in the Texas League during the 1930 season, while playing for Waco. He hit three home runs and drove in seven runs during one inning in a game against Beaumont, the first time that any professional baseball player had accomplished that feat.

Bret Saberhagen—an extraordinarily effective but injury-prone starting pitcher. Saberhagen had a long and impressive career before joining the Red Sox as a free agent in 1997. In 1985 he became the youngest pitcher to win the American League Cy Young Award (at age 21), and in 1989 he won the award again. After seven years with the Kansas City Royals and four with the New York Mets, Saberhagen was traded to the Colorado Rockies during the 1995 season. He suffered a shoulder injury and had surgery in May 1996, missing the entire season. Red Sox GM Dan Duquette signed the still-injured Saberhagen as a reclamation project, and Saberhagen spent most of 1997 rehabbing with several of the organization's minor league teams before joining the parent club late in the season. Saberhagen started six games for the Sox that year, but except for occasional flashes pitched ineffectively, finishing 0–1 with a 6.98 ERA. Most un-Saberhagen like were the 10 walks issued in just 26 innings (Saberhagen always had pinpoint control). Things turned around in 1998 and 1999, however. In 1998 Saberhagen had a 15–7 record with a good 3.92 ERA, and in 1999 he was 10–6, with an excellent 2.95 ERA. He issued only 11 walks in 119 innings pitched in 1999. This was very much like the Bret Saberhagen of old—who holds the major league record for fewest walks per nine innings at 1.66.

Unfortunately, he continued to be plagued by injury, first missing time after cutting his foot on a broken glass at a party he threw for his teammates, then pitching through shoulder pain in the 1999 playoffs, where he was not effective. The shoulder injury turned out to be serious, and Saberhagen's 2000 season was entirely lost to surgery and rehabilitation. He returned in mid-2001 and initially excited fans with a terrific first game, but was only able to pitch in two more games before injuries again curtailed his season. Saberhagen retired after the 2001 season.

Donnie Sadler—a diminutive infielder drafted by the Red Sox in 1994, some scouts considered Sadler a better shortstop prospect than Nomar Garciaparra. Gifted with extraordinary speed, defensive range, and a strong throwing arm, Sadler was heavily hyped in the media as "the most exciting player in the Red Sox organization." With Garciaparra blocking him as a shortstop, the Sox experimented with Sadler in center field and at second base in an attempt to find him a position. Sadler, a favorite of manager Jimy Williams, would play defensively at second base, shortstop, all three outfield positions, and occasionally third base but his lack of offensive production kept him from earning a permanent job with the Red Sox. Despite his small size Sadler seldom walked, and was unable to hit the ball on the ground to utilize his great speed. Sadler spent 1998–2000 shuttling between Boston and Pawtucket, hitting .242 over 156 games (with an awful .283 on-base percentage). After the 2000 season, with Sadler out of options that would allow the Red Sox to send him back to the minor leagues without the risk of losing him to another team, Boston traded Sadler to the Cincinnati Reds as part of a deal for infielder Chris Stynes. Although his physical gifts keep earning him major league chances, Sadler's offensive woes have continued: He has hit .162, .163, .198, and .130 for four different teams since leaving the Sox.

Joe Sambito—an elite relief pitcher with Houston for five years, from 1977 to 1981, Sambito was a 33-year-old coming off three injury-filled years when he joined the Red Sox for the 1986 season. He was expected to reinforce the Red Sox weakness in lefthanded relief pitching, possibly to assume the closer's role, and at least to stabilize the team's weak bullpen and take some of the pressure off overworked Bob Stanley. Sambito never fully regained his effectiveness, however; he had 12 saves in 1986, but was frequently hit hard and was unable to pitch consistently. By the end of the year, Calvin Schiraldi was the closer. Sambito pitched even worse in 1987 (a dreadful 6.93 ERA) before retiring. He is now a player agent, whose clients included Sox player David McCarty in 2004.

Freddy Sanchez—infield prospect who the Red Sox reluctantly traded in 2003, as part of a larger trade that went horribly wrong for nearly all the teams and players involved. Drafted out of Oklahoma City University in 2000, Sanchez posted a career minor-league average of .319 entering the 2003 season, and was widely seen as Boston's second baseman of the future. (Sanchez began his pro career as a shortstop, but concerns about his range—along with the presence of Nomar Garciaparra and Boston's lack of stability at second—eventually led the Red Sox to try him out at second and third.) After the Red Sox traded young pitchers Brandon Lyon and Anastacio Martinez to the Pirates for reliever Scott Sauerbeck and pitching prospect Mike Gonzalez in July 2003, Pittsburgh claimed Lyon was injured, while the Red Sox claimed he was healthy. After nine days of bickering, Boston agreed to take back Lyon and Martinez, send Gonzalez back to Pittsburgh, and trade Sanchez (who was hitting .341 for Pawtucket at the time of his trade) to the Pirates for starter Jeff Suppan. So Boston ended up with Suppan and Sauerbeck, who both pitched poorly during the Red Sox playoff drive, hurting both the Sox and their own careers; Lyon ended up traded again, this time to Arizona, where he *did* get hurt; and Sanchez ended up penciled in as the Pirates second baseman of the future until he also got hurt, missing three months after requiring ankle surgery. The Pirates sent him to the Arizona Fall League following the 2004 season, where he hit .364.

Rey Sanchez—light-hitting, slick-fielding middle infielder who inherited the starting second base job on the Red Sox when Jose Offerman was released in 2002. Sanchez was a 34-year-old veteran of 11 major league seasons whose glove was good enough to win him starting roles in the majors, but whose light bat prevented him from keeping them. (Sanchez hit for a resonably good average, but a hollow one, since he had little power and rarely walked.) He'd finally won a starting job with Kansas City in 1999 and had his three best seasons, only to see his career as a starter derailed by a disastrous stretch run in 2001. (He was traded to the Braves and hit only .227.) Signed by the Red Sox with the hope that he'd help their defensively challenged infield, Sanchez ended up playing far more than expected when Jose Offerman's deteriorating knees and bat lost cost him the second base job. Sanchez hit a hollow .286—better than expected, but not good enough to be brought back. He signed with the Mets to replace the similarly named (and similarly light-hitting but great-fielding) Rey Ordonez but soon lost that job and drifted to Seattle and then Tampa Bay, where he spent the 2004 season. Sanchez signed with the Yankees for 2005.

Jose Santiago—righthanded pitcher who played a key role on the 1967 Impossible Dream team. Santiago came to the Red Sox in 1966, after 3 years as a part-timer in Kansas City. Inserted into the rotation that year, the 26-year-old Santiago was mediocre on a mediocre team, winning 12 games and losing 13. He spent most of the next season in the bullpen, bailing out a pennant-winning team that had only one reliable starter. He finished with a 12–4 record, tied for second on the team in wins. The next year he was inserted back into the rotation and started the season brilliantly (9–4 with a 2.25 ERA) before blowing out his elbow. (This was before "Tommy John" surgery was developed to restore similar injuries, which has become almost routine today.) Santiago was able to pitch briefly in each of the next two years, but never won another game in the majors.

Scott Sauerbeck—sidearming lefty relief specialist who Boston acquired for its 2003 playoff run, but who turned into a major disappointment. Sauerbeck had been an inconsistent but generally effective reliever for Pittsburgh from 1999–2003 (3.55 ERA, 319 strikeouts and only 279 hits allowed in 308.2 innings, though he also issued 191 walks). In 2003, both the Yankees and Red Sox needed another bullpen lefty, and Sauerbeck was considered the best one on the trade market. Boston won the bidding war, sending relievers Brandon Lyon and Anastacio Martinez to Pittsburgh for Sauerbeck and minor league reliever Mike Gonzalez on July 22. The deal was later reworked due to Lyon's elbow injury, with Jeff Suppan joining Boston and Freddy Sanchez going to the Pirates, while Lyon, Martinez, and Gonzalez returned to their original teams. In retrospect, GM Theo Epstein probably wishes the entire trade had been revoked, since Suppan and Sauerbeck both pitched horribly for the Red Sox. Never a great control pitcher to begin with, Sauerbeck walked 18 batters in 16⅔ innings, allowed 17 hits, and had an unseemly 6.48 ERA. Instead of being a valuable weapon for manager Grady Little, Sauerbeck was a complete non-factor in the stretch drive and playoffs, and wasn't offered a contract for 2004. He signed a minor league contract with Cleveland in the spring of 2004, but had shoulder surgery and missed the entire season, though he recovered in time to pitch in the Dominican Winter League, and looked promising enough that the Indians re-signed him for 2005.

Wally Schang—underrated catcher who played semi-regularly with the 1918 World Champions. Schang hit .306 and .305 the next two years, before joining Babe Ruth and many other ex-Sox on the Yankees. He played in a total of six World Series with the Athletics, Red Sox, and Yankees, retiring with a .284 average in 19 seasons.

Curt Schilling—righthanded pitcher who played two major roles in Red Sox history, first as a a star who got away in the late 1980s, then as a grizzled veteran who returned to lead the Red Sox to the 2004 World Championship. Schilling was a top minor league pitching prospect who the Red Sox traded to Baltimore as part of the Mike Boddicker deal in 1988. Traded twice more, Schilling took years to establish himself as a major leaguer, but then became one of the best starting pitchers in the game—a six-time All Star and the MVP of the 2001 World Series, when he led Arizona to victory over the Yankees. For years Schilling was cited by fans as a future star who the Red Sox allowed to get away, but the criticism was unfair; Boston knew they were trading two good prospects to Baltimore for Boddicker, but they needed help in the pennant race that year and were willing to give up future talent to have a chance at winning in 1988.

Schilling went 22–6 for Arizona in 2001 and 23–7 in 2002, but in 2003 an injured 36-year-old Schilling went 8–9 (though his 2.95 ERA was fifth-best in the league) and the rebuilding Diamondbacks decided to trade him. The Red Sox managed to outbid the Yankees, who didn't have the young pitching that Arizona wanted in return, but the deal hinged on Schilling's agreeing to an extension— and he was reluctant to pitch in Fenway Park. A combination of pressure from fans (especially on the Sons of Sam Horn Internet forum, where the net-savvy Schilling still sometimes drops by . . . he calls into radio shows sometimes as well) and the team (general manager Theo Epstein came to Thanksgiving dinner with the Schillings in order to close the deal) convinced the pitcher that Boston would be a good fit. He negotiated his own extension, which guaranteed a $2 million bonus if the Red Sox won the World Series. (The commissioner's office approved the extension, then thought better of it and decreed that future extensions like it would be rejected.)

Schilling filmed a Ford Truck commercial in which he hitched a ride to Boston, saying "Got to end an 86-year-old curse," but it turned out not to be just talk. Schilling went 21–6 at age 37, leading the league in wins and finishing second in ERA (3.26), and third in strikeouts (203), finishing second in the Cy Young balloting for the third time in his career. He also tactfully deferred to tempestuous star Pedro Martinez, who was sensitive about being supplanted as ace by Schilling. A late-season ankle problem didn't slow him in his first playoff start, an ALDS victory against the Angels, but in Game 1 of the ALCS against the Yankees it affected his pitching motion; Schilling gave up six runs in three innings, and it was announced he would be unlikely to pitch again in the postseason, and would need surgery on the ankle. By Game 6, with the Red Sox backs to the wall for the third straight game, Schilling and the team's medical staff found a way to temporarily suture an tendon to the bone, stabilizing the ankle enough to allow Schilling to pitch. Schilling gave up only one earned run in seven innings, despite blood visibly seeping through his sock the whole game. He repeated the performance in Game 2 of the World series, playing through pain and deteriorating skin around the sutures to give up no earned runs in six innings. Conscious of the team's history, the first person he mentioned after the team's World Series victory was longtime Red Sox great Johnny Pesky.

Despite some postseason tension when Schilling wanted to put off surgery briefly in order to campaign for George Bush's reelection (the team owners and majority of its fans supported Massachusetts native son John Kerry), Schilling remains a hugely popular and articulate player in New England, and the team's undisputed ace entering the 2005 season, following the departure of Martinez. Hopefully Schilling's appearance on *Celebrity Poker Showdown*—in which he was doing well until one of his competitors donned a Yankees cap, after which Schilling didn't win another hand—isn't an omen of things to come.

Calvin Schiraldi—righthanded pitcher who came to the Sox in the winter of 1985 from the Mets in the Bobby Ojeda deal. Big, strong, and from Texas, Schiraldi was a much-hyped prospect who was envisioned as the Sox closer of the future. He appeared in 25 games down the stretch in 1986, earning nine saves and helping to bolster a collapsing bullpen. His terrific half-season was a crucial reason the Sox won their division, but the magic wore off in the playoffs. The still-inexperienced Schiraldi pitched poorly and couldn't hold the Mets in the World Series. The inability of Schiraldi and Bob Stanley to hold the lead against the Mets in Game 6 was perhaps the biggest factor in the Sox failure to win a World Series that they had all but wrapped up—and paved the way for Bill Buckner's infamous misplay that finally lost the game. Schiraldi was an average pitcher for the Sox the next year and was shipped off to Chicago (along with Al Nipper) for Lee Smith—one of the Sox great trades.

Pete Schourek—a lefthanded pitcher who spent two stints with the Red Sox. Schourek won 18 games for Cincinnati in 1995, but never won more than eight games in any of his other nine seasons in the major leagues. (In 1998, the Reds fielded an outfield behind Schourek of Dmitri Young, Mike Frank, and Chris Stynes. Movie fans should be quick to note that the outfield would be comprised of Young, Frank, and Stynes.)

Schourek was obtained by Boston in a trade from Cincinnati for the 1998 stretch run, and pitched decently for the Red Sox. His biggest moment with the Red Sox came during the 1998 American League Division Series against Cleveland, when he was named by manager Jimy Williams to start the deciding Game 4 (ahead of ace Pedro Martinez, who would have been working on short rest). The decision was widely criticized, but Schourek pitched well in a losing cause, throwing 5⅔ innings of scoreless ball against a potent Indians lineup.

Allowed to move on during the offseason, Schourek signed a two-year free agent contract with the Pittsburgh Pirates, who released him during spring training in 2000. Schourek then re-signed with the Red Sox (although because of the contract, the Pirates were still paying most of his salary). His 2000 record of 3–10 was somewhat deceptive; early in the year he pitched very well but received poor run support, and he had arm problems in the season's second half. In a valiant but ultimately vain move, Schourek put off surgery to try to help the team down the stretch, but was unable to pitch effectively. He had surgery after the season ended, and signed a minor league contract with the Red Sox for 2001. Schourek pitched 33 games for Boston that year (all in relief, which was all his rebuilt arm could tolerate), with a hard-luck 1–5 record and 4.45 ERA. In 2002, he signed with the Philadelphia Phillies but was released during spring training.

Don Schwall—a young pitching star who never matched his rookie promise, Schwall first made the big leagues in 1961, along with fellow rookie Carl Yastrzemski. Schwall had been a basketball star at the University of Oklahoma, and seemed to be on his way to baseball stardom as well; he went 15–7 as a 25-year-old rookie on a bad team, pitched in the All Star Game (there were actually two All Star Games that year), and was the second Boston player to win the Rookie of the Year award. (Walt Dropo was the first.) Schwall struggled with his control in his two seasons with Boston, and in 1962 his wildness caused him to fall to 9–15 for an equally bad Red Sox team. Still seen as a valuable pitcher, Schwall was traded to Pittsburgh for slugger Dick Stuart after the 1962 season. After an unsuccessful career as a starter Schwall was used mostly in relief, but while his control improved he never returned to the consistently dominant form of his rookie season.

Everett "Deacon" Scott—the prototypical good-field/no-hit shortstop, Scott is best-known for holding the consecutive game record broken by Lou Gehrig (and then Cal Ripken Jr.). Scott debuted in 1914, and his batting averages ranged from .201 to .241 in his first five years. He had no power, almost never walked, and didn't run well, but his glove enabled him to play regularly for three World Champions. In 1916, Scott began two streaks. He led American League shortstops in fielding percentage for the first of eight straight seasons, and, on June 30, played in the first of 1,307 consecutive games. Scott improved to a career-high .278 in 1919, and his average stayed in the .260s the next two years. But, like many of his teammates, Scott wound up on the Yankees, going to the Bronx with Joe Bush and Sad Sam Jones after the 1921 season. The Deacon was the shortstop on the first Yankees championship team (1923), but by 1925 his defense had begun to slip. On May 5, Scott was replaced by Pee-Wee Wanninger, ending his record streak. Ironically, less than a month later, teammate Lou Gehrig began his 2,130 game streak by pinch-hitting for Wanninger. Scott retired a year later, and his streak is currently third on the all-time list.

George Scott—"Boomer" was a slugging first baseman and excellent defensive player who spent nine years with the Red Sox in two tours of duty, but had most of his best years elsewhere. Scott had a good rookie year in Boston as a 22-year-old in 1966, hitting 27 home runs and driving in 90 runs (as well as leading the league in strikeouts). He was a key player in the Impossible Dream year of 1967, when he hit .303 (fourth in the league), although his power dropped off a bit. The next year his offense mysteriously fell apart. In a year when pitchers dominated,

Scott hit only .171 with three homers. He recovered somewhat over the next 3 years, when he split time between first base and third base, but never came close to matching the promise of his first two seasons. Traded to Milwaukee after the 1971 season, Scott finally became the consistent .280 hitter with the power the Sox had hoped for; Scott would lead the league in homers and RBI in 1975. The Red Sox tried to make up for their mistake by trading Cecil Cooper to Milwaukee to get Scott back in 1976, but that move backfired. Scott had only one good year left, while Cooper went on to become a star.

Although Scott is remembered as a slugger, he was a terrific defensive player at a position usually reserved for offense-first players. During his career he won eight Gold Gloves at first base, a record at the time.

Tom Seaver—a Hall of Fame pitcher who was great with the Mets in the 1970s and good with the Reds in the early 1980s. He was traded to the Red Sox by the Chicago White Sox for the 1986 stretch drive. He pitched in 16 games, going 5–7, but was injured and unable to play in the playoffs, which pushed the ineffective Al Nipper back into the World Series rotation. Seaver retired after the season.

Diego Segui—a journeyman pitcher who played for eight teams in a 15-year career, Segui was a reliever for the Red Sox in 1974–75, when he was near the end of the line. He led a 1974 team in transition with 10 saves and 108 innings of relief, and had six more saves on the 1975 American League pennant winners, where he was mostly a long reliever. Segui finished up his career with the expansion Seattle Mariners in 1977, which made him the only person to play for both the Seattle Pilots and the Seattle Mariners. Segui's son, David, is currently a major league first baseman.

Aaron Sele—a starting pitcher drafted by the Red Sox in the first round in 1991 (he and Sox catcher Scott Hatteberg were college teammates at Washington State), Sele was heralded as the best starting pitcher to come out of the Red Sox system since Roger Clemens. He made the majors in 1993, posting a 7–2 record with a 2.74 ERA in 18 starts in his rookie year, and displaying one of the best curveballs in baseball. After missing most of the 1995 season due to injury, Sele struggled in 1996 and 1997, posting ERAs above 5.00 in both seasons. Sele became a focus of controversy on the team; he failed to regain the consistent form he'd shown as a rookie and was accused of being "gutless" by Roger Clemens and others. The Red Sox had hoped Sele would succeed Clemens as the ace of the rotation, but he never reached the next level with Boston. He was traded to Texas in an offseason deal that brought role players Jim Leyritz and Damon Buford to the Sox before the 1998 season. Sele revived his career in Texas, winning a combined 37 games in two seasons (although his ERA remained high, he played for a terrific offensive team), and enjoyed similar success with the Seattle Mariners before signing a three-year deal with the Anaheim Angels, and seeing his career disintegrate amid a series of arm and shoulder injuries. He was left off Anaheim's 2004 playoff roster (after a deceptive 9–4 season, in which he pitched very poorly and had a shoulder injury but got great run support) and signed with Seattle after the season.

Jeff Sellers—a righthanded pitching prospect who never fulfilled his promise. He made four starts for the Sox as a 21-year-old in 1985, going 2–0 and looking like the future star he was supposed to become. It was the only winning record he would have in the major leagues. Sellers played for parts of three seasons but was never able to crack the starting rotation full-time despite many opportunities, given the lack of depth on the Sox pitching staff (he had ERAs around 5.00 each year, at a time when league average was about 4.20). After he went 1–7 in 1988 the Red Sox gave up on him, and his career was over at age 24.

Ernie Shore—a righthanded pitcher who pitched well for the Sox from 1914–1917 (65–42 and a 2.45 ERA over his seven-year career, at a time when the league average was about 2.70). His great moment came as a relief pitcher in 1917 (one of only two relief appearances that year) when he replaced Babe Ruth, who had been thrown out for arguing the umpire's ball four call on the first batter. Shore picked off the runner Ruth had walked, then retired the next 26 batters in order—a perfect game. (Major League Baseball retroactively decided this didn't count as a perfect game in the early 1990s, when they also took away Red Sox pitcher Matt Young's no-hitter). After World War I, Shore followed Babe Ruth to New York, where he pitched badly for two years. He was done as a major leaguer at age 29.

Sonny Siebert—curveball specialist whom the Red Sox acquired in the controversial Ken Harrelson trade. Siebert, whose real name was Wilfred, had several good years for the mediocre Cleveland Indians in the mid-to-late 1960s. (He chose baseball over basketball, having been drafted by the NBA's St. Louis Hawks.) In 1966, he pitched a no-hitter against Washington. Early in the 1969 season, the Red Sox sent Harrelson to Cleveland (though the slugger initially failed to report) in a six-player deal. The key player for Boston was Siebert and he pitched well, going 14–10 with a 3.80 ERA and five saves, while splitting his time between the rotation and bullpen. In 1970, Siebert focused exclusively on starting, and he won 15 games, with a fine 3.44 ERA. Part of the reason for his success was better control: in 45 more innings, he walked 16 fewer hitters than he had in 1969. He was even better in 1971 (16–10, 2.91 ERA, only 220 hits and 60 walks in 235 innings), and earned a spot on the American League All Star team. Siebert slipped into mediocrity the following season, however, as his record fell to 12–12, and his ERA went up nearly a run, to 3.80. After two ineffective relief appearances in 1972, Siebert was sold to Texas. He finished his career in 1975, retiring with a 140–114 lifetime record.

Al Simmons—a Hall of Fame outfielder who played 40 games with the Red Sox in 1943, at the age of 37. Simmons had driven in more than 100 runs in his first 11 seasons with the Athletics and White Sox, but hit only .203 for the Red Sox. He had 2,897 hits when he joined Boston, but only mustered 27 with the Sox and three more in his final season, finishing 73 hits shy of the 3,000-hit milestone. He was known as "Bucketfoot Al" for his peculiar batting stance.

Ted Sizemore—light-hitting second baseman who was the 1969 National League Rookie of the Year for the Los Angeles Dodgers. He spent his entire career in the National League, with four different teams, before the Red Sox traded catcher Mike O'Berry (and cash) to the Cubs for Sizemore in August of 1979. Sizemore actually caught two games for the Red Sox that season. He finished his career with five hits in 29 at-bats for the 1980 Red Sox before being released.

Heathcliff Slocumb—intimidating relief pitcher acquired prior to the 1996 season from the Philadelphia Phillies (where he'd been an All Star in 1995) in a six-player deal which sent young relief pitcher Ken Ryan and journeyman center fielder Lee Tinsley to the Phillies. The 6-foot–3, 220-pound Slocumb was a menacing figure on the mound, with a good fastball and a nasty slider. Though he was effective as the Sox closer in 1996, posting a 3.02 ERA with 31 saves, Slocumb constantly seemed to be in trouble because of his wildness on the mound. Although he was tough to hit, he allowed 55 walks in 83 innings of work, creating a dangerously high number of baserunners. The next year, his wildness caught up with him, leading to five losses and a 5.79 ERA—and losing the support of fans, who were terrified whenever he took the mound in a close game. Slocumb still threw hard and showed flashes of brilliance, however, and in one of the best Sox trades ever, GM Dan Duquette sent him to Seattle for catcher Jason Varitek and pitcher Derek Lowe—both of whom turned into All Stars.

Slocumb never did overcome his wildness, and was out of the majors following the 2000 season, after bouncing around to three more teams. He is now a Florida real estate developer.

Lee Smith—burly righthanded relief pitcher who spent three years with the Sox en route to becoming one of baseball's most accomplished closers. Smith came up in 1980 and spent the first eight seasons of his career with the Chicago Cubs, for whom he notched 180 saves. The Red Sox, desperately in need of bullpen stability, traded pitchers Al Nipper and Calvin Schiraldi to get Smith after the 1987 season—in what turned out to be a terrific trade.

Although Smith's debut with the Sox was tarnished when he surrendered a game-winning home run to Alan Trammell of Detroit on Opening Day 1988, he gave the Red Sox everything their bullpen had been lacking. In his two full seasons with the Sox he saved 29 and 25 games (he was among the league leaders both years; no one on the 1986 team had more than 16) with extraordinary strike-

Two players who don't get enough credit for their role in the Red Sox 2004 World Series Championship are Jim Smith and Derek Vinyard.

Neither ever played a day in the major leagues, but Derek Vinyard was the player-to-be-named-later that the Sox sent to Montreal for Glen Murray. Jim Smith was the player-to-be-named-later that the Sox sent to Seattle for Lee Tinsley.

Murray and Tinsley were later packaged with Ken Ryan, whom the Sox had signed as an amateur free agent, for Heathcliff Slocumb.

Slocumb was subsequently sent to Seattle for Derek Lowe and Jason Varitek.

Everyone remembers how much the Slocumb trade helped the Sox, but they forget how Slocumb himself was acquired for a pile of swag.

—Tim Savage

out numbers and almost unhittable power, although his sometimes erratic control led to some less-than-pretty performances. He was a major factor in 1988 as the Sox won their division, and he pitched nearly as well in 1989.

The signing of Massachusetts native Jeff Reardon before the 1990 season created a surplus of closers on the team. Early in the season the 32-year-old Smith was traded to the St. Louis Cardinals for disappointing right fielder Tom Brunansky. Smith continued his success with St. Louis and a string of other teams before retiring in 1997 with 478 saves, first on baseball's all-time list. He was a seven-time All Star (five times after the Sox traded him), led the league in saves four times, and was a three-time winner of the Rolaids Relief Man of the Year Award.

Reggie Smith—switch-hitting outfielder, Smith spent the first eight years of his career with the Red Sox, coming up in 1966 at the age of 21. He had been a shortstop in the Minnesota Twins minor league system but the Sox put him in the outfield (first in center, then in right). He hit over .300 three times, won a Gold Glove, and made the All Star team twice as a member of the Red Sox. He was traded (with Ken Tatum), to the Cardinals for Rick Wise and Bernie Carbo following the 1973 season. He was an All Star during his first two seasons in St Louis, then was traded to the Dodgers in June of 1976.

During the 1977 season, Smith combined with Steve Garvey, Ron Cey, and Dusty Baker to become the first set of four teammates to hit 30 or more home runs in the same season. Knee, ankle, neck, and shoulder injuries hampered the last five years of his career; Smith finished in 1982 at age 37, playing 99 games at first base for the Giants in his one season in San Francisco. At the time of his retirement, his 314 career home runs were second only to Mickey Mantle among switch-hitters, he was the only switch-hitter with 100 home runs in each league, and he was the only switch-hitter to homer from each side of the plate twice in each league. He was also, with Frank Robinson, one of only two players to appear in World Series and All Star games in each league.

Tris Speaker—spectacular center fielder for the dominant Red Sox teams of the early twentieth century, and one of the greatest all-around players in major league history. Nicknamed "The Grey Eagle" because of his prematurely grey hair, Speaker is best remembered today for his brilliant defense. He was regarded as the best center fielder of his era, and is considered one of the all-time greats at his position. Speaker probably played the shallowest center field ever (he made several unassisted double plays at second base), but had no problems running down fly balls over his head. In seven full seasons with Boston, he led AL center fielders in putouts five times, in assists three times, and in double plays four times. He holds the career records for assists and double plays by an outfielder. But Speaker was much more than a great fielder; he hit .345 in his 22-year-career, with 3,514 hits and a major league record 793 doubles, plus 432 stolen bases.

Like Babe Ruth and Stan Musial, Speaker began his minor league career as a lefty pitcher, but he was soon moved to the outfield. He joined the Red Sox in 1907 for a brief but unimpressive seven-game stint. Although he was only 19, the Red Sox didn't offer him a contract after the season. The young outfielder tried out for John McGraw's New York Giants, but was turned down, and returned to Boston. He didn't play full-time until 1909, when he hit .309, stole 35 bases, and set a league record with 35 outfield assists. Speaker continued to excel the next two years, batting .340 and .334, and he anchored what might be the best defensive outfield in history, with fellow youngsters Duffy Lewis and Harry Hooper. Ironically, Speaker didn't get along well with Hooper and hated Lewis. One day in St. Louis, Lewis shaved his head to get relief from the heat (a very unfashionable thing to do at the time). During batting practice, Speaker ran over and removed Lewis's cap, exposing his bald head to the fans, and legend has it that the two men never spoke to each other again, except when calling for fly balls.

Speaker was already a star, but he really came into his own in 1912. Only Ty Cobb and Shoeless Joe Jackson exceeded The Grey Eagle's .383 average, and Speaker also led the league in home runs (10—a high total for the "Dead Ball Era"), doubles (53), and on-base percentage (.464). He scored 136 runs, drove in 90, had 222 hits, slugged .567, stole a career-high 52 bases, and tied his own record with 35 assists. In the 1912 World Series, Speaker tied the deciding game with a hit off future Hall of Famer Christy Mathewson, and the Red Sox won the championship when the next batter, Larry Gardner, hit a sacrifice fly.

The Red Sox fell to fourth and second in the next two seasons, but Speaker maintained his incredible level of play. He hit .363 in 1913, with 46 steals and a career-high 22 triples. The following season, he led the league in hits and doubles, batted .338, scored 101 runs, drove in 90, and stole 42 bases. In both years, Speaker slugged over .500, which was a great achievement in an era when home runs were so rare, and had on-base percentages well over .400.

In 1915, Speaker's numbers declined a bit, but he was still outstanding. He didn't hit any homers, but finished fourth in the batting race (.322), scored 108 runs, and drew 81 walks—while striking out only 14 times. More importantly, he won his second World Series, batting .294 in an easy five-game victory over the Phillies. At this point, Speaker was only 27 years old and was clearly one of baseball's greatest players, even if 1915 hadn't been his best season. But the Sox decided to cut Speaker's salary in half, from $18,000 to $9,000. The superstar refused to sign a contract, and didn't report to spring training. Just before the 1916 season began, Boston sent Speaker to Cleveland for talented pitcher Sad Sam Jones, rookie third baseman Fred Thomas, and $55,000 cash.

Speaker hadn't been the most popular person in the Red Sox clubhouse, and the remaining players took great pride in winning the 1916 and 1918 World Series without him. But the trade was still terrible for Boston, and it set the stage for a series of player giveaways the next few years, mainly to the hated Yankees. Speaker won the batting title in 1916, and hit .340 or better in 8 of his 11 Cleveland seasons. In 1919, he was named player-manager, and in 1920 he hit .388 and led the Indians to a World Championship. Some of Speaker's success in the 1920s can be attributed to the lively ball, which increased hitting stats across the board, but his numbers are still eye-popping, including a .389 average and .479 on-base percentage at the age of 37.

Unfortunately, Speaker's career ended in a shroud of controversy. In 1926, former Red Sox star Dutch Leonard accused Speaker and Detroit player-manager

Ty Cobb of fixing a meaningless 1919 game. Leonard produced two letters (neither of which mentioned Speaker by name) as evidence, but later recanted his statement. Commissioner Landis decided to drop the matter, but American League President Ban Johnson was furious and decided that Speaker and Cobb could still play, but no longer be managers. Both players became free agents; Cobb went to the Philadelphia A's, while Speaker spent 1927 with the Washington Senators. In 1928, Speaker joined Cobb in Philadelphia, and both legends retired after the season.

After his career, Speaker became a minor league manager and owner. He also spent some time as a broadcaster for the Cubs and Indians. Speaker narrowly missed getting elected into the first Hall of Fame class in 1936, but made it in easily the next year. Today, Speaker is rarely mentioned as an all-time great, perhaps because he played much of his career in the Dead Ball Era—and often in the shadow of Cobb, who was a little better and a lot more famous. When fans choose all-time Red Sox teams, Jim Rice and Dwight Evans invariably get more votes than Speaker. But if one examines the record closely, it's hard to argue that The Grey Eagle doesn't belong in Boston's all-time outfield, surrounded by Yaz and Teddy Ballgame.

Bobby Sprowl—lefthanded pitcher thought to be a strong prospect, who was brought to the majors during the Red Sox swoon in September 1978. Pawtucket manager Joe Morgan thought that Sprowl wasn't ready, but lefty Bill Lee was buried in manager Don Zimmer's doghouse (for, among other things, calling the manager a "gerbil" in the press, an appellation that stuck in many corners of Red Sox Nation) and the Sox needed a pitcher. Sprowl made three starts for the Sox, going 0–2. His last appearance in a Red Sox uniform was the fourth and last game of the "Boston Massacre," when he never made it out of the first inning. Sprowl went on to become a college coach, and his son, Jon-Mark, is a minor league catcher.

Chick Stahl—a player-manager who killed himself under controversial circumstances. Charles Sylvester "Chick" Stahl was a good-hitting center fielder who became the club's manager late in 1906, replacing Jimmy Collins as player/manager of a truly dreadful team (the Red Sox lost 20 games in a row at one point, and 19 in a row at home). The following spring, Stahl reportedly told Collins that he couldn't take the strain of managing, before drinking carbolic acid. There's also been a persistent rumor, though never proven, that Stahl killed himself over romantic entanglements. Stahl had recently gotten married but supposedly learned that he had gotten another woman pregnant. He was 34.

Jake Stahl—a righthanded-hitting outfielder who came up with Boston in 1903 and played 28 games for the team that won the first World Series. He spent the next three seasons in Washington, managing the team in two of those seasons. Stahl was independently wealthy, and played only for the love of the game. After being out of baseball in 1907, he signed with the Yankees in 1908, and then was traded back to Boston in midseason. He played first base for the Sox in 1909 and 1910 before retiring. In 1912, Boston owner James McAleer hired him as player-manager, and Stahl came out of retirement. He played in 95 games for the 1912 team, and managed them to the World Series title. After being replaced in the middle of the 1913 season by Bill Carrigan, Stahl was out of baseball for good. Jake Stahl was not related to Chick Stahl, although some accounts mistakenly claim the two men were brothers.

Matt Stairs—once a top prospect with the Expos, Stairs had stalled in the Montreal system by the mid–1990s. Dan Duquette, who had signed Stairs while he was GM in Montreal, brought the lefthanded-hitting outfielder to Boston as a minor league free agent in 1995. Stairs was sent down to AA (the Sox AAA affiliate at Pawtucket had too many outfielders), where he thoroughly dominated the league. Stairs wasn't much of a fielder, and didn't look athletic, so he had trouble getting a chance to play in the major leagues, no matter how well he hit. He finally made the Red Sox as a pinch hitter late in the 1995 season, before moving on to Oakland as a minor league free agent. In Oakland he showed what all the hype had been about, hitting .298 with 27 home runs in 1997 and following with two more excellent seasons before an off year in 2000. Stairs has continued to hit well in a part-time role ever since (but never quite well enough to land himself a full-time job), playing for four teams over the last four years. Now 37 years old, he played for Kansas City in 2004.

Tracy Stallard—a mediocre righthanded starting pitcher who came up with the Sox in 1960. Stallard is best remembered for giving up Roger Maris's 61st home run on October 1, 1961, at Yankee Stadium. After three years in Boston, Stallard joined the woeful expansion Mets. He lost 37 games in two years before finishing his career with two years in St. Louis.

Lee Stange—Stange had a tough luck season for the Red Sox in the pennant-winning season of 1967, finishing with only an 8–10 record despite a fine 2.77 ERA. He was scheduled to start a pennant-deciding one-game playoff game that year, had the season ended in a tie. Instead he worked out of the bullpen during the World Series. He continued to relieve in 1968 and saved a staff-high 12 games. Stange's best major league year was in 1963 when he had a 12–5 record with the Senators. While with Cleveland in 1964 Stange performed the statistical oddity of striking out four men in one inning. (Tim Wakefield did the same thing for the Red Sox in 1999, after one of the batters he struck out reached on a wild pitch.) After retiring, Stange served as pitching coach for several teams, including the Red Sox.

Bob Stanley—while notorious for his wild pitch/passed ball in Game 6 of the 1986 World Series, Stanley was a valuable pitcher for many years. Stanley first pitched for the Sox in 1977, appearing in 41 games and starting 13. This swing man role would be his most effective with the Sox for the next 12 years, but he was used in many other roles as well. In 1978 Stanley went 15–2 with 10 saves and a 2.60 ERA. (He only started three games that year.) In 1979, Stanley was moved into the rotation, starting 30 games and going 16–12 with one save and a 3.99 ERA. After pitching poorly as a starter in 1980, he was moved into a relief and spot-starting role, where he thrived, setting a record by pitching 168⅓ innings in relief in 1982 (and finishing second in the league in ERA). In 1983, he was made the closer for a bad Red Sox team. That year Stanley appeared in 64 games and saved 33. He followed that up in 1984 with 22 more saves before moving back to being a middle reliever and part-time closer. In 1987 Stanley went back to starting most of the time and had his worst year (4–15 with a 5.01 ERA in 20 starts). After pitching in 1988 and 1989 exclusively as a reliever, the 34-year-old Stanley retired to care for a son who had cancer. He later became a pitching coach in the Mets system.

Stanley was known for his palm ball, which he threw almost every pitch; it was slow and looked very hittable, but its crazy action made the ball seem to dart and flutter like a butterfly. He never struck out very many batters, but he had good control and threw a lot of double play balls. Stanley is also one of two pitchers to have both 100 saves and 100 career wins.

During the Margo Adams scandal, Wade Boggs and Steve Crawford allegedly arranged for Stanley to be seduced by a stripper while the team was on the road. Boggs supposedly came into the hotel room in mid-seduction and took pictures of Stanley and the stripper, so Stanley—who had a reputation for gossiping—could be kept from talking about his teammates' extramarital escapades.

Never really a fan favorite, Stanley used to capture beach balls thrown around by fans and kill the balls with a rake in the bullpen. He also counts as a local kid done good; he was born in Portland, Maine.

Mike Stanley—for years a light-hitting backup catcher with the Rangers, Stanley blossomed into a good hitter for the Yankees at age 30, when he hit .305 with 26 homers. After four very good years in New York, he signed as a free agent with the Red Sox and was their catcher for most of 1996. He continued to hit well in Boston, posting solid but not great batting averages with good power and high walk totals. Stanley played 97 games at DH for the Red Sox in 1997 before being traded back to the Yankees. At the time it seemed a relatively minor matter. The Red Sox, out of the postseason picture, acquired minor league pitchers in exchange for a major league bat, as the Yankees prepared for the postseason. It turned out to be a very big deal on a couple of fronts, however. First, one of the pitchers obtained, Jim Mecir, never pitched for the Red Sox, but was selected in the expansion draft by Tampa Bay, enabling the Red Sox to avoid losing outfielder Trot Nixon (who would probably have been selected otherwise). The other big aspect was the acquisition of Tony Armas Jr. This minor league pitcher, son of former Red Sox outfielder Tony Armas, was a key reason why the Red Sox were able to put together a better trade for superstar pitcher Pedro Martinez than the Yankees were.

Stanley finished the 1997 season with New York and signed with Toronto in the offseason. The Red Sox re-acquired him in the middle of the 1998 season, trading minor league pitchers Peter Munro and Jay Yennaco, as they prepared to go to the playoffs after winning the wild card. He remained with Boston, playing first base and DHing (injuries prevented him from catching any longer), until midway through the 2000 season. In a move that caused some consternation among his teammates (Jeff Frye was particularly outspoken) and the media, the

Red Sox released Stanley, believing that his bat had slowed significantly. He signed on with Oakland, and finished the season better than he had started it, though not well.

At his best, Stanley was a disciplined hitter with decent power. He was always reputed to be an excellent teammate and a good clubhouse presence. These qualities were instrumental as Stanley was invited to return to Boston as the bench coach for the 2002 season. Regarded as a future manager, Stanley had a rough season as bench coach, left for undisclosed "personal reasons," and has not returned to baseball.

Mike Stanton—the Red Sox acquired Stanton, a lefthanded reliever, from the Atlanta Braves in a trading deadline deal in 1995, and he threw 21 solid innings for Boston, helping them win the American League East. At times during his stay in Atlanta, Stanton had been the Braves' closer, including 1993, when he saved 27 games. He was heavily used as a situational reliever for Boston 1996, until the Sox traded him to Texas late in the season. Following the 1996 season he signed with the New York Yankees, and returned to stardom as a significant part of the Yankees' strong bullpen for the next six years (including a rare All Star appearance for a middle reliever in 2001, when he went 9–4 with a 2.58 ERA). He moved to the Mets for the 2003 and 2004 campaigns, pitching about as well but to far less acclaim (and with a much weaker team). Stanton was traded back to the Yankees in exchange for Felix Heredia and cash after the 2004 season.

Dave Stapleton—pressed into emergency service in 1980 when Jerry Remy was injured, 26-year-old rookie Stapleton had the season of his life, hitting .321 in 449 at bats (although without many walks or much power). He had a solid second season as a utility player in 1981, hitting .285 in limited playing time (with more walks and home runs), and was inexplicably given the first base job for the next two years, where his limitations as a hitter were magnified. He stuck around as a rarely used defensive replacement for three more years, and is best remembered for a game when he was *not* on the field—in the sixth game of the 1986 World Series, when Stapleton was not substituted defensively for Bill Buckner, who let a ground ball go between his legs to allow the winning run to score. Stapleton accomplished the bizarre statistical feat of having his batting average go down every single year of his career—from .321 to .285 to .264 to .247 to .231 to .227 to .128.

Dernell Stenson—former phenom who never made it with the Red Sox, played briefly for Cincinnati, and was brutally murdered at age 25. Stenson was Boston's fourth-round pick in the 1996 draft, reached AAA before his twenty-first birthday, and was twice named the team's #1 prospect by *Baseball America*. He showed excellent plate discipline and power potential for a young player, earning comparisons to another big lefty, first baseman Mo Vaughn. In 1999, after Vaughn left as a free agent, Boston moved Stenson from left field to first base, but his 34 errors ended the experiment. The Sox called Stenson up for a week in 2000, but he didn't get into any games, and returned to Pawtucket. He stagnated there for two more years, putting up increasingly mediocre numbers. By the spring of 2003, Stenson was out of options—and out of the team's plans. Boston waived the disappointing slugger to make room for free agent Kevin Millar. Cincinnati claimed Stenson and sent him to AA, where he hit .306, though he struggled after a promotion to AAA. But the Reds had lots of injuries, and Stenson finally got his big chance: He hit .247 with three homers in 37 games, and was sent to the Arizona Fall League (a developmental league for top prospects), where he hit .394 for the Scottsdale Scorpions. But early in the morning of November 5, 2003, Stenson's body was found in a street in Chandler, Arizona. According to police, two men robbed Stenson after he left a bar, shot him in the head, bound his hands and feet, and ran him over with his own SUV. Both suspects are currently awaiting trial for murder. In tribute to a soft-spoken, friendly player who met a horrible fate, the Arizona Fall League renamed its sportsmanship award after Dernell Stenson.

Gene Stephens—an obscure backup outfielder who had one of the best innings in baseball history. On June 18, 1953, the Red Sox exploded for an American League-record 17 runs in the seventh inning against the Tigers. The Sox drew 6 walks and had 14 hits—three of them by Stephens, a 20-year-old rookie. Stephens is one of only two modern players ever to get three hits in an inning, earning him a place in the record books. (The second was also a Red Sox player, Johnny Damon, who did it in 2003.) Stephens only hit .204 in 1953, and spent the following season in the minors. He returned in 1955 and played for Boston until 1960, almost exclusively as a pinch-hitter or defensive caddy for Ted Williams. Stephens's only other claim to fame: He was later traded even-up for Marv Throneberry, a cult legend with the 1962 Mets.

Vern Stephens—a power-hitting shortstop known as "Junior" or "Buster" by most writers and fans, Stephens was already a four-time All Star when the Red Sox acquired him prior to the 1948 season. He went on to make the All Star team four more times during his five years in Boston. Before Ernie Banks came along, Vern Stephens was the best power-hitting shortstop in the history of the game. In 1945 (admittedly a war year, with many top players in the service), his 24 homers for the St. Louis Browns led the American League. During his first three years in Boston he hit 29, 39, and 30 home runs. In addition, he led the league in RBI during both 1949 and 1950, helped by having Ted Williams on base in front of him most of the time. His 159 RBI in 1949 is still the most by any big league shortstop. His 39 homers that year were a record at the time for a shortstop. (Ernie Banks broke it in the National League, but it stood in the American League until Sox player Rico Petrocelli hit 40 in 1969.)

Helped out by the manpower shortage, Stephens was a regular in 1942 at the age of 21. He came up with the St. Louis Browns and spent the first six years of his career with them—seven if you count the three games he got into in 1941. In 1946 he briefly jumped to the outlaw Mexican League, but came back after three games when his father and one of the Browns' scouts went down to get him. Commissioner Chandler suspended the players that remained in Mexico for up to five years.

In November of 1947 the Red Sox traded 10 players and $375,000 to the

Browns to get Stephens, along with pitchers Jack Kramer and Ellis Kinder and infielder Billy Hitchcock. Stephens was dropped into the lineup at shortstop, incumbent Johnny Pesky moved to third, and the Sox went on to win at least 94 games in each of the next three years—twice losing the pennant on the last day of the season.

There was some controversy when Stephens joined the Red Sox about who would play shortstop. Since Pesky was smaller and had no power, everyone assumed Stephens would play third base. Stephens was actually a solid defensive shortstop, but was perceived as poor—since he didn't fit the speedy, singles-hitting image of shortstops at the time. This perception led many people to think that Stephens typified the Red Sox lack of concern for the subtleties of the game. Phil Rizzuto wasn't in Stephens's league as a hitter, but was widely regarded as the top American League shortstop of the time, on the strength of his fielding, baserunning, and bunting. So Stephens, who would have been a big star today, was viewed in his era as a selfish, one-dimensional player.

The 1950 Red Sox were the last team to hit .300, and it was Stephens's last really good year, at the age of 29. By 1951 he was starting to show the results of injuries to his legs, and he played only 109 games, a number he wouldn't match again. His stats were still good, but he was on the way down. 1951 was the last season he ever slugged over .500 (.501) and it was the last time that his on-base percentage was over .350 (.364). The Red Sox released him after 1952, and he spent the next three years bouncing between the White Sox and the St. Louis Browns/Baltimore Orioles, playing some shortstop but mostly third base. In his five years in Boston he hit 122 home runs and drove in 562 runs, and was a key component of several Red Sox teams that were very good, though not quite good enough.

Stephens, who was said to be a heavy drinker, died in 1968 at age 48.

Jerry Stephenson—a minor league pitching phenom in the early 1960s, Stephenson wrecked his arm in AAA pitching off a wet mound and was never the same. He pitched one game for the Sox at age 19 and would pitch in parts of 5 seasons for the team without ever regaining the promise he showed before his injury. He later pitched for two other teams without any greater effectiveness, and was out of baseball at 26.

Stephenson's father, Joe, also played in the major leagues, and his son is a minor league pitching prospect who has also been set back by injuries. Stephenson is currently vice president of scouting for the Red Sox, after scouting for the Dodgers for many years.

Jeff Stone—a speedy outfielder who came up with the Phillies in 1983 but never developed as expected. After a stint with the Orioles he came over to the Sox during 1989, and was mainly used as a pinch-runner, getting only 15 at-bats in 18 games. He is mainly remembered for his only hit of the 1990 season, a late-inning pinch single that drove in the winning run of a game at Fenway against the Blue Jays, as the two flawed teams were battling for the American League East title. Stone's moment of glory came in the last week of the season, as the Red Sox held off Toronto to win the East by two games.

Stone was back in the news in January 2002, when he was allegedly stabbed by his wife in his Missouri home.

Dick Stuart—nicknamed "Stonefingers" for his poor fielding, Stuart was a slugging first baseman who spent two contentious years with Red Sox teams in the early 1960s. Obtained from Pittsburgh after the 1962 season as part of a deal for pitcher Don Schwall and catcher Jim Pagliaroni, Stuart hit 42 home runs and led the league in both RBI and errors. By the next year he was feuding constantly with manager Johnny Pesky, and although he continued to hit well (.279 with 33 homers at a time when the league average was less than .250), many people saw the clubhouse discontent as the source of the team's problems (the Sox lost 85 games in 1963 and 90 in 1964). After the 1964 season Pesky was fired as manager and Stuart was given away to the Philadelphia Phillies for pitcher Dennis Bennett, who would win only 12 games for the Sox over the next three years. The strategy failed; despite a happier clubhouse, the Sox hit 21 fewer home runs as a team and lost 100 games in 1965.

Frank Sullivan—a very good pitcher for the Red Sox during the 1950s. From 1955 through 1957, Sullivan pitched 742 innings, with ERAs of 2.91, 3.42, and 2.73 (league average was around 4.00). In all three years he appeared in the top 10 in innings pitched and ERA, and he was selected to the All Star team in 1955 and 1956. Unfortunately, after throwing over 240 innings for three straight years, Sullivan dipped to 199 innings in 1958, 177 innings in 1959, and 153 innings in 1960. His ERA similarly worsened, to 3.53, 3.95, and finally 5.10 in 1960. Having used up most of Sullivan's arm, the Red Sox traded him to the Phillies for pitcher Gene Conley. Sullivan would pitch 226 more innings for the Phillies and Twins over the final three years of his career, retiring after the 1963 season at age 33. Pitching his best years while the Red Sox were mediocre, Sullivan's name has rarely received the same recognition as players like Hughson, Ferriss, Kinder, or Lonborg—who did not pitch nearly as well as Sullivan, but were lucky enough to pitch for contending teams, helping them maintain better-remembered places in Sox lore than the superior but forgotten Frank Sullivan.

Marc Sullivan—a backup catcher during the mid-1980s, the suspicion was that Sullivan made the team only because his father was part-owner Haywood Sullivan, who had also been a backup catcher with the Sox. Marc struggled to hit .200 in the minor leagues, much less in the majors. His on-field highlight may have been a game in May 1986 when he provided the game-winning run by being hit in the rump with the bases loaded in the bottom of the ninth. He played in 137 games over a five-year career with the Red Sox, hitting .193 in his best season. (His father hit .161 in 1960, his only complete season with the Sox.)

Jeff Suppan—a righthanded pitcher and top Red Sox prospect, Suppan made his major league debut during the 1995 season. In 1997 he made 22 starts for the Sox, pitched badly, and was not protected during the expansion draft that stocked the Tampa Bay Devil Rays and the Arizona Diamondbacks. GM Dan Duquette was widely criticized for not protecting him, in a situation that was reminiscent of previous GM Lou Gorman's loss of popular Eric Wedge. By leaving him out, however, the Sox were able to pull back both Trot Nixon and minor league pitcher Tony Armas Jr., who was later the key to the Pedro Martinez deal.

Suppan pitched badly for Arizona before being traded to Kansas City during the 1998 season. In Kansas City, he became an average pitcher, who threw over 200 innings every year but wasn't outstanding. In 2003, Suppan signed a one year deal with Pittsburgh where he got off to a terrific start: 10–7 with a 3.57 ERA for a bad team. At the trade deadline, Suppan was dealt to Boston in one of the more bizarre trades ever. Boston had acquired Scott Sauerbeck and highly touted Mike Gonzalez from Pittsburgh for Brandon Lyon and Anastacio Martinez. However, the Pirates claimed Lyon had a bum elbow, so a week later they traded Suppan, Lyon, and Martinez to Boston for top infield prospect Freddy Sanchez and Mike Gonzalez, plus some cash. In essence, the Sox got Sauerbeck and Suppan for Sanchez plus cash. Suppan was lousy in his time with the Red Sox and was left off the postseason roster. He then signed a contract with St. Louis where he again was league average, but with a career-high 16 wins.

While Suppan's return to the Sox in 2003 clearly did not help their postseason run it can be argued that in 2004 he inadvertently assisted them in their World Series win. Suppan faced the Red Sox in Game 3 of the 2004 World Series and was shelled (giving up all four runs in a 4–1 loss). He did get a hit in his only at bat, with Boston up 1–0, in the third inning. Suppan advanced to third base with no outs, but when the next batter hit a groundball to second Suppan, instead of taking off for the plate (or even returning to third) inexplicably ran back and forth, starting and stopping a couple of times, and was thrown out at third.

Jim Tabor—a third baseman with the Sox from 1938–1944, Tabor had a reputation for hard drinking. He once stretched out to field a ball hit down the third base line and failed to get up. Everyone rushed over, thinking he had been hurt. He was drunk—he'd just passed out.

Tabor wasn't much of a power hitter (he hit more than 16 home runs in a season only once in his nine-year career), but in a July 4 doubleheader in 1939 he put on one of the most extraordinary power displays by a Sox player. After homering in the first game, Tabor hit three home runs (two of them grand slams, one of those an inside the park home run) in the second game. Tabor was out of baseball at 33, and died before he was 40.

Frank Tanana—a star pitcher with the California Angels before he hurt his arm, Tanana was a 28-year-old struggling to regain his effectiveness when the Sox obtained him as part of the desperation Fred Lynn trade before the 1981 season. He went 4–10 in his only season with the Sox. Although his fastball never did come back, Tanana eventually became an effective junkballer, and was able to pitch in the major leagues for more than 20 years.

Jesse Tannehill—a lefthanded pitcher whose career began in 1894 with Cincinnati in the National League. After two years out of the majors, he resurfaced with Pittsburgh in 1897. From 1898–1902, he won 18 to 25 games every year, while pitching very well for the Pirates. After commissioner Ban Johnson of the upstart American League helped the Yankees sign the established pitcher away from the National League, Tannehill went 15–15 for New York in 1903. The Sox traded Long Tom Hughes to the Yankees for Tannehill after they won the World Series in 1903. He won 21 games for Boston in 1904, and 22 the next year, despite not pitching quite as well. It was all downhill after that, however. After 4½ years in Boston, he was traded to Washington. In 1911, he finished his career at age 36 in Cincinnati, the same place where he'd started at age 18.

Jose Tartabull—a weak-hitting (even for the pitching-dominated 1960s) outfielder, Tartabull spent parts of three seasons with the Sox, including the 1967 Impossible Dream team. Jose ran for Tony C. the night that Conigliaro was beaned, but is best remembered for a throw he made against the Chicago White Sox, when he threw out Ken Berry who tried to score on a short line drive to right. Tartabull, who had a weak arm, made what might have been the best throw of his career. Elston Howard blocked the plate; the Red Sox won and moved into first place. Jose's son Danny was a power-hitting outfielder who later played in the major leagues for six teams.

Ken Tatum—righthanded reliever whose career was sidetracked by the emotional fallout from an on-field accident. Tatum was brilliant as a 25-year-old rookie for the Angels in 1969, saving 22 games with a 1.36 ERA, and started 1970 off the same way. Early in the season Tatum beaned Baltimore outfielder Paul Blair, however, ruining Blair's career (he was able to play again, but was never the same player). Tatum was unable to shake the incident, and began to pitch too tentatively. He finished the season with 17 saves, but gave up 12 home runs as well—after only giving up one in 1969. At the end of the season, the Angels decided he wouldn't recover and dealt him to a team that gambled that he would—the Red Sox. Ironically, Tatum was traded along with Doug Griffin—who would be seriously beaned with the Red Sox—for Tony Conigliaro, who had been nearly killed by a beaning in 1967. Tatum never did return to the dominant reliever he had been as a rookie. He saved only 13 games in three seasons with the Red Sox and was out of baseball at age 30.

Birdie Tebbetts—a popular, talented catcher on the "near-miss" Red Sox teams of the late 1940s, George "Birdie" Tebbetts spent over 60 years in Major League Baseball. He began his playing career in 1936 with the Tigers and quickly gained a reputation as a standout defensive catcher, though he was below-average offensively. Early in 1947 the Red Sox traded catcher Hal Wagner for Tebbetts, whose hitting improved after moving to Fenway. Catching had been a problem for Boston since Rick Ferrell was traded 10 years earlier, but Tebbetts filled the void. Ironically, he was very similar to Ferrell: he was strong defensively, had solid batting averages, not much power, good walk totals, and few strikeouts. Tebbetts hit .299 during the remainder of 1947, and made the All Star team in each of the next two seasons, batting .280 and .270 while driving in 126 runs (league average was about .260). Tebbetts set career highs with a .310 average and 8 homers in 1950, but he only played in 79 games. That December the Sox sold him to Cleveland, where he played his last two seasons. Tebbetts later spent 11 years as a big league manager (Reds, Braves, and Indians), and many more as a scout. In

1979, the Hall of Fame named Tebbetts to its Veterans Committee, which votes on old-time players, managers, executives, and umpires. He served on the Veterans Committee until his death in March 1999.

To celebrate baseball's centennial in 1969, each team held fan voting to select an all-time all star team. Red Sox fans elected Tebbetts as the team's best catcher. Another voting was held in 1982, and Tebbetts made the second team, behind Carlton Fisk. Rick Ferrell might have been a better selection, but Tebbetts was certainly one of the best catchers in Red Sox history.

Lee Thomas—an outfielder-first baseman who played for six teams in eight years. The lefthanded-hitting Thomas looked like a future star in his first two years in the league, when he averaged .287 with 25 homers, but he never matched those numbers again. He had a good year for a bad Boston team in 1965, hitting .271 with 22 homers. After retiring at age 32, he went into management, eventually becoming the general manager of the Philadelphia Phillies (where he was named executive of the year in 1993) and later an aide to Red Sox GM Dan Duquette. After Duquette was fired, and replaced by Theo Epstein (a job Thomas himself was interviewed for), Thomas agreed to remain with the organization in his original role as special assistant to the general manager, but has since left the organization. He is now a special assignment scout for the Milwaukee Brewers.

Luis Tiant—ask any Red Sox fan past a certain age to compile a list of their 10 most beloved Red Sox players, and Looie (the spelling is a Tiant nickname) Tiant's name would appear on the vast majority of them. Tiant, the son of one of Cuba's greatest pitchers (Luis Tiant Sr., who pitched in the Negro Leagues), started his big league career with the Cleveland Indians in 1964. He had a breakthrough season in 1968, when he developed his trademark pitching motion, in which he turned his back, showed the batter his uniform number, and hesitated before spinning to deliver the pitch to the plate. This motion was the antithesis of the way a pitcher should pitch, and could be used by any coach as an example of how *not* to pitch. (Former Sox starter Hideo Nomo had a pitching motion reminiscent of Tiant's.) The awkward windup worked nicely for Tiant, however. In 1968 Tiant had a 21–9 record with nine shutouts and a league-leading 1.60 ERA (albeit in a great year for pitchers). In a two-game stretch (one vs. the Red Sox), Looie struck out a then-record 32 batters.

The Indians wanted to protect their new superstar, and insisted that he skip his usual Winter League pitching. This proved disastrous; Tiant was dreadful in 1969. He was traded after that season, and a short but good turn with the Minnesota Twins ended with a hairline fracture shoulder injury and his release. Tiant signed a minor league deal with the Atlanta Braves, but was cut there and ended up with the Red Sox Louisville team. He made it to Boston that year but had an unimpressive 1–7 record. For all intents and purposes, he looked washed up.

Tiant started to put it back together in Boston, and in 1972 was 15–6 and won his second ERA title at 1.91 (again in a great pitching year, but still quite an accomplishment). He was 20–13 in 1973, and 22–13 in 1974, while racking up a league-leading seven shutouts (today, seven complete games of *any* type is a rarity). He was the ace of the 1975 pennant-winning team, going 18–14 and leading the team in innings pitched. In postseason play that year Tiant's Red Sox legend grew. He beat the three-time world champion Oakland A's in the first game of the ALCS with a three-hitter. He followed this with two vastly different wins against the Cincinnati Reds in the World Series. In the first game he was dominant in a five-hit 6–0 shutout. He followed this up in Game 4 with a 5–4 win in which he struggled, relying on guile and bullheadedness to prevail. After batting only once in the regular season (in only the third year of the DH), Tiant also had a hit in each of these games and provided some comic relief while trying to run the bases. He also pitched Game 6, which was delayed repeatedly, but was long gone before the twelfth-inning heroics that made it among the greatest Series games ever.

Tiant was 21–12 in 1976, but declined somewhat after that, though he still had 12 wins in 1977 and another 13 in 1978. In 1979 Tiant was a free agent, but amid the confused Red Sox ownership situation he was barely pursued, and ended up signing with the New York Yankees (an act that did little to tarnish Looie's legend—perhaps because it was seen as ownership's fault rather than Tiant's). He had one effective season with the Yankees, but faded fast after that.

Beyond his unorthodox motion, Tiant also hardly looked the part of an athlete—he was balding, overweight, and no one quite knew how old he was. (As with many Cuban players, Tiant was rumored to be years older than his listed age.) He spoke with a heavy Cuban accent and a high squeaky voice that had no business coming from a man of his age and size. He was also well known for smoking oversized cigars almost anywhere, including during interviews and while receiving whirlpool treatments. All of these quirks furthered his popularity with the fans, with his fellow players, and with the press. In his heyday, Tiant was one of the game's great pressure pitchers—a guy you'd want to pitch a must-win game. Fenway crowds would break out with a "Looie, Looie, Looie" refrain when he climbed the hill to pitch. Tiant was recently inducted into the Red Sox Hall of Fame, and in a nice turnabout, at the game where his longtime catcher Carlton Fisk's number was retired, Tiant caught the ceremonial first pitch thrown by Fisk. Fisk also gave Looie the ultimate compliment, by saying Tiant that was the best pitcher he ever caught. (Fisk also caught Tom Seaver, who was selected to the Hall of Fame with the highest vote percentage ever.)

Tiant played for years in the Mexican League after his career in the majors was over. He also served as pitching coach for Venezuela in the 2000 Olympics, and baseball coach at Savannah College of Art and Design. After the 2001 season he returned to the Red Sox as pitching coach for Boston's Sarasota and Lowell minor league affiliates. (Tiant lasted only one season in Lowell, where his celebrity status made it difficult to fulfill the duties of the position.) Tiant broadcast Red Sox games on the team's Spanish radio network in 2002–03, and is now an instructor in the Red Sox organization.

Mike Timlin—tough, rubber-armed reliever who's been an unsung hero for the 2003–04 Red Sox, helping to anchor an often chaotic bullpen. Timlin has spent 14 seasons in the major leagues. His 812 appearances rank 27th on the all-time list, and he has a solid 3.61 lifetime ERA, with 117 saves—and three World Series rings.

Timlin began his career with the Blue Jays in 1991, going 11–6 with a 3.16 ERA in long relief. As a sophomore, he saved the final game of the 1992 World Series, throwing out Otis Nixon (who later played for Boston) on a bunt back to the mound. Toronto repeated their title the following year, though Timlin wasn't a big contributor. He became the Blue Jays' closer in 1996, saving a career-high 31 games (though he was criticized for not being dominant, and for allowing big home runs). In an interesting link to Red Sox history, the Jays traded Timlin to Seattle for Jose Cruz Jr. on July 31, 1997—the same day the Mariners got Boston closer Heathcliff Slocumb for prospects Jason Varitek and Derek Lowe. (Seattle had a very talented team but desperately needed bullpen help, so they panicked, trading three talented young players for two closers with spotty resumes.)

He didn't help the Mariners much in 1997, but Timlin was an adequate closer in 1998, saving 19 games and posting a 2.95 ERA. Baltimore signed him as a free agent, and he had 38 saves in 1½ seasons, but also allowed an alarming 15 homers in 98 innings. Timlin's reputation as an unreliable closer was cemented, and he hasn't appeared in that role since leaving Baltimore. However, he pitched well as a middle reliever for St. Louis and Philadelphia from 2000–02, displaying excellent control and the ability to handle a large workload.

After the 2002 season, new Red Sox GM Theo Epstein didn't want to pay big bucks to Ugueth Urbina (a good, but not great, closer), and instead decided to try the now infamous "bullpen by committee." The goal was to pick up several quality relievers who didn't have gaudy save totals, but got outs and didn't cost a lot of money, giving manager Grady Little multiple relief pitching options in key game situations. The 37-year-old Timlin signed a three-year contract, and—unlike most members of "the committee"—was both healthy and productive. He appeared in 72 games, going 6–4 with two saves and a 3.55 ERA, while allowing only nine walks in 83⅔ innings. Timlin's best performances came in October, when Boston's shaky bullpen suddenly became flawless. In eight postseason appearances, Timlin allowed no runs and only one hit.

Timlin remained a solid contributor in 2004, though his numbers declined a bit because of the heavy workload he carried. (He pitched in a career-high 76 games, fourth in the AL). He struggled in the playoffs, most notably in Game 3 of the ALDS. Timlin gave up a game-tying grand slam to Anaheim's Vladimir Guerrero, wiping out what had once been a 6–0 Boston lead. But David Ortiz's walk-off homer took the veteran reliever off the hook, and the Red Sox completed their sweep, on the way to their remarkable championship run.

Denny Tomori—flamethrowing righthanded relief pitcher who the Red Sox signed in January 2005. The 37-year-old Yui "Denny" Tomori previously pitched with the Yokohoma Taiyo whales (for whom he was a first-round draft choice in 1987), the Yokohama Bay Stars, and the Seibu Lions of the Japanese league; he had a 3.96 ERA in 360 games, all but seven in relief. Although Tomori only pitched in 21 games in 2004, he throws a sidearm fastball that hits 95 MPH, along with a sinker and a variety of breaking pitches. Once Tomori decided to pitch in the U.S., he and his agent conducted an open practice session in Anaheim, which was attended by 22 teams (including three Red Sox scouts). After considering offers from the Reds, Blue Jays, and Dodgers, Tomori reportedly chose the Red Sox because GM Theo Epstein called him personally and told him that the Red Sox needed him.

Mike Torrez—a starting pitcher who will always be associated with the Sox failure to win in 1978. Torrez was an average starting pitcher, a workhorse who won a lot of games because he played for good teams and was seldom injured. He had poor control (he led the league three times in walks allowed) but in his best seasons did not give up a lot of hits. Torrez had his best season in 1975, winning 20 games for the Orioles, before being traded first to Oakland and then to the Yankees. Signed as a free agent by the Red Sox after the 1977 season, Torrez was trumpeted by Sox management as a pitcher who was going to help the team— with a great offense but thin starting pitching—close the gap between themselves and the Yankees. Torrez pitched solidly but unspectacularly in 1978, going 16–13 despite an ERA that was 20 points worse than league average. With the Red Sox and Yankees tied for first place on the last day of the season, manager Don Zimmer chose Torrez to start the one-game playoff which would decide who went to the league championship series and who went home (there was no wild-card team at this point). Torrez pitched well for six innings, but then gave up a three-run home run to light-hitting shortstop Bucky Dent (forever afterward known as "Bucky Bleeping Dent" by Boston fans), and walked another batter who scored as well in the Sox eventual 5–4 loss.

Torrez pitched three more years with Boston. He won 16 games again in 1979, but then was less effective as the Red Sox offense began to decline in the early 1980s (although he went 10–3 in an injury-filled 1981 season). After being traded to the New York Mets for a minor leaguer, Torrez's lack of control led to a scary moment in 1984, when he beaned Houston's shortstop Dickie Thon, nearly killing him. (Thon made it back to the major leagues but was never the same player again.)

John Tudor—one of a group of young Red Sox pitchers developed in the early 1980s. Although he actually made his debut in 1979, he didn't make the Red Sox full-time until 1982, when he went 13–10 with a 3.63 ERA. The next year he won 13 games again for a poor ballclub. The following winter Tudor was traded to Pittsburgh for hitting specialist Mike Easler (who was later traded for Don Baylor, an essential cog on the 1986 World Series team).

Tudor flowered in Pittsburgh (12–11 with a 3.27 ERA for a bad team) but was traded to the St. Louis Cardinals, where he spun 2 beautiful seasons. In 1985 he went 21–8 with a 1.93 ERA in 275 innings pitched (he outpitched Mets rookie Dwight Gooden down the stretch to help the Cardinals make the World Series that year). From 1987 on, Tudor was almost constantly injured, but pitched well when he was healthy. He continued to pitch for 5 more years with St. Louis and LA, still a quality pitcher, but was never able to pitch more than 150 innings in any of those seasons.

Ugueth Urbina—hard-throwing righthanded relief pitcher acquired from the cash-strapped Montreal Expos at the trading deadline of the 2001 season. Urbina took over the closer's role for the struggling Derek Lowe shortly after his arrival in Boston. In contrast to the boyish Lowe, Urbina pitched with a cocky swagger, ending his delivery with a pose reminiscent of Auguste Rodin's *The Thinker*, which was not always appreciated by opposing hitters. Although he pitched well, saving nine games for the Sox, it had little impact as the team quickly folded out of contention.

In 2002, Urbina (or UUU) was the Sox full-time closer and had a terrific year. He finished 55 of 61 games he appeared in, saving 40 and striking out 71 in 60 innings. Urbina was a free agent after that season and Sox GM Theo Epstein was reluctant to risk $7–8 million a year on a good but not great closer with a history of elbow injuries (including a mostly lost season in 2000). After helping the Florida Marlins surprise baseball by winning the 2003 World Series, Urbina signed with Detroit, only to see his season came to a bizarre end. On September 2, 2004, Urbina's mother was kidnapped from her home in Venezuela by four men disguised as police officers and held for a multimillion-dollar ransom.

Julio Valdez—once a great defensive shortstop prospect, Valdez ended up as a marginal infielder who shuttled between Pawtucket and the Red Sox from 1980 to 1983, playing a total of 65 games. In 1983 he was arrested in mid-game on a statutory rape charge involving a 14-year-old girl, and never resurfaced in the major leagues.

John Valentin—"Val" was never a superstar, but the former ninth-place hitter on his college team had a quietly remarkable career, marred by injury and a playing-related controversy, but featuring some wonderful highlights. Valentin came up in 1992 to replace the injured Tim Naehring, and quickly settled in at shortstop. He hit well (especially for a shortstop) his first two years, then broke through with a terrific .316 average and .505 slugging percentage in the strike-shortened 1994 season. He was even better the next year, hitting .298 with career highs in home runs (27), runs (108), RBI (102), walks (81), stolen bases (20), and slugging percentage (.533), all while playing very well at the most demanding defensive position on the field. After hitting .306 in 1997, a season in which he was moved first to second base and then to third base, Valentin began a long struggle with injuries that eventually ended his career.

Brief controversy erupted in spring training 1997 when Valentin was asked to move to second base to make way for shortstop phenom Nomar Garciaparra. This happened just a few days after being assured that he'd have a chance to compete to keep his job. Valentin left camp temporarily (with the club's permission) and threatened to quit. Eventually he accepted the move, as well as a subsequent move to third base to replace the injured Tim Naehring (who ironically he'd also replaced as a shortstop)—and Valentin played well defensively at both positions. The controversy fizzled out when it became clear just how extraordinary a player Garciaparra was.

Valentin had a career filled with highlights. His first home run in his rookie year of 1992 was a grand slam. In 1994, Valentin turned only the tenth unassisted triple play in major league history by catching a line drive for the first out, stepping on second for the second out, and tagging the runner heading for second for out number three. In 1995, Val and Mo Vaughn (his Seton Hall college teammate) each hit grand slams in an 8–0 win over the Yankees, the only time two grand slams were responsible for all the runs scored in a game. In another game that year, Val was 5-for-5, with three homers and four runs scored. He became the first shortstop to have 15 total bases in a game.

Valentin hit .467 in a losing cause in the 1998 American League Division Series. In the 1999 ALDS he was instrumental in the Red Sox coming back after falling behind 2 games to 0 to Cleveland, starting with a home run in Game 3. The next day, in a game in which the Red Sox scored a major league postseason-record 23 runs on 24 hits, Valentin had four of those hits, two of them home runs, while driving in seven runs. In Game 3 of the American League Championship Series, in which Pedro Martinez dominated the Yankees, Val contributed a home run and five RBI, hitting .348 overall in the series.

Early in 2000, after two injury-marred years, Valentin was making a routine play on a ground ball when his knee blew out and he went down in a heap. The injury required extensive reconstructive surgery and caused Valentin to miss the rest of the season. He came back in 2001, returning to shortstop because of an injury to Garciaparra, but was only able to play 20 games before injuries once again ended his season. Unwilling to give up on a playing career, Valentin signed with the Mets as a utility player for 2002, which proved to be his final season in the majors. In 2003, Valentin was released by Baltimore at the end of spring training. He then signed with Philadelphia, but turned down their offer of a minor league position and spent the rest of the summer out of baseball. In 2004, Valentin agreed to a minor league contract with Houston, but was bought out of his contract at the end of spring training. By the end of the season, he had reconciled himself to life after playing, appearing as a color commentator for Fox Sports New England during the World Series. He accepted a position as hitting coach of Toronto's AA New Hampshire Fisher Cats for the 2005 season.

Jason Varitek—a switch-hitting catcher acquired along with pitcher Derek Lowe from the Seattle Mariners in 1997 for closer Heathcliff Slocumb. Varitek was arguably the best catcher in NCAA history (and a teammate of Nomar Garciaparra at Georgia Tech). He was a first-round pick of Minnesota, but refused to sign for the amount of money they offered. Seattle took him in the first round a year later, but he waited nearly a year to sign, on the advice of agent Scott Boras. This greatly damaged Varitek's career, and he never put up good numbers in the minors. By the time the Red Sox got Varitek, he was considered a major bust. A strong spring performance in 1998 won him the right to platoon with left-handed-hitting catcher Scott Hatteberg instead of catcher/DH Jim Leyritz, who had been acquired during the off-season for that purpose. In 1999 Varitek was handed the starting catcher job when Hatteberg missed much of the season with an injury. Making the most of his opportunity, Varitek impressed many by hitting 20 home runs and playing well defensively, restoring his reputation as one of the game's top young catchers. In 2000 his power dropped due to a series of nagging injuries, but he retained his reputation for handling a pitching staff well.

Varitek got off to a tremendous start in 2001, hitting .293 with seven home runs in the first third of the season while playing excellent defense. In June, he fractured his elbow on a plastic mat while making one of those great defensive plays—sliding behind home plate to catch a popup. Although there was talk of him returning in August, due to recurring nerve problems Varitek never played again in 2001. Varitek came back from his injury in 2002 and played in 132 games, but with a diminished swing, largely due to the previous year's injury. His OPS of .724 was the lowest since his first year in Boston. However, Varitek's defense was outstanding, marking him as one of the top catchers in baseball. Varitek's fierce competitiveness was apparent and he quietly became the leader of the team. In 2003, completely recovered from the brokern elbow Varitek posted career highs in home runs, RBI, and slugging percantage, and made the All Star team. In 2004, Varitek held onto his place as one of the best catchers in the league, hitting a career high .296, and placing among the league leaders in on-base percentage. However, the highlight of Varitek's 2004 season may have been his late July confrontation with star infielder Alex Rodriguez of the Yankees. After being hit by a pitch, A-Rod started screaming at Bronson Arroyo and Varitek stepped between them. A-Rod taunted Varitek repeatedly, telling him to "bring it on," and Varitek did, shoving Rodriguez in the face with his glove hand and triggering the brawl cited as the moment when the 2004 team came together and started their remarkable run to the 2004 World Series. A possibly apocryphal story has Varitek telling A-Rod, who was slumping at the time, "We don't hit .260 hitters" before mashing him in the face. True or not, this is a good summary of Varitek's personality.

Varitek filed for free agency after the 2004 season, and since he was still represented by Scott Boras, who had arguably twice sidetracked Varitek's career by pushing too hard for more money, there was a fear that Boston would not be able to retain him. Although the Sox badly wanted to sign him and Varitek wanted to stay in Boston (to the point where Boras didn't seriously negotiate with other teams pending a resolution with the Sox) there were two major points of disagreement—money and Varitek's desire for a no-trade clause so he could end his career with the Red Sox. The team policy is never to give full no-trade clauses, but eventually Boras suggested a not-quite-no-trade clause (which will vest late in the 2005 season) and the catcher signed a four-year, $40 million deal.

Given the relative thinness of Red Sox catching over the years and Varitek's reputation for working with pitching staffs, Varitek has to be considered one of the team's all-time greats at the position. He is currently fourth among Red Sox catchers in games played with the team, behind only Rich Gedman, Sammy White, and Hall of Famer Carlton Fisk. After choosing to return to the Red Sox, Varitek was named team captain, only the third player since 1923 to be given the title. (Carl Yastrzemski and Jim Rice are the others.)

Mo Vaughn—a hulking first baseman nicknamed "The Hit Dog," Maurice Vaughn played college ball for three years at Seton Hall alongside future Red Sox teammate John Valentin before being drafted by the Boston Red Sox in 1989.

Vaughn was heavily hyped based on his minor league numbers and made it to the majors quickly. He did not hit well at first, however, and split 1991 and 1992 shuttling between AAA and the big leagues (and hitting .243 in the majors). Although the jury was still out on whether Vaughn would become the star he was projected to be, he was thrust into the starting role by a freakish injury that eventually ended fellow first baseman Carlos Quintana's career. Given a third chance at success, Vaughn played very well, hitting .297 with 29 home runs and 101 RBI. This would be the last year Vaughn would hit less than .300 for the Red Sox. In 1994 his batting average rose to .310. Vaughn was the bright spot in a rather impotent batting order in the final year of the mostly forgettable Hobson era. In 1995 Vaughn's 39 home runs, 126 RBI, and .300 batting average earned him the American League Most Valuable Player award in one of the closest votes ever. (Some Sox fans argue that teammate John Valentin should have won the award instead.) Vaughn followed with 44 homers, 143 RBI, and a .326 batting average in 1996, and 35 homers, 96 RBI and a .315 batting average in 1997. In 1998 Mo hit 40 home runs, drove in 115 runs, and batted a career high .337, losing the batting title to the Yankees' Bernie Williams on the final day of the season. Vaughn was a three-time All Star with the Red Sox.

As Vaughn matured as a player, his offensive numbers continued to improve, but he became prone to defensive lapses. Mo was also known on occasion not to run out ground ball outs, and looked heavier every year. These events brought some criticism from the press and fans, although Vaughn remained tremendously popular in Boston, as much for his larger-than-life personality and community involvement as for his hitting.

Vaughn exhibited a flair for the dramatic, both on and off the field. A couple of representative examples are Game 1 of the 1998 American League Division Series, when Vaughn blasted two home runs and drove in seven runs, and the

Jason Leader

The Red Sox tradition of lighting hope in the eyes of ailing youngsters struck a special note in 1993 for one young fan and his favorite player. On April 23 first baseman Mo Vaughn, only a few weeks into his breakout season, placed a telephone call to Jason Leader, a young patient at the Dana-Farber Cancer Institute. Jason, due to turn eleven the next day, was suffering from neuroblastoma, a cancer variant that attacks the adrenal glands and nervous system. That night the Sox were scheduled to play the California Angels at Anaheim Stadium. Jason, as a favor, asked Vaughn if he could hit a home run for him. Vaughn promised that he would try to do so. Indeed, in the seventh inning he launched a 3–1 pitch from Ken Patterson over the center field wall. Since the game was being played on the West Coast, Jason was already asleep when the homer was hit, and woke up on the morning of his birthday to the exciting news that Vaughn came through on his promise.

But the thrill for Jason didn't stop there. The fan in Anaheim who caught the home run heard about the story and sent the ball to Vaughn, who then invited Jason to meet him at Fenway Park and throw out the game's first pitch. Vaughn served as Jason's personal catcher during the ceremony and later signed the ball, "To Jason, stay strong, my friend, Mo Vaughn."

Jason Leader succumbed to cancer on August 15, 1994, at his home near Albany, New York. Since the baseball season had been suspended due to a players' strike, Vaughn was able to attend the funeral ceremonies for his young friend. Theirs was a heartwarming relationship that went beyond that of a sportsman and a fan, and truly exemplified the commitment of the Red Sox to fighting the debilitating disease and inspiring the children it affects.

home opener in that same year, when he hit a walk-off grand slam home run to beat the Seattle Mariners. Outside of the park he was also in the news, most notoriously when he was arrested for driving while intoxicated after hitting a disabled car on the shoulder of a highway, while on his way home from a Providence strip club. Vaughn publicly criticized the team for failing to support his side of the story and fought the charges in court—with his lawyer arguing that Vaughn failed field sobriety tests because he had gained so much weight in the offseason that it had affected his coordination. Vaughn won the case, but from that point on his relationship with the team—and with many fans—was strained. (The strip club— the Foxy Lady—took advantage of the publicity after Vaughn left the team, hiring a plane to tow a "Welcome Back" banner over Fenway when he returned with the Angels.)

As Vaughn approached free agency, several attempts to sign him to a longterm contract broke down acrimoniously, and communications went from strained to surreal. Vaughn first said that he would sign if the Red Sox locked the core of the team into longterm deals, but after GM Dan Duquette signed several players to rich deals, Vaughn accused him of lacking respect for Vaughn by signing other players before him. Vaughn also accused the team of hiring private investigators to follow him. Later, Vaughn would accuse the Red Sox of causing his father's urinary infection—claiming it was brought on by his father being upset at Vaughn's increasingly strained relationship with the team's management and fans.

After the 1998 season, Vaughn signed a lucrative multiyear contract with the Anaheim Angels, making him one of the game's best-paid players. Because of a lingering ankle injury in 1999, and because the Anaheim ballpark is less suited to his hitting style than Fenway Park is, Vaughn's numbers declined somewhat in California, although he remained a good hitter. Ironically, time healed some of the bitterness between Vaughn and the Sox, and some of his comments began to hint at a desire to return to the volatile Boston environment—where the passion for the game matches Vaughn's own intensity, unlike California, where he and the Angels were little fish in a big pond. After spending all of the 2001 season recovering from arm surgery Vaughn very publicly campaigned to return to Boston. The Red Sox showed little interest in taking on his huge salary, however. As 2001 neared an end, Vaughn was traded to the New York Mets. Vaughn played for the Mets in 2002, appearing in 139 games. But it was obvious that his skills were eroding and his physical condition was deteriorating. In 2002, Vaughn slugged 26 home runs, but only drove in 72 runs, his lowest totals since 1992. His averages were also the lowest since 1992. Vaughn only played in 27 games in 2003 before going on the DL with chronically arthritic knees, made worse by his weight and lack of conditioning. Following the 2003 season, Vaughn officially retired, but in the fall of 2004, Vaughn started rumbling about getting back into baseball.

Ramon Vazquez—Lefty-hitting utility infielder who was acquired (with outfielder Jay Payton and minor league RHP Dave Pauley) from San Diego for playoff hero Dave Roberts in December 2004. The 28-year-old Vazquez was born in Puerto Rico, and was drafted by the Mariners in 1995. He moved methodically through Seattle's system, putting up his best numbers in AAA Tacoma in 2001

(.300, 10 homers, 79 RBI, 76 walks, .397 OBP). The Mariners called up Vazquez in September 2001, but traded him to the Padres after the season. San Diego converted Vazquez to a second baseman in 2002, and he hit a respectable .274, though his OBP was unspectacular (.344), and he showed little power. Making room for Mark Loretta, Vazquez went back to shortstop in 2003, putting up similar offensive numbers, though his defensive stats were subpar. Rookie phenom Khalil Greene, a superior fielder, won the Padres' shortstop job last year, leaving Vazquez to split time between San Diego (.235) and AAA (.299, .402 OBP, .554 slugging). The Red Sox have reportedly been interested in Vazquez for a couple of years, even though his career doesn't seem too impressive on the surface, because his skills may be perfectly suited to a backup role. While he's no Gold Glove candidate, Vazquez can play all four infield positions, providing valuable injury insurance. He's also been a good hitter against righties, with solid averages and high walk totals.

Wilton Veras—a much-hyped third base prospect for the Red Sox who fell out of view after a terrible 2000 season. Veras was called up to Boston from Double-A Trenton, ahead of Triple-A third base prospect Cole Liniak, as a 21-year-old in 1999. Given significant playing time because of an injury to third baseman John Valentin, Veras fielded well and hit for a good average (.288) in 188 at bats, but with little power and virtually no walks. Still, his performance was seen as an important stepping stone to a permanent major league position. When Valentin was hurt again in 2000, Veras again was called up, but this time looked lost in the major leagues, rarely getting on base and making 13 errors in only 49 games before being returned to the minors (where he also played badly). Veras never resurfaced in the major leagues; in 2004, he played for the independent New Jersey Jackals in the Northeast league.

Mickey Vernon—a solid first baseman for 20 big league seasons, primarily with the Washington Senators, Vernon played for the Red Sox in 1956–57. The line-drive hitter won two batting titles and played in seven All Star Games, though chronic back problems limited his power. In the winter of 1955 Vernon was sent to Boston in a nine-player deal. The 38-year-old had a fine first season with the Red Sox, hitting .310 with a career-high .405 on base percentage. In only 403 at bats, Vernon hit 15 homers and drove in 84 runs. But he struggled in 1957, hitting .241 with 7 homers in limited playing time. Vernon was released after the season. After drifting to three teams over the next three seasons Vernon retired in 1960. He finished his career with a .286 lifetime batting average and 2,495 hits.

Frank Viola—star lefthanded pitcher who was a member of the Sox from 1992–94. "Sweet Music" Viola began his career with the Minnesota Twins, pitching badly for a couple of years before he blossomed in 1984 as a 24-year-old. He was the ace of the 1987 World Series champions, and won the World Series MVP award. In 1988 he pitched even better, going 24–7 and winning the American League Cy Young. After his agent made a "pay-me-or-trade-me" demand public, Viola was publicly criticized for his contract demands by teammates Gary Gaetti and Kent Hrbek, and Minnesota traded him to the Mets in 1989 on the July trading deadline. It was a huge deal at the time, the defending Cy Young winner traded for a large package of young pitchers (including future stars Rick Aguilera and Kevin Tapani).

In New York he became a teammate of Ron Darling—his opponent, and the losing pitcher, in one of the greatest games in NCAA playoff history. (Darling, pitching for Yale, had no-hit Viola's St John's team through 11 innings, but Viola shut Yale out as St. John's won 1–0 in 12 innings.) Viola, a native Long Islander, pitched very well for the Mets in 1990, winning 20 games while leading the league in innings pitched and finishing fourth in ERA. But the fickle New York fans turned on him as he faltered down the stretch in 1991, struggling with various nagging injuries. In the offseason he signed with the Red Sox as a free agent.

He pitched well for Boston in 1992–93, though these were among the weakest offensive teams in Sox history, so he didn't have very impressive won-lost records. He wasn't pitching at his previous Cy Young level, but he was a better-than-average American League starter. Then, in May of 1994 at Fenway, he threw a pitch to the backstop, clutched his pitching elbow awkwardly, and headed toward the dugout with the ball still in play. The injury required extensive reconstructive surgery, and he never pitched again for the Sox. In a long attempt to come back from the injury, Viola made three ineffective starts for the Cincinnati Reds in 1995, and six ineffective starts for the Toronto Blue Jays in 1996—winning only one—before retiring.

Clyde Vollmer—journeyman outfielder who came up with the Cincinnati Reds and played with the Red Sox from 1950–53. In a 10-year career that included Cincinnati, Boston, and two stints in Washington, he hit 69 home runs. Thirteen of them came during about a one-month stretch during July 1951, many of them winning games. One was a sixteenth-inning grand slam against Cleveland, the latest in a game that any major league grand slam had ever been hit. The power disappeared as quickly as it came, however, and "Dutch the Clutch" finished up his career at the age of 32 in 1954.

Hal Wagner—a light-hitting part time player before World War II, Wagner spent part of the war working in a defense plant during the days and catching for the Philadelphia A's on weekends. Boston acquired him and made him the starting catcher in 1944. The lefthanded-hitting Wagner was batting .332 and the Sox were in contention for a pennant until he, pitcher Tex Hughson, and second baseman Bobby Doerr were all drafted within two weeks of each other. After the war Wagner held on to the Red Sox catching job for a year, hitting .230 for the 1946 pennant winners, before spending the rest of his career as a part-timer.

Tim Wakefield—an entertaining but sometimes disgruntled knuckleball pitcher who has pitched for the Sox in a variety of roles since 1995. Wakefield had been a first baseman (he couldn't hit well enough to be a major leaguer) who began pitching in the minor leagues. His only effective pitch was the hard-to-control knuckleball, which would dance around the strike zone unpredictably (he did occasionally mix in not-very-fastballs or curves). Called up by Pittsburgh late in the 1992 season, the 26-year-old Wakefield went on an astonishing tear, going

8–1 and holding opposing hitters to a .232 average. The next season the magic was gone; Wakefield couldn't throw strikes with his knuckleball and hitters hammered his other pitches whenever he threw them. Pittsburgh sent him down to the minors, hoping he would regain his effectiveness, but by the next season he couldn't get anyone out in the minors either. The Pirates released Wakefield after a miserable year in AA ball, and Red Sox GM Dan Duquette signed him early in the 1995 season as a reclamation project.

Called up in May, Wakefield went on another extraordinary roll. With Sox ace Roger Clemens injured for long stretches, Wakefield was the team's best starting pitcher. He went 16–8 with a 2.95 ERA and, despite a late-season slump, finished second in the league in ERA. He was never as good again, but did pitch solidly for the next three years, winning 17 games in 1998. In 1999 he began the season poorly and lost his starting spot, but then pitched well in relief. Tom Gordon was injured, so manager Jimy Williams used Wakefield as his closer for the middle of the season. He was effective in that role, saving 15 games, although he frequently terrified fans by giving up walks and long fly balls in the late innings of close games. In 2000, he was shuttled between starting and relief, but never pitched consistently.

Like most knuckleball pitchers, he could be unhittable for long stretches and then would be completely ineffective. When the ball failed to break sharply enough or when he was forced to throw other pitches, Wakefield gave up enormous home runs. Although he pitched well at times, Wakefield never had a firm spot in the pitching rotation because of his inconsistency, and he sometimes complained when he felt he wasn't being used appropriately. As the Sox player representative, he spoke up on other issues as well, and he talked freely and indiscreetly to the press when players he considered important to the team were traded or not re-signed. As a result, he seemed to always be complaining. The Sox had given him a longterm contract through the 2000 season, but when they declined to guarantee his option year for 2001, Wakefield began complaining further. He did not like the way he was being switched between starting and relief, and told the media that he didn't consider it fair that the Red Sox took advantage of his flexibility by using him in so many different situations (his versatility was one of his greatest assets to the team). After Wakefield declined to start in the last game of the 2000 season (he considered it a meaningless game), his Red Sox career appeared to be over, but after testing the free agent market briefly he surprised everyone by signing a two-year contract to remain with the Red Sox.

In 2001–02 he again performed in a variety of roles, pitching solidly both years and eventually earning a permanent return to the starting rotation. In 2003 and 2004, Wakefield started almost full time, going 23–17. In 2003, Wakefield was a key starter on a Red Sox team known for their "Cowboy Up" rallying cry, which fought its way to the seventh game of the ALCS against the hated Yankees. After the Yankees tied the game and sent it to extra innings, Wakefield, who had already won 2 games in the series (had the Sox scored in the tenth, giving him a third win, he likely would have been series MVP), was brought into the game in relief, the rest of the bullpen depleted. After a scoreless tenth inning, Aaron Boone sent Wakefield's first pitch of the eleventh into the left field grandstands and the Yankees won the series. (Wakefield was concerned that the fans would turn on him as they had on Bill Buckner in 1986, but he remained popular.)

In the 2004 ALCS, Wakefield was also a key pitcher. Against the Yankees with the team down two games to none and losing big in Game 3, Wakefield gave up his scheduled start in Game 4 and pitched 3⅔ innings in Game 3 to avoid depleting the bullpen. This was a key moment in the Red Sox 2004 title run; the bullpen was not shot in the 19–8 blowout and over the next four games completely shut down the Yankees en route to the first ever comeback from a three-game deficit in a baseball playoff series. One of those wins belonged to Wakefield, who outdueled Yankee Esteban Loaiza in a dramatic Game 5 relief appearance, throwing three scoreless innings to win in the fourteenth inning of the longest postseason game ever played (almost six hours). The relief appearance was also dramatic because catcher Jason Varitek, unused to Wakefield's knuckleballs (Doug Mirabelli had caught all of Wakefield's starts that year) allowed three passed balls to get by him during the thirteenth inning without a run scoring. Entering the 2005 season, Wakefield is the Red Sox player with the longest continuous service to the team.

Todd Walker—the first major acquisition by wunderkind GM Theo Epstein, and a playoff hero for the Red Sox in 2003. The lefthanded hitting Walker played for LSU and had considerable success in the College World Series. Drafted eighth overall in 1994 by the Twins and brought to the majors two years later to replace star second baseman Chuck Knoblauch, Walker was highly touted but in his first season hit poorly and showed little defense (while Knoblauch led the Yankees to the World Series). In 1998, his first full season Walker had his best year, hitting .316 with a .372 OBP and stealing 19 bases. The following season he lost 30 points off his average and OBP. In the middle of 2000, Walker was traded to hitting heaven, Coors Field, in midseason. He did show some promise, but never had the monstrous numbers expected of hitters in Coors Field. In the middle of 2001 Walker was traded to Cincinnati where he actually hit better than he had in Colorado. Walker also showed greatly improved defense, but when his contract bacame too expensive for the Reds ($3.5 million for 2003), they shipped him to Boston for two minor leaguers.

Walker was a terrific fit in Boston, a scruffy, hard-nosed player whose uniform was always dirty by game's end, and fans loved him for it. Although his defense was erratic, he hit well for a second baseman (though nowhere near as well as in his best seasons), batting .283 with 13 homers and a career-high 85 RBI as the number-two hitter for a record-setting Red Sox offense. However unremarkable his season may have been, Walker's postseason was remarkable. In Game 1 of the ALDS against Oakland, Walker hit two home runs in a losing cause. In Game 4, with the Sox down 2–1 in the series, Walker hit a home run in the sixth against lefty Ricardo Rincon, to bring the Sox within one run in a game the Sox would come back to win. In Game 1 of the ALCS against the Yankees, Walker hit one of the more controversial home runs in postseason history in the top of the fifth. Walker hit a ball down the right field line that appeared to hit a fan before hitting the foul pole and was called foul, but the call was immediately overruled by the home plate umpire. (Replays clearly showed the ball was fair.) In Game 4,

Walker hit a home run in the bottom of the fourth, to put the Sox ahead for the first time in that game. For the 2003 postseason, Walker hit .349 with five home runs, a double, and a triple.

Although Walker was popular in Boston, the Red Sox weren't willing to pay the $3-million-plus it would have taken to re-sign him, so they chose not to tender him a contract. Walker signed with the Cubs, where he hit .274 with 15 homers, 50 RBI, and a .352 OBP. His replacement in Boston, Mark Bellhorn hit .264 with 17 homers, 82 RBI, and a .373 OBP . . . and was paid $490,000. Walker re-signed with the Cubs for 2005.

Bill Wambsganss—a second baseman who spent the 1924 and 1925 seasons with the Red Sox after 10 years in Cleveland. He's best known for being the only man to ever complete an unassisted triple play in the World Series, for Cleveland in Game 5 of the 1920 Series.

John Wasdin—talented righthanded pitcher who had limited success with the Red Sox, and is mostly remembered for giving up prodigious home runs, which earned him the nickname "Way Back Wasdin." (The nickname is based on announcer Jerry Trupiano's signature "way back . . . way back . . . home run" calls during Red Sox radio broadcasts.) Wasdin was a promising young starting pitcher when the Red Sox obtained him from Oakland in a trade for the disgruntled Jose Canseco in 1997. He had been a first-round draft choice for Oakland after pitching in two College World Series with Florida State University. Although Wasdin pitched very well at times with the Sox, mostly in relief, at other times he seemed to lose concentration, especially with runners on base. During the 2000 season, Wasdin was traded to Colorado, the easiest park in the major league to hit home runs in. After a short and predictably unsuccessful stay, he became a baseball nomad, moving on to Baltimore (where he pitched reasonably well) and then Philadelphia, which traded for him but then never offered him a contract, making him a free agent. He played in Japan in 2002, and has since pitched for Pittsburgh, Toronto, and Texas—still showing enough promise to keep landing major league jobs, but not enough consistency to keep them. Wasdin signed a minor league deal with Texas before the 2005 season.

Bob Watson—a good (but not great) hitting first baseman-outfielder for many years with the Houston Astros, Watson was traded to the Red Sox a third of the way through the 1979 season to replace the end-of-the-line George Scott. The 33-year-old Watson had started the season hitting .239 and the Astros dumped him, thinking he was in decline. Instead, Watson went on an incredible tear for the rest of the season, hitting .337 for a great-hitting Red Sox team that fell short of the pennant because of its thin pitching. After the season he went on to the Yankees as a free agent and played reasonably well for a year, then not so well for a couple of years afterward, but he is remembered for his great 1979 effort. Watson was briefly a celebrity in 1975, when he scored baseball's millionth run.

After finishing as a player, Watson went into baseball administration, and was general manager of the 1996 Yankees World Series winners. He is now the chief disciplinarian for Major League Baseball.

Earl Webb—outfielder who set a flukish major league record for doubles in 1931 that still stands. Webb only played two full seasons with the Red Sox, as the starting right fielder on dreadful teams, and played for five teams in seven years in the majors. He was a perfect fit for Fenway Park, a lefthanded line drive hitter who could take full advantage of the park's dimensions. He hit .323 and .333 in his two seasons with the Sox, but never hit above .301 elsewhere. Webb hit 67 doubles in his extraordinary 1931 season, but not more than 30 in any other year.

Eric Wedge—as a 24-year-old rookie catcher called up in 1992, Wedge excited Sox fans by hitting five homers in just 68 at bats for a team without much else to cheer for. Wedge needed surgery for an elbow injury in the off-season, and Boston left him off its protected list for the Expansion Draft, figuring no one would risk taking an injured player. There were howls from Boston fans when Colorado selected Wedge, but the Sox gamble turned out to be correct; Wedge was able to play in only nine games for Colorado because of his injury. He briefly returned to the Red Sox in 1994, but was finished as a player at age 26. Wedge is now considered one of the finest young managers in the game; his undermanned Cleveland Indians team finished a surprisingly good 80–82 in 2004.

David Wells—outspoken lefthanded pitcher with strikingly good control, signed by Boston as a free agent after the 2004 season. At age 41, Wells is a three-time All Star with 18 years of major league experience (212–136, 4.03 ERA). His baseball itinerary includes stops in Toronto, Detroit, Cincinnatti, Baltimore, New York, Toronto again, Chicago (AL), New York again, and San Diego. Along the way, he authored a colorful, outspoken, and funny autobiography *Perfect I'm Not: Boomer on Beer, Brawls, Backaches, and Baseball* and became a folk hero to many Yankees fans—although his signing with the Red Sox may affect that.

Wells's career began in the Blue Jays' bullpen but he evolved from a mediocre reliever to a successful starting pitcher. Although he gives up a lot of hits for a high-caliber pitcher, Wells has truly amazing control: He's allowed fewer than two walks per nine innings in his career (league average is about 3.4), and has been his league's best control pitcher in four of the last six seasons. He pitched a perfect game (later claiming to have been half-drunk) as a member of the Yankees in 1998. A great fan of Babe Ruth, he once wore the Bambino's Yankees hat during a regular season game, and was devastated by the trade that sent him back to Toronto for Roger Clemens.

Wells experienced chronic back pain in 2001 as a member of the White Sox. After surgery and rehab, he reached a handshake agreement to sign with the Diamondbacks. But a last-minute negotiation with George Steinbrenner put him back in Yankees pinstripes for two more seasons. Wells's reneging on the handshake deal led to bad feelings between Arizona owner Jerry Colangelo and George Steinbrenner, which may have indirectly given Boston an advantage over the Yankees when both were trying to trade for Arizona pitcher Curt Schilling.

Wells has an excellent 10–3, 3.18 record in the postseason, and 2 World Series rings (with Toronto in 1992 and the Yankees in 1998), but his bad back caused him to pull himself out of Game 5 of the 2003 World Series after only one inning. The Yankees lost that game and the Series to Florida (and much like Red Sox fans feel about ace Roger Clemens's blister that caused him to leave Game 6 of the 1986 World Series early, Yankees fans are divided over whether or not to blame Wells for the loss).

Wells's two-year contract with Boston came as something of a surprise, not just because of his strong relationship with Yankees fans, but also because he had real problems pitching at Fenway earlier in his career (once famously suggesting that the ballpark be blown up). He has been outstanding at Fenway the last three years, however (2.19 ERA in six starts).

Billy Werber—one of the first good players the Sox bought from the Yankees after Tom Yawkey put an end to 15 years of Harry Frazee's fire sales and Bob Quinn's penuriousness, Werber was as important as a symbol of how things had changed as he was as a player. Werber was a speedy 24-year-old rookie infielder who'd had two brief stints with the Yankees when the Sox got him in 1933. After spending the rest of that season splitting time between third base and shortstop, Werber took over at third in 1934, and had an extraordinary season—hitting .321 with 62 extra base hits, scoring 129 runs, and leading the league with 40 stolen bases. He would lead the league in steals again in two of the next three years. But he never had a season like 1934 again, although he remained a decent hitter (Werber didn't have more than so-so power, but he walked a lot and usually hit around the league average at a time of good offenses). He was sent to the Philadelphia A's in 1937, and played for two more teams before retiring in 1942.

Sammy White—the regular Red Sox catcher from 1952 through 1959. He averaged 120 games per year behind the plate during that stretch. His most notable career achievement came in June of 1953 when he became the first twentieth century player to score three runs in a single inning, as the Red Sox scored 17 in the seventh inning of a game against the Tigers. He wasn't a good hitter, but was considered to be a fine game-caller and framer of pitches.

White was traded to Cleveland with Jim Marshall for Russ Nixon in March 1960. White retired rather than go to Cleveland, and the trade was canceled. During the 1960 season, the Sox ended up getting Nixon and Carroll Hardy in another deal. White's rights were traded to the Milwaukee Braves in June 1961, and he came out of retirement. He spent the season backing up Joe Torre in Milwaukee, and the 1962 season in Philadelphia also as a backup, before retiring.

During his brief 1960–61 retirement, White operated a bowling alley called Brighton Bowling Alleys, which became famous as the site of a mass murder during the 1970s.

Ted Williams—Teddy Ballgame, The Splendid Splinter, The Kid. If there is any question that Babe Ruth was the greatest hitter in the history of baseball, it is raised by the performances of #9, Theodore Samuel Williams. There might be some debate over the order of the best two hitters in baseball history, but not the composition of the pair. The raw numbers are impressive enough. Williams was the last man to hit .400, hitting .406 in 1941, just his third season in the majors. (While the .406 batting average gets the bulk of the press, the most astounding thing that Williams accomplished in 1941 was his .553 on-base percentage, the

best in major league history until 2002 and now third, including the 1800s.)
Williams's 521 career home runs placed him third (behind Ruth and Jimmie
Foxx) when he retired after the 1961 season. His .344 lifetime batting average is
seventh on the all-time list, and the highest of any player whose career started
after 1920. He won the Triple Crown twice (leading the league in batting average, home runs, and RBI in the same season). He also won the MVP twice, and
deserved it several more times.

Looking beyond the traditional Triple Crown statistics, Williams was the best
hitter in history at the most important offensive baseball skill—getting safely to
first base. He is the all-time major league baseball leader in on-base percentage
at .482. He made outs in fewer than 52% of his plate appearances, the only player in baseball history to accomplish that. It is actually difficult to put Williams's
career on-base percentage into proper perspective. The single most important
skill that an offensive player has is the skill of not making outs. Williams did it
better than anyone else ever did. There have only been 44 single season on-base
percentages in major league history that were higher than Williams's *career* .482,
and they were compiled by only 18 players, including Ruth nine times, Williams
seven, and Barry Bonds four. And eight of the other players played predomi-
nantly in the nineteenth century. He's still second to Ruth on the all-time lists for
both slugging and OPS.

Williams played right field as a rookie in 1939 and then, with the exception of
about five seasons lost to military service, he was as much a fixture in left field at
Fenway as the Green Monster until 1960. He was an indifferent fielder, but a
passionate hitter. All evidence suggests that he was always ready, willing, and able
to talk hitting with anyone, anywhere. In 1971 he co-authored, with journalist
John Underwood, possibly the best book about hitting ever written, *The Science
Of Hitting*.

Beyond baseball, Williams lived life on a large scale. He was, in many ways,
the American that John Wayne played in the movies—the Hemingway hero
exemplifying grace under pressure. He was the greatest baseball player of his day,
and spent nearly five years of what should have been the prime of his baseball
career flying fighter planes in two different wars. He never made it overseas for
World War II, but flew 39 combat missions over Korea in 1953 (seven as wing-
man to future astronaut John Glenn, who once called Williams "the best jet pilot
I ever saw"). He was a skilled hunter and sportsman (who got in trouble for taking a shotgun to Fenway Park's pigeon population). He retired from baseball and
went on to acclaim as a master fly fisherman.

Williams always had a flair for the dramatic. In 1952, expecting to be called up
for active duty in Korea, he hit a home run in his last at bat at Fenway. In
September 1960, heading into retirement, he hit another home run in his last at
bat at Fenway.

Williams's relationship with the Boston media, the "knights of the keyboard,"
was very rough for many years, particularly with famed *Boston Daily Record*
columnist "Colonel" Dave Egan. Reporters' dislike for Williams cost him several
MVP awards, since some writers refused to vote for him altogether, no matter
how well he played. Indeed, Williams's feelings toward the fans and the city were

mixed during his career, and those mixed feelings were mutual. Williams received far more than his share of boos from the Fenway faithful. In return, he occasionally aimed foul balls at fans who were particularly vocal in their criticism.

Following a booing early in his career, Williams resolved never to tip his cap to the fans again. Not even the standing ovation following the home run that marked his last career at bat altered that. But in the years following his retirement, the frictions that remained between city, fans, and superstar gradually softened. Early in the 1990s, the street that runs behind the Green Monster was renamed from Lansdowne Street to Ted Williams Way. In 1995, the third harbor tunnel of the massive Boston Big Dig was named after Williams.

One of the lasting memories of the 1999 All Star Game, held at Fenway Park 38 years after Williams's retirement, will always be the appearance of Ted Williams on the Fenway Park infield. Major League Baseball chose the top 50 players of the twentieth century and the living members were introduced to the crowd on the Fenway infield prior to the All Star Game. The greats of the game were gathered, but when Williams came out in a golf cart, that was the feature attraction. All of the greats of baseball clustered around Williams, wanting to shake hands, or even to touch his arm. The All Stars of 1999, accustomed to being surrounded by smiling kids, were a group of smiling kids themselves around Williams. And in the broadcast booth Tim McCarver said "You find yourself asking, 'Can't this go on forever?' to nobody in particular." The sight of Ted Williams being surrounded by the great players of not only the 1999 season, but the entire twentieth century, is the lingering memory from the 1999 All Star Game.

Williams was troubled in his later years by a series of minor strokes and by heart problems (he had bypass surgery in 2000 and was hospitalized again in the winter of 2002), limiting his activities severely. Williams died July 5, 2002 after a series of strokes and congestive heart failure. After his death a bizarre series of incidents involving his son, John-Henry Williams, and daughter, Bobby-Jo Ferrell, led to Williams's body being cryogenically preserved. Williams's will had required his remains to be cremated and scattered over the waters of the Florida Keys where he loved to fish, but his son produced a highly dubious document—written on a napkin in handwriting disputed by experts—that he said proved Williams's desire to be preserved with his son and other daughter, Claudia. Ferrell disputed the validity of this napkin, but ran out of money fighting her brother over this issue, and dropped her legal challenge. In a strange twist of fate, John-Henry Williams himself died in 2004 from leukemia, at age 35.

Scott Williamson—flamethrowing reliever acquired by the Red Sox in midseason 2003 to bolster a flagging bullpen. Williamson struggled early with the Red Sox due to personal issues (his wife and newborn baby were having health problems), but once they improved so did Williamson's performance, and he was unhittable in the Red Sox 2003 postseason run. In eight innings, covering eight games, Williamson allowed only three hits while striking out 14; he was one of the main reasons the Sox pushed the Yankees to extra innings in Game 7 of the ALCS. Manager Grady Little's decision not to use him, or the rest of the bullpen, to bail ace Pedro Martinez out of a seventh-inning jam was widely criticized (although to be fair, the Sox bullpen, nearly perfect in the playoffs, had been erratic until that time).

Williamson began his career in the Cincinnati Reds organization. He came up to majors in 1999, two years after being drafted out Oklahoma State. Williamson was awesome in his first year, making the All-Star team and winning the Rookie of the Year award. In 62 games, Williamson went 12–7 with 19 saves. In 93⅓ innings, he allowed only 54 hits (but 43 walks), and struck out 107 batters. The following year, Williamson was instead the primary setup man to Danny Graves and also started 10 games, throwing a career high 112 innings. From that point on he was rarely injury free; the next season Williamson only pitched ⅔ of an inning over two games before going on the DL with torn elbow ligaments.

Williamson recovered and pitched the entire 2002 season, again striking out over a batter an inning. In 2003, the Reds decided to make Graves a starter and Williamson was annointed the closer. He pitched well in this role, saving 21 games before being traded to the Red Sox at midseason. In 2004, Williamson was never quite right but pitched extraordinarily well in extreme pain, making it into 28 games in which he gave up only 11 hits, with an extraordinary 1.26 ERA. He went on the DL multiple times, but kept coming back and trying to pitch through what was diagnosed as a frayed or partially torn elbow ligament. (Prior to the diagnosis, Curt Schilling railed at Williamson in the dugout for not being tough enough. After the diagnosis, it became apparent how tough Williamson really was.) He postponed surgery to pitch in September for the Sox, trying unsuccessfully to show that he was well enough to be on the playoff roster. After the postseason Williamson had surgery on his ailing elbow, which turned out to be even more severely injured than originally thought. His ability to pitch in the majors again remains in question; determined to make a quick comeback regardless of the odds, Williamson signed a minor league deal with the Cubs for the 2005 season.

Jim Willoughby—reliever whose removal from Game 7 of the 1975 World Series remains one of the most controversial decisions in Red Sox history. Willoughby was acquired from the Cardinals in 1975, in exchange for promising infielder Mario Guerrero. He began the season in the minors, but pitched well down the stretch for Boston (5–2, 8 saves, 3.54 ERA in 24 games). In the World Series, Willoughby was dominant. He didn't allow any earned runs in his 3 appearances covering 6⅓ innings. In Game 7, he cut off a Reds rally in the seventh inning, keeping the score tied 3–3, and pitched a perfect eighth. In the bottom of the eighth, manager Darrell Johnson pinch-hit for Willoughby, even though there were two outs and nobody on. Willoughby's replacement, Cecil Cooper, was an excellent hitter mired in a horrible 1-for-18 slump. Cooper fouled out to third baseman Pete Rose and rookie Jim Burton took over on the mound. The Reds scored off Burton in the top of the ninth, and the Sox came up empty in the bottom half, losing the game and the World Series. Fans continue to debate Johnson's decision to this day, especially since the obscure Burton had to be used in such a crucial spot.

Willoughby had a good year in 1976, despite a 3–12 record. He pitched 99 innings in relief, saving 10 games and posting an excellent 2.82 ERA. But, like his fellow Buffalo Heads, Willoughby didn't see eye-to-eye with Don Zimmer, who became manager in mid-1976. He wasn't used much in 1977 (31 games), and wasn't particularly effective (6–2, 4.94 ERA, only 2 saves). Right before Opening Day of 1978, the Red Sox sold Willoughby to the White Sox, where he pitched fairly well before injuries prematurely ended his career.

Earl Wilson—a righthanded pitcher, Wilson was the first black pitcher in Red Sox history. Drafted in 1953 as a catcher, he made his major league debut in 1959 against the Tigers. He allowed no hits but walked nine in his 3⅔ innings, leaving with a 4–0 lead. That lack of control led him to bounce up and down between Boston and the minors before sticking for good in 1962. In 1961, he didn't pitch at all in the majors. In June of 1962 Wilson became the first black pitcher to throw a no-hitter in the American League. He beat the Angels 2–0, and drove in the winning run with a third-inning home run off of California starter Bo Belinsky. Owner Tom Yawkey rewarded the feat with a $1,000 bonus.

The control difficulties were not behind Wilson, however. In 1963 he walked a league-high 105 batters, and tied the American League record with 21 wild pitches. In 1966, after complaining about unequal treatment with the Sox, he was traded to the Detroit Tigers, where he made the *Sporting News* all star team. He pitched four more seasons for the Tigers before finishing as a member of the San Diego Padres in 1970. He finished his career with a 121–109 won-loss record, and an ERA that was basically league average for his career. He wasn't a good hitter, but had excellent power for a pitcher, finishing his career with 35 home runs in only 740 career at-bats.

Wilson is now president and CEO of the Baseball Assistance Team (B.A.T.), which assists struggling former players.

Rick Wise—workhorse who won 19 games for the 1975 Red Sox, and had a solid but unspectacular 18-year career. Wise pitched for the Phillies and Cardinals from 1964–73, giving his teams lots of innings, ERAs around the league average, and about 13–17 wins a year (with nearly as many losses). He remains best-known for one of baseball's greatest single-game performances on June 23, 1971. In addition to no-hitting the powerful Cincinnati Reds, Wise also hit two home runs in the same game—a two-way feat that no other pitcher has ever accomplished.

In 1974, Wise and Bernie Carbo joined the Red Sox in the controversial Reggie Smith deal. The normally durable Wise missed most of 1974 with a sore arm but rebounded with a career-best 19–12 record in 1975, though good run support covered up for a so-so 3.95 ERA. Wise won Game 3 of the ALCS against Oakland, clinching the series. He was also the winning pitcher, in an emergency relief appearance, of Game 6 of the World Series—though Carlton Fisk deserves credit for that one.

Wise had a solid year in 1976 (14–11, 3.53 ERA), but ran into trouble when Don Zimmer took over as manager in the second half. Their personalities clashed, and Wise joined the infamous "Buffalo Heads," a clique (led by Bill Lee, Fergie Jenkins, and Carbo) that openly mocked Zimmer. Wise only started 20 games in 1977, and went 11–5 despite a poor 4.77 ERA. Before the 1978 season, he and three teammates were traded to Cleveland for rising star Dennis Eckersley. Wise lost 19 games for the Indians in 1978, and ended his career in 1982 with a 188–181 record. He is now pitching coach for the independent Nashua Pride, whose manager is former Sox teammate Butch Hobson.

Tony Womack—Speedy middle infielder who signed a minor league deal with Boston in 2004, but was traded to the Cardinals at the end of spring training. Womack had led the NL in steals for three straight years (1997–99) and usually had decent batting averages (though he rarely walked for a leadoff man). Yankees haters will always remember Womack's heroics for Arizona in the 2001 World Series. His clutch double against Mariano Rivera tied Game 7, setting up Luis Gonzalez's Series-winning bloop single. But by the spring of 2004, Womack looked like he was over the hill. His hitting had deteriorated, and Tommy John surgery had weakened his throwing. Red Sox doctors didn't think he was healthy enough to make the Opening Day roster, and the team thought Cesar Crespo could handle utility infield duties until injured shortstop Nomar Garciaparra returned from the DL. So Womack was traded to St. Louis for minor league reliever Matt Duff—and became one of the NL's biggest surprises. Not only did he win the Cardinals' starting second base job, but he set career highs in average (.307) and OBP (.349), while stealing 26 bases. Making matters worse, Nomar's injury lingered and Crespo flopped, so Womack might have been a valuable guy for the Red Sox to have around. Instead, he faced his spring training teammates in the World Series, where he hit only .182—and was nearly decapitated by a David Ortiz line drive in Game 1. Red Sox fans will see a lot more of Womack in the next two years: He signed a free agent contract with the Yankees.

Smoky Joe Wood—a pitcher and outfielder who at his peak was one of the best pitchers ever. Wood first appeared for the Sox in 1908 and moved into the rotation as part of a youth movement in 1909, when the aging Cy Young was traded. An above-average pitcher for the next two years, Wood became a workhorse in 1911, when he went 23–17 in 275 innings, with 231 strikeouts and a 2.02 ERA. In 1912, Wood had one of the finest seasons ever for a pitcher, and one of the very best for any Sox pitcher. He went 34–5 in 43 games. He threw 344 innings that year and struck out 258. His 1.91 was only the third lowest of his career. (He managed an astonishing 1.49 ERA in 1915, when he was throwing on fumes.) The toll the 1912 season took on Wood's arm was severe; he pitched for six more years, but only appeared in 73 games over that span, including only seven in the last three years. He continued to pitch well when he was available, winning the ERA title in his last full season as a pitcher in 1915, when he went 15–5 but could only start 25 games. Wood retired with a 2.03 career ERA (excellent, but not as astonishing as it would be today; the league average ERA was about 3.00 while he was pitching, while it's over 4.50 today).

Unable to pitch regularly after 1915, Wood resurrected his career as an outfielder and occasional pitcher for Cleveland, where he played until 1922. Wood's son, Joe Frank Wood, pitched briefly for the Red Sox in 1944.

John Wyatt—relief ace for the 1967 Impossible Dream team, Wyatt's career flamed out quickly at a time when almost all closers were overworked and ruined their arms in a few years (which is why people in the 1960s and 1970s used to complain about relief pitchers being inconsistent). Wyatt won 10 games as a Kansas City A's rookie in 1961, pitching mostly in relief. From then on he worked entirely out of the bullpen, saving between 10 and 20 games each year at a time when save totals were very low (since starting pitchers were expected to stay in games they were winning, even if they were tired), and leading the league in appearances in 1964, when he made the All Star team. He was traded to Boston after losing his first three games in 1966. As a 32-year-old in 1967 Wyatt had his best year, winning 10 games and saving 20 more while posting a 2.60 ERA. Although Wyatt didn't give up many hits he always struggled with his control. In 1967, however, he recorded the lowest walk total of any full season of his career. He blew a lead in Game 6 of the World Series, but won the game when the Red Sox rallied—becoming only the fourth black player to win a World Series game. The Sox sold Wyatt to the Yankees early the next season, his place in the bullpen lost to Sparky Lyle and Lee Stange, and Wyatt drifted to four teams over the next two years before retiring.

Carl Yastrzemski—in 1961, a year after the retirement of the immortal Ted Williams, the Red Sox turned to 21-year-old Long Island native Carl Yastrzemski, a second baseman in the minors, as the first candidate for the opening in left field. Yastrzemski had been signed by the Sox during his first year at the University of Notre Dame, and had put up explosive numbers at Raleigh and Minneapolis in the minor leagues.

Held up against nearly impossible expectations, Yaz's early performance was productive but not immediately reflective of his extraordinary predecessor, to whom he would be constantly compared. Both were sprightly lefthanded hitters who played left field and worked to adjust their swings and styles to the odd shapes and angles of Fenway Park. Yastrzemski was even assigned the number 8 by the Red Sox clubhouse manager because of its close association with Williams's #9. But Yastrzemski's hitting style, with a sprawled crouch and the bat held straight up with the hands behind the head, was more unorthodox than Williams's was, and it took a few years for Yastrzemski to mature from a young hitting threat to a home run force (especially in the pitching-dominated 1960s).

Yaz did not play for numbers, but his hard work finally showed off in that column during the Impossible Dream season of 1967. After adopting a new training regimen, Yastrzemski launched 44 home runs to go with a .326 average and 121 RBI, becoming the last player of the twentieth century to capture baseball's triple crown (leading the league in average, home runs, and RBI). Yaz carried the team almost by himself offensively at a time when it seemed like the dream was about to end. He had an incredible September, and in the last 12 games of the season hit .523 with 5 home runs and 16 runs batted in. At the end of the season the Red Sox needed to win their final two games against the Twins to win the pennant and avoid finishing in a three-way tie with Minnesota and Detroit. Yaz went 7-for-8 in the two Sox victories, including a home run and a terrific defensive throw that caught Bob Allison at second to end a rally.

He followed up his Triple Crown year by hitting a league-leading .301 (the lowest average ever to lead the league, in a year when the average hitter batted only .230). He would continue to hit well, but often sacrificed personal achievements for the good of the team. For instance, Yaz lost a batting title on the last day of the 1970 season because he refused to sit out the last game of a meaningless season, while California's Alex Johnson did sit out. Earlier in that strange season, Yaz became the only All Star to be named the game's MVP while playing for a losing team.

The key to Yaz's success was not so much a blessed ability as it was longevity, durability, and hard work. His 23 years with the Sox were the second most in baseball history for players who spent their careers with one team, behind only Baltimore's Brooks Robinson. As his hitting improved over his career, so did his defense in left field, one of Fenway's more demanding positions. Yastrzemski became known for the acrobatic catches he made in front of the Green Monster, despite the lack of modern finesse we see in some of today's highlight films. Because of his athleticism, Yaz was occasionally asked to fill in elsewhere, mostly at first base. In 1973 he made a valiant, but doomed, attempt to play third base, and as a 43-year-old he was forced to fill in briefly in center field. An aging Yastrzemski eventually moved to first base full-time (and finally to designated hitter in the last years of his career) when Jim Rice emerged as a talented left fielder in his own right.

Yaz was a gritty, feisty player. Although he was outwardly stoic (part of his popularity, since it came off as New England reserve), Yaz on more than one occasion exploded at an umpire when he felt he had a legitimate complaint. A frequently replayed clip of Yaz during his playing days was of him being called out on strikes, never saying a word to or looking at the umpire, but dropping the bat at the plate, then bending down to cover the plate with dirt. He was thrown out of the game before he stood back up.

In addition to being a fan favorite, Yaz was a favorite of owner Tom Yawkey. There was media criticism when Yastrzemski was suspected of having input on managerial decisions. Yaz was also criticized for being overpaid, at a time before free agency when baseball owners were notorious for underpaying players.

My first memory of the Red Sox dates back to the end of the '67 season. I was eight years old at the time, and it was one of those family cookout days which gave the men an excuse to watch baseball and drink beer. I can remember my dad, a longtime Sox fan, being absolutely thrilled by the pennant chase. He'd seen the '46 race, along with the disappointments of 1948–50 and the dreadful years since then. So 1967 was a reason to be excited about baseball again. I wasn't all that sure what baseball was all about, or what the big deal was about the final weekend series against the Twins. The things I remember most were seeing replays of the catch Yaz made in the final game, using the wall to aid his throw to second base, the homer Yaz hit to put him into a tie with Killebrew winning the Triple Crown, the catch of the popup by Rico to end the game, and the screams of joy from dad and my uncles as they saw their Sox win their first pennant in 20 years. I wasn't so sure what the game was all about or what the excitement was all about, but that was the day I became a lifelong Sox fan. I knew I wanted in on whatever it was all about. And Yaz became my childhood idol that day, because anyone named "Carl" had to be cool!

—Carl Bérubé

(Highly paid players were frequently criticized at the time, since players were supposed to play for the love of the game, with money being secondary.) Like fellow Sox star left fielders Ted Williams and Jim Rice, Yaz often didn't get along with the press, which may have been related to his being so close to Yawkey.

The combination of longevity and hard work contributed to some outstanding achievements reached near the twilight of his career. He topped the 100 RBI mark five times, picked up seven Gold Gloves for fielding excellence, and was an 18-time All Star. He finished his career leading the majors in games played, and third in at-bats. In 1979, he became the first American League player ever to reach both 3,000 hits and 400 home runs (only Willie Mays, Stan Musial, and Hank Aaron had done it in the NL). Hit number 3,000 came in September at Fenway against the Yankees, when the 40-year-old Yaz grounded a single past Willie Randolph that caused a frenzy in the stands. The game was halted for several minutes and a microphone was set up at first base for Yastrzemski to thank the Fenway crowd for their support—an unforgettable moment in Red Sox history.

Yaz retired after the 1983 season to another dramatic ovation; always reserved as a player, in his last game he trotted around the perimeter of the ballpark, greeting as many fans as he could. He repeated this ceremony when his number 8 was retired by the Red Sox in 1989, shortly after his induction into the Hall of Fame. His final totals included a .285 average (compiled at a time when pitchers dominated the game), 452 home runs, 1,844 runs batted in, and a countless number of thrills.

Rudy York—a slugger who spent most of his career with the Detroit Tigers. After playing first base for the 1940 and 1945 World Champion Tigers, York was acquired by the Red Sox before the 1946 season (in exchange for shortstop Eddie Lake) in order to bolster the team's lineup. Though his slugging percentage of .437 was a far cry from his peak years (.651 in 1937 and .583 in 1940), he hit two grand slams in the same game at one point during the season, and he drew enough walks that season to make up somewhat for his disappointing power numbers. In the 1946 World Series, York provided most of the power in the losing effort by the Sox, slugging home runs that led to wins in Games 1 and 3. The next season, as the Red Sox slipped in the standings, York was traded to the White Sox for first baseman Jake Jones. A seven-time All Star, York played only 202 mediocre games for the Sox, but his contributions in that 1946 World Series still cause him to be fondly remembered by Sox fans.

Kevin Youkilis—a much-heralded rookie third baseman who was called up to the Red Sox in May 2004 after Bill Mueller was sidelined with a knee injury. Before he ever saw a pitch in the majors, Youkilis had already developed a cult following among sabremetrics buffs and some observant baseball minds. Aside from his batting average and run production, they noticed that Youkilis drew a consistently high number of walks, which is particularly rare for a young hitter.

Among those who took notice of these statistics was Oakland Athletics general manager Billy Beane. In Michael Lewis's 2003 book *Moneyball*, which chronicles the day-to-day operations of the Oakland front office, Beane reveals his strategy for pursuing low-budget players who are adept at getting on base, and Youkilis, with his disciplined batting eye and high walk totals, is identified by Beane as the player who best fit that mold. Beane dubbed Youkilis "The Greek God of Walks," although it turned out Youkilis is not of Greek ancestry. (He's Jewish; the Red Sox were the only major league team with two Jewish players in 2004, in Youkilis and outfielder Gabe Kapler.)

In 2003, splitting time between Portland and Pawtucket in the Red Sox minor-league system, Youkilis reached base in 71 consecutive games, falling one game short of the minor-league record (held by future Boston teammate Kevin Millar). Youkilis hit a home run in his first major league game at Toronto. He was briefly sent back to the minors once Mueller returned from his injury, but did see action with the big club again near the end of the season. Youkilis finished the year with Boston with a .260 batting average, seven home runs . . . and a strong .367 OBP.

Oddly enough, shortly after the 2002 season, Beane had been courted by the Red Sox to fill their own vacant general manager position (a job that eventually went to Theo Epstein). Beane verbally agreed to a deal with the Sox, but within 24 hours had a change of heart and decided to stay with the A's. According to *Moneyball*, Youkilis was the player most likely to be offered to the A's in compensation for allowing Beane out of his contract.

Cy Young—righthanded pitcher whose career accomplishments became the standards by which pitching excellence is measured, and whose name graces the award bestowed upon the best pitchers in baseball each season. Denton True Young was nicknamed "Cyclone" in the minors because of how hard he threw, and the nickname stuck, and Cy is how he is known to all baseball fans. He spent eight of his 22 years in a Boston uniform, from 1901 when he joined the Boston Americans, through the 1908 season (the first year of the Red Sox.) He was one of the first big stars to make the jump from the established National League to the upstart, fledgling American League, and probably the biggest name.

The numbers that Young put up are difficult to comprehend for people watching today's game. He pitched in the dead-ball era, when players rarely hit home runs. All of the pitching statistics from Young's era are incompatible to today's game. There was almost no such thing as a bullpen—pitchers finished what they started. From 1891 to 1898 Young averaged more than 41 complete games per season, with a high of 48. (Only one pitcher had more than 5 in 2004.) Young did not lead the league in complete games in any of those seasons. In his career, he completed over 91% of the games that he started, starting 815 major league games and finishing a staggering 749.

But, while recognizing the context of his accomplishments, and the impossibility of comparing them to the pitching accomplishments of today, it is also important to recognize that, even in his own era, he stood out. Gehrig's consecutive games record, Cobb's hit record, and Ruth's home run record have all been broken, but Young's win record has never been challenged, even in the era when he set it. Second place on the all-time win record list is the Big Train, Walter Johnson—the only other man over 400, with 417 wins. Young had 511. His loss record is probably even farther out of reach, as he lost 316 games.

Young owed a large part of his success to his control. In his 22 major league seasons, he led the league in fewest walks per nine innings 14 times. Seven times he led in fewest baserunners (hits plus walks) per nine innings. He believed that an arm only had a certain number of pitches, and never threw more than a dozen warmups before a game.

In Boston, Young was the best pitcher on the staff of the first-ever World Series champions (1903). In his eight years with the Americans/Red Sox, he won 192 games, while finishing 275 of the 297 games that he started. He was 41 in 1908 during his last season in Boston, and he was almost done. He won only 33 games in the three years before his retirement, spent mostly in Cleveland, with a partial season back in Boston playing for the Boston Rustlers (who, in 1912, became the Boston Braves). Cy Young was elected into the Baseball Hall of Fame in 1937. In 1956, Major League Baseball created an award for the best pitcher in baseball, and named it the Cy Young Award.

Matt Young—a Sox pitcher in the early 1990s who was plagued by inconsistent control. Following Bruce Hurst's departure after the 1988 season, Young cashed in on general manager Lou Gorman's desperation to acquire lefthanded starting pitching. Young had terrific talent, but in 1990 was coming off an 8–18 season with the Seattle Mariners in which he posted high totals in both walks and strike-outs. Nevertheless, Gorman daringly signed Young to an expensive contract before the 1991 season, one of three handed out by the Sox that winter. Young's control problems with the Sox were no surprise, though he did show occasional flashes of dominance. His unpredictability made him unusually difficult to hit against, and he would frequently pitch himself both into and out of trouble, nervewracking as it was to watch.

Many critics felt that Young's control problems were psychological in nature, a theory that was supported by his erratic throws to bases. Most lefthanders, with first base in their line of sight when they prepare to pitch, are able to control baserunners more easily than righties. Young had an actual phobia about throwing the ball to bases, which led to horribly wild throws and baserunners taking advantage of him by confidently moving up. He experienced similar trouble whenever the ball was bunted or hit back to the mound and he had to throw out a runner. At one point he had regular consultations with a psychiatrist to help end this affliction, but it never led to any noticeable improvement.

Young's difficulties were epitomized in a heartbreaking game in Cleveland on April 12, 1992. Showing wild movement on his pitches, Young no-hit the Indians for eight innings but allowed two runs as a result of seven walks, six stolen bases (four by speedster Kenny Lofton) and an error by shortstop Luis Rivera. Sox hitters were no help, leaving 11 men on base. The final result was an unbelievable 2–1 loss. Because of a change in baseball rules, the game no longer counts as an official no-hitter., but it was only the second time in major league history that a pitcher lost a game without allowing a hit. (The first came from the Yankees' Andy Hawkins on July 1, 1990.)

Bob Zupcic—a young outfielder with strong defensive skills who spent parts of four seasons with the Sox in the early 1990s. While he hit 18 homers at AAA

Pawtucket, his swing seemed to slow down upon reaching the major leagues, and he never exhibited the consistent power that his early performance promised. He did, however, hit two late-inning grand slams in the week following his callup to the Sox in 1992, tying the major league record for most grand slams in a season by a rookie.

In 1975, for no apparent reason, Dutch TV decided to show some footage of a game called base-ball. A team called the Reds were playing a team called the Red Sox. Nobody in my part of Holland knew what *that* was all about, but those people on TV in America seemed pretty excited about it. They all went berserk when this guy used a big stick to hit this ball over a large green wall. The guy who hit that ball over the wall then started jumping up and down, his teammates ran toward him and started hugging him, and the crowd just kept cheering for like forever. It was 1975. I was nine years old and I got hooked on the Red Sox right there and then.

Now, in Holland, baseball is a small sport. It's hardly ever on TV. Less than 11,000 people are playing for official teams in "real" games. Sure, the Dutch National Team always ends up playing Italy for the European Baseball Championship, but who cares?

In Holland, if you want to talk about sports, you better talk about soccer, speed skating, or cycling. Anyone in Holland who knows more about Joe DiMaggio than the fact the Simon and Garfunkel mentioned him in a song and the fact that he was once married to Marilyn Monroe is considered to be either a dangerous freak or someone with way too much time on his or her hands.

Question: So, who are you going to talk to about this game called baseball and that team called the Red Sox in 1975 if you're living in the south of Holland?

Answer: Everyone.

Question: Who cares?

Answer: No one.

Question: Where are you going to learn more about those Red Sox?

Answer: Nowhere; you can't learn more about them.

Still, I never forgot the pictures on TV in 1975.

Fast forward to 1990: I'm 24. I played some high school softball (baseball is considered to be too difficult to learn and too dangerous to play for high school kids in Holland) and I'm at this baseball tournament in the west of Holland. They have this small fan shop. They sell baseball cards. They sell *Red Sox* baseball cards!

Suddenly I'm learning about this guy called Clemens, who seems to be a pretty good pitcher. It turns out in the old days a guy called Williams played for the Red Sox for just about forever. Then a guy called Yastrzemski got the job of playing there forever. There's this guy called Jody Reed, an outfielder called Plantier, a guy called Brunansky, another one called Boggs.

After that, things speeded up a lot. In 1994 or so CNBC started showing live MLB games for a year or two on Friday night. That is, until the World Series started. Then those Friday night games magically disappeared. But anyway, I'd be up from 2:00 A.M. until 5:00 A.M. watching Pettitte and the Yankees dominate the Red Sox the night after Mo Vaughn hit three dingers against the Yankees (which, of course, wasn't on TV).

Next, we got CNN and CNN text with their three-line game reports. As the season progressed, I was actually able to get a clue of the Red Sox lineup: Clemens, Wakefield, Sele, Vaughn, Valentin, Naehring, Greenwell, etc. . . . .

Then, August 1996. Two games in Fenway: Red Sox vs Angels and Red Sox vs. the A's and I was there. In person! Clemens won the game vs. the Angels and Wakefield beat the A's while giving me a heart attack every time Big Mac came to the plate. I wouldn't have left Fenway for the dura-tion of my holiday but my girlfriend kept telling me she wanted to stay in a hotel, not a ballpark.

It's now January 2005. I read about the Red Sox winning the World Series on the Internet in the bar of a hotel on the Spanish island Tenerife the day after it happened. That's okay, though. I still enjoyed it. I still cried, but only a bit (I didn't want to worry the people in the bar).

In a couple of days I expect to receive my 2004 World Series Highlights DVD. Next, I'm going to grab a sixpack and pretend it's October 2004. . . .

—Toine Otten

Quotes

"Boston has two seasons: August and winter." —former Red Sox manager (and Hall of Fame infielder) Billy Herman.

"All literary men are Red Sox fans. To be a Yankee fan in literary society is to endanger your life." —Author John Cheever.

"Baseball isn't a life-and-death matter, but the Red Sox are." —Boston columnist Mike Barnicle.

"A lyric little bandbox of a ballpark." —Novelist John Updike's description of Fenway.

"Will not play anywhere but Boston." —Text of a telegram from Babe Ruth as reported in the Boston Globe by Ruth's agent Johnny Igoe. At the time, Ruth had already agreed to terms with the Yankees.

"Ruth had simply become impossible and the Boston club could no longer put up with his eccentricities. While Ruth, without question, is the greatest hitter the game has ever seen, he is likewise one of the most selfish and inconsiderate men that ever wore a baseball uniform." —Harry Frazee after selling Ruth in 1920.

"The wrecking of this once famous ballclub is a crime and somebody ought to put an end to such methods." —A New York City newspaper in 1920 after the Red Sox kept selling players to the Yankees.

"I don't want my players to hustle too much in the spring." —Player/manager Joe Cronin, 1938.

"I'll be back soon and make more money than all three of you together." —Ted Williams to taunting Red Sox players after being sent to the minors in 1938.

"A man has to have goals and that was mine, to have people say, 'There goes Ted Williams, the greatest hitter who ever lived.' " —Ted Williams.

"I still think neckties are designed to get in your soup." —Ted Williams.

"Bobby Doerr and not Ted Williams is the number one man of the Red Sox in my book." —Babe Ruth in 1946.

"Hub Fans Bid Kid Adieu" —Title of an essay written by novelist John Updike upon the event of Ted Williams's final game. Updike was in the stands that day.

"He has muscles in his hair." —Lefty Gomez, describing Jimmie Foxx's strength.

"I'm in the twilight of a mediocre career." —Red Sox pitcher Frank Sullivan.

"Go crack me open a beer, I'll only be a minute." —Red Sox reliever Dick Radatz to starter Earl Wilson on the mound at Yankee Stadium. Radatz struck out Micky Mantle, Roger Maris, and Elston Howard on 10 pitches.

"There'll be no niggers on this ball club as long as I have anything to say about it." —Sox player, manager, and general manager Pinky Higgins.

"Good things happen to some people." —Earl Wilson, the first black player to pitch for the Red Sox, commenting on the death of former Sox manager and general manager Pinky Higgins.

"We'll win more than we lose." —New Red Sox manager Dick Williams at the end of spring training in 1967. The Sox had been at least 18 games under .500 in each of the previous three years, and hadn't had a winning record since 1957.

"He's an All Star from the neck down." —White Sox manager Eddie Stanky on Carl Yastrzemski in early 1967.

"lefthanded pitchers are the only people in their right minds." —Bill Lee.

"The Wall giveth and the Wall taketh away." —Roger Angell on the Green Monster.

"Do they leave it there during games?" —Bill Lee, the first time he saw the Green Monster.

"I loved the game. I loved the competition. But I never had any fun. I never enjoyed it. All hard work, all the time." —Carl Yastrzemski.

"Too much importance is placed on the starting pitchers. It's much more important to have a finishing pitcher." —Red Sox manager Joe McCarthy.

"25 players, 25 cabs." —Description of the lack of clubhouse unity on the Red Sox teams of the early 1970s.

"Go, go, go!" —What Denny Doyle heard in Game 6 of the 1975 World Series from third base coach Don Zimmer before being thrown out at the plate in the last of the ninth inning.

"No, no, no!" —What Zimmer claims to have said.

"No one's worth that, but if they want to pay me, I'm certainly not going to turn it down." —Bill Campbell after the Red Sox made the reliever one of the first big money free agents in 1977 by signing him to a five-year $1 million contract.

"The kid's got ice water in his veins." —Red Sox manager Don Zimmer about rookie pitcher Bobby Sprowl before the fourth game of a crucial series against the Yankees in 1978. Sprowl faced only six batters and gave up four walks and a hit.

"They killed our fathers and now the sons of bitches are coming after us." —Anonymous Sox fan after the 1978 playoff game loss to the Yankees.

"The worst curse in life is unlimited potential." —Ken Brett, a journeyman pitcher whose brother, Hall of Famer George Brett, said Ken was the best hitter in the family.

"That's what they get for building a ballpark next to the ocean." —Dennis "Oil Can" Boyd after the Red Sox win a fog-shortened game against the Indians at Municipal Stadium in Cleveland, on the shores of Lake Erie.

"My pitcher asked out of the game." —Red Sox manager John McNamara, following the sixth game of the 1986 World Series, about Roger Clemens who left in the eighth inning with a 3-2 lead. Clemens had a bleeding blister on his pitching hand, but denies that he asked to come out.

"The sun will rise, the sun will set, and I'll have lunch." —Sox GM Lou Gorman on Roger Clemens walking out of training camp in 1987 as part of a contract dispute.

"There are a lot of things that are a disadvantage to a family there." —Roger Clemens speaking of Boston in a live TV interview with Boston station WCVB in December 1988. Clemens was speaking in the wake of Bruce Hurst's decision to leave, and complained, among other things, of players having to carry their own bags through airports. It was the beginning of a big rift between Clemens and the Boston fans.

"The twilight of his career . . ." —General manager Dan Duquette's assessment of pitcher Roger Clemens after the 1996 season when Clemens signed with Toronto rather than re-sign with the Sox. Clemens won the National League Cy Young award in 2004.

"What would we do with Willie McGee?" —Sox GM Lou Gorman during the 1990 season, when the American League West-leading A's picked up former batting champion Willie McGee.

"Blow it up. Blow the damned place up." —Red Sox first baseman Mo Vaughn, talking about Fenway Park in a 1995 interview.

"I was worried about the horse." —Red Sox president John Harrington after being asked if he was concerned about seeing Mo Vaughn on a policeman's horse following the Sox clinching of the American League East in 1995.

"The price tag goes up every day." —Sox first baseman Mo Vaughn as he and the Sox were locked in a prolonged contract struggle before the 1998 season.

"If a frog had wings, he wouldn't bump his booty when he hopped." —Manager Jimy Williams at a press conference introducing him to the Boston media.

"When Georgie-Porgie speaks, I don't listen." —Sox manager Jimy Williams after being accused by Yankees owner George Steinbrenner of "inciting" the crowd during the fifth game of the 1999 American League Championship Series.

"One of my superstitions is I'm not allowed to talk about them." —Nomar Garciaparra, who had a reputation for following many rituals to keep his game focused.

"If the Lord were a pitcher, he would pitch like Pedro." —First baseman David Segui, son of former Red Sox pitcher Diego Segui, discussing Pedro Martinez.

"This team is starting to develop kind of a makeup of its own. Hopefully we can bring the mullets back and grow the hair out. I think you're starting to see baseball players who are going to be all about winning. You're going to have a lot of guys pulling from the same rope instead of three or four pulling from different ropes." —Kevin Millar during 2003 spring training.

"Cowboy up!" —Kevin Millar's rallying cry for the 2003 Red Sox.

"We played into the eleventh inning before losing Game Seven of the ALCS. . . . Yes, we came up short of our goal, and to the Red Sox Nation, I say I hurt with each of you. It was painful for all of us." —Grady Little, after the Red Sox lost the 2003 ALCS.

"If Grady Little is not back with the Red Sox, he'll be somewhere. I'll be another ghost fully capable of haunting." —Little, shortly before his firing.

"We will now seek a new manager for the long term to take us in a new direction, and, we hope, to the next level. . . . The decision to make a change resulted from months of thought about that long-term direction." —Red Sox president Larry Lucchino after firing Grady Little.

"We are not the cowboys anymore—we are just the idiots this year. So we are going to go out and try to swing the bats, find the holes, and, hopefully, good things happen." —Johnny Damon during the 2004 season.

"We're going to keep playing hard and we're going to blank out all the negativity. We are a bunch of idiots that we go out to have fun and we don't think—we eliminate thinking, and we have fun and pick each other up." —Manny Ramirez during the 2004 season.

"As a group, they are borderline nuts, but when they get out in the field, I think they try to play the game right. I just want them to be themselves, because I think we are a good team like that." —Manager Terry Francona on "The Idiots."

"What gets old is seeing that damn 1918 sign wherever you go and are playing a contending team. Every player wants to part of the team that wins so they won't be flashing that sign and talking about this curse. We totally understand the pain of the fans because the pain of the players is just as much." —Ellis Burks on "The Curse."

"I just tip my hat and call the Yankees my daddies." —Pedro Martinez after a crucial loss to the Yanks on September 26, 2004.

"Who's Your Daddy?" —Yankees fans' taunt when Pedro Martinez pitched against them in the 2004 ALCS.

"Who's your Papi?" —Red Sox fans counterchant, referring to ALCS hero David Ortiz

"Who's Your Caddy?" —Red Sox fans' response after the Yankees lost the 2004 ALCS.

"He's bulletproof, as far as I'm concerned. Whether there's a lefthander on the mound or a righthander on the mound, he beats us up pretty good." —Yankees manager Joe Torre on David Ortiz.

"One day I was driving from my house to the stadium . . . and I saw a big sign on the street that said, 'Keep the faith.' And I saw it was a photo of Manny, it had the big smile. I just parked in front of the photo and I just sat down for a minute and just thought about it, you know, we've been through the whole year. Then I went to the field and I just expressed myself to my teammates about what the Boston nation has been waiting for us and what they expect from us. So it doesn't matter if we are down 3-0. We just have got to keep the faith . . . because the game is not over till the last out." —David Ortiz after winning Game 4 of the 2004 ALCS with a walk-off homer.

"Ten years from now I think people are going to look back and say Willis Reed pulled a Curt Schilling. . . . Willis Reed scored four points. Curt Schilling went seven innings against one of the best offenses of recent memory. No offense to Willis Reed." —Theo Epstein after Schilling beat the Yankees in Game 6 of the ALCS.

"It's crushing for us. I don't have the words to describe how disappointed I am." —Alex Rodriguez after losing the 2004 ALCS.

"It was the most unbelievable day of my life. So many things happened. I woke up at seven o'clock this morning. I couldn't walk. I couldn't move. I don't know what had happened, but I knew when I woke up that there was a problem. I wasn't going to go out on the mound the way I felt . . . I don't know the medical science behind it . . . I honest-to-God did not think I was going to take the ball today." —Curt Schilling after winning Game 2 of the 2004 World Series.

"When you have an enemy hanging on the side of a cliff by one arm, you need to step on his arm." —Trot Nixon, explaining why the Red Sox didn't take the Cardinals for granted in Game 4 of the 2004 World Series.

"I wanted to be the guy on the mound with the ball in my hand at the end." —Keith Foulke after making the final play of the 2004 World Series.

"This is like an alternate reality. All of our fans waited their entire lives for this . . . We won't even need the airplane to fly home." —John Henry, Red Sox owner, after the 2004 World Series.

"We don't believe in no stinking curses." —Red Sox President Larry Lucchino after the 2004 World Series.

"Unbelievable. No more going to Yankee Stadium and having to listen to '1918!' " —Derek Lowe after the Red Sox won the 2004 World Series.

"We wanted to do it so bad for the city of Boston. To win a World Series with this on our chests—it hasn't been done since 1918. So rip up those '1918" posters right now." —Kevin Millar.

"I went through a lot of drama during the winter, but I keep my mind positive and I told my wife before the season started, 'Hey, baby, this is going to be my year. This is the year.' And we did it, man. We're the champs." —2004 World Series MVP Manny Ramirez.

"I'm so happy. I'm happy for the fans in Boston, I'm happy for Johnny Pesky, for Bill Buckner, for Stanley and Schiraldi and all the great Red Sox players who can now be remembered for the great players that they were." —Curt Schilling.

"I dreamt about this day. I said my prayers every night to the big guy: 'Bring us a World Series.' " —Johnny Pesky after the Red Sox won in 2004.

"I don't want to bring a downer on the whole situation because I'm very happy for the Boston Red Sox. . . . This whole thing about being forgiven and clearing my name, you know, I mean . . . cleared from what? What did I do wrong? It's almost like being in prison for thirty years and then they come up with a DNA test to prove that you weren't guilty." —Bill Buckner after the Red Sox won the 2004 World Series.

"In baseball, too many people try to discount someone like Theo, someone who could be the C.E.O. of a Fortune 500 company and probably will be. . . . Guys like Theo have really opened the door for other bright young guys who might otherwise go to Wall Street." —Oakland GM Billy Beane on Theo Epstein.

"He ain't going to no Mets" —Fellow Dominican David Ortiz on Pedro Martinez's free agency. Martinez signed a $53 million contract with the Mets shortly afterward.

"When they want someone to push the button, I want to be the guy to blow this place up." —Pitcher David Wells on Fenway Park in 2000

"I've been the bad guy coming into Boston. I guess I'm one of the good guys now." —Wells in 2004, after signing with the Red Sox

"I am no longer a fan. I am no longer that kid who was rooting for the Red Sox, and thank God! Because if I were, it would be impossible for me to do my job." —Red Sox GM Theo Epstein.

"I don't think we have to do it any better. I just think we have to do it again." —Curt Schilling, 2005

"[The 2005 Red Sox] will field the best bad team in baseball history."
—Pedro Martinez, after leaving the Red Sox to sign with the Mets.

"There's no place like it, and it's ours." —Stephen King on Fenway Park.

My family immigrated to Canada from Italy in March of 1955, near the end of the NHL season. By the time I could (barely) make myself understood in English, I was watching playoff hockey games at the home of the kid across the hall. His family had come to Ajax from Windsor (across the river from Detroit), so he was a Detroit Red Wing fan. So I became a Detroit Red Wing fan. Following his lead, Ted Lindsay was my favorite player.

When summer came I was astonished at how everybody was trying to hit a ball with a strange-looking stick, and when someone managed that, everyone tried to catch and throw it while others ran all over the place. In about ten minutes one afternoon I was introduced to the concept of base-ball. Perhaps it was its somewhat anarchic appearance, but as far as playing it, I was hooked. This sandlot variety was the only baseball I knew. The only time baseball was on television was on Saturday afternoons, and we were too busy playing to watch.

The following year (by this time I actually knew the rules!), I was learning the intricacies of playing second base (pretty good), hitting (lousy), and the English language. Another boy, John Brewer, with whom I made friends, was a Yankees fan. I had very little idea of who the Yankees were. I'm eight years old at this time, one year of English under my belt, quite bright and learning quick but I had a bit of difficulty reading newspapers, much less the sports pages. But I had, by absorption, learned most of the team names.

When John Brewer (pity he was a Yankees fan) asked me which was my favourite team, I con-sidered ingratiating myself by saying the Yankees, but I couldn't bring myself to do it (I had *no* knowledge of baseball history at this time). Thinking furiously, I ran down the names of the teams I knew and linked the Detroit *Red Wings* with the Boston *Red Sox*. Boston, I told him. The Red Sox.

Hmph, he replied. You only like them because they have Ted Williams. Well, I thought. Since the *Red Wings* had Ted Lindsay and the *Red Sox* had Ted Williams, my choice seemed obviously fated. No, I told him, I like them because they're my favourite team. The Yankees fan was disgusted and regaled me with tales of Babe Ruth, Lou Gehrig, Joe DiMaggio, Mickey Mantle, et al. I had no easy rejoinder, so I went to the library and pored through volumes of sports history for three evenings. When next we met I could hold up my end of the argument, having committed to memory pages of statistics and historical data. He knew a lot more about baseball than I did, so in order to continue arguing intelligently, I had to keep learning, with the accent on the Red Sox.

When Ted Williams retired I had saved my pennies to take a bus to Boston (I ran away from home, technically) to see him play for the only time in my life. I saw his last game. I was appre-hended and returned to Canada four hours after the game.

In '67 I attended all four games at Fenway and two in St. Louis. In '75 I saw both games against Oakland at Fenway. I saw the first two games of the Series and two games in Cincinnati. I saw all three games in Boston, and almost went broke. Due to the rain, I ran out of money (but had tickets) and spent a night in the park under three days' worth of newspapers until someone took me in for the rest of the week.

In '86 I had pretty well given up hope, but ended up in Fenway for the final game of the American League Championship Series. I saw the second game in New York against the Mets and two of the three games at Fenway. I went to New York but could not acquire tickets for the final two games. I cried, though.

—Mario Martinelli

The Fenway Experience

What is the Fenway experience?

Perhaps it begins in the dark of the offseason, walking down Landsdowne Street and looking up at the back of the Green Monster, the looming, stretching images of the lights, darkened for winter, waiting for spring. The nightclubs and shadowed streets do their business even when there is no baseball, when the ballpark hibernates. Crowds ebb and flow through Kenmore Square without any thought or concern for the sleeping park off to the side. It is different in the winter, when a person traveling up Commonwealth Avenue does not occasionally hear the roar of the crowd even over the traffic, like a wave sweeping through the Fens. Perhaps it begins with the opening of the box office, with the people lined up the length of the street in the cold, the children restless and chilled and keeping warm with games of tag, their parents peering at schedules and murmuring questions about whether or not the Yankees games will be sold out by the time they get to the head of the line, and discussing what other games they might want to get tickets to see.

But the Fenway experience is mostly the experience of game day, the gathering of the people and the slow, graceful unfolding of the game of baseball. The Fenway experience is the snarl of traffic through the Fens, the group of twenty Cub Scouts with baseball gloves tucked under their arms occupying half of a commuter rail car until they're herded out onto the Yawkey Station platform by the tall, broad-shouldered form of their Scout Leader, the tight-packed clusters of people in their blue jackets with the red lettering, their blue caps with the red B, exploding down out of the Green Line trolleys and surging up the steps and into the light of Kenmore Square.

The Fenway experience is climbing up over the bridge that spans the Pike and the rail line and being greeted by the vendors with their "Yankees Suck" t-shirts and their baseball caps, to the sound of one of the kids who turns over a few buckets and pans and beats on them with such skill and enthusiasm that the music of his drumming is far more powerful than the fact that his materials are makeshift. The Fenway experience is walking through the crowds along Brookline Avenue, past fast-moving men with sharp eyes who bob alone through the traffic muttering, "Tickets? Tickets? Tickets?" and past scared kids who are trying to sell off tickets while terrified of being caught by a cop, and past people desperately trying to get tickets or sell them if the game is sold out: if the Yankees are playing, or perhaps if Curt Schilling is pitching.

The Fenway experience is going with a group of people who have scrounged their money from the seats of college dorm sofas and their allowances from their parents to make the trip into Boston and getting tickets to claim a corner of the upper grandstand on a bright, sunny day in May. The Fenway experience is getting tickets to an early game and huddling in the cold in a clear spot in Section 18 with a perfect view of the field. The Fenway experience is an afternoon game spent over the triangle and the sunburn that follows as a souvenir. The Fenway experience is getting a ticket from one of those scared kids, and giving him more than he wanted because he couldn't make change—besides, getting the ticket and getting into the game matters more than the extra few dollars.

The experience is in waiting for the gates to open, in among the bustle and activity of the other people waiting: the vendors, the scalpers, the casual passers-by. Perhaps it's waiting in a nearby bar until close to game time; or then again perhaps it's browsing the Twins store and prowling among jerseys numbered 24 and 18 while watched by the figures on the posters. It's in picking up the current copy of *Boston Baseball* to get the articles and have a new scoresheet for the game and hearing, down the way, the cry of "Pizza! Fried Shrimp! Fried Clams! Steak and Cheese!"

It's in turning up early and watching batting practice, with equipment strewn across the field and each batter in turn popping a long sequence of baseballs into a scattered spray across the field. Sometimes, they fly over the Green Monster and earn a smattering of applause. It comes in seeing the clusters of children pressed up against the wall near the dugouts, hoping that the players were coming out to sign their cards, their pieces of paper, their baseballs and gloves. It comes in being there and pointing out the features of the park to someone who does not know them: The right field foul pole? That's Pesky's Pole, named for John Michael Paveskovich, shortstop. That red chair way up there? That's where Ted Williams's home run hit the man in the straw hat. The bullpens? That's Williamsburg.

The Fenway experience is coming into the park with a love of the team and only knowing the name of one of the players, and discovering that that player is the starting pitcher for the day. The Fenway experience is coming in to the park with a head full of stats and figures. The Fenway experience is keeping score in a program with a pen that keeps running out of ink, and explaining to the nearby people what the arcane markings mean. It's keeping track of the gameplay for the other fans in the bleachers, and rattling off who the runners on base are when they've lost track, and how they got there.

It's joining a section of some 30 people who are surrounding a visitor to the park who seems to speak not much English, and explaining to him what's happening in the game, listing off balls and strikes, the nuance of a foul ball after two strikes, the number of outs, the flow of the game: the entire group within earshot, not just the people who came with him, sharing the enthusiasm and the love of the game, sometimes in English a little too fast for him to follow.

It's in sitting in the bleachers up near the centerfield wall watching Pedro Martinez pitch against whatever team you most hate. It's in cheering the crowd of people wearing red—the K-Men—who post the big red Ks for Pedro's strike-outs, and after the first three are pressed up against the wall, and the stickum set by rubbing the corners with the end of a red umbrella, counting them off in a resounding chant that eventually is taken up by the entire upper bleachers: "One! Two! Three! Uno! Dos! Tres! Cuatro!" It's in seeing the six guys without shirts, who have NOMAR painted across their chests and PEDRO painted across their backs, and who were painting a K on their remaining companion with each strikeout as a living memorial to the game. It's in watching the wave sweep around Fenway until it stalls out in one strike against the Green Monster over in left field and just never makes the transition, or possibly even joining in. It's in seeing the signs that people make and wave at the cameras, the players, the other fans in the stadium.

The Fenway experience is meeting people one knows from elsewhere, finding them brought in for the sake of the game. Or coming with a friend (how better to get some hot chocolate in a cold game in March than to send the other person in the party to go stand on line?) and rattling discussion back and forth about the progress of the game. Or coming alone and talking game with the people nearby. The Fenway experience is razzing the Yankees fans who turn up—sometimes politely, sometimes not. The Fenway experience is being told to stop chanting at the Yankees fans because of the presence of the kids. The Fenway experience is taunting the players on the field with cries of "Bull-pen! Bull-pen!" when their pitchers struggle, or with the jubilant shout of "Wall ball!" when someone dou-bles off the Monster. The Fenway experience is the howl of "Youk!" as Youkilis comes to bat. The Fenway experience is singing "Sweet Caroline" with a few thousand fellow fans and knowing what it means to have good times.

The Fenway experience is a double down the line to left, landing fair by a hand's breadth and rolling to the wall. The Fenway experience is a Garciaparra leap to catch a ball that was surely gone otherwise, limbs windmilling, and a sud-den, breathless landing. The Fenway experience is a bang-bang double play, bases mysteriously empty of runners now, the pitcher on the mound catching his breath and going for the last out. The Fenway experience is a ball lobbed into the trian-gle and barely caught, a foul into the right field stands chased by the right fielder like a seeker missile, a skid on the grass and a three-base error. The Fenway expe-rience is a ball hit on what looks to be a perfectly straight line, rising, rising, ris-ing, and barely dropping over the Green Monster. The Fenway experience is a pitcher turned around with a look of dismay to watch that ball rise.

The Fenway experience is sometimes a blow-out victory, unadulterated tri-umph, glory for all told. Or perhaps it is an infuriating, heartbreaking loss, shut down by some pitcher who will never have a good game in the major leagues again. Or a game lost in a sudden implosion of defense in the eighth inning. Or a game won with yet another last-minute comeback—or lost because that comeback fell just a little short. The Fenway experience is remembering players who have gone, both those who left angrily and those who left quietly, and looking forward to tomorrow's stars, now hiding in Pawtucket, in Portland, in Lowell.

The Fenway experience is the ripples of "Dirty Water" played over the PA and sung, mostly on-key, by the fans as they file out and into the streets. The Fenway experience is also silence, and tomorrow's game.

The Fenway experience is standing in the frigid cold of an October midnight, standing and watching and knowing that three games down isn't out, and that just a little more hope and a little more faith could be just what's needed to tip the balance to victory. The Fenway experience goes home with you.

—Heather Anne Nicoll

Getting to Fenway

Fenway isn't the most convenient place to get to by mass transit, but it is accessible. The parking situation around Fenway Park is hideous, however. The easiest way to get to the park by car is to park near a subway or trolley line and take the train to the park. The Red Sox also have a discount ticket arrangement with the Prudential Center parking garage. For directions by car, train, bus, subway, or air, go to the team's website at www.redsox.com.

You can order Sox tickets by mail, fax, phone, through the team's touch-tone ticketing service, over the Internet, or in person. The best ways are usually by phone or in person—when you can talk to a staff member and ask questions about available seating before making your choice. Online, fax, and touch-tone tickets give you fewer options; you can pick an area of the park where you want to sit, but the team will assign you seats within that area, and you may end up with poor seats that you would not have chosen. For instance, if you're on the phone with a ticket agent and ask for a seat in section 15, the agent can tell you that the only seats left are obstructed view, and will suggest seats in another area if you ask. If you order online, by mail, or by fax, you will be assigned the obstructed view seats. Note that the Sox charge a handling fee on phone, fax, and online ticket orders.

No matter how you order, you'll want to specify what section of the park you want to sit in. If you don't have a preference, you may be steered to less-desirable seats in right field. If you want seats against the Yankees, be sure to order early; Yankees games tend to sell out quickly. Tickets usually go on sale in early January. In 2005, tickets ranged from $12–120, with most of the season selling out quickly. (If you know any season ticket holders, it's a good idea to cultivate their friendship, since they will be selling any tickets they can't use during the season.)

You can order Sox tickets by phone at 617-267-1700, or use 617-482-4SOX for the 24-hour touch-tone ticketing system (617-236-6644 is the TDD number). If you want more than 40 tickets, call 617-262-1915. To order online (or to download a form for a fax order) go to www.redsox.com. Tickets can be ordered by mail from Boston Red Sox Ticket Office, 4 Yawkey Way, Boston, MA 02215-3496.

Disabled fans can call 617-267-1700 or can order in person at the ticket window. Tickets for fans with disabilities must be purchased at least three days in advance. Or you can order in person at the Fenway ticket window from 9:00 A.M. to 5:00 P.M. Monday to Saturday.

If you want to buy tickets on the spur of the moment for that day's game you should go to the ticket office. Often very good seats are made available at the last minute, even for sold-out games. Be sure to check with the ticket office before buying tickets above face value from a scalper, since the ticket office may have better seats.

While the Boston police seem to tolerate some scalpers around the park, be very careful about selling tickets because of Massachusetts's strict ban on ticket sales by unlicensed agents. In one well-publicized case, a priest taking a youth group on an outing was arrested for trying to sell a spare ticket at face value. The DA's office usually won't prosecute these arrests, and they've been laughed out of court on the occasions they got that far, but you don't want to spend the game filling out paperwork at a police station.

Where to Sit

There are good and bad things about sitting in a 90-year-old ballpark. Many of the seats in Fenway are small and cramped, with metal armrests that may poke into you uncomfortably if you don't have the same dimensions as the typical World War I-era adult. On the other hand, most of the seats are close to the field and give you a better view of the game than in more modern parks, which are designed with more of an eye toward luxury box revenue than toward the needs of typical fans. And even though Fenway Park is close to full for most games, it's relatively easy to get good seats—without having to resort to ticket scalpers.

Most of the seats at Fenway are good, with the conspicuous exception of the right field box seats. Most of those seats face the right fielder, so if you sit in them you have to turn your neck to see the plate, and will have a stiff neck by the end of the game. During evening games, the setting sun will be in your eyes when you look toward home plate for the first few innings.

If you want the bleacher experience (the cheapest seats in the house), the best bleacher seats are in sections 34, 35, and 36. These seats look directly over the center fielder's shoulder and give a good view of all the action.

Several new sections of seating have been added recently, including the Green Monster seats (only 274 available), seats on the roof above the left field grandstand (a surprisingly good view, and access to uncrowded concession stands and restrooms), and right field roof seats with waiter service (variably priced depending on the popularity of the opponent; the price includes a food credit).

The View Inside Fenway

There's something magical about walking into Fenway Park, when the green of the field opens in front of you. Newcomers to the park are often astonished by how close to the action many of the seats are, especially compared with more recent facilities. The Boston region is captivated by history, and Fenway Park is no exception; fans glory in the field's legends and traditions, and every change or updating is cause for conversation and controversy. The most hated features are as much a part of history as the beloved ones, which is why you'll still here people talking about the long-gone horse trough style urinals that used to line the men's rooms under the bleachers, or about stadium advertisments from generations past. In New England, everything is woven into history, and Fenway Park and its features are very much a part of that fabric.

Some of Fenway's legends and traditions belie description, but here are a few swatches from fabric of Fenway Park.

THE GREEN MONSTER

"The Green Monster," also known simply as "The Wall," is the 37-foot wall that extends from the left field foul pole to almost dead center field and is perhaps Fenway Park's most famous feature. It was, for most of its life, topped by a 23-foot net that caught most home runs hit over it. When the new ownership group took over in 2002, one of the things that they were looking for was a way to increase the revenue stream the park was capable of generating. They added a couple of rows to the front around the back of the field, but the most visible change was the 2003 removal of the screen and the addition of seats to the top of the left field wall. Called the "Monster Seats," the 274 seats atop the wall have been sold out constantly since they were built.

The foul pole is marked as 310 feet from home where the wall starts in left field, but has been rumored for years to be even closer to the plate. The nickname "Green Monster" comes from the dark green paint that has adorned the wall for the past several decades. During the early days of the park, the wall was covered in advertisements, but it has been mostly clean for the past 40 years. The wall contains a real oddity in this day of multimillion-dollar electronic scoreboards: a simple scoreboard run by three people actually inside the wall. They keep score by listening to games on the radio and by looking through a small slit in the wall. And many pictures of the wall show something that is frequently associated with Fenway, though it is not part of the park. The view of the Green Monster from behind the plate and up the first base line shows, as a notable and prominent part of the skyline, the Citgo sign on top of a building in Kenmore Square. (When the Citgo sign had to be renovated recently, it was done in the offseason at the team ownership's request so as not to disrupt the fan experience.)

Another notable feature of the Green Monster is the ladder 13 feet up the wall in left center that was used by groundskeepers to retrieve balls hit into the screen during batting practice. Though the screen is gone, the ladder remains. Very rarely balls will be hit off the ladder, causing wild bounces that fielders have no way to anticipate. There is also a garage door in the center field area of the Green Monster. This door was once used by maintenance staff to drive a baseball-shaped golf cart onto the field and out to the bullpens to pick up and deliver relief pitchers to the pitching mound. This has been long since done away with, and relief pitchers now walk from the right field bullpens to the pitching mound, but the door is still used for a variety of other functions.

One of the greatest myths about the Green Monster is that it creates many cheap home runs. While the occasional "normal fly ball out" does indeed drift over the wall (most famously Bucky Dent's tragic home run that ended the Red Sox season in 1978), as many rising line drives will bang off the wall to become doubles, or even singles. What the wall does create is an unusually high number of doubles. As with Pesky's Pole, the wall can work for or against the home team. And contrary to what has become a fairly widespread belief, there is no such thing as a ground-rule triple at Fenway Park (although there once was, in the distant past).

LEFT FIELD STANDS

About halfway between the wall and third base the stands jut out to just a few inches from fair territory. This not only gives fans sitting in this area a birdseye view but can become a nightmare for baserunners inexperienced in Fenway's many quirks. Balls are known to be called fair as they pass third base, but bounce off the stands afterward—caroming within reach of the left fielder faster than in other parks. This results in many runners being thrown out while going for seemingly sure doubles. Where the wall and the stands meet is also a problem for left fielders, as there is almost no room to catch balls hit down the foul line. Fan interference can also cause problems here.

RIGHT FIELD FAÇADE

Over the right field grandstand, there is a façade on the roof where the retired numbers of past Red Sox greats are displayed. The numbers are red, like the numbers on the home uniforms, and displayed on circular fields of white. The team has specific rules on how numbers are retired. Players must be members of the Hall of Fame who played at least 10 seasons for—and finished their careers with—the Red Sox. From the time that Williams's #9 was retired until 1997, the numbers were displayed in the order that they were retired. 9 (Williams), 4 (Joe Cronin), 1 (Bobby Doerr), and 8 (Carl Yastrzemski). In 1997, they were re-ordered numerically. The team denied that any superstition was involved with the re-ordering, but believers in the "Curse of the Bambino" had long noted that the 9-4-1-8 on the façade was the eve of the last World Series win for the Sox (the 1918 World Series began on September 5, 1918—9-5-18.) Also in 1997, number 42 was added to honor Jackie Robinson. Major League Baseball retired Robinson's number for all teams in both leagues upon the fiftieth anniversary of Robinson breaking the color barrier, though the 12 players wearing the number (including Boston's Mo Vaughn) were allowed to keep wearing it. Number 42 is numbered in blue, and slightly separated from the red numbers representing Sox players. In 2000, the Red Sox retired Carlton Fisk's #27, bringing the total number of retired numbers on the façade to the current 6. In order to do this, the team needed to stretch the self-imposed rules somewhat, and Dan Duquette's hiring of Fisk as a special assistant was considered to meet the requirement that Fisk's career finish in Boston. If Jim Rice is elected to the Hall of Fame, his #14 will go up soon thereafter.

RIGHT FIELD ROOF SEATS

In their continuing effort to increase the number of people that they can fit into the park, the team added more seats prior to the 2004 season. The most prominent of these were 191 seats on the roof in right field, arranged in café fashion with tables.

THE PESKY POLE AND THE RIGHT FIELD CORNER

One of Fenway Park's most legendary quirks, Pesky's Pole is the right field foul pole that stands a scant 302 feet from home plate. Though right field continues to arc deeper (thus the quirk) beyond the pole, fly balls that would be outs—or at least stay in most parks—occasionally curl around this pole for home runs that can be considered cheaper than those over the notorious "Green Monster" in left. Whether this pole has resulted in more "good" (i.e., by the Sox) or "bad" (i.e., by their opponents) home runs will be forever debated. The nickname for the pole comes from 1950s Red Sox infielder Johnny Pesky, who curled several of his rare homers around the pole.

As noted above, though the foul pole is a relatively short distance from home plate, the field expands quickly. The effect of this is that the right field wall, starting at the foul pole, runs almost directly away from home plate. Whereas in most parks a ball that gets to the outfield wall will bounce back toward home plate, in Fenway's right field corner, balls can just follow the curve of the wall out toward the bullpens. This has a tendency to lead to inside-the-park home runs if the right fielder isn't careful.

MORSE CODE

On the left field scoreboard there are dots and dashes of green on two of the vertical white stripes. These are the initials TAY and JRY, for longtime owners Thomas A. Yawkey and Jean R. Yawkey, spelled out in Morse code.

DUFFY'S CLIFF

In the early years of Fenway Park, the 25-foot wooden wall in left field was fronted by a 10-foot slope. This feature was initially constructed to allow spectators to stand and see down onto the field over people in front of them. Sox left fielder George "Duffy" Lewis became adept at scrambling up the embankment to make plays. Cartoons of the day portrayed him as cavorting among mountain goats and snowcaps to field a fly ball; because of his prowess, the hill became known as "Duffy's Cliff." Unfortunately, Duffy's Cliff was flattened during the 1934 refurbishment of Fenway Park.

WILLIAMSBURG AND THE CENTER FIELD TRIANGLE

In 1940 the team constructed new bullpens at Fenway Park, ostensibly for the purpose of giving the pitchers a better place to warm up. Prior to that, they had to use the meager foul territory or loosen up under the grandstand. However, the main purpose was rumored to have been to move the right field wall 23 feet closer to home plate as a target for Ted Williams. The new bullpens were unofficially dubbed "Williamsburg." One of the interesting eccentricities of the playing field was formed by the addition of the bullpens. The end of the pen slants back to a point where it meets the center field wall. The area formed by these two walls meeting is triangular in shape and thus called the Center Field Triangle, or just The Triangle.

Above the triangle, in the center field bleachers, is a group of seats that the team only sells for night games. During day games, the glare off any light-colored clothing is in the hitter's line-of-sight, and the distraction can be dangerous to hitters who need to avoid 90 MPH pitches. So the seats are generally covered with a black tarp for day games. During one day game in April of 2004 the seats were filled, as the team had sold the seats for a night game, then had to use them during the day to make up the game when it was rained out. The team addressed the safety issue by handing out green t-shirts for everyone seated in that area, and asking them not to move during innings. There was mixed reaction from the players, and it seems unlikely to become a regular occurrence.

THE RED SEAT

There is, in the sea of green seats in the right field bleachers, a red seat. This is the seat located at the spot—502 feet from home plate—where Ted Williams is alleged to have hit a home run that ruined the straw hat of one of the patrons in

Since I was eight I have played baseball. My father dragged me to the club which he and some others friends started in 1954—the year I was born. I am a reasonable soccer player but a pathetic baseball player. I could not hit at all and as an outfielder I catch the occasional ball but also miss a lot. But we have fun and my friends are as bad as I and after the game we drink beer in our clubhouse and forget about the result. Dutch baseball is not as bad as my fellow Dutchman Toine Otten from Born suggests. At the last Olympics in Sydney the Dutch team beat Cuba! In 1994 I decided to go to the States to see some baseball and saved for three years. The strike cost me a year but in 1996 I visited New York, Chicago, and Boston and saw the Yankees, White Sox, Cubs, and Red Sox. I used to have a soft spot for the Yankees but during our ten-day trip I changed my mind. I like old-fashioned soccer stadiums in England and noticed that only the Cubs and the Red Sox came close.

In 1998 I get some frequent flyer miles from my brother in law who actually played on the Dutch national team and hear to my surprise that his aunt lives in Lexington and is prepared to share the house with me. The perfect combination: free flight and free lodgings! I see the Red Sox six times in August and love the area around Fenway Park. Fenway Park is baseball heaven for me although I have to admit I am a atheist! In such a stadium it is not that important to win. Just be there and enjoy the atmosphere!! I like Nomar and Mo but Pedro Martinez is my hero. I watch him against the Texas Rangers and he is in total control in a 4–1 win.

In 2000 another trip to Boston, now staying in the nearby YMCA and another six games. I walk to Fenway every day and love it. I freelance for a sports paper and produced a feature story about the Red Sox. Nomar does not hit at all and is in a slump, Carl Everett is good and very irritating at the plate but Pedro Martinez, my hero, is in great form again. Again versus Texas, a 9–0 win and he plays games with some of their best hitters. I buy the *Boston Globe* every day and love the articles. Back in the Netherlands: first thing in the morning, I check the Boston Red Sox results on the Internet.

One urgent request: Please never switch to a boring out-of-town soulless, modern, boring, expensive, multifunctional stadium. Create a new one a few hundred yards from Fenway Park and model it to the current one like the current plans are. Deep in my heart I say: NEVER LEAVE FENWAY PARK for anything else.

One everlasting memory: "Ladies and gentlemen, now at bat for the Red Sox, number 5: Nomarrrr Garciaparrahhh."

—Hans Akkerman

June of 1946. No one has ever hit a ball over the roof above the right field grandstand, where the retired numbers of Red Sox greats are displayed.

PAST FIRES

Twice in its early years, Fenway Park suffered serious fire damage. In May 1926 the bleachers along the foul line in left field burned down and were not initially replaced. This actually allowed—for a brief time—left fielders to make plays on foul balls behind the third base grandstand. Then in January 1934, fire swept through the park again, destroying nearly all of the construction then underway to refurbish the park. The refurbishment continued and the park reopened in April of 1934.

Where to Eat and Drink

There are dozens—if not hundreds—of bars and restaurants offering everything from the latest in fusion cuisine, to whatever sort of ethnic food one might desire to New England staples such as Boston's famous clam chowder, to various fast food chains, both in Boston and around Fenway Park itself. The following are some of the best and most popular places to eat in the Fenway Park area, listed alphabetically. Remember that the most popular bars and restaurants around Fenway Park get very crowded before games (and most restaurants don't accept reservations on game nights), so you may need to show up early to get a table. Restaurants around Fenway are generally open after games as well—and much less crowded. Prices listed are for a typical entree.

Ankara Cafe—a small cafe and student hangout next to the Kenmore Square T station at 472 Comm (Commonwealth) Ave. (617-437-0404, fax 617-437-1803, www.ankaracafe.com), Ankara Cafe features traditional and specialty pizzas, sandwiches, salads, and rollups ($5–14), along with almost 50 flavors of frozen yogurt. They also serve breakfast, if you're arriving especially early for a day game.

Bertucci's—the distinctive chain recently arrived in Kenmore Square, at 533 Comm Ave. (617-236-1030, www.bertucci's.com). Many entrees ($9-15) and all pizzas ($10–19) are cooked in an authentic Italian brick oven, and Bertucci's is the only American chain honored by Italy's L'Associazion Vera Pizza Napoletana. They're open until 11:00 Monday–Thursday, until midnight Friday–Saturday, sometimes later on game nights. Unlike most Fenway Park–area restaurants, you can call ahead for seating as you leave the game. Bertucci's also serves appetizers ($6–10), lunches ($7–9), and on game days, pizza by the slice.

Boston Beer Works—located across the street from Fenway at 61 Brookline Avenue (617-536-BEER, fax 617-536-3325, www.beerworks.net), Boston Beer Works boasts a large selection of specialty beers brewed on the premises or locally, as well as an extensive menu heavy on appetizers and out-of-the-ordinary pizzas (lunch $7–10, dinner $12–16). Favorite brews include Blueberry and Fenway Pale Ale. The Beer Works gets very crowded before games with a correspondingly high noise level. After 5:00 on a game night, expect waits of up to an hour (no reservations on game nights). If you have to wait for a table, the staff will give you a beeper and let you roam the restaurant (or sit at the bar section and get a start on perusing the beer special board) until your table is ready. The Beer Works also sells t-shirts and other souvenirs.

Boston Billiard Club—a cavernous restaurant, bar, and upscale billiard club, located a couple of blocks from Fenway at 126 Brookline Avenue (617-536-POOL, www.bostonbilliardclub.com). The menu leans toward appetizers and sandwiches ($7–9). There's a full bar along with a variety of draft beers. Pool tables are $8/hour for the first two players, and $2 for each additional player (slightly more after 5:00 P.M. and on weekends). Satellite TV and video games are available, and the club also has five private rooms and a lounge and café area for non–pool players. Get there early on game days—it gets very crowded after 5:00. The club opens at noon when there's a day game at Fenway. (If you don't have tickets to the game, the club broadcasts it over 33 TVs, including a six-foot big screen with surround sound and plasma flat screens.) The Boston Billiard Club also sells billiard supplies, t-shirts, and souvenirs.

Cask'N Flagon—a popular bar and gathering spot game-goers will pass on the way to the ballpark at 62 Brookline Avenue (617-536-4840); lines waiting to get in spill out the doors and mingle with the crowd heading for Fenway. The historic building was an auto dealership about the same time Fenway Park was built. In addition to the full bar, there's a full menu (heavy on sandwiches, burgers, and ribs, $8–15) but no reservations on game nights. The Cask'N Flagon's function room seats up to 172. The bar gets very crowded starting around 5:00 on game days, so expect a wait. The Cask'N Flagon also sells t-shirts.

Copperfield's—a large, comfortable bar, located about a block from Fenway at 98 Brookline Avenue (617-247-8605, www.2nite.com/copperfields). Copperfield's features live bands (check the website for who's playing) and entertainment both upstairs and downstairs. They serve 30 draft beer lines, including local microbrews. Function space is also available.

Cornwall's—a traditional British-style pub with a great beer selection, at 654 Beacon Street (617-262-3749). Cornwall's features pool tables, darts, 24 beers on tap (mainly English and local brews) as well as many bottled beers. Hours are noon to 2:00 A.M., 7 days a week, and the kitchen is open until 11:30 P.M. (sometimes later after night games). The menu combines traditional English pub food (shepherds pie, bangers and mashed, fish and chips, Welsh chicken pie) with burgers, salads, and other American fare. Lunch and dinner are both $8–15.

India Quality Restaurant—located at 484 Comm Ave. on the way to the ballpark (617-267-4499, fax 267-4477, www.indiaquality.com), India Quality is open both before and after the game, and provides good North Indian food ("highly recommended" in the 2002–05 *Zagat's Guide*) at a reasonable price for a Boston restaurant. There is a broad menu for both lunch ($6–8) and dinner ($9–14) including vegetarian, chicken, lamb, and fish, as well as a wide variety of breads, soups, and side dishes. India Quality also serves beer and wine. India Quality is usually less crowded than the more baseball-oriented restaurants in Kenmore Square.

Maluken—a Japanese restaurant in the Hotel Buckminster, just off the heart of Kenmore Square at 645 Beacon Street (617-859-8828, fax 617-859-8827). The hotel is rich in baseball and Red Sox history; Babe Ruth stayed there and frequented the bar, and the 1919 Black Sox scandal was reportedly hatched at the Buckminster. Maluken offers a sushi bar, Japanese appetizers ($5–9), lunches ($6–13), dinners ($9–37), and boxed specials ($8–9), as well as American breakfasts ($3–6). There's Karaoke on Monday through Saturday from 9:00 P.M. to 1:00 A.M. if you want to embarrass your friends after a game.

Pizzeria Uno—not your typical pizza joint, located in a stately building at 1 Brookline Avenue (617-262-4911, fax 617-859-7044, www.unos.com) where it crosses Comm Avenue. In addition to the usual deep-dish and thin crust pizza, sandwiches, and appetizers ($7–12), there is a full bar. This is one of the few places that will take advance seating over the phone on game days; it starts to fill up about three hours before the start of a game. Pizzeria Uno does promotions with local radio stations every game night.

Sol Restaurant—a Brazilian buffet at 636 Beacon Street (617-236-8666) that also grills meat, vegetables, and fruit to order and has a variety of homemade desserts. Both lunch and dinner are $5.50/pound, but Red Sox ticketholders get 20% off on game days.

FAST FOOD
Within a few blocks of Fenway you can find a **McDonald's**, **Bruegger's Bagel Bakery**, and **Burrito Max**, as well as a **Baskin Robbins** if you're in the mood for ice cream.

CASH MACHINES
Bank of America and Sovereign Bank both have locations at the corner of Commonwealth Avenue and Brookline Avenue, a few hundred yards from Fenway Park, and there's a Mercantile Bank branch even closer to Fenway on Brookline Avenue. There are also cash machines within the park itself.

OUTSIDE FENWAY PARK
Want roasted peanuts? Sausages? Kielbasa? Hot dogs? Buffalo wings? The various vendors set up on game days (or in some cases, permanently) outside the park can provide all those and more if you want to sit or stand on the curb outside Fenway munching on your food of choice and listening to the program hawkers trying to outshout the cries of "Tickets? Anybody need tickets?" Especially popular are the sausages from the **Best Sausage Co.**, directly across from the park on Yawkey Way.

INSIDE FENWAY PARK

If you don't want to sit in the stands and have bags of peanuts tossed to you by a vendor with a rifle arm or wait for his tireless leather-lunged cohorts to make their way up and down the ballpark with their cargoes of hot dogs, Cracker Jack, cotton candy, cold soda, or ice cream, venture into the concourse inside Fenway and choose from a large array of foods. Legal Seafoods has a stand in Fenway, as do several other chains; if you're in the mood for pizza, hot dogs, or fries, you can get it in the ballpark. Eating and drinking at the ballpark is not cheap, however. Beer drinkers should be aware that the only beers available (ID required; beer sales are cut off partway through the game) are domestic.

Souvenirs

The Souvenir Store (Twins Enterprises)—there is a sort of souvenir store monopoly across from the park, which includes three stores with slightly different specialties (800-336-9299, www.thesouvenirstore.com). For a long time, the stores were owned by the same family, but they are now owned by the Red Sox and have become the official Red Sox Team Store. This is the place to get Red Sox hats in dozens of patterns and colors, t-shirts, customized jerseys, bobblehead dolls, books, or anything else Red Sox-related. One of the three stores specializes in cards and collectibles. About ninety percent of the stores are reserved for Red Sox fan items (you name it, they have it), but there is a small corner with souvenirs for "other teams." You can also order by phone or over the Internet.

Street Vendors—vendors set up outside Fenway sell ballcaps, programs, and other baseball paraphernalia for the Red Sox as well as other teams. The prices are usually cheap, but the quality varies dramatically. If you really want a "Yankees Suck" t-shirt, odds are you can find it on the way to Fenway.

Other Things You Should Know

New England tends to be cool at night even during the summer. Daytime temperatures can be in the eighties and drop down to the fifties in the evening. It's wise to bring a sweater or light jacket if you're going to a night game—you'll be more comfortable in the late innings, and any non-fans with you won't be agitating to leave early.

As in any crowded surrounding, exercise sensible precautions: don't leave your wallet in a back pocket, keep an eye on your children and/or personal belongings, and be alert when using the ATMs on the way to, or inside, Fenway. There is a first aid station within Fenway; park personnel make periodic announcements as to where parents should look for lost children and/or where children finding themselves lost should go for help.

The Minor Leagues

There has been a dramatic resurgance in minor league baseball over the last decade or so. In the 1980s, the minor leagues had seemed to be dying; stripped of power, independence, and much of their personalities by major league baseball, there didn't seem to be much reason to see what was widely billed as an inferior product. What had been forgotton was that the minor leagues offer a very different experience for baseball fans—much closer to the action, more accessible, a chance to feel a personal connection with a local team, and to share the excitement of young players dreaming of glory.

During the strike-torn 1990s, the minor league resurgence gained momentum, as a tremendous audience disenchanted with major league baseball rediscovered its less-jaded cousin. Independent leagues like the Northern League started and thrived, and established minor league teams were able to wrest more freedom from their major league patrons. As a result, in many places minor league baseball today has evolved into a best-of-both-worlds combination: the small-town intimacy and carnival atmosphere of nineteenth-century baseball, combined with twenty-first century stadium amenities and big-city comfort. This is particularly true of the Red Sox, which as a regional franchise has tended to see strong New England-based minor league teams as a critical part of the Red Sox Nation.

The Red Sox minor league system has been reshaped and strengthened significantly over the last decade, both in terms of the quality of its players and in the location and strength of its teams. The longtime top (AAA) minor league team in Pawtucket, Rhode Island has been joined by New England affiliates in Portland, Maine (AA) and Lowell, Massachusetts (A), adding access to some form of the Red Sox experience to many fans who can't easily get to games in Boston, or can't afford the cost of bringing a family to Fenway Park. (Minor league tickets are typically less than $10—and often less than $5—with parking free or cheap.) The Red Sox also field teams in Delaware, South Carolina, and Fort Myers, Florida (which is also the team's spring training home) and sponsor a summer league team in the Dominican Republic.

What follows is a guide to the Red Sox minor league system: which players to watch, how to go about seeing a game, what to look for if you're visiting the various minor league teams or spring training.

Who Are the Red Sox Best Minor League Prospects?

Here are 50 of the players you may see on the Red Sox in the next few years: young players working their way up through the minor league system who have the best chance of playing for the Red Sox—or of being traded for other players. Each player's age as of July 1, 2005, is listed in parentheses, along with how the Red Sox acquired him. A few players who are likely to spend much of the season with the Red Sox or aren't really unknowns anymore (such as Kevin Youkilis and Lenny DiNardo) are listed in The Players chapter.

Why is age so important? The younger a minor leaguer is when he is good enough to play in the big leagues, the better his chances are of having a long career, since he will have longer to develop his skills before his reflexes begin to decline. Most players peak around age 27, and are out of the major leagues by their early thirties (so a player who doesn't make the majors until he's 27, like Lou Merloni, is likely to have a short career). Every once in a while a player peaks early and never gets any better (like Wil Cordero, who played briefly for the Sox), or shows a sudden improvement late in his career (like Dwight Evans did for the Red Sox). But most players continue to improve steadily until age 27 or 28 and then slowly decline. Of course, a superstar in decline may still be better than a younger—but less talented—player.

THE HITTERS

Stefan Bailie, first base (25, 4th round pick in 2001)—slugger who struggled in his first three seasons, but was one of the system's most productive hitters in 2004. Bailie hit only five homers in 2002–03, with averages in the .250s, and was hampered by injuries. But he found his power stroke in 2004, hitting .306 with 23 doubles, 11 home runs, and a .383 OBP in 58 games for Sarasota. This earned Bailie a promotion to Portland, where he continued to pile up big numbers (.309, 15 doubles, 8 homers, .364 OBP in 37 games). He's still considered a sleeper, but another good year could turn Bailie into a viable prospect.

Ian Bladergroen, first base (22; traded from Mets in 2005)—lefty power hitter who was one of the Mets' top prospects before being traded to Boston for first baseman Doug Mientkiewicz. "The Blade" was New York's 44th-round draft pick in 2002, out of obscure Lamar Community College in Colorado. The Mets let him play one more year of college ball (where he hit 32 homers), and signed him as a "draft and follow" in 2003. Bladergroen made his pro debut for the Brooklyn Cyclones (managed by ex-Red Sox catcher Roger LaFrançois) that summer, batting .285 with 6 home runs and 36 RBI in 74 games, while using his 6-foot–5 frame effectively in the field. Promoted to low-A Capital City in 2004, Bladergroen rivaled Boston prospect Brandon Moss as the South Atlantic League's top hitter: .342, .397 OBP, .595 slugging, 13 homers, and 74 RBI in only

72 games. Unfortunately, Bladergroen missed the second half of the season with torn ligaments in his wrist. (He's expected to recover fully.) Though scouts think Bladergroen needs to become more selective at the plate, they also feel that he has a chance to be a steady big league first baseman, and have compared him to a young John Olerud.

Alberto Concepcion, catcher-third base (24, 21st round pick in 2002)—versatile player who could become a valuable big league backup. Concepcion had a great career at USC, and was a finalist for the Johnny Bench Award (for best collegiate catcher) in 2002. After signing with Boston, Concepcion hit only .225 for Lowell—but had a solid .354 OBP, with 39 RBI in 56 games. After an awful 2003 season in Sarasota (.218), Concepcion rebounded last year to hit .281 with a .364 OBP, while splitting time between catcher and third base. Reports on his defense vary, but his ability to play several positions is impressive. Concepcion played four games for Portland late in 2004, and he's expected to be their main catcher this season.

Chris Durbin, outfield (23, 10th round pick in 2003)—solid all-around player who doesn't get much attention, but could be a sleeper. Durbin was a star center fielder for Baylor University, where fellow Red Sox prospect David Murphy played right field (they were also teammates of Kelly Shoppach in 2001). Boston drafted Murphy in the 1st round and envisioned him as a center fielder, so Durbin moved to right. He began his career in Augusta, where he hit just .229 in 29 games. But he improved in 2004, batting .279 for Sarasota, with a .344 OBP, 32 doubles, and 7 homers. Compared by scouts to Darren Bragg, Durbin projects to be a backup outfielder in the majors.

Jesus Garcia, catcher (19, free agent in 2003)—Hard-hitting catcher who was MVP of Boston's Venezuelan Summer League Team. Little is known about Garcia beyond his age and numbers, but both are impressive. The teenager hit .329 with a .401 OBP, a .519 slugging percentage, 9 home runs, and 41 RBI, and only struck out 19 times in 216 at-bats. He's also said to have a good arm. The quality of the VSL is suspect, but Garcia's stats are certainly encouraging. He'll have a chance to prove himself in a U.S.-based short-season league this year.

Mickey Hall, outfield (20, 2nd round pick in 2003)—one of the best athletes in the system, and a player with lots of potential—provided he learns how to hit breaking pitches. Although Theo Epstein and his scouts favor the "Moneyball" approach of drafting collegians, they made an exception for Hall, a high school star who planned to attend Georgia Tech. Boston loved Hall's sweet lefty swing, speed, and defense, and they gave him a sizable bonus. He began his career at the rookie level, batting only .227, though he drew 19 walks in 21 games. Hall spent his first full season in Augusta, where he had mixed success. On the downside, he hit only .242 and struck out 134 times in 118 games. But he also belted 13 homers, drew 58 walks, and stole 13 bases. For a 19-year-old in a pitcher-friendly league, Hall held his own. The Red Sox will be patient with the young outfielder, hoping he'll continue to refine his skills and make more consistent contact.

Christian Lara, shortstop (20, free agent in 2002)—slick-fielding speedster whose high on-base percentages have caught the front office's eye. Born in Venezuela, the switch-hitting Lara made his pro debut in the Dominican Summer League in 2003, batting .273 with a .365 OBP, 24 steals, and 52 runs in 65 games. He began 2004 in rookie-level Fort Myers, but was clearly too advanced for that league (.433 average, .493 OBP, 8 steals). Not only that, but Boston had another fine shortstop prospect at Fort Myers (Luis Soto). So Lara was promoted to Lowell, where his average dropped to .277. But he made up for it with an outstanding .404 OBP, plus 10 more steals. *Baseball America* ranked Lara as the ninth best prospect in both of his leagues, and he appears to have a bright future (either with the Red Sox or as trade bait, considering the team's glut of shortstop prospects).

Brandon Moss, outfield (21, 8th round pick in 2002)—the organization's most improved player and best hitter. Moss, drafted as a high school shortstop, didn't show much in his first two seasons. He played second base in rookie ball in 2002, batting .204 with a .295 OBP. The Red Sox shifted the Moss to right field in 2003, but he continued to struggle, posting a .237 average and .290 OBP at Lowell, though he led the team with 7 home runs. Flying under the radar of minor league mavens last spring, the lefty swinger made Augusta's roster, got off to a great start, and never cooled off. He wound up being voted MVP of the South Atlantic League, hitting .339 with 13 homers and 101 RBI in 110 games. Moss had a .402 OBP, .515 slugging percentage, and 19 steals. The Red Sox promoted him to Sarasota for the final month, and Moss was up to the challenge. In 23 games, he batted an ungodly .422 with a .462 OBP and .542 SLG. Despite his incredible stats, solid defense, and "Dirt Dog" intensity, most scouts don't see Moss as a star. Instead, he's often compared to Darin Erstad and Paul O'Neill. If Moss can match those players' success, not to mention their World Series rings, the Red Sox should be very satisfied.

Willy Mota, outfield (19, free agent in 2003)—rifle-armed, toolsy player who's impressed scouts more than statisticians so far. Mota hit only .237 in the Dominican Summer League in 2003, with a poor .312 OBP and embarrassing .292 slugging percentage, though he stole 22 bases in only 62 games. He spent 2004 in rookie-level Fort Myers, and while his numbers improved (.295 average, .328 OBP, .457 SLG), they were hardly eye-popping. But opposing managers raved about Mota's athleticism, power potential, and throwing arm. *Baseball America* ranked Mota as the Gulf Coast League's nineteenth best prospect, marking him as a player to watch.

David Murphy, outfield (23, 1st round pick in 2003)—the first—and most disappointing—draft choice of the Theo Epstein Era. Following the formula of Billy Beane's A's, Epstein wanted to replenish a weak farm system by selecting college players who'd quickly advance. Murphy, an All-American right fielder at Baylor, looked like a sure thing: a lefty line-drive hitter who drew walks, had power potential, ran well, and played good defense. The Red Sox converted Murphy to center field and sent him to Lowell. In 21 games, he hit .346 with an incredible .453 OBP. Not wasting any time, Boston promoted Murphy to Sarasota, but he didn't do much there (.242, 1 homer in 45 games, .329 OBP). Murphy returned to Sarasota in 2004, got off to a slow start, and missed two months with a foot injury. A late streak salvaged his batting average (.261), but his other stats were weak (.323 OBP, .346 SLG, 4 homers). Yet as disappointing as Murphy's been, it's too early to give up on him. The Red Sox still think he'll improve his offense and become a solid all-around center fielder.

Dustin Pedroia, shortstop-second base (22, 2nd round pick in 2004)—college superstar who has thrived as a pro despite limited tools. Pedroia, a .383 lifetime hitter at Arizona State University, was a 2004 finalist for the Golden Spikes Award (the Heisman Trophy of college baseball). In 2003, he was voted NCAA Defensive Player of the Year. But because Pedroia's only 5-foot–8 and lacks power, blazing speed, and a strong arm, some teams doubted his potential. The sabremetrically savvy Red Sox focused on his results more than his skills, and may have gotten the steal of the 2004 draft. Pedroia batted .357 for Augusta and Sarasota, with 19 extra base hits, 19 walks, and only 7 strikeouts in 157 at bats. Amazingly, he didn't make a single error in 42 games. (Most minor league parks have rough infields and bad lighting, which inflate error totals.) After the season, the Red Sox sent him to the prospect-laden Arizona Fall League, where he continued to hit and field well. With Edgar Renteria and Hanley Ramirez ahead of him at shortstop, Pedroia's future is probably at second base, a position scouts think he's better suited for. No matter where he plays, Pedroia is the type of guy any team would love to have—an ideal number–2 hitter and sure-handed fielder with tremendous leadership skills. He's most often compared to ex-Red Sox prospect David Eckstein, but could turn out to be much better.

Kenny Perez, shortstop-second base (23, 6th round pick in 2000)—sleeper who's been overshadowed by Boston's other shortstop prospects, but projects to be a decent utility player. The switch-hitter struggled at the plate in his first few seasons, batting around .250 with no power. Perez improved to .278 at Sarasota in 2003, and hit .280 in Portland last year. While his OBPs are too low (.319 and .323), Perez has begun to drive the ball, resulting in more doubles and a higher slugging percentage. He has decent speed and is solid defensively. Perez moved to second late last year to make room for top prospect Hanley Ramirez, and has also been learning how to play third base.

Hanley Ramirez, shortstop (21, free agent in 2000)—the top prospect in the organization, and the most eagerly anticipated young Red Sox player since Nomar Garciaparra. Ramirez began his career in the Dominican Summer League, batting .345 in 2001. He was a switch-hitter then, but the Red Sox loved his righty stroke and told him to bat exclusively from that side. Moving to Fort Myers in 2002, Ramirez hit .341 with a .402 OBP, .555 slugging percentage, 6 homers, and 8 steals in 45 games. While he made 20 errors, observers raved about his range and arm, and *Baseball America* named him the Gulf Coast League's best prospect. Amazingly, they also ranked him #1 in the NY-Penn League, where he hit .371 in 22 games at Lowell (.402 OBP, .536 SLG, 19 RBI, 4 steals, 7 errors). But the hype took a toll, and the teenage phenom was sent home from instructional league after an altercation with a staff member. The following spring, while playing for Augusta, Ramirez was suspended for making an obscene gesture at a fan. His play on the field suffered, too: .275 average, .327 OBP, .403 SLG, with 8 home runs and 36 errors in 111 games, though he stole 36 bases. Determined to turn his career around, Ramirez showed up to camp in 2004 with a new attitude. He began the year in Sarasota, where he hit .310, stole 12 bases, and improved his error rate (17 in 62 games). A wrist injury sapped his power (only one homer), but it healed in time for a promotion to Portland. Ramirez was a revelation in AA: .310, .512 slugging, 5 homers, 12 steals, and only 3 errors in 32 games. After the season, he joined Licey of the Dominican Winter League, which features many major leaguers, and ranked among the leaders in home runs, RBI, and runs. When the Red Sox signed All Star shortstop Edgar Renteria to a four-year deal, it led to speculation that they'll trade Ramirez for a front-line starting pitcher—or convert him to second base, third base, or center field (since Mark Bellhorn, Bill Mueller, and Johnny Damon could all leave as free agents after 2005).

Kelly Shoppach, catcher (25, 2nd round pick in 2001)—one of the better catching prospects in baseball, but his stock fell after a disappointing 2004 season. Shoppach was a star at Baylor University, where he won the 2001 Johnny Bench Award as the NCAA's best catcher. Known more for his defense and batting eye than for his hitting as a collegian, Shoppach began his pro career in the tough Florida State League in 2002. His hitting was a very pleasant surprise: .271, 35 doubles, 10 homers, 59 walks, .369 OBP. Shoppach had shoulder surgery after the season, but recovered in time to play 90 games for Portland in 2003. He improved his average to .282, with 30 doubles, 12 homers, a .488 SLG, and a .353 OBP. Minor league watchers compared Shoppach to Jason Varitek, who had a similar combination of skills and leadership. Since Varitek's contract would expire after 2004, many observers thought the Red Sox might let him go and hand Shoppach the starting job. But his average dipped to .233 at Pawtucket, and while his power continued to rise (22 home runs and 64 RBI in 399 at bats), so did his strikeouts (138). Additionally, some of Pawtucket's pitchers criticized his game-calling skills. Scouts don't think Shoppach's ready for the majors yet, and suddenly his future doesn't look as bright as it did a year ago. But catchers (like Varitek) often take longer than other players to develop, and Boston remains cautiously optimistic that Shoppach will do well in the majors.

Luis Soto, shortstop (19, free agent in 2003)—raw but talented switch-hitter who made a big splash in his first season. The Dominican-born Soto signed with the Red Sox on the same day they opened a new baseball academy in his homeland. Soto bypassed the Dominican Summer League and began his career in Fort Myers. Though his stats were mediocre (.261, 5 home runs, .289 OBP, .470 slugging percentage), scouts raved about his power potential, speed, arm, and work ethic. *Baseball America* named Soto the top prospect in the Gulf Coast League, saying he could eventually hit 30 homers a year. With that kind of power and prospects like Ramirez, Pedroia, and Lara ahead of him on the depth chart, Soto could eventually be shifted to third base.

Chad Spann, third base (21, 5th round pick in 2002)—promising line-drive hitter whose 2004 season was ruined by injuries. Like Moss, Spann was drafted as a shortstop out of a Georgia high school, shifted to an easier position, and had a surprise breakout season in Augusta. After a .222 debut in rookie ball, Spann won Augusta's third base job in 2003—and proceeded to hit .312. Though Spann's other numbers were so-so (5 homers, 40 walks, 9 steals), his season was a big success. Not many teens can hit .312 in the South Atlantic League, which favors pitchers (teammate Hanley Ramirez, who was the same age, hit only .275). Managers also voted him the league's best defensive third baseman. The Red Sox had high hopes for Spann last year, and he moved up to Sarasota. But knee surgery limited him to 61 games, and he only batted .248 with 4 homers and a .286 OBP. Spann remains Boston's best third base prospect, though he needs to be more patient at the plate and improve his power.

Adam Stern, outfield (25; Rule 5 Draft pick in 2004)—lefty-hitting speedster who's coming off a great year in AA, was taken from the Braves in the Rule 5 Draft, and hopes to make the Red Sox as a backup. The 25-year-old Stern was born in London, Ontario, attended the University of Nebraska, and was Atlanta's third-round draft pick in 2001. He stole 40 bases in low-A ball in 2002, but hit only .253 with a .298 on-base percentage, and missed most of 2003 with a serious hamstring injury. But he took a major step forward last season, hitting .322 for Greenville, with a .378 OBP, .480 slugging percentage, 8 homers, and 27 steals, while making only two errors in center field. He also spent a couple of weeks in Athens, playing for Canada's Olympic team. Stern could stand to draw more walks, but he doesn't strike out much—and is almost impossible to double up (only 7 GIDPs in 1,035 pro at-bats). He has an excellent defensive reputation, and if his offensive improvement is real, he could have a solid future. For now, the Red Sox hope Stern can be a cheaper, younger version of Dave Roberts, serving mainly as a pinch-runner and defensive sub.

Chris Turner, outfield (21, 15th round pick in 2003)—gifted athlete who hasn't translated his tools into results yet. Turner would have gone higher in the 2003 draft, but was regarded as "unsignable." Boston took a chance on him, offered a big bonus, and landed what they thought was a big prize. However, while scouts are impressed with his strong arm and power potential, Turner's stats have been mediocre. He hit .254 with only one homer and a .338 OBP in Lowell in 2003. Last season, Turner played 61 games for three farm teams, hitting .241 with 9 home runs and 39 RBI, but he struck out 74 times while drawing only 7 walks.

Matt VanDerBosch, outfield (23, 9th round pick in 2004)—speedy, lefty-hitting leadoff man who had an impressive pro debut. VanDerBosch was originally an infielder (like his cousin, 1979 AL Rookie of the Year John Castino), but converted to center field at Oral Roberts. He hit .271 at Lowell with a fine .376 OBP. In 60 games, VanDerBosch scored 52 runs and stole 28 bases in 29 attempts. He's also a good defensive outfielder with a strong arm. Like his heroes, Brett Butler and Lenny Dykstra, VanDerBosch is an undersized overachiever, and he'll have to keep proving the skeptics wrong as he climbs the ladder.

Jeremy West, first base (23, 7th round pick in 2003)—one of the best hitting prospects in the system, despite limited athleticism and shaky defense. West was a catcher at Arizona State University, but the Red Sox didn't think he could play the position at higher levels, so they converted him to first base. He was Lowell's MVP in 2003, hitting .280 with a .368 OBP and 43 RBI in 71 games, though he only had 4 homers. West spent 2004 in Sarasota, where he got off to an incredible start before cooling off to .293 with 18 home runs and 68 RBI. Strangely, despite a reputation for being patient, West drew only 37 walks and had a so-so .347 on-base percentage. Many observers compare West to Kevin Millar; they're both righty hitters with similar physiques, good power, and awkward defense. Like all 1B-DH types, West's chances of reaching the majors lie solely in his bat.

Scott White, catcher-third base (21, 3rd round pick in 2002)—good athlete who's trying to revive his career by converting to catcher. Like Moss and Spann, White was drafted out of a Georgia high school. He signed too late to make his pro debut in 2002, but the front office expected him to begin 2003 in Augusta. When Spann beat him out for that job, White was sent to Fort Myers—where he hit like an NL pitcher: .168; only one extra base hit (a double) in 131 at bats. The Red Sox put White on a weight-training program, and he showed lots of improvement with Augusta in 2004. He batted .281 with 34 doubles and 19 stolen bases, though his low on-base percentage (.333) and lack of power (6 homers) remained concerns. As a catcher, White's offense would be more valuable, but the big question is whether he can handle such a demanding position change.

THE PITCHERS

James Albury, RHP (19, free agent in 2003)—Aussie import who might be the most underrated pitching prospect in the organization. The Red Sox have heavily scouted Australia in recent years, and their biggest prize has been Albury, who signed a few days after his seventeenth birthday. He remained in his homeland in 2003, but made his pro debut last summer in rookie ball, going a perfect 5–0 with an outstanding 1.15 ERA. Albury allowed only 26 hits in 39 innings, though his peripheral stats (16 walks, 21 strikeouts) need improvement.

Abe Alvarez, LHP (22, 2nd round pick in 2003)—Boston's most advanced pitching prospect, a control specialist who reached the majors 13 months after being drafted. Amazingly, Alvarez has thrived despite being legally blind in his left eye. (He tilts his cap to shield his eye from the light, though some people mistakenly think he does it as a sign of disrespect.) Not only that, but his fastball only peaks at 85–87 MPH, which is well below average. But the Red Sox focused on Alvarez's positives: a 23–5 record at Long Beach State, impeccable command, an outstanding changeup. Boston sent Alvarez to Lowell in 2003, but kept him on a strict pitch count. While he only pitched 19 innings, his numbers were remarkable: 0.00 ERA, 19 strikeouts, only 11 baserunners allowed. Alvarez was expected to begin 2004 in Sarasota, but a strong spring (including mop-up work in big league exhibition games) landed him a ticket to Portland. Alvarez was consistently good, if not spectacular, going 10–9 with a 3.66 ERA. When the Red Sox needed an emergency starter for a July 22 game against Baltimore, they summoned Alvarez. (He didn't pitch well, even with his teammates affectionately tilting their caps in the dugout.) Alvarez returned to Portland after the start, finishing his solid season, and will begin 2005 as Pawtucket's ace. Most experts don't think Alvarez's stuff is good enough for him to be a star, but they project him as a steady starter, especially if he continues to improve his curveball.

Tim Bauscher, RHP (26, waiver claim in 2004)—hard-throwing sleeper grabbed from the Colorado Rockies last December. The Mariners drafted Bauscher in 2001 (27th round), but released him after the season. He didn't pitch professionally in 2002, but resurfaced in an independent league the following year. Late in 2003, Bauscher hooked up with Milwaukee and joined their low-A affiliate's bullpen. He made their AA rotation last season, but was claimed by Colorado on waivers in June, and finished the season with the Rockies' AA team. Overall, he went 5–14 in 2004, though he had a respectable 4.01 ERA and very good peripheral stats (138 strikeouts and 40 walks in 130 innings pitched). In his brief professional career, Bauscher has struck out 10.3 batters per 9 innings, and his fastball has been clocked at 97 MPH. He's probably more of a project than a prospect, but Bauscher's velocity and versatility may make him a pitcher to watch.

Randy Beam, LHP (23, 18th round pick in 2004)—reliever who had a tremendous pro debut, yet hasn't earned much respect from scouts. Despite a great college career at Florida Atlantic, Beam was ignored in the 2003 draft and a late-round afterthought last year. Boston sent Beam to Lowell, where he had two saves and a 1.62 ERA. With Augusta needing bullpen help, Beam got promoted—and became the best closer in the South Atlantic League. He saved 10 games, didn't allow an earned run in 23⅔ innings, gave up only 10 hits and 4 walks, and fanned 27 batters. Beam lacks great stuff, but he pounds the strike zone and gets ahead of hitters. He's not expected to remain a closer, but could be a lefty setup man.

Adam Blackley, LHP (20, free agent in 2003)—Australian who's put up good numbers, but isn't regarded as highly as Albury. Blackley, whose brother Travis is a Seattle prospect, had an 0.73 ERA in a cameo at Fort Myers in 2003. He started 12 games for Augusta last year, going 4–3 with a 3.39 ERA. But Blackley's below-average fastball and doughy physique leave most scouts skeptical.

Kyle Bono, RHP (22, 8th round pick in 2004)—hard-thrower who might be groomed as a future closer. Bono was expected to return to the University of Central Florida, where he had been an All-American, but the Red Sox lured him to the pros with a $432,000 signing bonus (a record for 8th round picks). He had a 3.00 ERA in 12 innings with Lowell, allowing only 9 baserunners and striking out 17 batters.

Juan Cedeño, LHP (21, free agent in 2001)—hard thrower who's coming off a disappointing season, but was still added to the 40-man roster. The Dominican native emerged as a prospect with Augusta in 2003 (7–9, 3.02, 87 strikeouts and only 87 hits allowed in 101⅓ innings). Other teams frequently asked about Cedeño in trade talks, but Theo Epstein didn't want to give up a young lefty with a mid–90s fastball and sharp curve. However, Cedeño was far less impressive at Sarasota last season. Though he improved his control and had a 7–6 record, his ERA jumped to 4.64, his strikeout rate fell, and he gave up 145 hits in 120⅓ innings. Due to his youth and raw ability, Cedeño remains a prospect, but he needs to get back on track in 2005.

Manny Delcarmen, RHP (23, 2nd round pick in 2000)—Bostonian who regained his blazing fastball after Tommy John surgery, and hopes to reclaim his status as a top prospect. Delcarmen, whose family emigrated from the Dominican Republic, attended West Roxbury High School and participated in the Red Sox RBI (Revitalizing Baseball in the Inner City) Program. Despite his local roots, it took Delcarmen a long time to sign with Boston, and his pro debut was pushed back to 2001. He immediately established himself as a blue chipper, dominating the Gulf Coast League. His numbers were less spectacular at Augusta in 2002, but he still struck out a batter per inning. The Red Sox loved Delcarmen's 95–97 MPH heater, top-notch curve, and competitive nature, and felt he just needed some time to learn more about the art of pitching. He appeared to be taking that next step in early 2003 (3.13 ERA at Sarasota)—until he blew out his elbow. The injury sidelined Delcarmen until mid–2004; he returned to Sarasota, where his results were mixed (3–6, 4.68, but 76 strikeouts and only 20 walks in 73 innings). After the season, the Red Sox sent him to the Arizona Fall League, where he pitched well and lit up the radar gun. Delcarmen was added to the 40-man roster, and there's been talk of the Red Sox converting him to the bullpen, where he might become a dominant setup man, and could reach the majors more quickly

Andrew Dobies, LHP (22, 3rd round pick in 2004)—crafty pitcher whose outstanding changeup and good control make up for a mediocre fastball. Dobies was drafted out of the University of Virginia and made his pro debut at Lowell. Boston likes to put their young hurlers on strict pitch counts in their first season, and Dobies was no exception. Even though he started 14 games, he only pitched 26⅔ innings. While that sample is tiny, Dobies's statistics were very promising: 2.03 ERA, 17 hits, 8 walks, 36 strikeouts.

Kason Gabbard, LHP (23, 29th round pick in 2000)—big starter who's shown flashes of brilliance, but has battled recurring elbow injuries. Gabbard signed a six-figure bonus as a draft-and-follow in 2001, but only totaled 59 innings pitched in his first three seasons. Healthy in 2004, he pitched very well for Sarasota (3–2, 2.70), though he got lit up after a promotion to Portland (3–6, 6.28). Gabbard doesn't throw very hard, but mixes his pitches well. If he can stay healthy and improve his control, Gabbard could be a sleeper.

Gary Galvez, RHP (21, free agent in 2003)—Cuban refugee who had a rough season, but still has lots of potential. Galvez, the ace of Cuba's national junior team, was the subject of a bidding war between the Yankees and Red Sox in early 2003. Though Boston won that battle (giving Galvez a $1million bonus), the signing was mocked in baseball circles. After all, the Yankees had just outbid Boston for Cuban star Jose Contreras, leading to Larry Lucchino's infamous "Evil Empire" comment (and allegedly causing Theo Epstein to smash a chair). Galvez was seen as a minor consolation prize, and making matters worse, a visa problem prevented him from entering the U.S. He pitched in the Dominican Summer League instead, and did very well (6–3, 1.64). Galvez made his belated American debut in Augusta last year, but didn't do well (7–10, 5.14, though he had 102 strikeouts and only 36 walks in 140 innings).

Jarrett Gardner, RHP (24, 19th round pick in 2003)—the Rodney Dangerfield of Red Sox prospects, a man who gets no respect despite great stats. Gardner was drafted from the University of Arkansas and had an interesting debut with Lowell in 2003. Though he had a 4.20 ERA and low strikeout rate, he only walked two batters in 60 innings. He made Augusta's rotation last year and was superb: 13–5, 2.51, 11 walks and 92 strikeouts in 136 innings. Gardner also won an emergency start for Portland. But as well as Gardner's performed, he hasn't appeared on many prospect lists, due to his age (a bit old for his level) and lack of dominating stuff. Scouts don't think he'll fool hitters at higher levels. Then again, they said that about ex-Red Sox prospect Justin Duchscherer (traded for Doug Mirabelli in 2001), who turned into a valuable pitcher for Oakland.

Tommy Hottovy, LHP (23, 4th round pick in 2004)—curveball specialist who dominated New York-Penn League hitters in his brief pro debut. If any pitcher typifies Theo Epstein's new draft philosophy, it's Hottovy. He was a successful college pitcher (Wichita State) despite an underwhelming fastball, throws strikes, and is a converted reliever (less wear and tear on his arm). Early returns on Hottovy are very promising. Limited to a strict pitch count at Lowell, he only threw 30⅓ innings in 14 starts, but was nearly unhittable: 0.89 ERA, 39 strike-outs, only 4 walks. His manager, former Red Sox infielder Luis Alicea, raved about Hottovy's command and maturity, and thinks he could be on a fast track to the majors.

Kyle Jackson, RHP (22, 32nd round pick in 2001)—New Hampshire native who's battled injuries and ineffectiveness, but has good stuff and remains a sleeper. Jackson signed in 2002 as a draft-and-follow, but was only healthy enough to pitch one game for Fort Myers. He returned there in 2003, was one of the Gulf Coast League's best pitchers (5–2, 1.85), and earned a promotion to Lowell (0.93 ERA in two starts). Jackson was expected to anchor Augusta's rotation last year, but he endured a nightmarish season (3–13, 4.64). However, a closer look reveals some encouraging signs: 130 strikeouts and only 36 walks in 142 innings.

Jimmy James, RHP (20, free agent in 2002)—talented Venezuelan who's shown promise in his first two seasons. James spent 2003 in the Dominican Summer League, where he went 3–2 with a 2.83 ERA. He was even better at Fort Myers in 2004 (5–1, 2.33), thanks in part to improved control. The Red Sox want James to improve his strikeout rate, but overall they're pleased with his progress.

Jon Lester, LHP (21, 2nd round pick in 2002)—inconsistent but often dominant starter who's regarded as one of Boston's best prospects. Lester was drafted out of high school a year before Theo Epstein became GM. Ironically, Epstein believes high school pitchers are too risky to draft early, yet Lester has thrived.

The Red Sox lured him away from Arizona State with a big bonus, but only let him pitch one inning in 2002 (at Fort Myers). Lester spent 2003 at Augusta, where he went 6–9, 3.65. Many teams covet Lester, whose velocity (92–96 MPH) is rare for a lefty. In fact, had the A-Rod trade gone through, Lester would have gone to Texas with Manny Ramirez. Sometimes the best trades are the ones that aren't made—not just because Manny outshined A-Rod in October, but also because Lester's value continued to rise. While he was a modest 7–6 in Sarasota last year, with a 4.28 ERA, his peripheral stats were mouth-watering: 90 innings, 82 hits, 37 walks, 97 strikeouts. (The inning total was low because of shoulder soreness, which wasn't regarded as serious.) He also excels at keeping the ball in the yard: only 9 homers in 198 innings as a pro. Lester seems like ideal trade bait, but could be a major part of Boston's rotation if he sticks around.

Anastacio Martinez, RHP (26, free agent in 1997)—Dominican reliever who's had a strange career, and is running out of time to stick in the majors. Martinez began as a starter, but didn't accomplish much in his first three seasons. In 2001 he had a breakthrough at Sarasota (9–12, 3.35) and vaulted up the prospect rankings. But 2002 was a disaster for Martinez, who got bombed in AA (5–12, 5.31)—and was found to be two years older than the age on his birth certificate. He went from a prospect to a nonentity, and was unceremoniously moved to the bullpen in 2003. The change worked wonders; Martinez saved 14 games for Portland, with a tidy 2.25 ERA. In July, he and Brandon Lyon were traded to Pittsburgh for Scott Sauerbeck. Martinez pitched three games for the Pirates' AA team (managed by current Sox coach Dale Sveum), but the deal was reworked and expanded due to Lyon's elbow injury. Martinez returned to the Boston system, moved up to Pawtucket, and had a 1.93 ERA as a setup man. He had the same role last year (3.74 ERA), and was called up twice when injuries hit Boston's pen. Martinez won two games for the Red Sox, but was wild and ineffective (8.44 ERA). He remains on the 40-man roster, but his future appears to be that of a "AAAA" player, biding time in Pawtucket between brief big league call-ups.

Luis Mendoza, RHP (21, free agent in 2000)—Mexican who was added to the 40-man roster, yet remains one of the team's most mysterious prospects. Mendoza made a name for himself at age 17, when he went 6–0 with a 2.27 ERA for Boston's affiliate in the Venezuelan Summer League. He came to the U.S. in 2002 and had an uneventful season in rookie ball, but posted an impressive 2.26 ERA in 13 appearances for Augusta the following year. The Red Sox placed him in Sarasota last season, and on the surface he did well: 8–7, 3.74. But Mendoza only struck out 51 batters in 137 innings, a dangerously low rate, and his walk total (54) was also less than ideal. What's even more confounding is the fact that Mendoza isn't a soft-tosser. He has a fastball that's been clocked at 94 MPH and a solid changeup. Though Mendoza hasn't made batters swing and miss, he's gotten outs, and the Red Sox must believe that he'll improve his peripheral stats.

Cla Meredith, RHP (22, 6th round pick in 2004)—sidearming reliever who had an excellent pro debut. Meredith, a co-closer at Virginia Commonwealth, remained in that role after signing with Boston. He reported to Augusta, where he pitched 15⅔ scoreless innings and notched 6 saves. A promotion to Sarasota ensued, and Meredith was up to the task: 12 saves, 2.20 ERA. Overall, he had 34 strikeouts and only 6 walks in 31⅔ innings. Meredith may not throw hard enough to be a big league closer, but could help Boston's pen one day.

Jon Papelbon, RHP (24, 4th round pick in 2003)—converted closer with great stuff who's become a legitimate prospect. Papelbon has a classic Roger Clemens/Curt Schilling build (6'4", 230 pounds), has been clocked as high as 98 MPH, and is developing an effective slider and changeup. Boston gambled that the Mississippi State reliever was suited to starting, and he showed positive signs in Lowell in 2003 (36 strikeouts, 9 walks in 32⅔ innings, despite an ugly 6.34 ERA). But nobody expected Papelbon to have such a brilliant season in Sarasota: 12–7, 2.64, 130 innings, 97 hits, 43 walks, 153 strikeouts. He got even better as the season progressed: 1.25 ERA in the last two months. *Baseball America* named Papelbon the team's third best prospect, saying he could be a frontline starter, and at worst should be a solid "innings eater" in the back of the rotation.

Dave Pauley, RHP (22, acquired in 2004 trade)—former San Diego prospect who was sent to Boston in the Dave Roberts trade. Pauley was the Padres' eighth round pick in 2001. He had a breakout season in 2002, going 6–1 with a 2.83 ERA in short-A ball, and followed that with an impressive year in low-A (7–7, 3.29). *Baseball America* named Pauley San Diego's seventh-best prospect after 2003, but he was somewhat disappointing in high-A Lake Elsinore last season (7–12, 4.17 ERA, with mediocre peripheral numbers). Known for an outstanding curveball, Pauley also has a pretty good fastball, though his changeup is said to need some work. He's an interesting sleeper who's been very young for his leagues, has already tasted some success as a pro, and certainly has the potential to be a major league starter one day.

Mike Rozier, LHP (19, 12th round pick in 2004)—big flamethrower who got a huge bonus to sign with Boston, but has yet to make his pro debut. The high school football star (just like another Mike Rozier, the 1983 Heisman Trophy winner) was headed to UNC until Boston offered $1.575 million (a record for players chosen after the tenth round). Had he not been deemed "unsignable," Rozier would surely have been a much higher pick, and the Red Sox consider him a first-round value. The 6-foot–5, 210-pound lefty is said to have electric stuff, and the organization can't wait to see if he'll justify the hype.

Anibal Sanchez, RHP (21, free agent in 2001)—Venezuelan phenom who went from virtual unknown to exciting prospect. Sanchez pitched in the Venezuelan Summer League in 2001–02, but missed all of 2003 with elbow problems. He made his U.S. debut in Lowell last summer and mystified hitters with his mid–90s fastball, tremendous curve, and rapidly improving changeup. Poor run support limited Sanchez to a 3–4 record, but he led the NY-Penn League in ERA (1.76) and strikeouts (101), while allowing only 43 hits and 29 walks in 76 innings. *Baseball America* ranked him as the league's #2 prospect. While Sanchez's smallish size and injury history raise some red flags, his skills, smarts, and maturity could make him a frontline starter in the majors one day. Sanchez was added to the 40-man roster last November, in order to avoid the risk of losing him in the Rule 5 Draft. Boston can only option him to the minors for the next three years, so they'll accelerate his development to have him ready for the majors by 2008.

Ryan Schroyer, RHP (23, 5th round pick in 2004)— another college closer who's being converted into a starter. Schroyer began his college career at Arizona State, but later transferred to San Diego State (coached by future Hall of Famer Tony Gwynn). He struggled at times in his new role, going 4–2 with a 4.44 ERA at Lowell, allowing 6 homers and 23 walks in 48⅔ innings. On the plus side, Schroyer struck out 57 batters, and the Red Sox like his competitiveness and ability to throw four pitches (fastball, slider, curve, circle changeup).

Chris Smith, RHP (24, 4th round pick in 2002)—promising starter whose career has been stalled by two major injuries. The California native had a 4.13 ERA in 56⅔ innings for Lowell in 2002, but the Red Sox loved his 50–14 strikeout-to-walk ratio. Smith was slated to pitch for Augusta or Sarasota in 2003, but broke his arm in a dune buggy accident before the season. Doctors inserted two steel plates and 12 screws into his arm, and he managed to pitch 13 games before the season ended. A strong spring landed him in Portland last year, and he was one of the team's top pitchers in the first half (5–2, 3.75). But he went on the DL in July with a partial tear in his labrum, and missed the rest of the season. Full labrum tears are career-threatening, though partial ones can be treatable. Smith's status for 2005 is iffy, but Boston added him to the 40-man roster, so they're optimistic that he'll return.

R.J. Swindle, LHP (21, 14th round pick in 2004)—the most extreme member of Boston's "Moneyball" crop of pitchers. If Beam, Dobies, Gardner, and Hottovy can be classified as "great results/limited stuff," then how would one describe Swindle? His fastball barely tops 80 MPH, but his 65 MPH changeups and sharp sliders drive hitters crazy. Swindle, a collegiate star at Charleston Southern, had a magnificent pro debut for Lowell: 5–1, 1.94, 56 strikeouts and only 4 walks in 51 innings pitched. If he keeps pitching like that, Swindle will be the steal of the 2004 draft, but he'll have to continually prove himself on each rung of the minor league ladder.

Jose Vaquedano, RHP (23, 35th round pick in 2002)—tall, lanky starter who was one of the system's top pitchers in 2004, yet hasn't gotten much attention. Vaquedano was born in Honduras (a country that's never had a major leaguer), but attended college in Texas. He struggled at Lowell in 2002, but returned the following season with better results (7–4, 3.30, 70 strikeouts and only 15 walks in 73⅔ innings). Vaquedano began 2004 in Augusta, where his dominant performance (4–2, 1.88) earned him a promotion to Sarasota. While his ERA rose to 3.95, he had a 5–1 record. Combined, Vaquedano allowed only 124 hits and 33 walks in 135 innings, while fanning 126 batters. Like many Red Sox prospects, he gets by more on smarts than velocity, though his sinking fastball and changeup are effective. Surprisingly, Vaquedano wasn't added to the 40-man roster, even though Boston had nine vacancies, and this could indicate that the organization isn't that high on him.

Beau Vaughan, RHP (24, 3rd round pick in 2003)—jumbo-sized hurler who's pitched well, but has been overshadowed by other draftees. Vaughan played for three different colleges before landing at Arizona State (where his teammates included Pedroia, Schroyer, and West). He had a 2.32 ERA for Lowell in 2003, with 30 strikeouts in 31 innings. He failed to make any full-season teams the following spring, but was eventually added to Augusta's roster. Vaughan went 7–3 with a 3.30 ERA; in 71 innings, he struck out 73 hitters and only allowed 58 hits. He also made one fill-in start in AA Portland. While scouts like Vaughan's repertoire (solid fastball, good change, excellent curve), they worry about his control and conditioning. He's also older than most of the prospects he's faced, and that's tempered experts' enthusiasm. Still, Vaughan is talented and competitive, and could have a bright future if he works hard and stays healthy.

Jon Wilson, RHP (22, 9th round pick in 2003)—yet another control pitcher with impressive stats in the lower minors. Wilson, drafted from a Colorado junior college, has spent most of the 2003–04 seasons in rookie ball, with a 2.23 ERA and only 21 walks in 84⅔ innings, though his strikeout ratio was only fair.

Charlie Zink, RHP (25, free agent in 2001)—knuckleballer who's trying to rebound from a horrible season. Zink's parents were Charles Manson's wardens at Folsom State Prison. He attended Savannah College of Art and Design, where his coach was the legendary Luis Tiant. Despite a mid–90s fastball, Zink was passed up in the MLB draft and signed with an independent team. But Tiant recommended him to the Red Sox, and Zink relieved for Augusta and Sarasota in 2002, posting a 1.41 ERA. Still, the front office wasn't impressed—until they learned that he fooled around with a knuckler on the side. Perhaps looking for a successor to Tim Wakefield, the Red Sox had Zink become a full-time knuckleballer in 2003, and he pitched well (7–9, 3.90 in Sarasota; 3–2, 3.43 in Portland, including two near no-hitters). The statistically inclined *Baseball Prospectus* even named him Boston's best prospect. But Zink never got untracked in 2004, and his season went from bad (1–8, 5.79 in Portland) to worse (0–2, 5.65 after a demotion to Sarasota). He walked 81 batters and struck out only 53 in 107⅔ innings. However, the Red Sox haven't given up on Zink, since it usually takes knuckleballers years to master the elusive pitch. (After all, Wakefield went 5–15 with a 5.84 ERA in the minors in 1994. A year later, he was a Cy Young candidate with Boston.)

I became peripherally interested in the Red Sox during the '67 World Series, just listening to my high school classmates talking about the series. The following summer I was working a boring, lonely job on Sundays pumping gas at a station owned by my father. The only real entertainment available was a radio, and as I was not really a fan of any music that played on the stations, the only other choices were the three AM stations that carried baseball. The choices were the Red Sox, the Expos, and the Yankees. Because of my interest in the '67 series, I started listening to the Sox. Kind of scary to think how it might have gone, eh? A sign of my initial ignorance was me telling someone that Yaz had just hit a grand slam home run with the bases loaded. Anyway, I was soon hooked, and two years later being a Sox fan was one reason I went to college in Boston. That was followed for several years by twice-a-summer overnight ballgame trips with several family members, which are among my most cherished memories.

—Don Violette

Visiting the Minor Leagues

If you're near one of the Red Sox minor league affiliates, or if you'd like to travel to watch some of the Sox players of the future in action, minor league games are a terrific value. Most games are inexpensive, with good seats and parking easy to come by. (Some minor league cities, like Pawtucket, are a hot ticket, so you'll want to call ahead to check availability.)

PAWTUCKET, RHODE ISLAND

The Pawtucket Red Sox are the highest level team in the Red Sox farm system. This AAA team plays in McCoy Stadium in Pawtucket, Rhode Island, and competes in the Northern Division of the International League. Located just 40 miles down I-95 from Fenway Park, the Pawtucket Red Sox enjoy a close and fruitful relationship with their parent club. The PawSox have served as Boston's Triple-A affiliate since 1973, and during that time the PawSox have become one of the most successful franchises in minor league baseball. The club finished the 2004 season with an all-time record attendance of 679,021. The 2004 seaon was highlighted by the nationally televised Triple-A All-Star Game at McCoy Stadium.

It wasn't always like that for the PawSox, a franchise that nearly folded prior to 1977. But that year Ben Mondor, a Rhode Island businessman, acquired the club and kept it in Pawtucket. That initial season, the PawSox drew 70,000 fans total. Since that time, more than 7 million have passed through the gates at McCoy, one of the more remarkable turnarounds in baseball history.

The PawSox are no longer just a Rhode Island team, either. PawSox faithful come from Massachusetts, Connecticut, New Hampshire, Maine and even points further to see future Boston stars. Over the last 30 years, just about every Red Sox star has spent time at McCoy Stadium (either on their way up to the majors or while rehabilitating from injuries). From current Red Sox like Trot Nixon, Tim Wakefield, Bronson Arroyo, and Kevin Youkilis to all-time greats Jim Rice, Wade Boggs, Roger Clemens, and Mo Vaughn, the PawSox have helped develop the top talent in Boston's organization. In 2004, PawSox fans were pleased to see Mark Bellhorn, Ellis Burks, Bill Mueller, and Trot Nixon along with other Red Sox rehabbers make appearances at McCoy.

Fans come to see the players, but they also come to visit historic McCoy Stadium. The PawSox park has been around since 1942 and has been home to the team since the inaugural season of 1973. The park was updated in 1999 in an award-winning renovation that expanded the capacity of McCoy to 10,031 and added brand new concourses, seating areas, concession and clubhouse facilities, and a grass outfield berm. But McCoy also still has the feel of a great old park. The stadium is perhaps best known as the home of the longest game in professional baseball history—a 33-inning contest in 1981 in which the PawSox defeated Cal Ripken and the Rochester Red Wings 3–2.

A game in Pawtucket is a must for Red Sox fans. But call ahead for tickets— most summertime games are sold out by game time. You can contact the team by phone at (401) 724-7300 and by e-mail at info@pawsox.com. Tickets can be purchased over the phone or through the team's website (www.pawsox.com). Ticket prices have remained virtually the same since 1977. Box seats are $9 and general admission tickets are $6 (adults) and $4 (senior or kids 12 and under).

PORTLAND, MAINE

The Portland Sea Dogs are Boston's Eastern League AA affiliate playing at Hadlock Field (capacity 6,975) in Portland, Maine. The Sea Dogs joined the Red Sox family in 2003 when Boston moved their Double-A affiliate from Trenton, New Jersey. The Sea Dogs had previously been affiliated with the Florida Marlins for nine years.

When you walk into Hadlock Field a green 37-foot-high wall complete with Coke Bottle and Citgo sign in left field immediately grabs your attention. The wall, a likeness of Fenway's Green Monster, was built in 2003 when the Red Sox affiliated with the Sea Dogs. Nicknamed the Maine Monster, the wall stands a mere 315 feet from home plate.

While Hadlock has many touches of Red Sox Nation, it is complemented by many touches of local small-town seaside flavor. A lighthouse rises above the center field fence after every Sea Dogs home run and victory. A fan favorite in between inning promotion is the "lobster toss," featuring two contestants working together to catch rubber lobsters in real lobster traps.

Current Red Sox stars Matt Mantei, Kevin Millar, Edgar Renteria, and Kevin Youkilis all came through Portland on their way to the big leagues. In the Sea

Directions to McCoy Stadium.

From the North: I-95 South to Exit 29 in Rhode Island (Route 1/Route 114-Downtown Pawtucket). Proceed straight off of the exit. Turn right onto Broadway (one way) after second stop sign. Continue straight through set of traffic lights and bear left at the fork in the road. Proceed over bridge (crossing over Route 95) and merge right at the next fork. Turn left at the Stop Sign onto Walcott Street. Proceed straight on Walcott to set of traffic lights. At the lights turn right onto South Bend Street. At next set of lights, turn left onto Division Street and follow signs for Game Day Parking.

From the South: I-95 North to Exit 27, 28, or 29 and follow directional signs to McCoy Stadium. All exits lead to available Game Day Parking Lots.

From the West (Worcester, MA): Route 146 South to route 295 North to I-95 South - then follow directions from the north.

From the East (Fall River, MA) : Route 195 West to I-95 North - then follow directions from the south.

Directions to Hadlock Field

From the North: Take I–295 South to exit 6A. Merge onto Forest Ave., follow Forest to the intersection with Park Avenue. Merge right onto Park Avenue. The ballpark will be about 1 mile down on the right.

From the South: Take I–295 North to exit 5A, and merge onto Congress Street. At the first set of lights take a left onto St John Street. At the next set of lights, merge right onto Park Avenue. The ballpark will be immediately on the left.

From the West: Follow either Route 302 West or Route 25 West into Portland. Route 25 West will turn into Brighton Avenue, which will intersect with Park Avenue. Take a right onto Park Avenue. Route 302 West will turn into Forest Avenue and will intersect with Park Avenue. Again, take a right onto Park Avenue.

Dogs' 11-year history more than 100 players have gone on to play in the major leagues. Other notables include World Series MVPs Livan Hernandez and Josh Beckett, as well as Charles Johnson, Mark Kotsay, and Luis Castillo.

Order tickets early, as most games from June through the end of the season sell out. Last season the Sea Dogs drew a franchise record 434,684 fans to the ballpark. Tickets range in price from $3–8, and can be ordered through the team website (www.seadogs.com) or by phone (207-879-9500 or 800-936-3647). The ballpark is located right off I-295 in Portland.

WILMINGTON, DELAWARE

The Wilmington Blue Rocks are a new addition to the Red Sox minor league system. This Advanced-A club competes in the Northern Division of the Carolina League. The Blue Rocks play their 70 home games at Frawley Stadium, located 30 miles south of Philadelphia off of I-95.

Baseball returned to Wilmington in 1993, when the franchise formerly known as the Peninsula Pilots was relocated there from Hampton, Virginia. The stadium, built by the construction company of Blue Rocks President Matt Minker, was named Legends Stadium (later changed to Judy Johnson Field at Daniel S. Frawley Stadium). The stadium originally seated 5,500 fans, but was expanded in 2001 and now holds 6,532. Frawley Stadium is located at the Wilmington Riverfront. The Riverfront district features a plethora of restaurants and outlet shopping stores, to enhance a visit before or after any Blue Rocks game.

The Blue Rocks have enjoyed great on-field and off-field success, obtaining the best winning percentage among all full season minor league clubs since 1993, with a record of 943–728 (.564). The Rocks have also led the league in attendance since 1998. The Blue Rocks have captured four Carolina League championships (1994, 1996, 1998, and 1999) and eight Northern Division titles in 12 years. A total of 75 former Blue Rocks have made it to the major league level.

In 2005, the Wilmington Blue Rocks will be welcoming their four-millionth

Directions to Frawley Stadium

From the South: I-95 North to Exit 6, Maryland Avenue. Right onto Maryland Avenue, then another right on Read Street. Right onto South Madison Street.

Alternate Route: I-95 North to Exit 6, Maryland Ave. Left onto Maryland Avenue, then another left onto Beech Street (second light). Right onto South Madison Street.

From the North: I-95 South to Exit 6. Go through 3 lights, make a left at the fourth light onto Martin Luther King Boulevard. Go through 2 lights. Make a right at the third light onto South Madison Street.

Alternate Route: I-95 South to Exit 6. Follow Jackson Street to Maryland Avenue. Turn right onto Maryland Avenue, then left onto Beech Street. Right onto South Madison Street.

(*Alternate routes are suggested for weekend games.*)

Directions to LeLacheur Park

From 495 and Route 3, take the Lowell Connector. Follow the Connector to exit 5B, Thorndike Street. Follow Thorndike Street onto Dutton Street. Go past City Hall and take a left on to Father Morrissette Street. At second set of lights take a right onto Aiken Street. LeLacheur Park will be on your left.

fan to the ballpark. At the conclusion of the 2004 season, the Blue Rocks finished their twelfth season with a total attendance mark of 3,956,675.

The Wilmington Blue Rocks pride themselves on offering fun, affordable family entertainment. Most nights offer giveaway items for fans as they walk through the gates. Patrons are entertained during inning breaks with in-game contests such as the Dizzy Bat Race and Mascot Mania. When the Blue Rocks score a run, minor league baseball's most famous vegetable "Mr. Celery" emerges onto the field to celebrate behind home plate. Rocky Bluewinkle, the team's official mascot, is out greeting fans throughout the game and signing autographs for the younger fans.

The Blue Rocks offer ticket prices of $9 for box/upper box seats, $8 for reserved seats, and $5 for general admission seats. The Wilmington Blue Rocks can be reached by phone at (302) 888-BLUE, or visit the team web site at www.bluerocks.com.

LOWELL, MASSACHUSETTS

The Lowell Spinners are a short-season class A team, playing in the New York-Penn League. The Spinners derive their name from the major activity in the formation of Lowell, a Merrimack River Valley mill city. (The city also has a textile museum, celebrating that heritage.) Because it is less than 30 miles from Boston, Lowell has been a good starting point for pitchers rehabilitating from injuries. In the last two years both Bret Saberhagen and Ramon Martinez have started games in Lowell. There are not yet any Lowell Spinners alumni Kevin Youkilis, Abe Alvarez, and Anastacio Martinez played for the Red Sox in 2004.

The Spinners began play in 1996 at Alumni Field. In 1998 they moved to Edward A. LeLacheur Park (capacity 5,000), on the shore of the Merrimack River. Although a small city (and not a particularly attractive one), LeLacheur Park is a beautiful ballpark, sitting on a lovely spot on the river.

Ticket prices range from $3.50 to $7.50 (call 978-459-2255 or visit the team's website at www.lowellspinners.com). As with most minor league facilities, Lowell is very fan friendly, with a variety of entertainment going on between innings (some featuring the Canaligator, the Spinners' mascot). For any baseball fans in the area, a night at LeLacheur Park would be an evening well spent.

COLUMBIA, SOUTH CAROLINA

This is a new affiliate for the Red Sox, who switched from the Augusta GreenJackets after the 2004 season. The Capital City Bombers, a former Mets affiliate, play in the South Atlantic League (A) at Capital City Stadium in Columbia, South Carolina. The Bombers have been in Columbia since 1983; the team changed its name in 1992 from the Columbia Mets to the Cap City Bombers to honor the Doolittle Raiders, who initiated the first American attack on Japan following the bombing of Pearl Harbor. The Raiders conducted their training for the mission in Columbia and their B–25 bomber inspired the team's new name.

The Bombers play from April to mid-September. Tickets are $4–6 ($2 for kids, seniors, and armed forces members). Contact the team at 803-254-HITS for ticket and team information or visit the team website at www.bomberball.com.

The team may be moving for the 2005 season, so call to confirm location before making travel plans.

FORT MYERS, FLORIDA

The Gulf Coast Red Sox, a short-season rookie ball team, play 70 games (35 home) from mid June through late August. They play in City of Palms Park, the same stadium where major league spring training is held. The facility is minutes away from the Edison-Ford Museum in Ft. Myers (on the Winter Estates of Henry Ford and Thomas Edison).

The roster is made up of first-year professional players or young Latin players being introduced to U.S. culture. (Most players are under age 20). It's also not unusual to see a major league player on a rehab stint. The games are during the day but don't let the heat scare you off; there is plenty of shade and seating, and admission is free. Call the team at 239-334-4799 for more information.

DOMINICAN REPUBLIC

The Dominican Summer League is a short season rookie league, playing 72 games from June through August. The Boston Red Sox entry in the league plays in the San Pedro de Macoris division. You can find out more information by visiting the league's website, www.dominicansummerleague.com (there is an English-language version, but it's quirkily translated) or calling 809-532-3619.

Visiting Spring Training

Since 1993 the Red Sox have held their annual spring training in the lush green surroundings of Fort Myers, Florida, on the southwest coast of the Florida peninsula. As part of the 20-team Grapefruit League, the Sox play an exhibition schedule of 32 games throughout the month of March (not including B-games and intrasquad games). The small season is usually kicked off with an exhibition contest against the Boston College Eagles. About 70 players show up for camp every year, hoping to impress team management with their skills and perhaps win a spot on the big league club (even though much of the roster is already determined before spring training starts). Nevertheless, the opportunity to be noticed is valued by an eager young player, since over the course of a long season a injuries or subpar performances by roster players will leave openings for additional players to be called up. (About 70 percent of major league players are injured at some point during the season.)

Red Sox spring training home games are played at City of Palms Park, at 2201 Edison Avenue in Fort Myers. Because the Minnesota Twins also hold their spring training in Fort Myers (on the other side of the city), they are scheduled as a frequent opponent for the Sox, to form a friendly series that the locals have dubbed "The Mayor's Cup." Spring training games are a popular attraction not only for local residents but also for fans from afar who want to see their Sox in a warm-weather environment without forking over the high price of admission to a major league park. Florida in March also serves as a warm, scenic, and life-affirming vacation spot for New Englanders who are tired of another arduous winter. In February the park also hosts the annual Red Sox Fantasy Camp, in which fans can fulfill their baseball dreams by receiving tips and coaching from former major leaguers. For more information on the Fantasy Camp call (888) 901-PLAY.

Tickets for games at City of Palms Park can be ordered starting in early December via phone, fax, or on the web (www.redsox.com or (617) 482-4SOX), or walk-up starting in the middle of January. Prices for the 2005 spring training season are $24 for box seats and $21 for reserved grandstand seating, with prices ranging down to $10 for standing room. The team has also added new home plate and dugout box seats, ranging from $36–44.

I had been married a couple years and my wife and I were expecting our first (and it turns out, only) child at any moment. At the beginning of World Series week, Paula let me know that she felt the baby would come before the end of the week. I earned very few points by telling her that if she HAD to have the baby THIS week, then it had better be on Friday as that was the off day between game 5 and 6 so that was the only time that would work for me. Now for all of you spouses-to-be who are mentioned in the subtitle of this book "... or to marry one," this is a good pointer for you. Make sure that whatever it is that you need to do, that it doesn't interfere with a Red Sox World Series appearance.

Somehow, Paula cooperated. Although married to a die-hard Sox fan, she really isn't what one might call a "fan" of the game. But just to make me happy I suppose, she took one for the team, enduring 36 hours of labor until our beautiful baby girl was born on October 24, on the day between games 5 and 6!

So, feeling on top of the world, I was ready the next night to see my second miracle in two days. With the Sox up three games to two, I just knew that Game 6 was going to be the one that finally made the Sox the Champs. And as you all know, it sure looked that way all night long. Even when Roger left the game, with a 3–2 lead, it still looked possible. I sat there stunned as Calvin Schiraldi came in from the pen. "NO," I thought, "anyone but him." But what was worse was that when the Sox took the 5–3 lead into the bottom of the tenth, Calvin was still in there! Then came a defining moment in my daughter's life. With two down in the bottom of the tenth, I did something that would forever place Katie in our "club." I called my wife at the hospital. "Honey, are you watching the game? No? Well put it on. Is Katie with you? She is? Well sit her up and face her toward the TV. She's about to see something I have waited nearly 20 years to see ... " Perhaps that had something to do with it, maybe I interrupted somebody's karma, maybe the Big Guy was watching from up there somewhere and said, "Not so fast, pal." I don't know, but I then watched in horror as Schiraldi choked, let up three hits and a run, and was replaced by Bob Stanley. I was starting to lose faith, but I still knew this had to be the year, didn't it? Then the wild pitch allowing the tying run happened, and my stomach flip-flopped. I knew we were doomed. The "hit" by Wilson was just an insulting way to make it happen, it wasn't Buck's fault. It was destiny. And the worst part of it was that I had doomed Katie to my fate. She was destined to see the Sox fail, but worse, she was destined to think that it somehow mattered. Never again will she be able to see the Sox make the World Series and be ambivalent about it. In future years, when they got there, or even got close, it is going to make a difference whether they win or lose to her. Oops!

—Carl Bérubé

The Red Sox Fan's Guide to Surviving Yankee Stadium

It happens every year—common sense to the contrary, Red Sox fans insist on going to New York–Boston games at Yankee Stadium, thus setting themselves up for several hours of vitriol and abuse. One can, perhaps, chalk this up to the masochism inherent in being a Red Sox fan, but still, you gotta wonder why anyone would subject themselves to this. . . .

Of course, some have no choice. For example, there are Red Sox fans who live in the New York Metropolitan Area, and view games at the Stadium as the only chance to see their team—especially now that the unbalanced schedule provides upwards of ten games a year between the two in the House that Ruth Built.

And there is the value inherent in seeing a game between these two teams regardless of venue. Many baseball fans are willing to put up with a little abuse—okay, a *lot* of abuse—to see a game like the Pedro Martinez–Roger Clemens pitchers' duel in May 2000 that Martinez won 2–0, or the two consecutive 9–8 Yankees wins in July 2002 that ended with Grady Little overmanaging his way to Ugueth Urbina walking Jorge Posada with the bases loaded to lose the final game, or the 2003 American League Championship Series, or pretty much any game the two teams played in 2004, from the Jason Varitek–Alex Rodriguez brawl game to the dramatic ALCS. Yankees–Red Sox matchups are incredibly exciting ballgames for any fan, regardless of affiliation.

So, as a public service to those fans who will attempt to run the gauntlet, herewith is a guide to surviving Yankee Stadium as a Red Sox fan.

1. DON'T SHOW UP.

This is the easiest and safest way to go. Why stick your head in the lion's mouth?

2. DON'T DISPLAY YOUR PLUMAGE.

Wearing clothing or paraphenalia that identify you as a Red Sox fan—or even as being in any way associated with the state of Massachusetts—is the functional equivalent of painting a bullseye on your chest. All those around you will immediately assume you to be a Red Sox fan and act accordingly, whether it's something as obvious as a Red Sox cap or as innocuous as an Amherst sweatshirt.

3. TAKE IT LIKE A FAN.

If you must disregard the first two rules, know that you will be subjected to verbal abuse. Epithets will be tossed your way with great assiduity and regularity throughout all nine innings. Major League Baseball's desire to keep things civil at the ballpark have resulted in attempts to punish those who cry "[fill in team] sucks!" but that won't always stop people, so expect lots of "Boston sucks!" leavened with bursts of "Manny sucks!" "Ortiz sucks!" "Schilling sucks!" and so on.

The absolute worst thing you can do is respond to this, as it is akin to pouring gas on a fire. Any attempts to reply in kind will just result in folks ganging up on you. Remember, you're in enemy territory, and you're seriously outnumbered. Plus, as the entire world learned in the last few years, New Yorkers tend to support each other when bashed, so crying, "Yankees suck!" in response to one beer-drinking yahoo may result in fifteen people (some of them even sober) screaming obscenities in your ear.

By the same token, if you sit there and take it, even revel in it, the Yankees fans will view that with respect and probably not harass you directly (unless something happens on-field to warrant a comment, like a Yankees home run or a Boston pitcher being removed or a Red Sox fielder letting a ball go between his legs).

4. FOR GOD'S SAKE, DON'T SIT IN THE BLEACHERS.

As a denizen of the right field bleachers, I can't emphasize strongly enough that, if you do show up, *don't sit in the bleachers*. Elsewhere in the Stadium you might luck out and be in an area where people are only paying partial attention to the game, or the fans are a bit less intense, or you've got families having an outing that are more interested in having a good time than abusing their fellow travelers.

The bleachers, however, especially the right field bleachers in Sections 37, 39, and 41 (right field corner), are all hardcore fans who are focused on nothing but

I was born in Brooklyn, NY, to a father who was a rabid Yankees fan despite growing up a few blocks from Ebbets Field. Even as an infant, there are photos of me wearing baby Yankees hats and outfits, and by the time I was four, he started taking me to games. The Yankees played at Shea Stadium in 1974–75, and I kept thinking it was weird to see them play in the Mets' park. Due to his talent and TV commercials, I had become interested in Tom Seaver, and kept begging my father to take me to a Mets game. He hated the Mets but relented, and I saw Seaver lose a brilliantly pitched 2–0 game to San Diego in 1975. Much to my father's dismay, I became a stone-cold Mets fan.

Meanwhile, I had also become a baseball card collector. The Topps cards back then had little banners to signify All Stars, and I used to put those cards in a special place—thinking they were more important than the others. I immediately noticed how many Red Sox players were All Stars: Fisk, Lynn, Rice, and this guy with a long, weird name. I asked my father about him, and was told that everyone called him "Yaz." I loved that nickname and the stories of his defense and Triple Crown, and Yaz began to rival Seaver as my favorite player. The Sox of 1977 had weak pitching, but the lineup was loaded, and while the Mets were slipping, these guys were hitting homers at a near-record pace. Their ballpark was more interesting than dumpy old Shea, they had more history, and I learned that they were much bigger rivals with the Yankees.

So from May 1977 until June 15, my loyalties were divided. I was still more of a Mets fan, but began following the Red Sox day-by-day. Then, on that fateful day, the Mets traded my two favorite players: Dave Kingman (at age seven, I didn't understand that he only had one skill) and Tom Seaver. Had it only been Kingman, I would've been able to handle it. But Seaver's departure was too much to take, and from that moment on, the Mets were on the back burner. Needless to say, it was an incredible thrill to see Seaver, even as elderly six-inning pitcher, play for Boston in 1986. I still follow the Mets and go to many of their games, but it hasn't been the same. As for the Sox, I managed to survive Bucky Dent (naively thinking, "We'll get 'em next year")—and all the taunts from Yankee fans. If you can make it through that, and 1986, you're a fan for life.

Living in New York City, I don't get to see many Sox games. I used to call "Sports Phone" for in-game updates, go to the library for day-old *Boston Globes*, and manipulate my radio to get WTIC-AM in Hartford (its signal faded every half hour or so). Today, with more cable coverage and the Internet, it's easier to follow the team. There are a few thousand Sox fans in NYC, including my younger brother, and while many people around here think we're crazy, the effort we put in just makes our loyalty stronger. And going to Fenway is like a religious pilgrimage for us. I first went in 1978, seeing Boston beat Chicago, and have been fortunate enough to watch 15–20 games there since.

—Dave Bismo

the game. There is no discussion going on that is not related to baseball in general and the game on the field in particular. For example, using one's cell phone at any time when the game is in progress will result in half a dozen people shouting, "Get off the phone!" at you in as loud a volume as possible.

If showing up at the Stadium is like painting a bullseye on your chest, going to the bleachers is like shooting yourself in the foot after painting the bullseye. The bleacher fans are particularly merciless. (They will also toss dozens of abusive verbal salvos at whoever plays right field for the Red Sox, so if the right fielder is your favorite player, be prepared.) Stadium Security knows better than to even attempt to enforce the theoretical ban on "Boston sucks!" chants in the bleachers, so that one will be flying fast and furious.

(It should also be noted that they don't serve beer in the bleachers. Of course, considering that the choices elsewhere in the Stadium are assorted watery tasteless brews, there's an argument to be made that they don't serve beer anywhere else in the Stadium, either. . . .)

5. AFTER THE GAME, KEEP YOUR HEAD DOWN AND MOVE OUT QUIETLY.

If the Yankees win, you can expect the sojourn from your seat to the street to include a lengthy serenade of "Boston sucks!" If the Red Sox win, that serenade is less likely. The temptation to act cocky and superior—especially given the results of the 2004 postseason—will be great, but resisting it would be wise. One of the best taunts—"1918!"—has been forevermore removed from Yankees fans' lexicon, and that is apt to make them twitchy and quick to anger. So don't push it.

DIRECTIONS AND GUIDELINES.

If it is at all possible to take public transportation to the Stadium, do it. You *can* get there by car via the Major Deegan Expressway (Interstate 87) to the 161st Street/Yankee Stadium exit (about halfway between the George Washington Bridge and Triboro Bridge exits), but if you do so, try to get there as early as possible (at least two hours before gametime). The closer to gametime, the worse the traffic and the more difficult it is to park in the area lots. Traffic after the game is also nightmarish.

Your best bet is the 4, B, or D train to the 161st Street/Yankee Stadium stop. (The 4 goes to Grand Central Station; the B and D stop near Penn Station.) If you're coming from north of New York City, a good way to avoid traffic is to take the Deegan to the 233rd Street exit (the first exit in the Bronx) and go straight on Jerome Avenue. There's a long stretch of Jerome between East 233rd and the Woodlawn stop on the 4 train where the Woodlawn Cemetery is on the left and Van Cortland Park is on the right, and there are *tons* of places to park. You can then walk to the 4 and take it to the Stadium.

In this post-9/11 world, security at the Stadium has been upgraded. Opaque bags larger than a purse or fannypack are not allowed (there are places to check your bag on River Avenue, alongside the bars and souvenir stands under the elevated subway), and some gate guards will do frisks and/or pat-downs (though that is inconsistently applied). It is possible that this will be relaxed for the 2005 season, but be warned that security is *always* higher at Red Sox games.

Further information, including ticket prices, more standard directions, schedules, and season ticket availability, can be found on the Web at www.yankees.com.

—Keith R.A. DeCandido

I was born in Boston. From as far back as I can remember, my father would take my brother and me to Red Sox games. Before I was out of grammar school we moved to California but this didn't stop the tradition. Every year when the Sox came to town to play the Oakland A's, we were there rooting for the Old Towne Team.

I have since moved back to the East Coast but this time to New York City. As you can imagine, being a Red Sox fan in this town can sometimes be tough but it's something I never hide. Each year, when the Sox come to New York, I board the D train wearing my Red Sox jersey and brace for anything. I get lots of stares and the occasional chant, "1918, 1918, . . . " However, mostly I get unspoken smiles of understanding from others going out to the Stadium to root for Boston.

My brother still lives in California but has now decided to make a tradition of coming out to New York to see the Sox play the Yankees. Last year we enjoyed together the May 2000 classic pitching duel between Pedro and Clemens. We were sitting in the second to last row of the upper deck of the stadium. However, this had no bearing on the wonder and magic of sharing with my brother something so steeped in tradition and history.

This year my brother will bring someone else with him when he joins me for the games—his two-year-old son. The tradition continues.

—Lisa Norcia

Questions and Answers

What are leagues, and which one do the Red Sox belong to? Are there big differences between the major leagues? Where do the minor leagues fit into things?

Major League Baseball is divided into the National League (NL) and American League (AL). The National League began play in 1876, and is regarded as baseball's first *major league*. (Some historians consider the National Association, which played from 1871–75, the first major league. Many of its teams and stars joined the National League in 1876.) The Chicago Cubs and Atlanta Braves (originally the Boston Red Stockings, before they changed their name several times and moved to Milwaukee and then Atlanta) are the only original National League teams still in existence. There were three other major leagues in the nineteenth century. The American Association lasted from 1882–91, and played World Series against the National League from 1884–90. (The National League had its top two teams play a form of the World Series from 1892–1900.) The AA is best remembered for allowing two black players, Moses and Welday Walker, to play in 1884— 63 years before Jackie Robinson. Two other major leagues lasted a season apiece: the Union Association (1884) and the Players League (1890). As its name suggests, the latter was formed by players involved in a labor dispute with National League owners, who wanted to limit salaries. Some things never change.

The American League became a major league in 1901. It evolved from the Western League, a high-quality minor league created by Ban Johnson a year earlier. Johnson wanted to compete with the National League, and he moved some teams into bigger cities, while raiding National League rosters for stars like Nap Lajoie, Cy Young, and Jimmy Collins. In the minds of most fans, the American League truly gained major league status in 1903, when the first modern World Series was played—the Boston Americans (soon to be the Red Sox) defeated the Pittsburgh Pirates. The loss so embarrassed the National League that the New York Giants refused to play in the 1904 World Series against Boston, but the Fall

Classic resumed the following year. In 1933, the National League and American League began playing an annual midseason All Star Game, with the best players in each league facing off for bragging rights. (From 1959–62 the leagues played two All Star Games a year, but the experiment was a failure.)

From 1903–52, the National League and American League had the same 16 teams (none of them west of the Mississippi). In 1953, the Boston Braves moved to Milwaukee, and the St. Louis Browns became the Baltimore Orioles in 1954. Later that decade the National League spread to the West Coast, with the Dodgers and Giants leaving New York City for California. In 1961 the American League added two teams, and the National League did the same in 1962. In 1969 both leagues expanded to 12 teams. Instead of having only two of 24 teams make the playoffs, each league split into an Eastern and Western Division, with the winners meeting in a playoff to qualify for the World Series.

The National League and American League played essentially the same game with the same rules from 1901–72, though players from different leagues only faced each other in the World Series and All Star Games. In 1973 the American League added the designated hitter rule (see page 329), changing its style of play dramatically.

The American League expanded to its current 14 teams in 1977, and the National League added two more teams in 1993. In 1994, a season ultimately ruined by a strike, baseball changed its playoff format. Each league went to a three-division setup. The winners of each division made the playoffs, along with a wild card team (the team with the best record of the non-division winners). Another round of playoffs was added, so a team now needed to win three series to become World Champions. Though the 1994 playoffs were wiped out, the system went into effect in 1995, and remains the same today. For example, in 2004, the New York Yankees, Minnesota Twins, and Anaheim Angels won the American League's three divisions. The Red Sox, who had the best record of the league's other teams, made the playoffs as a wild card team. It's not unusual to have a wild card team with a better record than one of the division winners, especially if one division has much stronger teams than the others.

In 1997 baseball made another radical change, incorporating some interleague games into regular season play. Traditionalists worried that interleague play would make the World Series less meaningful, while many others looked forward to new rivalries and the chance to see more star players. The next season, baseball added two more teams. Tampa Bay joined the American League, while Arizona entered the National League. To balance the schedules, the American League's Milwaukee Brewers moved to the National League.

Currently, American League teams are the Los Angeles Angels of Anaheim, Baltimore Orioles, Boston Red Sox, Chicago White Sox, Cleveland Indians, Detroit Tigers, Kansas City Royals, Minnesota Twins, New York Yankees, Oakland Athletics, Seattle Mariners, Tampa Bay Devil Rays, Texas Rangers, and Toronto Blue Jays.

The National League consists of the Arizona Diamondbacks, Atlanta Braves, Chicago Cubs, Cincinnati Reds, Colorado Rockies, Florida Marlins, Houston Astros, Los Angeles Dodgers, Milwaukee Brewers, New York Mets, Philadelphia

Phillies, Pittsburgh Pirates, St. Louis Cardinals, San Diego Padres, San Francisco Giants, and Washington Nationals.

Each major league team has several minor league affiliates in smaller cities throughout the United States and Canada. The minor leagues are as old as the major leagues, and began as a series of independently owned teams. The best players, such as Baltimore's Babe Ruth, were sold to major league teams for big profits. Some major league teams owned minor league teams, but St. Louis's Branch Rickey invented the "farm system" in 1921, when he bought several independent minor league ballclubs—and the rights to many future stars. The goal of the minor league teams gradually changed from winning games to developing young players for the big leagues (though they still want to win).

Today major league teams generally have six minor league affiliates. Most affiliates are independently owned, but subsidized by major league teams, who stock them with players and instructors. The players are owned and controlled by the major league teams, though most will never reach "The Show." Each team has an affiliate in class AAA, which is one step below the majors. Many class AAA players have big league experience, and can be called up to the majors in case of injury. Other players are younger, and are getting seasoning to develop their big league potential. Each team also has a class AA affiliate, and generally two in class A. These leagues aren't as good as AAA, but are important steps in a player's growth. Class A and AA teams are geared more toward development, and have very few ex-big leaguers or older players on their rosters. Big league teams typically have two more affiliates in short-season leagues (some are considered class A; others are called rookie league). These leagues only play from June to August, and consist of players just out of high school or college.

In the last decade, several independent minor leagues have begun play, and some have been quite successful. These leagues have no affiliation with the majors, and their players aren't owned by big league teams. Their players are looking to gain the attention of big league scouts, and some, like Red Sox first baseman Kevin Millar, have been signed by major league organizations.

Why do runners go back to the base if there's a fly ball, but not if there's a ground ball?

Fly balls can hang in the air for a long time, and it would be too easy for runners to score if they could advance as soon as the ball is hit. So baseball rules require runners to go back to the base and "tag up" if fly balls are caught. If the runner doesn't get back to the base the defense can throw the ball to a player at that base, and the runner is out. If the runner tags up he can try to make it to the next base as soon as the ball is caught (if it's dropped, he can advance anyway). With fewer than two outs, runners on second or third often advance a base by tagging up after long fly balls. When a runner scores after tagging up, the batter is credited with a "sacrifice fly" and an RBI. Runners rarely tag up from first base (since it's a short throw from the outfield to second base). On long flies they generally run halfway to second base so that if the ball's caught, they can easily make it back to first. If it's not caught, they have a better chance of scoring.

On ground balls, runners on first base are "forced" to run to second. (If it's first and second, both runners are "forced" to advance, and all three must run if the bases are loaded.) A defensive player with the ball only needs to tag the base before the runner reaches it to get an out, instead of having to tag the runner (just like first basemen on groundouts). So the runner has little choice but to run to the next base, where he might be able to prevent a double play by distracting the fielder (Ty Cobb was notorious for sharpening the metal spikes on his shoes and trying to drive them into the second baseman while sliding, but umpires frown on that today), or be safe if the fielder drops the ball. If a runner is on second or third, and there's no one on first, he doesn't have to run on a grounder. He can safely stay on his base, or try to advance at his own risk, depending on where the ball is hit.

Can you explain the infield fly rule?

The *infield fly rule* only applies with runners on first and second, or with the bases loaded, when there are fewer than two outs. If a batter hits a high pop-up in the infield or short outfield, the umpire can (but doesn't have to, if he doesn't feel it's necessary) call "infield fly." This means that the batter is automatically out, whether or not the fielder catches the ball. (If the ball is foul, the infield fly rule no longer applies, but the batter is out if it's caught.) The runners can advance at their own risk. They can tag up if the ball is caught, or can run if it's dropped—but they can be thrown out. The reason for the rule? Without it, an infielder can purposely drop the pop-up, pick up the ball, and start an easy double play. The runners would be forced to advance, and it would be easy to get force-outs at two bases.

How does pinch hitting work? What are double switches? What are some of the other kinds of in-game strategy I should look for?

Any players who aren't in the lineup—and haven't been used yet in a game—are eligible to *pinch hit*. A pinch hitter bats in place of someone in the lineup. Unlike in football or basketball, a baseball player who is replaced for any reason *can't* come back into the game. In the National League (and the American League before the DH rule), pitchers have to bat. Since they're normally weak hitters, they're often pinch hit for in close games but then can't pitch again. In the modern American League, pinch hitting isn't nearly as common, but it still happens quite a bit in the late innings of tight games. Some regular players aren't good hitters, but start because of their fielding ability. If the team is behind, the manager often pinch hits for those weak hitters. Sometimes, the opposing team brings in a tough righthanded pitcher to get a righty hitter out, and a lefty on the bench is summoned to pinch hit. (There's a rule that says every pitcher brought into a game has to face at least one batter, so teams can't keep switching back and forth until they run out of players.) Pinch hitting is difficult, since a player must enter a game cold, often facing a tough reliever in a crucial situation. Many great players have struggled in the role, while journeymen like Rick Miller and Manny Mota have been among the game's best pinch hitters.

After a player pinch hits, the manager has to change his lineup, unless the game ends during that half-inning. If the pinch hitter plays the same position as the guy he hit for, then he normally stays in the game at that position. If not, the manager puts another bench player in, and the pinch hitter leaves the game.

Sometimes a manager makes a *double-switch*, where a pinch hitter stays in the game, but another change is made simultaneously. Let's say Jason Varitek is catching and batting eighth, while Jay Payton is playing center field and batting leadoff (first). Suppose Johnny Damon pinch hits for Varitek in the bottom of the eighth, and Payton makes the last out that inning. Since Damon is also a center fielder, Terry Francona might leave him in the game, batting in Varitek's old #8 spot. He still needs to bring a catcher in, so Doug Mirabelli enters the game and bats in Payton's leadoff slot. Double-switches are far more common in the National League, where pitchers are often pinch hit for. Some National League managers also make double-switches during a pitching change, to avoid having to waste a pinch hitter the next time the pitcher bats (conserving spare players, since a manager usually has only five or six extra non-pitchers on his roster during a game).

In addition to pinch-hitting, managers can *pinch run* for players who get on base. The same rules as pinch-hitting apply; the pinch runner takes his predecessor's place in the lineup. Teams generally pinch run late in games, when a faster player might be able to steal a key base, or score a run more easily. Managers also pinch run for players who have minor leg injuries that prevent them from running effectively.

Though Red Sox fans haven't seen much of this over the years, the *hit-and-run* is a common baseball strategy. This occurs with a runner on first, or sometimes with runners on first and second. The baserunner will run with the pitch, as he would in a stolen base attempt. But the goal isn't a steal; instead, the batter tries to hit the ball to the area vacated by the fielder covering second base. When a hit-and-run works properly, the runner easily makes it from first base to third base, often leading to a big inning. But if the batter hits a fly ball or line drive, it could turn into an easy double play. The invention of the hit-and-run is often credited to the National League's Baltimore Orioles (1890s), but may have actually been invented by that league's Boston Beaneaters.

A variation of the hit-and-run is the *run-and-hit*. The difference is that the batter has an option. He can swing, like a hit-and-run, or he can let the pitch go, hoping the runner can steal second.

Managers often try to foil hit-and-runs, run-and-hits, and stolen bases by calling *pitchouts*. The catcher signals to the pitcher, who throws way outside, where the batter can't hit the ball. If the runner is on the move, the catcher has an excellent chance of throwing him out. If the runner isn't going, though, the failed pitchout increases the batter's odds of getting on base via a walk (because the pitchout counts as a ball, not a strike).

Another common managerial strategy is the *sacrifice bunt*, used with runners on base and fewer than two outs. The batter squares to the pitcher, puts the bat parallel to home plate, and taps the ball a short distance. The fielders can usually throw the batter out at first base, but a good bunt allows the other runners to advance a base. National League pitchers bunt frequently, since most are weak hitters. In the American League bunts are less frequent, and almost always occur with no outs. Studies have suggested that bunting increases a team's chances of scoring one run (because it moves up the runner) but *decreases* the chances of scoring two or more runs in an inning (because it typically gives up an out). For that reason, bunting is comparatively rare in today's high-scoring game, except in cases when one run may make the difference in the game (such as late in a close game, or in extra innings). In the 1960s, when games were much more low-scoring, there were many more bunts, because every run was more valuable.

A *squeeze bunt* is a sacrifice with a runner on third base. In a *suicide squeeze*, the runner breaks for home (as if he were trying to steal), and the batter tries to bunt the ball. As long as the batter makes contact, the run will almost always score, but if he misses, the runner is a dead duck. If the batter gives away the bunt too early, the pitcher will throw the ball where he can't bunt it, letting the catcher tag the runner. In a *safety squeeze*, the runner doesn't break for the plate until he knows that the batter has made contact with the ball. This makes it harder to score, but also cuts down on the risk.

In certain crucial situations, some managers opt to *intentionally walk* a batter. This normally occurs when first base is empty and a weaker hitter is on deck. The catcher stands up and puts his arm out, and the pitcher lobs four balls far off home plate. The idea is to prevent the tougher hitter from beating you, while hoping the pitcher can get the lesser batter out. It can also be used to set up a potential double play grounder. This strategy often backfires, as the Indians learned in Game 5 of their 1999 playoff series against Boston. Twice in that deciding game the Indians intentionally walked Nomar Garciaparra to face Troy O'Leary—who responded with a three-run homer and a grand slam to help the Red Sox win, 12–8.

What is the designated hitter (DH)?

In American League (as well as minor league and most amateur) games, the designated hitter (or DH) is a player who bats instead of the pitcher. The DH doesn't play the field, and can stay in the game as long as the manager wants, regardless of how many pitching changes are made. The pitcher is not required to bat. (If the DH is forced to move into a defensive position, the pitcher is then required to bat, and the team loses the DH for the rest of the game.) The DH is fixed in whatever lineup spot the manager selects at the start of the game; unlike other positions, the manager can't move the DH around the lineup by using double switches (see page 328). A manager can pinch hit or pinch run for the DH, but the new player then becomes the DH; if the manager wants him to play a position in the field, the DH is lost and the pitcher will have to bat.

The DH Rule was adopted by the American League in 1973 as a response to the low-offense, pitching-dominated baseball of the 1960s and early 1970s. Fearful of losing popularity to football, American League owners decided that this radical change would spice up the game and add scoring. The National League decided against the rule, making the two leagues extremely different. The DH concept had been kicked around for decades, and was rejected at a National League meeting as far back as 1928.

Traditionalists were furious over the new rule, saying it tampered with the offense/defense balance of the game. Others disagreed, pointing out that it was a good way to let stars like Hank Aaron and Orlando Cepeda extend their careers. Early DHs tended to be that sort of player: slow, aging sluggers who could barely play the field. Later, teams were more likely to DH younger players like Jim Rice, or rotate several players in the role. The DH spot is also frequently used to keep an injured player who can still hit but can't field in the lineup, or to rest a player without taking his bat out of the lineup.

The World Series presented a problem, however, since both leagues had different rules. In 1976 they decided to alternate years (DH in even years, no DH in odd years). This gave National League teams an advantage. In even years, they got to add a bat, and in odd years, the American League team had to bench one of their top hitters. In 1986 baseball changed the rule. All games in the American League park use the DH, but pitchers have to hit in National League parks. This compromise is also used in regular season Interleague games. The All Star Game uses a DH, regardless of ballpark, to make substitutions easier.

Explain to me about stats. What do some of the terms people throw around mean? Why can't everybody agree on which stats are important?

"A single death is a tragedy, a million deaths is a statistic." —Joseph Stalin

"When you can measure what you are speaking about, and express it in numbers, you know something about it; but when you cannot measure it, when you cannot express it in numbers, your knowledge is of a meagre and unsatisfactory kind." —Lord Kelvin

"Numbers serve to discipline rhetoric. Without them it is too easy to follow flights of fancy, to ignore the world as it is and to remold it nearer the heart's desire." —Ralph Waldo Emerson

For its entire history, baseball has been a game of numbers. Most newspapers, when listing players, sort them by *batting average*, from highest to lowest, and have done so for decades now. Why is that? Is that the best way to rank players? Is someone hitting .314 necessarily hitting better than someone hitting .278? More importantly, is there any way to know for sure?

These questions are at the center of a debate that has raged for years. How do we measure performance on the baseball diamond? How do we determine which is the best *metric*, the best measurement, for identifying the activities that are valuable in assisting a team to win games? Answering these questions is one of the functions of the Society for American Baseball Research, or SABR. The general term for the mathematical, statistical evaluation of player performance has derived from this acronym, and is called sabremetrics. Bill James, one of the first and best known of the modern sabremetricians, has referred to sabremetrics as "the search for objective knowledge about baseball."

It is easy to demonstrate ways in which the traditional measures have fallen short of the mark when evaluating individual player contributions. Picture the following example:

Player A leads off an inning with a walk. Player B follows with a ground ball. Player A is forced out at second, and Player B is safe at first. Player C then doubles, leaving men on second and third. Finally Player D hits a medium depth fly ball to right, and Player B scores.

So what has happened? By traditional credit assignment metrics, Player A and Player C, the two players who really helped the team, get no statistical credit for the run. Player B gets a run scored and Player D gets an RBI, yet both of them made outs. It is frequently said that baseball is a game without a clock and that's true. But it does have a virtual clock, in the form of outs. Each team starts the game with 27 of them. As a general rule, hitters that don't use up those outs are more productive than hitters that do. Therefore, for the most part, offensive statistics that fail to take into account outs made are flawed at measuring offensive performance.

Following is a brief glossary of the best-known traditional statistics, and of some sabremetric tools for statistical evaluation:

Counting stats: statistics which consist of just raw numbers—hits, home runs, runs batted in, etc. on the offensive side and wins, strikeouts, etc. on the pitching side. They are strictly a measurement of events that happened, and are heavily influenced by playing time. For instance, the Pirates' Jack Wilson got 201 hits in 2004 (third in the league) because he played almost every game, never got hurt (at least not seriously enough to remove him from the lineup), and rarely walked. But he was not a very good hitter that year because he made almost 500 outs in the process of getting those hits. A very productive player who doesn't play as much may not have totals as good as a poor player who plays every day. That doesn't mean totals aren't useful and important—just that you have to look at them in context.

Rate stats: statistics that are adjusted for playing time. For instance, earned run average (ERA) is earned runs per nine innings, and batting average (BA) is hits per at bat.

Traditional statistics:
Batting Average (BA or AVG): Batting average is computed by dividing a player's hits by his total times at bat. Batting average is one of the most commonly used traditional statistics, and one of the most useful. However, there are two weaknesses (from a sabremetric point of view) with batting average as a metric for performance—it fails to distinguish between singles and home runs, and it gives a hitter no credit for drawing walks. Fans therefore have to look at stats like slugging percentage and on-base percentage to tell how impressive a player's batting average really is. To go back to the previous example, Jack Wilson hit .308 in 2004, which would normally be a good average. However, he walked only 26 times in almost 700 plate appearances. Despite his good batting average, he still made outs about two-thirds of the time—which isn't very good. By contrast, Boston's Manny Ramirez had the same batting average, but was on base over 30

times more than Wilson (because he walked a lot more) and made more than 80 fewer outs.

Runs Batted In (RBI): Maybe the most maligned offensive statistic from a sabremetric point of view, RBI are still viewed as important in much of the baseball press. One of the most overused terms in baseball talk is "he's a big RBI man." The problem is that RBI are a heavily team-dependent stat. In other words, someone who plays for a team that puts a lot of players on base ahead of him will drive in a lot of runs, whether he's a good hitter or not. Despite the fact that large sections of the baseball media are contemptuous of this position, this is not a new revelation. In 1954, Branch Rickey wrote that "as a statistic, RBIs were not only misleading but dishonest. They depended on managerial control, a hitter's position in the batting order, park dimensions and the success of his teammates in getting on base ahead of him."

For example, Hideki Matsui drove in 108 runs in 2004 (tenth in the league) while batting fourth in the Yankees lineup. Does this mean he was a good RBI man, as he was called in the papers? Actually, no, it does not. Matsui batted behind Derek Jeter (.352 on-base percentage), Alex Rodriguez (.375 OBP), and Gary Sheffield (eighth in the league with a .393 on-base percentage). He had almost 700 plate appearances with two of the best players in the league in getting on base hitting in front of him. For the number of outs he made, his RBI total is pretty ordinary. Hank Blalock of Texas had a batting average more than 20 points lower than Matsui and played behind hitters who were much worse at getting on base than A-Rod and Sheffield—but Blalock drove in more runs.

Home Runs: A pure counting stat, this may be the least misleading of the traditional stats. A player who hits a lot of home runs is probably a useful player, unless his batting average and on-base percentage are truly awful. In the 1970s and 1980s, when offensive levels were lower, a player who hit 20 homers in a year was a pretty good power hitter. These days, with the surge in offense, 20-homer hitters are more common (although it's still pretty good), but a player who hits 30 or more in a year is definitely a power threat. Home run numbers can still be deceptive, however. Nomar Garciaparra and Doug Mirabelli both hit 9 homers in 2004—comparable numbers on the surface—but Nomar took 348 plate appearances to hit his 9 (so-so home run power), while Mirabelli hit his in only 179 plate appearances (a very good total). Also remember that some parks are easier to hit home runs in—like Coors Field in Colorado, because of the thin air at the park's high altitude. Fenway Park used to be a very good home run hitter's park, until the 1980s, when the 406 Club was built, cutting off wind currents that used to help the ball carry. Now Fenway is a little harder than average to hit home runs in, although it still helps batting average.

Win-Loss Record (usually written as two numbers separated by a dash, i.e., 3–2 for 3 wins and 2 losses): A *win* is awarded to the pitcher who is in the game when his team takes a lead that it holds for the rest of the game. A starting pitcher has to pitch at least 5 innings to get a win, while relievers have no restrictions in how long they have to be in the game. Conversely, the pitcher who lets the other team take a lead that they never give up ends up with a *loss*. A few examples:

> Curt Schilling pitches 7 innings and leaves the game with a 5–1 lead. The Red Sox eventually win the game 5–3. Schilling is given a win.

> Curt Schilling pitches 7 innings and leaves the game with a 2–1 lead. Alan Embree comes in to pitch and gives up the tying run. Mike Timlin comes in with the game still tied and the Red Sox come back to win. Timlin is given a win.

> Bronson Arroyo pitches 6 innings and leaves trailing 5–3. The Red Sox never catch up, and he is given a loss.

> Bronson Arroyo pitches 6 innings and leaves trailing 5–3. The Red Sox catch up to tie the game, but Keith Foulke later gives up the winning run. Foulke is the losing pitcher.

Someone once, back in the murky depths of time, decided to award team victories to pitchers, based on a fairly straightforward set of rules. And, in the days when pitchers always pitched complete games, it made some sense. Unfortunately, this has misled generations of baseball fans on the relative quality of pitchers. There are two components that determine the outcome of a baseball game—the runs a team scores, and the runs a team allows. The pitcher has responsibility for only one of these and it isn't even solely his responsibility, as a bad defensive team can give up runs even if he pitches well. To award wins and losses to pitchers is so silly that no one would dare suggest it now if it hadn't been done for the last 120 years. But it has, and there's no getting away from it.

Why is it so silly? Here's an example. On July 26, 2004, Pedro Martinez pitched 6⅔ innings and gave up 5 runs. In the next game, Curt Schilling pitched 7 innings and gave up 4 runs. Who pitched better? Obviously Schilling did, pitching more innings and allowing fewer runs. He also got a loss, because the Red Sox offense was held to 1 run by the Orioles. Martinez, however, got a win, as the Red Sox had put 12 on the board. Tim Wakefield had a loss in a game in which he gave up 2 runs in 7 innings, and he had a win in a game in which he gave up 7 runs in 5 innings. Possibly the greatest starting pitching performance in major league history ended in a loss, as Harvey Haddix threw 12 perfect innings against the Milwaukee Braves of Joe Adcock and Hank Aaron. Haddix took the loss in the thirteenth inning when his defense fell apart, because the Pirates were shut out all night.

Does that mean won-lost records are meaningless? No, but they have to be taken with a grain of salt. Most of the time a pitcher wins games by pitching well. But sometimes people have great won-lost records even though they didn't pitch particularly well, because they play for great-hitting teams or are just lucky. The opposite can happen as well. In 1987, Nolan Ryan was one of the very best pitchers in baseball, leading the National League in earned run average and strikeouts.

His won-lost record? 8–16. In 2003, Curt Schilling was 8–9 for Arizona, even though his 2.95 ERA was fifth in the league.

Earned Run Average (ERA): For starting pitchers, this is usually the best judge of quality. ERA measures how many runs a pitcher gives up per 9 innings—in other words, how many runs a game will be scored against your team with a certain pitcher in there. If a run scores as a result of a fielding error, it's called an *unearned run* and doesn't count toward a pitcher's ERA. Sometimes this leads to pitchers who play for teams that make a lot of errors looking better than they really are, since they give up a lot of runs that aren't counted against their ERAs. Another way that ERAs can be skewed is in the case of relief pitchers. If a reliever comes into a game with runners on base and allows those runners to score, they are charged to the starter (who originally let them get on base). A reliever who lets in a lot of other people's runs can have a good ERA, while a good starting pitcher can have a bad ERA if he plays for a team with poor relievers, who can't help him out if he starts to tire.

As time has gone on and the game has changed, so has the level at which an ERA is considered good. In the 1960s, offensive levels were very low, and the unadjusted pitching numbers look excellent compared to today. In 1968, the American League average ERA was 2.98, and 5 pitchers had ERAs below 2.00. The AL average in 2004 was 4.63, and only one starting pitcher, Minnesota's Johan Santana, had an ERA under 3.25.

For me, it started in 1986 as a 15-year-old on the other side of the pond, in England. A group of us had become crazy about the NFL, which had just started to be televised over here and had picked up a hardcore following. Taking the tried and trusted policy of sticking with my best friends, I went with the Washington Redskins, Riggins and all, as we started a lifelong passion for football, and American sports in general.

    At about the same time, Channel 4 also started showing some baseball on TV, and although I didn't pay much attention, I did catch the highlights of something called "The World Series" featuring the Boston Red Sox and the New York Mets. My friends had some kind of allegiance with the Red Sox, so I followed suit, I remember there was some kind of logic in there, since we were all fans of the Red-Skins, it seemed perfectly natural to root for the Red-Sox. Thank goodness there was no baseball team in DC that year or else an entire history of allegiance might have taken a different path. I'll be honest, I don't remember much about the World Series that year, or the Red Sox, or even baseball. I remember the name Darryl Strawberry being highlighted a lot, and I remember a lot of focus on a young pitcher called Roger Clemens. I do recall them going over the Buckner error, and while they surely highlighted the plight of Red Sox nation and their wait for satisfaction, it didn't particularly stick out in my memory at that time.

    One of the things that I really remembered were the amazingly complex array of numbers and letters that formed the scoreboards. While it seemed like an almost random, haphazard array of hieroglyphyics, there was always something in there that appealed to the part of me that loved to while away time doodling basic dice and card based games and simulations (this was before such things as PlayStation and the computer, remember!). While some of my friends knew certain aspects of the rules and scoring, it was almost an unspoken wish that one day maybe it would all make sense! I also clearly remember one of the coolest things about the game was the whole "Strike three" thing. I don't know why, it seems pretty silly now, but when talking about the game it seemed to make sense to do the pointing thing and grunt out "Strike threeeeee" in as an American-sounding voice as possible.

—Lee Harris

Saves: Saves were officially sanctioned by Major League Baseball in 1969, to recognize that relievers had become an integral part of the game. (Before the 1960s, most relievers were broken-down starters, and the few really good ones—like Boston's Ellis Kinder in the 1940s—were treated as flukes. You'll see saves from earlier years in stat books, but that's because they were figured out retroactively.) A save is awarded to a pitcher who finishes a close game (at the time he comes in his team has to be leading by three runs or less, or the tying run has to be on deck), assuming he isn't the *pitcher of record*. The pitcher of record is the one who stands to be awarded the win or loss (a pitcher can get a win or a save, but not both in the same game). In other words, a save generally goes to a pitcher who finishes a close victory for another pitcher (though a save can also be awarded to a pitcher who pitches the last three innings in a winning game, regardless of the size of the lead).

The knock on saves is that a pitcher doesn't always have to pitch very well to get one. In the 1960s and 1970s, relievers tended to be used for two or more innings at a time, and the team's best reliever would be used whenever he was most needed, not just at the end of the game. A terrific reliever might have 20 saves in a season. In the 1980s and early 1990s, bullpens began to get much more specialized, with long relievers, middle relievers, and closers. Top relievers, now called *closers*, usually were only used for an inning at a time at the end of a game. This led to huge save numbers for the top relievers, many of which were cheaply earned. In the last few years, the pendulum has swung back again. Because of the high levels of offense, a three-run lead is a much closer game than it was in 1985, so a closer's job is more difficult today. At the same time, the best relief pitchers are occasionally being used earlier in the game now.

Less Traditional Stats:
On-base percentage (OBP): A measure of the total times a runner gets on base, whether via base hit, walk, or being hit by a pitch. A .400 on-base percentage is very good, while anything below around .350 is not. A player with a .330 OBP may still be a useful player if he does other things well, such as hitting for excellent power, but he's going to make a lot of extra outs over the course of the season. A player who walks a lot may have a good on-base percentage even if his batting average is mediocre—and a player with a good batting average who never walks may not be a very good player. In 2004, for example, Red Sox second baseman Mark Bellhorn and Red Sox shortstop Orlando Cabrera each finished the season with a .264 batting average. (Two-thirds of Cabrera's season took place with the Expos.) But Bellhorn reached base safely in 37% of his plate appearances while Cabrera only did so in about 32% of his. This is because Bellhorn walked 81 times on the year, while Cabrera only drew 39 walks, and, consequently, made more outs.

If you only had one statistic available to judge offensive players, in most cases, OBP is the most important one. The single most important thing an offensive player can do is not make an out. Teams score runs by not making outs, and on-base percentage tells you how often a player makes an out and how often he gets on base. There are lots of people, particularly in the media, who talk about teams making "productive" outs, but in general, any out hurts a team's chances of scoring more runs. There are occasional times when a bunt makes sense, and with a tie game in the last of the ninth and a runner on third and less than two outs, a deep fly ball is as good as a hit, since either ends the game. But for the most part, trading sacrifice flies for walks would lead to a lot more runs.

Slugging Percentage (SLG): While batting average tells you what percentage of the time a player got a hit, slugging percentage tells you how much power a hitter has. It is calculated by dividing a hitter's total bases (a single is 1 base, a double is 2, etc.) by the total number of at-bats. A slugging percentage of .500 is good, even in today's high-offense baseball.

In general, on-base percentage is more important than slugging in winning games—even though home run hitters will appear more frequently in the highlight shows. A player who slugs .500 is good. A player who gets on base half the time (an OBP of .500) is outstanding. A guy who slugs .500 for his career is someone like Jim Rice—a near Hall of Famer. Not even Ted Williams, the best player ever at getting on base, got on base at a .500 clip (though he came close). If you could slug .600 for a season you'd have had a really good season. If you could get on base at a .600 level, you'd be Barry Bonds, who's the only one in baseball history to accomplish it. Because each point of OBP is that much rarer than each point of SLG, each point of OBP is more valuable. In heavy-slugging years, like the current era, OBP becomes even more important in comparison—because it's easier to find a slugger who's good at driving in runs than it is to find people who are good at getting on base. And even without home runs, a team that gets a lot of players on base will score a lot of runs; because they aren't making as many outs they will have big innings. In low-scoring times such as the 1960s and the 1900s, the relationship comes pretty close to being even.

OPS: OPS is a statistic created by a simple addition of the two previous statistics, OBP and SLG. So what does OPS stand for? *On-base percentage Plus Slugging*. OPS does not correlate quite as well to runs as some of the more advanced sabremetric measures, but it is very close, and has the advantage of being easy to calculate, particularly as the SLG and OBP numbers have become more widely used. Ranking players by OPS gives you a list that is much closer to actual value than a list of batting averages. One of the problems with OPS, however, is that the relative value of OBP and SLG vary at different times. In a very low-scoring environment, like the early 1960s, OBP is less valuable relative to SLG than it is in a high-scoring era. In low-offense eras, the ability to drive yourself in (slugging) is more important, because your teammates are less likely to do it for you. In a high-offense era, someone's going to get a hit, so just getting on base gives you an excellent chance to score.

Holds: A *hold* is designed as a way to measure the effectiveness of relievers who aren't closers. A middle reliever may come into a game when it is technically a save situation (for instance, when his team is nursing a two-run lead in the sixth inning), but he doesn't really have much chance to get a save. If he pitches well, the game will be turned over to the closer in the ninth inning (and the closer will get the save), but if he pitches poorly, the middle reliever is still charged with a blown save. So a hold is awarded if a reliever enters the game in a save situation and pitches effectively before turning the game over to another pitcher.

All right, I know that there are some stranger statistics out there. What are some of the measurements that the "statheads" use, and where do I find out about them?

Linear weights:A method of evaluating a player's offensive contribution to his team run production, developed by John Thorn and Pete Palmer, the authors of *Total Baseball*.

Equivalent Average: Sabremetric evaluation of a player's offensive contribution, scaled to yield averages that look like batting averages. Includes adjustment for home ballpark effects and league level. Developed by Clay Davenport, EQA reports are available at www.BaseballProspectus.com.

DIPS ERA: DIPS was a concept developed by Voros McCracken (now a Red Sox consultant), and stands for "Defense-Independent Pitching Statistics." While looking at the problem of separating pitching performance from defensive performance, McCracken stumbled upon a fact which has significantly changed the way that many people look at pitching evaluation. He went through the process of separating those events that were independent of the defense (strikeouts, walks, home runs, hit by pitch) from those that the defense was involved with (balls in play, both hits and outs). In doing so, he discovered that once a ball is put in play, the pitcher has very little influence over whether it becomes a hit or an out. This shocked many people, but many have looked at this conclusion since he announced it, and the evidence strongly supports his position. There's very little correlation, year-to-year, on what percentage of balls in play become hits for any given pitcher, and the better pitchers in baseball don't necessarily allow fewer hits on balls in play than worse pitchers do. The reason that certain pitchers are more effective than others are that they allow fewer walks, fewer home runs and strike out more batters.

This revelation led to the development of what McCracken called DIPS. It attempts to separate out the defense-independent, or pitcher-responsible, events from the defense-dependent events. It then normalizes pitcher performance, assuming average defense, to determine what a pitcher's ERA would be if it were solely dependent on his performance. DIPS, while not something that you'll see in the newspapers yet, has a substantial following in the "stathead" community.

SNWL: Support-Neutral Won-Loss record. Developed by Michael Wolverton (and also available at www.BaseballProspectus.com) the idea behind SNWL is to take a bad metric (pitcher won-loss record) and massage it into something useful. Basically, SNWL looks at starting pitchers on a game-by-game basis and awards partial wins and partial losses, based on how often the average team could expect to win or lose with that pitching performance, assuming average run-support. One of the keys to understanding SNWL is the concept that all runs given up are not equal. A pitcher who gives up 20 runs in one game and 0 in the next has got the same ERA as the pitcher who gives up 10 in each. But the first pitcher's team is likely to win that second game, and the second pitcher's team is very likely to be 0–2.

VORP: Value Over Replacement Player—attempts to value players against what a typically available major league replacement would be able to produce. Developed by Keith Woolner, VORP rankings can now be found at www.BaseballProspectus.com.

Pythagorean Winning Percentage: This is one of formulas developed by Bill James, the most famous of the modern sabremetricians. James was looking for the relationship between a team's runs scored and runs allowed, and its winning percentage. He discovered that the ratio of the square of the runs scored to the sum of the square of the runs scored and the square of the runs allowed, very closely approximates the winning percentages for nearly all teams. (Runs Scored^2) / (Runs Scored^2 + Runs Allowed^2). Due to its similarity to Pythagoras' theorem describing the relationship of the sides in a right triangle, James dubbed this relationship the "Pythagorean Winning Percentage."

Win Shares: In 2002, Bill James released a book that statheads had been anticipating for years. The eponymously named *Win Shares* outlined James's newest metric, by which he attempted to sum up the value of every player and every pitcher in a single number. This number encapsulated all aspects of the game—offense, defense, and pitching.

The system is fairly long and complicated. At its heart, James is trying to give credit to players for their contributions to team wins. Each team gets 3 "Win Shares" for each victory that it achieved, and those shares are divided among all of the team's players based upon their performances. So people have loved it, others have hated it, but it stimulated a lot of conversation.

And there are others. This is just a brief sampling of what's available out in the baseball research universe. But the things that you're most likely to see thrown around are still on-base percentage, slugging, and OPS.

What does it mean to score a baseball game? How is it done?

For some fans, *scoring* a game adds to their enjoyment and understanding; others prefer just to watch the game. Scoring a baseball game is more than keeping track of the number of runs each team has; it involves keeping track of the plays throughout the game to present a detailed picture of how each inning progressed. With even a basic record of the game it is possible to reconstruct how many hits each team had, which fielders made which plays, and some of the internal strategy of the game; more detailed scoring includes such things as pitch counts, distinguishing between a play made deep and a play made shallow, and other nuances. Game programs and some informational magazines sold at the park generally have scoresheets printed in them for the convenience of people who want to score games.

Basically a scoresheet is just a chart; a column runs down the left side for players' names, and then nine (and a few extra) columns that represent innings.

Players are written down in the appropriate column, often by number and position. What each player does at the plate in each inning is entered in the appropriate place in a somewhat standardized shorthand. There are two charts, one for each team, and therefore the fielding plays for one team are noted on the batting chart for the other.

The basic shorthand for fielding is also used by sports announcers, though it is rarely explained: each position on the field has a number. If the fielder touches the ball, his position number is part of the play. The pitcher is position number 1, the catcher 2; the infield is first base, 3, second base, 4, third base, 5, shortstop, 6; the outfield is 7–8–9 from left to right. Therefore, a ball hit to left field and caught is recorded as "7"; a ball hit to the shortstop, who makes the successful throw to first, is recorded as "6–3." Strikeouts are recorded as a K, if the batter is out swinging, or a backward K for out looking; walks are recorded as BB (or IBB if intentional), and hit batsmen as HBP. If the batter-runner reaches on an error, the play is recorded with E-number; if a fly is bobbled by the center fielder, for example, it is E8. A double play is recorded with the addendum "DP," so a shortstop-second base-first base play is "6–4–3 DP." Sacrifice flies get scored as "SF" in addition to marking down the out, and bunts as "SH."

Hits are recorded with lines in the box on the chart; a clean single to center gets an 8 and a single diagonal mark, where a double to the same location would get an 8 and two such lines. The plays that allow the runners to advance are marked in the corners of the square that correspond to passage around the bases, with home plate at the bottom. For the abovementioned single an 8 and diagonal would be noted in the lower right hand corner, and if the runner later advanced to second on a wild pitch, the "WP" note would be written in the upper right hand corner, and so on around the bases. When the player has advanced around the bases, a run has scored, of course; at the bottom of the column on a pre-printed chart, there are sometimes boxes to check off runs scored, hits, and sometimes men left on base.

There are separate charts for keeping track of the pitchers; pitching changes are difficult to note on a lineup chart, especially if they happen frequently in a game. The pitching chart has columns for the player's number, name, and the game-related stats: innings pitched, hits and runs given up, earned runs given up, walks, and strikeouts. As many of these are cumulative stats that can only be written down conclusively after the pitcher is pulled from the game, they can be tabulated after he is relieved, or with tally-marks rather than numbers. You can make your own chart, or use one that comes with a program you buy at a game.

How does the manager decide on a lineup? What is platooning?

Several decisions go into a lineup, and a manager must ask himself a series of questions: What kinds of hitters do I have? Who's healthy? Who needs rest? Who needs to get into more games? Who's on a hot streak, and who's cold? Do any of my hitters do unusually well or poorly against the opposing pitcher? Does my pitcher throw a lot of ground balls, necessitating better infield defense? Can I sacrifice defense for offense at certain positions?

Some managers, like John McNamara and Ralph Houk, are more apt to set a basic lineup in spring training and stick with it as long as possible. They prefer to let their best eight regulars play nearly every game, while the bench players rarely appear. When Houk managed Boston in 1982, catcher Roger LaFrançois was on the roster all season, yet only played in eight games, with 10 at bats. This runs the risk of tiring the regulars, or having an unprepared reserve if there's an injury. Other managers, like Jimy Williams, like to rest regulars and use bench players frequently. (Williams used 140 different lineups in 162 games during the 2000 season.) While this may keep the stars fresh over the long season, it can also backfire on a game-by-game basis—because the best players aren't on the field to help the team win, and because players are unsure of their roles on the team.

In a traditional lineup, the leadoff hitter is someone who gets on base and has good speed, but lacks power. Speed used to be the primary qualification for a leadoff man, but many managers have learned the importance of on-base percentage. Players like Dwight Evans and Wade Boggs scored many runs as leadoff men despite little speed, thanks to high OBPs. Evans was a rare power-hitting leadoff man, but he drew lots of walks—and the Sox had plenty of power hitters to drive him in. Most managers prefer not to "waste" power hitters in that slot, since leadoff hitters bat with the bases empty at least once a game.

Traditionally, #2 hitters have been good bunters and hit-and-run artists, with the goal of moving the leadoff man into scoring position. But in today's high-offense game, many managers prefer a less passive, more skilled hitter in that slot. Many #2 hitters are similar to leadoff men (speed, high OBP), while others have more power. If the leadoff man steals lots of bases, a lefty hitter gains an advantage batting second. The first baseman holds the leadoff man on, opening a big hole on the right side of the infield for a lefty pull hitter (who is likely to hit the ball that way, toward right field).

The #3 hitter is generally the team's best: someone who hits for a high average, has power, gets on base, and drives in runs. The #4 (or *cleanup*) hitter typically has the most power, but isn't quite as good as the #3. The #5–6 batters are generally good hitters with power, but a notch or two below the #3–4.

The #7–9 slots are the best of the rest. In the National League (and the American League before 1973), the pitcher, almost always the weakest hitter in the lineup, customarily bats ninth—since the ninth spot will bat the fewest times. In the American League, the ninth hitter is usually the worst one in the lineup. But some managers like to make the ninth slot a "second leadoff," putting a fast player with some on-base ability in there. That way, if the ninth hitter leads off an inning, you have two speedsters setting the table for the #2, 3, and 4 hitters.

One of the oldest and most-criticized lineup strategies is platooning, where a lefty and righty hitter share playing time at a position. Since most lefties hit better against righties, and most righties hit better against lefties, platooning lets a manager combine the best skills of two flawed players. Some managers platoon at several positions, while others will only do so at one or two. It depends not only upon the manager's strategic bent, but also on the personnel. A star player like Ted Williams or Nomar Garciaparra will never be platooned. But lesser players (like Reggie Jefferson and Mike Stanley, or Rick Miller and Reid Nichols) have been very useful in platoon roles. Many young players (like Trot

Nixon) begin their careers in platoons, and their managers are often urged to play them every day.

Some forms of platooning date back to the nineteenth century, but the practice was popularized by Boston's other team in 1914. The "Miracle Braves," a last-place club in July, won the World Series with platoons in all three outfield positions. Manager George Stallings was hailed as a genius, and many teams copied his strategy. The practice died down somewhat in the 1930s and 1940s, and Casey Stengel is credited with making it popular again.

As statistics have gotten more precise, some analysts have criticized the typical lefty-righty platoon system. They've urged managers to go deeper into the numbers, and select hitters based on such factors as players who hit better at home or on the road, during the day or at night, against fly ball pitchers or ground ball hitters, and other categories. (For instance, former Red Sox catcher Scott Hatteberg hit much better during the daytime, while catcher Jason Varitek hit much better at night.) But managers have been reluctant to use this sort of complex platoons, and platooning remains largely a lefty-righty phenomenon.

What's a pitching rotation? What's an ace? How about a closer? What's more valuable, a great starting pitcher or a great reliever?

Unlike every other position on the field, the stress of pitching is such that no one can do it every day without significant damage to the shoulder and arm. There was a time in the late 1800s, the very early days of professional baseball, when the object of the pitcher was not to strike someone out, but rather to put the ball where the hitter could put the ball in play. Under these conditions, playing with balls that couldn't be hit out of the ballpark under most conditions (the so-called "deadball era"), the stress on the shoulder and arm of the pitcher was significantly different than it is today, and many teams had just one starting pitcher. But starting shortly before the turn of the century, that changed, and teams began to have multiple starting pitchers, each of whom would start in turn. In other words, they'd "rotate" their pitchers from game to game. For most of the twentieth century, a typical starting rotation consisted of four pitchers, pitching on about three days' rest. In the early 1970s the transition began to a five man rotation, each going on four days' rest. (In practice, the best starter gets more turns than the other pitchers, and the weakest pitcher gets skipped if there is a day off.)

As to what an "ace" is, there is no strict definition, but generally an ace is the best starting pitcher on a staff. However, some people think that an ace is a top-level pitcher, and that most teams don't have an ace at all. In the 2004 season Curt Schilling clearly was an ace, and Randy Johnson, Johan Santana, and Roger Clemens wouldn't draw much debate either. Beyond that, people disagree, based on different usages of the term. Broadcasters typically use the looser definition, defining the best starter on a team, or sometimes even the best over the last couple of starts, as the "ace of the staff."

A closer is a relatively new phenomenon, not seen much before the 1960s, and assuming its current form and stature within the past decade or so. The closer is a pitcher who starts the game in the bullpen and is brought into a game as a reliever, when the team is leading by a small margin late in the game, to close out the game. The typical manager brings the closer into the game in situations where the closer is eligible to receive a *save*. That ordinarily means to pitch the last half-inning with a lead of three runs or less.

As to which is more valuable, there isn't any real debate over that. A great starting pitcher is of more value to a team than a great reliever, simply due to the number of innings pitched. Keith Foulke, who generally pitches more than a typical closer, pitched 83 innings in 2004, while all five Red Sox starters had more than twice as many innings pitched.

While it is clear that a great starter is the more valuable commodity, there is some debate over the actual value of a closer. Some think that anyone can pitch the ninth inning, and that there isn't any reason to designate someone for that job. In addition, there are people who believe that closers would be more valuable to the team by pitching more innings—either starting the game, or coming into games earlier and being available out of the bullpen less often. On the other hand, there is a case to be made for having a great or near-great pitcher available to pitch in situations where the outs are determinative—that is, when a perfect inning guarantees a victory. But the exact value of the closer is still unclear, and frequently debated.

How can I tell a good defensive player from a bad one when I'm watching a game? Why do people say defensive stats are unreliable?

How can I tell a good defensive player from a bad one when I'm watching a game? The short answer is, you can't. A trained scout who has been watching for years can make a guess, but the reality is, no one can actually tell from watching a game whether someone is good, bad, or indifferent. There are certain aspects of defensive baseball that we can evaluate, but the bottom line on defense is this—the goal of position players is to turn batted balls into outs, and there is no way to say for sure who is good at it, and who isn't. There are some exceptions, mostly on the downside, where it is obvious that a player is just incapable of getting to balls, or incapable of fielding them. But at the typical level of major league competence (even the worst major leaguer is one of the top 1,000 or so baseball players in the world), it is just not possible for human beings to make the comparisons that a rigid assessment of defensive abilities would require.

Scouts certainly want to see how fast a player is. They want to know how well a player catches the ball and throws it. There are drills that they'll watch and things they'll look for in games to try to make a judgment on how well the player reacts to a batted ball. How quickly does he react? Does he go in the right direction immediately? Every time? How do his reactions compare to the other players in the game? How do his reactions compare to the other players available to the team? One of the biggest things that is tough to quantify is instinct—was the player standing in the optimal spot when the pitcher released the ball?

All of these questions are useful criteria in trying to determine a player's potential. They are things that a scout with a stopwatch and some time to observe and interact with a player can use to perform some high level evaluation. Unfortunately for the fan in the stands, the human brain is not constructed to make rational assessments and comparisons between two similar events separated by time. Observation can make you think that two events are similar, but can't quantify the similarities and differences. Consider, for example, that a ball is hit to a Red Sox second baseman's left and he handles it. A similar ball is hit to an Indians second baseman two weeks, or two days, or even two innings, earlier. Were the balls hit at the same speed? Were the second basemen playing at the same spot on the diamond? Did the balls spin off the bats the same way? Was the terrain the same? There just isn't any way to tell even by close observation.

Frankly, the same holds for offense as well. If you only watched games and didn't take numbers into account you'd look at what happened and form opinions, but very possibly those opinions would cause you to think that Derek Jeter is a better hitter than Alex Rodriguez, or Sammy Sosa is more valuable than Barry Bonds. But how a player looks at bat or in the field doesn't always reflect how good he really is. It is only by objective analysis of what they've accomplished in their at-bats that we know that Jeter doesn't compare to Rodriguez over time, and that Sosa's home runs don't match up to Bonds's overall offensive game. Sometimes scouts *do* make judgments based on this sort of appearances, and they can lead to disaster; for instance Wade Boggs was stuck in the minor leagues for years because he didn't fit the perception of what a good hitter should *look* like, even though he hit well every year. Similarly, Phil Plantier wasn't given much of a chance as a major league hitter because he had an unorthodox batting stance, and scouts decided that he couldn't hit that way, instead of paying attention to his actual results.

When the same comparisons come up while talking of defense, there is no objective standard to fall back upon to measure the actual accomplishments of the defensive players. The one standard that is typically used is one of the most misleading statistics of all—fielding percentage. Fielding percentage is a simple rate statistic, where the number of errors that a players has made is divided by the total number of chances that the player has. (A *chance* is any time a player handles the ball during a play.) The problem with fielding percentage is that it's only half of fielding, and doesn't tell you anything about a player's range—how many balls a player gets to. An outfielder that stood in one place would be a horrible defender, but would almost never make an error. By contrast, before his heel injury, Nomar Garciaparra got to a lot of balls that other shortstops wouldn't, but made an above-average number of throwing errors on those balls. None of this is going to be discernible by someone watching a single game, or even several.

One way to try to judge a player's range is to see how many total chances he has per game—does he make a lot more plays than his peers at that position? This is useful in figuring out what kind of range players have, but it's not infallible. A team whose pitchers yield a lot of ground balls will inflate the stats of the infielders, while a team with a lot of flyball pitchers will make the outfielders look better. Different ballparks can affect range as well; for instance, Fenway Park left fielders always seem to have terrible range, because left field in Fenway is small, and many potential outs in other parks turn into hits off the Green Monster.

Frequently, defensive skills are judged much as figure skating is judged—people watch and assign higher rankings to the people that look the smoothest. There is also often a mental "bonus" applied to players who make spectacular plays, diving to the left or the right. A player will get praise for making a play with a diving catch that a faster, or more reactive, or better-positioned player will make standing upright. But there has not yet been, despite some very good attempts, an objective means of rating defense.

There are currently a couple of sabremetric attempts to quantify defense. Project Scoresheet has observers at every single major league game, tracking the balls that are hit. They divide the fields into different areas, and every batted ball becomes the responsibility of a fielder. They compute a Defensive Average, which is analogous to batting average—every fielder gets a DA, computed by dividing outs produced by total opportunities. STATS, Inc. also has observers, whose data they use to compute a rating called Zone Rating (ZR). Zone Rating is similar to DA but does not have zones overlapping, so there are balls in right field that are no one's responsibility, while every ball has a zone of responsibility for DA. There is also a more advanced version of ZR, called Ultimate Zone Rating (UZR), that closely examines the difficulties of the plays within each zone and attempts to measure how many runs a fielder saves or costs his team. But while each has adherents in parts of the "stathead" or sabremetric community, none has been embraced by the mainstream yet.

How much effect does Fenway Park have on the Red Sox players' stats? Do other parks have the same kind of impact?

Fenway has always been known as a park that greatly favors hitters, leading to more runs and home runs. Since the late 1980s Fenway has actually hurt home run hitters, but most media members still think of it as a "launching pad," because of its longtime reputation. In terms of overall offense, Fenway isn't as much of a factor as it once was, but it still favors hitters.

As any fan or player can attest, Fenway has the oddest dimensions of any big league stadium. For one thing, there is almost no foul territory. This is to the hitter's advantage, since popups that would be foulouts anywhere else fall harmlessly into the stands. (By contrast, Oakland has acres of foul ground, helping its staff's ERAs and saving them from throwing a few extra pitches.)

For example, the Green Monster is an inviting target in left field, and several righty hitters (Bobby Doerr, Felix Mantilla) tailored their swings to loft flies into the screen. On the other hand, hitters like Nomar Garciaparra and Jim Rice lost several homers a year, since the Wall turned their long liners into singles and doubles. What's worse, some righty batters try too hard to hit homers at Fenway, ruining their swings (and batting averages) in the process. Because of the Monster, managers have been reluctant to use lefthanded pitchers at Fenway, since righty batters can turn mistakes into homers. The stereotype isn't entirely true, however, since Lefty Grove, Bill Lee, and Bruce Hurst all pitched very well at Fenway.

Right field is another story, however. Once you get past Pesky's Pole, it takes a monstrous shot to hit a homer to right (before the bullpen was installed in 1940, it was even tougher). Lefty pull hitters routinely lose home runs at Fenway. Most of the Red Sox best hitters, however, have been lefthanded line drive hitters who learned how to hit to the opposite field (including Fred Lynn and Mo Vaughn, both of whose stats declined tremendously when they moved to the Angels).

In 1988 the Red Sox added the 406 Club seats behind home plate, a huge structure that is widely believed to have cut down the wind that normally blew out to left field—thus reducing homers. The statistics clearly indicate that Fenway is now one of the more difficult parks to hit a home run in. Other teams have moved into smaller parks that favor homers, and this makes Fenway look like even less of a launching pad—while also reducing the overall offensive impact of the ballpark.

One of the charms of baseball is the uniqueness of its stadiums; each park has a different effect on statistics. Coors Field, in the Mile High City of Denver, increases offense more than any park in baseball. The thin air makes the ball carry about 10% further than it does at sea level. The park has deep fences to compensate, but this results in more base hits—since there is more area for the ball to drop in where an outfielder can't reach. Shea Stadium (Mets), Dodger Stadium, and the Tigers' Comerica Park are all parks that help pitchers. On the other hand, some parks favor certain types of players. Yankee Stadium has a very short right field, but a deep left field. Lefty hitters who master the art of pulling fly balls hit more homers there, but righties are often frustrated by the deep fences in left-center.

What happens if the umpires can't agree on a call?

The umpires will privately huddle and discuss the disputed play. Each ump will discuss what he saw, and they'll try to come up with the most fair (or foul) solution. The umpires usually let the one who had the best view make the final decision. For example, umpires are often blocked by fielders on tag plays, and another ump may have a better angle. Umpires are divided into 4-man crews who work together all season, so they usually communicate with each other pretty well. But if they still can't agree on a call, the crew chief (generally the one with the most experience) has the final say.

One frequent complaint of former Red Sox manager Jimy Williams was that major league umpires frequently don't ask for help from another umpire if they don't have a clear view (and for years umpires almost never overruled calls once they had been made—even if they realized the call was wrong). Once in a while the crew chief will overrule another member of the crew on a call, and Major League Baseball has been encouraging umpires to confer more frequently. Jimy Williams was no longer around in Game 6 of the 2004 ALCS when the umpires twice conferred and (correctly) overturned calls.

While the idea of using instant replay has been brought up from time to time, there is a general consensus that it doesn't fit with the character and pacing of the game.

Are players allowed to steal the other team's signals? How about doctoring the ball or the bat? What's considered legal and illegal?

Players, coaches, and managers have stolen signs from opponents since the game began. Though it may not be ethical, certain kinds of sign-stealing are condoned as "part of the game," while more blatant efforts have been outlawed. Runners on second base have a great view of the catcher's signals, and may try to relay them to the batter. The catcher, in turn, frequently sends bogus signals to the pitcher, to trip up the baserunning spy. This is considered fair, but if a batter turns around to peek at the catcher's signals, the pitcher will sometimes throw the next pitch at his head. People in the dugout can try to decode the third base coach's signs, but other forms of spying are no-nos. Several teams have been accused of putting hidden cameras in the center field scoreboard (monitored from within the clubhouse), in order to decipher the catcher's signs. This is completely illegal, though few of these allegations are ever proven.

Other forms of cheating include spitball pitching and corking bats. Before 1920, pitchers could put spit, grease, and other substances on the ball. This made pitches move sharply and unpredictably, and drove hitters crazy. After the 1920 season baseball made rules to increase hitting (due largely to the fallout of the 1919 Black Sox gambling scandal, and also the popularity of Babe Ruth's homers). The spitball was outlawed, but 17 known spitballers were allowed to keep throwing it until they retired. Though illegal today, many pitchers (most notably Hall of Famer Gaylord Perry) have used it, or been accused of using it. There are many other ways to doctor a ball, such as using a hidden piece of sandpaper or a sharpened belt buckle to mar or scuff the ball. Players caught doctoring the ball are ejected from the game and suspended.

The hitting version of the spitball is the corked bat. Some batters have been known to drill holes in their bats and fill the holes with cork or rubber. This makes the ball go further than it would when hit by an unaltered wooden bat, but the illegal contents are easily revealed if the bat breaks. Players caught with corked bats are also ejected and suspended. One famous incident occurred in the Red Sox–Indians playoff series in 1995. Manager Kevin Kennedy accused Cleveland slugger Albert Belle of corking his bat. After a home run, Belle taunted Kennedy by pointing to his muscles. At another time, earlier in Belle's career, his bat shattered during a time at bat and a bunch of rubber balls fell out.

What is salary arbitration? How does it work?

All but a few players with less than three years of service time have to play for whatever salary the team wants to pay them (although there are minimum salaries for major league players). Teams will negotiate to a certain extent, because they don't want their players to be unhappy, but players have very limited leverage until after their third year in the big leagues. After a player has about three years of major league service time (the top 17 percent of players with more than two years are included as well) he is eligible for *salary arbitration*. If a player with three or more years of experience and his team can't agree on a salary, the team can offer arbitration. If the player accepts (and players with less than six years of service time don't have a choice), he is considered signed to a one-year contract, leaving just the amount of his salary to be worked out. Teams can also offer their own free agents arbitration. If a team refuses to offer arbitration to an unsigned player who is eligible, he becomes a free agent. (This is common when a team wouldn't mind signing a player at a low salary, but doesn't think he is worth the high salary an arbiter might award.)

Before the arbitration period in February, the team and player exchange salary figures. If they can't compromise before the hearing is held, each side gets a chance to argue before an arbitrator why their figure is more in line with the major league salary for comparable players. The argument often centers on whom the player in arbitration is most comparable to. The arbiter can pick either the team's proposed salary or the player's proposed salary—he is not allowed to compromise. Often arbitration is offered because if a player declines arbitration and signs elsewhere, the team who loses him may get up to two high-round draft choices, depending on how good the player is. Every once in a while a team offers arbitration to a player it doesn't really want for this reason and gets burned when the player accepts.

Because even players who lose generally get huge raises (and players who win increase the salary scale to which other players in arbitration are compared) arbitration was seen as a huge factor in driving up player salaries in the 1980s and early 1990s, and was a major sticking point in the negotiations to end several strikes. More recently owners have reacted by either signing young players to long-term contracts before they are arbitration-eligible (as the Red Sox did with Trot Nixon) or releasing arbitration-eligible players who they feel can be replaced more cheaply. (Many of these players then have to sign more cheaply elsewhere or settle for minor league deals, so the effect has been mainly to increase the salary gap between the stars and the lesser players.)

How many times can you send a player to the minor leagues? What does it mean to "option" someone? What are waivers?

When a player is first signed the club who signs him gets three *options*, each one good for a year. If the player is under 19 when first signed, he needn't be protected from the Rule 5 Draft (see page 352) until four seasons after he signs. If he is over 19 he must be protected by being placed on the team's 40-man roster (a team can protect up to 40 players, but only 25 players can be on the major league roster at a time) after three seasons or the Red Sox risk losing him. As long as a player has options remaining, the team can call him up and send him down as much as they want (although a player who is sent to the minors can't be recalled for 10 days, to keep clubs from shuttling different pitchers through their roster every night, which would make the 25-player roster meaningless). A player who isn't ready for the major leagues is usually optioned to the minors at the end of spring training. That uses up one option, but he can be recalled and sent back to the minors any number of times during the year that option is in effect. Remember that most players who make the major leagues spend about five years in the minors. The option rule is designed to allow teams to send players back and forth for a reasonable amount of time while they are developing, but not to keep them indefinitely in the minor leagues when they could be playing in the majors somewhere else.

After the three options are used up, a player has to pass through *waivers* to be sent down to the minors, meaning that any other club can put in a claim for him, and if the team doesn't pull the player back off waivers, the claiming team gets him. They get his salary, too, so you don't want to claim an overpriced player whom you don't want. You have to pass a player through waivers for certain kinds of trades, too—about half of all major league players are put on waivers every year. The list is supposed to be secret (so players don't feel like their teams are trying to get rid of them).

When the Red Sox send down a marginal veteran player like Cesar Crespo, for example, any other team can claim him. If nobody wants him, he is sent to the minors.

After you have five years in the majors, you can refuse an assignment to the minor leagues and become a free agent if the team tries to send you down, even if you still have options. Once a player passes through waivers (it takes 72 hours) and is officially released, any new team that signs him only has to pay the major league minimum salary (or a prorated portion of it). The rest of his contract is paid by the team who signed him to the contract. So in 2000 the Red Sox only paid Pete Schourek $200,000. The rest of his $2 million salary was being borne by the Pittsburgh Pirates, who had released him in spring training.

When does a player become a free agent?

After six years of major league service a player whose contract expires can become a *free agent*, and is free to sign with any team in baseball (including his current team). Players who are released and clear waivers also become free agents, as do players who have been in the minor leagues for six years and are not put on a team's 40-man major league roster (these players are usually called *minor league free agents*).

Sometimes players become free agents for other reasons, such as when a team breaks a rule. The Red Sox lost Carlton Fisk to free agency (and would have lost Fred Lynn if they hadn't quickly traded him for much less than his true value) after the 1980 season when they didn't mail them contracts by the deadline. The Red Sox signed minor league first baseman Carlos Diaz in 2000 after he was made a free agent because the Dodgers went into Cuba to sign him, violating the American embargo on Cuba.

A team can offer arbitration to a player who is eligible for free agency, but players—who want the security of a guaranteed contract lasting more than one year—seldom accept.

Star free agents command the highest salaries in baseball, but they aren't always a good deal. It may be popular with sportswriters and casual fans when a team signs a big-name player for millions of dollars, but when Red Sox general manager Lou Gorman signed a bunch of pricey free agents in the late 1980s and early 1990s, it led to disastrous teams filled with old, frequently hurt players.

Remember that baseball players typically make the major leagues when they are 23 to 25 years old, and don't become free agents until they have six full years of major league experience. As a group, baseball players peak around age 27 (some say a little older), and decline rapidly after age 30. While there are exceptions to this (and a very few players have played into their fifties), most players end their careers before they are 35. So as a general manager, you have to think long and hard about whether you want to sign a superstar player to the seven-year contract he wants when he may only have two or three good years left.

If a Red Sox player signs with another team as a free agent, do the Sox get any kind of compensation for losing him?

It depends. Each year, the Elias Sports Bureau ranks all players based upon their stats in certain categories over the past two seasons. Many statisticians ridicule these results, which even Elias admits are pretty arbitrary, but they're used by major league baseball to determine free agent compensation.

The top 30% of all players at each position are classified as Type A. If the Red Sox lose a Type A free agent, they get the other team's first- or second-round pick in the next draft. If the other team has one of the 15 best records in the major leagues, it must surrender its first rounder. If they're one of the bottom 15 teams, they can keep their #1, but must give up their #2. In addition, the Red Sox would get a "supplemental" or "sandwich" pick between the first and second rounds. For example, when Mo Vaughn left Boston in 1999, the Sox got the Angels' first rounder (used to select outfielder Rick Asadoorian) and a supplemental pick (pitcher Brad Baker).

Players ranked in the 31–50% range are Type B. If the Red Sox lose a Type B free agent, they get the other team's first- or second-round pick (same rules as Type A). However, they do not get the supplemental pick. In 2000, Type B Rheal Cormier signed with the Phillies, so Boston got the Phillies' second round pick (the Phils were one of the bottom 15 teams, so they keep their first rounder). They selected catcher Kelly Shoppach (see p. 304) with that pick.

Players ranked in the 51–60% range are Type C. If the Red Sox lose a Type C free agent, they get a supplemental pick between the second and third rounds. Type C free agents are very rare. Tom Gordon, who signed with the Cubs in 2000, is the only Type C free agent the Red Sox have lost in recent years.

Any players ranked in the lowest 40% do not require compensation.

Before a team can get compensation, it must formally offer arbitration (see page 346) to a free agent by an early December deadline. If the player accepts, he is considered signed, and returns to his original team at a salary determined by an arbitrator. If a team doesn't offer arbitration to a free agent, it doesn't get compensation if he leaves—even if he's a Type A, B, or C player. Since draft picks are involved, one might think teams that would always offer arbitration. But sometimes they're afraid that other teams won't make good offers, forcing the free agent to accept arbitration and return. If the team doesn't want to get stuck with a big contract, or just wants the player gone at any cost, they might play it safe and not offer arbitration.

After the 2004 season, the Red Sox lost three Type A free agents (Pedro Martinez, Derek Lowe, and Orlando Cabrera), and signed two Type A free agents (Edgar Renteria and David Wells) and a Type B (Matt Clement). Even though they won the World Series, the Red Sox personnel moves guaranteed them six of the first 60 picks in the next draft.

I've heard people say that big-name free agents don't like to sign with the Red Sox. Why is that?

Boston has a poor reputation with many athletes who grew up in the Southern or Western United States or the Caribbean (as the majority of them do). It's about as far culturally from what they are used to as can exist in the United States. Besides, Boston's climate is cold in April and May and too overcast and rainy for many Southern, Western, or Caribbean athletes' taste all year round—especially for those players who have grown up in a hot climate and would prefer to play and live somewhere warmer than New England.

Whether it fully deserves it or not, Boston has a reputation as a snooty, academic town with its share of racism, which alienates many ballplayers. The Boston Red Sox were the *last* team in major league baseball to have a black ballplayer on their roster (the very limited Pumpsie Green). They passed on signing both Jackie Robinson and Willie Mays. Despite the systematic eradication of the Sox racist legacy over the last decade, the reputation persists to a certain extent even though Boston fans of all races and creeds have welcomed Pedro Martinez, Nomar Garciaparra, Manny Ramirez, David Ortiz, Rich Garces, Troy O'Leary, Carl Everett, Sang-Hoon Lee, Hideo Nomo, and Tomokazu Ohka—to name just a few recent players who happen not to be white. In fact, Manny Ramirez was advised by friends and family to sign with the Red Sox in late 2000 in part because of Boston's thriving Dominican population and friendliness to Dominican athletes. He also shopped in the Dominican areas of Boston for years when he came to town on road trips and so already had firsthand experience with the community.

Unfortunately, despite Fenway Park's fabled history, it has some of the worst major league clubhouse and ballpark facilities in baseball, especially when compared to sleek new corporate parks in other cities. For instance, the clubhouse is small, cramped, and visited by the occasional rat. (The new ownership is in the process of replacing it, although finding space to renovate and expand a park as old as Fenway in a dense urban area requires a lot of creativity.) Boston traffic—including traffic to and from Fenway Park—is infamous for its frustrating density. Therefore a multimillionaire free agent, given the choice, might pick a team with more modern clubhouse and ballpark facilities over the quirky and historical but aging Fenway Park.

The good news and the bad news is that Red Sox fans are passionate about their team. Since Fenway Park is tiny, the fans are very close to the playing field. A player on the field can hear everything some drunk fan is shouting from Section 14—which makes for an unpleasant working environment for a personally struggling player or a struggling Red Sox team. (Ted Williams once tried to silence a heckler by repeatedly fouling the ball into the left field stands where the heckler was sitting, for example.) There is really no designated place for players' families to sit and watch a game without sitting in the stands and hearing often-personally vitriolic tirades directed against their loved ones by aggravated fans. This can make a free agent concerned about not only his own working environment at Fenway but the safety of his family in the stands.

In terms of media relations, the Boston media is very intense and actively investigative in its coverage of the Red Sox. Some players are happy with this and some players find this uncomfortable, depending on what kind of relationship they have traditionally had with media as well as their own communication style. Players who are not natural communicators can get themselves into trouble with the Boston media through simple misunderstandings on both sides. Some players might prefer not to be put under the enormous combined media and fan pressure of playing in Boston.

These are a number of potentially daunting negatives to work against, and agents aren't above bringing up any or all of them during negotiations. While most teams start at zero, and a few teams—like the Yankees, the Giants, the Diamondbacks, and the Braves—may start on the plus side, the Red Sox have to start at a minus on the player likeability scale.

To sum up: Boston is not an ideal place to play as far as many baseball players are concerned, although the job has been easier in the last few years, since the Red Sox have been a very strong team, and many free agents want the chance to play for a potential World Champion. Some things—like the weather, the traffic, and the culture—the Red Sox general manager can't do much about. So when the team isn't championship-caliber, the general manager may end up overpaying for Grade B free agents and having to acquire most of the best players through the system (Nomar, Nixon, Hatteberg) or in trades (Pedro, Everett, Lowe, Varitek). The general manager may give former stars second chances (Saberhagen, Beck, Fassero) which they appreciate and find young players who've had arm troubles or weren't great fits elsewhere (Ortiz, Garces) and give them a chance. The general manager may go to the Frontier League and find a Morgan Burkhart or give career minor leaguer Brian Daubach a last shot. In short, the Boston Red Sox general manager will do the best he can. That may or may not include being able to sign big-name free agents.

How does the amateur draft work? What happens if a player doesn't want to sign with the team that drafts him? How do players from foreign countries get signed by teams?

The Amateur Draft was created in 1965. Baseball wanted to stop big-budget teams from signing the best amateur players, while giving the worst teams the first shot at top prospects. The draft is held every June. (There was once a January draft too, but it was discontinued.) Picks are alternated between American League and National League teams, in reverse order of their records the previous year. If a team loses 100 games, they'll have one of the top picks in each round, while the World Series winner will have one of the last picks. The draft generally lasts about 50 rounds, though very few late-round picks make the major leagues.

Only players born in the United States, Canada, and Puerto Rico are eligible for the Amateur Draft. All high school seniors are eligible, as are all players at two-year "junior" colleges. Players at four-year colleges are eligible if they turn 21 within 45 days of the draft.

Not all drafted players sign right away, especially if they're picked in later rounds. High school players often choose to go to college, either for an education or to increase their value in future drafts (for example, the Mets drafted Roger Clemens in 1981, but he decided to go to the University of Texas, and was redrafted by Boston). College players sometimes return to school (an example is Red Sox catcher Jason Varitek, who refused to sign with the Twins in 1993) if they don't like the team's offer and think they will be able to get more money later—although this is risky, since a player who gets hurt or plays badly may see his value go *down*. If a drafted player goes to (or returns to) a four-year college, the team loses their rights to sign him. But if a drafted player goes to (or returns to) a two-year college, the team can still sign him up to a week before the next Amateur Draft. Teams often let late-round picks from high schools play a year at junior college before deciding whether to sign them; this practice is called *draft-and-follow*.

Amateur players from other countries (again, except for Cuba, because of the United States' embargo on Cuba) can be signed as free agents by big league teams as long as they're at least 16 years old. The Dominican Republic, despite its tiny size, has produced some of the game's greatest stars, including Pedro Martinez, Manny Ramirez, and Vladimir Guerrero. Other foreign sources of big league talent include Venezuela, Mexico, Japan, Korea, and Australia. Many Cubans have signed with major league clubs in recent years *after* defecting to the United States.

What is the Rule 5 Draft? Is it good for a player to be selected?

The Rule 5 Draft is held every December at baseball's Winter Meetings. Teams must submit a 40-man major league roster by a certain date in November. Minor leaguers who have played more than three professional seasons (four if they were signed before age 19) who are not placed on the 40-man roster can be lost in the Rule 5 Draft. Since there are only 40 roster spaces available, including 25 major leaguers, only the most promising minor league players can be protected from the Rule 5 Draft. Hundreds of minor leaguers are eligible, but few are strong candidates to be drafted.

Like the Amateur Draft, teams pick in reverse order of their records. Teams can only select players in the Rule 5 draft if they have an opening on their 40-man roster. They can take any eligible player from any organization (they pay $50,000 to the team who loses the player). But there's a big catch: whomever they select *must* be on the major league roster for the entire season. Before a Rule 5 draftee can be sent to the minor leagues, he must be offered back to his old team for $25,000. (The original team usually takes the player back.) Relatively few players are selected in the Rule 5 draft, which usually lasts one or two rounds—and all but a handful are given back to their old clubs by the end of Spring Training. In 2003, 20 players were taken in the draft (16 in the first round, three in the second, one in the third), and none of them made a major impact on the major league team that selected him. The Red Sox didn't lose any players in 2003, though Detroit plucked LHP Wil Ledezma (now a good prospect) in 2002. Boston selected two players in 2003: LHP Lenny DiNardo, who pitched pretty well in limited duty, and RHP Colter Bean, who was returned to the Yankees after a poor spring training. Other recent Rule 5 players on the Red Sox include veteran outfielder Adrian Brown and young pitchers Matt White, John Trautwein, and Mike Trujillo, none of whom went on to have successful careers.

Although Rule 5 players have a golden opportunity to make the majors ahead of schedule, the draft is often bad for their careers in the long run. Most Rule 5 players are very raw (often coming from Class A ball) and far from ready for the majors. Big league teams are often forced to bury these players at the end of the bench, depriving them of valuable at bats or innings pitched. After a season in the majors, many Rule 5 players go back to the minors, and most are never heard from again. Notable exceptions include 2004 AL Cy Young winner Johan Santana (who had a 6.49 ERA as a rookie in 2000); George Bell and Kelly Gruber, who became stars with Toronto in the 1980s; and journeyman shortstop Deivi Cruz. Fortunately for the Red Sox, Wade Boggs was never lost in the Rule 5 Draft; he was eligible in 1980 and 1981, but 25 teams passed him up twice.

How do trades work? Why is there a trading deadline? What's the 10-and-5 rule? Are there other ways that teams or players can block trades?

Trades can occur during the season (pending some deadlines and rules), or in the offseason (often during the December Winter Meetings). Sometimes teams don't get a player in return right away; instead, they'll trade someone for a "player to be named later" or "future considerations," and the deal is completed within six months. Teams can also trade players for cash, but baseball (unlike other sports) does not allow teams to trade draft picks, and any trades involving large amounts of cash must be approved by the commissioner.

Broadly speaking, there are three types of trades. Teams with bad records and/or payroll restrictions often trade high-priced players before they can declare free agency. The idea is to get some young, cheap players in return, instead of simply losing the player for draft picks. The Red Sox did this in 1997, getting Derek Lowe and Jason Varitek for Heathcliff Slocumb, who had worn out his welcome in Boston. Other times teams do the opposite, trading young players for veterans they hope can get them into the playoffs, as the Sox did in the Curt Schilling deal. Or a team might have a surplus at one position, but a weakness at another. They'll try to find a team with the opposite problem, and work out a deal to help both teams. The Red Sox did this in 1989, trading Lee Smith—one of two good closers—for outfielder Tom Brunansky, who the Cardinals easily replaced.

During the season, there are two main trading deadlines. From Opening Day through July 31, teams can freely trade players. After July 31, only players who have cleared waivers (see page 347) can be traded. Because of this rule, teams often put players on recallable waivers (if the player is claimed, the team can pull him back) before July 31, hoping to sneak them through and make them eligible for a trade. August 31 is, for all intents and purposes, the second trading deadline. After that date, players acquired in trades aren't eligible for the playoffs (see page 354). So playoff contenders tend to make deals in late August to firm up playoff rosters, but trades after September 1 are rare.

Players have some control over whether they're traded. The "10-and-5 Rule" gives all players with 10 years of big league service, the last five on their current team, the right to veto trades. (on the 2005 Red Sox, only Tim Wakefield is a "10-and 5-Man.") Other players negotiate no-trade clauses in their contracts (the Red Sox have a club policy prohibiting this, but give trade approval to players with eight consecutive years of service with the team). Some no-trade clauses give the player veto power on all trades. Others specify teams the player can or can't be traded to. Trades can also be vetoed by the commissioner if he feels they violate "the best interests of baseball." In 1976, the Red Sox gave Oakland $2 million for Rollie Fingers and Joe Rudi, but Commissioner Bowie Kuhn overturned the deal, essentially banning the longtime practice of poor clubs selling their stars to better-off teams for quick cash.

What's the difference between the 25-man roster and the 40-man roster? How about the playoff roster?

During the offseason, teams are required to set a 40-man major league roster. All players with three or more years in professional baseball (four years if they signed before age 19) must either be placed on the 40-man roster, or else be subject to the Rule 5 Draft (see page 353). The 40-man roster will have established big leaguers, several players from the AAA team, and a few other prospects. Teams often leave a few spaces open for free agents or players acquired in trades. By spring training, the 40-man roster is usually completely filled.

Players on the 40-man roster and selected minor league invitees fight for spots on the 25-man roster during spring training. From Opening Day through August 31, big league teams carry 25 active players. During spring training, some players from the 40-man roster are sent to the minors or released, and the active roster is cut to 25 before the regular season begins (with the other players on the 40-man roster playing in the minor leagues).

If a player on the 25-man roster is hurt, he can be placed on the disabled list. Most injured players go on the 15-day DL, meaning they can't play for a minimum of 15 days and are temporarily off the 25-man roster. During this time the team can call up a replacement from the minors. When the injured player returns, someone must be taken off the 25-man roster (usually by sending him to the minors). Seriously injured players often go on the 60-day DL. Players on the 60-day DL are also taken off the 40-man roster until they're reactivated, so they're easier to replace.

Any player on the 40-man roster can join the 25-man roster without any problems. Sometimes players who aren't on the 40-man roster are called up. If there aren't any vacancies on the 40-man roster, someone must be taken off. Any player taken off the 40-man roster goes on waivers, giving all other teams the right to claim him for cash. For example, Troy O'Leary was removed from the Brewers' 40-man roster at the end of 1995 spring training. He went on waivers, and the Red Sox claimed him.

On September 1, teams can expand their 25-man roster to 40 players, and they bring up several minor leaguers (generally 5–8 players, rather than the maximum 15). Teams in contention call up players to fill specific roles (pinch-runner, extra lefty reliever, third catcher). Teams lower in the standings like to give minor leaguers auditions for the following season. Most callups are already on the official 40-man roster, so they can be added to the active roster. If not, they can only join if there's a vacancy on the 40-man roster, and the same waiver rules apply.

If a team makes the playoffs, it submits a 25-man roster prior to each round. Only players on the 25-man roster or the DL on August 31 are eligible for the playoff roster (so a team can have a few more than 25 players available). Players acquired in September trades—and those still in the minors on August 31—are ineligible, unless the league grants special permission. However, the team can submit a different roster before each playoff round, provided they have more than 25 eligible players. Sometimes a team omits a player from the first round roster, but decides he'd be a better fit than someone else in the next round.

How do the playoffs work in baseball? How many games do the Sox have to win to become world champions?

Four teams in each league make the playoffs. The three division winners (East, Central, and West) qualify, as does a *wild card* team (the non-division winner with the best record). The first round of playoffs is a best-of-five (called the Divisional Series). The division winner with the best record plays the wild card team, and the other two division winners play each other. (If the wild card winner is in the same division as the team with the best record, the team with the best record plays the division winner with the worst record.) The winners of the first round play each other in a best-of-seven League Championship Series (LCS). The winner of the LCS goes to the World Series, where it plays a best-of-seven against the other league's champion.

If the Red Sox make the playoffs, they'll need to win 11 games to be World Champions. (They'll probably need to win more than 90 regular season games first, in order to make the playoffs.) In the 2004 ALCS, the Red Sox were on the brink of elimination before winning eight games in a row (the last four games of the ALCS and all four World Series games).

What does "games behind" mean? What's a "magic number?"

Games behind (sometimes abbreviated GB in newspapers) is a way of measuring how hard it is to catch up to a team that's ahead in the standings. A team gains a game in the standing anytime it wins and the team in first place loses (meaning that each win or opponent's loss is worth half a game). So if the Yankees are 54–47 and the Red Sox are 51–50, the Sox would be 3 games behind—meaning that the Sox need to win 3 games while the Yankees lose 3 for the Sox to catch up (at 54–50). If teams have played different numbers of games, the number of games behind may not be even. For instance, if the Sox are 88–60 and Baltimore in 85–60, Baltimore would be 1½ games behind the Red Sox.

It's not unusual for a team to come from 6 or 7 games behind at midseason, but late in the season it's hard to make up more than a few games in the standings. It does happen, though. In 1949 the Sox were 12 games behind the Yankees in July, but came back to pull a game ahead on the last weekend of the season—only to lose the last two games to the Yankees and finish a game out of first place. In 1978 the Red Sox were in first place by 14 games at midseason, only to fall hopelessly behind the Yankees amid a string of injuries and mismanagement—and then stormed back into a short-lived tie for first by winning eight games in a row at the end of the season.

Toward the end of the season people will start talking about a first-place team's *magic number*. That's the combination of wins and opponent losses that it will take to clinch the division title. For instance, if the Red Sox are 98–58 and the

Yankees are in second place at 95–61 (3 games behind, with six to play in the 162-game season), the Sox magic number is 3. Any combination of Boston wins or Yankees losses totaling three will guarantee at least a tie for first in the division. (If the Sox win three games, the Yankees can only tie them at 101–61, even if New York wins all six of its remaining games. Another Boston win or New York loss would guarantee an outright win for the division title.)

How do you get into the Hall of Fame?

Practice, practice, practice.

The most common route to induction to the Baseball Hall of Fame is via election by the Baseball Writers Association of America (BBWAA). In order to be elected, a player must be selected on 75% of the ballots cast by the writers during the annual voting. During the voting process, each member of the BBWAA (active or honorary) who has at least 10 years' experience may submit a ballot naming up to 10 eligible players. (Most writers name fewer than 10 on their ballots.)

To be eligible for election by the BBWAA, a player must have played parts of at least 10 seasons in the major leagues (at least some of that time during the previous 20 seasons), and must have been retired for five seasons. No player who is listed on Major League Baseball's permanently ineligible list may be selected—with the two best-known names on that list being "Shoeless" Joe Jackson and Pete Rose. In addition, any player failing to receive at least 5% of the BBWAA vote during any voting year ceases to be eligible for selection by the BBWAA. In other words, a player with at least 10 years in the major leagues goes on the ballot after being retired for five years (usually around 20 players each year). If he gets 75% of the votes (like Carlton Fisk did in 2000), he is elected to the Hall of Fame. If he gets fewer than 75% (but more than 5%), he stays on the ballot and has another chance. (Jim Rice is a former Red Sox star who is currently in this sort of holding pattern). Players who aren't elected can stay on the ballot for up to 15 years. Many players are not selected the first time they are eligible, since some sportswriters think only the most elite players deserve a vote in their first year of eligibility.

The other traditional route to the Hall was via the Baseball Hall of Fame Committee on Baseball Veterans (affectionately known as the Veterans Committee, the source of many of the least-qualified members of the Hall), but also of many players whose perceived value rose over time. The 15-member Veterans Committee, made up of Hall of Fame players, baseball executives, and/or broadcasters, had the ability to address players that the BBWAA chose not to induct, as long as they met certain requirements. The first criteria for Veterans Committee selection was that the players had been retired for over 23 years and played in at least 10 seasons. Because there was a perception that Veterans Committee members were selecting their old cronies to the Hall based on marginal qualifications (such as Phil Rizzuto), the rules for who the Veterans Committee could select were tightened, but that created even greater problems. Under the revised rules, players whose careers started after 1945 had to have received at least 60% of the BBWAA vote or received at least 100 votes in the one season's BBWAA voting. (The Veterans Committee could also consider players who played 10 years in the Negro Leagues prior to 1946, or whose service in the Negro Leagues prior to 1946 and in the Major League from 1946 on totalled at least 10 seasons.) Unfortunately, this meant that the Veterans Committee could no longer do what it was originally created for—select players for the Hall of Fame whose greatness only becomes apparent after a number of years have passed, or who are deserving but unpopular with the BBWAA. For instance, Dwight Evans would never be eligible for selection to the Hall of Fame, despite his long and excellent career—because he was overshadowed and quickly dropped off the ballot without receiving 100 votes from the BBWAA. To remedy this, the Veteran's Committee was replaced by a vote of all living Hall of Famers.

Over the years, the Veterans Committee also considered the selection of managers, umpires, and baseball "pioneers/executives" who have been retired for five years. The waiting period was reduced to six months after the persons in question reached 65 years of age. The Veterans Committee selected about 150 members of the Hall of Fame, as opposed to fewer than 100 selected by the BBWAA. Veterans Committee selections include all of the managers, umpires, executives, and broadcasters in the Hall, in addition to most of the Negro Leaguers.

From 1971 through 1977, there was also a Negro League Committee that elected nine players to the Hall, including Satchel Paige, Josh Gibson, and Cool Papa Bell.

How does a player get put onto the permanently ineligible list? Can players be banned from baseball for committing crimes or having drug problems, or only for gambling?

In theory, the Commissioner of Baseball has wide-ranging powers to act for the "good of the game." Practically speaking, the commissioner isn't generally going to do anything without fairly widespread support among the owners (who hire and pay the commissioner). While it is theoretically possible that a player could be put on the list for committing crimes, or repeated drug suspensions, in reality it is only gambling that has gotten players into trouble. In the early days of baseball there were many gambling scandals, and the game itself, at the professional level, was endangered by the perception that the games were not honest. This culminated in 1920 when eight members of the Chicago White Sox team that lost the 1919 World Series were put on trial for intentionally throwing the series in exchange for payoffs from gamblers. The eight have been known as the "Black Sox" ever since. Though eventually acquitted (largely due to the fact that signed confessions disappeared from the courthouse), Judge Kenesaw Mountain Landis, hired by the owners as Commissioner of Baseball, banned the eight (including Joe Jackson and former Red Sox pitcher Ed Cicotte) permanently from major league baseball. Since then gambling on baseball games has been expressly forbidden.

While players have been suspended for up to a year for drug-related offenses, the commissioner is very unlikely to ban a player permanently for personal problems that don't affect the integrity of the game (even in cases where the player commits a violent crime, as with Wil Cordero's spousal abuse). This is partly because the Players Association would be likely to challenge such a suspension through arbitration or in court, and would probably win, undermining the commissioner's power. In a similar case in the 1980s, the Chicago White Sox tried to void the contract of pitcher Lamarr Hoyt, who was caught selling drugs, based on a standard good conduct clause in his contract—and lost the case.

What was the "Curse Of The Bambino"? Why did people say there was a curse on the Red Sox?

Baseball is a game of superstitions and traditions. The influence of fate is given great weight in the game and its legends, and there are speculations and theories, supernatural and otherwise, about many of the trends and patterns in the history of the game.

One of those superstitions was the "Curse of the Bambino," the supposed reason that the Red Sox had not won the World Series from 1918 until they finally "reversed the curse" in 2004. The curse was alleged to be the lasting influence of the departed Babe Ruth, and blamed on Harry Frazee, the owner who sold him.

Ruth was only one of a number of Red Sox players who eventually turned up in pinstripes, and an alternate history could well look at the Yankees rosters of the beginning of their dynasty and see a golden age of Red Sox championships. It is commonly said that Harry Frazee, then owner of the Sox, sold Ruth to finance his Broadway productions, specifically *No, No, Nanette*, but this is not precisely the case. Ruth was a discipline problem who was demanding to have his salary literally doubled (he *was* being dramatically underpaid), and Frazee was financially strapped from his purchase of the ballclub. Frazee, in justifying the sale, blamed Ruth's boisterous and difficult behavior for the team's failure to follow up on their championship year with anything better than a sixth-place finish. Ruth was sent south in 1919, and *No, No, Nanette* didn't hit the big time until 1925.

The years after the Ruth sale and the other departures of players to the Yankees were dark ones for the Red Sox. Many of the transfers were cash sales rather than trades, so comparatively unskilled, or at least untried, players needed to be brought up to fill out the Boston roster. In fact, the Red Sox did not appear in the World Series again until 1946. It was after 1946, in fact, that the notion of a "curse" first appeared. With World War II over, the Sox war heroes came home again, and baseball as it was meant to be played lived in Boston again. Ted Williams, Dom DiMaggio, Bobby Doerr, Johnny Pesky, and a number of other players came back from the war, and it seemed the Red Sox dynasty was finally back on track. Before 1946, the Sox had never yet lost a World Series, and they were favored to win it all over the Cardinals.

It came down to a seventh game, though. Dom DiMaggio left the game with a limp in the eighth inning, and weak-throwing Leon Culberson had to go into center field. Enos Slaughter led off the bottom of the eighth with a single, and was still on first with two outs—when Harry Walker popped a shot into left center field, which was chased by Culberson and relayed in a lob throw to Johnny Pesky. The shortstop turned in short left center, prepared to throw the ball into the infield so it wouldn't be mishandled, and saw Slaughter a few strides from home plate, scoring from first on the double.

"Pesky held the ball" became the anguished cry after the Sox failed to rally in the ninth, despite mounting a threat. Accused of hesitating on the throw, of losing Bobby Doerr's call of "HOME" in the crowd noise (though Doerr doesn't remember calling anything), or of losing the runner in the sun's glare, Johnny Pesky became the goat of the 1946 Series. After the loss in the "sure thing" World Series, rumors of a curse inflicted by the loss of Babe Ruth began to surface, though it would be 40 years before they'd become a significant public topic of conversation.

In 1948 the Red Sox tied the Cleveland Indians for first place on the last day of the season, but lost a one-game playoff when manager Joe McCarthy inexplicably started journeyman Denny Galehouse instead of one of his four stronger starting pitchers.

The next year the Sox went into Yankee stadium with a one-game lead and two games to play, and 20-game winners Mel Parnell and Ellis Kinder ready to take the mound. They lost both, and the Yankees went to the World Series.

In 1967 the Impossible Dream team, which had come out of nowhere to win one of the closest and most exciting pennant races in history, stretched another World Series to seven games—and lost in heartbreaking fashion. One of the team's rising young stars, Tony Conigliaro, was hit in the head by a pitch in August and lost for the year. (It effectively ended his career.) After the season, pitching ace Jim Lonborg destroyed his knee in a skiing accident. The team was no longer a contender the next season.

In 1972 a players strike caused the season to start a week late, and the missed games were not replayed. The Red Sox missed seven games, and the Detroit Tigers six. When the dust cleared, the Red Sox lost the division title by the margin of that single game: 85–70 to the Tigers' 86–70.

Boston was forced to play the 1975 World Series without rookie star Jim Rice, who'd had his wrist broken by a pitch the month before. What has been called the greatest baseball game ever, the legendary Game 6 of the 1975 World Series, was won by Carlton Fisk's wave-it-fair home run off the left field foul pole. These explosive heroics were followed by yet another Game 7 loss, reinforcing the highs-and-lows feel of Red Sox championship hopes.

In early 1978 Boston looked like the dominant team in the AL. At the close of play on July 19, they had built a lead of nine games over second place Milwaukee, while the Yankees were 14 games out in fourth. However, Rick Burleson, the shortstop cited as a sparkplug for the team, had injured his ankle just before midseason. And injuries started to catch up with them, as the Red Sox lost 9 of their next 10, and the lead dropped to 4½ games, and the Yankees got back within 8. Their lead was still strong enough that not many people worried—especially as the Yankees lineup and pitching was also full of injuries.

By the end of the season, however, the Yankees team was cobbled back together. The Boston pitching staff, perhaps frustrated by manager Don Zimmer, seemed almost to implode, and several major players were on the disabled list. Some weren't who should have been, such as third baseman Butch Hobson, who kept rearranging the bone chips in his throwing elbow when it locked, and throwing balls into the dugout and stands. Others, such as Carl Yastrzemski, missed time with injuries but didn't go onto the DL, meaning that the team was playing

shorthanded for long stretches. After several series between the teams, the
Yankees were up 3½ games in the division, and the Red Sox needed to win 12 out
of the 13 remaining games to make the postseason.

The last day of the season, the Red Sox won, the Yankees lost, and a tie was
forced: another single-game playoff, just like in 1948, to be held in Fenway Park.
(The Red Sox won a coin toss). Down by two in the seventh, two outs, two on,
light-hitting Yankees shortstop Bucky Dent came to the plate. He fouled the second pitch off his shin, replaced his cracked bat in the pause in game play, then
lofted a perfect Fenway Park home run over the Green Monster, a piddling pop-
fly down the left field line, aided by a shift in the wind.

Bucky Dent had four home runs and a .243 batting average on the season, and
had previously been 0-for-2 that game. Rumors circulated years later that the bat
he hit the home run with was one of Mickey Rivers's that had been corked.

The Sox cut the lead to 5–4, and had a chance in the ninth, but Yankees right
fielder Lou Piniella's blind stab (with the sun in his eyes) of Jerry Remy's one-out
single held Rick Burleson at second, so he couldn't score the tying run on Rice's
fly ball. The game ended when Yaz just missed a Goose Gossage fastball, popping
up to third to end the Red Sox season.

After being one pitch away from elimination in a hard-fought and dramatic
competition against the Angels, the 1986 Red Sox managed to stage a comeback,
claim the pennant, and get into the World Series, where they faced the New York
Mets. Boston won the first game in a 1–0 duel, the second handily, and then
dropped the next two to New York before winning Game 5. There was a theory
that the jinx had been broken; the Sox, after all, were one game away from victory and their rings.

The game was knotted 2–2 by a Mets rally in the fifth, but the Sox took a one-
run lead in the seventh. In the eighth, Roger Clemens, who had torn a blister in
the fifth and ripped a fingernail in the seventh, was pulled for a pinch hitter, who
struck out. A lefthanded pitcher was brought in to face Bill Buckner (who didn't
hit lefties well) with the bases loaded, and Don Baylor, who was told to be ready
to pinch hit, was not called in. Buckner flied out, and then took his place at first
base for the bottom of the eighth.

Calvin Schiraldi was brought in to pitch and seemed rattled, rushing a throw
and failing to get an out, throwing balls, and eventually blowing the save. The
game eventually went into extra innings.

In the tenth, Dave Henderson led off for the Sox with a home run. After two
strikeouts, Wade Boggs got a double and scored on a following single, pushing
the score to 5–3. Buckner was hit by a pitch, but Jim Rice lined out, leaving
Buckner stranded on first. With victory seemingly assured, Buckner (who'd had
ankle problems all year) stayed at first for the bottom of the tenth rather than giving up his place to the usual defensive replacement, Dave Stapleton.

Unlike the previous two innings, Schiraldi managed to get two outs quickly in
the tenth. The third batter reached on a single. The fourth, a pinch-hitter for the
pitcher, also reached. The next Mets player, Ray Knight, took a called strike and
fouled the next pitch off; the following pitch was blooped off his handle into short
center. A run scored, 5–4, runners on first and third, two outs.

A new pitcher was called in to face Mookie Wilson: Bob Stanley—the Red Sox career saves leader. Wilson fouled it off, took two pitches for balls, and fouled off another, leaving the Sox again one strike away from winning the Series. Two more foul balls heightened the tension, then a wild pitch allowed the runner on third to score. Tie game.

Wilson fouled off two more balls before hitting a tapper down the first base line. Buckner moved to intercept the ball as Stanley moved to cover the bag. The ball took a bounce, slipped under the first baseman's glove, and rolled through his legs into right field. Ray Knight rounded third, saw the error, and ran home. Game 6 was over, with the Mets winning.

The Sox had a three-run lead in Game 7, but eventually lost, 6–3.

It was after the 1986 World Series that the "curse of the Bambino" first made it into print, in the column of New York sportswriter George Vecsey. Just like everyone else covering the game, Vecsey had to do a quick rewrite of his column when the Mets came back to win Game 6. He had been working on a "redemption" theme, and when the Mets won, he turned it on its head, remaking it in to a "haunting" theme. When the Red Sox lost Game 7, he tied it to Ruth and Frazee—"Babe Ruth Curse Strikes Again." And there the matter rested, until 1990, when Dan Shaughnessy's book, *The Curse Of The Bambino*, was published. Suddenly, people who hadn't been alive when Denny Galehouse took the mound against Cleveland in 1948 were tying Bill Buckner to Johnny Pesky, and blaming them both on Harry Frazee.

In both 1988 and 1990, the Oakland Athletics swept the Red Sox in the ALCS. Ace Roger Clemens was inexplicably rattled in 1988, and was even thrown out of one game for cursing at an umpire whose calls he disagreed with. The Red Sox lost in both of those seasons to a better team, but now that the "curse" was in wide circulation, everything was shoehorned in to the storyline.

In the 1998 Division Series manager Jimy Williams chose to start sore-armed Pete Schourek in the crucial fourth game, despite fan clamoring for ace Pedro Martinez. (Boston needed to win two in a row to take the series.) Schourek pitched very well, but Tom Gordon, who'd been the best reliever in baseball all year, blew his first save since May, and the futility continued.

The 1999 American League pennant came down to a competition between the Red Sox and the Yankees after the Sox mounted a stunning comeback against the Indians in the Division Series. The games were plagued by controversy, as a single umpire botched several calls—cutting short potential Red Sox rallies in very close games. When another bad call in the fourth game had Nomar Garciaparra out at first, the crowd at Fenway bordered on riot, sensing another chance at a pennant cut short by perverse circumstance.

In 2003, the Red Sox had an opportunity to end all of the curse talk, when Pedro Martinez started Game 7 of the ALCS against Roger Clemens in Yankee Stadium. Clemens was knocked out in the fourth but Martinez was outstanding, allowing only two solo home runs to steroid-enhanced Jason Giambi through seven innings. With a bullpen that had been outstanding in the postseason, the situation looked great for the Sox as they took a 5–2 lead to the bottom of the eighth. Unfortunately, the only man in America who didn't realize that Martinez was gassed was Red Sox (soon to be ex-) manager Grady Little. Pedro retired the first batter of the eighth inning on a pop-up, and that was the last out he recorded. Jeter hit a hard line drive double to right-center, and Little left Martinez in the game. Williams drove Jeter in with a hard line drive. Matsui hit a hard line drive double down the right field line. Matsui's was the sixth hit, and the third extra-base hit, from the last eight Yankees batters. The next batter was Posada, who did not hit the ball hard, but his pop-up fell just out of reach of second baseman Todd Walker, and the game was tied. At which point Little finally removed Martinez.

But it was too late, and everyone watching knew it. At that point the question wasn't who would win, but when and how. The "when" was the bottom of the eleventh, the "how" was the Tim Wakefield knuckleball that didn't knuckle, deposited into the left field stands by Yankees third baseman Aaron Boone. And the talk of the curse intensified, yet again . . .

. . . until the Red Sox finally ended it in 2004. At the end of the 2003 season, fans and team alike were consumed with what had become a familiar feeling: "Why us?" Curse believers wrapped themselves in stoicism to protect themselves from the failure of their hopes in another year; nonbelievers wondered if there might be something to it after all. The hot stove season was tense and fraught with drama, with rumors surrounding the failed trade for A-Rod and the eventual landing of Curt Schilling. In some ways Schilling managed to turn the tone with his attitude of "Why not us?"—a slogan he had put on a t-shirt.

After sweeping the Anaheim Angels in the first round, the Red Sox met the Yankees for the third time in six years in the ALCS, this time with what appeared to be a clear pitching advantage. Until Curt Schilling was bombed in Game 1, unable to pitch effectively on a badly injured right ankle. When Martinez was outpitched by Jon Lieber in Game 2, the Red Sox were down 2–0 headed back to Boston. At which point things got very ugly. Game 3 was rained out on Friday night, and when the teams took to the field on Saturday, none of the pitchers seemed to show up. When the dust cleared, the Yankees had a 19–8 win, and a 3–0 series lead. No team had ever come back from a 3–0 deficit in baseball history.

In Game 4, the Yankees had closer Mariano Rivera on the mound in the ninth to protect a 4–3 lead, but Kevin Millar walked, pinch-runner Dave Roberts stole second, and Bill Mueller singled him home to tie the game, eventually won by the Sox in the twelfth on a David Ortiz walk-off home run. In Game 5, the Yankees had a 4–2 lead in the eighth, but Ortiz led off with a home run, Millar walked, Roberts pinch-ran and Nixon singled him to third, all off of setup man (and former Red Sox pitcher) Tom Gordon. Mariano Rivera's second consecutive blown save came when Varitek drove Roberts in with a fly ball. The Red Sox finally won it on a fourteenth inning single by David Ortiz, to send the Series back to New York with the Yankees up 3–2 for the second consecutive year.

Curt Schilling, who would require off-season surgery, took the mound for Game 6 with stitches holding the skin of his ankle down to anchor his damaged tendon in place, and was outstanding. A fourth-inning three-run home run from Mark Bellhorn (initially called a double by the left field umpire, and overturned by a meeting of all of the umps) gave the Red Sox a 4–0 lead, which they took into the late innings. The lead was 4–2 in the eighth when one of the signature plays of the series occurred. With Jeter at first and one out, Alex Rodriguez hit a weak, spinning ground ball off the end of the bat down the first base line. The ball was fielded by Sox pitcher Bronson Arroyo, who went to tag Rodriguez, but the ball went flying down the right field line, past first base, while Jeter scored and Rodriguez went to second. As Fox announcer Joe Buck (accurately) called it, "I know when that ball was trickling down the right field line, Red Sox fans were thinking 'here we go again.' " And most were. This was exactly the kind of thing that had happened over the years in their games against the Yankees.

But not this time. As the Yankee Stadium crowd roared, for the tying run was now at second base with one out, the Red Sox came out to argue the play—and replays showed exactly why. As Rodriguez approached Arroyo, he had reached out with his left hand and slapped the ball out of the pitcher's glove. Again, the umpires huddled together, finally calling Rodriguez out and sending Jeter back to first base. The crowd tossed baseballs and rubbish onto the field, prompting Terry Francona to call his team back to the dugout. With riot police on the field, the Red Sox held their lead through the bottom of the eighth, and brought closer Keith Foulke—who had pitched four innings and 72 pitches over the previous two games—in to finish. He did not have his best command, walking two, and blood pressure throughout Red Sox nation was elevated as Tony Clark, a power hitter who had been atrocious for Boston two years earlier, faced Foulke with two on and two out. With a full count, and people envisioning a home run that would put 2004 on a par with 2003 in Red Sox lore, Clark struck out to end the game.

With the pitching staffs of both teams depleted, Derek Lowe took the mound for Boston in Game 7 on only two days' rest. His outstanding performance was made much more comfortable for Boston fans by Ortiz's two-run homer in the top of the first, and Damon's grand slam in the top of the second. The only drama from that point on came when Pedro Martinez, on one day's rest, pitched the bottom of the seventh, allowing two runs, as the Red Sox finally beat the Yankees in a winner-take-all/loser-go-home game, for the first time since the Ruth trade.

If it was necessary for the Red Sox to come back from 3–0 against the Yankees, and to win the ALCS in Yankee Stadium, for the "curse" to be lifted, it was appropriate that they faced the St. Louis Cardinals—who had beaten the Sox in 1946 and 1967—in the World Series. But after the Yankees series, even a competetive World Series would have been anti-climactic, and this was not a competetive series. The Red Sox scored in the first inning of each game; the Cardinals never led, and the Sox swept the Series in four games.

The "Curse Of The Bambino" was finally over.

There have been other teams that haven't won. The Cubs and White Sox have each had World Series droughts longer than Boston's, but no one speaks seriously about "curses" (though there is a "nanny-goat" curse that gets joked about with the Cubs). Some people have said that there was no "curse of the Bambino"— the Red Sox were just collateral damage from the "Black Sox" scandal, as the 1919 White Sox threw the World Series, and from then until 2004, no team from Chicago and no team nicknamed "Sox" had won. But most Red Sox fans have decried the "curse" as a myth.

People in other parts of the country pointed to Cleveland, and the Cubs, and other teams that were perpetually bad, and said that Red Sox fans shouldn't complain. Which missed the key feature of the curse: It isn't that the Red Sox were always bad. On the contrary, the focus of the "curse" was that the Sox had frequently been good or very good, and found excruciating ways to lose.

The Chicago Cubs may have been "lovable losers"—the Boston Red Sox were not. From 1967 through 2003, only two major league teams had better records than the Red Sox—the New York Yankees, who won six World Series in that span, and the Arizona Diamondbacks, who won one World Series, despite being in existence for only six seasons. The Red Sox had a better cumulative winning percentage than Oakland (four World Series), Cincinnati (three World Series), the nine teams (including expansion teams Florida and Toronto) that won two and the five teams that won one. No other team had as many winning seasons (30) over that span as the Boston Red Sox.

From the sixth game in 1986 until the first game in 1998, the Red Sox lost 13 consecutive postseason games. Six of those 13 games were started by Roger Clemens, one of the greatest pitchers in baseball history. Assuming that they had a 50–50 chance of winning any one of them, the odds of randomly losing 13 in a row are 1 in 8,192. It isn't surprising that fans sought supernatural explanations.

People pointed to language and symbols as evidence for the curse. Bruce Hurst is an anagram for *B Ruth Curse*, and Peter Schourek can be rearranged as *Ruth Keep Score*. The retired numbers 9–4–1–8, re-arranged in 1997, on the facade in right field were also the date of the eve of the 1918 World Series, the last victorious World Series for the Sox before 2004.

In the half-century since the notion of the curse was spawned, the notion of suffering had become part of the culture of baseball fandom in New England. Fans who were merely thought of as long-suffering in 1946 came to see themselves as profoundly afflicted by this long drought in championships. It became a badge of pride, to carry on in loyalty despite the lack of consummation.

The feeling of almost supernatural persecution also flavored individual games. A short series in the middle of the summer could be charged by one incredible come-from-behind win, as if in tribute to Carlton Fisk and the good Game 6, and then let down again by a late-innings squander. There was always the hope that somehow, someway, the Sox would pull something out of a hat and come back to win, and always the fear (and sometimes the conviction) that something would go wrong, somewhere, leaving the team and its fans let down again.

Before 2003, 1986 stood alone, but only in the slope of fall, not in the type. From losing the 14-game lead in 1978 to Bucky Bleepin' Dent; from "Pesky held the ball" in '46 to losing to Gibson three times in 1967; from Parnell and Kinder losing in Yankee Stadium in 1949 to Posada's bloop extending the game for Boone's home run, the particular magic of the curse was to "snatch defeat from the jaws of victory," to turn well-earned victory into heartrending loss. It's tradition, it's superstition; it's part of the flavor of Red Sox fandom.

And now, thankfully, it's a part of history.

Although the Yankees minor league team in Trenton (which was a Red Sox affiliate until a bitter parting a few years back) has threatened to hold a "restore the curse" day in 2005. . . .

A Red Sox Bibliography

Here is an annotated list of some of the best and most interesting books written about the Red Sox over the years, along with a few key reference books about baseball. Many of the older books are out of print, but used copies are readily (and usually inexpensively) available through search services such as www.bibliofind.com or www.half.com.

Babe: The Legend Comes to Life, by Robert Creamer. One of the best sports biographies ever, it gives excellent info on Ruth's years with the Red Sox (1914–19, including 3 championships). There's a lot more to Ruth's story, of course, and the whole book is a must-read.

The Babe in Red Stockings, by Kerry Keene, Raymond Sinibaldi, and David Hickey. An exploration of Babe Ruth's time with the Red Sox, including a lot of new material that refutes some of the longstanding legends surrounding Ruth's time in Boston and his sale to the Yankees.

The Ballplayers, edited by Mike Shatzkin. A mammoth book containing brief biographies and essays about more than 6,000 players, teams, leagues, and other baseball topics. The book appeared in 1990.

Beyond the Sixth Game, by Peter Gammons. This book shows why Gammons built a reputation as one of the finest local sportswriters in the country, long before he moved to ESPN. Gammons uses the 1975 Red Sox as a microcosm of how baseball changed in the free agency era. The descriptions of the great 1970s teams and how the team lost its way in the early 1980s clarifies a confusing time.

Blood Feud, by Bill Nowlin and Jim Prime. A complete history of the rivalry between the Red Sox and Yankees, from the inception of both teams through the 2004 World Series and beyond.

The Boston Red Sox, by Donald Honig. A coffee table book with lots of great photos and a basic history of the team.

Boston Red Sox 100 Years: The Official Retrospective. Glossy coffee table book put out by the *Sporting News.* Lots of pretty pictures, not a whole lot of text—and not the place to look for controversy.

The Boys of October: How the 1975 Red Sox Embodied Baseball's Ideals—and Restored Our Spirits, by Doug Hornig. Hornig, a New Englander better known for his suspense writing, uses the 1975 team as a metaphor for heroism in troubled times. Includes interviews with Yaz, Tiant, Bernie Carbo, Don Zimmer, and many of the others involved with the team.

Broadcast Rites and Sites: I Saw It on the Radio With the Boston Red Sox, by Joe Castiglione with Douglas B. Lyons. Collection of vignettes by the longtime radio broadcaster.

The Bronx Zoo, by Sparky Lyle with Peter Golenbock. This diary of the infamous 1978 season is a must-read for masochistic Sox fans, though it's told from the perspective of the hated Yankees. We're not crazy about the ending, but Lyle's descriptions of clubhouse pranks and fights are often hilarious. Lyle briefly discusses his days as a Red Sox reliever, prior to his disastrous trade.

The Catcher Was a Spy, by Nicholas Dawidoff. A biography of Moe Berg, the brilliant Red Sox catcher who also served as a World War II–era intelligence agent.

The Curse of the Bambino, by Dan Shaughnessy. A dark and pessimistic, but funny, history of the Red Sox. Includes a lot of gossip about who was sleeping with whom on the 1980s teams. Also worth picking up is Shaughnessy's *At Fenway.*

Faithful, by Stewart O'Nan and Stephen King. A day-by-day account of the 2004 World Championship season told through the correspondence of two writers. King's second foray into Red Sox writing, following the fictional *The Girl Who Loved Tom Gordon.*

Fear Strikes Out, by Jimmy Piersall and Al Hirshberg. Later turned into a powerful, if not particularly accurate movie, this 1955 baseball classic recently was brought back into print. A moving account of baseball and mental illness, co-written by the popular but troubled outfielder and noted sportswriter Hirshberg.

Feeding the Green Monster, by Rob Neyer. Neyer, an ESPN website columnist and former assistant to Bill James, spent the entire 2000 season in Boston, attending every Red Sox home game. Writing mainly from a fan's perspective, Neyer describes his impressions of Fenway, baseball, and a controversial, disappointing Red Sox season.

Fenway, by Peter Golenbock. Entertaining team history, aided by many interviews of players and fans. Very similar to the author's acclaimed histories of the Yankees (*Dynasty*) and Brooklyn Dodgers (*Bums*). Nitpickers may be distracted by the surprising number of errors.

Fenway: A Biography in Words and Pictures, by Dan Shaughnessy, with photographs by Stan Grossfeld, and introduction by Ted Williams. A history and commentary on the ballpark, with some tremendous photographs.

Fenway Lives: The Team Behind the Team, by Bill Nowlin. Interviews with and recollections by the people who work in and around Fenway during a ballgame.

The Fenway Project, edited by Bill Nowlin and Cecilia Tan. One night in the life of Fenway Park, as chronicled by 64 different writers and photographers under the auspices of the Society for American Baseball Research in 2002.

The First World Series, by Roger Abrams. The story of baseball fans and the first World Series, won by Boston in 1903.

A Funny Thing Happened on the Way to Cooperstown, by Mickey McDermott with Howard Eisenberg. Lighthearted memoir by the charismatic Red Sox pitcher, published just before his death in 2003.

The Girl Who Loved Tom Gordon, by Stephen King. A short novel about a girl lost in the woods who depends on the Red Sox pitcher—listened to over her Walkman—for support. A novel written as a tribute to the Sox by one of the team's greatest fans—even if catcher Jason Varitek's name is misspelled throughout, and Gordon had to have arm surgery as soon as the book came out.

The Glory of Their Times, by Lawrence Ritter. Many say it's the best baseball book ever written. The book is made up of interviews with a wide variety of players from the early twentieth century, told in the first person. This style has been copied many times, but there's something magical about the way Ritter edited the players' stories; you feel like you're on the field with them. Two Red Sox greats are included, Harry Hooper and Smoky Joe Wood, so you'll learn a lot about the old-time teams.

Idiot, or How I Learned to Stop Thinking and Avoid the Curse, by Johnny Damon with Peter Golenbock. The beloved and outspoken center fielder's take on the 2004 World Championship, written in the irreverent style of Golenbock's famed collaborations with Sparky Lyle and Billy Martin.

Images of Baseball: The Pawtucket Red Sox. The book includes more photos (over 200) than text, tracing the history of baseball in Pawtucket back to the Slaters and Indians in the pre-Mondor decades. It also includes pictures from the longest game, McCoy Stadium's 1999 renovation, and of former PawSox greats like Jim Rice, Wade Boggs, Mo Vaughn, and Nomar Garciaparra. It's available in paperback from the Pawtucket Red Sox.

Lefty Grove: An American Original, by Jim Kaplan. An excellent biography published by the Society for American Baseball Research in 2000.

The Long Ball, by Tom Adelman. Like *The Boys of October*, another good book on the 1975 season.

Lost Summer, by Bill Reynolds. The story of the 1967 "Impossible Dream" season.

Mr. Red Sox: The Johnny Pesky Story, by Bill Nowlin. A recent biography of the Red Sox great by a well-known Red Sox historian.

My Turn At Bat, by Ted Williams. Still one of the best autobiographies by a ballplayer.

Moneyball: The Art of Winning an Unfair Game, by Michael Lewis. An in-depth study of Oakland GM Billy Beane, who was coveted by the Red Sox and who pioneered a view of baseball shared by Boston management, during the 2002 season. A hugely influential and important book with a number of Red Sox tie-ins, such as a Bill James profile, Scott Hatteberg disagreeing with the old Red Sox coaching philosophy, Kevin Youkilis described as the Greek God of Walks, and an analysis of Johnny Damon's defensive value.

1918: Babe Ruth and the World Champion Red Sox, by Alan Wood. Extensive, well-researched look at the Red Sox championship season. Wood's book covers Ruth's transition to the outfield, the effects of World War I on the season, and Boston's World Series victory over the Cubs.

One Day at Fenway, by Steve Kettman. With the assistance of a corps of researchers, this book attempts to capture a single Red Sox game.

One Pitch Away: The Players' Stories of the 1986 League Championships and World Series, by Mike Sowell. The history of the events leading up to the 1986 World Series, as well as accounts by the key players involved, drawn from records and interviews.

The Progress of the Seasons, by George Higgins. Covers the years 1946–86.

Real Grass, Real Heroes, by Dom DiMaggio with Bill Gilbert. Light, but very interesting look at the last prewar season, 1941, written by the man who was a teammate of Ted Williams and the brother of Joe DiMaggio.

Red Sox Century, by Glenn Stout and Richard Johnson. Comprehensive account of the team's first 100 years, written by two prominent sports historians. Gained attention for contradicting the prevailing accounts about Babe Ruth's sale and Boston's delay in signing black players. Stout also edited *Impossible Dreams*, a reader on the Red Sox.

Red Sox Heroes of Yesteryear, by Herb Crehan. A massive collection of interviews with former Red Sox players and managers, previously published in *Red Sox Magazine*. The word "heroes" is used loosely—Don Zimmer, never a hero to Red Sox Nation, is included—but the soft-focus remembrances of the team's past are fascinating.

The Red Sox Reader, edited by Dan Riley. A cross-section of articles about the team through the years, including the famous John Updike piece on Ted Williams.

A Rooter's Guide to the Red Sox, by Harold Kaese. An odd 1974 collection of facts and tidbits compiled from 41 years of the longtime sportswriter's notes.

The Science of Hitting, by Ted Williams and John Underwood. Possibly the best book ever written about hitting a baseball. First published in 1971.

Shut Out: A Story of Race and Baseball in Boston, by Howard Bryant. Critically acclaimed study of Boston's racial dynamics as played out in the history of the Red Sox and their minority players. It provides insight into the history of race relations in Boston, segregation, busing and politics. Written by a noted sports-writer who grew up as a black baseball fan in Boston.

Tales from the Red Sox Dugout, by Jim Prime with Bill Nowlin. A collection of anecdotes and strange stories, with something of a greater focus on recent play-ers. An overview of the historical and current wackiness of the team. There's also a sequel, *More Tales from the Red Sox Dugout: Yarns from the Sox* and the two writers have done a number of other Red Sox-related books, such as *Fenway Saved* (with Mike Ross).

The Teammates, by David Halberstam. A study of the relationship between four all-time Red Sox greats, who were also longtime friends: Ted Williams, Bobby Doerr, Johnny Pesky, and Dom DiMaggio.

Ted Williams, by Leigh Montville. Widely acclaimed as the definitive biography of the Splendid Splinter. Montville tells great stories of Williams's success on the ballfield, heroism in the military, and battles with the "knights of the keyboard," while also detailing Teddy Ballgame's complex personal relationships (including the sad details of his later years). Neither a whitewash nor a hatchet job, Montville's biography humanizes a legend—yet doesn't make him any less com-pelling.

Ted Williams: The Pursuit of Perfection, by Jim Prime and Bill Nowlin. A tribute to Ted, drawn from over 200 interviews, including Hank Aaron, Bobby Knight, Stan Musial, George Bush, Bobby Doerr, Cleveland Amory, Bill Lee, Curt Gowdy, and Bud Leavitt. Many of the illustrations come from Nowlin's vast col-lection of Williams memorabilia.

Ted Williams: reflections on a Splendid Life, edited by Lawrence Baldassaro. A collection of original newspaper and magazine articles judging, analyzing, vilify-ing, and adulating Ted Williams, from the beginning of his career in Boston, right up through his retirement 50 years later. An earlier version was titled *The Ted Williams Reader.*

Ted Williams: The Seasons of the Kid, by Richard Ben Cramer. Large format cof-fee-table book, featuring a fabulous collection of photos with relatively brief biographical text. Currently out of print and hard to find, but well worth having if you can track it down. Other notable Ted Williams books include *Teddy Ballgame: My Life in Pictures*, by Ted Williams and David Pietrusza; *Hitter: The Life and Turmoils of Ted Williams*, by Ed Linn; and *A Baseball Life*, by Michael Seidel.

This Time, Let's Not Eat the Bones, by Bill James. A best-of compilation by a writer who redefined baseball analysis with his *Baseball Abstract* (and who now works for the Red Sox). There are articles on a number of Red Sox players and teams included, as well as many other fascinating bits (including what may be the best and clearest article ever written about the salary arbitration process). James's *Historical Baseball Abstract* (extensively revised in 2001) is a terrific study of how the game, teams, and players evolved over the years, and his *Whatever Happened to the Hall of Fame* is a fascinating look at the players who were selected (as well as many who weren't) and the shifting politics of the Hall of Fame. Actually, anything by Bill James is worth reading. Don't be put off by the stathead reputation; James is a lively and incisive sportswriter.

Total Baseball, edited by John Thorn, Pete Palmer, and others, is the official encyclopedia of Major League Baseball. Like the legendary but out of print *Baseball Encyclopedia*, *Total Baseball* has a complete record of major league players, but instead of a season-by-season record of teams, the book has a more anecdotal approach to each season. *Total Baseball* also includes essays on key players and topics, and features many newer statistical categories.

Watching Baseball: Discovering the Game Within the Game, by Jerry Remy with Corey Sandler. Recent book by the longtime Red Sox broadcaster and second baseman, who's become a New England favorite.

What Do You Think of Ted Williams Now? A Remembrance, by Richard Ben Cramer. Adapted from Cramer's acclaimed 1986 profile in *Esquire* magazine, updated to cover Williams's struggles in his last years. Contains rare, moving insights about The Splinter's personal life, without diminishing the traits that made him a hero to millions.

Why Not Us?, by Leigh Montville. A collection of stories from Red Sox fans about what the 2004 World Championship meant to them personally. The genesis of Montville's book came from a post on the Sons of Sam Horn online message board, when dozens of fans implored the Red Sox to "Win it For" various long-suffering relatives and friends. Many of those touching, emotional posts are included in this book.

The Wrong Stuff, by Bill Lee with Dick Lally. A quirky autobiography from one of the Red Sox's quirkiest players. Also worth reading is Lee's *Little Red (Sox) Book*.

Yaz: Baseball, The Wall, and Me, by Carl Yastrzemski with Gerald Eskenazi. Better than most "as told to" sports autobiographies, with insights on what it took for Yaz to play so well for so long. Has some interesting anecdotes about Yaz's relationship with Ted Williams, Tom Yawkey, and many of his teammates.

The Year of the Gerbil, by Con Chapman. About the 1978 season.

The Red Sox on the Internet

The Internet Revolution has been a wonderful development for baseball fans. Instead of waiting for the morning paper or the 11 o'clock news, fans can access instant boxscores, game broadcasts, stats, news stories, rumors, and just about anything else they want to know about their favorite team. They can chat with other fans at any hour, and from anywhere in the world.

Here are a few of the Net's best resources for Red Sox fans.

General Baseball Information

Major League Baseball (www.mlb.com): Baseball's official website. In addition to the standard news, scores, and stats, this site lets fans listen to teams' radio broadcasts. It also features lots of officially licensed baseball merchandise, plus links to every team's official website. The MLB site is somewhat generic and sanitized, but is a good starting point for fans.

ESPN (http://baseball.espn.go.com): Probably the most popular baseball website. This site provides instant updates of game action, detailed boxscores, lots of stats, and columns by Peter Gammons, sabremetrician Rob Neyer, and others. Its writers also have frequent chat sessions with fans. Some of the content, such as Neyer's column, requires a paid "premium" membership.

CBS SportsLine (www.cbs.sportsline.com): Information-heavy site similar to ESPN, but with more of a focus on Rotisserie/Fantasy Leagues. It also features pitch-by pitch updates of games with a wealth of instantly available stats. (It's the site that announcers tend to keep up on their laptops during games.)

Fox Sports (www.foxsports.com): Another good, wide-ranging source of baseball info. This site is particularly good on business-related issues, and features lots of well-known columnists.

CNN/Sports Illustrated (http://sportsillustrated.cnn.com): Combines two excellent resources, giving fans lots of content, including top columnists and a fine historical section.

The Sporting News (www.sportingnews.com): No longer "The Bible of Baseball," but the website features outstanding team-by-team coverage.

USA Today (www.usatoday.com/sports): Lots of info, including team updates and articles from the *Baseball Weekly* newspaper. This site is particularly valuable for Rotisserie/Fantasy players.

Baseball America (www.baseballamerica.com): Online version of the newspaper, which is the top source of information on minor league and amateur baseball. In addition to many articles about future prospects, its minor league and winter league stats are updated daily.

RotoWorld (www.rotoworld.com): This is probably the best site for diehard Rotisserie/Fantasy players to visit. Even if you're not a Rotisserie fan, this is a good source for the latest baseball news, including up-to-the minute reports on injuries, trades, and rumors—even for obscure players.

Sportspages.com (www.sportspages.com): Contains links to every major newspaper's sports section. Fans can also pick any pro team and read recent articles from a wide variety of sources.

John Skilton's Baseball Links (www.baseball-links.com): Extremely well-organized warehouse of baseball sites, divided by categories (players, teams, leagues, rules, history, etc.). If you can't find a baseball site on Skilton's page, it probably doesn't exist. It's a great starting point for any baseball-loving websurfer.

Sean Lahman's Baseball Links (www.baseball1.com): Not quite as extensive as Skilton's site, but still a terrific source for baseball stats and analysis. Fans can download Lahman's free database, which has stats on every big league player.

Baseball Reference (www.baseball-reference.com): Outstanding statistical resource on teams and players; it's like having *Total Baseball* at your fingertips. It includes conventional and sabremetric stats, plus the addictive "similarity scores," which finds the most comparable careers to any big league player.

Bill Simmons (http://sports.espn.go.com/espn/page2/simmons/index): The home of the former Boston Sports Guy, and a frequent commentator on the Red Sox and other Boston area sports teams. Simmons can still hit the home run, although his column is as much about pop culture as about Boston sports these days.

The Dead Ball Era (www.thedeadballera.com) is a macabre site devoted to dead ballplayers. It includes obituaries, pictures of gravesites, and stories about accidents, murders, suicides, etc. involving major league baseball players.

Official Red Sox-Related Sites

Official Site (www.redsox.com): Much to the chagrin of many fans, Major League Baseball decided to take over each team's official website, giving all of them a uniform look and feel. While this has improved some teams' sites, others have lost a certain individuality and charm. Nevertheless, the official site remains one of the best sources for Red Sox information. Features include full game-day coverage, minor league info, player bios, audio/video, historical articles, and official press releases that make even the worst utilityman seem like a future Hall of Famer. The site also includes information on buying tickets and merchandise, as well as community service links.

Minor League Sites: Each affiliate has its own website (see Visiting the Minor Leagues section on page 314 for details).

The Jimmy Fund (www.jimmyfund.com): Information on the Red Sox favorite charity, special programs, success stories, and donations.

The Boston Globe (www.boston.com/sports/baseball/redsox/) and *The Boston Herald* (http://redsox.bostonherald.com/redSox.bg): The two most prominent local newspapers post each day's stories and columns, and are great resources for out-of-town fans.

Providence Journal-Bulletin (www.projo.com/redsox): In addition to Red Sox coverage, ProJo extensively covers the nearby Pawtucket Red Sox, so it's a great source on prospects.

Red Sox Player Websites

In the early days of the Internet, some visionary big leaguers, like pitcher C.J. Nitkowski and former Sox coach Wendell "Wave 'Em In" Kim, created their own quirky, fun websites. But today, such sites are very rare; the few remaining ones are rarely updated. Later on, many players had generic "official" sites that were usually under the umbrella of bigger corporations, with the primary goal of selling merchandise and ads. Most of these companies have gone belly-up, and as a result, few current Red Sox players have official sites.

Manny Ramirez has a pretty attractive site (www.mannyramirez.com) with a message board, Manny's comments on select games, and information on Manny's charitable foundation.

Curt Schilling, one of the game's most net-savvy players, has two charitable sites: Curt's Pitch (www.als-ma.org/curtspitch) is dedicated to ALS research/funding, and he and his wife Shonda's Shade Foundation (www.shade-foundation.org) is dedicated to research and prevention for melanoma (which Shonda was diagnosed with three years ago).

Two former Red Sox greats also have official sites. Ted Williams's site (www.tedwilliams.com) includes career highlights, memorabilia, and information on his Florida museum, although the site is seldom updated. It might be most interesting for its coverage of Williams's other careers: military pilot and world-class fisherman. Carl Yastrzemski's site (www.yaz8.com) is run by his agent and primarily exists to sell merchandise.

Broadcaster and cult favorite Jerry Remy has an interactive, frequently updated site (www.TheRemyReport.com) as well.

Fan-Run Red Sox Websites

Sons of Sam Horn (http://sonsofsamhorn.com): Named for the cult legend and former Boston DH, this has become one of the leading sites for Red Sox discussion. An estimated 5,000 readers a day visit SOSH's message boards, which feature intelligent, on-topic discussion about the team (owner John Henry and players Curt Schilling and Kevin Youkilis are occasional participants). The website also has columns, articles, pictures, and links, plus some of the Web's best coverage of Red Sox minor leaguers.

Royal Rooters (www.redsoxnation.net/forums/) has also become very prominent; it's probably the #2 message board behind SOSH right now. It appears to have grown out of two sources: *Providence Journal-Bulletin* message board posters who were tired of trolls, and people who find SOSH too "elitist." The site also has some excellent interviews and features.

Red Sox Diehard (www.redsoxdiehard.com): A comprehensive site with history, information, quirky articles, polls, message boards, Fenway photos, and a Red Sox store. This site is updated frequently by webmaster Kristen Cornette, a Sox fan from Atlanta.

The Buffalo Head Society (www.buffalohead.org): Excellent articles on Red Sox players past and present, including an outstanding piece on Tony Conigliaro. Named for the anti-Don Zimmer faction of Red Sox players in the 1970s. Also contains a comprehensive list of Red Sox radio and TV announcers, and of uniform numbers—every player, coach, and manager who wore each number. You'll find plenty of fun, oddball trivia here.

Boston's Dirt Dogs (www.bostondirtdogs.com): Before the team's late-season collapse, the 2001 Red Sox acquired the "Dirt Dogs" nickname for their gritty play. This site borrows the nickname and gritty tone, and is filled with cynical but often funny analysis of the Red Sox as well as news, links, and merchandise with a Dirt Dogs logo.

Red Sox Connection (www.redsoxconnection.com): Contains good original articles on topics ranging from the minors to the Hall of Fame, plus oddball factoids and updated links to news articles about the Red Sox.

Our Red Sox (www.ourredsox.com): Site that bills itself as "All Red Sox, All the Time." Its highlights include tributes to current stars plus updated news items and fan-written columns.

The Sox Prospects Site (www.soxprospects.com): has lots of great information on Red Sox farmhands, former prospects, major and minor league transactions, and draft history.

Darkhawk's Boston Red Sox Page (http://aelfhame.net/~darkhawk/baseball/): A personal site with essays and commentary and a little bit of creative work.

The Bosox Babes Network (www.bosoxbabes.com): Articles, essays, and a blog all "dedicated to female fans of the Boston Red Sox and showing that baseball is NOT solely a guys' sport."

Fenway Nation (www.fenwaynation.com): Contains news, links, and fan columns.

1918 Red Sox (www.1918redsox.com): Operated by Alan Wood, who wrote *1918: Babe Ruth and the World Champion Boston Red Sox*. It contains information and links on the team and its players, plus box scores of every game. Wood also runs a daily blog on the team, The Joy of Sox (http://joyofsox.blogspot.com).

The Fan's Choice (www.allsports.com/mlb/redsox/): Has articles, photos, stats, quizzes, and links to buy Red Sox merchandise.

Save Fenway Park (www.savefenwaypark.com): Site for a nonprofit group of fans dedicated to preserving and renovating Fenway in its current location.

The Miserable Red Sox Fan Forum (http://kelly.jefferson.net/soxforum/): Site for Red Sox fans to vent when the team or a player does something especially exasperating. Gives out a monthly "Harry Frazee Award for making us cry."

Not all Red Sox fans are English-speaking, of course. Among the many foreign language Red Sox sites are Daigo's Red Sox blog (www.go-redsox.com) and http://redsox.japaneseballplayers.com, both in Japanese

Newsgroups and Mailing Lists

Red Sox Newsgroup (Usenet: alt.sports.baseball.bos-redsox): Forum for fans to post their thoughts on the team, analyze stats, argue about the manager and GM, and reminisce about Sox history. Like many unmoderated newsgroups, it has its share of "flame wars" between overzealous Red Sox and Yankees fans, but there's plenty of intelligent, provocative discussion. Regular posters include most of the contributors to this book. Newcomers are welcomed, provided they participate in a reasonably polite and intelligent fashion.

Red Sox Mailing List (apple.ease.lsoft.com/archives/bosox.html): Created in 1991 and currently operated by Keith Woolner. Same basic idea as the newsgroup, but the mailing list keeps discussions more focused by discouraging off-topic posts and "flaming." Members can follow a simple procedure to subscribe (there are about 600 subscribers), and the list is received via e-mail. The site also includes an FAQ (Frequently Asked Questions) section on the Red Sox.

Many of the sites listed in this section have their own message boards, which follow similar procedures as the Newsgroup. The most prominent of these are Sons of Sam Horn and ProJo.

Tell Your Own Story

Do you have your own story that you'd like to see included in the next edition of this book? Is there something you'd like to see added to a player entry, or a piece of history that you'd like to clarify? Is there a question you've always been dying to ask? Do you think it's a travesty that Scott Fletcher and Randy Kutcher aren't included in the player entries? Or would you just like to comment to the people who worked on this book? To reach the editors, e-mail soxfan@swordsmith.com, or write to:

Leigh Grossman
Attn: Red Sox Fan Handbook
PO Box 242
Pomfret, CT 06258

About the Contributors

Carl Bérubé has been a Sox fan since the Impossible Dream season of 1967. Raised in central Massachusetts, he lost his mind after graduating high school and enlisted in the USMC. Regaining his senses four years later, he decided to relocate to Beaufort, South Carolina, where he met his wife Paula (who agreed to marry him despite the fact that he was a "damnyankee"). Nowadays, Carl makes his living as a multitasking computer geek for a manufacturing company based in Ohio. He and Paula currently live on a barrier island off the coast of South Carolina with their teenaged daughter Katie, six cats, and whatever wildlife happens to happen by.

Lyford Beverage, a native of Maine, is a 1985 graduate of Worcester Polytechnic Institute and has worked as a computer engineer—writing software, designing hardware and analyzing system performance since then. Some of his fondest childhood memories are of lying in bed on North Haven listening to the Red Sox on the radio. He is neither a lawyer nor a statistician, though he occasionally portrays one or the other on the Internet. He is a member of the choir at historic Park Street Church on the Boston Common, with a particular fondness for Handel's *Messiah*. He lives in Lawrence, Massachusetts, with his wife Lori and their children, Lyf, Lisa, Sam, and Ben.

Dave Bismo is a writer/researcher for a television news organization in New York City. He has also written freelance reviews for several websites. Bismo has a bachelor's degree in math from Binghamton University, where he worked as a radio disc jockey, and a master's degree in broadcasting from Brooklyn College. He lives in Brooklyn, New York, and listens to Red Sox games on Hartford's WTIC—at least until the signal fades.

Keith R.A. DeCandido has been a Yankees fan since birth (his paternal grandfather attended the first game at Yankee Stadium on 18 April 1923, forty-six years *to the day* before Keith was born; his maternal grandfather was part of the construction crew that refurbished the Stadium in the 1970s; it was genetically inevitable). In 2002 and 2003, he wrote an Internet column on the Yankees called "Bleacher Creature Feature," which is archived at his website at DeCandido.net, and he continues to do occasional baseball commentary on his LiveJournal under the username "kradical." When he's not rooting for the Yankees and incurring the wrath of Red Sox fans everywhere, he is a science fiction author with over a dozen novels to his credit, including many in the *Star Trek* universe, and also a musician, editor, anthologist, and book packager.

Leigh Grossman is a writer, editor, college instructor, and reviewer. He teaches writing, science fiction, and book publishing at the University of Connecticut, and runs Swordsmith Productions, a book production company that works on several hundred books per year for various publishers. Grossman is the author of nine books from six different publishers, and has reviewed books for *Absolute Magnitude, Horror* magazine, and *Wavelengths*. He lives in northeast Connecticut.

Joe Kuras was raised as a Red Sox fan in Grafton, Massachusetts and never left his hometown. As a youth in the 1960s, Saturday and Sunday afternoons were spent faithfully in front of the black and white TV, watching the Red Sox and listening to the play-by-play with Curt Gowdy, Ned Martin, and Art Gleason. Commercials for Narragansett Beer, Atlantic Oil, and White Owl Cigars were a trademark of Red Sox games, along with the Johnny Most postgame scoreboard show. The first Red Sox game he attended was in 1961 against the Washington Senators and the results were typical of the team back then. The Sox lost, Jackie Jensen hit two home runs for Boston, and Red Sox fans booed their own Billy Muffett who came into the game to pitch in relief.

From there Joe took the customary route of many youths in America, playing Little League baseball, junior high and high school baseball, capped off with 20 consecutive years on the same team in a men's softball league. Joe was an officer of the softball league, coached youth baseball and was also the president of the local Little League for several seasons. For ten years, Joe was the minor league correspondent and Webmaster for *A Red Sox Journal*, a publication of the Buffalo Head Society. He is currently the general manager and coach of the Grafton Lake Sox, a summer league team for high school and college age ballplayers.

A graduate of Nichols College in Dudley, Kuras still resides in Grafton with his wife Maryellen. He has three grown children and manages a software test lab for a Massachusetts-based investment company. Kuras co-authored *A History of the Polish American Community of South Grafton, Massachusetts* in 1999 and is the treasurer of the Polish National Home in South Grafton.

Robert Machemer grew up in the suburbs of Philadelphia. He attended Amherst College, but claims that he would like Dan Duquette even if the latter were a graduate of another school, perhaps even Williams. While honing his skills as a poet both on stage and in rugby drink-ups, he earned his BA in the double major of mathematics and Classical languages (because they both seemed so darned practical). After teaching math and Latin (and coaching soccer) in private high schools on the East Coast for four years, Bob moved to Los Angeles.

Longtime Red Sox fan **Mario Martinelli** was born in Venice, Italy and tried to grow up in Ajax, Ontario. His life-long affair with the Boston Red Sox began months after immigrating to Canada and continues to this day. He maintains that a Roman Catholic upbringing steeled him to the vicissitudes of Red Sox (mis)fortunes through the years.

He has worked professionally in theater (principally provo street groups), was a local star as a folksinger in the 1960s and 1970s, and managed, after 15 years of ambivalence, to acquire a BFA and most of a MFA in Creative Writing and Film. He has attended all Red Sox Series appearances in his lifetime, and is convinced that he jinxed them in 1986 when he set the VCR to tape the last out in the sixth game.

Mario lived on the West Coast (Vancouver, Victoria) for 20 years before returning to Toronto, where he works as a Technical Writer when he can't get away with doing nothing. A musician and writer, he has produced seven CDs of his original music, and is currently working on his third (soon to be unpublished) novel: *The Anything Machine, Vol. 2: Wearing Yellow to the Wake*.

Heather Anne Nicoll comes from a long line of generic New Englanders and variously improper Bostonians, and has for years claimed, "I was born in Fenway—the region, not the ballpark." Despite her parents' moving to Maryland when she was a baby, the Red Sox have always been her true baseball love. She is a writer, potter, perpetual student, amateur musician, and sometime activist, and lives on the North Shore with her husband, Kevin Marsh (who converted to Red Sox fandom in self-defense), and a miscellaneous assortment of animals.

Bill Nowlin is first and foremost a lifelong Sox fan. A co-founder of Rounder Records in Cambridge, MA, when he turned age 50, he also turned to writing. He has written about a dozen books—all on the Red Sox or Sox-related topics—and over 100 articles for various publications. Among his works are *Mr. Red Sox: The Johnny Pesky Story*, *Fenway Lives*, and *The Kid*. He has co-authored several books with Jim Prime, including *Ted Williams: The Pursuit of Perfection*, *Tales From the Red Sox Dugout*, and *Blood Feud: The Red Sox, the Yankees and the Struggle of Good Versus Evil*. Bill still lives in Cambridge, and is still hoping his son Emmet develops a greater interest in the Red Sox. Winning it all in 2004 certainly helped.

Toine Otten lives in the small town of Born in the south of The Netherlands with his girlfriend

Pauline, their 7½-year-old daughter Judith, and Josh, the cat. Toine works as a Human Resource Manager. He got hooked on baseball and the Red Sox at the age of nine, after watching the 1975 World Series. After playing baseball himself for 15 years, Toine now focuses on teaching kids about baseball in a country in which baseball is still a very unknown sport.

Paul Ryan is a young Mechanical Engineering graduate from Worcester Polytechnic Institute. Currently he spends his days working temp jobs, and his free time surfing the Internet, especially keeping abreast of all the latest baseball news. He lives in northeast Connecticut with his family, and enjoys being able to see his nephew Patrick on a regular basis.

Neil Serven was born and raised in Lynn, Massachusetts, where he lived for 25 years. He earned his BA in English from Merrimack College, where he wrote, edited and illustrated for two literary magazines, one of which he co-founded. Since graduation in 1997 he has enjoyed careers in book sales, electronic publishing, and journalism. He now resides in Florence, Massachusetts, working as a writer, painter, and lexicographer.

Colin Smith was born in 1968 and lives in North West London. He works as an Emergency Medical Technician for the London Ambulance Service and following his first visit to Boston in 1999 has become a regular visitor, taking in both Red Sox and Bruins games in recent years. At home he follows the fortunes of Sunderland Football Club (soccer) and his local ice hockey team, the London Racers.

Jim Tiberio graduated from the University of Connecticut in 1994 and has worked in sales since then. He is currently licensed and working in the investment services industry and also has several years experience working as a loan officer in the mortgage industry. He has been a Red Sox fan all of his life. He lives in southwest Connecticut, a.k.a. Yankeeville, and gets to listen to the Sox on 1080 WTIC out of Hartford while also catching an occasional game on TV.

Eric M. Van is best known for the wealth of statistical analysis he has posted to Sons of Same Horn and, previously, to the Red Sox and general baseball Internet newsgroups. In the world at large, he is equally well known as the longtime Program Chair of Readercon, the country's leading literary science fiction conference, and as the official historian of Boston's reunited indy-rock legends Mission of Burma. He recently began work as a player evaluation consultant for the Red Sox.

Donald Violette is a lifetime resident of central Vermont. He spent many years working in the video game/vending machine industry. With the help of friends and family, Don is continuing to recover from a debilitating illness. Besides being a near-fanatical Red Sox fan, Don has recently discovered the Internet, is a bowling league Secretary-Treasurer, has collected comic books most of his life, and is a voracious reader of several fiction genres. Don presently lives in Barre, Vermont, with his parakeets, Pedro and B.B.

Edward Zartler was born in Cambridge in 1970, which is where he caught The Bug. It lay dormant through the fitful 70s, but sprang up after his Bar Mitzvah . . . musta been puberty. It raged full blown in 1986, and he blames Stanley not Buckner for the loss. Getting progressively worse, it followed him to Baltimore where in 1988 he enrolled at Goucher College and was able to watch a young Curt Schilling pitch for the O's after he was traded along with Brady Anderson for Mike Boddicker. Four years later he graduated in a roaring state of infection; the O's sucked, but his beloved team came to play nine games a year. His choice for graduate school was dominated by the need to at least be in a major league city, and he chose Penn over Cornell. Six years of exile in a National League city was made tolerable by interleague play and meeting his wonderful wife. Zartler was married in 1997, and graduated, painfully, in 1998. He moved to Athens, Georgia, a wonderful town, but no major league baseball. The Bug was the most painful in this time; Braves on TBS is like *USA Today* after the *New York Times*. Two years later he moved to Indianapolis, going from no baseball to AAA. The Indianapolis Indians at least play the PawSox. He is employed by Eli Lilly where he keeps bugging management to work on a cure for The Bug, but to no avail. He and his wife have two Cardigan Welsh Corgis, Clyde and Owen, and a son, Ben. He assures his wife The Bug is not genetic, but the Red Sox mobile he constructed in his son's room should help in passing on the disease.

Index